Anonymous

Angliiskaia Khrestomatiia

S prilozheniem anglo-russkago slovaria

Anonymous

Angliiskaia Khrestomatiia
S prilozheniem anglo-russkago slovaria

ISBN/EAN: 9783337173074

Printed in Europe, USA, Canada, Australia, Japan

Cover: Foto ©Andreas Hilbeck / pixelio.de

More available books at **www.hansebooks.com**

АНГЛІЙСКАЯ

ХРЕСТОМАТІЯ,

СЪ ПРИЛОЖЕНІЕМЪ

АНГЛО-РУССНАГО СЛОВАРЯ,

СОСТАВЛЕННАЯ

ФЛОТА КАПИТАНОМЪ 1-ГО РАНГА

А. Паукеромъ,

Инспекторомъ воспитанниковъ и классовъ Императорскаго
Александровскаго лицея, авторомъ „Англійской Морской
Хрестоматіи“, „Французской Морской Хрестоматіи“ и
„A Manual of Russian Conversation“.

—◦◇◦—

2-ое ИЗДАНІЕ,

ИСПРАВЛЕННОЕ И ЗНАЧИТЕЛЬНО ПОПОЛНЕННОЕ

СAНКТПЕТЕРБУРГЪ.
—
1869.

Типографія Р. Голике, Толмазовъ переулокъ домъ Ильина № 16 —2.

ПРЕДИСЛОВІЕ

КЪ ПЕРВОМУ ИЗДАНІЮ.

———

Хрестоматія эта имѣетъ цѣлью дать начинающимъ учиться англійскому языку средства усвоить себѣ практическимъ путемъ такое число словъ, выраженій и оборотовъ языка, которое составляетъ достаточный матеріалъ для того, чтобъ свободно выражаться по англійски.

Для достиженія сего руководство это раздѣлено на 4 отдѣленія: 1) Первыя 15 страницъ содержатъ легкіе разговоры и другія статьи, знакомящія учащагося съ большимъ числомъ словъ и выраженій. Къ этому отдѣленію принадлежитъ помѣщенный въ концѣ книги особый краткій словарь, въ которомъ, для облегченія начинающимъ, слова и цѣлыя фразы расположены въ томъ же порядкѣ, въ какомъ слѣдуютъ въ текстѣ. — 2) Второе отдѣленіе заключаетъ въ себѣ 88 статей повѣствовательной прозы, къ каждой изъ которыхъ присоединены вопросы. Учащійся, пріискавъ отвѣты на нихъ въ текстѣ и выучивъ ихъ наизусть, усвоиваетъ себѣ главные очерки статьи, которую онъ потомъ передаетъ учителю изустно, дополняя упомянутые отвѣты собственными выраженіями. — 3) Третье отдѣленіе составляютъ 20 легкихъ стихотвореній, назначенныхъ для выучиванія наизусть. — 4) Послѣднее отдѣленіе содержитъ полный подробный лексиконъ всѣхъ словъ и выраженій, встрѣчающихся во всей книгѣ.

Почти всѣ статьи 2-го отдѣленія повѣствовательны, для того, чтобъ сдѣлать ихъ болѣе занимательными и удобными для разсказыванія. Онѣ почти исключительно касаются исторіи и народнаго быта Англіи, представляя такимъ образомъ характеристическіе очерки того народа, коего языкъ изучается, и вмѣстѣ съ этимъ доставляя англійскимъ учителямъ (бóльшая часть которыхъ природные Англичане) достаточный матеріалъ для поучительныхъ разговоровъ о томъ, что имъ болѣе всего знакомо и ближе къ сердцу.

ПРЕДИСЛОВІЕ

КО ВТОРОМУ ИЗДАНІЮ.

Въ настоящемъ второмъ изданіи хрестоматіи прибавлены многіе отрывки изъ исторіи Англіи, извлеченные изъ сочиненій лучшихъ англійскихъ историковъ и расположенные въ хронологическомъ порядкѣ. Въ дополненіе къ сему присоединены краткіе очерки Англіи, знакомящіе учащагося съ современнымъ географическимъ состояніемъ Британской имперіи.

Второй отдѣлъ — поэзія — также значительно пополненъ новыми стихотвореніями, въ томъ числѣ нѣкоторыми любимыми народными англійскими балладами.

Слова „для Начинающихъ“, стоявшія въ заглавіи перваго изданія, выпущены, такъ какъ въ настоящемъ видѣ учебникъ этотъ можетъ быть употребляемъ въ продолженіе нѣсколькихъ курсовъ.

СОДЕРЖАНІЕ.

Стр.

Предисловіе . . . . III.
Elementary Sentences 1

Connected Phrases.

General Remarks on the World 6
Productions of Various Countries 7
Of the Difference and Distance of a Mile in Different Countries. 8
Varieties of the Human Species . . . . —
Useful Knowledge 9
Languages of the World 10

Anecdotes, Narrative and other Pieces.

1. Laconic Answers 11
2. Friend Charles, Put on thy Hat. . . . . —
3. The Duke of Marlborough . . . . —
4. Hogs, the Only Gentlemen 12
5. I Will no More Verses Make . . . . —
6. The Origin of the Term Sandwich . . . . —
7. The Origin of the Term Grog. 13
8. The First Smoker . . . . —
9. A Resolute Boy 14
10. Scarce Articles . . . . —
11. The Note of Interrogation 15
12. Doctor Goldsmith . . . . —
13. The Quaker 16
14. Effect of Music . . . . —
15. Honesty the Best Policy 17
16. An Enemy's Courtesy . . . . —
17. Humanity 18
18. The Bagpiper Revived 19
19. Newton's Command of His Temper . . . . —
20. Abstraction . . . . —
21. Oliver Cromwell . . . . —
22. Canute's Reproof 21
23. Dr. Johnson and Mrs. Thrale 22
24. Shut the Door . . . . —
25. Dean Swift 23
26. Swift Teaching Good Manners . . . . —

Стр.

27. Jonathan Swift 24
28. Sir Walter Scott 25
29. Walter Scott at School 26
30. Sheridan 27
31. The Value of Time . . . . —
32. Peter the Great 28
33. Newton and the Shepherd Boy 29
34. Almanac Weather Wisdom 30
35. Singular Cases of Inability to Distinguish Colours . . . 31
36. Alick 32
37. Professor Porson . . . . —
38. The Travelling Library 33
39. The National Debt of England 34
40. Doing Justice to the Consonants 35
41. Vulgar Pronunciation . . . . —
42. Lying Punished 36
43. Mr. Dodd 37
44. Private Prayer . . . . —
45. The Praying Little Girl . . . . —
46. A Better Rule than «Expediency» 38
47. The Missionary Money-box 39
48. Dr. Franklin on Prayer . . . . —
49. Washington 40
50. An Illustration of a Special Providence and of the Power
    of Prayer 41
51. The Bible a Shield for Soul and Body 42
52. Honesty the Best Policy 43
53. Remarkable Escape from Danger 44
54. Newfoundland Dogs 45
55. A Priceless Dog 46
56. Canine Sagacity 48
57. More Faithful than Favoured 49
58. Bill, the Fire-escape Dog 50
59. The Strictness of Discipline Rewarded 52
60. Thomson and Quin 53
61. The Whistle 54
62 A Trait of Lord Byron's Generosity, Humanity, and Tender-
    heartedness 55
63. The Chimney-sweepers' Feast, or the Lost Child. Found 58
64. A Nobleman and his Noble Servant 60
65. Miss Burney 62
66. The Generous Cateran 64
67. Singular Instance of Generosity 65
68. Bradford the Innkeeper 68

69. Fingal outwitting the Scotch Giant 71
70. The Adventure of My Aunt 72
71. James V. Travelling in Disguise 75
72. James Chrichton 77
73. Sir Sidney Smith's Escape 80
74. A Dangerous Journey in Labrador 82
75. Over the Rapids 85
76. A Visit to a Famous Island 91
77. The Sedar, and Leopard Hunt 96
78. A Princess Royal 100
79. Anecdote of Rev. John Wesley 108
80. Nelson 112
81. The Loss of the Royal George 115
82. Anecdotes of Discoveries 123

Historical Extracts.

1. Ancient England and the Romans 129
2. The Scots and Picts 137
3. The Saxons 139
4. King Alfred the Great 143
5. The Story of Macbeth 146
6. The Battle of Hastings 154
7. Bold Robin Hood 157
8. Death and Character of Richard I. 163
9. Chivalry 165
10. Henry II. Conquest of Ireland 166
11. Magna Charta 169
12. Edward I.'s Conquest of Wales and Scotland . . 170
13. Robert Bruce 172
14. Battle of Crecy 176
15. The War of Roses 183
16. Henry VII. 187
17. Henry VIII. 188
18. King Edward VI. 191
19. The Invincible Armada 192
20. The Gunpowder Plot 194
21. The Petition of Right 199
22. The Puritans 200
23. Habeas Corpus Act (1679) 203
24. Earl of Nithsdale 204
25. Stratagem Signally Defeated 206
26. The Country Gentlemen, Clergy, and Yeomanry . . 208
27. Difficulty of Travelling 220
28. England in 1685, and England in 1857 223

Sketches from the British Empire.

Стр.

I. General Physical Features of England 239
II. Civil and Ecclesiastical State 243
III. National Character — Language, Literature, Arts, and Sciences 245
IV. The City of London 247
V. The Streets of London 252
VI. The River Thames 254
VII. Life and Manners of the Inhabitants of Scotland . . . 256
VIII. Colonies and Dependencies of Great Britain 258
IX. Commerce and Manufactures of Great Britain 265

POETRY.

1. The Busy Bee 267
2. The Lazy Fly . . . . —
3. The Field Daisy 268
4. The Little Coward . . . . —
5. The Evening Bells . . . . —
6. The Disobedient Little Fish 269
7. The Idle Boy . . . . —
8. The Monkey 270
9. Questions and Answers 271
10. A Morning Hymn . . . . —
11. An Evening Hymn 272
12. The Great Shepherd . . . . —
13. The Glow Worm 273
14. God Provideth for the Morrow . . . . —
15. Paraphrase on Psalm XXIII 274
16. We are Seven 275
17. The Bundle of Sticks 276
18. The Hare and the Tortoise 279
19. Destruction of Sennacherib 280
20. Pity for Poor Africans 281
21. My Heart's in the Highlands 283
22. Rule Britannia . . . . —
23. The Inchcape Rock 284
24. Sir Lancelot du Lake 286
25. King Leir and His Three Daughters 289
26. King John and the Abbot of Canterbury 294
27. Chevy-Chase 298
28. The Diverting History of John Gilpin 301
29. The Cataract of Lodore 305
Словарь къ первымъ 10 страницамъ . . . 313
Алфавитный словарь ко всей книгѣ 325

Elementary Sentences.

I.

There is a knock at the door. — Somebody knocks at the door. — Go and see who it is. — Go and open the door. — It is Mr. B.— Good morning to you.—I am very glad to see you.— I am very happy to see you.—I have not seen you this age.— You are quite a stranger.— Pray be seated. — Do, pray, sit down.—Please to sit down.— Give a chair to Mr. B.—Fetch a seat.— Will you stay and take dinner with us? — I cannot stay.—I only came in to ask how you did. — I must go.—You are in a great hurry. — I have a good many things to do.— Surely you can stay a little longer. — I have many places to call at. — I will stay longer another time.— I thank you for your visit.— I hope I shall see you soon again.

II.

Have you breakfasted?—Not yet.— You come just in time. —You will breakfast with us.—Breakfast is ready.—Come to breakfast. —Do you drink tea or coffee?— Would you prefer chocolate?—I prefer coffee?— What shall I offer you? — Here are rolls and toast. — Which do you like best? — I will take a roll. — I prefer some toast. — How do you like the coffee? —I hope your coffee is as you like it. — Is the coffee strong enough? — It is rather too strong. — It is excellent. — It is sweet enough.— It is not clear. — If it is not, I beg you will say so.

III.

What time do we dine to-day? — We are to dine at four o'clock. — Dinner will not be ready before five o'clock. — Is any one coming to dinner, besides our own family? — Do you expect company?—I expect

1

Mr. T. — If the weather is fine, Mr. N. has promised to take dinner with us. — Have you given orders for dinner? — What have you ordered for dinner? — What have we got for dinner? — Have you sent for any fish? — I could not get any fish. — There was not any fish in the market. — I fear we shall have a very plain dinner. — We must manage as well as we can.

IV.

What shall I help you to? — Would you like to taste the soup? —. Will you take some soup? — I thank you, I will trouble you for a little beef. — It looks very nice. — What part do you like best? — Will you have it well done or underdone? — Rather well done, if you please. — I prefer it rather underdone, if you please. — I like it rather well done. Have I helped you as you like?—It is excellent. — Will you let me send you a piece of this pie?—I thank you, I perfer a piece of that pudding. — Try them both. — You had better take some of both. — Will you taste a slice of this mutton, what shall I send you? — Do you choose any of the fat? — A little of the lean, if you please? — This piece, I hope, will suit your taste.

V.

You have no gravy. — You have no sauce on your plate. — I have plenty, I thank you. — I have as much as I wish for, I thank you. — How do you like the boiled veal? — It is delightful. — It is remarkably fine meat. — What will you take with your meat? — Shall I help you to some vegetables? — Here is some spinage and some brocoli, and there are new potatoes. — Will you have peas, or cauliflower? — The asparagus is extremely tender and very sweet. — Do you eat salad? — Here are both carrots and turnips. — Have you any bread? — We have both brown bread and white. — The brown bread is home-made.

VI.

Shall I help you to some of this? — Allow me to help you to a piece of this fish. — Shall I send you a slice of this leg of mutton? — It is very full of gravy. — You have not tasted any of this tart. — This ham is delicious. — Shall I help you to some of it? — I will thank you for a very small piece, just to taste it. — Give me but a little bit. — You have no appetite. — You eat nothing. — I beg your pardon, I have eaten very heartily. — A small piece of this partridge cannot hurt you. — Will you try the plum sauce? — Shall I give you a wing or a leg? — You have helped me rather too plentifully. — Will you please to cut it in two? — The half will be sufficient for me.

VII.

Have you carried in the tea things?—Every thing is on the table.— Does the water boil? — Tea is quite ready. — They are waiting for you. —I am coming.—I will follow you.— You have not put a basin on the table. — We have not cups enough. — We want two cups more. — Bring another spoon, and a saucer.— You have not brought in the sugar-tongs. — Do you take sugar? — Do you like cream? — I will thank you for a little more milk.— The tea is too strong.— Will you fill up my cup with water? — Shall I give you black tea or green? — I have both here. — What will you take to eat? — Here are cakes and muffins. — Do you prefer bread and butter? — I will take some. — Get some more bread and butter.— Will you take a small piece of cake? — Do pray taste it. — Not any more, I thank you. — Had you rather not? — Much rather not, I assure you.

VIII.

Will you be so kind as to pull the bell. — Pray ring the bell. — We want some more water. — Make more toast. — Bring it as soon as possible. — Take the plate along with you. — Is your tea sweet enough? — Have I put sugar enough in your tea? — Do you find your tea sweet enough? — It is excellent, I do not like it so very sweet.— Your tea is very fine. — This is most excellent tea. — Where do you get it? — A friend has procured me a small chest. — It is the only way to get it good and cheap. — You will take another cup? — I will pour you out only half a cup. — I had much rather not, I thank you. — I never take more than three cups. — Call the servant to take everything away.

IX.

Will you stay and sup with us? — Pray take your bread and cheese with us. — I am much obliged to you, but I am afraid it will be too late. — We shall sup directly. — We have only a little cold meat to offer you, and a few oysters. — Are you fond of oysters? — I like them very much. — Here is some ham and cold beef; which shall I offer you first? — I will try a few oysters. — I hope they are quite fresh.— They are very good. — Pray take a few more. — No, I thank you, I will take a slice of cold ham. — Will you taste the apple pie? — It looks very good. — No, I have supped very heartily. — I have done extremely well.

X.

Will you take a glass of wine with me? — I thank you, with much pleasure. — Which do you prefer, claret or portwine or a glass of sherry? — A glass of white wine. — What do you drink with your dinner? — We have table beer, and porter, and Scotch ale. — I will taste a glass of porter. — The porter is extremely fine. — It is quite ripe. — How long has it been in the bottle? — I think I never drank better.

XI.

Have you written your exercise? — Where is your translation? — I am very sorry, but I have quite forgotten to make it.— I was prevented from making it, I had a very bad tooth ache.—Let me see your copy.— It is very badly written. — It is scarcely legible. — You must write it better, or I shall expect you to make it over again.—Have you learnt your vocabulary. — Repeat your dialogues. — Let me hear the irregular verbs.—Have you learnt the rules?—Repeat your lesson. — You hardly know a single word, you must learn it again after school. — I will have it said perfectly, without missing a word.

XII.

Where shall I sit? — Take your seat on that form. — Sit a little higher up. — Do not make such a noise. — Spell that word again. — Do not shake the table, I cannot write unless you sit still. — Lend me your knife. — I have lost my pen. — Can you lend me one? — I have none to spare. — I want to use mine myself. — I can't find my copy-book. — Where did you leave it? — Upon the desk, under my other books. — I put it into my desk. — I laid it on the shelf, just by my seat. — Go and fetch it. — Have you got your slate? — Have you got it? — Look for it. —I have found it. —Where was it? — It was under the form.

XIII.

Do you know what o'clock it is?— I don't know exactly. —I can't tell you to a quarter of an hour. — Look at your watch.—It is not wound up.— I forgot to wind it up.—It does not go.— It has stopped. — My watch does not go well. — It loses a quarter of an hour every day. — Mine gains as much. — The main spring is broken. — It must be sent to the watchmaker. — Are you up already? — I have been up this hour. — You got up very early. — I generally rise early. — Have you slept well? — I never woke all night. — I could not sleep a wink. — I never closed my eyes the whole night. — Oh! what a fine morning. — What do you think of taking a short walk? — Shall we have time before breakfast? — They won't breakfast this hour. — We have full an hour before us. — The walk will give us an appetite.

XIV.

It begins to grow very late. — It is almost time to go to bed. — Mr. B. is not yet come home. — I hear a knock. — Very likely he is there already. — Go and see. — Ha, there he is! — I hope I have not kept you up. — Oh, not at all. — It is only ten o'clock. — Have you had a pleasant walk? — Very much so. — It is a charming evening. — Are you not tired? — Not much. — Pray sit on the sofa, and rest yourself a little. — I fear we shall have a very hot summer. — We have had no summer this year. — We have had a fire even in the month of July. — There will be a great deal of hay. — They have begun the harvest. — The crop will be plentiful. — There is wheat cut down already. — The corn will all be housed next week. — No wonder it is so warm, we are in the dog days.

XV.

The summer is over. — We must not expect many more fine days. — The leaves begin to fall. — The mornings are cold. — We have already begun fires. — A fire begins to be comfortable. — The days are very much shortened. — The evenings are long, we cannot see at five o'clock. — It is hardly day light at four in the afternoon. — It is soon dark. — The winter draws near, we shall have the shortest day in three weeks. — Christmas will soon be here. — I wish it were here already. — The days begin to lengthen. — The fire is very low. — Here is a poor fire. — Put some more turf and wood into the stove. — You have not kept up a good fire. — You have let the fire go out. — It must be lighted again. — What are you looking for? — I am looking for the tongs. — Now put in two or three pieces of wood. — It will soon draw up.

Here is another new book. — What is it about? — A little of every thing. — Is it entertaining? — Yes, very, for young people; it is full of anecdotes, serious and sad, lively and laughable. — Very well, I am sure I shall like it; shall we read a page or two?—If you please, I have some time to spare before I go out. — Are you going to walk this evening?— Yes, if the weather continues fine, but I think it will rain, it is dark and cloudy. — Oh! I think not, the wind is too high. — Which way is the wind? — East, this morning it was west. — This has been a cold month. I have taken a great deal of exercise, and I am now quite strong and well.

Good morning! I was just wishing to meet with you, which way are you going? will you go home with me? — I have something very beautiful to show you. — Come! it is not late, I have not seen you for a long time, where have you been? I thought you had left town, you never go out. — Why don't you oftener visit us? — We walk or ride into the country every day. — We sail or row up the river. — We went out shooting yesterday. — Next week we are going to the races, on Wednesday or on Thursday we shall see the balloon ascend.

Connected Phrases.

General Remarks on the World.

The coldest country in the world is Greenland, and the hottest, the Burmese empire. The largest empire in Europe and the world, is Russia, and the smallest kingdom in Europe is Saxony. The tallest people in the world are the Patagonians, and the shortest people, the Laplanders. The most polished people in the world are in Europe, the most savage in Africa, the most numerous in Asia; and the thinnest population in the world is in America. The most numerous people in the world are the Chinese. The freest country in Europe is England, and the most enslaved is Turkey. The oldest empire in the world is China, and the newest is the Brazils. The most mountainous country in Europe is Norway, and the flattest is Russia. The highest mountain in Europe is Mont Blanc, in Savoy, in France; and the highest mountain in the world is Mont Everest, one of the Himalaya mountains, in Asia. — The largest river in the world is the Maranon, or Amazon, in South America. Great Britain has the largest fleet of ships in Europe. France, Austria, and Russia have the largest armies. England is the most trading country in the world, and the United States next to it. South America is remarkable for its gold and silver mines. Arabia is famed for fine horses. Egypt and Palestine were civilized, when Europe was all barbarous; now Europe is civilized, and they are in a rude state. Greece was once the mightiest of nations, and it is now the weakest. The Italians and Germans are the most musical people in the world, and the Chinese the least so. He who speaks the French language can travel all over Europe, and he who speaks the English can trade all over the world.

_____

Productions of Various Countries.

Anchovies come from the Mediterranean. The best brandy is distilled in France. Butter is carried to England from Ireland, Holland, and Holstein. Carpets of the best sort are manufactured in Persia and Turkey. Cheese of one kind, called Dutch cheese, comes from Holland. Cocoa grows in the East Indies, and in Polynesia; coffee in Arabia, the East and West Indies, Persia, and America. Cork comes from France, Spain, and Italy. Cotton is brought from the United States, the East and West Indies, where it grows on a tree; it is also brought from Egypt, Cyprus, Smyrna, etc. Deal wood comes from Sweden, Norway, and America. Diamonds are found in Brazil and India. Figs grow in Turkey, chiefly Smyrna. Codfish is brought from Newfoundland. Gin, called Hollands, is distilled in Holland. Gloves of the best sort are made in France. Gold for the most part comes from Siberia, California, Australia, and South America. Ivory, made of elephants' teeth, is sent from Africa, but the best is from the island of Ceylon. The best lace is made in Belgium and France. Muslin of the best sort is manufactured in Bengal. Oil of the finest kind for eating is imported from Italy. Oranges grow in Italy, Portugal, Spain, the Cape Verd islands, Madeira, and the Azores. Pearls are found by diving near Ceylon. Plums and raisins are dried, and sent from Turkey and Spain. Rice is cultivated in China and the East Indies. Rum is made from sugar in Jamaica. Silk worms are bred in Italy, China, the Caucasus, and Persia. Silver is found in Mexico and South America. Spices, such as cinnamon, cloves, pepper etc.

grow in Ceylon, and the Moluccas. Sponge is found in the Mediterranean Sea, near the Archipelago islands. Tallow comes from Russia. Timber chiefly comes from Sweden and the United States. Cigars of the best kind come from Cuba and Manilla, and tabacco from Virginia, and Turkey. Toys are mostly made in Germany. Whalebone is made out of the bone of whales, a huge fish caught off Greenland. Whisky comes from Scotland and Ireland. Wines are made in Portugal, Madeira, Spain, France, Sicily, Cape of Good Hope etc. Wool of the finest kind comes from Saxony and Spain.

Of the Difference and Distance of a Mile in Different Countries.

Is the length of a mile the same in every country? No, very different; for the English mile is much less than the Indian; the Indian, than the Spanish; the Spanish, than the German. What is an English mile? An English statute mile consists of 5280 feet, or 1760 yards. What nations agree nearly in this measure? The Turkish, Italian and old Roman mile is nearly one English. What is a Russian verst? Very little more than three quarters of an English mile. What is an Indian mile? Three English miles. What is a Spanish, Polish, and Dutch mile? About three miles and a half English. What is a Scotch and Irish mile? About a mile and a half English. What is an Arabian mile? A mile and a quarter English. What is a German mile? Little more than four English miles. What is a Swedish, Danish, and Hungarian mile? From five to six English miles.

Varieties of the Human Species.

There are five grand varieties of the human race; but they imperceptibly approach, and are lost in each other. First: the white and brownish nations of Europe, western Asia, and the north coast of Africa; who, according to our notions of beauty, are the handsomest and best formed of the human race. Next: the yellow or olive coloured Chinese, Monguls, Calmucs, and other eastern nations of Asia, with whom may be reckoned the most northerly American Indian tribes, having flat foreheads, little eyes, and wide mouths. Thirdly: the copper coloured American Indians, dispersed over the entire continent; with broad faces, bristly hair, and stout masculine limbs. Fourthly: the jet black negroes and other Africans of various shades of black, having woolly hair, thick lips, flat noses, prominent chins, and downy skins. Fifthly: the dark brown Australians, on the continent, and in the islands of the Pacific and Indian oceans, with large features, strong hair, broad nostrils and great mouths.

But all men are the offspring of one common parent; and among the varieties, the swarthy negro and the delicate European are brethren, descended from the same ancestor.

Useful Knowledge.

One is often surprised, when talking with little boys, to find them so ignorant of many things, which they ought to have known as well as their own names. I was questioning one, at least eight years old, the other day, who knew neither the number of days, weeks, or months there are in the year. He could not tell whether the sun rose in the east or the west, and was equally ignorant whether his pocket was made of hemp, flax, or wool. There are things certainly more important for him to know than these, but he should make himself better acquainted with things of this nature.

Every boy ought to know, that he has five senses, seeing, hearing, smelling, feeling, and tasting;—that the year has four seasons, spring, summer, autumn, and winter;—that the earth turns round, and travels round the sun;—that the world is composed of land and water, and divided into six parts, Europe, Asia, Africa, America, Australia, Oceania or Polynesia;—that there are four cardinal points, east, west, north, and south;—that gold, silver and other metals, and coal are dug out of the earth; diamonds are found on the land, and pearls are found in the sea. That boy must be ignorant indeed, who does not know, that bread is made of the flower of wheat; butter from cream, and cheese from milk; that when flour is mingled with yeast, it makes leavened, or light bread, and that when no yeast is used, the bread is heavy or unleavened. The passover cakes of the Jews, the biscuits eaten by sailors, and the barley bread of Scotland are all unleavened. A boy ought, at an early age, to be acquainted with such things as are in common use; but I have frequently found it necessary to explain to young people, that sugar is made from the juice of the sugar cane in the Indies; that tea is the dried leaves of a shrub which grows in China, about the size of a currant bush; that coffee is the berry of a bush growing in Arabia and the West Indies; and that chocolate is manufactured from cacao and vanilla. Many boys know very well that ale and beer are made with malt and hops, cider from apples, and perry from pears; who do not know, that wine is the juice of the grape; that brandy is distilled from wine, rum from sugar, and gin from juniper berries. And they have been equally ignorant that oranges, citrons, and lemons grow in Spain and the western islands; and spices in in the East Indies, and other parts; that pepper and cloves are fruits of shrubs; nutmegs, the kernels of a fruit like a peach; cinnamon, the bark of a tree; and ginger and rhubarb, the roots of plants. A great deal of this kind of knowledge may be obtained in a little time by young people, if they keep their eyes and ears open, and now and then ask a question of those who are wiser than themselves. I know a father who is very anxious that his children should obtain useful knowledge, and I heard him explain to them the other day, that salt is sea water, or salt water dried; glue, the sinews, feet, and skins of animals, boiled down; cork, the bark of a tree; flax, the fibres of the stalk of a plant resembling a nettle; and tow, the refuse of hemp. He told them also, that paper is made principally from linen rags, torn to pieces, and formed into a pulp; and lastly, that glass is made of sand, flint, and alkaline salt.

Languages of the World.

According to the enumeration of Professor Adelung, there are in the world three thousand and sixty-four different languages; of which five hundred and eighty-seven are spoken in Europe, nine hundred and thirty-seven in Asia, two hundred and seventy-six in Africa, and one thousand two hundred and sixty-four in America. The Professor probably includes in this enumeration many provincial corruptions of the same general languages.

Anecdotes, Narrative and other Pieces.

1. Laconic Answers.

The following conversation is one that happened to take place in the backwoods of America.
«What is the land?» «*Bogs*». — «The atmosphere?» «*Fogs.*» — «What do you live on?» «*Hogs*». — «What are your draught animals?» «*Dogs*». — What do you build your houses of?» «*Logs*». — Is there any fish in the ponds?« «*Frogs*». — «What do you travel by? «*Clogs*». — Many honest people there?» «*Rogues*».

2. Friend Charles, Put on thy Hat.

Mr. Penn, the proprietor of Pennsylvania, and the most considerable man among the Quakers, once went to Court to pay his respects to King Charles II. When that merry Monarch observed that the Quaker did not take off his hat, he took off his own, and stood uncovered before Penn. «Prithee, friend Charles», said the Quaker, «put on thy hat». «No, friend Penn», said the King, «it is usual for only one man to stand covered here».

Questions.
1. Who was Mr. Penn? — 2. Where did he once go? — 3. What did Charles II observe? — 4. What did he take off?
4. What did the Quaker say? — 6. What was the King's reply?.

3. The Duke of Marlborough.

The Duke of Marlborough admiring the fine figure and warlike air of a French soldier taken prisoner in the battle of Hochstett, said to him: «If the French had but fifty thousand such men as you, we should not have gained the battle so easily». — «Morbleu, Milord», said the solider, «we have plenty such men as I, we only want one like you».

Questions.
1. What did the Duke of Marlborough admire? — 2. At what battle had this solider been taken prisoner? — 3. How was the figure and air of the soldier? — 4. What did the Duke of Marlborough say to him? — 5. What did the soldier answer?

4. Hogs, the Only Gentlemen.

Dr. Franklin, when last in England, used to repeat an observation which was made by his negro servant, on a tour in Lancashire etc.

«Oh! Massa», said the negro, «every thing is working in this country: water works, wind works, fire works, smoke works, dogs work, men work, oxen work, horses work, asses work — every thing works here but the hog: it eats, it drinks, it sleeps, it does nothing all the day, but walks about like a gentleman».

Questions.

1. What did Dr. Franklin use to repeat?
2. What did the negro say?

---

5. I Will no More Verses Make.

It was so natural for Dr. Watts, when a child, to speak in rhyme, that even at the very time he wished to avoid it, he could not.

His father was displeased with this propensity, and threatened to whip him, if he did not leave off making verses.

One day, when he was about to beat his son for again speaking in rhyme, the child burst out into tears, fell on his knees, and said:

«Pray, father, do some pity take,
And I will no more verses make».

Questions.

1. What was natural for Dr. Watts, when a child? — 2. Was his father pleased with this propensity? — 3. What did he threaten to do to the boy? -- 4. What was he about one day? — 5. What did the child do and say?

---

6. The Origin of the Term Sandwich.

Not many years ago, Lord Sandwich, Minister of state, spent twenty-four hours in a gaming-house. He was so occupied by the passion of gaming, that during the whole time he had only some slices of fried beef between toast, which he ate without leaving the gaming-table.

This new kind of viand obtained the name of the Minister, who had invented it for the purpose of economizing his time.

Questions.

1. Who spent twenty-four hours in a gaming house? — 2. What did he eat there during the whole time?
3. What name did this new kind of viand obtain?

---

7. The Origin of the Term Grog.

Until the time of Admiral Vernon the British sailors had their allowance of brandy or rum served out to them unmixed with water.

This plan was found to be attended with inconveniences on some occasions. The Admiral, therefore, ordered that in the fleet he commanded, the spirit should be mixed with water before it was given to the men.

This innovation, at first, gave great offence to the sailors, and rendered the Commander very unpopular.

The Admiral, at that time, wore a grogram coat, and was nicknamed «Old Grog». This name was afterwards given to the mixed liquor he compelled them to take; and it has hence universally obtained the name of grog.

Questions.

1. How did the British sailors take their brandy or rum until the time of Admiral Vernon?
2. How did this plan prove? — 3. What order did the Admiral accordingly give? — 4. What was the consequence?
5. What did the Admiral wear, at that time, and how was he nicknamed? —
6. To what was this name afterwards given?

---

8. The First Smoker.

Tobacco was first brought into repute in England by Sir Walter Raleigh. By the caution he took in smoking it privately, he did not intend it should be copied. But sitting one day, in deep meditation, with a pipe in his mouth, he inadvertently called to his man to bring him a tankard of small-beer. The fellow, coming into the room, threw all the liquor into his master's face, and running down stairs, bawled out: «Fire! Help! Sir Walter has studied till his head is on fire, and the smoke bursts out at his mouth and nose!»

Questions.

1. By whom was tobacco first brought into repute in England? — 2. Why did he smoke it privately? — 3. What was he doing one day? — 4. What did he tell his man to do? — 5. What was the consequence?

9. A Resolute Boy.

A boy, who had sold a cow at the fair of Hereford in the year 1766, was waylaid by a highwayman on horseback, who, at a convenient place, demanded the money.

On this the boy took to his heels, and ran away. But being overtaken by the highwayman, who dismounted, the boy pulled the money out of his pocket, and strowed it about on the ground.

While the robber was picking it up, the boy jumped upon the horse, and rode home. When he was searching the saddle-bags, there were found twelve pounds in cash, and two loaded pistols.

Questions.

1. Who had sold a cow at the fair of Hereford? — 2. By whom was he waylaid, and what did the highwayman demand?

3. What did the boy do on this? — 4 When the boy was overtaken by the highwayman, what did he do with his money?

5. What followed?

10. Scarce Articles.

George I, King of England, being once on a journey to Hanover, stopped at a little village in Holland, and being hungry asked for two or three eggs, which he ate while the postillions were changing horses. When they were going away, the servant told his Majesty that the inn-keeper had charged two hundred florins; on which the King sent for him, and said: «How is it, Sir, that you charge me two hundred florins for three eggs? are they so scarce here?» «No», replied the host, «eggs are abundant enough, but Kings are excessively rare here, and we must make the most of them, when fortune does us the favour of throwing them into our way». — The King smiled, bade the postillions drive on, telling the landlord, «qu'il donnait ses oeufs pour avoir des boeufs».

Questions.

1. On what journey was George I? — 2. Where did he stop?— 3. What did the king ask for? — 4. How many eggs did he eat? — 5. What did the servant tell his Majesty? — 6. Whom did the King send for, and what did he say to him? — 7. Were eggs very scarce in that country? — 8. What was there very rare? — 9. What did the King say to the landlord?

11. The Note of Interrogation.

When Pope was one evening at Burton's coffee house, and with Swift poring over a Greek manuscript of Aristophanes, they found one sentence which they could not comprehend. As they talked pretty loud, a young officer, who stood by the fire, heard their conference, and begged leave to look at the passage. «Oh», said Pope, sarcastically, «by all means! Pray, let the young gentleman look at it». Upon which the officer took up the book, and considering a while, said, there wanted only a note of interrogation, to make the whole intelligible. «And, pray Sir», said Pope, piqued, perhaps, at being outdone by a red coat, «what is a note of interrogation?» «A note of interrogation», replied the youth, with a look of the utmost contempt, «is a little crooked thing that asks questions». (It must be remembered that Pope was slightly hump-backed).

Questions.

1. Where was Pope one evening. — 2. With whom was he there? — 3. What were they doing? — 4. What did they find in that manuscript? — 5. How did they talk? — 6. What did a young officer do, when he heard their conference? — 7. What did Pope answer, and in what manner? — 8. What did the officer do, after he had taken up the book? — 9. What would make the whole intelligible? — 10. By whom was Pope outdone, and how did he feel on that account? — 11. What did he say. — 12. What was it the youth replied?

12. Doctor Goldsmith.

A poor woman, understanding that Dr. Goldsmith was a physician, and hearing of his great humanity, solicited him, by letter, to send her something for her husband, who had lost his appetite, and was reduced to a most melancholy state. The good-natured poet waited on her instantly, and, after some discourse with his patient, found him sinking with sickness and poverty. The doctor told the honest pair that they should hear from him in an hour, when he would send him some pills which, he believed, would prove efficacious. He immediately went home, and put ten guineas into a pill-box, with the following label: «These must be used as necessities require: be patient and of good heart». He sent his servant with this prescription to the comfortless mourner, who found it contained a remedy superior to any thing Galen, or his disciples, could ever administer.

1. Who believed Dr. Goldsmith to be a physician? — 2. Was he indeed a physician? — 3. What did this woman solicit from him by letter? — 4. What had her husband lost, and to what was he reduced? — 5. What did Dr. Goldsmith immediately do? — 6. How did he find his patient? — What did Dr. Goldsmith tell the patient? — 8. What did he put into a pill-box, and how was this box labelled? — 9. How was this remedy found?

---

13. The Quaker.

A Quaker, driving in a one-horse chaise, happened to meet with a young fop, who was also in a one-horse chaise. There was not room enough for them to pass each-other, unless one of them would back his carriage, which they both refused. «I will not make way for you», said the fop, «no, I will not». «I think I am older than thou art», said the Quaker, «and therefore have a right to expect thee to make way for me». «I will not», resumed the first. He then pulled out a news-paper, and began to read, as he sat still in his chaise. The Quaker observing him, pulled a pipe and some tobacco from his pocket, and with a convenience which he carried about him, struck a light, lit his pipe, and sat and puffed away very comfortably. «Friend», said he, «when thou hast read that paper, I should be glad, if thou wouldst lend it me».

Questions.
1. Whom did a Quaker happen to meet? — 2. How was this Quaker driving? — 3. Was there room enough for them to pass each other? — 4. What was necessary? — 5. Why was the youth not willing to make way? — 6. Which was the elder of them? — 7. What did the Quaker expect? — 8. What did the young blood pull out of his pocket? — 9. What did the Quaker pull out of his pocket? — 10. With what did he strike a light? — 11. How did he smoke his pipe? — 12. What did the Quaker at last say to the young man?

---

14. Effect of Music.

A Scotch bag-piper, traversing the mountains of Ulster, was one evening encountered by a starved Irish wolf. In his distress the poor man could think of nothing better, than to open his wallet, and try the effect of his hospitality; he did so, and the savage swallowed all that was thrown to him, with so improving a voracity, as if his appetite was but just returning to him. The whole stock of provisions was, of course, soon spent, and now his only recourse was to the virtues of his bag-pipe, which the monster no sooner heard, than he took to the mountains with great precipitation. The poor piper could not so perfectly enjoy his deliverance, but that with an angry look at parting he shook his head, saying: «Ay, are these your tricks? Had I known your humour, you should have had your music before supper».

Questions.

1. Who was traversing the mountains of Ulster? — 2. By whom was he encountered? — 3. What did the poor man do in his distress? — 4. What did the savage do? — 5. What was soon spent? — 6. To what had the bag-piper recourse now? — 7. What did the monster do, as soon as he heard the bag-pipe? — 8. What did the bag-piper say, as he shook his head?

---

15. Honesty the Best Policy.

A nobleman travelling in Scotland, about six years ago, was asked for his alms in the High Street in Edinburgh by a little ragged boy. He said, he had no change; upon which the boy offered to procure it. His Lordship, in order to get rid of his importunity, gave him a piece of silver, which the boy conceiving to be changed, ran off for the purpose. On his return, not finding his benefactor, whom he expected to wait, he watched for several days in the place where he had received the money. At length, the nobleman happened again to pass that way; the boy accosted him, and put the change he had procured into his hand, counting it with great exactuesss. — His Lordship was so pleased with the boy's honesty, that he placed him at school, with the assurance of providing for him.

Questions.

1. Where and when did a nobleman travel? — 2. Where was he asked for his alms, and by whom? — 3. Why did his Lordship give the boy a silver piece, and what was the consequence? — 4. When the nobleman happened again to pass that way, what did the boy do? — 5. What was the result of the boy's honesty?

---

16. An Enemy's Courtesy.

When the crusaders under King Richard of England defeated the Saracens, the Sultan seeing his troops fly, asked what was the number of the Christians who were making all this slaughter? He was told, that it was only King Richard and his men, and that they were all on foot. «Then», said the Sultan, «God forbid, that such a noble fellow as King Kichard should march on foot»! and sent him a noble-charger. The messenger took it, and said: «Sire, the Sultan sends you this charger, that you may not be on foot». The King was as cunning as his enemy, and ordered one of his squires to mount the horse in order to try him. The squire obeyed; but the animal proved fiery, and the squire being unable to hold him in, he set off, full speed, to the Sultan's pavillion. The Sultan expected, he had got King Richard, and was not a little mortified to discover his mistake.

Questions.

1. When the Sultan saw his troops fly, what did he ask? — 2. What was he told? — 3. What did the Sultan say and do? — 4. What were the words of the messenger? — 5. What did the King order one of his squires to do?— 6. What was the consequence? — 7. What did the Sultan expect, and how did he feel on discovering his mistake?

17. Humanity.

Sir Philip Sidney, at the battle near Zutphen, displayed the most undaunted courage. He had two horses killed under him; and, while mounting a third, was wounded by a musket-shot out of the trenches, which broke the bone of his thigh. He returned about a mile and a half on horseback to the camp, and being faint with the loss of blood, and, probably, parched with thirst through the heat of the weather, he called for drink. It was presently brought him; but, as he was putting the vessel to his mouth, a poor wounded soldier, who happened to be carried by him at that instant, fixed his eye eagerly upon it. The gallant and generous Sidney took the bottle from his mouth just when he was going to drink, and delivered it to the soldier, saying: «Thy necessity is yet greater than mine»!

Questions.

1. What did Sir Philip display at the battle near Zutphen? — 2. What happened to him, while mounting a third horse? — 3. What did he call for, and why? — 4. As he was putting the vessel to his mouth, what occurred? — 5. What did the generous Sidney do and say?

18. The Bagpiper Revived.

The following event happened in London during the great plague which, in 1665, carried off nearly 100,000 of the inhabitants.

A Scotch bagpiper used to get his living by sitting and playing his bagpipes every day on the steps of St. Andrew's church, in Holborn. In order to escape the contagion he drank a great deal of gin; and, one day, having taken more than usual, he became so drunk that he fell fast asleep on the steps. It was the custom, during the prevalence of that terrible disease, to send carts about every night to collect the dead, and carry them to a common grave, or deep pit, of which several had been made in the environs of London.

The men passing with the cart up Holborn-hill, and seeing the piper extended on the steps, naturally thought it was a dead body, and tossed him into the cart among the others, without observing that he had his bagpipes under his arm, and without paying any attention to his dog, which followed the cart, barking and howling most piteously.

The rumbling of the cart over the stones, and the cries of the poor dog, soon awoke the piper from his drunken lethargy, and, not being able to discover where he was, he began squeezing his bag and playing a Scotch air, to the great astonishment and terror of the carters who immediately fetched lights, and found the Scot sitting erect amid the dead bodies, playing his pipes. He was soon released, and restored to his faithful dog. The piper became, from this event, so celebrated, that one of the first sculptors of that epoch made a statue of him and his dog, which is still to be seen at London.

Questions.

1. How many people died of the plague in London in 1665? — 2. How did the Scotch bagpiper get his living? — 3. What did he do in order to escape the plague, and what were the consequences? — 4. What was the custom at that time in London? — 5. What did the men do with the piper? — 6. What awoke the piper? — 7. What did he do on awaking? — 8. What became of him afterwards?

19. Newton's Command of his Temper.

Newton had a favorite little dog called «Diamond». One winter's morning, while attending early service, he inadvertently left his dog shut up in his room. On returning from chapel, he found that the animal, by upset-

ting a taper on his desk, had set fire to the papers on which he had written
down his experiments; and thus he saw before him the labors of so many
years reduced to ashes. It is said, that on first perceiving this great loss,
he contented himself by exclaiming: «Oh Diamond! Diamond! thou little
knowest the mischief thou hast done».

Questions.

1. When had Newton inadvertently left his dog shut up in his room? —
2. What did the animal upset on his desk? — 3. What papers had the animal
set fire to? — 4. To what was the labor of many years reduced? — 5. What
did Newton content himself to exclaim?

20. Abstraction.

Sir Isaac Newton, finding himself extremely cold one winter's evening,
drew a chair very close to the grate, in which a fire had recently been
lighted. By degrees the fire having completely kindled, Sir Isaac felt the
heat intolerably intense, and rang his bell with unusual violence. His
servant was not at hand in the moment, but soon made his appearance.
By this time Sir Isaac was almost literally roasted. «Remove the grate,
you lazy rascal»! he exclaimed in a tone of irritation, very uncommon
with this amiable and mild philosopher, «remove the grate before I am
burned to death»! On the servant's remarking that it would be easier for
him to draw back his chair; «upon my word», said he, smiling, «I never
thought of that»!

Questions.

1. How did Sir Isaac find himself one winter's evening, and what did he do?
— 2. What did he feel and do when the fire had completely kindled? — On the
servant's appearing, what did Sir Isaac exclaim, and how? — 4. What remark
did the servant make? — 5. What did Sir Isaac say?

21. Oliver Cromwell.

Oliver Cromwell was born at Huntingdon, and of the younger branch
of a good family. There is a curious story told of a narrow escape he had,
when an infant, from the mischievous tricks of a monkey. He had been
taken by his father and mother to his grandfather's, old Sir Henry Cromwell's at Hinchinbroke; and, while his nurse was out of the way, a great
monkey, which was allowed to run loose about the house, snatched him

out of the cradle, and ran with him to the roof of the house, where it was seen dancing about with the child in its arms, to the great terror of the whole family, particularly, as you may suppose, of his father and mother. It was impossible to attempt to catch the animal; the only thing that could be done was to place feather-beds and carpets all round the house, for the child to fall on in case the monkey should let him drop. However, after some time, the creature returned down into the house by the way it had got up, and brought the child back in safety.

Questions.

1. Where was Oliver Cromvell born? — 2. Of what is there a curious story told? — 3. To whom had he been taken by his parents? — 4. Who snatched young Oliver out of the cradle? — 5. What was this monkey allowed to do? — 6. Where was the nurse? — 7. Whither did the monkey run with the child in its arms? — 8. What was impossible? — 9. What was placed round the house, and why? — 10. Whither did the monkey return, and by what way? — 11. How was the child brought back?

22. Canute's Reproof.

Canute, the greatest and most powerful monarch of his time. sovereign of Denmark and Norway as well as of England, could not fail of meeting with adulation from his courtiers, a tribute which is liberally paid even to the meanest and weakest princes. Some of his flatterers, breaking out one day in admiration of his grandeur, exclaimed that every thing was possible for him. Upon which the monarch ordered his chair to be set on the seashore while the tide was rising, and, as the waters approached, he commanded them to retire, and to obey the voice of him who was lord of the ocean. — He feigned to sit some time in expectation of their submission. — But when the sea still advanced towards him, and began to wash him with its billows, he turned to his courtiers, and remarked to them, that every creature in the universe was feeble and impotent — and that power resided with one Being alone, in whose hands were all the elements of nature; who could say to the ocean, *thus far shalt thou go and no farther*; and who could level with his nod the most towering piles of human ambition.

Questions.

1. What did Canute's flatterers exclaim? — 2. What did the Monarch order to be done? — 3. When the sea advanced, what did Canute remark to his courtiers?

23. Dr. Johnson and Mrs. Thrale.

.The first time Johnson was in company with Mrs. Thrale, neither the elegance of his conversation, nor the depth of his knowledge could prevent that lady from being shocked at his manners. Among other pieces of in-decorum, his tea not being sweet enough, he dipped his fingers into the sugar-basin, and supplied himself with as little ceremony and concern, as if there had not been a lady at the table. Every well bred cheek was tinged with confusion; but Mrs. Thrale was so exasperated, that she ordered the sugar-basin immediately from the table, as if its contents had been contaminated by the Doctor's fingers. The Doctor prudently took no notice, but peaceably swallowed, as usual, his dozen cups of tea. When he had done, instead of placing his cup and saucer upon the table, he threw them both calmly under the grate. The whole tea-table was thrown into confusion. Mrs. Thrale screamed out: «Why, Doctor, what have you done? You have spoiled the handsomest set of china I have in the world!» «I am very sorry for it, madam», answered Dr. Johnson, «but I assure you I did it out of good breeding; for from your treatment of the sugar-basin, I supposed you would never touch any thing again that I had once soiled with my fingers».

Questions.

1. At what was Mrs. Thrale shocked? — 2. Into what did Dr. Johnson dip his fingers?—3. How did Mrs. Thrale feel, and what did she order to be done?— 4. How did Dr. Johnson act? — 5. When the Doctor had finished his tea, what did he do? — 6. What was Mrs. Thrale's exclamation, when Dr. Johnson threw the cup and saucer unter the grate? — 7. What was the Doctor's reply?

---

24. Shut the Door.

Dean Swift, though a good master, was very strict with his servants. The task of hiring them was always entrusted to his housekeeper; but the only two positive commands he had for them, he generally de-livered himself: these were, to shut the door whenever they came into, or went out of a room. One of his maid-servants one day asked permission to go to her sister's wedding, at a place about ten miles distant. Swift not only consented, but lent her one of his own horses, and ordered his servant to ride before her. The girl, in the ardour of joy for this favour, forgot to shut the door after her, when she left the room. In about a quarter of an hour after her departure, the Dean sent a servant after her, to order her immediate return. The poor girl obeyed; and entering his presence, begged to know in what she had offended, or what her master wished. «Only shut the door», said the Dean, «and then resume your journey».

Questions.

1. What was Dean Swift? — 2. What two positive commands had he for his servants? — 3. Where did one of his maidservants ask permission to go? — 4. How did the Dean grant this request? — 5. What did the girl forget to do? — 6. What was the consequence? — 7. On the girl's entering the Dean's presence, what did he say?

25. Dean Swift.

As the late Dean Swift was once upon a journey, attended by a servant, they put up at an inn, where they lodged all night. In the morning, the Dean called for his boots; the servant immediately took them to him. When the Dean saw them, «How is this, Tom», says he, «my boots are not clean?» «No, Sir», replied Tom; «as you are going to ride, I thought they would soon be dirty again, so I did not clean them». Very well», said the Doctor, «go and get the horses ready». In the mean time the Dean ordered the landlord to let his servant have no breakfast. When the servant returned, he asked if the horses were ready. «Yes, Sir», was the answer. «Go, bring them out», said the Doctor. «I have not had my breakfast yet», replied Tom. «Oh, no matter for that», said his master, if you had, you would soon be hungry again». They mounted, and rode off.

Questions.

1. Where was the late Dean Swift once, and what did he do? — 2. For what did he call in the morning? — 3. What did he say to his servant? — 4. What was Tom's reply? — 5. What did the Doctor say to this, and what did he do in the mean time? — 6. What did the servant say, when the Doctor bade him bring out the horses? — 7. What was his master's reply?

26. Swift Teaching Good Manners.

A friend of Dean Swift one day sent him a turbot, as a present, by a servant who had frequently been on similar errands, but had never yet received the most trifling mark of the Dean's generosity. Having gained admission, he opened the door of the study, and abruptly putting down the fish, cried very rudely: «Master has sent you a turbot». «Heyda! young man», said the Dean, rising from his easy chair, «is that the way you deliver your message? Let me teach you better manners; sit down in my chair, we will change situations, and I will show you how to ·behave in future». The boy sat down, and the Dean, going to the door, came up to the table with a respectful pace, and making a low bow, said: «Sir, my master presents his kind compliments, hopes your Reverence is well, and begs your acceptance of a turbot».—«Does he», replied the boy. «Here John, take this honest lad down into the kitchen, and give him as much as he can eat and drink; then send him up to me, and I will give him half a crown».

Questions.

1. What present had a friend of Dean Swift sent him one day, and by whom? — 2. Had this servant ever received any mark of the Dean's generosity? — 3. What did the servant do and say, when he had gained admission?—4. What did the Dean say? — 5. Whither did the Dean go, when the boy was sitting down, and what did he say, when he had made a low bow? — 6. What did the boy reply?

27. Jonathan Swift.

In one of his letters, Pope gives the following illustration of Dean Swift's eccentricity:

Dean Swift has an odd, blunt way, that is mistaken by strangers for ill nature: it is so odd that there is no describing it but by facts. I'll tell you one that first comes into my head.

One evening, Gay and I went to see him: you know how intimately we were all acquainted. On our coming in, «Heyday, gentlemen», says the doctor, «what's the meaning of this visit? How came you to leave all the great lords that you are so fond of, to come hither to see a poor dean?» «Because we would rather see you than any of them». «Ay, any one that did not know you so well as I do might believe you. But since you have come I must get some supper for you, I suppose». «No, doctor, we have supped already». «Supped already? That's impossible: why, it is not eight o'clock yet. That's very strange: but if you had not supped, I must have got something for you. Let me see; what should I have had? A couple of lobsters? Ay, that would have done very well—two shillings; tarts, a shilling».

«But you will drink a glass of wine with me, though you supped so much before your usual time, only to spare my pocket». «No, we had rather talk with you than drink with you». «But if you had supped with me, as in all reason you ought to have done, you must then have drunk with me. A bottle of wine, two shillings. Two and two are four, and one is five; just two and sixpence a piece. There, Pope, there's half a crown for you; and there's another for you, Sir; for I won't save any thing by you, I am determined».

This was said and done with his usual seriousness on such occasions; and, in spite of every thing we could say to the contrary, he actually obliged us to take the money.

Questions.

1. What does Pope give in one of his letters? — 2. What had Dean Swift about him, and how can it only be described?

3. Where did Gay and Pope go one evening? — 4. What did the Doctor say on their coming in? — 5. What did the two poets answer? — 6. What did the Dean reply to this? — 7. What did he say when told that they had supped already?

8. How did he invite his friends to take a glass of wine with him? — 9. On being told that they had rather talk with him than drink with him, what did he say?

10. How was all this said and done, and what did he actually oblige them to do?

---

28. Sir Walter Scott.

When Sir Walter Scott was a schoolboy, between ten and eleven years of age, his mother one morning saw him standing still in the street, and looking at the sky, in the midst of a tremendous thunderstorm. She called to him repeatedly, but he did not seem to hear: at length he returned into the house, and told his mother that if she would give him a pencil, he would tell her why he looked at the sky. She acceded to his request, and in a few minutes he laid on her lap the following lines:

«Loud o'er my head what awful thunders roll!
What vivid lightnings flash from pole to pole!
It is thy voice, O God, that bids them fly;
Thy voice directs them through the vaulted sky;
Then let the good thy mighty power revere;
Let hardened sinners thy just judgments fear.»

4

Questions.

1. When Walter Scott was between ten and eleven years of age, what did his mother see him doing? — 2. Did he take notice, when she called him? — 3. When he returned into the house, what did he tell his mother? — 4. What lines did he present to her a few minutes after?

---

29. Walter Scott at School.

It appears that when this celebrated author was at school, though very laborious, his intelligence was not brilliant, and his great success in after-life was owing to his indefatigable perseverance.

The following anecdote is found in his autobiography published some years since.

«There was», says Walter Scott, «a boy in my class, who stood always at the top, and I could not with all my efforts supplant him. Day came after day, and still he kept his place; till at length I observed that, when a question was asked him, he always fumbled with his fingers at a particular button on the lower part of his waistcoat while seeking an answer. I thought, therefore, if I could remove the button slily, the surprise at not finding it might derange his ideas at the next interrogation of the class, and give me a chance of taking him down. The button was therefore removed without his perceiving it. Great was my anxiety to know the success of my measure, and it succeeded but too well.

«The hour of interrogation arrived, and the boy was questioned: he sought, as usual, with his fingers, for the friendly button, but could not find it. Disconcerted he looked down, the talisman was gone, his ideas became confused, he could not reply. I seized the opportunity, answered the question, and took his place, which he never recovered, nor do I believe he ever suspected the author of the trick.

«I have often met with him since we entered the world, and never without feeling my conscience reproach me. Frequently have I resolved to make him some amends by rendering him a service; but an opportunity did not present itself, and I fear I did not seek one with as much ardour as I sought to supplant him at school».   W. S.

Questions.

1. To what was Sir Walter indebted for his great success? — 2. What could Sir Walter not do with regard to a boy in his class? — 3. What did Sir

Walter observe regarding the boy above him in the class?— 4. What did Walter Scott do to the boy? — 5. What did the boy seek? — 6. What was the consequence, when the boy did not find the button? — 7. What did Walter Scott do, when the boy could not answer the question? — 8. What did Sir Walter feel, and what did he resolve to do?

30. Sheridan.

Sheridan was one day much annoyed by a fellow member of the House of Commons, who kept crying out every few minutes: «Hear! hear!» During the debate he took occasion to describe a political cotemporary who wished to play the rogue, but had only sense enough to act the fool. «Where», exclaimed he, with great emphasis, «where shall we find a more foolish knave or a more knavish fool than he?» «Hear! hear!» was shouted by the troublesome member. Sheridan turned round, and, thanking him for the prompt reply, sat down amid a general roar of laughter.

Questions.

1. By whom was Sheridan one day much annoyed? 2. — 2. Whom did he describe during the debate? — 3. What did he exclaim? — 4. What was shouted by the troublesome member? — 5. What followed?

31. The Value of Time.

King Alfred, who ascended the throne of England in 871 (eight hundred and seventy one), and who, like Charlemagne, by his magnanimity and wise government, acquired the title of the Great, was a prudent economist of time, well knowing that a moment lost can never be recovered. Alfred wished to divide the day into equal proportions, in order to appropriate a certain space of time to the accomplishment of the different objects he had in view.

This was not an easy matter, as clocks were at that time nearly unknown in Europe, and quite so in England. It is true that in fine weather the flight of time could be marked, in some degree, by the course of the sun; but in the night, and when the sun was hidden by clouds, there were no means of judging.

The King, after much reflection, and many experiments, ordered a certain quantity of wax to be made into six candles of equal length and thickness, which being lighted one after the other, as he had found by experience, would last from mid-day to mid-day. On each of these candles, he marked twelve divisions or inches, so that he knew nearly how the day was going, as the consumption of each candle marked the expiration of a sixth part, or about four hours, and each division or inch denoted the lapse of twenty minutes.

By these means Alfred obtained what he desired, an exact admeasurement of time; and the improvements which took place during his reign show that both the King and his people had learned to appreciate its value.

Questions.

1. When did King Alfred ascend the throne of England? — 2. What title has he acquired? 3. By what virtues has he aquired this title? — 4. Of what was he a prudent economist, and why?—5. What did Alfred wish to divide, and for what purpose?
6. Why was this not an easy matter? — 7. When can the flight of time be marked by the course of the sun, and when is it impossible to do so?
8. What did the King, after many experiments, order to be made, and how long did the candles last?— 9. What did the King mark on each of the candles? —10. What mas marked by the consumption of them?—11. What was denoted by each division?— 12. What did Alfred obtain by these means? — 13. What do the improvements during his reign show?

---

32. Peter the Great.

It was the custom of Peter the Great to visit the different workshops and manufactories, not only to encourage them, but also to judge what other useful establishments might be formed in his dominions. Among the places he visited frequently, were the forges of Mr. Muller at Istia, ninety versts from Moscow. The Czar once passed a whole month there, during which time, after giving due attention to the affairs of state, which he never neglected, he amused himself with seeing and examining every thing in the most minute manner, and even employed himself in learning the business of a blacksmith. He succeeded so well, that on one of the last days of his remaining there, he forged eighteen poods of iron, and put his own particular mark on each bar. The boyars, and other noblemen of his suite were employed in blowing the bellows, stirring the fire, carrying coals, and performing the other duties of a blacksmith's assistant.

When Peter had finished, he went to the proprietor, praised his manufactory, and asked him how much he gave his workmen per pood.

«Three copeeks, or an altina», answered Muller. «Very well», replied the Czar, «I have then earned eighteen altinas». Muller fetched eighteen ducats, offered them to Peter, and told him, that he could not give a workman like his Majesty less per pood. Peter refused. «Keep your duc·ats», said he, «I have not wrought better than any other man; give me what you would give to another; I want to buy a pair of shoes, of which I am in great need». At the same time he showed him his shoes. which had been once mended, and were again full of holes. Peter accepted the eighteen altinas, and bought himself a pair of new shoes, which he used to show with much pleasure, saying: «These I earned with the sweat of my brow».

One of the bars of iron forged by Peter the Great, and authenticated by his mark, is still to be seen at Istia, in the forge of Muller. Another similar bar is preserved in the cabinet of curiosities at St. Petersburgh.

Questions.

1. What custom had Peter the Great? — 2. Why did he visit workshops and manufactories?—3. Whose forges did Peter frequently visit?—4. How long did the Czar stay at Istia? — 5. With what did he amuse himself during this time? — 6. What business did he learn? — 7. Did he neglect his affairs of state? — 8. How many poods of iron did Peter the Great forge in one of the last days of his remaining at Istia, and what did he put on each bar he had forged? — 9. What duties were the Boyars obliged to perform?

10. To whom did Peter go, when he had finished, and what did he praise? — 11. How much did Mr. Muller use to give his workmen per pood? — 12. How many altinas had the Czar earned? — 13. What did Mr. Muller tell the Czar? — 14. Did Peter accept the ducats? — 15. What did he say to Mr. Muller? — How were his shoes? — 17. What did Peter buy for his eighteen altinas? — 18. Why did he always show these shoes with so much pleasure?

19. What is still to be seen at Istia? — 20: Where is another similar bar preserved?

---

33. Newton and the Shepherd Boy.

This illustrious philosopher was once riding over Salisbury plain, when a boy keeping sheep called to him: «Sir, you had better make haste on, or you will get a wet jacket». Newton, looking around, and observing neither clouds nor a speck on the horizon, jogged on, taking very little notice of the rustic's information. He had made but a few miles, when a storm, suddenly arising, wet him to the skin. Surprised at the circumstance, and determined, if possible, to ascertain how an ignorant boy had attained a precision and knowledge in the weather, of which the wisest philosopher would be proud, he rode back, wet as he was. «My lad», said Newton, «I'll give thee a guinea, if thou wilt tell me how thou canst foretell the weather so truly». «Will ye, Sir? I will, then», said the boy, scratching his head, and holding out his hand for the guinea. «Now, Sir» (having received the money, and pointing to the sheep), «when you see that black ram turn his tail towards the wind, 'tis a sure sign of rain within an hour». «What!» exclaimed the philosopher, «must I, in order to foretell the weather, stay here and watch which way that black ram turns his tail?» «Yes, Sir». Off rode Newton, quite satisfied with his discovery, but not much inclined to avail himself of it, or to recommend it to others.

Questions.

1. Where was Newton once riding? — 2. What did a boy call to him? — 3. Did Newton take any notice of the rustic's information?—4. When he had made but a few miles, what happened? — 5. What did the philosopher then do, and what did he say to the shepherd? — 6. What was the boy's reply? — 7. What did Newton exlaim? — S. What did he think of his discovery?

34. Almanac Weather Wisdom.

An English paper tells a pleasing anecdote of Partridge, the celebrated almanac maker, about one hundred years since. In travelling on horseback into the country, he stopped for his dinner at an inn, and afterwards called for his horse, that he might reach the next town, where he intended to sleep.

If you will take my advice, Sir,» said the hostler, as he was about to mount his horse, «you will stay where you are for the night, as you will surely be overtaken by a pelting rain».

«Nonsense, nonsense», exclaimed the almanac maker»; «there is a sixpence for you, my honest fellow, and good afternoon to you».

He proceeded on his journey, and sure enough he was well drenched in a heavy shower. Partridge was struck by the man's prediction, and being always intent on the interest of his almanac, he rode back on the instant, aud was received by the hostler with a broad grin.

«Well, Sir, you see I was right after all».

«Yes, my lad, you have been so, and here is a crown for you; but I give it to you on condition that you tell me how you knew of this rain».

«To be sure, Sir», replied the man; «why, the truth is we have an almanac at our house called Partridge's *Almanac*, and the fellow is such a notorious liar, that whenever he promises us a fine day, we always know that it will be the direct contrary. Now, your Honour, this day, the 21st of June, is put down in our almanac indoors as «settled fine weather; no rain». I looked at that before I brought your Honour's horse out, and so was enabled to put you on your guard».

Questions.

1. Of whom does an English paper tell a pleasant anecdote? — 2. When and why did he stop? — 3. What did he do afterwards?

4. What did the hostler say to him, as he was about to mount his horse?

5. What did the almanac maker exclaim?

6. While proceeding on his journey, what happened? — 7. What did Partridge do on the instant, and how was he received by the hostler?

8. What did the hostler say, and what was Patridge's answer?

9. What was the man's reply?

---

35. Singular Cases of Inability to Distinguish Colours.

Mr. Harris, a shoemaker at Allonby, was unable from infancy to distinguish the cherries of a cherrytree from its leaves, in so far as colours were concerned. Two of his brothers were equally defective in this respect, and always mistook *orange* for *grass green*, and *light green* for *yellow*. Harris himself could only distinguish black from white. Mr. Scott, who describes his own case in the «Philosophical Transactions», mistook *pink* for a *pale blue*, and a full *red* for a full *green*. All kinds of yellows and blues, except sky blue, he could discern with great nicety. His father, his maternal uncle, one of his sisters, and her two sons, had all the same defect. A tailor at Plymouth, whose case is described by Mr. Harvey, regarded the solar spectrum as consisting only of *yellow* and *light blue*; and he could distinguish with certainty only *yellow*, *white*, and *green*. He regarded indigo and Prussian blue as black.

Questions.

1. What was Mr. Harris from infancy unable to do? — 2. For what did his brothers mistake *orange* and *light green*? — 3. What could Harris himself only distinguish? — 4. For what did Mr. Scott mistake *pink*, and a full *red*?

— 5. What colours could he discern correctly? — 6. Who had all the same defect? — How did a tailor at Plymouth regard the solar spectrum, and what could he distinguish with certainty? — 8. What did he regard as black?

36. Alick.

There is still living at Stirling a blind old beggar, known to all the country round by the name of Alick, who possesses a memory of almost incalculable strength. It was observed with astonishment, that when he was a man, and obliged by the death of his parents to gain a livelihood by begging through the streets of his native town of Stirling, he knew the whole of the Bible, both Old and New Testaments, by heart; from which you may repeat any passage, and he will tell you the chapter and verse; or you may tell him the chapter and verse, and he will repeat to you the passage, word for word. Not long since, a gentleman, to puzzle him, read, with a slight verbal alteration, a verse of the Bible. Alick hesitated a moment, and then told where it was to be found, but said it had not been correctly delivered. He then gave it as it stood in the book, correcting the slight error that had been purposely introduced. The gentleman then asked him for the ninetieth verse of the seventh chapter of Numbers. Alick was again puzzled for a moment, but then said hastily: «You are fooling me, Sir! there is no such verse. That chapter has only eighty-nine verses». Several other experiments of the sort were tried upon him with the same success. He has often been questioned the day after hearing any particular sermon or speech; and his examiners have invariably found that, had their patience allowed, blind Alick would have given them the sermon or speech.

Questions.

1. Who is still living at Stirling, and what does he possess? — 2. What was observed with astonishment? — 3. What did a gentleman do to puzzle him? — 4. What answer did Alick give? — 5. What did the gentleman then ask him for? — 6. What was Alick's reply? — 7. When questioning him the day after hearing any particular sermon or speech, what have his examiners invariably found?

37. Professor Porson.

Professor Porson, when a boy at Eton School, discovered the most astonishing powers of memory. In going up to a lesson one day, he was accosted by a boy on the same form, «Porson, what have you got there?» «Horace». Let me look at it». Porson handed the book to the boy, who, pretending to return it, dexterously substituted another in its place, with which Porson proceeded. Being called on by the master, he read and construed Carm. I, X. very regularly. Observing the class to laugh, the master said: «Porson, you seem to be reading on one side of the page, while I am looking at the other; pray, whose edition have you?» Porson hesitated. «Let me see it», rejoined the master who, to his great surprise, found it to be an English Ovid. Porson was ordered to go on, which he did easily, correctly and promptly, to the end of the ode.

Questions.

1. What did Professor Porson discover when a boy? — 2. What did a boy on the same form say to thim? — 3. When Porson handed his «Horace» to him, what did the boy do with it? — 4. Being called on by the master, what did he read and construe? — 5. On observing the class to laugh, what did the master say? — 6. When the master had looked at the book, what did he find it to be? — 7. What was Porson ordered to do, and how did he succeed?

---

38. The Travelling Library.

Professor Porson, the celebrated Grecian, was once travelling in a stage-coach, where a young Oxonian, fresh from college, was amusing the ladies with a variety of talk, and amongst other things, with a quotation, as he said, from Sophocles. A Greek quotation, and in a coach too, roused the slumbering professor from a kind of dog-sleep, in a snug corner of the vehicle. Shaking his ears and rubbing his eyes, «I think, young gentleman», said he, «you favoured us just now with a quotation from Sophocles; I do not happen to recollect it there». «O, Sir», replied the tyro, «the quotation is word for word as I have repeated it, and from Sophocles, too; but I suspect, Sir, it is some time since you were at college». The professor, applying his hand to his great-coat pocket, and taking out a small pocket edition of Sophocles, quietly asked him if he would be kind enough to show him the passage in question in that little book. After rummaging the pages for some time, he replied: «Upon second thoughts, I now recollect that the passage is in Euripides». «Then, perhaps, Sir», said the professor, putting his hand again into his pocket, and handing him a similar edition of Euripides, «you will be so good as to find it for

5

me in that little book«. The young Oxonian again returned to his task, but with no better success, muttering, however, to himself a vow never again to quote Greek in a stage-coach. The tittering of the ladies informed him plainly that he had got into a hobble. At last, «Why, Sir», said he, «how dull I am! I recollect now; yes, now I perfectly remember that the passage is in Aeschylus». The inexorable professor returned to his inexhaustible pocket, and was in the act of handing him an Aeschylus, when our astonished freshman vociferated: «Coachman! holloa, coachman! let me out; I say instantly let me out! There's a fellow here has the whole Bodleian library in his pocket».

Questions.

1. Who was once travelling in a stage-coach? — 2. With what was a young Oxonian amusing the ladies? — 3. What effect had the Greek quotation on the professor? — 4. What did he say to the young gentleman? — 5. What did the tyro reply? — 6. What did the professor take out of his pocket, and what did he ask his fellow traveller? — 7. What did the latter reply? — 8. What did the professor then do and say? — 9. Had the young Oxonian better success now? — 10. Of what did the tittering of the ladies inform him? — 11. What did he say at last? — 12. What followed?

39. The National Debt of England.

If a man was employed to count the national debt of England, supposing he reckoned 100 pieces every minute for 12 hours a day, it would require 30 years to count it in sovereigns, 600 years to count it in silver, and 14,400 years to count it in copper.

In shillings placed in a line, it would reach ten times round the earth, or once to the moon (240,000 miles).

Its weight in gold is 5,625 tons, in silver 89,000 tons, in copper 2,140,000 tons.

It would take 100 barges, 56 tons burden each, to carry it in gold, 1600 barges to carry it in silver, or 382,000 barges to carry it in copper. These would reach 5000 miles, if placed close to one another.

To carry it in copper, it would take upwards of 2,100,000 of carts, each one ton; to carry it in silver, nearly 90,000 carts, and to carry it in gold, 5,625 carts.

Questions.

1. How many years would it take to count the national debt of England in sovereigns, in silver, and in copper?
2. If it were placed in a line in shillings, how far would that line reach?
3. What is its weight in gold, in silver, and in copper?
4. How many barges would it take to carry it in gold, in silver, and in copper? — 5. How far would these barges reach?
6. How many carts would be required to carry it in copper, in silver, and in gold.

---

40. Doing Justice to the Consonants.

Mr. Jones, in his life of Bishop Horne, speaking of Dr. Hinchcliffe, Bishop of Peterborough, says, that in the pulpit he spoke with the accent of a man of sense, such as he really was in a superior degree; but it was remarkable, and, to those who did not know the cause, mysterious, that there was not a corner of the church, in which he could not be heard distinctly. The reason which Mr. Jones assigned was, that he made it an invariable rule *to do justice to every consonant, knowing that the vowels would speak for themselves.* And thus he became the surest and clearest of speakers; his elocution was perfect, and never disappointed his audience.

Questions.

1. What does Mr. Jones say of Dr. Hinchcliffe? — 2. What reason is assigned, why the Bishop could be heard distinctly in every corner of the church? —3. What did he thus become? — 4. How was his elocution?

---

41. Vulgar Pronunciation.

One of the peculiarities of vulgar English pronunciation is to put the letter *r* at the end of words ending with a vowel. Some of the inhabitants of London, if they had to speak the following sentence, «A fellow broke the window, and hit Isabella on the elbow, as she was playing a sonata on the piano», would give it in the following manner: «A fellor broke the windor, and hit Isabellar on the elbor, as she was playing a sonatar on the pianor». Others adopt the contrary plan, and leave out the *r* as often as they can. There are magistrates of high pretensions to education, who would say, «The conduct of the prisna' and his general characta' render it propa' that he should no longa' be a memba' of this community». Equally glaring is the taking away of *h* from places where it is required, and giving it where its absence is desirable. The termination of words ending in *ing* with a *k*, as *somethink*, is not less incorrect or less disagreeable. It is worth while accasionally to point out these errors, as many must be disposed to correct them, on being made aware of their existence.

Questions.

1. Mention one of the peculiarities of vulgar English pronunciation? — 2. How would some of the inhabitants of London give the following sentence: «A fellow broke the window, and hit Isabella on the elbow, as she was playing a sonata on the piano?» — 3. What plan do others adopt? — 4. What would magistrates of high presentions to education say? — 5. What mistake is equally glaring, and what not less incorrect? — Why is it worth while occasionally to point out these errors?

42. Lying Punished.

One day there happened a tremendous storm of lightning and thunder as Archbishop Leighton was gcing from Glasgow to Dunblane. He .was descried, when at a distance, by two men of bad character. They had not courage to rob him; but, wishing to fall on some method of extorting money from him, one said: «I will lie down by the wayside as if I were dead, and you shall inform the archbishop that I was killed by the lightning, and beg money of him to bury me». When the archbishop arrived at the spot, the wicked wretch told him the fabricated story. He sympathised with the surviver, gave him money, and proceeded on his journey. But, when the man returned to his companion, he found him really lifeless! Immediately he began to exclaim aloud: «Oh, Sir, he is dead! Oh, Sir, he is dead!» On this the archbishop, discovering the fraud, left the man with this important reflection: «It is a dangerous thing to trifle with the judgments of God!»

Questions.

1. What happened one day, as Archbishop Leighton was going to Dunblane? — 2. By whom was he descried?— 3. What method did they find out of extorting money from the Archbishop?— 4. What did he do, when the fabricated story was told him? — 5. What did the man find on returning to his companion, and what did he immediately exclaim? — 6. With what important reflection did the Archbishop leave the man?

43. Mr. Dodd.

Mr. Dodd, an eminent minister, being solicited to play at cards, arose from his seat, and uncovered his head. The company asked him what he was going to do. He replied: «To crave God's blessing». They immediately exclaimed : «We never ask a blessing on such an occasion». «Then», said he, «I never engage in anything but what I beg of God to give his blessing».

Questions.

1. What did Mr. Dodd do, when solicited to play at cards? — 2. What did the company ask him, and what was his reply?—3. What did they immediately exclaim? — 4. What did he say?

---

44. Private Prayer.

«*Acknowledge the Lord in all thy ways, and he shall direct thy paths*». Prov. An English clergyman, preaching from this text, observed as follows:

«Archbishop Cranmer, who died a martyr, said that the day he signed his recantation back to popery he omitted private prayer in the morning. This brought to my recollection the two memorable occurrences of my life, when I omitted private prayer, and went to my business. On each day I had an accident that nearly cost me my life; but in mercy I was spared to my family. Private prayer is a high privilege. I cannot neglect it any more than I can neglect my food. It is my grand stay for each day; and I feel that, unless I acknowledge God herein, I have no right to expect his guidance and protection».

Questions.

1. From what text did an English clergyman preach? — 2. What did he observe of Archbishop Cranmer? — 3. What two memorable occurrences did this circumstance bring to the clergyman's recollection?— 4. What is said of private prayer?

---

45. The Praying Little Girl.

A little girl in London, about four years of age, was one day playing with her companions. Taking them by the hand, she led them to a shed in the yard, and asked them all to kneel down, as she was going to pray to God Almighty; «but don't you tell my mamma», said she, «for she never prays, and would beat me, if she knew that I do».

Instead of keeping the secret, one of her playmates went directly, and told this little girl's mother, who was very much struck, but for the present took no notice. Some time after, on her going in doors, her mother asked her what she had been doing in the yard; she tried to avoid giving a direct answer. The question being repeated, the answer was the same; when her mother, however, promised not to be angry with her, and pressed the inquiry by very kind words, she said: «I have been praying to God Almighty». «But why do you pray to him»? «Because I know he hears me, and I love to pray to him». «But how do you know he hears you»? This was a difficult question, indeed, but mark her reply; putting her little hand to her heart, she said: «Oh, I know he does». This language pierced her mother's heart, who was a stranger to prayer, and she wept bitterly.

Let good children, therefore, do as this little girl did, bow their knees before God Almighty; and, however short and feeble their little prayers, they may be sure he hears them if they are offered in earnest; for he says: «I love them that love me; and they that seek me early shall find me».

Questions.

1. What was a little girl doing one day. — 2. Where did she lead them, and what did she ask them to do? — 3. Why were her companions not to tell her mamma?

4. What did one of her playmates do? — 5. What did her mother ask her some time after, and what did the little girl try to do? — 6. When the inquiry was pressed by very kind words, what did she say? — 7. Why did the little girl pray?—8. When asked how she knew God heard her, what did she say?— 9. What effect had these words on her mother?—10. What does God Almighty say?

---

46. A better Rule than «Expediency».

Lord Erskine, when at the bar, was always remarkable for the fearlessness with which he contended against the bench. In a contest he had with Lord Kenyon, he explained the rule and conduct at the bar in the following terms: «It was», said he, «the first command and council of my youth, always to do what my conscience told me to be my duty, and leave the consequences to God. I have hitherto followed it, and have no reason to complain that obedience to it has been even a temporal sacrifice; I have found it, on the contrary, the road to prosperity and wealth, and I shall point it out as such to my children».

Questions.

1. For what was Lord Erskine remarkable? — 2: With whom had he a contest?— 3. In what terms did he explain his rule and conduct at the bar?

---

47. The Missionary Money-box.

A few weeks since a trading vessel, laden with corn, from Cardigan, in Wales, was taken in the channel by an American privateer. When the captain went into the cabin to survey his prize, he espied a little box, with a hole in the top, similar to that which tradesmen have in their counters, through which they drop their money; and at the sight of it he seemed a little surprised, and said to the Welsh captain: «What is this?» pointing to the box with his stick. «Oh», said the honest Cambrian, « 'tis all over now.» «What?» asked the American. «Why, the truth is», replied the Welsh captain, «that I and my poor fellows have been accustomed, every Monday, to drop a penny each into that box, for the purpose of sending out missionaries *to preach the gospel to the heathen*, but it is all over now»! «Ah»! said the American, «that is very good»; and, after pausing a few minutes, he said: «Captain, I'll not hurt a hair of your head, nor touch your vessel». The pious Welshman was accordingly allowed to pursue his voyage unmolested.

Questions.

1. What happened to a trading vessel from Cardigan? — 2. What did the captain of the privateer espy in the cabin? — 3. What explanation did the Welsh captain give, when asked what the box was? — 4. What did the American say to this, and what did he add after a few minutes? — 5. What followed?

---

48. Dr. Franklin on Prayer.

When the American Convention was framing their constitution, Dr. Franklin asked them how it happened that, while groping, as it were, in the dark to find political truth, they had not once thought of humbly applying to the Father of lights to illumine their understandings. »I have lived, Sir», said he, «a long time, and the longer I live, the more convincing proofs I see of this truth, that God governs in the affairs of men;

and if a sparrow cannot fall to the ground without his notice, is it probable that an empire can rise without his aid? We have been assured, Sir,
in the Sacred Writings, that, except the Lord build the house, they labour in vain that build it. I firmly believe this; and I also believe that without his concurring aid we shall succeed in this political building no better
than the builders of Babel. We shall be divided by our little partial local
interests; our project will be confounded, and we ourselves become a
reproach and a byword down to future ages». He then moved that prayers
should be performed in that assembly every morning before they proceeded
to business.

Questions.

1. What did Dr. Franklin ask the American Convention? — 5. What statements
did he make? — 3. What did he then move?

---

49. Washington.

One Reuben Rouzy, of Virginia, owed the general about one thousand
pounds. While President of the United States, one of his agents brought
an action for the money; judgment was obtained, and execution issued
against the body of the defendant who was taken to jail. He had a considerable landed estate; but this kind of property cannot be sold in Virginia
for debts unless at the discretion of the person. He had a large family,
and for the sake of his children preferred lying in jail to selling his land.
A friend hinted to him that probably General Washington did not know
anything of the proceeding, and that it might be well to send him a petition, with a statement of the circumstances. He did so, and the very
next post from Philadelphia after the arrival of his petition in that city
brought him an order for his immediate release, together with a full discharge, and a severe reprimand to the agent for having acted in such a
manner. Poor Rouzy was, in consequence, restored to his family, who
never laid down their heads at night without presenting prayers to Heaven for their «beloved Washington». Providence smiled upon the labours of the grateful family, and in a few years Rouzy enjoyed the exquisite pleasure of being able to lay the one thousand pounds, with the
interest, at the feet of this truly great man. Washington reminded him that
the debt was discharged; Rouzy replied, the debt of his family to the
father of their country and preserver of their parent could never be discharged; and the General, to avoid the pleasing importunity of the grateful

Virginiau, who would not be denied, accepted the money, only, however, to divide it among Rouzy's children, which he immediately did.

Questions.

1. How much did Reuben Rouzy owe General Washington?—2. What did one of the general's agents do, and what was the consequence?— 3. What did the defendant possess? — 4. Why did he not sell his property to pay his debts?— 5. What did a friend hint to him? — 6. What did the next post bring him?— 7. What was the consequence? — 8. What was Rouzy enabled to do in a few years? — 9. What followed?

---

50. An Illustration of a Special Providence and of the Power of Prayer.

Captain H. and crew sailed some time since from the port of.— After having been at sea for several days they were assailed by an unusually severe storm, which continued forty-five days and nights in succession. They were driven far from their course by the violence of the wind. Nature had become nearly exhausted by hard and long toiling; and, to add to their affliction, famine began to threaten them with a death far more appalling than that of a watery grave.

The captain had with him his wife, two daughters, and ten persons besides. As their provisions grew short, his wife became provident and careful of the pittance that fell to their family share. She would eat but little lest her husband should starve. The children would eat but little for fear the mother would suffer, and the captain refused to eat any, but left his portion for his suffering family. At length they were reduced to a scanty allowance for twenty-four hours, in the midst of a storm and one thousand miles from land. Captain H. was a man who feared God. In this his extremity he ordered his steward to bring the remaining provision on deck, and spread the same on the tarpawling which covers the hatch; and, falling down beside the fragments of bread and meat before him, he lifted up his voice in prayer to Him who heareth out of the deep, and said: «O thou who didst feed Elijah by a raven while in the wilderness, and who commandedst that the widow's cruise of oil and barrel of meal should not fail, look down upon us in our present distress, and grant that this food may be so multiplied that the lives now in jeopardy may be preserved». After this he rose from his knees, went to the companion way, and found his

6

wife and children engaged in the same holy exercise. He exhorted them to pray on, and assured them that God had answered his prayer, and that not one soul then on board should perish. Scarcely had he uttered these words when his mate, who had been at the masthead for some time on the look-out, exclaimed: «Sail ahoy, sail ahoy! » At this crisis the captain shouted with swelling gratitude: «What, has God sent the ravens already!» and in one hour from that time, through the friendly sail, barrels of bread and meat were placed upon the deck.

Questions.

1. By what were Captain H.. and crew assailed? — 2. What had nature become, and with what did famine threaten them? 3. Whom had the captain with him? — 4. How did they care for each other? — 5. To what were they at length reduced? — 6. What was Captain H., and what did he do in this extremity? — 8. Where did he go after his prayer, and how did he find his family? — 8. What did he assure them of?—9. What happened immediately afterwards, and what exclamation did the captain make?

---

51. The Bible a Shield for Soul and Body.

When Oliver Cromwell entered upon the command of the parliament's army against Charles I, he ordered, all his soldiers to carry a Bible in their pockets. Among the rest there was a wild, wicked young fellow, who ran away from his apprenticeship in London for the sake of plunder and dissipation. This fellow was obliged to be in the fashion. Being one day ordered out upon a skirmishing party, or to attack some fortress, he returned back to his quarters in the evening without hurt. When he was going to bed, pulling the Bible out of his pocket, he observed a hole in it. His curiosity led him to trace the depth of this hole into his Bible; he found a bullet was gone as far as Ecclesiastes XI, 9. He read the verse: «Rejoice, oh young man, in thy youth, and let thy heart cheer thee in the days of thy youth, and walk in the ways of thy heart, and in the sight of thine eyes; but know thou that for all these things God will bring thee into judgment». The words were set home upon his heart by the Divine Spirit, so that he became a sound believer in the Lord Jesus Christ, and lived in London many years after the civil wars were over. He used pleasantly to observe to Dr. Evans, author of the Christian Temper, that the Bible was the means of saving both his soul and body.

What did Oliver Cromvell order all his soldiers to do? — 2. What sort of person was there among the rest? — 3. Where was he ordered out one day, and in what condition did he return to his quarters? — 4. What did he observe, when he was going to bed? — 5. How far was the bullet gone into the Bible? — 6. What effect did the words produce on him? — 7. What did he use to observe to Dr. Evans?

---

52. Honesty the Best Policy.

Some years since there resided in a country village a poor but worthy clergyman who, with the small stipend of forty pounds per annum, supported himself, a wife, and seven children. At one time, walking and meditating in the fields, in much distress from the narrowness of his circumstances, he stumbled on a purse of gold. Looking round, in vain, to find its owner, he carried it home to his wife, who advised him to employ at least a part of it in extricating them from their present difficulty; but he conscientiously refused until he had used his utmost endeavours to find out its former proprietor, assuring her *that honesty is always the best policy.* After a short time it was owned by a gentleman who lived at some little distance, to whom the clergyman returned it without any other reward than thanks. On the good man's return, his wife could not help reproaching the gentleman with ingratitude, and censuring the over-scrupulous honesty of her husband; but he only replied as before, *honesty is the best policy.* A few months after this the curate received an invitation to dine with the aforesaid gentleman; who, after hospitably entertaining him, gave him the presentation to a living of three hundred pounds per annum, to which he added a bill of fifty pounds for present necessities. The curate, after making suitable acknowledgements to his benefactor, returned with joy to his wife and family, acquainting them with the happy change in his circumstances, and adding that he hoped she would now be convinced that *honesty was the best policy;* to which she readily assented.

1. Who resided in a country village? — 2. What was he doing one day, and on what did he stumble — 3. On being advised to employ part of the money in extricating himself from his present difficulty, what did he reply? —

4. Was the purse owned by any one? — 5. Did the clergyman return the money, and what reward did he receive? — 6. What could the good man's wife, on his return, not help doing? — 7. What was his reply? — 8. What happened to the curate a few months after? — 9. How did the curate feel, and what did he say to his family?

---

53. Remarkable Escape from Danger.

There is a singular adventure, recorded by the Captain of a Guinea-man, and as it is not very long, it will be here related in the Captain's own words, for the amusement and advantage of our readers.

The ocean was very smooth, and the heat very great, which made us so languid, that almost a general wish overcame us on the approach of the evening. to bathe in the waters of the Congo. However, I and Johnson were deterred from it by an apprehension of Sharks, many of which we had observed in the progress of our voyage, and those very large. — Campbell alone, who had been drinking too much, was obstinately bent on going over board, and although we used every means in our power to persuade him to the contrary, he dashed into the water, and had swum some distance from the vessel, when we on board discovered an alligator, making towards him behind a rock that stood a short distance from the shore. — His escape I now considered impossible, and I applied to Johnson to know how we should act, who, like myself, affirmed the impossibility of saving him, and instantly seized upon a loaded carbine, to shoot the poor fellow, ere he fell into the jaws of the monster. I did not, however, consent to this, but waited, with horror, the event; yet, willing to do all in my power, I ordered the boat to be hoisted, and we fired two shot at the approaching alligator, but without effect; for they glided over his scaly covering, like hail stones on a tiled penthouse, and the progress of the creature was by no means impeded. The report of the piece, and the noise of the blacks from the sloop, soon made Campbell acquainted with his danger: he saw the creature making-towards him, and with all the strength and skill he was master of, he made for the shore. And now the moment arrived, in which a scene was exhibited, beyond the power of my humble pen perfectly to describe. On approaching within a very short distance of some canes and shrubs, that covered the banks, while closely pursued by the alligator, a fierce and ferocious tiger sprang towards him, at the instant the jaws of his first enemy were extended to devour him. —At this awful moment Campbell was preserved. The eager tiger, by overleaping, fell into the gripe of the alligator. A horrible conflict then ensued.—The water was coloured with the blood of the tiger, whose efforts to tear the scaly covering of the alligator were unavailing, while the latter had also the advantage of keeping his adversary under water, by which the victory was presently obtained; for the tiger's death was now effected. They both sunk to the bottom, and we saw no more of the alligator. Campbell was recovered, and instantly conveyed on board; he spoke not, while in the boat, though his danger had sobered him: but the moment he leaped on the deck, fell on his knees, and returned thanks to the Providence which had so protected him; and what is most singular, from that moment to the time I am now writing, he has never been seen the least intoxicated, nor has been heard to utter a single oath.

Questions.

1. What general wish overcame the persons on board the Guineaman?— 2. What deterred the Captain and Johnson from bathing?—3. On what was Campbell obstinately bent, and what did he do?—4. When he had swum some distance, what did those on board discover?—5. What did Johnson seize upon, and for what purpose? — 6. What did the captain order to be done, and how many shot did they fire, and with what effect? — 7. With what was Campbell made acquainted, and what did he see?—8. What happened on Campbell's approaching the bank? — 9. Describe the conflict between the tiger and the alligator?—10 Where was Campbell conveyed, and what effect had his remarkable escape on him?

54. Newfoundland Dogs.

A vessel was once driven by a storm on the beach, in the county of Kent, in England. Eight men were calling for help, but not a boat could be got off for their assistance... at length a gentleman came on the beach accompanied by his Newfoundland dog. He directed the attention of the noble animal to the vessel, and put a short stick into his mouth. The intelligent and courageous dog at once understood his meaning, and sprang into the sea, fighting his way through the foaming waves. He could not, however, get close enough to the vessel to deliver that with which he was charged, but the crew joyfully made fast a rope to another piece of wood, and threw it towards him... The sagacious dog saw the whole business in an instant, he dropped his own piece, and immediately seized that which had been cast to him; and then, with a degree of strength and resolution almost incredible, he dragged it through the surge, and delivered it to his master... By this means a line of communication was formed, and every man on board saved.

Sometimes the dog is rather officious in his demonstrations of affection, as the following story will show. — A boatman once plunged into the water to swim with another man for a wager. His Newfoundland dog, mistaking the purpose, and supposing that his master was in danger, plunged after him, and dragged him to the shore by his hair, to the great amusement of the spectators.

Questions.

1. Where was a vessel once driven by a storm? — 2. Who were calling for help, and why could they not be assisted?—3. Who came on the beach?— 4. To what did the gentleman direct the attention of the dog, and what did he put into his mouth? — 5. What did the intelligent dog then do, and how did the crew act?— 6. What did the dog at once see, and what did he do with the rope thrown towards him? — 7. What followed? — 8. What is the Newfoundland dog said sometimes to be?—9. What is related of a boatman and his Newfoundland dog?

55. A Priceless Dog.

A gentleman was lately returning from a visit to New - Orleans, in a steamer, with but a few passengers. Among the ladies, one especially interested him. She was the wife of a wealthy planter, returning with an only child to her father's house; and her devotion to this child was touching.

While passing through the canal of Louisville, the steamer stopped for a few moments at the quay. The nurse, wishing to see the city, was stepping ashore, when the child suddenly sprang from her arms into the terrible current that swept towards the falls, and disappeared immediately. The confusion which ensued attracted the attention of a gentleman who was sitting in the fore part of the boat, quietly reading. Rising hastily, he asked for some article the child had worn. The nurse handed him a tiny apron she had torn off in her efforts to save the child as it fell. Turning to a splendid Newfoundland dog that was eagerly watching his countenance the gentleman pointed first to the apron, and then to the spot where the child had sunk.

In an instant, the noble dog leapt into the water, and disappeared. By this time the excitement was intense, and some person on shore supposing that the dog was lost, as well as the child, procured a boat, and started to search for the body.

Just at this moment the dog was seen far away with something in his mouth. Bravely he struggled with the waves, but it was clear his strength was failing fast, and more than one breast gave a sigh of relief as the boat reached him, and it was announced that he was still alive. They were brought on board—the dog and the child.

Giving a single glance to satisfy herself that the child was really living, the young mother rushed forward, and sinking beside the dog, threw her arm around his neck, and burst into tears. Not many could bear the sight unmoved, and as she caressed and kissed his shaggy head, she looked up to his owner, and said:

«Oh, sir, I must have this dog, take all I have — everything — but give me my child's preserver».

The gentleman smiled, and patting his dog's head, said: «I am very glad, madam, he has been of service to you, but nothing in the world could induce me to part with him».

The dog looked as though he perfectly understood what they were talking about, and giving his sides a shake, laid himself down at his master's feet, with an expression in his large eyes, that said plainer than words: «No! nothing shall part us».

Questions.

1. From what place was a gentleman lately returning, and with whom? — 2. Who was the lady that especially interested him? — 3. What is said of her devotion to her only child?

4. Where did the steamer stop for a few moments? — 5. What happened as the child's nurse was stepping ashore? 6. Whose attention did the confusion attract? — 7. What did the gentleman ask for? — 8. What did the nurse hand him? — 9. What did the gentleman then do?

10. On the dog's disappearing in the water, what did a person on shore do? · 11. Where was the dog at this moment seen, and with what? — 12. Were the child and the dog saved?

13. How did the young mother act on finding that her child was really alive?

14. What did she say to the owner of the dog?

15. What did the gentleman answer?

16. How did the dog look, and what did he do?

56. Canine Sagacity.

The following story, which illustrates in a singular manner the communication of ideas between dogs, was told by a clergyman, as an authentic anecdote.

A surgeon of Leeds found a little spaniel who had been lamed. He carried the poor animal home, bandaged up his leg, and, after two or three days, turned him out. — The dog returned to the surgeon's house every morning, till his leg was perfectly well. At the end of several months, the spaniel again presented himself, in company with another dog, who had also been lamed; and he intimated, as well as piteous and intelligent looks could intimate, that he desired the same kind assistance to be rendered to his friend, as had been bestowed upon himself. A similar circumstance is stated to have occurred to Morant, a celebrated French surgeon.

The following instance also affords a remarkable proof of the sagacity of these animals. — A British officer in the 44th regiment, who had occasion when in Paris, to pass one of the bridges across the Seine, had his boots, which had been previously well polished, dirtied by a poodle dog rubbing against them. — He in consequence, went to a man who was stationed on the bridge, and had them cleaned. — The same circumstance having occurred more than once, his curiosity was excited, and he watched the dog. He saw him roll himself in the mud of the river, and then watch for a person with well polished boots, against which he contrived to rub himself. — Finding that the shoe black was the owner of the dog, he taxed him with the artifice; and after a little hesitation, he confessed, that he had taught the dog the trick in order to procure customers for himself. The officer being much struck with the dog's sagacity, purchased him at a high price, and brought him to England. He kept him tied up in London for some time, and then released him. The dog remained with him a day or two, and then made his escape. A fortnight afterwards he was found again in Paris playing his old tricks on the bridge as before.

Questions.

1. What does the above story illustrate? — 2. What did a surgeon of Leeds find, and what did he do to the dog? — 3. What did the dog do every morning? — 4. Who presented himself again at the end of several months, and with whom? — 5. What did he intimate?

6. What happened to a British officer on one of the bridges across the Seine? — 7. What did he do in consequence? —8. What did he see on watching the dog? — 9. What did the owner of the dog confess? — 10. What did the officer then do? — 11. How long did the dog, when released, remain with the officer, and where was he found a fortnight afterwards?

57. More Faithful than Favoured.

Sir Harry Lee of Ditchley, in Oxfordshire, ancestor of the Earls of Lichfield, had a mastiff which guarded the house and yard, but had never met with the least particular attention from his master, and was retained for his utility alone, and not from any particular regard. One night as his master was retiring to his chamber, attended by his valet, an Italian, the mastiff silently followed him up stairs, which he had never been known to do before, and, to his master's astonishment, presented himself in his bed room. Being deemed an intruder he was instantly ordered to be turned out; which being done, the poor animal began scratching at the door, and howling loudly for admission. The servant was sent to drive him away. Discouragement could not check his intended labour of love, or rather providential impulse; he returned again, and was more importunate than before to be let in. Sir Harry weary of opposition, bade the servant to open the door, that they might see what he wanted to do. This done the mastiff with a wag of his tail, and a look of affection at his Lord, deliberately walked up, and crawling under the bed, laid himself down, as if desirous to take up his night's lodging there. To save farther trouble, but not from any partiality for his company, the indulgence was allowed. About the solemn hour of midnight the chamber door was opened, and a person was heard stepping across the room: Sir Harry started from his sleep; the dog sprung from his covert, and seizing the unwelcome disturber, fixed him to the spot! All was dark; and Sir Harry rang his bell in great precipitation, in order to procure a light. The person who was pinned to the floor by the courageous mastiff, roared for assistance. It was found to be the valet, who little expected such a reception. He endeavoured to apologize for his intrusion, and to make the reasons, which induced him to take this step, plausible; but the importunity of the dog, the time, the place, the manner of the valet, all raised suspicion in Sir Harry's mind; and he determined to refer the investigation of the business

7

to a magistrate. The perfidious Italian, alternately terrified by the dread of punishment, and soothed with the hopes of pardon, at length confessed, that it was his intention to murder his master, and then rob the house, which design was only frustrated by the instinctive attachment of the dog to his master, which seemed to be directed on this occasion by the interference of Providence. A full length picture of the dog and his master, and the words «More faithful than favoured» are still to be seen at the family seat at Ditchley.

Questions.

1. What is said of Sir Harry's mastiff? — 2. What did he do one night? — 3. What followed? — 4. When Sir Harry bade the servant open the door, what did the mastiff do? — 5. What happened about the solemn hour of midnight?— 6. What did the perfidious Italian at last confess? — 7. What picture is still to be seen at the family seat at Ditchley, and what words are under it?

---

58. Bill, the Fire-escape Dog.

There is a fine band of men in London, who have charge of the fire-escapes: which are immense movable ladder-machines, by which people descend of themselves, or are conveyed, from the windows of a house on fire. Samuel Wood, one of the bravest of those men, has saved more than one hundred men, women, and children, from the flames! Much of Wood's success, however, is justly due to his wonderful little dog «Bill». Around his neck the parishioners of Whitechapel have placed a silver collar, in token of his valuable services during the nine years that he has filled the important post of «Fire-escape Dog».

Bill, like his master, has to be very wakeful, and at his post of duty during the whole of the night, and therefore he sleeps during the day close to his master's bed. He never attempts to run out of doors until the hour approaches at which they must go to the «Station».

Bill does not allow his master to sleep too long. He is sure to wake him, if he is likely to be late! How the dog knows the time is a puzzle, but know it he does! When the fire-escape is wheeled out of the Whitechapel Churchyard, at nine o'clock, Bill is promptly at his post. When an alarm of fire is heard, Bill, who is at other times very quiet, now begins to bark most furiously. Wood has no occasion to spring his rattle; for the policemen all around know Bill's bark so well that they at once come up to render help.

Il the alarm of fire takes place, when but few people are in the streets, Bill runs round to the coffee-honses near, and pushing open the doors, gives his well-known bark, as much as to say: «Come and help, men! come and help!» Bill has not to bark in vain. His call is cheerfully obeyed.

In dark nights the lantern has to be lit, when Bill seizes hold of it, and like a herald, runs on before his master. When the ladder is erected, Bill is at the top before his active master has reached half way! He jumps into the rooms, and amid thick smoke and the approaching flames. runs from room to room, helping his master to find and bring out-the poor inmates.

On one occasion, the fire burned rapidly, and the smoke in the room became so thick, that Wood and another man were unable to find their way out. They feared that escape was now hopeless. Bill seemed at once to understand the danger, in which his kind master was placed, and he began to bark. Half suffocated, Wood and his comrade knowing this to be the signal «Follow me», at once crawled after Bill, and in a few minutes they were led to the window, and thus their lives were saved.

Richly does Bill deserve his silver collar. It bears this inscription:

> I am the Fire-escape's man dog. My name is Bill.
> When «Fire» is called, I'm never still.
> I bark for my master; all danger I brave,
> To bring the escape, man's life for to save.

Poor Bill, like human beings, has had his trials and sufferings, as well as honours. At one fire, he fell through a hole burnt in the floor, into a tub of scalding water, from which he suffered dreadfully, and narrowly escaped a painful death. On three other occasions he had the misfortune to be run over; but, with careful doctoring, he was soon able to return to his duties *).

Questions.

1. What fine band of men is there in London? — 2. What are the fire-escapes? — 3. What is said of Samuel Wood and of his little dog Bill?

4 Where has Bill to be during the whole of the night, and where does he sleep during the day?

---

*) This famous dog died in 1861.

5. What is said of Bill's waking his master and knowing the time? — 6. When is Bill promptly at his post, and when does he begin to bark most furiously? — 7. Why has Wood no occasion to spring his rattle?

8. If the alarm of fire takes place, when but few people are in the streets, what does Bill do? — 9. Has he to bark in vain?

10. What is Bill's duty in dark nights? — 11. Where is Bill as soon as the ladder is erected? — 12. What does he then do?

13. What happened on one occasion, and how did Bill save his master and the other man?

14. What inscription does Bill's silver collar bear?

15. Describe some of poor Bill's trials and sufferings?

59. The Strictness of Discipline Rewarded.

The Empress Catherine being sick, the Czar went to the Fortress to perform his devotions; but it being midnight he found the gate shut. The sentinel cried out: «Who goes there?» «The Emperor!» «That is impossible; no one can know him at present, and we have strict orders not to allow any person whomsoever to come in». Peter at first did not recollect that this order had been given; he was not, however, displeased with the refusal of this brave soldier, and secretly congratulated himself, that discipline was so well attended to. «My friend», said he to the sentinel, «it is true that the prohibition does exist, but as sovereign I can revoke it». «You endeavour in vain to persuade me: you shall not enter». The monarch was delighted with this perseverance, and asked: «Who gave you this order?» «My corporal». «Call him». He came; the Prince, without saying who he was, ordered him to open the gate. «That is impossible; no one can enter, not even the emperor». «Who gave that order?». «My officer». «Let him be fetched; the Emperor wants to speak to him». The officer of the guard appeared, and Peter desired him also to open the gate. He ordered the sentinel to hold a lantern to the face of the unknown, and being convinced of the presence of his master, he suffered him to pass. The Czar, without speaking, went forward, and said his prayers; on his return from the church he entered the guardhouse, and announced to the soldier, the corporal, and the officer, whose denial he had received, that he promoted each of them to a higher rank. «Continue, my friends», said he on quitting them, «to observe the same strictness of discipline, and be assured you will always find me ready to recompense it».

Questions.

1. Where did the Czar go? — 2. What did the sentinel cry out, and what was the answer? — 3. What did the sentinel reply to it? — 4. On what did the Czar secretly congratulate himself? — 5. What did he say to the sentinel? — 6. What was the sentinel's reply? — 7. Whom did the Prince order to call, and what did he bid him do? — 8. To whom did the Emperor want to speak, and what did he desire him to do? — 9. How did the officer act? — 10. What did the Czar, on his return from the church, announce to the soldier, the corporal, and the officer, and what did he say on quitting them?

---

60. Thomson and Quin.

Thomson the poet, when he first came to London, was in very narrow circumstances, and was very often at a loss, where, or how to procure himself a dinner. Upon the publication of his Seasons, one of his creditors had him arrested, thinking that a proper opportunity to get his money. The report of this misfortune reached the ears of Quin, who had read the Seasons, but never seen their author: and he was told that Thomson was in a Spunging-house in Holborn. Thither Quin went, and being admitted into his chamber: «Sir», said he, «you do not know me, but my name is Quin». Thomson said, «that, though he could not boast of the honour of a personal acquaintance, he was no stranger either to his name or his merit»; and invited him to sit down. Quin then told him he was come to sup with him, and that he had already ordered the cook to provide supper, which he hoped he would excuse. When supper was over, and the glass had gone briskly about, Mr. Quin told him «it was now time to enter upon bnsiness». Thomson declared he was ready to serve him as far as his capacity would reach, in anything he might command (thinking he was come about some affair relating to the drama). «Sir», says Quin, «you mistake me. I am in your debt. I owe you a hundred pounds, and I am come to pay you». Thomson, with a disconsolate air, replied, that, as he was a gentleman whom he had never offended, he wondered he should seek an opportunity to banter with his misfortune. «No», said Quin, raising his voice: «I say I owe you a hundred pounds, and there it is» (laying a bank note of that amount before him). Thomson, astonished, begged he would explain himself. «Why», says Quin, «I will tell you. Soon after I had read your Seasons, I took it into my head, that, as I had something to leave behind me when

I died, I would make my will: and among the rest of my legatees I set down the author of the Seasons far a hundred pounds; and this day hearling that you were in this house, I thought I might as well have the pleasure of paying the money myself, as order my executor to pay it, when perhaps you might have less need of it; and this, Mr. Thomson, is my business». Of course Thomson left the house in company with his benefactor.

Questions.

1. For what was Thomson often at a loss? — 2. What happened to him after the publication of his Seasons? — 3. Who went to visit Thomson in the Spunging-house, and how did he introduce himself? — 4. What was Thomson's reply? — 5. What did Quin order? — 6. After supper what did Quin say? — 7. What did Thomson reply? — 8. How much did Quin say he owed Thomson? — 9. On Thomson's begging an explanation, what explanation did Quin give him?

---

61. The Whistle.

A true story — Written to his Nephew by Dr. Franklin.

When I was a child, at seven years old, my friends on a holiday filled my pockets with coppers. I went directly to a shop where they sold toys for children; and, being charmed with the sound of a *whistle*, that I met by the way in the hands of another boy, I voluntarily offered him all my money for one. I then came home, and went whistling all over the house, much pleased with my *whistle*, but disturbing the whole family. My brothers, and sisters, and cousins unterstanding the bargain I had made, told me I had given four times as much for it as it was worth. This put me in mind what good things I might have bought with the rest of the money; and they laughed at me so much for my folly, that I cried with vexation, and the reflection gave me more chagrin than the whistle gave me pleasure.

This, however, was afterwards of use to me, the impression continuing on my mind; so that often when I was tempted to buy some un- necessary thing, I said to myself, *Don't give too much for the whistle*; and so I saved my money.

As I grew up, came into the world, and observed the actions of men, I thought I met with many, very many, *who gave too much for their whistle*.

When I saw any one too ambitious of court favours, sacrificing his time in attendance on levees, his repose, his liberty, his virtue, and perhaps his friends, to attain it, I have said to myself: *This man gives too much for his whistle.*

When I saw another full of popularity, constantly employing himself in political bustles, neglecting his own affairs, and ruining them by that neglect: *He pays indeed*, say I, *too much for his whistle.*

If I knew a miser who gave up every kind of comfortable living, all the pleasures of doing good to others, all the esteem of his fellow citizens, and the joys of benevolent friendship, for the sake of accumulating wealth: *Poor man*, say I, *you do indeed pay too much for your whistle.*

Whe I meet a man of pleasure, sacrificing every laudable improvement of the mind, or of his fortune, to mere corporeal sensations: *Mistaken man*, say I, *you are providing pain for yourself instead of pleasure — you give too much for your whistle.*

If I see one fond of fine clothes, fine furniture, fine equipages, all above his fortune, for which he contracts debts, and ends his career in prison: *Alas!* say I, *he has paid dear, very dear, for his whistle.*

When I see a beautiful, sweet-tempered girl, married to an ill-natured brute of a husband: *What a pity it is*, say I, *that she has paid so much for a whistle.*

In short, I conceived that great part of the miseries of mankind were brought upon them by the false estimates they had made of the value of things, and by their giving too much for their *whistles.*

Questions.

1. When Franklin was a child, what did his friends do? — 2. What did F— do with the money? — 3. What did his brothers, etc. tell him?—4. What did the observation of F —'s brothers, etc. put him in mind of?—5. What use did F. derive from the remarks of his brothers, etc.? — 6. What did F — say to himself when he saw an ambitious man? — 7. And what, when he saw a man full of popularity? — 8. And what to the miser? And what to the man of pleasure?

62. A Trait of Lord Byron's Generosity, Humanity, and Tender-heartedness.

At Ellora, a sea-port very little known to Europeans, situate on the coast of Barbary, Lord Byron was leaning over the gangway of a vessel, looking at the sea serpents playing along-side, and enjoying the evening rays of the sun: these animals are, to all appearance, from six to twelve feet long, and proportionably large in circumference. While in this situation, his Lordship's gold watch fell from his jacket-pocket into the sea, and was plainly seen at the bottom, although in five fathoms of water. His Lordship said, «he would not have lost it for ten times its value». A sailor immediately undressed, and, diving down, succeeded in bringing up the watch, though sharks were very numerous round the vessel at the time, and so very ravenous, that several of them were caught with bait.

Lord Byron was not aware of the man's intention, or he never would have allowed him to run such a risk; he offered the man thirty dollars and a gallon of rum; the sailor said, «He would take the rum to drink his Lordship's health, but he never would take money for going over-board in a calm, for the watch of a man who would jump overboard in a gale of wind, to save a poor fellow's life!» The honest tar recollected the following noble trait of his Lordship's humanity: The ship had encountered a severe gale of wind off Cape Bon, that carried away her maintopmast in a heavy, deep, high rolling sea. A man stationed at the masthead fell with the mast, and, holding by one of the ropes floated about 20 fathoms from the ship's stern. He was hailed to hold fast, and the boat would be sent for him; the vessel, however, was nearly unmanageable, and the boat difficult to hoist out, being covered with part of the topmast. The man got weak, and at last called out that he could hold no longer, but must let go and submit. Every exertion to get out the boat seemed fruit-less, when Lord Byron stripped, and, taking a small rope in his hand, dashed into the waves, then running very high. Just as the poor fellow was sinking, he caught him by the hair of the head, and fastened the small rope round his arms; he was then hauled on board, and his life was saved. His Lordship, being an excellent swimmer, by help of the rope which the rescued man had hold of, made shift to get along-side, and was taken on board quite exhausted. The exertion threw him into a high fever, and he was confined to his bed for a week in a doubtful state. The poor fellow, whose life he had saved, stood sentinel at his cabin door, wishing he had been drowned rather than anything should have happened to his preserver; and the vessel exhibited the extraordinary spectacle of a dejected British crew. Not a word was to be heard but in whispers; and every one offered up prayers for Lord Byron's recovery. When he became so well as to reappear upon deck, they hailed it as a day of jubilee, and expressed their joy by three hearty cheers. The captain ordered them grog to drink his Lordship's health, and never did the cango merrier round. Every heart was filled with joy; and at the evening's dance, the preserved mariner presided, as master of the ceremonies, with grateful delight sparkling in his eyes.

The heart of Lord Byron was peculiarly tender. When at Genoa, he was in the practice of going on board the Blossom, sloop of war, without ceremony, at all hours. One day he climbed up the side, the crew were all arranged, and Captain Stewart was directing the punishment of an of·fender against discipline. No sooner did the poor fellow's cries, and the sound of the lash, reach his Lordship's ears, than he tottered to a gun for support, and was seized with a violent sickness. The lash was sus·pended, and the officers crowded round, anxious to know the cause. When a little recovered, he inquired if the man's crime was theft, mutiny or lying. «Drunkenness!» was the reply. «Then let me beg of you to pardon him this time». Captain Stewart read the man a lecture, and complied with his Lordship's request, who privately sent him some mon·ey, and a message enjoining him sobriety in future. He was several days affected with this painful circumstance, and said «he would not have heard the punishment for a thousand pounds».

Questions.

1. Where was Lord Byron? — 2. What was he doing? — 3. What is the length of the sea-serpents? —· 4. What happened to Lord Byron? — 5. What did His Lordship say? — 6. What did a sailor do?

7. What did Lord Byron offer the man? — 8. What did the man say? — 9. What had happened to the ship off Cape Bon? — 10. What became of the man at the mast·head, and what did Lord Byron do? — 11. What were the consequences to Lord Byron? — 12. What were the poor fellow's thoughts, and what did the vessel exhibit? — 13. How did the crew, on Lord Byron's reappearance upon deck, express their joy, and what did the captain order? — 14. Who presided at the evening's dance, and in what quality?

15. What did Lord Byron find, one day, on arriving on board «the Blos-som»? — 16. What happened to Lord Byron, when the poor fellow's cries and the sound of the lash reached his Lordship's ears? — 17. What did he inquire? — 18. What did he beg of the captain, and what was the consequen-ce? — 19. What did Lord Byron afterwards do, how did he feel, and what did he say?

8

63. The Chimney-sweepers' Feast, or the Lost Child Found.

There was formerly at London, on the first of May of every year, a superb feast given to the chimney-sweepers of the metropolis, at Montagu-House, Cavendish-Square, the town residence of the Montagu family. The custom is said to have taken its origin from the following circumstance:

Lady Montagu, being at her country-seat as usual in the summer, used to send her little boy Edward to walk every day with the footman, who had strict orders never to lose sight of him. One day, however, the servant, meeting an old acquaintance, went into an alehouse to drink, and left the little boy running about by himself. After staying some time drinking, the footman came out to look for the child to take him home to dinner, but he could not find him. He wandered about till night, enquiring at every house, but in vain, no Edward could be found. The poor mother, as may well be imagined, was in the greatest anxiety about the absence of her dear boy; but it would be impossible to describe her grief and despair, when the footman returned, and told her he did not know what had become of him. People were sent to seek him in all directions; advertisements were put in all the newspapers; bills were stuck up in London, and in most of the great towns of England, offering a considerable reward to any person who would bring him, or give any news of him. All endeavours were, however, unsuccessful, and it was concluded that the poor child had fallen into some pond, or that he had been stolen by gipsies, who would not bring him back for fear of being punished.

Lady Montagu passed two long years in this miserable uncertainty: she did not return to London as usual in the winter, but passed her time in grief and solitude in the country. At length one of her sisters married, and, after many refusals, Lady Montagu consented to give a ball and supper on the occasion at her town-house. She arrived in London to superintend the preparations, and while the supper was cooking, the whole house was alarmed by a cry of, fire!

It appears that one of the cooks had overturned a saucepan, and set fire to the chimney. The chimney-sweepers were sent for, and a little boy was sent up; but the smoke nearly suffocated him, and he fell into the fire-place. Lady Montagu came herself with some vinegar and a smelling-bottle; she began to bathe his temples and his neck, when suddenly she screamed out, Oh! Edward! — and fell senseless on the floor. She soon recovered, and taking the little sweep in her arms, pressed him to her bosom, crying: «It is my dear Edward! It is my lost boy»!

It appears she had recognised him by a mark on his neck. The master-chimney-sweeper, on being asked where he had obtained the child, said he had bought him about a year before of a gipsy woman, who said he was her son. All that the boy could remember was, that some people had given him fruit, and told him they would take him home to his mamma; but that they took him a long way upon a donkey, and after keeping him a long while, they told him he must go and live with the chimney-sweep who was his father: that they had beaten him so much whenever he spoke of his mamma and of his fine house, that he was almost afraid to think of it. But he said his master, the chimney-sweeper, had treated him very well.

Lady Montagu rewarded the man handsomely, and from that time she gave a feast to all the chimney-sweepers of the Metropolis on the first of May, the birth-day of little Edward, who always presided at the table, which was covered with the good old English fare, roast beef, plum pudding, and strong beer. This circumstance happened many, many years ago, and Lady Montagu and Edward are both dead; but the first of May is still celebrated as the chimney-sweepers' holiday, and you may see them on that day in all parts of London, dressed in ribbons and all sorts of finery, dancing to music at almost every door, and beating time with the implements of their trade.

Questions.

1. What was formerly at London? — 2. What used Lady M. to do? — 3. What did the servant do, and what was the consequence? — 4. How did the poor mother feel? — 5. What was the result of all the endeavours to find the boy, and what was concluded? — 6. How did Lady M. pass her time, and how long? — 7. By what was the house alarmed? — 8. Who were sent for, and what was the consequence?— 9. What did Lady M. do? — 10. What happened to Lady M., and what did she do afterwards? — 11. How did she recognise her son? — 12. What did the chimney-sweeper say about the child? — 13. What could the boy remember? — 14. How did Lady M. reward the man? — 15. What did she always give? — 16. Who presided at the feast, and of what did it consist? — 17. How is the first of May still celebrated in London?

64. A Nobleman and his Noble Servant.

A Russian nobleman was travelling in the early part of the winter over a bleak plain. His carriage rolled up to an inn, and he demanded a relay of horses to go on. The innkeeper entreated him not to proceed, for there was danger abroad; the wolves were out. He thought the object of the man was to keep him as a guest for the night; and saying it was too early in the season for wolves, ordered the horses to be put to. In spite of the continued warnings of the landlord, the carriage drove away, with the nobleman, his wife, and their only daughter.

On the box of the carriage was a serf, who had been born on the nobleman's estate, and who loved his master as he loved his life. They rolled on over the hardened snow, and there seemed no signs of danger. The moon began to shed her light, so that the road appeared like polished silver. At length the little girl said to her father: «What is that strange dull sound that I just heard»? Her father replied: «Nothing but the wind sighing through the trees of the forest we have just passed». The child shut her eyes, and was quieted for the time; but in a few minutes, with a face pale with affright, she turned to her father, and said: «Surely, that was not the wind; I heard it again, did you not hear it too? Listen!» The nobleman listened, and far, far away in the distance behind him, but distinct enough in the clear, frosty air, he heard a sound, which he knew the meaning of, though they did not.

He put down the glass, and speaking to the serf, said: «I think they are after us; we must make haste; tell the post-boy to drive faster, and get your musket and pistols ready; I will do the same; we may yet escape».

The man drove faster; but the mournful howling, which the child had first heard, began to come nearer and nearer, and it was perfectly clear to the nobleman that a pack of wolves had got scent, and were in pursuit of them. Meanwhile he tried to calm the anxious fears of his wife and child. At last the baying of the pack was distinctly heard, and he said to his servant: «When they come up with us, single you out the leader, and fire; I will single out the next, and, as soon as one falls, the rest will stop to devour him: that will be some delay at least.

By this time they could see the pack fast approaching with their long measured tread, a large dog-wolf leading. They singled out two, and they fell; the pack immediately turned on their fallen comrades, and soon tore them to pieces. The taste of blood made the others advance with more fury, and they were again soon baying at the carriage. Again the nobleman and his servant fired, and two more fell, which were instantly devoured as before; but the next post-house was still far distant.

The nobleman then cried to the post-boy: «You must let one of the horses loose from the carriage, iu order that, when the wolves come up to him, their destruction of the horse may gain us a little time». This was done, and the horse was left on the road: «in a few minutes they heard the loud agonizing shriek of the poor animal as the wolves tore him down. Again they urged on the carriage, but again their enemies were in full pursuit. A second horse was sent adrift, and shared the same fate as his fellow.

At length the servant said to his master: «I have served you since I was a child, and I love you as I love my own life; it is perfectly clear to me that we cannot all reach the post-house alive; I am quite prepared, and I ask you to let me die for you». «No», said the master, «we will live together, or die together; it must not be so». But the entreaties of the man at length prevailed. «I shall leave my wife and children to you; you will be a father to them; you have been a father to me; when the wolves next reach us, I will jnmp down and do my best I can to arrest their progress».

The carriage rolls on as fast as the two remaining horses can drag it! the wolves are close on their track, and almost dash against the doors of the carriage. Presently is heard the discharge of the servant's pistols as he leaps from his seat. Soon the door of the post-house is reached, and the family is safe.

They went to the spot the following morning, where the wolves had pulled the devoted servant to pieces. There now stands a large wooden cross, erected by the nobleman, with this text upon it: «Greater love has no man than this, that one lay down his life for his friend».

Questions.

1. When and where was a Russian nobleman travelling? — 2. What did he demand, when arrived at the inn? — 3. What did the innkeeper entreat him not to do, and why? — 4. What did the nobleman think, and what followed?

5. Who was on the box of the carriage? — 6. What did the little girl say to her father? — 7. What did the father reply? — 8. What did the child do, a few minutes after, and what did she say? — 9. What did the nobleman hear?

10. What did the nobleman then say to the serf?

11. What did the nobleman tell his servant to do, when the baying of the pack was distinctly heard?

12. Describe the shooting of the four wolves?

13. What did the nobleman then cry to the post-boy, and what followed?

14. Mention the words, and describe the death of the devoted servant?

15. What words were written on the wooden cross erected by the nobleman to the memory of his servant?

---

65. Miss Burney.

Miss Burney, afterwards Madame D'Arblay, wrote her celebrated novel of *Evelina* when only seventeen years of age, and published it without the knowledge of her father who, having occasion to visit the metropolis, soon after it had issued from the press, purchased it as the work then most popular, and most likely to prove an acceptable treat to his family.

When Dr. Burney had concluded his business in town, he went to Chessington, the seat of Mr. Crisp, where his family were on a visit. He had scarcely dismounted and entered the parlour, when the customary question of «What news»? was rapidly addressed to him by the several personages of the little party. «Nothing», said the worthy doctor, «but a great deal of noise about a novel which I have brought you».

When the book was produced, and the title read, the surprised and conscious Miss Burney turned away her face to conceal the blushes and delighted confusion which otherwise would have betrayed her secret; but the bustle which usually attends the arrival of a friend in the country, where the monotonous but peaceful tenor of life is agreeably disturbed by such a change, prevented the curious and happy group from observing the agitation of their sister.

After dinner, Mr. Crisp proposed that the book should be read. This was done with all due rapidity; when the gratifying comments made during its progress, and the acclamations which attended its conclusion, ratified the approbation of the public. The amiable author, whose anxiety and pleasure could with difficulty be concealed, was at length overcome by the delicious feeling of her heart; she burst into tears, and throwing herself on her father's neck, avowed herself the author of *Evelina*.

The joy and surprise of her sisters, and still more of her father, cannot easily be expressed. Dr. Burney, conscious as he was of the talents of his daughter, never thought that such maturity of observation and judgment, such fertility of imagination and chasteness of style, could have been displayed by a girl of seventeen — by one who appeared a mere infant in artlessness and inexperience, and whose deep seclusion from the world had excluded her from all visual knowledge of its ways.

Soon after 1774, she settled at Rome, and was admitted a member of the Academy of the Arcadi, under the name of Corilla Olympica, and for some time continued to charm the inhabitants of Rome by her talents in improvisation. At length, when Pius VI became Pope, he determined that she should be solemnly crowned—an honour which had been granted to Petrarch only.

Twelve members of the Arcadian Academy were selected out of thirty, publicly to examine the new edition of the «Tenth Muse», which has so often been dedicated to ladies of poetical and literary talents. Three several days were allotted for this public exhibition of poetical powers, on the following subjects: — sacred history, revealed religion, moral philosophy, natural history, metaphysics, epic poetry, legislation, eloquence, mythology, fine arts, and pastoral poetry.

In the list of examiners appeared a prince, an archbishop, three monseigneurs, the Pope's physician, *abati*, *avocati*, all of high rank in literature and criticism. · These severally gave her subjects which, besides a readiness at versification in all the measures of Italian poetry, required science, reading, and knowledge of every kind.

In these severe trials she acquitted herself to the satisfaction and astonishment of all the personages, clergy, literati, and foreigners then resident at Rome. Among the latter was the brother of George III, the Duke of Gloucester. Nearly fifty sonnets, by different poets, with odes, canzoni, terze rime, attave, canzonetti, etc., produced on the subject of the event, are inserted at the end of a beautiful volume containing the description of the order and ceremonials of this splendid, honourable, and enthusiastic homage paid to poetry, classical taste, talents, literature, and the fine arts.

Questions.

1. At what age did Miss Burney publish her *Evelina*, and without whose knowledge? — 2. What book did her father purchase, and why?

3. Where did Dr. Burney go, when he had concluded his business in town? — 4. What question was adressed to him, when he had entered the parlour, and what was his answer?

5. When the book was produced, what effect had it on Miss Burney, and what prevented the happy group from observing the agitation of their sister?

6. What did Mr. Crisp propose after dinner, and how was the approbation of the public ratified? — 7. How did the amiable author feel, and what avowal did she make to her father?

8. What is said of the joy and surprise of her father and sisters?

9. Where did she settle soon after 1774, and of what was she admitted a member?

10. What did Pius VI determine?

11. Who were selected to examine the new edition of the «Tenth Muse»? — 12. On what subjects did this public exhibition take place.

13. Who appeared in the list of examiners, and what did the subjects they gave her require? — 14. How did she acquit herself in these severe trials?

66. The Generous Cateran.

Early in the last century, John Gunn, a noted Cateran, or Highland robber, infested Inverness-shire, up to the walls of the provincial capital. A garrison was then maintained in the castle of that town; and their pay was usually transmitted in specie, under the guard of a small escort. It chanced that the officer who commanded this little party was unexpectedly obliged to halt, about thirty miles from Inverness, at a miserable inn. About night-fall, a stranger, in the Highland dress, and of a very prepossessing appearance, entered the same house. Separate accommodation being impossible, the Englishman offered the newly-arrived guest a part of his supper, which was accepted with reluctance. By the conversation he found his new acquaintance knew well all the passes of the country, which induced him eagerly to request his company on the ensuing morning. He neither disguised his business and charge, nor his apprehensions of that celebrated freebooter, John Gunn. The Highlander hesitated a moment, and then frankly consented to be his guide. Forth they set in the morning; and in travelling through a solitary and dreary glen, the discourse again turned on John Gunn. «Would you like to see him?» said his guide; and, without waiting for an answer to this alarming question, he whistled, and the English officer, with his small party, were surrounded by a body of well armed Highlanders, whose numbers put resistance out of question. «Stranger», resumed the guide, «I am that very John Gunn by whom you feared to be intercepted, and not without cause; for I was come to the inn last night with the express purpose of learning your route, that I and my followers might ease you of your charge by the road. But I am incapable of betraying the trust you reposed in me, and having convinced you that you were in my power, I can only dismiss you un-plundered and uninjured». He then gave the officer directions for his journey, and disappeared with his party, as suddenly as they had presented themselves. (Walter Scott).

Questions.

1. What did John Gunn infest? — 2. What was maintained in the castle of Inverness, and how was the pay of the garrison transmitted? — 3. What happened to the officer who commanded the little party? — 4. Who entered the inn at night-fall, and what did the Englishman offer the newly-arrived guest? — 5. What did the officer find, and whose company did he request? — 6. Did the Highlander consent? — 7. What did he say to the English officer, as they were travelling through a solitary glen, and what followed? — 8. What explanation did the guide then give to the stranger, and how did he act afterwards?

----

67. Singular Instance of Generosity.

About thirty years ago, Mr. B. having at that time newly commenced business in Edinburgh, was returning on horseback from the city to a cottage he had near Cramond. It was a wild night in November, and though he usually took the shortest way home, he resolved, this evening, on account of the increasing darkness, to keep on the high road. When he had proceeded about three miles from the town, and had come to the loneliest part of the way, he was suddenly arrested by a man who sprang out of a small copse at the road side, and seized the bridle of his horse. Mr. B. was a man of great calmness and resolution, and asked the man the reason of his behaviour, without betraying the smallest symptoms of agitation. Not so that assailant. He held the bridle in his hand, but Mr. B. remarked that it trembled excessively. After remaining some time, as if irresolute what to do, and without uttering a word, he let go his hold of the bridle, and said in a trembling voice: «Pass on, Sir, pass on!» — and then he added: »Thank God, I am yet free from crime». Mr. B. was struck with the manner and appearance of the man,

9

and said: «I fear you are in distress, is there any thing in which a stranger can assist you?» «Strangers may, perhaps», replied the man in a bitter tone: for nothing is to be hoped from friends». «You speak, I hope, under some momentary feeling of disappointment». «Pass on, pass on!» he said impatiently: «I have no right to utter any complaints to you. Go home and thank God, that a better spirit withheld me from my first intention, when I heard you approach — or this might have been» — he suddenly paused. «Stranger», said Mr. B. in a tone of real kindness: «you say, you have no right to utter your complaints to me; I have certainly no right to pry into your concerns, but I am interested, I confess, by your manner and appearance, and I frankly make you an offer of any assistance I can bestow». «You know not», replied the stranger, «the person to whom you make this generous proposal — a wretch stained with vices — degraded from the station he once held, and on the eve of becoming a robber — aye», he added with a shudder, «perhaps a murderer». I care not, I care not, for your former crimes, — sufficient for me that you repent them — tell me wherein I can stand your friend». «For myself I am careless», replied the man; «but there is one who looks to me with eyes of quiet and still unchanged affection, though she knows that I have brought her from a house of comfort to share the fate of an outcast and a beggar. I wished for her sake once more to become respectable, to leave a country where I am known, and to gain character, station, wealth — to all which she is so justly entitled — in a foreign land; but I have not a shilling in the world». He here paused, and Mr. B. thought, he saw him weep. He drew out his pocket book, and unfolding a bank bill, he put it into the man's hand, and said: «Here is what I hope will ease you from present difficulties, it is a note for a hundred pounds». The man started as he received the paper, and said in a low subdued tone: «I will not attempt to thank you, Sir — may I ask your name and address?» Mr. B. gave him what he required. «Fare well, Sir», said the stranger, «when I have expiated my fault, by a life of honesty and virtue, I will pray for you: till then, I dare not». Saying these words, he bounded over the hedge and disappeared. Mr. B. rode home wondering at the occurrence; and he has often said since, that he never derived so much pleasure from a hundred pounds in his life. He related the adventure to several of his friends, but as they were not all endowed with the same liberality of spirit as himself, he was rather laughed at for his simplicity; and in the course of a few years, an increasing and very prosperous business drove the transaction almost entirely from his mind. One day, however, about twelve years after the adventure, he was sitting with a few friends after dinner, when a note was put into his hand, and the servant told him, that the Leith carrier had brought a hogshead of claret into the hall. He opened the note, and found it to contain an order for a hundred pounds, with interest up to that time, accompanied with the strongest expression of gratitude for the service done to the writer long ago. It had no date, but informed him that he was happy, that he was respected, and that he was admitted partner in one of the first mercantile houses in the city where he lived. Every year the same present was continued, always accompanied by a letter. Mr. B., strange to say, made no great effort to discover his correspondent. At last he died, and the secret of, who the mysterious correspondent might be, seemed in a fair way of dying along with him. But the story is not yet done. When the funeral of Mr. B. had reached the Grey-friars church yard, the procession was joined by a gentleman, who got out of a very elegant carriage at the door of the church. He was a tall, handsome man about five and forty years of age, dressed in the deepest mourning. There were no armoreal bearings on the panels of his carriage, he was totally unknown to all the family, and after the ceremony, during which he appeared to be deeply affected, he went up to the chief mourner, and said: «I hope, Sir, you will excuse the intrusion of a stranger; but I could not refrain from paying the last tribute of respect to an excellent gentleman who was, at one time, more my benefactor than any person living». Saying this he bowed, stepped quickly into his carriage, and disappeared. There can be no doubt, that this was the individual, who had been rescued, by the prompt benevolence of Mr. B. — from sin and misery.

Questions.

1. What was Mr. B. doing about thirty years ago? — 2. Why did he keep on the high road? — 3. What happened when he had come to the loneliest part of the way? — 4. What did Mr. B — ask the man, and what did the latter say? — 5. What did Mr. B— then say, and what was the man's reply? — 6. Give a further account of their conversation? — 7. On receiving the bank note from Mr. B—; what did the man say and do? — 8. What were Mr. B's feelings with regard to the hundred pounds? — 9. What happened one day,

when Mr. B. was sitting with a few friends after dinner? — 10. What was every year continued? — 11. Describe the appearance of the gentleman who joined the funeral procession? — 12. What did he do and say after the ceremony?

---

68. Bradford the Innkeeper.

Jonathan Bradford kept an inn in Oxfordshire, on the London road to Oxford. He bore a respectable character. Mr. Hayes, a gentleman of fortune, being on his way to Oxford on a visit to a relation, put up at Bradford's. He there joined company with two gentlemen, with whom he supped, and in conversation unguardedly mentioned that he had then about him a considerable sum of money. In due time they retired to their respective chambers; the gentlemen to a two-bedded room, leaving, as is customary with many, a candle burning in the chimney corner. Some hours after they were in bed, one of the gentlemen being awake, thought he heard a deep groan in an adjoining chamber; and this being repeated, he softly awoke his friend. They listened together, and the groans increasing, as of one dying and in pain, they both instantly arose, and proceeded silently to the door of the next chamber, from which the groans had seemed to come. The door being ajar, they saw a light in the room. They entered, but it is impossible to paint their consternation on perceiving a person weltering in his blood in the bed, and a man standing over him with a dark lantern in one hand, and a knife in the other! The man seemed as much petrified as themselves, but his terror carried with it all the appearance of guilt. The gentlemen soon discovered that the murdered person was the stranger, with whom they had that night supped, and that the man, who was standing over him, was their host. They seized Bradford directly, disarmed him of his knife, and charged him with being the murderer. He assumed by this time the air of innocence, positively denied the crime, and asserted that he came there with the same humane intentions as themselves; for that, hearing a noise, which was succeeded by a groaning, he got out of bed, struck a light, armed himself with a knife for his defence, and had but that minute entered the room before them. These assertions were of little avail: he was kept in close custody till the morning, and then taken before a neighbouring justice of the peace. Bradford still denied the murder, but with such

apparent indications of guilt, that the justice hesitated not to make use
of this extraordinary expression, on writing his mittimus, «Mr. Bradford,
either you or myself committed this murder».

This remarkable affair became a topic of conversation to the whole
country. Bradford was condemned by the general voice of every company.
In the midst of all this predetermination, came on the assizes at Oxford.
Bradford was brought to trial; he pleaded not guilty. Nothing could be
stronger than the evidence of the two gentlemen. They testified to the
finding Mr. Hayes murdered in his bed, Bradford at the side of the body
with a light and a knife, and that knife, and the hand which held it,
bloody. They stated that, on their entering the room, he betrayed all the
signs of a guilty man; and that, but a few minutes preceding, they had
heard the groans of the deceased.

Bradford's defence on his trial was the same as before: he had heard
a noise; he suspected that some villainy was transacting; he struck a light,
snatched up the knife, the only weapon at hand, to defend himself, and
entered the room of the deceased. He averred that the terrors he betrayed
were merely the feelings natural to innocence, as well as guilt, on beholding so horrid a scene. The defence, however, could not but be considered as weak, contrasted with the several powerful circumstances
against him. Never was circumstancial evidence so strong, so far as it
went. There was little need for comment from the judge in summing up
the evidence, no room appeared for extenuation; and the prisoner was
declared guilty by the jury, without their even leaving the box.

Bradford was executed shortly after, still declaring that he was not
the murderer, nor privy to the murder, of Mr. Hayes; but he died, dis-
believed by all.

Yet were these assertions not untrue! The murder was actually committed by the footman of Mr. Hayes; and the assassin, immediately on
stabbing his master, rifled his pockets of his money, gold watch, and
snuff-box, and then escaped back to his own room. This could scarcely
have been effected, as after-circumstances showed, more than two seconds
before Bradford's entering the unfortunate gentleman's chamber. The world
owed this information to remorse of conscience on the part of the footman
(eighteen monhts after the execution of Bradford), when laid on a bed
of sickness. It was a death bed repentance, and by that death the law
lost its victim.

It were to be wished that this account could close here, but there is more to be told. Bradford, though innocent of the murder, and not even privy to it, was nevertheless a murderer in design. He had heard, as well as the footman, what Mr. Hayes had declared at supper, having a sum of money about him ; and he went to the chamber of the deceased with the same intentions as the servant. He was struck with amazement on beholding himself anticipated in the crime. He could not believe his senses; and in turning back the bed clothes to assure himself of the fact, he in his agitation dropped his knife on the bleeding body, by which means both his hands and the weapon became bloody. These circumstances Bradford acknowledged to the clergyman who attended him after sentence, but who, it is extremely probable, would not believe them at the time.

Besides the graver lesson to be drawn from this extraordinary case, in which we behold the simple intention of crime so signally and wonderfully punished, these events furnish a striking warning against the careless, and, it may be, vain display of money or other property in strange places. To heedlessness on this score the unfortunate Mr. Hayes fell a victim. The temptation, we have seen, proved too strong for two persons out of the few who heard his ill timed disclosure.

Questions.

1. Where did Jonathan Bradford keep an inn, and what character did he bear ? — 2. What is said of Mr. Hayes? — 3. What did the two gentlemen do on hearing the groans in the abjoining chamber ? — 4. What did they perceive on entering the chamber? — 5. What is said of the man with the dark lantern and the knife? — 6. What did the gentlemen discover, and what followed?

7. When the assizes at Oxford came on, what did the two gentlemen testify and state ?

8. What is said of Bradford's defence on his trial, and what was he declared by the jury?

9. By whom was the murder actually committed, and to what circumstance did the world owe this information?

10. In what sense was Bradford nevertheless a murderer, and what circumstances did he acknowledge to the clergyman who attended him after sentence?

11. What lesson may be drawn from this extraordinary case, and what warning do these events furnish ?

69. Fingal outwitting the Scotch Giant.

Fingal was a giant, and no fool of one, and any one that affronted him was sure of a beating. But there was a giant in Scotland as tall as the mainmast, more or less, as we say when we a'n't quite sure. This Scotch giant heard of Fingal, and how he had beaten every body, and he said: «Who is this Fingal? I'll just walk over and see what he's made of». So he walked across the Irish channel, and landed within half a mile of Belfast, and I suspect that he was not dry-footed.

When Fingal heard that this great chap was coming over, he was in a devil of a fright, for they told him that the Scotchman was taller by a few feet or so. So Fingal kept a sharp look-out for the Scotchman, and one fine morning, there he was, sure enough, coming up the hill to Fingal's house. If Fingal was afraid before, he had more reason to be afraid, when he saw the fellow; for he looked for all the world like the Monument *) upon a voyage of discovery. So Fingal ran into his house, and called to his wife Shaya, «my vourneen **)», says he, «be quick now; there's that big bully of a Scotchman coming up the hill. Cover me up with the blankets, and if he asks who is in bed, tell him it's the child». So Fingal lay down on the bed, and his wife had just time to cover him up, when in comes the Scothman, and though he stooped low, he broke his head against the portal. «Where's Fingal?» says he, rubbing his forehead; show him to me, that I may give him a beating». «Whist, whist»! cries Shaya, «you'll wake the baby, and then him that you talk of beating will be the death of you, if he comes in». «Is that the baby?» cried de Scotchman with surprise, looking at the great carcass muffled up in the blankets. «Sure it is», replied Shaya, «and Fingal's baby too; so don't you wake him, or Fingal will twist your neck in a minute». «By the cross of St. Andrew», replied the giant, then it's time for me to be off; for if that's his baby, I'll be but a mouthful to the fellow himself. Good morning to ye». So the Scotch giant ran out of the house, and never stopped to eat or drink until he got back to his own hills; foreby he was nearly drowned in having mistaken his passage across the Channel in his great hurry. Then Fingal got up and laughed, as well as he might, at his own acuteness; and so ends my story about Fingal.   (Marryat).

---

*) Здѣсь подразумѣвается монументъ, воздвигнутый въ Лондонѣ въ память великаго пожара въ 1666 году.

**) My vourneen или mavourneen (по ирландски), моя возлюбленная!

Questions.

1. What is said about Fingal? — 2. How tall was the Scotch giant? — 3. What did he hear of Fingal, and what did he say? — 4. Which channel did he walk across, and where did he land? 5. When Fingal heard that this great chap was coming over, what did he feel? — 6. What did he then do, and what happened? — 7. How did the Scotch fellow look? — 8. What did Fingal say to his wife Shaya? — 9. What did the Scotchman say on coming in? — 10. What was Shaya's answer? — 11. What did the Scotchman say to this, and what did Shaya reply? — 12. What did the giant then say and do? — 13. What did Fingal do, after the Scoth giant had gone? .

70. The Adventure of My Aunt.

My aunt was a lady of large frame, strong mind, and great resolution; she was what might be termed a very manly woman. My uncle was a thin, puny, little man, very meek and acquiescent; it was observed that he dwindled and dwindled gradually away, from the day of his marriage. My aunt, however, took all possible care of him; all was in vain. My uncle grew worse and worse the more dosing and nursing he underwent, until in the end he added another to the long list of matri‑monial victims who have been killed with kindness. My aunt took on mightily for the death of her poor dear husband. Perhaps she felt more compunction at having given him so much physic and nursed him into his grave. At any rate, she did all that a widow could do to honour his memory. She spared no expense in either the quantity or quality of her mourning weeds: she wore a miniature of him about her neck as large as a little sundial; and she had a full-length-portrait of him always hang‑ing in her bedchamber. All the world extolled her conduct to the skies; and it was determined that a woman, who behaved so well to the me‑mory of one husband, deserved soon to get another. It was not long after this that she went to take up her residence in an old country-seat in Derbyshire, which had long been in the care of merely a steward and a housekeeper. She took most of her servants with her; intending to make it her principal abode. The house stood in a lonely, wild part of the country, among the gray Derbyshire hills, with a murderer hanging in chains on a bleak height in full view. The servants from town were half

frightened out of their wits at the idea of living in such a dismal pagan-
looking place, especially when they got together in the servants' hall in
the evening, and compared notes on all the hobgoblin stories they had
picked up in the course of the day. They were afraid to venture alone
about the gloomy, black-looking chambers. My aunt herself seemed to
be struck with the lonely appearance of the house. Before she went to
bed, therefore, she examined well the fastnesses of the doors and windows, locked up the plate with her own hands, and carried the keys,
together with a little box of money and jewels, to her own room; for she
was a notable woman, and always saw to all things herself. Having put
the keys under her pillow, and dismissed her maid, she sat by her toilet,
arranging her hair; when all of a sudden she thought she heard something move behind her. — She looked hastily round, but there was nothing to be seen, nothing but the grimly painted portrait of her poor dear
man, which had been hung against the wall. She gave a heavy sigh to
his memory, as she was accustomed to do, whenever she spoke of him
in company, and then went on adjusting her night-dress. Her sigh was
re-echoed, or answered by a long-drawn breath. She looked round again,
but no one was to be seen. She ascribed these sounds to the wind oozing
through the rat-holes of the old mansion, and proceeded leisurely to put
her hair in papers, when, all at once, she thought she perceived one of
the eyes of the portrait move.

So strange a circumstance, as you may well suppose, gave her a
sudden shock. To assure herself of the fact, she put one hand to her
forehead as if rubbing it; peeped through her fingers, and moved the
candle with the other hand. The light of the taper gleamed on the eye,
and was reflected from it. She was sure it moved. Nay more, it seemed
to give her a wink, as she had sometimes known her husband to do when
living. It struck a momentary chill to her heart; for she was a lone woman, and felt herself fearfully situated.

The chill was but transient. My aunt became instantly calm and collected; she went on adjusting her dress. She even hummed an air, and
did not make a single false note. She casually overturned a dressing box,
took a candle, and picked up the articles one by one from the floor, pursued a rolling pincushion that was making the best of its way under the
bed, then opened the door, looked for an instant into the corridor, as if
in doubt whether to go, and then walked quietly out. She hastened down

stairs, ordered the servants to arm themselves with the weapons that first came to hand, placed herself at their head, and returned almost immediately. Her hastily levied army presented a formidable force. The steward had a rusty blunderbuss, the coachman a loaded whip, the footman a pair of horse-pistols, the cook a huge chopping-knife, and the butler a bottle in each hand. My aunt led the van with a red-hot poker, and, in my opinion, she was the most formidable of the party. The waiting-maid, who dreaded to stay alone in the servants' hall, brought up the rear, smelling to a bottle of volatile salts, and expressing her terror of the ghosts.

«Ghosts!» said my aunt resolutely. «I'll singe their whiskers for them!»

They entered the chamber. All was still and undisturbed as when she had left it. They approached the portrait of my uncle. «Pull me down that picture!» cried my aunt. A heavy groan, and a sound like the chattering of teeth, issued from the portrait. The servants shrunk back; the maid uttered a faint shriek, and clung to the footman for support.

«Instantly!» added my aunt, with a stamp of the foot. The picture was pulled down, and from a recess behind it, in which had formerly stood a clock, they hauled forth a round-shouldered, black-bearded varlet, with a knife as long as my arm, but trembling all over like an aspen leaf. The vagabond was a loose idle fellow of the neighbourhood, who had once been a servant in the house, and had been employed to assist in arranging it for the reception of its mistress. He confessed that he had stolen into her chamber to violate her purse, and rifle her strong box, when all the house should be asleep. He had contrived his hiding-place for his nefarious purposes, and had borrowed an eye from the portrait by way of a reconnoitring hole.

My aunt was a woman of spirit, and apt to take the law in her own hands. She had her own notions of cleanliness also. She ordered the fellow to be drawn through the horsepond, to cleanse away all offences, and then to be well rubbed down with an oaken towel.

Questions.

1. Describe my aunt? — 2. Give a description of my uncle and his illness? — 3. What is said of my aunt's conduct after her husband's death? — 4. Where did she go to take up her residence? — 5. Where did the house stand? — 6.

What did the servants do in the evening? — 7. What did my aunt do before she went to bed? — 8. What did she think she heard? — 9. What followed? — 10. What did she do to assure herself of the fact, and what was the result? — 11. When my aunt had become calm and collected, what did she do? — 12. Describe her hastily collected army?

13. When the waiting-maid expressed her terror of the ghosts, what did my aunt say?

14. What did my aunt cry on approaching my uncle's picture, and what followed?

15. Who was hauled forth from a recess behind the picture? — 16. Who was the vagabond, and what did he confess?

17. What punishment did my aunt assign to the varlet?

---

71. James V travelling in Disguise.

James V, King of Scotland, had a custom of going about the country disguised as a private person, in order that he might hear complaints which might not otherwise reach his ears, and, perhaps, that he might enjoy amusements which he could not have partaken of in his avowed royal character.

Upon such an occasion King James fell into a quarrel with some gipsies, or rather vagrants, and was assaulted by four or five of them. This chanced to be very near the Bridge of Cramond; so the King got on the Bridge which, as it was high and narrow, enabled him to defend himself with his sword against the number of persons by whom he was attacked. There was a poor man thrashing corn in a barn near by, who came out on hearing the noise of the scuffle, and seeing one man defending himself against numbers, gallantly took his part with his flail to such purpose, that the gipsies were obliged to flee. The husbandman then took the King into the barn, brought him a towel and water to wash the blood from his face and hands, and finally walked with him a little way towards Edinburgh, in case he should be again attacked. On the way, the King asked his companion what and who he was. The labourer answered that his name was John Howieson, and that he was a bondsman on the farm of Braehead, near Cramond, which belonged to the King of Scotland. James then asked the poor man, if there was any wish in the world, which he would particularly desire to see gratified; and honest John confessed, he should think himself the happiest man in Scotland, were he but proprietor of the farm on which he wrought as a labourer. He then asked the King, in return, who he was; and James replied, as usual, that he was the Goodman of Ballengiech, a poor man, who had a small appointment about the palace; but he added, that if John Howieson would come to see him on the next Sunday, he would endeavour to repay his manly assistance, and, at least, give him the pleasure of seeing the royal apartments.

John.put on his best clothes, and appearing at a postern gate of the palace, inquired for the Goodman of Ballengiech. The King had given orders that he should be admitted; and John found his friend, the Goodman, in the same disguise which he had formerly worn. The King, still preserving the character of an inferior officer of the household, conducted John Howieson from one apartment of the palace to another, and was amused with his wonder and his remarks   At length he asked him if he should like to see the King; to which John replied, nothing would delight him so much, if he could do so without giving offence. The Goodman of Ballengiech, of course, undertook that the King would not be offended. «But», said John, «how am I to know his Grace from the nobles who will be about him?» — «Easily», replied his companion; «all the others will be bare-headed — the King alone will wear his hat or bonnet.»

So speaking, King James introduced the countryman into a great hall which was filled by the nobility and officers of the crown. John was a little frightened, and drew close to his attendant, but was still unable to distinguish the King. «I told you that you should know him by his wearing his hat», said his conductor. «Then», said John, after he had again looked around the room, «it must be either you or me, for all but us two are bare-headed.»

The King laughed at John's fancy; and, that the good yeoman might have occasion for mirth also, he made him a present of the farm of Braehead, on condition that John Howieson, or his successors, should be ready to present a ewer and basin for the King to wash his hands, when his Majesty should come to Holyrood palace, or should pass the Bridge of Cramond. Accordingly, in the year 1822, when George IV came to Scotland, the descendant of John Howieson of Braehead, who still possesses the estate which was given to his ancestor, appeared at a solemn festival, and offered his Majesty water from a silver ewer, that he might perform the service by which he held his lands.   (Walter Scott).

Questions.

1. What was James V accustomed to do, and for what purpose?
2. By whom was King James assaulted? — 3. Where did this happen, and how was the King enabled to defend himself? — 4. Who took the King's part, and what was the conseqnence? — 5. Where did the husbandman then take the King, and what else did he do? — 6. What question did James V put to his companion? — 7. What was the labourer's answer? — 8. What did James then ask the poor man, and what did honest John confess? — 9. What did the latter ask the King, in return. and what was James's reply?

10. For whom did John inquire on the next Sunday? — 11. What orders had the King given, and in what disguise did John find his friend? — 12. What did the King then do, and with what was he amused? — 13. What did the King ask John, and what was the answer? — 14. What did John then say? — 15. What did his companion reply?

16. Where did King James introduce the countryman? — 17. What did the King then say, and what answer did John give?

18. What present did the King make the yeoman, and on what condition? — 19. What happened in the year 1822?

---

72. James Crichton.

Among the favourites of nature, that have from time to time appeared in the world, none seems to have been more exalted above the common rate of humanity, than the man. known by the appellation of the Admirable Crichton; whatever we may suppress of his history as surpassing credibility, yet we shall relate enough to rank him among prodigies.

«Virtue», says Virgil, «is better accepted when it comes in a pleasing form»; but his beauty was consistent with such activity and strength, that in fencing he would spring at one bound the length of twenty feet upon his antagonist; and he used the sword in either hand with such force and dexterity, that scarce any one had courage to engage him.

Having studied at St. Andrew's in Scotland, he went to Paris in his twenty-first year, and affixed on the gate of the college of Navarre a kind of challenge to the learned of that university to dispute with him on a certain day, offering to his opponents, whoever they should be, the choice of ten languages, and of all the sciences. On the day appointed three thousand auditors assembled, four doctors of the church and fifty masters appeared against him; and one of his antagonists confesses that the doctors were defeated, that he gave proofs of knowledge above the reach of man, and that a hundred years, passed without food or sleep, would not be sufficient for the attainment of his learning. After a disputation of nine hours, he was presented by the president and professors with a diamond and a purse of gold, and dismissed with repeated acclamations.

From Paris he went to Rome, where he made the same challenge, and had in the presence of the Pope and cardinals the same success. He then visited Padua, where he engaged in another public disputation, beginning his performance with an extemporal poem in praise of the city and the assembly then present, and concluding with an oration equally unpremeditated in commendation of ignorance.

Besides these stupendous acquisitions of learning, Crichton practised in great perfection the arts of drawing and painting; he was an eminent performer in both vocal and instrumental music; he danced with uncommon gracefulness, and on the day after his disputation at Paris exhibited his skill in horsemanship before the court of France, where at a public match of tilting, he bore away the ring upon his lance fifteen times together.

He excelled likewise in games of less dignity and reputation: in the interval of his challenge and disputation at Paris, he spent so much of his time at cards, dice, and tennis. that a lampoon was fixed upon the gate of the Sorbonne, directing those who would see this monster of erudition, to look for him at the tavern.

So extensive was his acquaintance with life and manners, that in an Italian comedy composed by himself, and exhibited before the court of Mantua, he is said to have acted fifteen different characters. He had such power of memory, that once hearing an oration of an hour, he would repeat it exactly, and in the recital follow the speaker through all his variety of tone and gesticulation.

Nor was his skill in arms less than in learning, or his courage inferior to his skill. There was a prize-fighter at Mantua, who travelled about the world, according to the barbarous custom of that age, as a general challenger, and had defeated the most celebrated masters in many parts of Europe. In Mantua where he then resided, he had killed three that appeared against him. The Duke repented that he had granted him protection; when Crichton, looking on his sanguinary success with indignation, offered to stake fifteen hundred pistoles, and mount the stage against him. The Duke with some reluctance consented, and on the day fixed the combatants appeared: their weapon seems to have been the rapier which was then newly introduced into Italy. The prize-fighter advanced with great violence end fierceness, and Crichton contented himself calmly to ward his passes, and suffered him to exhaust his vigour by his own fury. Crichton then became the assailant, and pressed upon him with such force and agility, that he thrust him thrice through the body, and saw him expire: he then divided the prize he had won among the widows whose husbands had been killed.

The Duke of Mantua having received so many proofs of his various merits, made him tutor to his son Vincentio of Gonzaga, a prince of loose manners and turbulent disposition. But his honour was of short continuance: for as he was one night, in the time of carnival, rambling about the streets, with his guitar in his hand, he was attacked by six men masked. Neither his courage nor his skill in this exigence deserted him: he opposed them with such activity and spirit, that he soon dispersed them, and disarmed their leader who, throwing off his mask, discovered himself to be the Prince, his pupil. Crichton, falling on his knees, took his own sword by the point, and presented it to the Prince who immediately seized it, and instigated, as some say, by jealousy, according to others only by drunken fury and brutal resentment, thrust him through the heart.

Thus was the Admirable Crichton brought into that state, in which he could excel the meanest of mankind only by a few empty honours paid to his memory: the Court of Mantua testified their esteem by a public mourning, the contemporary wits were profuse of their encomiums, and the palaces of Italy were adorned with pictures, representing him on horseback, with a lance in one hand, and a book in the other.

(Samuel Johnson).

Questions.

1. What is said about the Admirable Crichton, and his history?

2. What does Virgil say? — 3. Give a description of Crichton's beauty, strength, and dexterity?

4. Where did he go in his twenty-first year, and what did he affix on the gate of the college of Navarre? — 5. How many auditors assembled, and who appeared against Crichton? — 6. What does one of his antagonists confess? —

7. With what was Crichton presented after the disputation, aud how was he dismissed?

8. What is mentioned about Crichton's residence at Rome? — 9. State his performances at Padua?

10. Mention Crichton's attainments in drawing, painting, music, dancing, and horsemanship?

11. What is stated about his excellence in games of less dignity?

12. Give proofs of his extensive acquaintance with life and manners, and of his power of memory?

13. What do we read of the prize-fighter at Mantua, and how many pistoles did Crichton offer to stake? — 14. Describe Crichton's combat with the prize-fighter, and his generous conduct to the widows whose husbands had been killed?

15. To what place was Crichton appointed by the Duke of Mantua? — 16. Describe the unfortunate death of Crichton?

17. How did the court of Mantua and the public honour the memory of the Admirable Crichton?

---

73. Sir Sidney Smith's Escape.

Sir Sidney Smith, who was charged by Admiral Hood with the duty of burning the French fleet at Toulon, in 1793, fell into the hands of the French two years later, and was treated with considerable severity as a prisoner of war. Confined in the Temple, that gloomy prison in Paris, in which the unfortunate Louis the Sixteenth and Marie Antoinette spent their last days, the unwholesome closeness of his dungeon brought on an illness which for a time threatened to put an end to his career. In this condition, prompted by the impulses of his own generous nature, he wrote a letter to Napoleon Bonaparte, imploring him to order that he, a dying prisoner, might be allowed to breathe the air beyond his prison walls. No answer was returned to this request; but Sir Sidney soon after reviving, a plan was successfully devised, by which he effected his escape.

A friend had provided him with a false passport, a sword, a pistol, and a loose great-coat; and thus provided, sleeping by night in obscure road-side cabarets, and by day proceeding cautiously by bye-roads, he made his way through Normandy. Following the windings of the Seine, and avoiding Rouen and other great cities, he finally got to the coast in the neighbourhood of Havre. This was a dangerous spot, for it was here

that he had been captured, and consequently his person was known to
the authorities; but he was aware that a number of British ships of war
were blockading that port, and if he could only communicate with these,
he knew that his escape would be easy. Having secreted himself in a little
town at a considerable distance from the coast, he walked to the sea shore,
where he arrived in the dusk of the evening and here, at length, he was
so fortunate as to find a solitary fisherman in charge of several boats.
Sir Sidney, who had spoken French from a child with the fluency of a
native, told the man that he had a particular reason for wishing to visit
one of the English ships lying off the harbour, and that he would give a
handsome reward to be conveyed aboard. The poor fisherman consented
on condition that the stranger would wait till it was later, and meanwhile
invited him to his cottage to take rest before starting. Sir Sidney accepted
his offer, and followed him to a cottage, where a poor old woman, the
fisherman's wife, spread a cloth and laid before them a good supper. But
their guest was too unwell to eat, and was not unnaturally anxious lest
the man should only have asked for delay in order to betray him. He was
now, however, in their power, and it was useless to hesitate; so he
merely asked for leave to lie down and sleep until the time to depart had
arrived. The woman accordingly gave him a clean mattress in the room
in which they sat; and here, worn out with a long day's walk, he wrapped himself in his cloak and slept.

At the appointed hour the fisherman awoke his guest, and bade him
follow him. Sir Sidney started from his place and obeyed, and with a
joyful heart stepped into the boat which lay waiting for them in a little
cove. Feeling himself once more upon his native element, after so many
wanderings, the gallant sailor drew his cloak around him with an involuntary gesture of satisfaction, which the man observed, but mistook its
meaning. To Sir Sidney's surprise, he laid his hand upon his shoulder,
and said, «Do not hide yourself, Sir, from me; for I have known you
all along». Sir Sidney was scarcely alarmed by this speech; for they were
alone, and he was armed. «If you indeed know me», he said calmly,
«who am I?» «You are Commodore Smith», replied the man; «you more
than once gave me a glass of spirits with your own hands, when I have
come in my boat, the Diamond, on wet nights, to sell fish to your crew;
and I should be a scoundrel if I betrayed you».

In telling this anecdote to a friend, long afterwards, Sir Sidney re-

11

marked, «You see by this occurrence that no man can be aware how the most apparently trifling events may influence his future safety, nor how humble may be the individual who may have his life or liberty in his hands. And thus, my friend, Almighty Providence appears to weave together all his creatures in a mutual kindly dependence, so that none may say, 'I can have no need of you?'» The little fishing-boat conveyed its freight safely to the side of a British man-of-war, the «Argo» frigate, which joyfully took him aboard, and without loss of time brought him to England, where the return from his perilous adventures, of this great favourite of the people, was welcomed with almost a national rejoicing.

(The Temple Anecdotes).

Questions.

1. Into whose hands did Sir Sidney Smith fall, and how was he treated? — 2. Where was he confined, and what was the consequence?—3. What did Sir Sidney do, and what followed?

4. With what had a friend provided him, and how did he proceed through Normandy?— 5. Was he safe in the neighbourhood of Havre? — 6. What did he tell the fisherman, and what condition did the latter make?—7. How was Sir Sidney treated at the fisherman's cottage?

8. How did Sir Sidney feel in the boat, and what did he do?—9. Give an account of Sir Sidney's conversation with the fisherman?

10. In telling this anecdote, what did Sir Sidney remark? — 11. Where did the boat convey Sir Sidney, and was his return welcomed in England?

---

74. A Dangerous Journey in Labrador.

Samuel Liebisch was required by the duties of his office, to visit Okkak, the most northern of the settlements, and about one hundred and fifty English miles distant from Nain, the place where he resided. Another European, named Turner, being appointed to accompany him, they left Nain on March 11th, 1782, early in the morning with very clear weather, the stars shining with uncommon lustre. — The sledge drawn by dogs, in which the brethren travelled, was driven by the baptized Esquimaux, Mark; and another sledge carrying some heathen Esquimaux joined company.

The two sledges contained five men, one woman, and a child. All were in good spirits, and appearances being much in their favour, they

hoped to reach Okkak in safety, in two or three days. The track over
the frozen sea was in the best possible order, and they went with ease
at the rate of six or seven miles an hour. After they had passed the islands in the bay of Nain, they kept at a sonsiderable distance from the
coast, both to gain the smoothest part of the ice, and to weather the high
rocky promontory of Kiglapeit. About eight o'clock they met a sledge
with Esqimaux, turning in from the sea. After the usual salutations, the Esquimaux alighting, held some conversations, as is their general practice,
the result of which was, that some hints were thrown out by the strange
Esquimaux, that it might be as well to return. — However, as the Missionaries saw no reason whatever for it, and only suspected that the És-
quimaux wished to enjoy the company of their friends a little longer,
they proceeded. — After some time, their own Esquimaux hinted that
there was a ground swell under the ice. It was then hardly perceptible,
except on lying down and applying the ear close to the ice, when a hollow disagreeable, grating and roaring noise was heard, as if ascending
from the abyss. The weather remained clear, except towards the east,
where a bank of light clouds appeared, interspersed with some dark
streaks. But the wind being strong from the north west, nothing less than
a sudden change of weather was expected.

The sun had now reached its height, and there was as yet little or
no alteration in the appearance of the sky. But the motion of the sea
under the ice had grown more perceptible, so as rather to alarm the
travellers, and they began to think it prudent to keep closer to the shore.
The ice had cracks and large fissures in many places, some of which
formed chasms of one or two feet wide; but as they are not uncommon,
even in its best state, and the dogs easily leap over them, the sledge
following without danger, they are only terrible to new comers, inexpe-
rienced in the peculiarities of Labrador travelling.

As soon as the sun declined towards the west, the wind increased,
and rose to a storm, the bank of clouds from the east began to ascend,
and the dark streaks to put themselves in motion against the wind. The
snow was violently driven about, by partial whirlwinds both on the ice,
and from the peaks of the high mountains, and filled the air. At the
same time the ground swell had increased so much, that its effect upon
the ice became very extraordinary and alarming. The sledges, instead of
gliding along smoothly, upon an even surface, sometimes ran with vio-

lence after the dogs, and shortly after seemed with difficulty to ascend
the rising hill; for the elasticity of so vast a body of ice, of many
leagues square, supported by a troubled sea, though in some places three
or four yards in thickness, would, in some degree, occasion an undulatory motion, not unlike that of a sheet of paper, accommodating itself to
the surface of a rippling stream. Noises were likewise distinctly heard
in many directions, like the report of a cannon, owing to the bursting of
the ice at some distance.

The Esquimaux, therefore, drove with all haste towards the shore,
intending to take up their night quarters on the south side of Uivak. But,
as it plainly appeared that the ice would break and disperse in the open
sea, Mark advised to push forward to the North of Uivak, from whence
he hoped the track to Okkak might still remain entire. To this proposal
the company agreed; but when the sledges approached the coast, the prospect before them was truly terrific. The ice having broken loose from
the rocks, was forced up and down, grinding and breaking into a thousand pieces against the precipices with a tremendous noise which, added
to the raging of the wind and the snow driving about in the air, deprived
the travellers almost of the power of hearing and seeing any thing distinctly. To make the land at any risk, was now the only hope left, but
it was with the utmost difficulty the frightened dogs could be forced forward, the whole body of ice sinking frequently below the surface of the
rocks, and then rising above it. As the only moment to land was that,
when it gained the level of the coast, the attempt was extremely nice and
hazardous. However, providentially, it succeeded: both sledges gained
the shore, and were drawn up the beach with much difficulty.

The travellers had hardly time to reflect with gratitude to God, on
their safety, when that part of the ice, from which they had just now
made good their landing, burst asunder, and the water forcing itself from
below, covered and precipitated it into the sea. In an instant, as if by a
signal given, the whole mass of ise, extending for several miles from
the coast, and as far as the eye could reach, began to burst and to be
overwhelmed by the immense waves. The sight was tremendous and
awfully grand, the large fields of ice raising themselves out of the water,
striking against each other and plunging into the deep with a violence
not to be described, and a noise like the discharge of innumerable batteries of heavy guns. The darkness of the night, the roaring of the wind

and sea, and the dashing of the waves and ice against the rocks, filled
the travellers with sensations of awe and horror, so as almost to deprive
them of the power of utterance. They stood overwhelmed with astonishment at their miraculous escape, and even the heathen Esquimaux expressed gratitude to God for their deliverance.

Questions.

1. What was Samuel Liebisch required to do? — 2. Who was appointed to
accompany him? — When did they leave Nain, and what was the state of the
weather? — 4 By whom was the sledge driven, and who joined them? — 5.
Whom did the two sledges contain? — 6. At the rate of how many miles an
hour did they go over the frozen sea? — 7. What did they meet at eight
o'clock, and what was the result of the conversation of the Espuimaux? — 8.
How did the Missionaries act, and why? — 9. What did their own Esquimaux
hint after some time, and how was the ground swell only to be perceived? —
10. To whom are the chasms in the ice terrible?

11. What happened as soon as the sun declined towards the west? — 12.
What filled the air, and how much had the ground swell increased?—13. What
occasioned an undulatory motion, and what was it like?

14. Where did the Esquimaux drive to, and what was their intention? —
15. What was Mark's advice? — 16. Give a description of the terrific prospect
before them? — 17. What was now the only hope left? — 18. Did they succeed in this?

19. What happened as soon as they had gained the shore?— 20. Describe
the sight presented by the sea and ice? — 22. What were the feelings of the
travellers at their miraculous escape?

---

75. Over the Rapids.

On the 29-th of April, 1810, a party of Englishmen embarked at
Pointe du Lac, on Lake St. Frances, in Canada, in an American barge,
or broad flat-bottomed boat, deeply laden with wood ashes, passengers,
and baggage, with the intention of proceeding down the River St. Lawrence. The adventures of this little river vessel and its passengers have
been related by one of the party in a narrative which, for exciting interest, may be compared with any of the most thrilling stories of disaster
by wreck.

Above Montreal, for nearly a hundred miles, the River St. Lawrence,
as is well known, is interrupted in its course by rapids which are occa-

sioned by the river being confined within comparatively narrow, shallow, rocky channels. Through these it rushes with great force and noise, and is agitated like the ocean in a storm. By some, these rapids have been admired for grandeur and appearance more than the Falls of Niagara. They are from half a mile to nine miles long each, and require regular pilots. On the 30-th of April, the party arrived at the village of the Cedars, immediately below which are three sets of very dangerous rapids— the Cedars, the Split Rock, and the Cascades — distant from each other abought eight miles. On the morning of the 1-st of May, they set out from here. Their barge was very deep and very leaky; and the captain, a daring, rash man, refused to take a pilot. After they had passed the Cedar Rapid, not without danger, the captain called for some rum, declaring, at the same time, that all the powers could not steer the barge better than he did. Soon after this, the boat entered the Split Rock Rapids by a wrong channel, and, to their horror, the passengers found themselves advancing rapidly towards a dreadful watery precipice, down which they went. The barge slightly grazed her bottom against the rock, and the fall was so great as nearly to take away their breath. They here took in a great deal of water, which was mostly baled out again before they hurried on to what the Canadians call the «grand bouillie», or great boiling. In approaching this place, the captain let go the helm, saying, «Now for it; here we fill». The barge was almost immediately overwhelmed in the midst of immense foaming breakers, which rushed over the bows, carrying away planks, oars, and other articles. «About half a minute elapsed between the filling and going down of the barge», says the narrator of this story, during which I had sufficient presence of mind to strip off my three coats, and was loosening my braces when the barge sunk, and I found myself floating in the midst of people and baggage. Each man caught hold of something: one of the crew seized me, and kept me down under the water, but, contrary to my expectation, let me go again. On rising to the surface, I got hold of a trunk, on which two other men were then holding. Just at this spot, where the Split Rock Rapids terminated, the bank of the river is well inhabited, and we could see women on shore running about much agitated. A canoe put off, and picked up three of our number, who had gained the bottom of the barge which had upset and got rid of its cargo; these they landed on an island. The canoe put off again, and was approaching near to where I was, with two others, holding on the trunk; when, terrified with the vicinity of the cascades, to which we were approaching, it put back, notwithstanding my exhortations in French and English to induce the two men on board to advance. The bad hold which one man had of the trunk to which we were adhering subjected him to constant immersion, and in order to escape his seizing hold of me, I let go the trunk, and, in conjunction with another man, got hold of the boom which, with the gaff and sails, had been detached from the mast to make room for the cargo, and floated off. I had just time to grasp this boom, when we were hurried into the cascades; in these I was instantly buried, and nearly suffocated. On ris · ing to the surface, I found one of my hands still on the boom, and my companion also adhering closely to the gaff. Shortly after descending the cascades, I perceived the barge, bottom upwards, floating near me. I succeeded in getting to it, and held by a crack in one end of it; the vio- lence of the water, and the falling out of the casks of ashes, had quite wrecked it. For a long time I contented myself with this hold, not daring to endeavour to get upon the bottom, which I at length effected, and from this my new situation I called out to my companion who still preserved his hold of the gaff; he shook his head, and when the waves suffered me to look again he was gone. He made no attempt to come near me, being unable or unwilling to let go his hold, and trust himself to the waters which were then rolling over his head.»

The Cascades are a kind of fall, or rapid descent, in the river, over a rocky channel below; going down is called by the French, «sauter», to leap the Cascades. For two miles below the channel continues in an uproar, just like a storm at sea; and he was frequently nearly washed off the barge by the waves which rolled over it. «I now», continued the writer,» entertained no hope whatever of escaping; and although I con- tinued to exert myself to hold on, such was the state to which I was reduced by cold, that I wished only for a speedy death, and frequently thought of giving up the contest as useless. My hands felt as if dimin- ished in size one half, and I certainly should (after I became very cold and much exhausted) have fallen asleep, but for the waves that were passing over me, which obliged me to attend to my situation. I had never de- scended the St. Lawrence before; but I knew there were more rapids ahead, perhaps another set of cascades, but at all events La Chine Rapids whose situation I did not exactly know. I was hourly in expectation of these putting an end to me, and often fancied some points of ice extending from the shore to the head of foaming rapids. At one of the moments in which the succession of waves permitted me to look up, I saw, at a distance, a canoe with four men, coming towards me, and waited in confidence to hear the sound of their paddles; but in this I was disappointed. The men, as I afterwards learned, were Indians who, happening to fall in with one of the passengers' trunks, picked it up, and returned to the shore for the purpose of pillaging it, leaving, as they since acknowledged, the man on the boat to his fate. Indeed, I am certain I should have more to fear from their avarice, than to hope from their humanity; and it is more than probable that my life would have been taken, to secure them in the possession of my watch and several coins which I had about me.»

The accident happened at eight o'clock in the morning; in the course of some hours, as the day advanced, the sun grew warmer, the wind blew from the south, and the water became calmer. The shipwrecked man then got upon his knees, and found himself in the small lake of St. Louis, which is about three to five miles wide, and with which he happened to be familiar. With some difficulty he got upon his feet, but was soon convinced, by cramps and spasms in all his sinews, that he was incapable of swimming any great distance, and he was then two miles from the shore. He was now going, he thought, with wind and current, to destruction; and though cold, hungry, and fatigued, was obliged again to sit down to rest, when an extraordinary circumstance greatly relieved him.

On examining the wreck, to see if it were possible to detach any part of it by which to steer, he perceived something loose entangled in a fork of the wreck, and so carried along. This he found to be a small trunk, bottom upwards, which, with some difficulty, he dragged up upon the barge. After near an hour's work, in which he broke a penknife whilst trying to cut out the lock, he made a hole in the top, and, to his great satisfaction, drew out a bottle of rum, a cold tongue, some cheese, and a bagful of bread and cakes all wet. Of these he made a seasonable, though very moderate use; and the trunk answered the purpose of a chair to sit upon, elevated upon the surface of the water. After in vain endeavouring to steer the wreck, or direct its course to the shore, and having made every signal in his power, with his waistcoat and other

things, to the several headlands which he had passed, he fancied he was
driving into a bay which, however, soon proved to be the termination of
the lake and the opening of the river, the current of which was carrying
him rapidly along. He passed several small uninhabited islands; but the
banks of the river appearing to be covered with houses, he again renewed
his signals with his waistcoat and a shirt which he took out of the trunk,
hoping, as the river narrowed, they might be perceived; but the distance
was too great. The velocity with which he was going now convinced him
of his near approach to the dreadful rapids of La Chine. Night was drawing
on; his destruction appeared certain, but it did not, he said, disturb him
very much; the idea of death had lost his novelty, and had become quite
familiar. He even felt more provoked at having escaped so long to be
finally sacrificed, than alarmed at the prospect. «Finding signals in vain,»
he continues, «I now set up a cry or howl, such as I thought best calculated to carry a distance, and, being favoured by the wind, it did,
although at above a mile distant, reach the ears of some people on shore.
At last I perceived a boat rowing towards me, which, being very small
and white - bottomed, I had for some time taken for a fowl with a white
breast, and finally I was taken off the barge by Captain Johnstone, after
being ten hours on the water. I found myself at the village of La Chine,
twenty-one miles below where the accident happened, having been driven
by the winding of the current a much greater distance. I received no
other injury than bruised knees and breast, with a slight cold. The accident took some hold of my imagination, and for seven or eight succeeding
nights, in my dreams, I was engaged in the dangers of the Cascades,
and surrounded by drowning men. My escape was owing to a concurrence
of fortunate circumstances. I happened to catch hold of various articles
of support, and to exchange each article for another just at the right
time. Nothing but the boom could have carried me down the Cascades
without injury, and nothing but the barge could have saved me below
them. I was also fortunate in having the whole day; had the accident
happend one hour later, I should have arrived opposite the village of
La Chine after dark, and, of course, would have been destroyed in the
rapids below, to which I was swiftly advancing. The trunk, which furnished me with provisions and a resting-place above the water, I have
every reason to think was necessary to save my life. Without it, I must
have passed the whole time in the water, and have been exhausted with

12

cold and hunger. When the people on shore saw our boat take the wrong channel, they predicted our destruction; the floating luggage, by supporting us for a time, enabled them to make an exertion to save us; but as it was not supposed possible to survive the passage of the Cascades, no further exertions were thought of, nor indeed could they well have been made.» Of the eight men who passed down the Cascades, none escaped or were seen again but the writer, who some time afterwards published his singular narrative in a Liverpool newspaper, by the editor of which it was vouched for as true in every particular.

It was at this place that General Amherst's brigade, coming to attack Canada, were lost in September, 1760, the French at Montreal receiving the first intelligence of the invasion by the dead bodies floating past the town. It was said that the pilot who conducted their boats, being secretly favourable to the French, had committed the same error as the captain of the barge in the above narrative. He had intentionally taken the wrong channel, and the other boats, following mechanically and close upon him, were all involved in the same destruction. No less than forty-six barges, seventeen whale-boats, one row-galley with eighty men, besides artillery, stores, and ammunition, were then swept down these terrible rapids, and entirely lost. (The Temple Anecdotes).

Questions.

1. What happened on the 29-th of April, 1810 ? — 2. What is said of the adventures of the little river vessel and its passengers?

3. Give a description of the rapids in the River St. Lawrence? — 4. Name the three sets of very dangerous rapids ? — 5. After the party had passed the Cedar Rapid, what did the captain do? — 6. What happened soon after this? — 7. On approaching the «grand bouillie», what did the captain say? — 8. What did the narrator do between the filling and going down of the barge? — 9. How were three of the passengers saved? — 10. Give a further account of the story ?

11. What are the Cascades, and what is the meaning of the French term «sauter»? — 12. To what state was the writer reduced, and what did he wish for? — 13. What do we read about the canoe with the four Indians in it?

14. Where did the shipwrecked man find himself, and what did he do and think ?

15. What did the writer perceive, and what followed? — 16. Were his signals successful? — 17. What did he set up, and what was the consequence? —

18. Did the writer receive any injury?—19. To what was his escape owing? —
20. What is said about the people on shore?
   21. Give an account of the destruction of General Amherst's brigade?

76. A Visit to a Famous Island.

According to a well-known tradition, the story of «Robinson Crusoe»
was suggested to De Foe by the adventures of Alexander Selkirk who was,
early in the last century, cast away on the desert island of Juan Fernandez, off the coast of South America, in the Pacific Ocean; and there seems
little doubt that De Foe, though placing his imaginary island off a far
distant part of the South American coast, had really in his mind the island
described in the narrative of the Scottish sailor's experiences. Among
sailors this island will probably always be known as «Crusoe's Island»;
and as long as the adventures of Robinson Crusoe are read, voyagers in
those seas will feel some curiosity about the traditional scene of that
famous story. Something of this feeling, mixed with a natural longing
for going ashore after long beating about at sea, seems to have actuated
Mr. Ross Browne and ten companions to pay a visit to Selkirk's island,
under the singular circumstances related in his narrative of «A Ramble
in the Footsteps of Alexander Selkirk», recently published.

   It was early in the morning of the 19-th of May, 1849, that the
ship «Anteus», in which Mr. Browne was sailing as a passenger to San
Francisco, came in sight of the highest peak of the mountains on the
island. The weather was mild and clear; as the sun rose it fell calm, and
the vessel lay nearly motionless. A light blue spot, which might have
passed for a cloud, but for the indistinctness of its outline, was all that
appeared in the horizon. «Weary of the gales we had encountered off Cape
Horn», says Mr. Browne, »it was a pleasant thing to see a spot of earth
once more, and there was not a soul on-board but felt a desire to go
ashore». For some days past Mr. Browne and a few others had talked
about making the attempt, in case they came near enough; but now there
seemed to be every prospect of a long calm, and there was no other chance
but to lower a boat, and row for the distant land. A party of the passengers, headed by Mr. Browne, agreed to do this, provided they could get
a boat; and Mr. Bingham, a fellow-passenger, who happened to be owner

of one of the quarter - boats , fell with their scheme , together with his partner and some friends. They were sanguine of being able to row to the island before dusk, and return the following day, and the dead calm which prevailed promised them ample time for a still longer expedition; but knowing that their captain would probably endeavour to dissuade them from their project , they resorted to a little strategy to accomplish it. They had been in the habit of rowing about the ship whenever it was calm , and this provided a good excuse for lowering the boat. Being in great haste to launch it, they only thought of a few necessary articles in case they should be cast away or driven from the island. Not knowing but that there might be outlaws or savages ashore, they armed themselves with a double-barreled gun, a fusee, and an old harpoon, which was all that they could smuggle into the boat in the excitement of starting. At this time the captain , happening to come on deck , heard the rumour of their expedition; but he appears to have thought that the matter was a mere frolic, though he warned them that the peak which they could see in the horizon was fully seventy miles off. But Browne and his compan- ions had no doubt that he told them this only to deter them , and they had made up their minds that the island was not in fact at more than half that distance. Captain Brooks appears to have still regarded the pro- ject as having more of bravado than reality in it, and as the boat pushed off, called out good-humouredly, «Be sure not to forget the peaches; you will find plenty of them in the valleys. Only do not lose sight of the ves- sel». The boat's crew promised they would take care of themselves, and come back safely, if they were not foundered.

It was about nine in the morning as, with three cheers, they pushed off from the ship. Their boat was only twenty-two feet long, and was made of sheet-iron, and very narrow. The proper number of men for it was six, but, in consideration of the distance and the necessity for a change at the oars, five more were crowded into it. Most of them, except Browne and a whaleman, named Paxton, were unused to rowing, so that the prospect of reaching land depended upon the day remaining calm, and upon keeping the boat trimmed. «There was no excuse», says Mr. Browne, «for this risk of life, save that insatiable thirst for novelty, which all experience, to some extent, after the monotony of a long voy- age. I will only say, in regard to myself, that I was too full of joy at the idea of a ramble in the footsteps of Robinson Crusoe to think of risk at all. If there was danger, it merely served to give zest to the adventure».

. By their calculation of the distance and the rate of going, they expected to reach the land by sundown, or soon after; and their plan was then to make a tent of the boat sail, and sleep under it till morning, when, by rising early, they thought they could take a run over the island, and perhaps get some fruit and vegetables. Should a light breeze spring up during the night, they thought it likely the ship would be well up by the land, when they could pull out, and get on board without difficulty. But before long they began to find that distances at sea are deceptive. About noon, when they ate their first meal, their ship had disappeared behind them; but still there was but a single peak visible on the horizon, rising blue and dim in the distance, and apparently not much higher than when they had seen it from the masthead of their ship. A ripple beginning to show upon the water, they hoisted their sail to catch the breeze, and found that it helped them onwards. All of them, having gone so far, were now in favour of going on, though in secret they felt that there was a great deal of danger, for the sides of their iron boat were only an eighth of an inch thick, and it was so loaded that the gunwales rose scarcely more than ten inches out of the water. At sunset the land had risen over the sea from end to end, and they hoped to reach it in about three hours; but none of them knew anything about the shores, whether they abounded in bays or not, and, if so, where any place of landing could be found, which made them doubtful how to steer. «Clouds», says Mr. Browne's narrative,» were gathering all over the horizon, a few stars shone out dimly overhead, and the shades of night began to cover the island. Swiftly, yet with resistless power, the clouds swept over the whole sky, and the horizon in all the grandeur of its vast circle, was lost in the shades of night. No sail was near; no light shone upon us now but the dim rays of a few solitary stars through the rugged masses of clouds; no sound broke upon the listening ear save the weary stroke of our oars; a gloom had settled upon the mighty wilderness of waters, and we were awed and silent».

The wind soom began to increase, and all cowered down in the boat to keep her balanced. The spray washed over them fearfully, and the sail shook so in the wind that, having let go all, they thought it would tear the mast out. At this time they were about three leagues from the south-east end of the island, which was the nearest point then in sight. As the clouds spread by the attraction of the land, the whole island became wrapped in a dark mist, and in half an hour they could discern nothing but the gloom of the storm around them, as they bore down towards the darkest part. Their lamp was now quenched by a heavy sea, and being unable to distinguish the points of the compass, they were fearful that they should miss the island, and be carried off so far that they could never reach it again. Whenever there was a lull they tried to haul in their sheet, but a sudden flaw striking them once, the boat lay over till she buried her gunwales, and the sea broke heavily over the lee side; and the crew at the same time springing in a body to the weatherside to balance her, brought her over suddenly so that it was a miracle that they were not capsized, which, had it happened so far out at sea in the darkness, would have made an end of them. It was as much as they could do, by bailing continually, to keep her afloat, and every moment they expected to be submerged. They knew it was four hundred miles to the coast of Chili, and they had neither water nor provisions left At best their position was perilous. Ignorant of the bearings of the harbour, they were at a loss what to do, even if they should be able to reach the lee of the island, for they had seen that it was chiefly rock-bound and inaccessible to boats.

About two in the morning, as well as they could judge, they found themselves close under the lee of a high cliff, upon the base of which the surf broke with a tremendous roar. Some of the party, reckless of the consequences, were in favour of running straight in, and attempting to gain the shore at all hazards. The more prudent protested against the folly of this course, well knowing that they would be inevitably capsized in the surf, and dashed to pieces upon the rocks. They accordingly endeavoured to lay off and wait for daylight. It was a wild and awful place in the dead of the night, it being so dark that they scarcely knew where they steered. Once they stopped to listen, fancying they heard voices on the shore, but it was only the moaning of the tempest upon the cliffs, and the frightful beating of the surf below. Having pulled, as they believed, about twelve miles along the shore, and seeing no sign of a cove or bay, they despaired of getting ashore before daylight, when they were startled by one of their number crying out that he saw a light. The light disappeared and appeared again. It seemed at first to be on the shore, but finally they discovered that it hung in the rigging of a large vessel, which they were enabled to hail. To the inquiry, «Boat ahoy! where are you from?» the boat's crew replied, «The ship 'Anteus', bound for California: what ship is this?» The answer was «The 'Brooklyn', bound for California». No longer able to suppress their joy, the boat's crew gave three hearty cheers, and after a little while they found means of getting safely aboard the «Brooklyn», where they met with a kind welcome from the master, Captain Richardson, and his crew.

To endeavour to regain the ship by their boat was hopeless; and the adventurous boat's crew spent some days in exploring the island, which they found to be inhabited only by sixteen persons consisting of an American and four or five Chilian men with their wives and children. Mr. Ross Browne gives an interesting description of the condition of the island, and pleasantly interweaves with his narrative some fanciful adventures, such as may be supposed to haunt the dreams of cast-aways, full of the associations of the place. Fortunately for them, three days later the «Anteus» hove in sight of the island, and the boat's crew were once more enabled to resume their voyage with no worse result from their adventure than a reprimand from the captain for their rashness and disobedience to his orders.   (The Temple Anecdotes).

Questions.

1. By what was the story of «Robinson Crusoe» suggested to De Foe? — 2. By what name is the island of Juan Fernandez known to sailors?

3. Where, when, and in what ship did Mr. Browne sail? — 4. How was the weather, and what desire did all on board feel? — 5. Of what was there every prospect, and what did a party of the passengers agree to do? — 6. What articles did they take with them. — 7. What warning did the captain give them, and what did he exclaim good-humouredly?

8. What does Mr. Browne say in excuse of the danger, to which the party was exposed?

9. What did they find with regard to distances at sea? — 10. What does Mr. Browne's narrative say?

11. Give a further description of the weather, and of the state in which the boat was?

12. What happened when they had pulled about twelve miles along the shore?

13. How did the boat's crew spend some days, and of what does Mr. Browne give an interesting description? — 14. What happened three days later?

77. The Sedar, and Leopard Hunt.

I received a letter addressed to me at Calcutta, from a friend at Ber-hampore, stating that several robberies had taken place in my household during my absence, and that my sedar-bearer, on whom I could rely, had begged of my friend to write to me to return as soon as possible.

This information reached me as I lay on my couch, completely worn with the fatigues of the day previous; for I had been with some brother-officers to Barrackpore, to see a hunt by leopards — a sight the most curious that I ever beheld in India. These animals are so tame, that they range at large, and actually sleep beside their keeper. This I can vouch for, as I have seen it. They protect him with the same fidelity that a dog would defend his master, if any stranger should approach him during his slumbers. This I particularly know, as I unfortunately went to awake him, unaware of his faithful guardians, and nearly paid the penalty of my folly. The keeper, however, started up, aud called them off. They obeyed with the docility of domestic animals, and fell behind at his word of command. They belong, I believe, to the Governor-General for the time being, and are kept in the park of the government-house. It was here that I saw them run down a deer. Never in my life have I beheld any-thing so graceful in their movements, or so rapid as their speed. Consi-derably swifter than greyhounds, they bounded-along, and soon brought down their game. Fatigued with the excitement of this beautiful sport, I returned to Calcutta, and, as I have mentioned, was lying on my couch when the information, conveyed by my friend at Berhampore arrived. No time, however, was to be lost; so starting up, I ordered my palanquin to be brought to the door, determined on travelling up the one hundred and sixteen miles by bearers. This mode of proceeding may appear strange to Europeans, who will scarcely believe the rapidity with which such a journey is accomplished. By the river, on account of the current, seven days are required to arrive at Berhampore; by land, it only takes twenty-eight hours. The bearers, like post-horses, are relived every twelve or fifteen miles. Each relay consists of eight men, who shift the burden to each other at the end of about every league. The others trot alongside to rest themselves, the whole party singing and jolting on at the rate of about four miles and a half an hour. During the night the disengaged bearers carry torches, to scare away the wild beasts. The fire-flies buz-zing about, like innumerable stars, add to the beauty of the picture, and

render this scene most romantic and picturesque; though I must confess
the uneasy motion, the broiling of the sun in this luxurious, coffin-like
conveyance, and the fear of a voracious tiger, or other savage monster,
take away, in my opinion, all the charms which would otherwise gild
this mode of travelling.

At day break on the second morning, (for I had halted a few hours
at Aghardeep), I arrived in the cantonments, and entered my house, which
stood in an extensive barrack-square.

After breakfasting most luxuriously on Bombay ducks, (a small salt
fish, something like the European caplin), the sable fish, (closely resembling our salmon) and snipes, which are here far more plentiful than
sparrows in England, I secretly sent for the *wise man* of the place to
come and discover the thief; then, ordering the servants to fall in, in a
row under the verandah, I quietly and confidently awaited his arrival. I
had often seen his powers tested, and never knew them fail. I am aware
that my country-men will smile at my credulity; but, as I have the conviction from personal and constant observation, I do not hesitate to assert,
that his manner of discovering crime, though the simplest, was the most
wonderful that I ever beheld. The present instance served to strengthen
my belief.

In every bazaar or village in India exists a *wise man*, a sort of half-
priest, half-conjurer, who predicts events, tells fortunes, secures families,
and discovers crimes. These individuals are looked upon with great awe
by the natives, and are often found useful in the last instance by Europeans.

On the arrival of the magician, he made the men form circle around
him; then uttering some prayers, he produced a small bag of rice, and
taking out a handful, gave it to the man nearest to him, and desired him
to chew it, while he continued to recite certain prayers or incantations.
In a moment or two he held a plate to the man, and desired him to spit
out the grain. He did so; it was well chewed, and the man instantly declared innocent. Another and another succeeded. At length, he came to
one of my favourite servants — one whom I never suspected. On taking
the rice, the man seemed dreadfully convulsed. He ground his teeth, and
worked hard to masticate it; but all in vain. When he rendered it on the
plate, the grain was uncrushed, unchewed. The *wise man* instantly proclaimed him to be the thief: upon which, the servant falling on his knees,

13

confessed the crime and detailed a series of thefts, for which I had suspected, and even punished, others. By his own showing, he must have been the greatest rascal, the greatest scoundrel alive. He had, however, lived long with me; so I contented myself with instantly dismissing him.

In the evening I was sitting at whist, when I was called out by my sedar-bearer, whom I before mentioned as one of the most faithful creatures in existence. He begged of me instantly to set out for Moorshedabad — a distance of about ten miles, in order to see a cousin of mine, who had sent me a verbal message by a *punee* (a foot-runner), requesting my instant attendance, as he had met with a serious accident. When I asked to see the servant. I found he was already gone; and, when I expressed my astonishment that he had not even sent me a *chit* (note), my bearer assured me the accident had deprived him of the power of writing; but that he earnestly solicited me to lose no time in setting out. Of course I did not hesitate ordering my palanquin out once more. Though sadly tired, I started off, after making an apology to my friends for thus abruptly leaving them. On my arrival at Moorshedabad, I hurried to the bungalow of my relative. Here I found the world fast asleep; and, amongst others, my cousin. He was perfectly well, and slumbering most comfortably. On being awoke, he positively denied having sent any messenger whatever to me, and had met with no accident, nor was ever better in his life.

The deception thus practised on me staggered me so much, that, in spite of every remonstrance, I borrowed a relay of bearers, and set out on my instant return home.

On re-entering my quarter I found all quiet and still as the grave. I aroused some of the sleeping servants; and, having obtained a light, asked for the sedar-bearer, determined to make an example of the rascal for having thus played off a practical joke on me. None of the others, however, knew where he was; so I proceeded to my bed-room, resolved to punish him in the morning. As I passed through my dressing-room, I perceived my drawers open; I examined them, and found that a suit of my clothes had been extracted; and, by a turban I found lying near, I discovered that they had been taken by the sedar. That a man, whom I had hitherto looked upon as incorruptibly honest, should thus act, was a matter of the greatest surprise. That one, who had ever been considered as the most faithful of my servants, should thus, suddenly turn thief, annoyed, and disappointed me. But, what puzzled me more than all was, that my people declared he had been seen to enter this room early in the evening, but most positively had not passed out again. Tired with conjecture, I went into my sleeping apartment.

I started back with surprise. Upon the bed lay a figure, the very counterpart of myself! My heart misgave me as I rushed forward, and tore a handkerchief from the features of my other self, who so closely resembled me, as he appeared stretched on my bed, that my followers kept staring at me, and at the figure before them, as if doubtful of my identity.

As the covering was removed, I perceived the countenance of my sedar. He was fast asleep. I attempted in anger to awake him. He was a corpse. Stone dead before me·was stretched my late favourite servant. On a close examination I found a sharp-pointed instrument (probably poisoned) thrust into his heart, from which it was still undrawn. I could not decipher the dreadful mystery.

Presently one of my kidmutgars rushed up. He held a leaf in his hand on which some characters in Hindoostanee had been traced (as usual) with a pin. I sent for my *munchee* (interpreter), who thus translated them:

«Beloved master! a plot was formed this day by the man whom you this day discovered to be a thief, to murder you. It was too well planned for you to escape. I was too solemnly sworn to dare to reveal it to you! Pardon me, beloved master! but I ventured to deceive you. I took your place: and have felt happy to die for you! May the God of the white man make you happy»!

The riddle was solved. The delinquent, thinking he had completed his deed of blood, had fled. I provided for the family of my attached servant. Not one of his fellows, however, seemed astonished at the act. They appeared to look upon such devotion as a matter of course. For myself, I never can, I never will, forget the fidelity of my devoted «sedar».

H. R. A d d i s o n.

Questions.

1. What did the letter which Mr. A. received state? — 2. Where had Mr. A. been, and what had he seen? — 3. Where did the leopards sleep, and what do they do? — 4. How long does it take from Calcutta to Berhampore by water, and how long by land? — 5. Describe the mode of travelling by bearers? — 6. What takes away the charms of travelling? — 7. Whom did Mr. Addison send

for? — 8. Who exists in every bazaar or village? — 9. What did the magician do on his arrival, and what did he give to the man next him? — 10. How did the favourite servant act on taking the rice?—11. When the wise man proclaimed him to be the thief, what did he do? — 12. What happened in the evening as Mr. Addison was sitting at whist?—13. What did Mr. Addison find on arriving at Moorshedabad?—14. What did he find on returning to his quarters, and what did he determine to do? — 15. What did he perceive on passing through his dressing room?—16. What did Mr. A. do on entering his sleeping apartment?— 17. What lay upon the bed, and what did Mr. A. do?— 18. What did Mr. A. perceive when the covering was removed? — 19. What did he find on a close examination? — 20. What did the *kidmudgar* bring? — 21. What were the contents of the letter?—22. How did the other servants regard this act?

---

78. A Princess Royal.

I remember to have fallen in once with certain American captains, and colonels, and men-at-arms, in a small place on the Brazos river, a few miles north of Jose Maria, in Texas. I had paid a visit to this place, near which a dear companion of my youth had been murdered. We were school-fellows, and for five years we had been brother officers in the same regiment. He went to the United States just when the war broke out with Mexico, and became captain of a company of Kentucky rifle-men. A few months after the battle of Vera Cruz, he was deputed by the officers of his brigade to present to General Taylor — who was on leave of absence at New-Orleans — a gold medal as token of their re-spect. Choosing the nearest way from the camp across the country, he set out on his errand with a guide and two servants, all on horseback, armed to the teeth. In Jose Maria, my poor friend unwisely exhibited the medal to a crowd of respectable-looking persons, calling themselves colonels, majors, and captains, who seemed to take great pleasure in studying its engravings. He did not then remark in what a hurry some of those colonels were to start before him. But the medal has, in ten years, never more been heard of, and my old comrade and two of his companions were found shot dead in a ravine.

It was near this place that I also fell among colonels. There was one of them who took a great liking to my horse, when he saw me giving it to the ostler. He tapped it repeatedly on the neck, declaring it, with an oath, to be a nice hanimal and no mistake — which assertion he repeated afterwards over and over again to his fellow-men in the coffeeroom, who, when they had been out to satisfy their curiosity, agreed with him upon the matter. «Now, would'nt that be a nag for you, major?» he said to a tall, powerful man, with a rough beard and disgusting features, who sat a little apart from the rest, and wore a large grey coat. The major said nothing, but stalked out of the room, soon afterwards, followed by the colonel. The others had again taken up their old topic of conversation, and were talking politics, rather vehemently as I thought, when the waiter — a German — came up to me, and told me in our own language, that I had better take care, as those two ruffians outside had set eyes upon my horse, and would be sure to steal it, if I gave them the slightest chance. Annoyed at this intelligence, I asked my countryman what he thought it would be best for me to do.

«Why», said he, «you have fallen in with a bad set, and, if you want to keep your horse, I should advise you to escape as soon as possible». After a little reflection, I resolved to start at once, and made for the stable. There I found the colonel again, most urgently talking to the ostler, who only looked at me in a rather impudent manner, when I told him to bring out my horse, and paid me no further attention. I therefore began to bridle for myself.

«I say, captain!» said the colonel, coming up to me after a while, and tapping me on the shoulder.

«Sir!»

«Come on, man! don't make a fool of yourself! I want to buy that 'ere 'osse, captain!»

«Do you?»

Thank heaven'! I was in the saddle by that time.

«Do I? Am I the man to be put out of my way by one of these 'ere chawed up Germans?»

He laid both his hands upon the bridle of my horse. My blood generally boils at an insulting word against my countrymen, especially when I am far from home in foreign lands. In a trice, the stick of the riding-whip came down upon the colonel's head, whilst the horse urged to a powerful leap, threw him ten yards away upon the ground. As I knew very well that, according to the customs of the country, this was a revolver affair now, and as I had no wish to become entangled in such a business, I did not wait until the colonel had picked himself up, but rode forward without delay.

I was stopped by the waiter, whom I heard calling after-me, and who was out of breath when he came up to me at last. The honest fellow gave me a direction, which I was afterwards glad to have followed. He said that the colonel, though a coward, was a most desperate villain, not at all likely to give way so soon, but that the worst of the whole set was that tall fellow, the major, whom he suspected to have gone in search of some of his companions. «You will be chased by a couple of these ro-gues», he said, «as sure as I am a Saxon! Let me advise you. Follow your way. up to the north until you are out of sight, then do you turn back to the south, as far as Jose Maria. At the ravine south-east of that place turn to the left, and, following the course of the brook, ride for your life. Twenty miles up the stream you will come to a settlement, called the Wood Creek. Old Delamotte lives there, and he's the man for you to trust».

I offered the waiter a few pieces of money, but he would not take them, then a hearty shake of the hand, and this he took most cordially.

«Stop!» he said when I had already set spurs to my horse. He lifted up each of the horse's legs, and looked carefully at the shoeing. «All right», he said; «I thought the ostler might have played you one of his tricks, but he has not yet had time, I suppose. Now, go a head, and don't forget the Frenchman!»

I darted off.

It was eleven o'clock in the morning. I had to make twenty miles to the ravine which my countryman had pointed out to me. But my horse was worthy of the colonel's admiration, and, in spite not only of the round-about way I had taken in accordance with my friend's advice, and half-an-hour's delay for rest at Jose Maria, it was but five in the evening, when I reached this melancholy spot.

I stopped and looked about me. The surrounding country was all barren and desolate, the soil sterile. There was a wooden cross erected on the spot of the murder, and beneath it lay the mortal remains of the man whom I had known in the full glow and joy of youth.

A strange feeling made me linger in that place. The little rivulet smoothly gliding eastward showed me the way I was to go. I could follow its course with my eyes to a far distant forest, the high grass of the prairie having burnt a track down, as it always does at this time of the year. Yet still I lingered.

The horse began to neigh softly, and to prick up his ears. He was familiar with these prairies, as I had bought him but a few months ago at Little Rock, in Arkansas. There was something the matter.

I listened, but heard absolutely nothing. I alighted, and, pressing my ear to the ground, listened again. The earth trembled faintly with the tread of horses yet at a long distance; but, when I mounted again, I could hear the sound. It was rapidly approaching from the direction of Jose Maria, and, although the woods on that side of me prevented me from seeing anything, I had but little doubt who were the horsemen. Now, colonels, majors, captains, let us see what can be done! My horse gave such a sudden and vigorous jump, when I merely touched him with my whip, that I was almost thrown from my seat. I lost my cap, and a gust of wind threw it against that very mound by which I had been bound to the ravine. To pick it up would have been waste of time; and, as I wished to be out of sight before my pursuers had set foot upon the prairie, I left it and sped away, taking as straight a line as possible in the direction of the distant forest, to avoid the windings of the little brook, yet without losing sight of it.

In the brave horse there was no slackening of pace; there was no stumbling. I turned round three or four times during my rapid course, but, except a long thin cloud of dust and ashes, raised by myself, I saw nothing whatever. In an hour or so, the forest was before me, and then, reining up a little, I again made for the brook.

I had traced its windings for about another hour, when I arrived at a cleared space in the wood, and got sight of a block-house.

«Qui va là?» asked a deep voice.

«Un ami!» was the answer.

There were two men near the house, one with grey hair and weather-beaten features, the other in the prime of youth, both Frenchmen. The old man looked, with some astonishment, at my panting horse covered with foam, at his dilated nostrils and quick beating flanks.

«Why, it seems you are in a hurry», he said. In a few words I explained the motives of my visit, and told him my adventures at Santa Madre; not forgetting to report the advice of the German waiter at the coffee-house, that I should trust in him for help.

He listened eagerly to my narrative, and when I gave him a minute description of the colonel and the major, his attention grew to be intense.

«Again those two scoundrels!» he said. «Well, man, step into the house. Never mind the horse, the lad will rub him dry. We have a few hours before us yet. They know by this time where you are, and will consider twice before they call here; though we are quite sure to hear of them at nightfall».

I expressed regret for the trouble I was bringing on him; but he only laughed and replied: «Never mind, we are their match».

«But we are only three, and after all we don't know how many ruffians that tall fellow may bring with him».

«Let him bring a score, we are their match, I tell you! Do you account the Princess Royal nobody?»

«The what?»

«The Princess Royal: la Princesse Royale!» he laughed again. «Don't stare at me, you'll see her by-and-by».

The block-house had a very durable appearance; it was two stories high, and the upper room was neatly furnished. On the wall I observed a portrait of General Moreau. My host was no friend of the Emperor of the French: the present Emperor he mentioned only once during our conversation, and I had better not say what he said.

He lighted a candle and began to block the windows up, whilst I was eating and drinking what he had placed on the table. The lad made all safe on the ground floor, and secured the door.

«Now, we are all right!» said the old man, taking his seat at the table, and mixing rum and water in a large bowl.

«Au triomphe de la bonne cause!» he said, touching glasses with me.

«But I don't see any arms», I presently suggested.

«Arms? I have plenty of that stuff. How do you think a man could get on in these woods without arms? But we shan't want them to-night». Again he laughed. «We have the Princess Royal!»

He removed the candle with the other things from the table, and went out of the room.

The door was opened again about five minutes afterwards. I heard the crack of a whip. I saw a rapid flash before my eyes; and, with a mighty bound, that made my very blood run cold, a large jaguar leaped in alighting with a heavy pounce upon the table.

«La princesse royale!» announced my host. I do not know exactly what figure I may have presented at that moment; but I should not wonder, if anybody were to tell me that I looked like a craven.

«Don't be afraid of her», said the laughing Frenchman, when he saw me still as a mouse, scarcely venturing to turn my looks to her bright cruel eyes. «She is as decent as a cat, when I am by. Caress her, she likes to be fondled, it's the weak side of the sex, you know».

I touched her delicate fur but slightly with my hand, stroking it softly down her strong and beautiful back, the right way of the fur, you may be sure.

She bent her powerful and elastic limbs under my frail hand, and fanning the air with her curved tail, seemed to encourage me to bestow more caresses.

«Well, how do you like the Princess?» asked my host.

«Why, she is indeed handsome, and I have seen none in the old world more majestic».

«Take her down-stairs, George», he said to the lad, handing the whip over to him, «and keep a look out yourself; but mind you don't give her any supper. She shall help herself to-night».

He placed the candle and our glasses again upon the table, and began to sip his grog quite leisurely.

«By heavens, man», I said, after a pause, «it cannot be your real purpose to set the tiger on those people?»

«Eh, parbleu!» replied he, «and why not? What else do they deserve? Are they not also tigers? You don't know them, as I do! The tall rascal is a convicted felon, and ought to have been hanged two years ago at San Francisco. He contrived an escape and fled to Kansas. As to the other rogue, there is hardly a crime he has not stained his hands with. Make your mind easy about that».

A sudden thought came into my mind, and I asked him, whether he knew anything about that murder of my friend ten years ago in the ravine near Jose Maria?

No, he knew nothing about that. It was before his time; only he should not wonder, if the major had a hand in it; it looked very like him.

We were interrupted by a loud knocking at the door. The lad came in soon afterwards, telling us that he could descry five of them, all on horseback.

14

The old man rose, and moving one of the mattresses a little aside, he looked cautiously through the window. It was about nine o' clock, and the darkness began to set in with the rapidity, peculiar to southern climates.

The knocks were repeated more vehemently accompanied now with a loud summons to open the door.

«Here they are, sure enough!» said the old man.

«I wonder why this major does not go to Kansas: he is the very man for Kansas politics».

«If you don't open now, you French dog», said a coarse voice, «we'll break the door!»

The eyes of the old man flashed fire, but he spoke never a word.

«You know me, Delamotte», said another voice, which I had heard before. «You know colonel Brown. But though we'ave to settle an old account. I 'ave no business with you this time: it's the stranger I want, he has stolen a orse; give him up to us, and we'll be off in a minute».

«No use talking to that old miser», said the former voice, with an oath. «Come on, boys, break that door in, and end it!»

He seemed to suit the action to the word, for a tremendous crash came.

«En avant!» said the old man to the lad, and they both went downstairs.

I rose and paced up and down the room with rapid steps. Something terrible, awful was going on.

The whole block-house shook and trembled with the violent kicks and blows which were dealt at the door; but nevertheless I could hear distinctly when the iron bar was removed from it, and then I felt as if all my blood were rushing suddenly to my heart, leaving not one single drop in any limb of my whole body.

A roar, not at all like those you may hear in the Zoological Gardens, Regent's Park, at feeding-time — but a hundred times wilder, sharper, more piercing, more furious: then human cries of horror and despair — the trampling of flying horses — the quick report of fire-arms — then again the roar, but this time much louder, more savage, more ferocious, more horrible — then a heavy fall and a confused noise of grinding of teeth — then nothing more, because I stopped my ears with both my hands.

When I turned round, my host sat at the table again, sipping his grog, as if nothing had happened.

«I am afraid», he said after a while, «the Princess has been wounded. I have never heard her roaring in that way. Well, we must see after this to-morrow. It would be a dangerous job for any man to go near her to-night!»

Next morning, I stood by his side, when he opened the door. My first glance fell upon the tiger cowering in a thick brown-red pool. She was licking at a red spot upon her left flank, which seemed to have bled profusely; but with both her powerful fore-paws she clung to a deformed and shapeless mass which bore no likeness to anything I had ever seen. The corpse of a horse, frightfully mutilated, lay close by, and the whole ground was strewn with fragments of a horrible appearance. My host having examined them all with intense curiosity, cracked his whip, and moved straight towards the tiger.

A hollow menacing roar warned him off; the savage creature showed her formidable range of long and powerful teeth, and hast lost all signs of her old tameness. «She is thirsty for more blood; the Princess Royal is», said the Frenchman, «that's nature, you know. She can't help it, I suppose, and as I should be grieved to kill her, we must wait till she comes round again».

We had to wait long. After three days the old man himself beginning to doubt whether she ever would come round again, was forced to kill her after all.

When we were thus enabled to examine at leisure that horrible battle-field, he drew my attention to some remnants of a coat in which the grey colour was still to be distinguished.

«He has had his reward!» said the old man, «though it costs me dear. Better than all those majors was my poor old Princess Royal».

Questions.

1. With whom did the author once fall in? — 2. Who was murdered near the place to which the author paid a visit? — 3. Give an account of the murder?

4. Who took a great liking to the author's horse, and what did he say to the major? — 5. When the major and the colonel had left the room, what did the German waiter tell the author?

6. What happened to the author in the stable, and how did he make his escape?

7. When the waiter had stopped the author, what directions did he give him?

8. When the author's horse began to neigh softly, and to prick up his ears, what did he do?

9. Describe the author's reception at the blockhouse?

10. What appearance had the house?

11. How was the Princess Royal introduced?

12. What account did the host give of the major and the colonel?

13. Who were knocking at the door, and what did they threaten to do?

14. When the old man and the lad had gone down-stairs, what did their guest hear?

15. Describe the appearance of the tiger on the next morning?

16. What was the old man forced to do after all?

17. What did he say while turning the author's attention to some remnants of a grey coat?

79. Anecdote of Rev John Wesley.

Dr. Dudley was one evening taking tea with that eminent artist, Mr. Culy, when he asked him whether he had seen his gallery of busts. Mr. Dudley answering in the negative, and expressing a wish to be gratified with a sight of it, Mr. Culy conducted him thither, and after admiring the busts of the several great men of the day, he came to *one* which particularly attracted his notice, and on inquiry found it was the likeness of the Rev. John Wesley. «This bust», said Mr. Culy, «struck Lord Shelbourne in the same manner it does you, and there is a remarkable fact connected with it, which, as I know you are fond of anecdote, I will relate to you precisely in the same manner and words that I did to him». On returning to the parlour, Mr. Culy commenced accordingly: «I am a very old man; you must excuse my little failings, and, as I before observed, hear it in the very words I repeated it to his Lordship. «My Lord», said I, «perhaps you have heard of John Wesley, the founder of the Methodists?» «Oh, yes», he replied; «*he — that race of fanatics!*» «Well, my Lord; Mr. Wesley had often been urged to have his picture taken, but he always refused, alleging as a reason that he thought it nothing but vanity; indeed, so frequently had he been pressed on this point that his friends were reluctantly compelled to give up the idea. One day he called on me on the business of our church. I began the old sub ject of entreating him to allow me to take off his likeness. «Well», said I, «knowing you value money for the means of doing good, if you will grant my request, I will engage to give you ten guineas for the first ten minutes that you sit, and for every minute that exceeds that time you shall receive a guinea». «What», said Mr. Wesley, «do I unterstand you aright, that you will give me ten guineas for having my picture taken! Well, I agree to it». He then stripped off his coat, and lay on the sofa, and in eight minutes I had the most perfect bust I had ever taken. He then washed his face, and I counted to him ten guineas into his hand. «Well», said he, turning to his companion, «I never till now earned money so speedily; but what shall we do with it?» They then wished me a good morning, and proceeded over Westminster Bridge. The first object that presented itself to their view was a poor woman crying bitterly, with three children hanging round her, each sobbing, though apparently too young to understand their mother's grief. On inquiring the cause of her distress, Mr. Wesley learned that the creditors of her husband were dragging him to prison, after having sold their effects which were inadequate to pay the debt by eighteen shillings, which the creditors declared should be paid. One guinea made her happy! They then proceeded on, followed by the blessings of the now happy mother. On Mr. Wesley's inquiring of Mr. Barton, his friend, where their charity was most needed, he replied he knew of no place where his money would be more acceptable than in Giltspur-street Compter. They accordingly repaired thither, and on asking the turnkey to point out the most miserable object under his care, he answered, if they were come in search of poverty, they need not go far. The first ward they entered they were struck with the appearance of a poor wretch who was greedily eating some potato skins. On being questioned, he informed them that he had been in that situation, supported by the casual alms of compassionate strangers, for several months, without any hope of release, and that he was confined for the debt of half a guinea. On hearing this, Mr. Wesley gave him a guinea, which he received with the utmost gratitude; and he had the pleasure of seeing him liberated with half a guinea in his pocket. The poor man, on leaving his place of confinement, said: «Gentlemen, as you come here in search of poverty, pray go up stairs, if it be not too late». They instantly proceeded thither, and beheld a sight which called forth all their compassion. On a low stool, with his back towards them, sat a man, or rather a skeleton, for he was literally nothing but skin and bone; his hand supported his head, and his eyes seemed to be riveted to the opposite corner of the chamber, where lay stretched out on a pallet of straw, a young woman, in the last stage of consumption, apparently lifeless, with an infant by her side, which was quite dead. Mr. Wesley immediately sent for medical assistance; but it was too late for the unfortunate female, who expired a few hours afterwards from starvation, as the doctor declared. You may imagine, my Lord, that the remaining eight guineas would not go far in aiding such distress as this. No expense was spared for the relief of the now only surviving sufferer. But so extreme was the weakness to which he was reduced, that six weeks elapsed before he could speak sufficiently to relate his own history. It appeard that he had been a reputable merchant, and had married a beautiful young lady, eminently accomplished, whom he almost idolized. They lived happily together for some time, until, by failure of a speculation in which this whole property was embarked, he was completely ruined. No sooner did he become acquainted with his misfortune than he called all his creditors together, and laid before them the state of his affairs, showing them his books which were in the most perfect order. They all willingly signed the dividend, except the lawyer who owed his rise in the world to this merchant: the sum was two hundred and fifty pounds, for which he obstinately declared he should be sent to jail. It was in vain the creditors urged him to pity his forlorn condition, and to consider his great respectability: that feeling was a stranger to his breast, and, in spite of all their remonstrances, he was hurried away to prison, followed by his weeping wife. As she was very accomplished, she continued to maintain herself by the use of her pencil in painting small ornaments on cards; and thus they managed to put a little aside for the time of her confinement. But so long an illness succeeded this event, that she was completely incapacitated from exerting herself for their subsistence, and their scanty savings were soon expended by procuring the necessaries which her situation then required. They were driven to pawn their clothes, and their resources failing, they found themselves at last reduced to absolute starvation. The poor infant had just expired from want, and the hapless mother was about to follow it to the grave when Mr. Wesley and his friend entered; and, as I before said, the husband was so reduced from the same cause, that, without the utmost care, he must have fallen a sacrifice; and as Mr. Wesley, who was not for doing things by halves, had acquainted himself with this case of extreme misery, he went to the creditors and informed them of it. They were beyond measure astonished to learn what he had to name to them; for so long a time had elapsed without hearing anything of the merchant, or his family, that some supposed him to be dead, and others that he had left the country. Among the rest he called on the lawyer, and painted to him, in the most glowing colours, the wretchedness he had beheld, and which he (the lawyer) had been instrumental in causing; but even this could not move him to compassion. He declared the merchant should not leave the prison without paying him every farthing! Mr. Wesley repeated his visit to the other creditors who, considering the case of the sufferer, agreed to raise the sum and release him. Some gave one hundred pounds, others two hundred pounds, and another three hundred pounds. The affairs of the merchant took a different turn : God seemed to prosper him, and in the second year he called his creditors together, thanked them for their kindness, and paid the sum so generously obtained. Success continuing to attend him, he was enabled to pay all his debts, and afterwards realized considerable property. His afflictions made such a deep impression upon his mind, that he determined to remove the possibility of others suffering from the same cause, and for this purpose advanced a considerable sum as a foundation fund for the relief of small debtors. And the very first person who partook of the same was *the inexorable lawyer!*»

This remarkable fact so entirely convinced Lord Shelbourne of the mistaken opinion he had formed of Mr. Wesley, that he immediately ordered a dozen of busts to embellish the grounds of his beautiful residence.

Questions.

1. With whom was Mr. Dudley one evening taking tea? — 2. Where did Mr. Culy conduct him? — 3. Whose bust particularly attracted Mr. Dudley's attention?—4. What did Mr. Culy say?—5. What exclamation did Lord Shelbourne make, when asked whether he had heard of John Wesley? — 6. Give an account of Mr. Culy's persuading Mr. Wesley to have his bust taken? — 7. On leaving Mr. Culy, who was the first object that presented itself to Mr. Wesley and his companion? — 8. What was the cause of the poor woman's distress, and how did Mr. Wesley make her happy? — 9. On entering the first ward in Giltspur-street Compter, with what was Mr. Wesley struck?— 10. Of

what did the poor wretch inform him, and how did Mr. Wesley relieve him?—
11. What did the poor man say, on leaving his place of confinement? — 12.
What sight did Mr. Wesley and his companion next behold? — 13. Give the
story of the merchant? — 14. What effect had the above remarkable fact on
Lord Shelbourne?

80. Nelson.

This darling hero of his country, when eighteen years of age, was
obliged to return from sea, on account of the bad state of his health, and
leave his brother officers, then, like himself, beginning their career, in
the full enjoyment of health and hope. This depressed his spirit very
much; and long afterwards, when the fame of Nelson was known as that
of England itself, he spoke of the feelings, which he at that time endured. «I felt impressed», said he, «that I should never rise in my profession. My mind was staggered with a view of the difficulties which I
had to surmount, and the little interest I possessed. I could discover no
means of reaching the object of my ambition. After a long and gloomy
reverie, in which I almost wished myself over board, a sudden glow of
patriotism was kindled within me, and presented my King and country
as my patrons» — «Well then», I exclaimed: «I will be a hero; and con-
fiding in Providence, I will brave every danger». From that hour, as he
often declared to captain Hardy, a radiant orb was suspended before his
mind's eye, which urged him on to renown; and he spoke of these aspi-
rations of his youth, as if they had in them a character of divinity, as
if — «the light which led him on, was light from Heaven». Although
the promotion of Nelson was as rapid as it could be, yet it was much too
slow for his ardent ambition. He was never happy for a moment, when
not on actual service. In a letter to the Lords of the Admiralty, in 1792,
requesting a ship he adds: «if your Lordships will only be pleased to
appoint me to a *cockle boat*, I shall feel grateful».

After the sieges of Calvi and Bastia, in 1793, in which Nelson displayed military talents which would not have disgraced a general, his
services, by an unpardonable omission, were altogether overlooked; his
name did not even appear in the list of wounded, although he had lost
an eye. «One hundred and ten days», said he: «I have been actually
engaged at sea and on shore against the enemy; three actions against

ships, two against Bastia in my own ship, four boat actions, two villages taken, and twelve sail of vessels taken. I do not know that any one has done more; I have had the comfort to be always applauded by my own commander in chief, but never to be rewarded; and, what is more mortifying, for service in which I have been wounded, others have been praised, who, at the same time, were actually in bed, far from the scene of action. They have not done me justice; but never mind — I'll have a gazette of my own». How amply was this second sight of glory realized!

Previous to his attack on Teneriffe, after having failed in an attempt to take it before, he wrote to his commander in chief: «This night I command the whole force destined to land under the batteries of the town; and to-morrow my head will probably be crowned either with laurel or cypress». Perfectly aware how desperate a service this was likely to prove, he called his son-in-law, Lieutenant Nisbet, into his cabin, that he might assist in arranging and burning his mother's letters. Perceiving that the young man was armed, he earnestly begged him to remain behind. — «Should we both fall, Josiah», said he, «what will become of your poor mother? The care of the Theseus falls to you; stay, therefore, and take care of her». Nisbet replied: «Sir, the ship must take care of herself. I will go with you to-night, if I never go again».

The boats landed amidst powerful discharges of forty or fifty pieces of cannon, with musketry from one end of the town to the other. Nelson, when in the act of stepping out of the boat, received a shot through the right elbow, and fell; Nisbet, who was close to him, placed him at the bottom of the boat. He then examined the wound, and taking a silk handkerchief from his neck, bound it above the lacerated vessels, which saved his life. One of the bargemen tore his shirt into shreds, and made a sling for the wounded arm; Nisbet took one of the oars, and collecting four or five seamen, rowed back towards the vessel. Nelson desired to be raised up, that he «might look a little about him»; when a general shriek was heard from the Fox, which had received a shot under water, and gone down. Ninety seven men sank with her, and eighty three were saved, many by Nelson himself, whose exertions on this occasion materially increased the pain and danger of the wound. The first ship which the boat could reach, happened to be the Seahorse; but nothing could induce him to go on board, though he was assured that the attempt to row to another ship might be at the risk of his life. «I had rather suffer

15

death», said he, «than alarm Mrs. Freemantle, by letting her see me in this state, when I can give her no tidings of her husband». He was then rowed alongside the Theseus, and peremptorily refused all assistance in getting on board: so impatient was he that the boat should return, in hopes of saving a few more men from the Fox. He desired to have only a single rope thrown over the side, which he twisted round his left hand. «Let me alone»! said he, «I have yet my legs left, and one arm. Tell the surgeon to get his instruments; I know I must lose my right arm, so the sooner it is off the better».

It was Nelson's practice during a cruise, whenever circumstances would permit, to have his captains on board, and fully explain to them his plans. He had done this previous to the battle of the Nile; and when Capt. Berry, on comprehending the design of doubling on the enemy's ships, exclaimed with transport: «If we succeed, what will the world say?» — There is no *if* in the case», replied Nelson: «that we shall succeed is certain: who may live to tell the story is a very different question».

In this battle the French had a superiority over the British of one hundred and eighty four guns, and three thousand and eighty two men; yet they lost five sail taken, three sail burnt, one driven on shore and fired, and three frigates. «A victory», said the gallant Nelson, «is not a word strong enough for such an achievement: it should be called a conquest». From Bonaparte it drew this acknowledgement: «The destinies have wished to prove by this event, as by all others, that if they have given us a preponderance on the Continent, they have given the empire of the sea to our rivals».

Of all the engagements in which Nelson had been engaged, that off Copenhagen was said to have been the most terrible; when it was terminated, and Nelson had landed, some difficulty occurred in adjusting the duration of the armistice. Nelson required sixteen weeks, giving like a seaman the true reason, that he might have time to act against the Russian fleet and return. This not being acceded to, a hint was thrown out by one of the Danish commissioners of the renewal of hostilities. «Renew hostilities»! said he to one of his friends, for he understood French enough to comprehend what was said, though not to answer it in the same language: «Tell him we are ready at a moment! Ready to bombard this very night» !

Questions.

1. What was Nelson obliged to do, when eighteen years of age, and why?—
2. What effect had it on his mind, and what did he afterwards say of his feelings at that time? — 3. What did he often declare to Captain Hardy? — 4. What words did he add in a letter to the Lords of the Admiralty?

5. On what occasion were his services altogether overlooked? — 6. What did he say of it?

7. What did he write to his commander in chief,-previous to his attack on Teneriffe? — 8. Whom did he call into his cabin, and for what purpose? — 9. What did he say to Lieutenant Nisbet, and what was Nisbet's answer?

10. What happened to Nelson, when stepping out of the boat,-and what assistance did Nisbet and one of the bargemen give him?—11. Give an account of the disaster that happened to the Fox, and of Nelson's noble conduct on the occasion?

12. What was Nelson's practice during a cruise? — 13. What did Capt. Berry exclaim, on comprehending the design of doubling on the enemy's ships, and what did Nelson reply?

14. What superiority had the French, in this battle, over the British, and what did they lose?—15. What did the gallant Nelson say of it? — 16. What acknowledgement did it draw from Bonaparte?

17. What is said of Nelson's engagement off Copenhagen? — 18. What did Nelson require, and what reason did he give for it? — 19. What were his words, when a hint was thrown out of the renewal of hostilities?

---

81. The Loss of the Royal George.

The Royal George was a three-decker, a ship of one hundred and twenty guns, 24 and 31 pounders, with a crew of one thousand men. The length of her gun-deck was 210 feet, the breadth 56; her main-mast was 124 feet high, fore-mast 112, mizen-mast 112, and the main yard one hundred and six feet long. She measured sixty-six feet from the kelson to the taffrail; and being a flag-ship her lanterns were so big, that the men used to go into them to clean them.

In August, 1782, the Royal George had come to Spithead. She was in a very complete state, with hardly any leakage, so that there was no occasion for the pumps to be touched oftener than once in every three or four days. By the 19th of August she had got six months' provision on board, and also many tons of shot. The ship had her gallants up, the blue flag of Admiral Kempenfeldt was flying at the mizen, and the ensign

was hoisted on the ensign-staff, — and she was in about two days to have
sailed to join the grand fleet in the Mediterranean. It was ascertained that
the water-cock must be taken out, and a new one put in. The water-cock
is something like the tap of a barrel, — it is in the hold of the ship on
the starboard side, and at that part of the ship called the well. By turning
a thing which is inside the ship, the sea-water is let into a cistern in the
hold, and it is from that pumped up to wash the deck. In some ships
the water is drawn up the side in buckets, and there is no water cock.
To get out the old water-cock it was necessary to make the ship heel so
much on her larboard side as to raise the outside of this water-cock above
water. This was done at about 8 o'clock on the morning of the 19th of
August. To do this the whole of the guns on the larboard side were run
out so far as they would go, quite to the breasts of the guns, and the
starboard guns drawn in a midship and secured by tackles, two to every
gun, one on each side. This brought the water nearly on a level with
the port-holes of the larboard side, of the lower gundeck. The men were
working at this water-cock on the outside of the ship for nearly an hour,
the ship remaining on one side.

At about 9 o'clock A. M., or rather before, we had just finished our
breakfast, — says the narrator, — and the last lighter, with rum on board,
had come alongside: this vessel was a sloop of about fifty tons, and belonged
to three brothers, who used her to carry things on board the men-of-war.
She was lashed to the larboard side of the Royal George, and we were
piped to clear the lighter, and get the rum out of her, and stow it in the
hold of the Royal George. I was in the waist of our ship, on the larboard
side, bearing the rum-casks over, as some men of the Royal George were
aboard the sloop to sling them.

At first no danger was apprehended from the ship's being on one side,
although the water kept dashing in at the port-holes at every wave; and
there being mice in the lower part of the ship, which were disturbed by
the water which dashed in, they were hunted in the water by the men,
and there had been a rare game going on. However, by about 9 o'clock
the additional quantity of rum on board the ship, and also the quantity of
sea-water – which had dashed in at the port-holes, brought the larboard
port-holes of the lower gun deck nearly level with the sea.

As soon as that was the case, the carpenter went on the quarter-deck
to the lieutenant of the watch, to ask him to give orders to right ship,

as the ship could not bear it any longer. However, the lieutenant made him a very short answer, and the carpenter then went below. The captain's name was Waghorn. He was on board, but where he was I do not know; — however, captains, if anything is to be done when the ship is in harbour, seldom interfere, but leave it all to the officer of the watch. The lieutenant was, if I remember right, the third lieutenant; he had not joined us long; his name I do not recollect; he was a good-sized man, between thirty and forty years of age. The men called him «Jib-and-Foresail-Jack», for, if he had the watch in the night, he would be always bothering the men to alter the sails, and it was «up jib», and «down jib», and «up foresail» and «down foresail», every minute. However, the men considered him more of a troublesome officer than a good one; and, from a habit he had of moving his fingers about when walking the quarter-deck, the men said he was an organ-player from London, but I have no reason to suppose that that was the case. The admiral was either in the cabin or in his steerage, I do not know which; and the barber, who had been to shave him, had just left. The admiral was a man upwards of seventy years of age; he was a thin tall man who stooped a good deal.

As I have already stated, the carpenter left the quarter-deck and went below. In a very short time he came up again, and asked the lieutenant of the watch to right the ship, and said again that the ship could not bear it; but the lieutenant replied: «D— ye, sir, if you can manage the ship better than I can, you had better take the command». Myself and a good many more were at the waist of the ship and at the gangways, and heard what passed, and as we knew the danger, we began to feel aggrieved; for there were some capital seamen on board, who knew what they were about quite as well as the officers.

In a very short time, a minute or two I should think, the lieutenant ordered the drummer to be called to beat to right ship. The drummer was called in a moment, and the ship was then just beginning to sink. I jumped off the gangway as soon as the drummer was called. There was no time for him to beat his drums, and I don't know that he had even time to get it. I ran down to my station, and by the time I had got there, the men were tumbling down the hatchways one over another to get to their stations as soon as possible to right ship. My station was at the third gun from the head of the ship on the starboard side of the lower gun-deck, close by where the cable passes, indeed it was just abaft the bight of the cable. I said to the lieutenant of our gun, whose name was Carrel, for every gun has a captain and a lieutenant (though they are only sailors): «Let us try to house our gun out without waiting for the drum, as it will help to right ship». We pushed the gun, but it ran back upon us. and we could not start it. The water then rushed in at nearly all the port-holes of the larboard side of the lower gun-deck, and I directly said to Carrel: «Ned, lay hold of the ring-bolt, and jump out at the port-hole; the ship is sinking, and we shall all be drowned». He laid hold of the ring-bolt, and jumped out at the port-hole into the sea: I believe he was drowned, for I never saw him afterwards. I immediately got out at the same port-hole, which was the third from the head of the ship on the starbord side of the lower gun-deck, and when I had done so, I saw the port hole as full of heads as it could cram, all trying to get out. I caught hold of the best bower-anchor, which was just above me, to prevent my falling back again into the port-hole, and seized hold of a woman who was trying to get out at the same place,— I dragged her out. The ship was full of Jews, women, and people selling all sorts of things. I threw the woman from me, — and saw all the heads drop back again in at the port-hole; for the ship had got so much on her larboard side, that the starboard port-holes were as upright as if the men had tried to get out at the top of a chimney with nothing for their legs and feet to act upon. I threw the woman from me, and just the moment after the air that was between decks drafted out at the port-holes very quickly. It was quite a huff of wind, and it blew my hat off, for I had all my clothes on, including my hat. The ship then sank in a moment. I tried to swim, but I could not swim a stroke, although I plunged as hard as I could with both hands and feet. The sinking of the ship drew me down, — indeed I think I must have gone down within a yard as low as the ship did. When the ship touched the bottom, the water boiled up a great deal, and I felt that I could swim.

When I was about half way up to the top of the water, I put my right hand on the head of a man that was nearly exhausted. He wore long hair, as many of the men at that time did; he tried to grapple me, and he put his four fingers into my right shoe alongside the outer edge of my foot. I succeeded in kicking my shoe off, and, putting my hand on his shoulder, I shoved him away, — I then rose to the surface of the water.

At the time the ship was sinking, there was a barrel of tar on the starboard side of her deck, and that had rolled to the larboard and staved as the ship went down; and when I rose to the top of the water, the tar was floating like fat on the top of a boiler. I got the tar about my hair and face, but I struck it away as well as I could, and when my head became above water, I heard the cannon ashore firing for distress. I looked about me, and at the distance of eight or ten yards from me, I saw the main-topsail-halyard-block above water; — the water was about thirteen fathoms deep, and at that time the tide was coming in. I swam to the main-topsail-halyard-block, got on it, and sat upon it, and there I rode. The fore, main, and mizen tops were all above water, as were part of the bowsprit and part of the ensign staff, with the ensign upon it.

In going down, the main-yard of the Royal George caught the boom of the rum-lighter and sunk her, and there is no doubt that this made the Royal George more upright in the water when sunk than she otherwise would have been, as she did not lie much more on her beam-ends than small vessels often do when left dry on a bank of mud.

When I got on the main-topsail-halyard-block I saw the admiral's baker in the shrouds of the mizen-topmast, and directly after that the woman whom I had pulled out of the port-hole came rolling by. I said to the baker, who was an Irishman named Robert Cleary: «Bob, reach out your hand and catch hold of that woman; — that is the woman I pulled out at the port-hole. I dare say she is not dead». He said: «I dare say she is dead enough; it is of no use to catch hold of her». I replied, «I dare say she is not dead». He caught hold of the woman and hung her head over one of the ratlins of the mizen-shrouds, and there she hung by her chin, which was hitched over the ratlin; but a surf came and knocked her backwards, and away she went rolling over and over. A captain of a frigate which was lying at Spithead came up in a boat as fast as he could. I dashed out my left hand in a direction towards the woman as a sign to him. He saw it, and saw the woman. His men left off rowing, and they pulled the woman aboard their boat, and laid her on one of the thwarts. The captain of the frigate called out to me: «My man, I must take care of those that are in more danger than you». I said: «I am safely moored now, Sir».

There was a seaman, named Hibbs, hanging by his two hands from the main-stay; and as he hung there, the sea washed over him every now and then as much as a yard deep over his head; and when he saw it coming he roared out: however, he was but a fool for that; for if he had kept himself quiet, he would not have wasted his strength, and would have been able to take the chance of holding on so much the longer. The captain of the frigate had his boat rowed to the main-stay; but they got the stay over part of the head of the boat, and were in great danger be· fore they got Hibbs on board. The captain of the frigate got then all the men that were in the different parts of the rigging, including myself and the baker, into his boat, and took us on board the Victory, where the doc· tors recovered the woman; but she was very ill for three or four days. On board the Victory I saw the body of the carpenter, lying on the hearth before the galley fire; some women were trying to recover him, but he was quite dead.

The captain of the Royal George, who could not swim, was picked up and saved by one of our seamen. The lieutenant of the watch — who was the principal cause of the misfortune — I believe was drowned. The number of persons who lost their lives I cannot state with any degree of accuracy, because of there being so many Jews, women and other persons on board, who did not belong to the ship. The complement of the ship was nominally 1000 men, but it was not quite full. Some were ashore, and sixty marines had gone ashore that morning.

The government allowed L5 each of the seamen who were on board, and not drowned, for the loss of their things. I saw the list, and there were only seventy-five. A vast number of the best men were in the hold stowing away the rum casks: they must all have perished, and so must many of the·men who were slinging the casks in the sloop. Two of the three brothers belonging to the sloop perished, the other was saved. I have no doubt that the men caught hold of each other, forty or fifty to· gether, and drowned one another — those who could not swim catching hold of those who could; and there is also little doubt that as many got into the launch as could cram into her, hoping to save themselves in that way, and went down in her altogether.

In a few days after the Royal George sunk, dead bodies would come up, thirty or forty nearly at a time. Nothing was more frightful than, when at a little distance, when the moon shed her tender beams over the placid water, where so many brave men had lost their.lives, to see the heads popping up from under the water. A body would sometimes rise up so suddenly as to make one's hair stand on end. The watermen, there is no doubt, made a good business of it: they took from the bodies of the men their buckles, money and watches, and then made fast a rope to their heels, and towed them to land.

The water-cock ought to have been put to rights before the great quantity of shot was put on board; but if the lieutenant of the watch had given the order to right ship a couple of minutes earlier, when the carpenter first spoke to him, nothing amiss would have happened; as three or four men at each tackle of the starboard guns would very soon have boused the guns all out and righted the ship. At the time this happened, the Royal George was anchored by two anchors from the head. The wind was rather from the north-west, — not much of it, — only a bit of a breeze; and there was no sudden gust or puff of wind, which made her heel just before she sunk; it was the weight of metal, and the water which had dashed in through the port-holes, which sunk her, and not the effect of wind upon her. Indeed, I do not recollect that she had even what is called a stitch of canvass, to keep her head steady as she lay at anchor.

I am now seventy-five years of age, and was about twenty-four when this happened.

The foregoing curious and highly interesting narrative has been communicated by *Mr. James Ingram*, who was on board at the time the Royal George sunk. We have considered it better to give it in his own simple language, as affording a more graphic description of this extraordinary and melancholy catastrophe than more beautiful language could do. At the same time it may serve the young reader as an exercise in sea terms. J. S. S. Rothwell.

The following interesting lines have been written on the above unhappy event, by which 800 souls, with the unfortunate Admiral Kempenfeldt, perished:

> •Toll for the brave!
> The brave that are no more,
> All sunk beneath the wave
> Fast by their native shore.

«Eight hundred of the brave,
  Whose courage well was tried;
Had made the vessel heel,
  And laid her on her side.

«A land breeze shook the shrouds,
  And she was overset;
Down went the Royal George
  With all her crew complete.

«Toll for the brave!
  Brave Kempenfeldt is gone;
His last sea fight is fought,
  His work of glory done.

«It was not in the battle;
  No tempest gave the shock:
She sprang no fatal leak;
  She ran upon no rock.

«His sword was in his sheath,
  His fingers held the pen,
When Kempenfeld went down
  With twice four hundred men.

«Weigh the vessel up,
  Once dreaded by our foes;
And mingle with our cup
  The tear that England owes.

«Her timbers yet are sound,
  And she may float again,
Full charged with distant thunder,
  And plough the distant main.

«But Kempenfeldt is gone;
  His victories are o'er;
And he and his eight hundred
  Shall plough the wave no more». —

                        Cowper.

Questions.

1. What was the length and breadth of the Royal George, and what the height of her masts? — 2. Where was the Royal George to have sailed to? — 3. What was ascertained? — 4. What was necessary to be done to get out the old water-cock? — 5. What was not apprehended at first? — 6. What were in the lower part of the ship? — 7. What did the carpenter do? — 8. What sort of an answer did he get? — 9. What was the Lieutenant called, and why? — 10.

What did the men say he was? — 11. Where was the Admiral, what was his name, and what sort of man was he? — 12. What orders did the Lieut. give respecting the drummer, and what followed? — 13. Where did the water rush in, and what did the narrator say to Carrell? — 14. What did the narrator see on getting out of the port-hole? — 15. Of what was the ship full? — 16. What did narrator do with the woman? — 17. As the ship sank, what did the narrator try to do? — 18. When he was about half way to the top of the water, what did he do? — 19. When his head came above water, what did he hear and see? — 20. How deep was the water? — 21. What did the Royal George do in going down? — 22. What did the Admiral's baker do with the woman, and what happened to her afterwards? — 23. Who came in a boat? — 24. Where was the seaman named Hibbs, and what did he do? — 25. Whom did the narrator see on board the Victory? — 26. What can he not state? — 27. What was the complement of the ship? — 28. What did the government allow? — 29. Of what has the narrator no doubt? — 30. What would come up a few days after the Royal George sunk? — 31. What should have been done before the shot was put on board?

82. Anecdotes of Discoveries.

The love of knowledge will itself do a great deal towards its acquisition; and if it exist with that force and constancy which it exhibits in the characters of all truly great men, it will induce that ardent, but humble spirit of observation and inquiry, without which there can be no success. Sir Isaac Newton, of all men that ever lived, is the one who has most extended the territory of human knowledge; and he used to speak of himself as having been all his life but «a child gathering pebbles on the seashore» — probably meaning by that allusion, not only to express his modest conviction how mere an outskirt the field of his discoveries was, compared with the vastness of universal nature, but to describe likewise the spirit in which he had pursued his investigations. That was a spirit, not of selection and system building, but of childlike alacrity, in seizing upon whatever contributions of knowledge Nature threw at his feet, and of submission to all intimations of observation and experiment. On some occasions, he was wont to say, that, if there was any mental habit or endowment in which he excelled the generality of men, it was that of patience in the examination of the facts and phenomena of his subject. This was merely another specimen of that teachableness which constitutes the character of a wise man. He loved Truth, and wooed her with the unwearying ardour of a lover. Other speculators had consulted the book of nature principally for the purpose of seeking in it the defence of some favourite theory; partially, therefore, and hastily, as one would consult a dictionary: Newton perused it as a volume altogether worthy of being studied for its own sake. Hence proceeded both the patience with which he traced its characters, and the rich and plentiful discoveries with which the search rewarded him. It is, indeed, most instructive to all who are anxious to engage in the pursuit of know-ledge, (and is therefore properly introductory to the general subject we are about to treat), to consider the manner in which both this great man and many others, possessing a portion of his observant and inventive genius, have availed themselves, for the enlargement of the boundaries of philosophy, of such common occurrences as, from their very common-ness, had escaped the attention of all less active and original minds.

From one of these simple incidents did Sir Isaac Newton give to the world, for the first time, the system of the universe. It was in the twenty third year of his age, that this extraordinary man was sitting, as we are told, one day in his garden, when an apple fell from a tree beside him. His mind was perhaps occupied, at that fortunate moment, in one of those philosophical speculations on space and motion, which are known to have, about this time, engaged much of his attention; and the little incident, which interrupted him, was instantly seized upon by his active spirit, and, by that power which is in genius, assimilated with thought. The existence of gravitation, or a tendency towards the centre of the earth, was already known, as affecting all bodies in the imme-diate vicinity of our planet; and the great Galileo had even ascertained the law, or rate, according to which their motion is accelerated, as they continue their descent. But no one had yet dreamed of the gravitation of the heavens, — till the idea now first dimly rose in the mind of Newton. The same power, he said to himself, which has drawn this apple from its branch, would have drawn it from a position a thousand times as high. Wherever we go, we find this gravitation reigning over all things. If we ascend even to the tops of the highest mountains, we discover no sensible diminution of its power. Why may not its influence extend far beyond any height, to which we can make our way? Why may it not reach to the moon itself? Why may not this be the very power which retains that planet in its orbit, and keeps it revolving as it does around our own earth? It was a splendid conjecture, and we may be sure, that Newton instantly set all his sagacity at work to verify it.

Another very beautiful example, in the way in which some of the most valuable truths of philosophy have been suggested for the first time, by the simplest incidents of common life, is afforded by Galileo's discovery of the regularity of oscillation in the pendulum. It was while standing one day in the metropolitan church of Pisa, that his attention was first awakened to this important fact, by observing the movements of a lamp suspended from the ceiling, which some accident had disturbed and caused to vibrate. Now this or something exactly similar, was a phenomenon which, of course, every one had observed thousands of times before. But yet nobody had ever viewed it with the philosophic attention, with which it was on this occasion examined by Galileo. Or if, as possibly was the case, any one had been half unconsciously struck for a moment by that apparent equability of motion, which arrested so forcibly the curiosity of Galileo, the idea had been allowed to escape the instant it had been caught, as relating to a matter not worth a second thought. The young philosopher of Italy (for he had not then reached the twentieth year) saw at once the important application which might be made of the thought that had suggested itself to him. He took care, therefore, to ascertain immediately the truth of his conjecture, by careful and repeated experiment, and the result was the complete discovery of the principle of the most perfect measure of time which we yet possess.

Another example which may be given, is that of the famous Prince Rupert's supposed discovery of the mode of engraving, called mezzotinto, which is said to have been suggested to him by observing a soldier, one morning, rubbing off from the barrel of his musket the rust which it had contracted from being exposed to the night dew. The prince perceived, on examination, that the dew had left on the surface of the steel a collection of very minute holes, so as to form the resemblance of a dark engraving, part of which had been here and there already rubbed away by the soldier. He immediately conceived the idea that it would be practicable to find a way of covering a plate of copper in the same manner with little holes. Pursuing this thought, he at last after a variety of experiments, invented a species of steel roller, covered with points or salient teeth, which being pressed against the copper plate, indented it in the manner he wished; and the roughness thus occasioned had only to be scraped down, where necessary, in order to produce any gradation of shade that might be desired.

The celebrated modern invention of the balloon is said to have had an origin still more simple. According to some authorities, the idea was first suggested to Stephen Montgolfier, one of the two brothers to whom we owe the contrivance, by the waving of a linen shirt, which was hanging before the fire, in the warm and ascending air. Others tell us, that it was his brother Joseph who first thought of it, on perceiving the smoke ascending his chimney one day during the memorable siege of Gibraltar, as he was sitting alone, musing on the possibility of penetrating into the place, to which his attention had been called at the moment by a picture of it, on which he had accidentally cast his eyes. It is known, however, that the two brothers had, before this, studied and made themselves familiar with Priestley's work on the different kinds of air; and it is even said, that Stephen had conceived the idea of navigating the heavens, by the employment of a gas lighter than common atmospheric air, on his way home from Montpelier, where he had purchased that book. Newton, too, is well known to have been indebted for the first hint of certain of his great optical discoveries to the child's amusement of blowing bubbles out of soap; and as Dr. Pemberton has ingeniously observed, in his account of that great man's philosophy, «it is suitable to this mode of thinking that he has, in his «Observations on Daniel», made a very curious as well as useful remark, that our Saviour's precepts were all occasioned by some ordinary circumstance of things then especially before him». — The year 1815 is rendered memorable by the discovery of the safety lamp, one of the most beneficial applications of science to economical purposes yet made, by which hundreds, perhaps thousands, of lives have been preserved. Davy was led to the consideration of this subject by an application from Dr. Gray, the chairman of a society established in 1813, at Bishop Wearmouth, to consider and promote the means of preventing accidents by fire in coal pits. Being then in Scotland, he visited the mines on his return southward, and was supplied with specimens of fire damp, which, on reaching London, he proceeded to examine and analyze. He soon discovered that the carbonated hydrogen gas, called fire damp by the miners, would not explode when mixed with less than six, or more than fourteen times its volume of air; and further, that the explosive mixture could not be fired in tubes of small diameters and proportionate lengths.

Gradually diminishing these, he arrived at the conclusion, that a tissue of wire, in which the meshes do not exceed a certain small diameter, which may be considered as the ultimate limit of a series of such tubes, is impervious to the inflamed air; and that a lamp, covered with such tissue, may be used with perfect safety even in an explosive mixture, which takes fire, and burns within the cage, securely cut off from the power of doing harm. Thus when the atmosphere is so impure that the flame of the lamp itself cannot be maintained, the Davy still supplies light to the miner, and turns his worst enemy into an obedient servant. This invention, the certain source of large profit, he presented with characteristic liberality to the public. The words are preserved in which, when pressed to secure himself the benefit of it by a patent, he declined to do so: «I have enough for all my views and purposes, more wealth might be troublesome, and distract my attention from those pursuits in which I delight».

Questions.

1. What will the love of knowledge itself do, and what, if it exist with that force and constancy which it exhibits in the characters of all truly great men?— 2. Who has most extended the territory of human knowledge, and what did he say of himself? — 3. What was he wont to say, on some occasions? — 4. For what purpose had other speculators consulted the book of nature, and how did Newton peruse it? — 5. What is most instructive to all who are anxious to engage in the pursuit of knowledge?

6. What happened, when Sir Isaac Newton was sitting one day in his garden, and what effect did it produce on his mind? — 7. What was already known, and what law had the great Galileo ascertained? — 8. What did Newton say to himself?

9. On what occasion was Galileo's attention first awakened to the discovery of the regularity of oscillation in the pendulum? — 10. What did the young philosopher of Italy at once see, and what was the result of his careful and repeated experiment?

11. What other example may be given, and how is it said to have been suggested to Prince Rupert? — 12. What did the prince perceive, on examination, and what idea did he immediately conceive? — 13. What did he at last invent?

14. What is said of the origin of the invention of the balloon? — 15. What work had the two brothers studied before this, and what is Stephen said to have conceived? — 16. To what has Newton been indebted for certain of his great discoveries, and what has Dr. Pemberton ingeniously observed? — 17. By what is the year 1815 rendered memorable? — 18. Give an account of Davy's invention? — 19. What were his words, when pressed to secure himself the benefit of it by a patent?

Historical Extracts.

1. Ancient England and the Romans.

If you look at a Map of the World, you will see, in the left-hand upper corner of the Eastern Hemisphere, two islands lying in the sea. They are England and Scotland, and Ireland; England and Scotland form the greater part of these Islands, Ireland is the next in size. The little neighbouring islands which are so small upon the Map as to be mere dots, are chiefly little bits of Scotland — broken off, I dare say, in the course of a great length of time, by the power of the restless water.

In the old days, a long, long while ago, before Our Saviour was born on earth and lay asleep in a manger, these Islands were in the same place, and the stormy sea roared round them, just as it roars now. But the sea was not alive, then, with great ships and brave sailors, sailing to and from all parts of the world. It was very lonely. The Islands lay solitary, in the great expanse of water. The foaming waves dashed against their cliffs, and the bleak winds blew over their forests; but the winds and waves brought no adventurers to land upon the Islands, and the savage Islanders knew nothing of the rest of the world, and the rest of the world knew nothing of them.

It is supposed that the Phoenicians, who were an ancient people famous for carrying on trade, came in ships to these Islands, and found that they produced tin and lead; both very useful things, as you know, and both produced to this very hour upon the sea-coast. The most celebrated tin mines in Cornwall are, still, close to the sea. One of them, which I have seen, is so close to it that it is hollowed out underneath the ocean; and the miners say that in stormy weather, when they are at work down in that deep place, they can hear the noise of the waves thundering above their heads. So, the Phoenicians, coasting about the Islands, would come, without much difficulty, to where the tin and lead were.

The Phoenicians traded with the Islanders for these metals, and gave the Islanders some other useful things in the exchange. The Islanders were, at first, poor savages, going almost naked or only dressed in the

17

rough skins of beasts, and staining their bodies, as other savages do, with coloured earths and the juices of plants. But the Phoenicians, sailing over to the opposite coasts of France and Belgium, and saying to the people there, « We have been to these white cliffs across the water, which you can see in fine weather, and from that country, which is called Britain, we bring this tin and lead, » tempted some of the French and Belgians to come over also. These people settled themselves on the south coast of England, which is now called Kent; and, although they were a rough people too, they taught the savage Britons some useful arts, and improved that part of the Islands. It is probable that other people came over from Spain to Ireland, and settled there.

Thus, by little and little, strangers became mixed with the Islanders, and the savage Britons grew into a wild bold people, almost savage, still, especially in the interior of the country away from the sea where the foreign settlers seldom went; but hardy, brave, and strong.

The whole country was covered with forests and swamps. The greater part of it was very misty and cold. There were no roads, no bridges, no streets, no houses that you would think deserving of the name. A town was nothing but a collection of straw-covered huts, hidden in thick wood, with a ditch all round, and a low wall, made of mud, or the trunks of trees placed one upon another. The people planted little or no corn, but lived upon the flesh of their flocks and cattle. They made no coins, but used metal rings for money. They were clever in basket-work, as savage people often are; and they could make a coarse kind of cloth, and some very bad earthenware. But in building fortresses they were much more clever.

They made boats of basket-work, covered with the skins of animals, but seldom, if ever, ventured far from the shore. They made swords, of copper mixed with tin; but these swords were of an awkward shape, and so soft that a heavy blow would bend one. They made light shields, short pointed daggers, and spears — which they jerked back after they had thrown them at an enemy, by a long strip of leather fastened to the stem. The butt-end was a rattle to frighten an enemy's horse. The ancient Britons, being divided into as many as thirty or forty tribes, each commanded by its own little King, were constantly fighting with one another, as savage people usually do; and they always fought with these weapons.

They were very fond of horses. The standard of Kent was the picture of a white horse. They could break them in and manage them wonderfully well. Indeed, the horses (of which they had an abundance, though they were rather small) were so well taught in those days that they can scarcely be said to have improved since; though the men are so much wiser. They understood and obeyed every word of command; and would stand still by themselves, in all the din and noise of battle, while their masters went to fight on foot. The Britons could not have succeeded in their most remarkable art, without the aid of these sensible and trusty animals. The art I mean, is the construction and management of war-chariots or cars, for which they have ever been celebrated in history. Each of the best sort of these chariots, not quite breast high in front, and open at the back, contained one man to drive, and two or three others to fight — all standing up. The horses who drew them were so well trained, that they would tear, at full gallop, over the most stony ways, and even through the woods; dashing down their masters' enemies beneath their hoofs, and cutting them to pieces with the blades of swords, or scythes, which were fastened to the wheels, and stretched out beyond the car on each side, for that cruel purpose. In a moment, while at full speed, the horses would stop, at the driver's command, the men within would leap out, deal blows about them with their swords like hail, leap on the horses, on the pole, spring back into the chariots anyhow; and, as soon as they were safe, the horses tore away again.

The Britons had a strange and terrible religion, called the Religion of the Druids. It seems to have been brought over, in very early times indeed, from the opposite country of France, anciently called Gaul, and to have mixed up the worship of the Serpent, and of the Sun and Moon, with the worship of some of the Heathen Gods and Goddesses. Most of its ceremonies were kept secret by the priests, the Druids, who pretended to be enchanters, and who carried magicians' wands, and wore, each of them, about his neck, what he told ignorant people was a Serpent's egg in a golden case. But it is certain that the Druidical ceremonies included the sacrifice of human victims, the torture of some suspected criminals, and, on particular occasions, even the burning alive, in immense wicker cages, of a number of men and animals together. The Druid Priests had some kind of veneration for the Oak, and for the miseltoe — the same plant that we hang up in houses at Christmas Time now — when its white berries grew upon the Oak. They met together in dark woods, which they called Sacred Groves; and there they instructed, in their mysterious arts, young men who came to them as pupils, and who sometimes stayed with them as long as twenty years.

These Druids built great Temples and altars, open to the sky, of which some are yet remaining. Stonehenge, on Salisbury plain in Wiltshire, is the most extraordinary of these. Three curious stones, called Kits Coty House, on Bluebell Hill, near Maidstone in Kent, form another. We know, from examination of the great blocks of which such buildings are made, that they could not have been raised without the aid of some ingenious machines, which are common now, but which the ancient Britons certainly did not use in making their own uncomfortable houses. I should not wonder if the Druids, and their pupils who stayed twenty years, knowing more than the rest of the Britons, kept the people out of sight while they made these buildings. and then pretended that they built them by magic. Perhaps they had a hand in these fortresses too; at all events, as they were very powerful, and very much believed in, and as they made and executed the laws, and paid no taxes, I don't wonder that they liked their trade. And, as they persuaded the people that the more Druids there were, the better off the people would be, I don't wonder that there were a good many of them. But it is pleasant to think that there are no Druids now, who go on in that way, and pretend to carry Enchanters' Wands and Serpents' Eggs — and of course there is nothing of the kind any where.

Such was the improved condition of the ancient Britons, fifty-five years before the birth of Our Saviour, when the Romans, under their great General, Julius Caesar, were masters of all the rest of the known world. Julius Caesar had then just conquered Gaul; and hearing, in Gaul, a good deal about the opposite Islands with the white cliffs, and about the bravery of the Britons who inhabited it — some of whom had been fetched over to help the Gauls in the war against him — he resolved, as he was so near, to come and conquer Britain next.

So, Julius Caesar came sailing over to this Island of ours, with eighty vessels and twelve thousand men. And he came from the French coast between Calais and Boulogne, «because thence was the shortest passage into Britain;» just for the same reason as our steamboats now take the same track, every day. He expected to conquer Britain easily: but it was not such easy work as he supposed — for the bold Britons fought most bravely; and, what with not having his horse-soldiers with him (for they had been driven back by a storm), and what with having some of his vessels dashed to pieces by a high tide after they were drawn ashore, he ran great risk of being totally defeated. However, for once that the bold Britons beat him, he beat them twice; though not so soundly but that he was very glad to accept their proposals of peace, and go away.

But in the spring of the next year, he came back; this time, with eight hundred vessels and thirty thousand men. The British tribes chose, as their general-in-chief, a Briton, whom the Romans in their Latin language called Cassivellaunus, but whose British name is supposed to have been Caswallon. A brave general he was, and well he and his soldiers fought the Roman army! So well, that whenever in that war the Roman soldiers saw a great cloud of dust, and heard the rattle of the rapid British chariots, they trembled in their hearts. Besides a number of smaller battles, there was a battle fought near Cherstey, in Surrey; there was a battle fought near a marshy little town in a wood, the capital of that part of Britain, which belonged to Cassivellaunus, and which was probably near what is now Saint Albans, in Hertfordshire. However, brave Cassivellaunus had the worst of it, on the whole; though he and his men always fought like lions. As the other British chiefs were jealous of him, and were always quarrelling with him, and with one another, he gave up, and proposed peace. Julius Caesar was very glad to grant peace easily, and to go away again with all his remaining ships and men. He had expected to find pearls in Britain, and he may have found a few for anything I know; but, at all events, he found delicious oysters, and I am sure he found tough Britons — of whom, I dare say, he made the same complaint as Napoleon Bonaparte, the great French general, did eighteen hundred years afterwards, when he said they were such unreasonable fellows that they never knew when they were beaten. They never did know, I believe, and never will.

Nearly a hundred years passed on, and all that time there was peace in Britain. The Britons improved their towns and mode of life: became more civilised, travelled, and learnt a great deal from the Gauls and Romans. At last, the Roman Emperor Claudius sent Apulius Plautius, a skilful general, with a mighty force, to subdue the Island, and shortly afterwards arrived himself. They did little; and Ostorius Capula, another general, came. Some of the British Chiefs of Tribes submitted. Others resolved to fight to the death. Of these brave men, the bravest was Caractacus, or Caradoc, who gave battle to the Romans, with his army, among the mountains of North Wales. «This day,» said he to his soldiers, «decides the fate of Britain! Your liberty, or your eternal slavery, dates from this hour. Remember your brave ancestors who drove the great Caesar himself across the sea.» On hearing these words, his men, with a great shout, rushed upon the Romans. But the strong Roman swords and armour were too much for the weaker British weapons in close conflict. The Britons lost the day. The wife and daughter of the brave Caractacus were taken prisoners; his brothers delivered themselves up; he himself was betrayed into the hands of the Romans by his false and base stepmother; and they carried him, and all his family, in triumph to Rome.

But a great man will be great in misfortune, great in prison, great in chains. His noble air, and dignified endurance of distress, so touched the Roman people who thronged the streets to see him, that he and his family were restored to freedom. No one knows whether his great heart broke, and he died in Rome, or whether he ever returned to his own dear country. English oaks have grown up from acorns, and withered away, when they were hundreds of years old—and other oaks have sprung up in their places, and died too very aged—since the rest of the history of the brave Caractacus was forgotten.

Still, the Britons would not yield. They rose again and again, and died by thousands, sword in hand. They rose on every possible occasion. Suetonius, another Roman general, came, and stormed the Island of Anglesey (then called Mona) which was supposed to be sacred, and he burnt the Druids in their own wicker cages, by their own fire. But, even while he was in Britain with his victorious troops, the Britons rose. Because Boadicea, a British queen, the widow of the King of the Norfolk and Suffolk people, resisted the plundering of her property by the Romans who were settled in England; she was scourged by order of Catus, a Roman officer, and her two daughters were shamefully insulted in her presence, and her husband's relations were made slaves. To avenge this injury, the Britons rose, with all their might and rage. They drove Catus into Gaul; they laid the Roman possessions waste; they forced the Romans out of London, then a poor little town, but a trading place; they hanged, burnt, crucified, and slew by the sword, seventy thousand Romans in a few days. Suetonius strengthened his army, and advanced to give them battle. They strengthened their army, and desperately attacked his, on the field where it was strongly posted. Before the first charge of the Britons was made, Boadicea, in a war-chariot, with her hair streaming in the wind, and her injured daughters lying at her feet, drove among the troops, and cried to them for vengeance on their oppressors, the licentious Romans. The Britons fought to the last; but they were vanquished with great slaughter, and the unhappy queen took poison.

Still, the spirit of the Britons was not broken. When Suetonius left the country, they fell upon his troops, and retook the Island of Anglesey. The Emperor Agricola came, fifteen or twenty years afterwards, and retook it once more, and devoted seven years to subduing the country, especially that part of it which is now called Scotland; but its people, the Caledonians, resisted him at every inch of ground. They fought the blodiest battles with him; they killed their very wives and children, to prevent his making prisoners of them; they fell, fighting, in such great numbers that certain hills in Scotland are yet supposed to be vast heaps of stones piled up above their graves. The Emperor Hadrian came, thirty years afterwards, and still they resisted him. The Emperor Severus came, nearly a hundred years afterwards, and they worried his great army like dogs, rejoiced to see them die by thousands in the bogs and swamps. Caracalla, the son and successor of Severus, did the most to conquer them, for a time; but not by force of arms. He knew how little that would do. He yielded up a quantity of land to the Caledonians, and gave the Britons the same privileges as the Romans possessed. There was peace, after this, for seventy years.

Then new enemies arose. They were the Saxons, a fierce, seafaring people from the countries to the North of the Rhine, the great river of Germany, on the banks of which the best grapes grow to make the German wine. They began to come, in pirate ships, to the sea coast of Gaul and Britain, and to plunder them. They were repulsed by Carausius, a native either of Belgium or of Britain, who was appointed by the Romans to the command, and under whom the Britons first began to fight upon the sea. But after his time they renewed their ravages. A few years more, and the Scots (which was then the name for the people of Ireland), and the Picts, a northern people, began to make frequent plundering incursions into the South of Britain. All these attacks were repeated, at intervals, during two hundred years, and through a long succession of Roman Emperors and chiefs; during all which length of time, the Britons rose against the Romans, over and over again. At last, in the days of the Roman Emperor Honorius, when the Roman power all over the world was fast declining, and when Rome wanted all her soldiers at home, the Romans abandoned all hope of conquering Britain, and went away. And still at last, as at first, the Britons rose against them, in their old brave manner; for, a very little while before, they had turned away the Roman magistrates, and declared themselves an independent people.

Five hundred years had passed, since Julius Caesar's first invasion of the Island, when the Romans departed from it for ever. In the course of that time, although they had been the cause of terrible fighting and bloodshed, they had done much to improve the condition of the Britons. They had made great military roads; they had built forts; they had taught them how to dress, and arm themselves, much better than they had ever known how to do before; they had refined the whole British way of living. Agricola had built a great wall of earth, more than seventy miles long, extending from Newcastle to beyond Carlisle, for the purpose of keeping out the Picts and Scots; Hadrian had strengthened it; Severus, finding it much in want of repair, had built it afresh of stone. Above all, it was in the Roman time, and by means of Roman ships, that the Christian Religion was first brought into Britain, and its people first taught the great lesson that, to be good in the sight of God, they must love their neighbours as themselves, and do unto others as they would be done by. The Druids declared it was very wicked to believe any such thing, and cursed all the people who did believe it, very heartily. But when the people found that they were none the better for the blessings of the Druids, and none the worse for the curses of the Druids, but that the sun shone and the rain fell without consulting the Druids at all, they just began to think that the Druids were mere men, and that it signified very little whether they cursed or blessed. After which, the pupils of the Druids fell off greatly in numbers, and the Druids took to other trades.

Thus I have come to the end of the Roman time in **England**. It is but little that is known of those five hundred years; but some remains of them are still found. Often, when labourers are digging up the ground, to make foundations for houses or churches, they light on rusty money that once belonged to the Romans. Fragments of plates from which they ate, of goblets from which they drank, and of pavement on which they trod, are discovered among the earth that is broken by the plough, or the dust that is crumbled by the gardener's spade. Wells that the Romans sunk, still yield water; roads that the Romans made, form part of our highways. In some old battle-fields British spearheads and Roman armour have been found, mingled together in decay, as they fell in the thick pressure of the fight. Traces of Roman camps overgrown with grass, and of mounds that are the burial-places of heaps of Britons, are to be seen in almost all parts of the country. Across the bleak moors of Northumberland, the wall of Severus, over-run with moss and weeds, still stretches, a strong ruin; and the shepherds and their dogs lie sleeping on it · in the summer weather. On Salisbury Plain, Stonehenge yet stands: a monument of the earlier time when the Roman name was unknown in Britain, and when the Druids, with their best magic wands, could not have written it in the sands of the wild sea-shore.

(Dickens).

2. The Scots and Picts.

During the interval of blessed historic oblivion Adrian, who visited the island, thought fit to abandon the northern extremity, and erected a new rampart from the Solway to the Tyne, many miles south of the rampart of Agricola. Severus, likewise, who found his presence necessary in Britain to repel the incursions of the Caledonians and Meatae, erected a stone-wall almost parallel with that of Adrian; and so firmly was it constructed, that its remains are still visible. The Caledonians were a fierce and hardy tribe, supposed to have emigrated from Ireland into Scotland, the wild and mountainous region of which they occupied. The Meatae were the inhabitants of the northern part of England, who, though equally as barbarous as the Caledonians, yet not possessing a country so difficult of access were more easily subdued.

When Constantius ascended the imperial throne of Rome, he placed Britain under the Prefect of the Gauls and divided it into three provinces.

The first, called Britannia prima, comprehended all that portion of Britain, which lies south of the Thames. London was its capital. The second was named Britannia secunda. It comprehended that part of the country, which lies between the river Severn and the Irish sea, and which is now called Wales. Isca, or Caerleon, was its chief-town. The third named Maxima Caesariensis, included all the remaining part of Britain, east and north of the Thames and the Severn. York was its principal city. Towards the close of the fourth century the Britons engaged in the party of Maximus, a pretender to the imperial sceptre, and multitudes of them accompanied him into Gaul. His enterprize failed, but his British soldiers retreating to Armorica, settled there. The name Bretagne, Britany, and evident traces of their language are standing proofs of this event.

In the year of Christ 412 the weakened conditions of the empire obliged Honorius to withdraw the Roman troops from distant stations, in order to streng then the more central parts of his dominions. The Picts, so called from the term Pictich, a plunderer, together with the Scots, who derived that appellation from the Celtic word Scuite, a wanderer, quickly forced the rampart which had been raised by Roman skill, and defended by Roman bravery, and overwhelmed the unwarlike Britons, like a torrent. Twice the Roman emperor sent them aid from Gaul. Gallio of Ravenna, who commanded the last detachment of auxiliaries, having driven back the savage plunderers to their woods and fastnesses, assembled the chiefs of the island and informed them that they could not longer hope for the assistance of the Romans, but must depend for their safety upon their own exertions. The repairing of the wall of Severus, arms and military engines, with instructions how to use them, were the last kind offices the Britons received from their friendly conquerors. But arms and military engines are of little avail, without courage and experience, to use them. — Britain had been a Roman province nearly 400 years.

The Scots and Picts soon poured in again upon the effeminated Britons; who instead of uniting to oppose their dreaded foes, wasted the little strength they had in absurd disputes with one another. So wretched was the condition to which they were reduced, that they implored succour from Aëtius, the celebrated commander, whose courage and skill was the sole support of the empire against the attack of the dreadful Attila and his savage Huns, in most lamentable and bewailing language. « Come to our aid», said they, «for the barbarians drive us to the sea, and the sea repels us upon the weapons of the barbarians; so that the only choice left us is that of perishing in the waves, or by the swords of our ene- mies». Aëtius, having need of all his force to oppose his terrible foe, could afford them no succour. The Britons abandoned the open lands, and sought an asylum in the recesses of their forests. In 445 a prince, named Vortigern, apparently an ambitious, worthless man, gained the ascendancy over the Britons. Vortigern induced his countrymen to seek for aid against the Picts and Scots in Germany. For this purpose, the Britons sent an embassy to the Saxons, the people destined completely to enslave them.   (Holt).

3. The Saxons.

Off all the barbarous nations, known either in ancient or modern times, the Germans seem to have been the most distinguished both by their manners and political institutions, and to have carried to the highest pitch the virtues of valour and love of liberty; the only virtues which can have place among an uncivilized people, where justice and humanity are commonly neglected. Kingly government, even when established among the Germans (for it was not universal), possessed a very limited authority, and though the sovereign was usually chosen from among the royal family, he was directed in every measure by the common consent of the nation over whom he presided. When any important affairs were transacted, all the warriors met in arms, the men of greatest authority employed persuasion to engage their consent; the people expressed their approbation by rattling their armour, or their dissent by murmurs: there was no necessity for a nice scrutiny of votes among a multitude who were usually carried with a strong current to one side or the other; and the measure, thus suddenly chosen by general agreement, was executed with alacrity and prosecuted with vigour. Even in war, the princes go- verned more by example than by authority; but in peace the civil union was in a great measure dissolved, and the inferior leaders administered justice after an independent manner, each in his particular district. These were .elected by the votes of the people in their great councils; and though regard was paid to nobility in the choice, their personal qualities, chiefly their valour, procured them from the suffrages of their fellow-citizens that honourable, but dangerous distinction. The warriors of each tribe attached themselves to their leader with the most devoted affection and most unshaken constancy. They attended him as his ornament in peace, as his defence in war, as his council in the administration of justice. Their constant emulation in military renown dissolved not that inviolable friendship which they professed to their chieftain and to each other; to die for the honour of their band was their chief ambition: to survive its disgrace, or the death of their leader, was infamous. They even carried into the field their women and children, who adopted all the martial sentiments of the men: and being thus impelled by every human motive, they were invincible, where they were not opposed either by the similar manners and institutions of the neighbouring Germans, or by the superior discipline, arms, and numbers of the Romans.

The leaders and their military companions were maintained by the labour of their slaves, or by that of the weaker and less warlike part of the community, whom they defended. The contributions which they levied went not beyond a bare subsistence; and the honours, acquired by a superior rank, were the only reward of their superior dangers and fatigues. All the refined arts of life were unknown among the Germans: tillage itself was almost wholly neglected: they even seem to have been anxious to prevent any improvements of that nature; and the leaders, by annually distributing anew all the land among the inhabitants of each village, kept them from attaching themselves to particular possessions, or making such progress in agriculture as might divert their attention from military expeditions, the chief occupation of the community.

The Saxons had been for some time regarded as one of the most warlike tribes of this fierce people, and had become the terror of the neighbouring nations. They had diffused themselves from the northern parts of Germany and the Cimbrian Chersonesus, and had taken possession of all the sea-coast from the mouth of the Rhine to Jutland; whence they had long infested by their piracies all the eastern and southern parts of Britain, and the northern of Gaul. In order to oppose their inroads, the Romans had established an officer, whom they called *Count of the Saxon shore*; and as the naval arts can flourish among a civilized people alone, they seem to have been more successful in repelling the

Saxons, than any of the other barbarians by whom they were invaded. The dissolution of the Roman power invited them to renew their inroads; and it was an acceptable circumstance, that the deputies of the Britons appeared among them, and prompted them to undertake an enterprise, to which they were of themselves sufficiently inclined.

Hengist and Horsa, two brothers, possessed great credit among the Saxons, and were much celebrated both for their valour and nobility. They were reputed, as most of the Saxon princes, to be sprung from Woden, who was worshipped as a god among those nations, and they are said to be his great-grandsons; a circumstance which added much to their authority. We shall not attempt to trace any higher the origin of those princes and nations. It is evident what fruitless labour it must be to search, in those barbarous and illiterate ages, for the annals of a peo ple, when their first leaders, known in any true history, were believed by them to be the fourth in descent from a fabulous deity, or from a man exalted by ignorance into that character. The dark industry of an-tiquaries, led by imaginary analogies of names, or by uncertain tradi-tions, would in vain attempt to pierce into that deep obscurity which covers the remote history of those nations.

These two brothers, observing the other provinces of Germany to be occupied by a warlike and necessitous people, and the rich provinces of Gaul already conquered or overrun by other German tribes, found it easy to persuade their countrymen to embrace the sole enterprise which pro-mised a favourable opportunity of displaying their valour and gratifying their avidity. They embarked their troops in three vessels, and about the year 449 or 450, carried over 1600 men, who landed in the isle of Thanet, and immediately marched to the defence of the Britons against the northern invaders. The Scots and Picts were unable to resist the val-our of these auxiliaries; and the Britons, applauding their own wisdom in calling over the Saxons, hoped thenceforth to enjoy peace and security under the powerful protection of that warlike people.

But Hengist and Horsa perceiving from their easy victory over the Scots and Picts, with what facility they might subdue the Britons them-selves, who had not been able to resist those feeble invaders, were de-termined to conquer and fight for their own grandeur, not for the defence of their degenerate allies. They sent intelligence to Saxony of the fertility

and riches of Britain; and represented as certain the subjection of a people so long disused to arms, who, being now cut off from the Roman
empire, of which they had been a province during so many ages, had
not yet acquired any union among themselves, and were destitute of all
affection to their new liberties, and of all national attachments and re-
gards. The vices and pusillanimity of Vortigern, the British leader, were a
new ground of hope; and the Saxons in Germany, following such agreeable prospects, soon reinforced Hengist and Horsa, with 500 men, who
came over in seventeen vessels. The Britons now began to entertain
apprehensions of their allies, whose numbers they found continually aug-
menting; but thought of no remedy, except a passive submission and
connivance. This weak expedient soon failed them. The Saxons sought
a quarrel, by complaining that their subsidies were ill paid, and their
provisions withdrawn: and immediately taking off the mask, they formed
an alliance with the Picts and Scots, and proceeded to open hostility
against the Britons.

The Britons, impelled by these violent extremities, and roused to
indignation against their treacherous auxiliaries, were necessitated to
take arms; and having deposed Vortigern, who had become odious from
his vices, and from the bad event of his rash counsels, they put themselves under the command of his son, Vortimer. They fought many battles with their enemies; and though the victories in these actions be
disputed between the British and Saxon annalists, the progress still made
by the Saxons proves that the advantage was commonly on their side.
In one battle, however, fought at Eaglesford, now Ailsford, Horsa, the
Saxon general, was slain, and left the sole command over his countrymen in the hands of Hengist. This active general, continually reinforced
by fresh numbers from Germany, carried devastation into the most remote corners of Britain; and being chiefly anxious to spread the terror
of his arms, he spared neither age. nor sex, nor condition, wherever he
marched with his victorious forces. The private and public edifices of
the Britons were reduced to ashes: the priests were slaughtered on the
altars by those idolatrous ravagers; the bishops and nobility shared the
fate of the vulgar: the people, flying to the mountains and deserts, were
intercepted and butchered in heaps: some were glad to accept of life and
servitude under their victors: others, deserting their native country, took
shelter in the province of Armorica, where, being charitably received by

a people of the same language and manners, they settled in great numbers, and gave the country the name of Britanny,

(David Hume).

---

4. King Alfred the Great.

Alfred was a young man, three and twenty years of age, when he
became King. Twice in his childhood he had been taken to Rome, where
the Saxon nobles were in the habit of going on journeys which they supposed to be religious; and, once, he had staid for some time at Paris.
Learning, however, was so little cared for, then, that at twelve years
old he had not been taught to read; although, of the four sons of King
Ethelwulf, he, the youngest, was the favourite. But he had — as most
men who grow up to be great and good are generally found to have
had — an excellent mother; and, one day, this lady, whose name was
Osburgha, happened, as she was sitting among her sons, to read a book
of Saxon poetry. The book was what is called «illuminated» with beautiful bright letters richly painted. The brothers admiring it very much,
their mother said, «I will give it to that one of you four princes, who
first learns to read.» Alfred sought out a tutor that very day, applied
himself to read with great diligence, and soon won the book. He was
proud of it all his life.

This great King, in the first year of his reign, fought nine battles
against the Danes. He made some treaties with them too, by which the
false Danes swore that they would quit the country. They pretended that
they had taken a very solemn oath, in swearing this upon the holy brace-
lets that they wore, and which were always buried with them when
they died. But they cared little for it: one fatal winter, they spread
themselves in great numbers over the whole of England, and so dispersed
and routed the King's soldiers, that the King was left alone, and was
obliged to disguise himself as a common peasant, and to take refuge in
the cottage of one of his cowherds, who did not know his face.

Here, King Alfred, while the Danes sought him far and wide, was
left alone, one day, by the cowherd's wife, to watch some cakes which
she put to bake upon the hearth. But being at work upon his bow and
arrows, with which he hoped to punish the Danes when a brighter time

should come, his noble mind forgot the cakes, and they were burnt. «What», said the cowherd's wife, who scolded him well when she came back, «You will be ready enough to eat them by-and-by, and yet you cannot watch them, idle dog?»

At length, the Devonshire men made head against a new host of Danes who landed on their coast, killed their chief, and captured their flag, on which was represented the likeness of a Raven. The loss of their standard troubled the Danes greatly, for they believed it to be enchanted— woven by three daughters of one father in a single afternoon — and had a story among themselves, that when they were victorious in battle, the Raven stretched his wings and seemed to fly; and that when they were defeated, he would droop. King Alfred joined the Devonshire men, made a camp with them on a piece of firm ground in the midst of a bog in Somersetshire, and prepared for a great attempt for vengeance on the Danes, and the deliverance of his oppressed people.

But, first, as it was important to know how numerous the Danes were, and how they were fortified, King Alfred, being a good musician, disguised himself as a gleeman or minstrel, and went, with his harp, to the Danish camp. He played and sung in the very tent of Guthrum, the Danish leader, and entertained the Danes, and they caroused. While he seemed to think of nothing but his music, he was watchful of their tents, their arms, their discipline, everything that he desired to know. And right soon did this great King entertain them to a different tune: for summoning all his true followers to meet him at an appointed place, where they received him with joyful shouts and tears, he put himself at their head, marched on the Danish camp, defeated the Danes with great slaughter, and besieged them for fourteen days to prevent their escape. But, being as merciful as he was good and brave, he then proposed peace, on condition that they should altogether depart from that western part of England, and settle in the East; and that Guthrum should become a Christian, in remembrance of the divine religion which now taught his conqueror, the noble Alfred, to forgive the enemy who had so often injured him. This Guthrum did. At his baptism, King Alfred was his godfather. And Guthrum ever afterwards was loyal and faithful to the King. The Danes plundered and burned no more, but worked like honest men; they ploughed, and sowed, and reaped, and led good honest English lives.

As great and good in peace, as he was great and good in war, King Alfred never rested from his labours to improve his people. He loved to talk with clever men, and with travellers from foreign countries, and to write down what they told him, for his people to read. He had studied Latin, and now another of his labours was, to translate Latin books into the Anglo-Saxon tongue, that his people might be interested and improved by their contents. He made just laws, that they might live more happily and freely; he turned away all partial judges, that no wrong might be done them; he was so careful of their property, and punished robbers so severely, that it was said that under the great King Alfred, golden chains and jewels might have hung across the streets, and no man would have touched one. He founded schools; he patiently heard causes himself in his court of justice; the great desires of his heart were, to do right to all his subjects, and to leave England better, wiser, happier in all ways, than he found it. Every day he divided into certain portions, and in each portion devoted himself to a certain pursuit. That he might divide his time exactly, he had wax torches or candles made, which were all of the same size, were notched across at regular distances, and were always kept burning. Thus, as the candles burnt down, he divided the day into notches, almost as accurately as we now divide it into hours upon the clock.

Alfred was afflicted with a terrible unknown disease, which caused him violent and frequent pain that nothing could relieve. He bore it, as he had borne all the troubles of his life, like a brave and good man, until he was fifty-three years of age. Having reigned thirty years, he died in the year 901; but long ago as that is, his fame, and the love and gratitude with which his subjects regarded him, are freshly remembered to the present hour.

Under the great Alfred, all the best points of the Anglo-Saxon character were first encouraged, and in him first shown. It has been the greatest character among the nations of the earth. Wherever the descendants of the Saxon race made their way, even to the remotest regions of the world, they have been patient, persevering, never to be broken in spirit, never to be turned aside from enterprises on which they have resolved. In Europe, Asia, Africa, America, the whole world over; in the desert, in the forest, on the sea; scorched by a burning sun, or frozen by ice that never melts: the Saxon blood remains unchanged. Whereso-

19

ever that race goes, there law, and industry, and safety for life and property, and all the great results of steady perseverance, are certain to rise.   (Charles Dickens).

---

5. The Story of Macbeth.

Soon after the Scots and Picts had become one people, as I told you before, there was a King of Scotland called Duncan, a very good old man. He had two sons; one was called Malcolm, and the other Donaldbane. But King Duncan was too old to lead out his army to battle, and his sons were too young to help him.

At this time Scotland, and indeed France and England and oll other countries of Europe, were much harassed by the Danes. These were a very fierce, warlike people, who sailed from one place to another, and landed their armies on the coast, burning and destroying every thing wherever they came. They were heathens, and did not believe in the Bible, but thought of nothing, but battle, and slaughter, and making plunder. When they came to countries where the inhabitants were cowardly, they took possession of the land, as I told you the Saxons took possession of Britain. At other times, they landed with their soldiers, took what spoil they could find, burned the houses, and then'got on board, hoisted sails, and away again. They did so much mischief, that people put up prayers to God in the churches, to deliver them from the rage of the Danes.

Now, it happened in King Duncan's time, that a great fleet of these Danes came to Scotland, and landed their men in Fife, and threatened to take possession of that province; so a numerous Scottish army was levied, to go to fight with them. The King, as I told you, was too old to command his army, and his sons were too young. So he sent out one of his near relations, who was called Macbeth; he was the son of Finel, who was Thane, as it was called, of Glamis. The governors of provinces were at that time, in Scotland, called Thanes; they were afterwards termed Earls.

This Macbeth, who was a brave soldier, put himself at the head of the Scottish army, and marched against the Danes. And he carried with him a relation of his own, called Banquo, who was also a very brave man. So there was a great battle fought between the Danes and the Scots, and Macbeth and Banquo defeated the Danes, and drove them back to their ships, leaving a great many of their soldiers both killed and wounded. Then Macbeth and his army marched back to a town in the North of Scotland, called Forres, rejoicing on account of their victory.

Now, there lived at this time three old women in the town of Forres, whom people thought were witches, and supposed they could tell, what was to come to pass. Nobody would believe such folly now-a-days, except low and ignorant creatures, such as those who consult gipsies, in order to have their fortunes told; but in those early times the people were much more ignorant, and even great men like Macbeth believed, that such persons as these witches of Forres could tell, what was to come to pass afterwards, and listened to the nonsense they told them, as if the old women had really been prophetesses. The old women saw that they were respected and feared, so that they were tempted to impose upon people, by pretending to tell what was to happen to them, and they got presents for doing so.

So the three old women went, and stood by the wayside, in a great moor or heath near Forres, and waited till Macbeth came up. And then stepping before him, as he was marching at the head of his soldiers, the first woman said: «All hail, Macbeth — hail to thee, Thane of Glamis»! The second said: «All hail, Macbeth — hail to thee, Thane of Cawdor»! Then the third, wishing to pay him a higher compliment than the other two, said: «All hail, Macbeth, that shall be King of Scotland»! Macbeth was very much surprised to hear them give him these titles; and while he was wondering, what they could mean, Banquo stepped forward, and asked them whether they had nothing to tell about him, as well as about Macbeth. And they said, that he should not be so great as Macbeth; but that, though he himself should never be a king, yet his children should succeed to the throne of Scotland, and be Kings for a great number of years.

Before Macbeth was recovered from his surprise, there came a messenger to tell him, that his father was dead, so that he was become Thane of Glamis by inheritance. And there came a second messenger from the King, to thank Macbeth for the great victory over the Danes, and tell him, that the Thane of Cawdor had rebelled against the King, and that the King had taken his office from him, and had sent to make

Macbeth Thane of Cawdor as well as Glamis. Thus the two first old women seemed to be right in giving him these two titles. I dare say, they
knew something of the death of Macbeth's father, and that the government of Cawdor was intended for Macbeth, though he had not heard of it.

However, Macbeth seeing a part of their words come to be true,
began to think, how he was to bring the rest to pass, and make himself
King, as well as Thane of Glamis and Cawdor. And Macbeth had a wife,
who was a very ambitious wicked woman, and when she found out,
that her husband thought of raising himself up to be King of Scotland,
she encouraged him by all the means in her power, and persuaded him,
that the only way to get possession of the crown was to kill the good
old King Duncan. Macbeth was very unwilling to commit so great a
crime; for he knew, what a good king Duncan had been, and he recollected, how he was his relation, and had been always very kind to him,
and had intrusted him with the command of his army, and had bestowed
on him the government or Thanedom of Cawdor. And his wife continued
telling him, what a foolish, cowardly thing it was in him, not to take
the opportunity of making himself king, when it was in his power to
gain what the witches promised him. So the wicked advice of his wife,
and the prophecy of these wretched old women, at last brought Macbeth
to think of murdering his King and his friend. The way in which he accomplished his crime, made it still more abominable.

Macbeth invited Duncan to visit him, at a great castle near Inverness; and the good King, who had no suspicion of his kinsmann, accepted the invitation very willingly. Macbeth and his lady received the
king and all his retinue with much appearance of joy, and made a great
feast, as a subject would do, to make his King welcome. About the
middle of the night, the King desired to go to his apartment, and Macbeth conducted him to a fine room, which had been prepared for him.
Now it was the custom in those barbarous times, that wherever the King
slept, two armed men slept in the same chamber, in order to defend his
person in case he should be attacked by any one during the night. But
the wicked Lady Macbeth had made these two watchman drink a great
deal of wine, and had besides put some drugs into the liquor, so that
when they went to the King's apartment, they both fell asleep, and slept
so soundly, that nothing could awaken them.

Then the cruel Macbeth came into King Duncan's bedroom, about two ln the morning. It was a terrible stormy night; but the noise of the wind and of the thunder could not awaken the King, as he was old, and weary with his journey; neither could it awaken the two sentinels. They all slept soundly. So Macbeth having come into the room, and stepped gently over the floor; he took the two dirks, which belonged to the sentinels, and stabbed poor old King Duncan to the heart, and that so effectually, that he died without giving even a groan. .Then Macbeth put the bloody daggers into the hands of the sentinels, and he daubed their faces over with blood that it might appear, as if they had committed the murder. Macbeth was frightened at what he had done, but his wife made him wash his hands and go to bed.

Early in the morning, the nobles and gentlemen, who attended on the King, assembled in the great hall of the Castle, and there they began to talk of what a dreadful storm it had been the night before. But Macbeth could scarcely understand what they said, for he was thinking on something much worse and more frightful than the storm, and was wondering what would be said, when they heard of the murder. They waited for some time, but finding the King did not come from his apartment, one of the noblemen went to see, whether he was well or not. But when he came into the room, he found poor King Duncan lying stiff, and cold, and blody, and the two sentinels, with their dirks or daggers covered with blood, both fast asleep. As soon as the Scottish Nobles saw this terrible sight, they were greatly astonished and enraged, and Macbeth made believe, as if he were more enraged than any of them, and drawing his sword, before any one could prevent him, he killed the two attendants of the King, who slept in the bedchamber, pretending to think, they had been guilty of murdering King Duncan.

When Malcolm and Donaldbane, the two sons of the good King, saw their father slain in this manner, within Macbeth's castle, they became afraid, that they might be put to death likewise, and fled away out of Scotland; for notwithstanding all the excuses which he could make, they still believed, that Macbeth had killed their father. Donaldbane fled into some distant island, but Malcolm, the eldest son of Duncan, went to the court of England, where he begged for assistance from the English King to place him on the throne of Scotland, as his father's successor. .

In the meantime Macbeth took possession of the kingdom of Scotland, and thus all his wicked wishes seemed to be fulfilled. But he was not happy. — He began to reflect, how wicked he had been, in killing his friend and benefactor, and how some other person, as ambitious as he was himself, might do the same thing to him. He remembered, too, that the old women had said, that the children of Banquo should succeed to the throne after his death, and therefore he concluded, that Banquo might be tempted to conspire against him, as he had himself done against King Duncan.

The wicked always think other people as bad as themselves. In order to prevent this supposed danger, he hired ruffians to watch in a wood, where Banquo and his son Fleance sometimes used to walk in the evening, with instructions to attack them, and kill both father and son. The villains did as they were ordered by Macbeth; but while they were killing Banquo, the boy Fleance made his escape from their wicked hands, and fled from Scotland into Wales. And it is said, that long afterwards his children came to possess the Scottish crown.

Macbeth was not the more happy that he had slain his brave friend and cousin Banquo. He knew that men began to suspect the wicked deeds which he had done, and he was constantly afraid, that some one would put him to death, as he had done his old sovereign, or that Malcolm would obtain assistance from the King of England, and come to make war against him, and take from him the Scottish kingdom. So in this great perplexity of mind, he thought he would go to the old women, whose words had first put into his mind the desire of becoming a king. It is to be supposed, that he offered them presents, and that they were cunning enough to study how to give him some answer, which should make him continue in the belief, that they could prophesy what was to happen in future times. So they answered him, that he should not be conquered or lose the crown of Scotland, until a great forest, called Birnam wood, should come to attack him in a strong castle, situated on a high hill called Dunsinane. Now, the hill of Dunsinane is upon the one side of a valley, and the forest of Birnam is upon the other; there are twelve miles distance betwixt them, and besides that, Macbeth thought it was impossible that the trees could ever come to the assault of the castle. He therefore resolved to fortify his castle on the hill of Dunsinane very strongly, as being a place in which he would always be sure to be safe. For this purpose, he caused all his great nobility and thanes to send in stones, and wood, and other things, wanted in building, and to drag them with oxen up to the top, of the steep hill, where he was building the castle.

Now, among other nobles who were obliged to send oxen, and horses, and materials, to this laborious work, was one, called Macduff, the Thane of Fife. Macbeth was afraid of this Thane, for he was very powerful, and was accounted both brave and wise: and Macbeth thought he would most probably join with Prince Malcolm, if ever he should come from England with an army. The King, therefore, had a private hatred against the Thane of Fife, which he kept concealed from all men, until he should have some opportunity of putting him to death, as he had done Duncan and Banquo. Macduff, on his part, kept upon his guard, and went to the King's court as seldom as he could, thinking himself never safe unless while in his own castle of Kennoway, which is on the coast of Fife, near to the mouth of the Frith of Forth. It happened, however, that the King had summoned several of his nobles, and Macduff the Thane of Fife, among others, to attend him at his new castle of Dunsinane; and they were all obliged to come, none dared stay behind. Now, the King was to give the nobles a great entertainment, and preparations were made for it. In the meantime, Macbeth rode out with a few attendants, to see the oxen drag the wood and the stones up the hill, for enlarging and strengthening the castle. So they saw most of the oxen trudging up the hill with great difficulty, for the ascent is very steep, and the burdens were heavy, and the weather was extremely hot. At length, Macbeth saw a pair of oxen so tired, that they could go no farther up the hill, but fell down under their load. Then the King was very angry, and demanded to know who it was among his Thanes that had sent oxen so weak and so unfit for labour, when he had so much work for them to do. Some one replied, that the oxen belonged to Macduff, the Thane of Fife. «Then», said the King in great anger, «since the Thane of Fife sends such worthless cattle as these, to do my labour, I will put his own neck into the yoke, and make him drag the burdens himself».

There was a friend of Macduff, who heard these angry expressions of the King, and hastened to communicate them to the Thane of Fife, who was walking in the Hall of the King's castle, while dinner was preparing. The instant that Macduff heard what the King had said, he knew he had no time to lose in making his escape; for whenever Macbeth threatened to do mischief to any one, he was sure to keep his word.

So Macduff snatched up from the table a loaf of bread, called for his horses and his servants, and was gallopping back to his own Province of Fife, before Macbeth and the rest of the nobility were returned to the castle. The first question which the King asked was, what had become of Macduff? and being informed, that he had fled from Dunsinane, he ordered a body of his guards to attend him, and mounted on horseback himself to pursue the Thane, with the purpose of putting him to death.

Macduff, in the mean time, fled as fast as horse's feet could carry him; but he was so ill provided with money for his expenses, that, when he came to the great ferry over the river Tay, he had nothing to give to the boatmen, who took him across, excepting the loaf of bread, which he had taken from the King's table. The place was called, for a long time afterwards, the Ferry of the loaf.

When Macduff got into his province of Fife, which is on the other side of the Tay, he rode on faster than before, towards his own castle of Kennoway, which, as I told you, stands close by the sea side; and when he reached it, the King and his guards were not far behind him. Macduff ordered his wife to shut the gates of the castle, draw up the drawbridge, and on no account permit the King, or any of his soldiers to enter. In the meantime, he went to the small harbour belonging to the castle, and caused a ship which was lying there, to be fitted out for sea in all haste, and got on board himself, in order to escape from Macbeth.

In the meantime, Macbeth summoned the lady to surrender the castle, and to deliver up her husband. But Lady Macduff, who was a wise and brave woman, made many excuses and delays, until she knew that her husband was safely on board the ship, and had sailed from the harbour. Then she spoke boldly from the wall of the castle to the King, who was standing before the gate, still demanding entrance, with many threats of what he would do, if Macduff was not given up to him.

«Do you see», she said, «yon white sail upon the sea? Yonder goes Macduff to the court of England. You will never see him again, till he comes back with young Malcolm, to pull you down from the throne, and to put you to death. You will never be able to put your yoke, as you threatened, on the Thaue of Fife's neck».

Some say, that Macbeth was so much incensed at this bold answer, that he und his guards attacked the castle and took it, killing the brave lady and all whom they found there. But others say, and I believe more truly, that the King seeing, that the castle of Kennoway was very strong, and that Macduff had escaped from him, and was embarked for England, departed back to Dunsinane, without attempting to take Macduff's castle of Kennoway. The ruins are still to be seen.

There reigned at that time in England a very good king, called Edward the Confessor. I told you, that Prince Malcolm, the son of Duncan, was at his court soliciting assistance, to recover the Scottish throne. The arrival of Macduff greatly aided the success of his petition; for the English King knew, that Macduff was a brave and a wise man. As he assured Edward, that the Scots were tired of the cruel Macbeth, and would join Prince Malcolm, if he were to enter Scotland at the head of an army; the king ordered a great warrior, called Siward, Earl of Northumberland, to enter Scotland with an army, and assist Prince Malcolm in the recovery of his father's crown. Then it happened, as Macduff had said; for the Scottish Thanes and Nobles would not fight for Macbeth, but joined Prince Malcolm and Macduff against him; so that at length he shut himself up in his castle of Dunsinane, where he thought himself safe, according to the old women's prophecy, until Birnam wood should come against him. He boasted of this to his followers, and encouraged them to make a valiant defence, assuring them of certain victory. By this time, Malcolm and Macduff were come as far as Birnam wood, and lay encamped there, with their army. The next morning, when they were to march across the broad valley, to attack the castle of Dunsinane, Macduff advised that every soldier should cut down a bough of a tree and carry it in his hand, that the enemy might not be able to see, how many men were coming against them. Now, the sentinel, who stood on Macbeth's castlewall, when he saw all these branches, which the soldiers of Prince Malcolm carried, ran to the King, and informed him, that the wood of Birnam was moving towards the castle of Dunsinane. The King at first called him a liar, and threatened to put him to death; but when he looked from the walls himself, and saw the appearance of a forest, approaching from Birnam, he knew the hour of his destruction was come. His followers, too, began to be disheartened, and to fly from the castle, seeing their master had lost all hopes. Macbeth, however, recollected

20

his own bravery, and sallied desperately out, at the head of the few followers, who remained faithful to him. He was killed after a furious resistance, fighting hand to hand with Macduff, in the thick of the battle. Prince Malcolm mounted the throne of Scotland, and reigned long and prosperously. He rewarded Macduff by declaring, that his descendant, should lead the vanguard of the Scottish army in the battle, and place the crown on the King's head, at the ceremony of coronation. King Malcolm also created the Thanes of Scotland, Earls, after the title adopted in the Court of England.

6. The Battle of Hastings.

The English and Normans now prepared themselves for the important decision; but the aspect of things on the night before the battle was very different in the two camps. The English spent the time in riot, and jollity, and disorder; the Normans in silence, and in prayer, and in the other functions of their religion. On the morning, the duke called together the most considerable of his commanders, and made them a speech suitable to the occasion. He represented to them, that the event which they and he had long wished for was approaching; the whole fortune of the war now depended on their swords, and would be decided in a single action; that never army had greater motives for vigorous courage, whether they considered the prize which would attend their victory, or the inevitable destruction which must ensue upon their discomfiture; that if their martial and veteran bands could once break those raw soldiers, who had rashly dared to approach them, they conquered a kingdom at one blow, and were justly entitled to all its possessions as the reward of their prosperous valour: that, on the contrary, if they remitted in the least their wonted prowess, an enraged enemy hung upon their rear, the sea met them in their retreat, and an ignominious death was the certain puishment of their imprudent cowardice: that by collecting so numerous and brave a host, he had insured every human means of conquest; and the commander of the enemy, by his criminal conduct, had given him just cause to hope for the favour of the Almighty, in whose hands alone lay the event of wars and battles: and that a perjured usurper, anathematized by the sovereign pontiff, and conscious of his own breach of faith, would be struck with terror on their appearance, and would prognosticate to himself that fate which his multiplied crimes had so justly merited. The duke next divided his army into three lines: the first, led by Montgomery, consisted of archers and light armed infantry: the second, commanded by Martel, was composed of his bravest battalions, heavy armed, and ranged in close order: his cavalry, at whose head he placed himself formed the third line, and were so disposed, that they stretched beyond the infantry, and flanked each wing of the army. He ordered the signal of battle to be given; and the whole army, moving at once, and singing the hymn or song of Roland, the famous peer of Charlemagne, advanced, in order and with alacrity, towards the enemy.

Harold had seized the advantage of a rising ground, and having likewise drawn some trenches to secure his flanks, he resolved to stand upon the defensive, and to avoid all action with the cavalry, in which he was inferior. The Kentish men were placed in the van; a post which they had always claimed as their due: the Londoners guarded the standard: and the king himself, accompanied by his two valiant brothers, Gurth and Leofwin, dismounting, placed himself at the head of his infantry, and expressed his resolution to conquer, or to perish in the action. The first attack of the Normans was desperate, but was received with equal valour by the English, and after a furious combat, which remained long undecided, the former, overcome by the difficulty of the ground, and hard pressed by the enemy, began first to relax their vigour, then to retreat; and confusion was spreading among the ranks, when William, who found himself on the brink of destruction, hastened with a select band to the relief of his dismayed forces. His presence restored the action; the English were obliged to retire with loss; and the duke, ordering his second line to advance, renewed the attack with fresh forces, and with redoubled courage. Finding that the enemy, aided by the advantage of ground, and animated by the example of their prince, still made a vigorous resistance, he tried a stratagem, which was very delicate in its management, but which seemed advisable in his desperate situation, where, if he gained not a decisive victory, he was totally undone: he commanded his troops to make a hasty retreat, and to allure the enemy from their ground by the appearance of flight. The artifice succeeded against those unexperienced soldiers who, heated by the action, and sanguine in their hopes, precipitately followed the Normans into the plain. William gave orders, that at once the infantry should face about upon their pursuers, and the cavalry make an assault upon their wings, and both of them pursue the advantage, which the surprise and terror of the enemy must give them in that critical and decisive moment. The English were repulsed with great slaughter, and driven back to the hill; where being rallied by the bravery of Harold, they were able, notwithstanding their loss, to maintain the post, and continue the combat. The duke tried the same stratagem a second time with the same sucess; but even after this double advantage, he still found a great body of the English, who, maintaining themselves in firm array, seemed determined to dispute the victory to the last extremity. He ordered his heavy-armed infantry to make an assault upon them; while his archers, placed behind, should gall the enemy, who were exposed by the situation of the ground, and who were intent on defending themselves against the swords and spears of the assailants. By this disposition he at last prevailed: Harold was slain by an arrow, while he was combating with great bravery at the head of his men: his two brothers shared the same fate: and the English, discouraged by the fall of those princes, gave ground on all sides, and were pursued with great slaughter by the victorious Normans. A few troops, however, of the vanquished, had still the courage to turn upon their pursuers; and attacking them in deep and miry ground, obtained some revenge for the slaughter and dishonour of the day. But the appearance of the duke obliged them to seek their safety by flight; and darkness saved them from any further pursuit by the enemy.

Thus was gained by William, Duke of Normandy, the great and decisive victory of Hastings, after a battle which was fought from morning till sunset, and which seemed worthy, by the heroic valour displayed by both armies, and by both commanders, to decide the fate of a mighty kingdom. William had three horses killed under him; and there fell near fifteen thousand men on the side of the Normans: the loss was still more considerable on that of the vanquished; besides the death of the king and his two brothers. The dead body of Harold was brouhgt to William, and was generously restored without ransom to his mother. The Norman army left not the field of battle without giving thanks to Heaven in the most solemn manner for their victory: and the prince, having refreshed his troops, prepared to push to the utmost his advantage against the divided, dismayed, and discomfited English.   (David Hume.)

7. Bold Robin Hood.

The famous Robin Hood, whose real name was Robert Fitzooth, and who flourished during the reigns of Henry the Second and Richard Coeur de Lion, was born in the town of Locksley, in Nottinghamshire, about the year 1160. He was a handsome youth, and the best archer in the county, and regularly bore away the prizes at all the archery meetings, being able to strike a deer five hundred yards off. In truth, he was just fit to be one of the royal archers, and would no doubt have turned out better, had not his uncle been persuaded by the monks of Fountain Abbey to leave all his property to the church; and thus poor Robin being sent adrift into the world, took refuge in Sherwood Forest, where he met with several other youths who had been driven into the woods by the oppression of the Norman nobles and the great severity of the forest laws. They soon formed themselves into a band under his leadership, and commenced leading the life of outlaws. Robin Hood and his men adopted a uniform of Lincoln green, with a scarlet cap, and each man was armed with a dagger and a basket-hilted sword, and a bow in his hand, and a quiver slung on his back, while the captain always had a bugle horn with him to summon his followers about him.

One day, when Robin Hood set out alone, in hopes of meeting with some adventure, he reached a brook, over which a narrow plank was laid to serve for a bridge, and, just as he was going to cross it, a tall and handsome stranger appeared on the other side, and as neither seemed disposed to give way, they met in the middle of the bridge.

«Go back», cried the stranger to Robin Hood, «or it will be the worse for you.»

But Robin Hood laughed at the idea of his giving way to anybody, and proposed they should each take an oak branch, and fight it out, and that, whoever could manage to throw the other into the brook should win the day. Accordingly they set-to in right earnest, and after thrashing each other well, the stranger gave Robin Hood a blow on his head, which effectually pitched him into the water. When Robin Hood had waded back to the bank, he put his bugle to his lips, and blew several blasts till the forest rang again, and his followers came leaping from all directions to see what their captain wanted. When he had told them how he had been served by the stranger, they would fain have ducked him, but Robin Hood, who admired his bravery, proposed to him to join their band.

«Here's my hand on it,» cried the stranger, delighted at the proposal, «though my name is John Little, you shall find I can do great things.»

But Will Stutely, one of Robin's merrymen, insisted upon it that he must be re-christened. So a feast was held, a barrel of ale broached, and the new-comer's name was changed from John Little to Little John, which nick-name, seeing that he was near seven feet high, was a perpetual subject for laughter.

Not long after this, as Robin Hood sat one morning by the wayside, trimming his bow and arrows, there rode by a butcher, with a basket of meat, who was hastening to market. After bidding him good-morrow, Robin asked him what he would take for the horse and the basket? The butcher, somewhat surprised, answered he would not care to sell them for less than four silver marks. «Do but throw your greasy frock into the bargain,» said Robin, «and here's the money.» Delighted at having concluded so good a bargain, the butcher lost no time in dismounting and throwing off his smock frock, which the outlaw instantly put on over his clothes, and then galloped away to Nottingham.

On reaching the town, Robin Hood put up his horse at an inn, and then went into the market, and, uncovering his basket, began to sell its contents about five times cheaper than all the other butchers; for Robin Hood neither knew nor cared about the price usually paid for meat, and it amused him vastly to see his stall surrounded by customers. The other butchers could not at first understand why everybody flocked to purchase his goods in preference to theirs; but when they heard that he had sold a leg of pork for a shilling, they consulted together, and agreed that he must be some rich man's son who was after a frolic, or else a downright madman, and that they had better try and learn something more about him, or else he would ruin their business. So when the market was over, one of them invited Robin Hood to dine with their company. The sheriff of Nottingham presided at the head of the table, while at the other end sat the innkeeper. The outlaw played his part as well as the rest of them, and, when the dishes were removed, he called for more wine, telling them all to drink as much as they could carry, and he would pay the reckoning.

The sheriff then turned to Robin Hood, and asked him whether he had any horned beasts to sell; for he was a miser, and hoped to profit by the new butcher's want of experience, and drive a good bargain with him. Robin Hood replied he had some two or three hundreds; whereupon the sheriff said that, as he wanted a few heads of cattle, he would like to ride over and look at them that same day. So Robin Hood flung down a handful of silver on the table, by way of farewell to his astonished companions, and set out for Sherwood Forest with the sheriff, who had mounted his palfrey, and provided himself with a bag of gold for his purchase. The outlaw was so full of jokes and merriment as they went along, that the sheriff thought he had never fallen in with a pleasanter fellow. On a sudden, however, the sheriff recollected that the woods were infested by Robin Hood and his band, and he said to his companion he hoped they would not meet with any of them; to which he only answered by a long laugh. Presently they reached the forest, when a herd of deer crossed their path. «How do you like my horned beasts, Master Sheriff?» inquired Robin. «To tell you the truth», replied the sheriff, «I only half like your company, and wish myself away from hence.» Then Robin Hood put his bugle to his mouth and blew three blasts, when about a hundred men, with Little John at their head, immediately surrounded them, and the latter inquired what his master wanted. «I have brought the Sheriff of Nottingham to dine with us,» said Robin Hood. «He is welcome,» quoth Little John, «and I hope he will pay well for his dinner.» They then took the bag of gold from the luckless sheriff, and, spreading a cloak on the grass, they counted out three hundred pounds, after which Robin asked him if he would like some venison for dinner. But the sheriff told him to let him go, or he would rue the day; so the outlaw desired his best compliment to his good dame, and wished him a pleasant journey home.

But if Robin loved a joke, he often did a good turn to those who needed his assistance. Thus, he lent four hundred golden pounds to Sir Rychard o' the Lee, who had mortgaged his lands of Wierysdale for that sum to St. Mary's Abbey, and who happened to pass through Sherwood Forest on his way to York, to beg the abbot to grant him another year. Robin Hood, moreover, bid Little John to accompany him as his squire. When they reached the city, the superior was seated in his hall, and declared to the brethren, that if Sir Rychard did not appear before sunset his lands would be forfeited. Presently the knight of Wierysdale came in, and pretended to beg for mercy; but the proud abbot spurned him, when Sir Rychard flung the gold at his feet and snatched away the deed, telling him, if he had shown a little christian mercy, he should not only have returned the money, but made a present to the abbey. And indeed, the monks had to rue their mercilessness in the end, as Robin Hood levied a toll of eight hundred pounds upon them as they once passed through Sherwood Forest, which enabled him to forgive Sir Rychard's debt, when that trusty knight came to discharge it at the appointed time.

Another time as Robin Hood was roaming through the forest, he saw a handsome young man, in a very elegant suit, who was passing over the plain, singing blithely, as he went. On the following morning, he was surprised to see the same young man coming along with disordered clothes and dishevelled hair, and sighing deeply at every step, and saying: «Alack! and well-a-day!» Robin Hood having sent one of his men to fetch him, inquired what lay so heavy on his heart, and why he was so gladsome yesterday and so sorry to-day. The young man pulled out his purse, and showed him a ring, saying: «I bought this yesterday to marry a maiden I have courted these seven long years, and this morning she is gone to church to wed another.» «Does she love you?» said Robin. «She has told me so a hundred times,» answered Allen-a-Dale, for such was the youth's name. «Tut man! then she is not worth caring for, if she be so fickle!» cried Robin Hood. «But she does not love him,» interrupted Allen-a-Dale; «he is an old cripple quite unfit for such a lovely lass.» «Then, why does she marry him?» inquired Robin Hood. «Because the old knight is rich, and her parents insist upon it, and have scolded and raved at her till she is as meek as a lamb.» «And where is the wedding to take place?» said Robin. «At our parish, five miles from hence», said Allen, «and the Bishop of Hereford, who is the bridegroom's brother, is to perform the ceremony.»

Then without more ado, Robin Hood dressed himself up as a harper with a flowing white beard, and a dark coloured mantle, and bidding twenty-four of his men follow at a distance, he entered at the church, and took his place near the altar. Presently the old knight made his appearance, hobbling along, and handing in a maiden as fair as day, all tears and blushes, accompanied by her young companions strewing flow-

ers. «This is not a fit match», said Robin Hood aloud, «and I forbid
the marriage,» And then, to the astonishment of the Bishop and of all
present, he blew a blast on his horn, when four-and-twenty archers came
leaping into the church-yard, and entered the building. Foremost among
these was Allen-a-Dale, who presented his bow to Robin Hood. The
outlaw by this time had cast off his cloak and false beard, and turning
to the bride, said: «Now, pretty one, tell me freely whom you prefer for
a husband — this gouty old knight, or one of these bold young fellows?»
«Alas!» said the young maid, casting down her eyes, «Allen-a-Dale has
courted me for seven long years, and he is the man I would choose.»
«Then, now my good lord bishop,» said Robin, «prithee unite this loving pair before we leave the church.» «That cannot be,» said the bishop;
«the law requires they should be asked three times in the church.» «If
that is all,» quoth Robin Hood, «we'll soon settle that matter.» Then,
taking the bishop's gown, he dressed Little John up in it, and gave him
the book, and bid him ask them seven times in the church, lest three
should not be enough. The people could not help laughing, but none attempted to forbid the bans, for the bishop and his brother walked indignantly out of the church. Robin Hood gave away the maiden, and the
whole company had a venison dinner in Sherwood Forest; and from that
day Allen-a-Dale was a staunch friend to Robin Hood as long as he
lived.

Robin Hood had often heard tell of the prowess of a certain friar
Tuck who, having been expelled from Fountain Abbey for his irregular
conduct, lived in a rude hut he had built himself amidst the woods, and
who was said to wield a quarter-staff and let fly an arrow better than
any man in Chistendom. So, being anxious to see how far this was true,
Robin set off one morning for Fountain's Dale, where he found the friar
rambling on the bank of the river Shell. The friar was a burly man at
least six feet high, with a broad chest, and an arm fit for a blacksmith.
The outlaw walked up to him saying: «Carry me over this water, thou
brawny friar, or thou hast not an hour to live.» The friar tucked up his
gown and carried him over without a word; but when Robin seemed to
be going, he cried out: «Stop, my fine fellow, and carry me over this
water, or it shall breed you pain.» Robin did so, and then said: «As
you are double my weight, it is fair I should have two rides to your one;
so carry me back again.» The friar again took Robin on his back; but

on reaching the middle of the stream he pitched him into the water, saying: «Now, my fine fellow, let's see whether you'll sink or swim.» Robin swam to the bank, and said: «I see you are worthy to be my match;» and then summoning his foresters by a blast of his bugle, he told the friar he was Robin Hood, and asked him to join his band.

«If there's an archer amongst you that can beat me at the long bow, then I'll be your man,» quoth Friar Tuck. Then pointing to a hawk on the wing, he added: «I'll kill it, and he who can strike it again before it falls, will be the better man of the two.» Little John accepted the challenge. The shafts flew off, and when the dead bird was picked up, it was found that the friar's arrow had pinioned the hawk's wings to his sides, and that Little John's had transfixed it from breast to back. So friar Tuck owned himself outdone, and joined Robert's merry men.

The whole country now rang with Robin Hood's lawless pranks, when one morning six priests passed through Sherwood Forest, on richly caparisoned horses, and thinking a good prize was in the wind, the outlaws bid them halt, and Friar Tuck seized the bridle of the one whom he judged to be the abbot, and bid him pay the toll. The abbot got down and gave him a cuff that made his ears tingle, and, flinging him on his knees, plucked him by the beard. Quoth Friar Tuck: «We don't take that sort of coin.» «But we are going on a message from King Richard,» said the abbot. Then Robin bid the friar desist saying: «God save the King, and confound all his foes!» «You are a noble fellow,» quoth the abbot, «and if you and your men will give up this lawless life and become my archers, you shall have the king's pardon.» He then opened his gown, and Robin Hood and his archers, guessing at once that Richard himself stood before them, bent their knees to their liege lord, crying: «Long live King Richard!»

· So Robin Hood accompanied the King to London, followed by fifty of his most faithful adherents; and here he assumed the title of Earl of Huntingdon; but he soon grew tired of the confinement of court, and asked permission to revisit the woods. The King granted him seven days; but when once he breathed the pure air of Sherwood again, he could not tear himself away; and when from old habit he sounded his bugle, he was surprised to see the signal answered by fourscore youths. Little John soon joined him, and he again became the leader of a band. Richard was so enraged on hearing this, that he sent two hundred soldiers to reduce the rebel, and a desperate fight took place on a plain in the forest, when Robin Hood was wounded by an arrow, and removed to Kirkley's Nunnery, where the treacherous prioress suffered him to bleed to death. Seeing his end fast approaching, he called to Little John, and begged him to remove him to the woods, and there poor Robin Hood died as he had lived, beneath the green trees, and was buried according to his wish. The stone that marked the spot bore the following inscription:

«Here underneath this little stone
Lies Robert, Earl of Huntingdon.
Ne'er archer was as he so good;
And people called him Robin Hood.
Such outlaws as he and his men
Will England never see again.»

8. Death and Character of Richard I.

Vidomar, Viscount of Limoges, a vassal of the king's, had found a treasure, of which he sent part to that prince as a present. Richard, as superior lord, claimed the whole; and, at the head of some Brabançons, besieged the viscount in the castle of Chalus, near Limoges, in order to make him comply with his demand. The garrison offered to surrender; but the king replied, that since he had taken the pains to come thither and besiege the place in person, he would take it by force, and would hang every one of them. The same day, Richard, accompanied by Marcadée, leader of his Brabançons, approached the castle in order to survey it; when one Bertrand de Gourdon, an archer, took aim at him, and pierced his shoulder with an arrow. The king, however, gave orders for the assault, took the place, and hanged all the garrison, except Gourdon, who had wounded him, and whom he reserved for a more deliberate and more cruel execution.

The wound was not in itself dangerous; but the unskilfulness of the surgeon made it mortal: he so rankled Richard's shoulder in pulling out the arrow, that a grangrene ensued, and that prince was now sensible that his life was drawing towards a period. He sent for Gourdon, and asked him, *Wretch, what have I ever done to you, to oblige you to seek my life? — What have you done to me?* replied coolly the prisoner; *You killed with your own hands my father and my two*

*brothers; and you intended to have hanged myself: I am now in
your power, and you may take revenge, by inflicting on me the most
severe torments; but I shall endure them all with pleasure, provided
I can think that I have been so happy as to rid the world of such a
nuisance.* Richard, struck with the reasonableness of this reply, and
humbled by the near approach öf death, ordered Gourdon to be set at liberty, and a sum of money to be given him: but Marcadée, unknown to
him, seized the unhappy man, flayed him alive, and then hanged him.
Richard died in the tenth year of his reign, and the forty-second of his
age; and he left no issue behind him.

The most shining parts of this prince's character are his military talents. No man, even in that romantic age, carried personal courage and
intrepidity to a greater height; and this quality gained him the appellation of the lion-hearted, *coeur de lion.* He passionately loved glory,
chiefly military glory; and as his conduct in the field was not inferior to
his valour, he seems to have possessed every talent necessary for acquiring it. His resentments also were high; his pride unconquerable; and his
subjects, as well as his neighbours, had therefore reason to apprehend,
from the continuance of his reign, a perpetual scene of blood and violence.
Of an impetuous and vehement spirit, he was distinguished by all the
good as well as the bad qualities, incident to that character; he was open,
frank, generous, sincere, and brave; he was revengeful, domineering,
ambitious, haughty, and cruel; and was thus better calculated to dazzle
men by the splendour of his enterprises, than either to promote their happiness or his own grandeur, by a sound and well-regulated policy. As
military talents make great impression on the people, he seems to have
been much beloved by his English subjects; and he is remarked to have
been the first prince of the Norman line that bore any sincere regard to
them. He passed however only four months of his reign in that kingdom:
the Crusade employed him near three years; he was detained about fourteen months in captivity; the rest of his reign was spent either in war,
or preparations for war, against France; and he was so pleased with the
fame which he had acquired in the East, that he determined, notwithstanding his past misfortunes, to have further exhausted his kingdom,
and to have exposed himself to new hazards, by conducting another expedition against the infidels.   (David Hume.)

9. Chivalry.

Chivalry was introduced into England under the Norman princes. Noble youths intended for the profession of arms were placed, as pages or valets, in the families of great barons, where they were instructed in the rules of courtesy and politeness, and in martial exercises. The courts of princes and barons became schools of chivalry, in which young men were taught dancing, riding, hawking, hunting, tilting, and other accomplishments, to qualify them for the honours of knighthood. From pages they were advanced to the rank of esquires.

Once on a week in Lent, crowds of sprightly youth, mounted on horseback, rode into the fields in bands, armed with lances and shields, and exhibited representations of battles. Many of the young nobility, not yet knighted, issued from the houses of their princes, bishops, earls, and barons, to make trial of their skill and strength in arms. The hope of victory rouses their spirits; their fiery steeds neigh, prance, and champ · their foaming bits. The signal given, the sports begin; the youth divided into bands, encounter each other. Some flee, others pursue without overtaking them; while in another quarter, one band overtakes and overthrows another.

After spending seven or eight years in these schools, in the station of esquires, these youths received the honours of knighthood, from the prince or baron. To prepare for this ceremony, they were obliged to submit to severe fastings, to spend nights in prayer in a church, to receive the sacrament, to bathe and put on white robes, confess their sins, and hear sermons, in which Christian morals were explained. Thus prepared, the candidate went to church, and advanced to the altar with his sword slung in a scarf about his neck. This sword he presented to the priest, who blessed and returned it. When the candidate approached the person who was to perform the ceremony, he fell on his knees and delivered him his sword.

The candidate having taken an oath, was adorned with the armour and ensigns of knighthood, by the knights and ladies attending the ceremony. First they put on his spurs, beginning with his left foot; next his coat of mail; then his cuirass; then the armour for his legs, hands and arms; and lastly, they girt on his swoord. Then the prince or baron descended from his throne or seat, and gave him the *accolade,* which was three gentle strokes with the flat of his sword on the shoulder, or with the palm of his hand on the cheek, pronouncing in the name of St. George, «I make thee a knight, be brave, hardy and loyal.» The young knight then rose, put on his shield and helmet, mounted his horse without the stirrup, and displayed his dexterity in the management of his horse, amidst the acclamations of a multitude of spectators.

(Noah Webster.)

10. Henry II. Conquest of Ireland.

Ireland was at the time of Henry II. nearly in the same situation in which England had been after the first invasion of the Saxons. Its in- habitants had been early converted to Christianity; and, for three or four centuries after, possessed a very large proportion of the learning of the times: being undisturbed by foreign invasions, and perhaps too poor to invite the rapacity of conquerors, they enjoyed a peaceful life which they gave up to piety, and such learning as was then thought necessary to promote it. Of their learning, their arts, their piety, and even their polished manners, too many monuments remain to this day for us to make the least doubt concerning them; but it is equally true, that in time they fell from these advantages, and their degenerate posterity, at the period we are now speaking of, were involved in the darkest barba- rity. This may be imputed to the frequent invasions which they suffered from the Danes and Norwegians, who overran the whole country, and every where spread their ravages, and confirmed their authority: the natives, kept in the strictest bondage, grew every day more ignorant and brutal; and when at last they rose upon their conquerors, and totally expelled them from the island, they wanted instructors to restore them to their former attainments. Henceforward they long continued in the most deplorable state of barbarism. The towns that had been formerly built were suffered to fall into ruin; the inhabitants exercised pasture in the open country, and sought protection from danger by retiring into their forests and bogs. Almost all sense of religion was extinguished; the petty princes exercised continual outrages upon each other's territories; and strength alone was able to procure redress.

At the time when Henry first planned the invasion of the island, it was divided into five small kingdoms, namely, Leinster, Meath, Mun·ster, Ulster, and Connaught. As it had been usual for one or other of the five kings to take the lead in their wars, he was denominated monarch of the island, and possessed a power resembling that of the early Saxon monarchs in England. Roderic O'Connor, king of Connaught, then enjoyed this dignity, and Dermont M'Morrogh was king of Leinster. This last-named prince, a weak, licentious tyrant, had carried off and ravished the daughter of the king of Meath, who, being strengthened by the alliance of the king of Connaught, invaded the ravisher's dominions, and expelled him from his kingdom. This prince, thus justly punished, had recourse to Henry, who was at that time in Guienne, and offered to hold his kingdom of the English crown, if he should recover it by the king's assistance. Henry readily accepted the offer; but being at that time embarrassed by more near interests, he only gave Dermont letters patent, by which he empowered all his subjects to aid the Irish prince in the recovery of his dominions. Dermont, relying on this authority, repaired to Bristol, where, after some difficulty, he formed a treaty with Richard, surnamed Strongbow, earl of Pembroke, who agreed to reinstate him in his dominions, upon condition of his being married to his daughter Eva, and declared heir of all his territory. He at the same time contracted for succours with Robert Fitzstephen and Maurice Fitzgerald, whom he promised to gratify with the city of Wexford, and the two adjoining districts, which were then in possession of the Easterlings, or descendants of the Norwegians. Being thus assured of assistance, he returned privately to Ireland, and concealed himself during the winter in the monastery of Fernes, which he had founded. Robert Fitzstephen was first able, the ensuing spring, to fulfil his engagements, by landing with thirty knights, sixty esquires, and three hundred archers.' They were soon after joined by Maurice Prendergast, who, about the same time, brought over ten knights and sixty archers; and with this small force they resolved on besieging Wexford, which was to be theirs by treaty. This town was quickly reduced; and the adventurers, being reinforced by another body of men, to the amount of a hundred and fifty, under the command of Maurice Fitzgerald, composed an army that struck the barbarous natives with awe. Roderic, the chief monarch of the island, ventured to oppose them, but he was defeated, and soon after the prince

of Ossory was obliged to submit, and give hostages for his future conduct.

Dermont, being thus reinstated in his hereditary dominions, soon
began to conceive hopes of extending the limits of his power, and making himself master of Ireland. With these views he endeavoured to
expedite Strongbow, who, being personally prohibited by the king had
not come over.

Dermont tried to inflame his ambition by the glory of the conquest,
and his avarice by the advantages it would procure: he expatiated on
the cowardice of the natives, and the certainty of his success. Strongbow first sent over Raymond, one of his retinue with ten knights and
seventy archers; and receiving permission shortly after for himself, he
landed with two hundred horse and a hundred archers. All these English
forces, now joining together, became irresistible, and though the whole
number did not amount to a thousand, yet, such was the barbarous state
of the natives, that they were every where put to the rout. The city of
Waterford quickly surrendered; Dublin was taken by assault; and Strongbow, marrying Eva, according to treaty, became master of the kingdom
of Leinster upon Dermont's decease.

The island being thus in a manner wholly subdued, for nothing was
capable of opposing the progress of the English arms, Henry became
jealous of the success of the adventurers, and was willing to share in
person those honours which they had already secured. He therefore
shortly after landed in Ireland (1171) at the head of five hundred knights
and some soldiers; not so much to conquer a disputed territory, as to
take possession of a subject kingdom. In his progress through the country, he received the homage of the petty chieftains, and left most of them
in possession of their ancient territories. In a place so uncultivated and
so ill peopled, there was still land enough to satisfy the adventurers who
had followed him: Strongbow was made seneschal of Ireland; Hugh de
Lacey was made governor of Dublin, and John de Courcy received a
patent for conquering the province of Ulster, which yet remained unsubdued, The Irish bishops very gladly admitted the English, as they expected from their superior civilization a greater degree of reverence and
respect. Pope Adrian IV. had, in the beginning, encouraged Henry to
subdue the Irish by his bull, granting him the kingdom. Pope Alexander III.
now confirmed him in his conquest; and the kings of England were ac-

knowledged as lords over Ireland for ever. Thus, after a trifling effort, in which very little money was expended, and little bloodshed, that beautiful island became an appendage to the English crown, and as such it has ever since continued with unshaken fidelity.

(Oliver Goldsmith).

11. Magna Charta (1215).

The famous document known to us under the name of Magna Charta was originally drawn up in the reign of King John. It professed to contain all that was valuable in the laws of Edward the Confessor, and consequently in those of Alfred the Great; for Edward's code was merely a repetition and an enlargement of Alfred's. The necessity for a revival of those laws arose from the harsh and cruel manner in which the Norman Kings used their power. They would exact money from their subjects, and give no account of the way in which it was spent. They would commit them to prison, without showing any cause for the act; and even refuse them the privilege of trial by jury . . . . These and many other wrongs the people were determined to bear no longer; and to prevent John and all his successors from committing like injuries to the people, the barons compiled a number of laws, rules, and clauses, which together make up the Magna Charta. It was signed by John, on a little island in the Thames, between Windsor and Staines, called Runnymede, 1215.

Many of its clauses related to facts and circumstances interesting only to those who lived in that age, but some few of them were of so much importance that to this day they are justly regarded as one of the most precious portions of an Englishman's birthright . . . . Of those which bear that character, the following is the substance: 1) No man shall be imprisoned without just cause being shown. 2) Every man committed to prison shall have a right to a trial by a jury of his peers. 3) Taxes should not be laid upon the people without the consent of parliament. 4) The courts of justice should be stationary, instead of following the King's person.

So much importance did the people attach to this charter, that in the course of John's reign, and those succeeding it, it was solemnly read

22

and confirmed upwards of thirty times; but at length it was found that many portions of it had become so inoperative, that it was disregarded by kings, and useless to the people. It was subsequently superseded by the «Petition of Right», presented to Charles I in 1628.

---

12. Edward I.'s Conquest of Wales and Scotland.

In 1274 Edward I., and Eleanor, his amiable and truly worthy queen, were crowned at Westminster. His virtues and talents had rendered him a favourite of the nation. By means of this popularity he curbed the insolence of the barons, and by the equable administration of justice he maintained tranquillity among the people. Had not the love of war and the thirst of conquest counterbalanced his good qualities, and impelled him to arbitrary and cruel acts, Edward I. would, probably, have been a blessing to his subjects. But he too soon began, and too long continued, the career of false glory. Scarcely did he find himself firmly seated on the throne, when he determined to subdue Wales, and to tame the hitherto untameable fierceness of the descendants of the ancient Britons.

Safe under the shelter of their mountains, and animated with the love of liberty, these aboriginal inhabitants of Britain had preserved themselves from the yoke of the Saxons, the Danes, and the Normans; but at last, internal discord began the process of their subjugation, and the great military abilities of Edward completed it. He subdued Wales, after a doubtful and severe struggle; annexed it to the English crown, and determined that the title of Prince of Wales should be borne by the eldest sons of his successors. It is asserted by the most historians of England, though denied by some, that Edward commanded all the Welsh bards who could be found to be put to death, lest by their enthusiastic songs they should rouse the ancient British spirit, and renew the struggle for liberty. Ambition is a restless, insatiable passion. Seven years after he had effected this conquest, Edward proceeded to another still more important. Alexander III., king of Scotland, dying without children, the crown was claimed by several competitors among whom Bruce and Baliol were the principal, being descended on the female side from the royal house. The flames of civil war were about to burst forth and rage. To prevent this, the nobles of Scotland chose Edward as umpire between the rivals. But by this, they brought upon their country an evil, worse than that which they wished to avoid. The monarch of England accepted the office; marched at the head of a powerful army; caused several fortresses to be put into his hands as pledges of obedience to his award; and obliged the Scotch barons to acknowledge him as their liege lord. He then pronounced sentence in favour of Baliol. Baliol soon found the yoke of Edward too galling to be borne; and making a league with Philip le Bel, king of France, he and his countrymen endeavoured to throw it off. This alliance had the unexpected effect of giving political existence to the common people of England. The Earl of Leicester had, indeed, invited them to send representatives to parliament; but the invitation of a rebel had been but little regarded. Edward, surrounded by a factious nobility, and threatened with two wars at once, perceived that he could not hope for external success, nor internal peace, unless the nation at large were interested in his favour; he accordingly, summoned the people to choose their deputies, in order to give their consent to the imposition of taxes, saying, «It is but just that what interests all, should be approved of by all.»

With the supplies granted by these representatives of the people, Edward raised a large army, and quickly subdued the Scotch, made Baliol prisoner, and sent him to finish his days as a private individual in France. In vain did Bruce and Wallace, heroic patriots, strive to resist the mighty power of Edward. They strove in vain; and had the English sovereign governed the Scotch with equity, their union with England would probably have taken place at that time. But his governors exercised shameful oppression, and harassed the nation with grievous vexations. Again and again did the Scotch rise against their oppressors, and sometimes by the wonderful valour of William Wallace, their efforts were crowned with success. Yet, finally, they failed; and Wallace, their noble hero, being betrayed into the hands of Edward, instead of being treated with that respect which his laudable through fruitless efforts merited, he was, contrary to all justice, executed as a traitor. Robert Bruce, son of the rival candidate with Baliol for the crown, then formed the design of delivering his country. He was living in London, a kind of prisoner at large, when intentions were betrayed to the king, by Comyn, a treacherous friend. Of this the Earl of Gloucester is said to have warned Bruce, by sending him a purse of gold and a pair of spurs. Though the roads were covered with snow, having caused his horse's shoes to be reversed, that he might not be tracked, he arrived safely in his own country, and roused the

Scotch once more to arms. At first, his bold attempt promised well, and he was crowned king of Scotland at Scone. But the scene soon changed. Three English armies invaded his territories at the same time. Bruce was defeated, and obliged to fly to concealment in one of the smallest of the western islands. His kinsmen and friends were taken prisoners and inhumanly massacred; and Edward, whose indignation had now risen to the highest pitch, threatening to exterminate the whole nation, marched early in the spring of the year 1307 towards the north, with a most formidable force of veteran soldiers and experienced commanders. But death arrested him in his sanguinary course. On the sands not far from Charlisle, he sank under the overpowering influence of a rapid disease. The immediate view of death did not quell his savage sentiments of revenge; for just before he expired, he exhorted his son to complete his schemes of vengeance, and commanded, that his bones should be carried in the front of the army, asserting that the Scotch would fly at the mere sight of his remains. — Edward had lived sixty-eight years, and reigned thirty-four. His stature was majestic, and his whole figure commanding. His legs. were long, out of proportion to the rest of his body; which circumstance gave him the name of Longshanks. (Holt.)

---

13. Robert Bruce.

The celebrated Robert Bruce was crowned king of Scotland, March 19-th 1306. On the 18-th of May, he was excommunicated by the Pope, a sentence which excluded him from all the benefits of religion, and authorised any one to kill him. Finally, on the 19-th June, the new king was completely defeated near Methven by the English Earl of Pembroke. Robert's horse was killed under him in the action, and he was for a moment a prisoner. But he had fallen into the power of a Scottish knight, who, though he served in the English army, did not choose to be the instrument of putting Bruce into their hands, and allowed him to escape.

Bruce, with a few brave adherents, among whom was the young Lord Douglas, who was afterwards called the Good Lord James, retired into the Highland mountains, where they were chased from one place of refuge to another, placed in great danger, and underwent many hardships. Bruce's wife, now Queen of Scotland, with several other ladies,

accompanied her husband and his followers during their wanderings.
There was no other way of providing for them save by hunting and
fishing. It was remarked, that Donglas was the most active and successful in procuring for the unfortunate ladies such supplies as his dexterity
in fishing, or in killing deer could furnish to them.

Driven from one place in the Highlands to another, Bruce endeavoured to force his way into Lorn, but he found enemies every where.
The M'Dougal, a powerful family, then called the Lords of Lorn, were
friendly to the English, and putting their men in arms, attacked Bruce
and his wandering companions, as soon as they attempted to enter their
country. The chief of these M'Dougal, called John of Lorn, hated Bruce
on account of his having slain the Red Comyn in the church at Dumfries,
to whom this M'Dougal was nearly related. Bruce was again defeated by
this chief, through force of numbers, at a place called Dalry, but he
shewed, admist his misfortunes, the greatness of his strength and courage. He directed his men to retreat through a narrow pass, and placing
himself last of the party, he fought with, and slew such of the enemy
as attempted to press hard on them. Three followers of M'Dougal, a
father and two sons, called M'Androsser, all very strong men, when they
saw Bruce thus protecting the retreat of his followers, made a vow, that
they would either kill him or make him prisoner. The whole then rushed
on the king at once. The king was on horseback, in the strait pass we
have described, betwixt a steep hill and a deep lake. He struck the first
man, who came up and seized his bridle, such a blow with his sword
as cut off his hand and freed his bridle. The man bled to death. The
other brother had seized him in the mean time by the leg, and was
attempting to throw him from horseback. The king, setting spurs to his
horse, made the animal suddenly spring forward, so that the Highlander
fell under the horse's feet, and as he was endeavouring to rise again,
the king cleft his head in two with his sword. The father, seeing his
two sons thus slain, flew at Robert Bruce, and grasped him by the
mantle so close to his body, that he could not have room to wield his
long sword. But with the heavy pommel, or, as others say, with an
iron hammer, which hung at his saddle bow, the king struck this third
assailant so dreadful a blow, that he dashed out his brains. Still, however, the Highlander kept his dying grasp on the king's mantle, so
that, to be free of the dead body, Bruce was obliged to undo the broach

or clasp, by which it was fastened, and leave that and the mantle itself behind him. The broach, which fell thus into the possession of M'Dougal of Lorn, is still preserved in that ancient family as a memorial, that the celebrated Robert Bruce once narrowly escaped falling into the hands of their ancestor. Robert greatly resented this attack upon him; and when he was in happier circumstances, did not fail to take his revenge on M'Dougal, or, as he is usually called, John of Lorn.

At last, dangers increased so much around the brave King Robert, that he was obliged to separate himself from the ladies and his queen, for the winter was coming on, and it would be impossible for the women to endure this wandering sort of life, when the frost and the snow should arrive. So he left his queen, with the countess of Buchan and others, in the only castle which remained to him, which was called Kildrummie, and is situated near the head of the river Don in Aberdeenshire. The king also left the youngest brother, Nigel Bruce, to defend the castle against the English; and he himself, with his second brother Edward, who was a very brave man, but still more rash and passionate than Robert himself, went over to an island called Rachrin, on the coast of Ireland, where Bruce and the few men that followed his fortunes passed the winter of 1306. In the meantime, ill luck seemed to pursue all his friends in Scotland. The castle of Kildrummie was taken by the English, and Nigel Bruce, a beautiful and brave youth, was cruelly put to death by the victors. The ladies who had attended on Robert's queen, as well as the queen herself, and the countess of Buchan, were thrown into strict confinement, and treated with the utmost severity. This news reached Bruce while he was residing in a miserable dwelling at Rachrin, and reduced him to the point of despair.

It was probably about this time that an incident took place, which, although it rests only on tradition in the family of the name of Bruce, is rendered probable by the manners of the times. After receiving the last unpleasing intelligence from Scotland, Bruce was lying one morning on his wretched bed, and deliberating with himself, whether he had not better resign all thoughts of again attempting to make good his right to the Scottish crown, and, dismissing his followers, transport himself and his brothers to the Holy Land, and spend the rest of his life in fighting against the Saracens: by which he thought, perhaps, he might deserve the forgiveness of Heaven for the great sin of stabbing Comyn in the church of Dumfries.

But then, on the other hand, he thought it would be both criminal and cowardly to give up his attempts to restore freedom to Scotland, while there yet remained the least chance of his being successful in an undertaking which, rightly considered, was much more his duty, than to drive the Infidels out of Palestine, though the superstition of his age might think otherwise.

While he was divided betwixt these reflections, and doubtful of what he should do, Bruce was looking upward to the roof of the cabin in which he lay, and his eye was attracted by a spider, which, hanging at the end of a long thread of its own spinning, was endeavouring, as is the fashion of that creature, to swing himself from one beam in the roof to another, for the purpose of fixing the line on which he meant to stretch his web. The insect made the attempt again and again, without success, and at length, Bruce counted that it had tried to carry its point six times, and been as often unable to do so. It came into his head, that he had himself fought just sixt battles against the English and their allies, and that the poor persevering spider was exactly in the same situation with himself, having made as many trials, and been as often disappointed in what it aimed at. «Now», thought Bruce, «as I have no means of knowing what is best to be done, I will be guided by the luck that shall attend this spider. If the insect shall make another effort to fix its thread, and shall be successful, I will venture a seventh time to try my fortune in Scotland; but if the spider shall fall, I will go to the wars in Palestine, and never return to my native country again».

While Bruce was forming this resolution, the spider made another exertion with all the force it could muster; and fairly succeeded in fastening its thread on the beam which it had so often in vain attempted to reach. Bruce seeing the success of the spider, resolved to try his own fortune; and as he never before gained a victory, so he never afterwards sustained any considerable check or defeat. I have often met with people of the name of Bruce, so completely persuaded of the truth of this story, that they would not on any account kill a spider, because it was such an insect, which had shown the example of perseverance, and given a signal of good luck, to their namesake.

14. Battle of Crecy.

The intelligence of Edward's unexpected invasion soon reached Paris, and threw Philip into great perplexity. He issued orders, however, for levying forces in all quarters; and despatched the Count of Eu, Constable of France, and the Count of Tancarville, with a body of troops, to the defence of Caën, a populous and commercial but open city, which lay in the neighbourhood of the English army. The temptation of so rich a prize, soon allured Edward to approach it; and the inhabitants, encouraged by their numbers, and the reinforcements which they daily received from the country, ventured to meet him in the field. But their courage failed them on the first shock: they fled with precipitation: the Counts of Eu and Tancarville were taken prisoners: the victors entered the city along with the vanquished, and a furious massacre commenced, without distinction of age, sex, or condition. The citizens, in despair, barricadoed their houses, and assaulted the English with stones, briks, and every missile weapon: the English made way by fire to the destruction of the citizens: till Edward, anxious to save both his spoil and his soldiers, stopped the massacre; and having obliged the inhabitants to lay down their arms, gave his troops licence to begin a more regular and less hazardous plunder of the city. The pillage continued for three days: the king reserved for his own share the jewels, plate, silks, fine cloth, and fine linen; and he bestowed all the remainder of the spoil on his army. The whole was embarked on board the ships, and sent over to England, together with three hundred of the richest citizens of Caën, whose ransom was an additional profit, which he expected afterwards to levy. This dismal scene passed in the presence of two cardinal legates, who had come to negociate a peace between the kingdoms.

The king moved next to Rouen, in hopes of treating that city in the same manner; but found that the bridge over the Seine was already broken down, and that the King of France himself was arrived there with his army. He marched along the banks of that river towards Paris, destroying the whole country, and every town and village which he met with on his road. Some of his light troops carried their ravages even to the gates of Paris; and the royal palace of St. Germains, together with Nanterre, Ruelle, and other villages, was reduced to ashes within sight of the capital. The English intended to pass the river at Poissy, but found the French army encamped on the opposite banks, and the bridge at that place as well as all others over the Seine, broken down by orders from Philip. Edward now saw that the French meant to enclose him in their country, in hopes of attacking him with advantage on all sides: but he saved himself by a stratagem from this perilous situation. He gave his army orders to dislodge, and to advance further up the Seine; but immediately returning by the same road, he arrived at Poissy, which the enemy had already quitted in order to attend his motions. He repaired the bridge with incredible celerity, passed over his army, and having thus disengaged himself from the enemy, advanced by quick marches towards Flanders. His vanguard, commanded by Harcourt, met with the townsmen of Amiens, who were hastening to reinforce their king, and defeated them with great slaughter: he passed by Beauvais, and burned the suburbs of that city: but as he approached the Somme, he found himself in the same difficulty as before: all the bridges on that river were either broken down or strongly guarded: an army, under the command of Godemar de Faye, was stationed on the opposite banks: Philip was advancing on him from the other quarter, with an army of a hundred thousand men: and he was thus exposed to the danger of being enclosed, and of starving in an enemy's country. In this extremity he published a reward to any one that should bring him intelligence of a passage over the Somme. A peasant, called Gobin Agace, whose name has been preserved by the share which he had in these important transactious, was tempted, on this occasion, to betray the interests of his country; and he informed Edward of a ford below Abbeville, which had a sound bottom, and might be passed without difficulty at low water. The king hastened thither, but found Godemar de Faye on the opposite banks. Being urged by necessity, he deliberated not a moment; but threw himself into the river, sword in hand, at the head of his troops; drove the enemy from their station; and pursued them to a distance on the plain. The French army under Philip arrived at the ford, when the rear-guard of the English were passing. So narrow was the escape which Edward, by his prudence and celerity, made from this danger! The rising of the tide prevented the French king from following him over the ford, and obliged that prince to take his route over the bridge at Abbeville; by which some time was lost.

It is natural to think that Philip, at the head of so vast an army, was impatient to take revenge on the English, and to prevent the disgrace to which he must be exposed, if an inferior enemy should be allowed, after ravaging so great a part of his kingdom, to escape with impunity. Edward also was sensible that such must be the object of the French monarch; and as he had advanced but a little way before his enemy, he saw the danger of precipitating his march over the plains of Picardy, and of exposing his rear to the insults of the numerous cavalry, in which the French camp abounded. He took, therefore, a prudent resolution: he chose his ground with advantage, near the village of Crecy; he disposed his army in excellent order; he determined to await in tranquillity the arrival of the enemy; and he hoped that their eagerness to engage, and to prevent his retreat, after all their past disappointments, would hurry them on to some rash and ill concerted action. He drew up his army on a gentle ascent, and divided them into three lines: the first was commanded by the Prince of Wales, and under him, by the Earls of Warwick and Oxford, by Harcourt, and by the Lords Chandos, Holland, and other noblemen: the Earls of Arundel and Northampton, with the Lords Willoughby, Basset, Roos, and Sir Lewis Tuftòn, were at the head of the second line: he took to himself the command of the third division, by which he purposed either to bring succour to the two first lines, or to secure a retreat in case of any misfortune, or to push his advantages against the enemy. He had likewise the precaution to throw up trenches on his flanks, in order to secure himself from the numerous bodies of the French, who might assail him from that quarter; and he placed all his baggage behind him in a wood, which he also secured by an intrenchment.

The skill and order of this dispositon, with the tranquillity in which it was made, served extremely to compose the minds of the soldiers; and the king, that he might further inspirit them, rode through the ranks with such an air of cheerfulness and alacrity, as conveyed the highest confidence into every beholder. He pointed out to them the necessity to which they were reduced, and the certain and inevitable destruction which awaited them, if, in their present situation, enclosed on all hands in an enemy's country, they trusted to any thing but their own valour, or gave that enemy an opportunity of taking revenge for the many insults and indignities which they had of late put upon him. He reminded them of the visible ascendant which they had hitherto maintained over all the bodies of French troops, that had fallen in their way; and assured them, that the superior numbers of the army which at present hovered over them, gave them not greater force, but was an advantage easily compensated by the order in which he had placed his own army, and the resolution which he expected from them. He demanded nothing, he said, but that they would imitate his own example, and that of the Prince of Wales; and as the honour, the lives, the liberties of all were now exposed to the same danger, he was confident that they would make one common effort to extricate themselves from the present difficulties, and that their united courage would-give them the victory over all their enemies.

It is related by some historians, that Edward, besides the resources which he found in his own genius and presence of mind, employed also a new invention against the enemy, and placed in his front some pieces of artillery, the first that had yet been made use of on any remarkable occasion in Europe. This is the epoch of one of the most singular discoveries that has been made among men; a discovery which changed by degrees the whole art of war, and by consequence many circumstances in the political government of Europe. But the ignorance of that age in the mechanical arts rendered the progress of this new invention very slow. The artillery first framed were so clumsy, and of so difficult management, that men were not immediately sensible of their use and efficacy: and even to the present times, improvements have been continually making on this furious engine, which, though it seemed contrived for the destruction of mankind, and the overthrow of empires, has in the issue rendered battles less bloody, and has given greater stability to civil societies. Nations by its means have been brought more to a level: conquests have become less frequent and rapid : success in war has been reduced nearly to be a matter of calculation: and any nation overmatched by its enemies, either yields to their demands, or secures itself by alliances against their violence and invasion.

The invention of artillery was at this time known in France as well as in England; but Philip in his hurry to overtake the enemy, had probably left his cannon behind him, which he regarded as a useless encumbrance. All his other movements discovered the same imprudence and precipitation. Impelled by anger, a dangerous counsellor, and trusting to the great superiority of his numbers, he thought that all depended on forcing an engagement with the English; and that, if he could once reach the enemy in their retreat, the victory on his side was certain and inevitable. He made a hasty march, in some confusion, from Abbeville; but after he had advanced above two leagues, some gentlemen, whom he had sent before to take a view of the enemy, returned to him, and brought him intelligence, that they had seen the English drawn up in great order, and awaiting his arrival. They therefore advised him to defer the combat till the ensuing day, when his army would have recovered from their fatigue, and might be disposed into better order than their present hurry had permitted them to observe. Philip assented to this counsel; but the former precipitation of his march, and the impatience of the French nobility, made it impracticable for him to put it in execution. One division pressed upon another: orders to stop were not seasonably conveyed to all of them; this immense body was not governed by sufficient discipline to be manageable: and the French army, imperfectly formed into three lines, arrived, already fatigued and disordered, in presence of the enemy. The first line, consisting of 15,000 Genoese crossbow men, was commanded by Anthony Doria and Charles Grimaldi: the second was led by the Count of Alençon, brother to the king: the king himself was at the head of the third. Besides the French monarch, there were no less than three crowned heads in this engagement: the King of Bohemia, the King of the Romans, his son, and the King of Majorca; with all the nobility and great vassals of the crown of France. The army now consisted of above 120,000 men, more than three times the number of the enemy. But the prudence of one man was superior to the advantage of all this force and splendour.

The English, on the approach of the enemy, kept their ranks firm and immovable; and the Genoese first began the attack. There had happened, a little before the engagement, a thunder shower, which had moistened and relaxed the strings of the Genoese crossbows; their arrows, for this reason, fell short of the enemy. The English archers, taking their bows out of their cases, poured in a shower of arrows upon this multitude who were opposed to them, and soon threw them into disorder. The Genoese fell back upon the heavy-armed cavalry of the Count of Alençon; who, enraged at their cowardice, ordered his troops to put them to the sword. The artillery fired amidst the crowd; the English archers continued to send in their arrows among them; and nothing was to be seen in that vast body but hurry and confusion, terror and dismay.

The young Prince of Wales had the presence of mind to take advantage of this situation, and to lead on his line to the charge. The French cavalry, however, recovering somewhat their order, and encouraged by the example of their leader, made a stout resistance; and having at last cleared themselves of the Genoese runaways, advanced upon their enemies, and by their superior numbers began to hem them round. The Earls of Arundel and Northampton now advanced their line to sustain the prince, who, ardent in his first feats of arms, set an exemple of valour which was imitated by all his followers. The battle became, for some time, hot and dangerous, and the Earl of Warwick, apprehensive of the event from the superior numbers of the French, despatched a messenger to the king, and entreated him to send succours to the relief of the prince. Edward had chosen his station on the top of the hill; and he surveyed in tranquillity the scene of action. When the messenger accosted him, his first question was, whether the prince were slain or wounded? On receiving an answer in the negative, *Return*, said he, *to my son; and tell him that I reserve the honour of the day to him: I am confident that he will show himself worthy of the honour of knighthood which I so lately conferred upon him: he will be able, without any assistance, to repel the enemy.* This speech, being reported to the prince and his attendants, inspired them with fresh courage: they made an attack with redoubled vigour on the French, in which the Count of Alençon was slain: that whole line of cavalry was thrown into disorder: the riders were killed or dismounted: the Welsh infantry rushed into the throng, and with their long knives cut the throats of all who had fallen; nor was any quarter given that day by the victors.

The King of France advanced in vain with the rear to sustain the line commanded by his brother: he found them already discomfited; and the example of their rout increased the confusion which was before but too prevalent in his own body. He had himself a horse killed under him:·he was remounted; and though left almost alone, he seemed still determined to maintain the combat; when John of Hainault seized the reins of his bridle, turned about his horse, and carried him off the field of battle. The whole French army took to flight, and was followed and put to the sword, without mercy, by the enemy; till the darkness of the night put an end to the pursuit. The King, on his return to the camp, flew into the arms of the Prince of Wales, and exclaimed, *My brave son! Per-*

severe in your honourable course: You are my son; for valiantly have you acquitted yourself to-day: You have shown yourself worthy of empire!

This battle, which is known by the name of the battle of Crecy, began after three o'clock in the afternoon, and continued till evening. The next morning was foggy; and as the English observed that many of the enemy had lost their way in the neight and in the mist, they employed a stratagem to bring them into their power: they erected on the eminences some French standards which they had taken in the battle; and all who were allured by this false signal were put to the sword, and no quarter given them. In excuse for this inhumanity, it was alleged that the French king had given like orders to his troops; but the real reason probably·was, that the English, in their present situation, did not choose to be encumbered with prisoners. On the day of battle and on the ensuing, there fell, by a moderate computation, 1200 French knights, 1400 gentlemen, 4000 men at arms, besides about 30,000 of inferior rank: many of the principal nobility of France, the Dukes of Lorraine and Bourbon, the Earls of Flanders, Blois, Vaudemont, Aumale, were left on the field of battle. The kings also of Bohemia and Majorca were slain: the fate of the former was remarkable: he was blind from age ; but being resolved to hazard his person, and set an example to others, he ordered the reins of his bridle to be tied on each side to the horses of two gentlemen of his train; and his dead body, and those of his attendants, were afterwards found among the slain, with their horses standing by them in that situation. His crest was three ostrich feathers, and his motto these German words, *Ich dien, I serve*: which the Prince of Wales and his successors adopted in memorial of this great victory. The action may seem no less remarkable for the small loss sustained by the English than for the great slaughter of the French; there were killed in it only one esquire and three knights, and very few of inferior rank; a demonstration, that the prudent disposition planned by Edward, and the disorderly attack made by the French, had rendered the whole rather a rout than battle; which was indeed the common case with engagements in those times.

(David Hume.)

15. The War of Roses.

As Henry VI. advanced in years, he manifested a mild and gentle disposition, but an utter incapacity for steering the vessel of the state through
the waves of a stormish sea. By the influence of the Earl of Suffolk, an ambitious and unprincipled man, Henry married Margaret, daughter of Réné,
of Anjou, titular king of Naples, a woman of great energy of mind, and
unbounded love of power, who, consequently, governed him with absolute
sway. the enthusiasm, excited in the French nation by Joan of Arc, who imagined herself to be commissioned by the Almighty to deliver her country
from a foreign yoke, of which Charles and his commanders skilfully made
use — the disputes which took place among the English captains; and
the defection of the Duke of Burgundy, together with the loss of Talbot,
the illustrious Earl of Shrewsbury, and several other brave warriors, gradually transferred the conquests made by Henry V., to their lawful pos-
sessors. The nation murmured; the barons quarrelled with one another,
till at last blazed forth that dreadful flame of civil war which raged for
thirty years — produced twelve pitched battles — sacrificed upwards of
one hundred thousand lives — and nearly destroyed the ancient nobility
of England.

Richard, Duke of York, was descended, by the female line, from
Lionel, the second son of Edward III., and was, therefore, nearer the
throne, in regular succession, than Henry VI., who derived his descent
from the Duke of Lancaster, the third son of that mighty monarch.
Richard was endowed with considerable abilities, great valour, and popular qualities. His party was sustained by the Earl of Salisbury and the
Earl of Warwick, the most potent baron and formidable warrior of his
age. The Lancastrian cause was espoused by the Dukes of Suffolk and
Somerset, the Earl of Northumberland, Clifford, and many other famous
nobles. The latter assumed the *red rose* as their emblem, while the
Yorkists adopted the *white rose* as the sign of their faction. Various
were the changes of fortune, which took place in these unhappy and most
destructive dissensions. Henry was alternately in the hands of both parties, and by each played as a mere puppet. His queen Margaret manifested astonishing activity and fortitude, but disgraced by cruel and implacable revenge. The Duke of York himself perished in the conflict with
his youthful son, the Duke of Rutland; but Warwick and the other sons of

York sustained their cause. Edward, the eldest son of Richard, was crowned at London, under the title of Edward IV. Henry, captive for the third
time, was lodged in the Tower of London. Margaret and his son took
refuge in France. To all appearances, the struggle was now over; but it
proved to be not so. Another storm was raised by pride and anger, which
produced another change. Warwick was sent by Edward to the French
Court, to demand for him in marriage Bona of Savoy, the sister-in-law
of Louis XI. The illustrious envoy succeeded in his commission, and obtained the Princess. But in the intervening time, the capricious Edward
had espoused and crowned a beautiful and accomplished woman, daughter
of the Duchess of Bedford, and widow of Sir John Grey. This imprudent
act naturally displeased the French monarch, and filled the high spirited
Warwick with indignation. This, however, he concealed in his own bosom
for some years, till he found an opportunity of displaying it effectually.

George, Duke of Clarence, one of Edward's brothers, being prevented
by him from marrying a rich heiress, who was given to the queen's brother, was impelled, by the rage of disappointment, to an open rupture
with the king; and with him Warwick united. Their firsts movements
were unsuccessful. They were obliged to fly to France: where the desire
of vengeance reconciled them to Queen Margaret. Louis furnished them
with troops, vessels, and money. Warwick arrived in safety at Dart-
mouth; declared himself the avenger of the house of Lancaster; and soon
saw himself at the head of sixty thousand men. Taken by surprise, and
unable to resist such a torrent, Edward fled into Holland, after having
narrowly escaped being taken prisoner. Henry VI. was released from the
Tower, and, for the fourth time, reseated on the throne. But the unfortunate sovereign did not remain long in that dangerous situation. Edward
returned with a small force, furnished for him by his ally, the Duke of
Burgundy. Landing in Yorkshire, the adherents to his cause crowded to
his standard by thousands; he led them to London, and was well received
in that city. At length the hostile armies met near Barnet, and a sanguinary battle took place. In the heat of the fight the fickle Duke of Clarence went over to his brother with the body of men which he commanded; and Warwick, wo had been styled the king-maker, was slain. In
another battle near Tewkesbury, the unhappy Margaret vainly endeavoured
to support her falling cause. The Lancastrians were again defeated; their
leader, the Duke of Somerset, was slain; and the queen, with her son

Edward, a high-minded and gallant young prince, fell into the power of the victors, who cruelly murdered the latter, and kept the former in captivity, till she was ransomed by the king of France. Almost all the friends of the Lancastrian family had now perished in battle or on the scaffold. Henry VI. did not long survive his irremediable misfortunes. After a miserable reign of fifty two years he died in the Tower, A. D. 1472; — according to most English historians, assassinated by Richard, Duke of Gloucester, the valiant, fierce, and pitiless brother of Edward IV.

Edward IV. may be regarded as being established on the throne of England, A. D. 1472. A profound calm now succeeded the dreadful tempest which had raged so long, and scattered desolation so widely from its wings. Edward was remarkable for the beauty of his form, and for active valour. But there ends his praise. He was vindictive, cruel, and shamefully intemperate, indulging all his passions, without scruple, or limit. In him it clearly appeared that the love of pleasure by no means tends to soften the angry and inhuman feelings. Though he had apparently pardoned Neville, Archbishop of York, for having deserted him, he sent him to perish in prison in a foreign land. Though his brother Clarence, by deserting Warwick in the midst of the fight, had probably given victory to Edward, yet mindful only of that prince's former defection, he impeached him before the parliament and procured his condemnation and death. Scarcely had he satisfied his thirst of revenge, when he yielded to the temptations of ambition, and formed the project of attacking France in conjunction with the Duke of Burgundy. He actually passed into that country at the head of a formidable army, but not being supported by his ally, he accepted an annual tribute which Louis offered for the sake of peace. In seven years after, death delivered the world from this pernicious monarch, A. D. 1483. He was forty three years of age.

The deceased monarch left two sons and six daughters. The eldest son, Edward V. was immediately acknowledged as king of England, but as he was only thirteen years old, Richard, Duke of Gloucester, his uncle, governed under his name as Protector. This ambitious and crafty man gradually gained possession of the supreme power, and destroyed his rivals and opponents, the relations of the queen. He seized the person of the young sovereign, and of his brother, Richard, Duke of York, and under pretext of securing them from sudden violence, placed them in the Tower. Afterwards he caused reports of their illegitimacy to be

24

spread, asserting that the late king was married to another woman, when he took Elizabeth Grey to wife; and that he himself was the only lawful heir of the crown. Endeavouring to engage Hastings, the lord chamberlain, to destroy the young princes, and finding him faithful to the royal house, he procured his condemnation and death. By means of the Duke of Buckingham, he then obtained the apparent choice of the people, and their invitation to assume the sceptre. In this manner, Richard of Gloucester ascended the throne; and soon after this event, his innocent nephews were murdered, A. D. 1485. It is supposed that they were stifled by his command, and buried beneath a heap of stones. In the reign of Charles II. the rubbish which was imagined to cover the remains of the unfortunate princes, being removed in order to make a new entrance to the chapel of thp white tower, in the great Tower of London, two-skeletons were found, answering in size and position, the tradition concerning the interment of the royal children. The bones were transported to Westminster Abbey, and there deposited under a marble monument. •

Wicked associates seldom live long in friendship: Richard and Buckingham, the vile instrument of his exaltation, soon quarrelled. There existed a branch of the house of Lancaster, Henry, Earl of Richmond, by the paternal line, grandson of Owen Tudor, whom Catherine of France had married after the decease of her noble husband, Henry V., and descended by the female side from Edward III. He was, at that time, living in Brittany, rather guarded than protected by its duke. Him Buckingham invited to wrest the sceptre from the hands of the tyrant Richard; while he himself appearing in arms prematurely, was taken and beheaded. In the mean time, Richmond obtained a small supply of troops from the French king; and, landing in Wales, was there joined by Vere, Earl of Oxford, and many remaining friends of the Red Rose. Thence he marched forwards to Bosworth in Leicestershire, where Richard met him with a far superior force. An engagement ensued; at the very commencement of which, Lord Stanley, who had married the mother of Richmond, and who had suffered under the oppressive sway of the usurper, deserted from him with a considerable body of troops. The rest of the royal army was speedily routed, and Richard, rushing among his enemies with desperate fury, was slain, after having killed Sir Robert Brandon, who bore Richmond's standard. Together with him fell the Duke of Norfolk and four thousand common men, fighting in a cause of little importance to their welfare, A. D. 1485. Upon the field of battle, the victorious army, with loud shouts, saluted Richmond king of England, and he ascended the throne without further opposition. The contest between the white and red roses was now terminated for ever. The families of York and Lancaster were united by the marriage of Richmond, now Henry VII., with Elizabeth, eldest daughter of Edward IV.; and an end was happily put to those dreadful civil wars, which had sacrificed multitudes of valuable citizens, and almost broken the strength of the nation. (Holt).

16. Henry VII.

Henry Tudor was a wise and prudent monarch, who knew how to appreciate the value of peace, and felt its necessity for reviving the strength of the nation. His reign of nearly four and twenty years was fortunate and tranquil, rather than brilliant, and was so much the more beneficial to his subjects. Toward its commencement he suppressed two dangerous insurrections by his activity and vigour; one raised by Simnal, the son of a baker, who pretended that the unfortunate Duke of Clarence was his father; the other by Perkin Warbeck, who asserted himself to be Richard, Duke of York, escaped from the assassins employed by his inhuman uncle; and who had actually murdered his brother Edward V. Henry VII. found the royal treasury nearly exhausted by the extravagance of his predecessors. Habits of strict economy were, therefore, absolutely necessary. Unfortunately those habits became immoderately strong and finally degenerated into rapacity and avarice. By Elizabeth of York, Henry had two sons; the elder of whom, Arthur, a prince whose talents and conduct raised the most pleasing expectations, died before his father, to the great regret of the whole nation; especially as Henry, the second son, did not afford such cheering hopes. Henry VII., by wise and cautious measures, endeavoured to destroy the overgrown and pernicious power of the nobles. Till his time, the great lords had the use of their possessions for their lives only, and had not the liberty of alienating or selling them; in consequence of which, such accumulations took place in some high families, that, by degrees, they became proprietors of the greater part of the lands of the whole kingdom. To remedy this evil, the king granted these great landholders permission to sell. They took advantage of this permission, and parted with their lands, or portions of them, to supply the cravings of dissipation and luxury. Private individuals, who had enriched themselves by industry, purchased them, and thus the lower orders of citizens acquired that influence which the barons lost; and a more even balance was established between the two orders.

This monarch patronized commerce and voyages of discovery, and invited the illustrious navigator Columbus to enter into his service, which was prevented only by an unlucky accident. In his reign Sebastian Cabot, sailing from Bristol, discovered that part of America, called Newfoundland. He caused to be constructed an enormously large vessel, named «the Great Henry», and by maintaining ships of his own, in fact laid the foundation of that navy which is the grand bulwark of Britain. Before his time, if the exigencies of the state required a fleet, the monarch had no other means of providing one than hiring, or forcibly seizing the vessels of the merchants. Henry died of consumption in the fifty-third year of his life, A. D. 1509, and was buried in a magnificent chapel, which he had built in Westminster Abbey, and which is still one of the greatest ornaments of that venerable edifice. The favourite maxim of this sovereign was, «When Christ came into the world, peace was sung, and when he left it, peace was bequeathed», and had this been the ruling principle of preceding and successive sovereigns, much less bloodshed and animosity, much less natural and moral evil, would have existed in the world. (Holt).

---

17. Henry VIII.

Upon the decease of his father, Henry VIII. ascended the throne without a rival, flourishing in youthful vigour and personal beauty, the object of the best hopes and most pleasing expectations of his subjects. Listening to the advice of his prudent grandmother, the countess of Richmond, and Derby, he selected a wise and respectable council; he completed his marriage with Catherine, who having been espoused to his brother Arthur, upon the prince's lamented death was retained in England to become his wife; he gave np to the resentment of the nation, Dudley and Empson, the odious ministers of the exactions of Henry VII. Adorned with manly and literary accomplishments, the young monarch attracted the attention of civilized Europe, and his friendship was courted by its greatest potentates. But this bright prospect was too soon obscured by threatening clouds. Henry became extravagant, luxurious, intemperate, and quickly lavished in useless and vain pomp, the immense treasures which the late king had amassed. These he might have applied to public benefit, and it was surely his duty so to do. In his alliances and attachments he was extremely fickle and capricious. Sometimes he was the friend of the gallant and romantic Francis I. of France, and at other times he united himself with the cautious and crafty Charles V., Emperor of Germany.

Youthful effervescence and activity of mind degenerated into violence and cruelty, and he finally became an odious tyrant! Wolsey, a priest of great abilities and learning, but cunning and ambitious, by flattering the passions of Henry, and administering to his absurd and extravagant pleasures, gained almost his exclusive favour. He rose rapidly to the highest rank and offices; and was graced by the pope with the title of Cardinal. This man, for a season, ruled insensibly the fiery monarch, and consequently the whole realm. The parliaments were submissive, the king was absolute, and English liberty appeared to be expiring. At this period, Luther, a German ecclesiastic, began to attack the corruptions introduced, or at least countenanced by the Roman Pontiffs. Henry VIII., having been intended for an ecclesiastical life, and destined to the archbishopric of Canterbury, before his brother's death, had been educated in the knowledge and practice of polemical theology. Proud of his attainment Henry entered the lists with Luther, and defended the power of the popes, and the seven Catholic sacraments. Pope Leo X. conferred upon the royal disputant, the title of «Defender of the Faith,» little expecting that this defender would finally sever England from the Holy See.

The passions of Henry VIII. were impetuous, and he had not acquired the power of commanding them. But from what was a personal evil to Henry himself and doubtless an apparent evil to those around, the infinitely wise and benevolent disposer of all events educed good. From this source arose the freedom of England from ecclesiastical tyranny. The king indulging a capricious fancy for Anne Boleyn, a beautiful and accomplished young woman, one of the queen's attendants, in order to marry her wished to obtain a divorce from Catherine. For this purpose he applied to Pope Clement VII. to annul his union with his brother's widow, as being unlawful, and pretending great scruples of conscience on that account. Catherine of Arragon was the aunt of the powerful Charles V. of Germany, whose menaces deterred Clement from complying with the request of Henry. Finding that he could not accomplish his plan, the impatient spirit of the king burst forth into a flame. He disgraced Cardinal Wolsey, who dared not support his temporal sovereign against his spiritual lord; and the fallen favourite died of grief and mortified pride.

Cranmer, a learned ecclesiastic, who was soon after created archbishop of Canterbury, devised the fortunate expedient of consulting the most celebrated universities of Europe upon the legality of the marriage with his brother's widow. The greater part of those learned bodies condemned such a union, and declared that the pope himself had not authority to sanction it. Whereupon, Henry repudiated Catherine, and substituted the object of his fickle affection in her place. Despising a bull of excommunication which Clement published against him, the king induced his compliant Parliament to declare him head of the English church instead of the pope, and to break off all connection with the Holy See. Henry proceeded to expel the monks from their convents and to take possession of their wealth, an act of cruel injustice. He persecuted to death both protestants and papists who denied his supremacy over the church, or presumed to profess religious opinions different from those which he pretended to hold. He created six new bishoprics, caused the Bible to be translated into English, and adopted partly the Romish and partly the Reformed creed. Sir Thomas More, a man of solid learning, great abilities and admirable character, who had succeeded Wolsey in the office of Chancellor and had executed the duties of that important office with undeviating integrity, together with Fisher, bishop of Rochester, who deservedly enjoyed high reputation, were sacrificed by Henry's indiscriminating anger. In comparatively a short time, Henry's affections were alienated from Anne Boleyn, and he caused her to be tried, condemned, and beheaded, though evidently innocent of the charges brought against her.

Immediately after her death, Henry married Jane Seymour, who became the mother of Edward VI. Death removing her, this capricious sovereign espoused Anne of Cleves, a Garman princess; but her he speedily divorced, and disgraced Cromwell, an able statesman and zealous friend of the reformation, for having advised that marriage. The tyrant caused him to be impeached of high treason and beheaded. Catherine Howard next succeeded to the dangerous dignity of queen, and experienced the fate of Anne Boleyn. Catherine Parr, widow of Lord Latimer, Henry's sixth wife, fortunately survived this sanguinary husband, though she had a narrow escape; for the king began to suspect that she presumed to differ from his religious opinions, and her enemies were urging him to her destruction. In the mean time, Henry had absurdly engaged in successive wars of no long duration, nor of great consequence; he gained some advantages in France, and while he was in that country, James IV. of Scotland, who had embraced this opportunity of attacking England, was defeated and killed by the Earl of Surrey at Flodden field. Henry VIII., rendered still more irritable than ever by disease, fortunately for his subjects at large, and yet more fortunately for those immediately about his person, died A. D. 1547.   (Holt).

18. King Edward VI.

Though considerable talents and attainments have not always been associated with eminent stations, a goodly number of the great are to be found in the list of those who have been richly endowed by their Creator, and have diligently improved his gifts. The young king Edward VI. stands among the most prominent of these examples.

This aimiable prince was born in 1537, at Hampton Court. His mother was Jane Seymour, the third wife of Henry VIII. At the early age of six years, he was committed to the care of Sir Anthony Cook, and other learned preceptors, who were intent on his improvement in spiritual knowledge, as well as in science and learning. The manner in which these gentlemen performed their duties, and in which the prince improved, may be ascertained from an account written by William Thomas, a learned man, who was afterwards clerk of the council. He says —

«If ye knew the towardness of that young prince, your hearts would melt to hear him named, and your stomach abhor the malice of them that would him ill. The beautifulest creature that liveth under the sun, the wittiest, the most amiable, and the gentlest thing of all the world. Such a capacity in learning the things taught him by his schoolmaster, that it is a wonder to hearsay. And, finally, he has such a grace of posture, and gesture in gravity, when he comes into a presence, that is should seem he were already a father, and yet passes he not the age of ten years. A thing, undoubtedly, much rather to be seen than believed».

In his ninth year he wrote letters in Latin and French; and in the British Museum are themes and orations in Latin, which he then composed. Curio, the Italian reformer, told his tutors, «that by their united prayers, counsels, and industry, they had formed a king of the highest, even divine hopes».

His ardent attachment and reverence to the Holy Scriptures are well known; and Foxe tells us «that he was not wanting in diligence to receive whatever his instructors would teach him; so that, in the midst of all his play and recreation, he would always keep the hours appointed to study, using the same with much attention, till time called him again from his book to pastime.

«In this, his study and keeping of his hours, he so profited, that Cranmer, beholding his towardness, his readiness in both tongues, in translating from Greek to Latin, from Latin to Greek again, in declaiming, with his schoolfellows, without help of his teachers, and that extempore, wept for joy, declaring to Dr. Fox, his schoolmaster, that he would never have thought it to have been in the prince, except he had seen it himself».

He became acquainted with seven languages, and well understood logic and theology.

19. The Invincible Armada.

Philip, King of Spain, threatened to do greater things than ever had been done yet, to set up the Catholic religion and punish Protestant England. Elizabeth, hearing that he and the Prince of Parma *) were making great preparations for this purpose, in order to be before hand with them, sent out Admiral Drake (a famous navigator who had sailed about the world, and had already brought great plunder from Spain) to the port of Cadix, where he burned a hundred vessels full of stores. This great loss obliged the Spaniards to put off the invasion for a year, but it was none the less formidable for that, amounting to 130 ships, 19000 soldiers, 8000 sailors, 2000 slaves, and between 2000 and 3000 great guns.

---

*) The Prince of Parma, главнокомандующій Филиппа.

England was not idle in making ready to resist this great force. All the men between 16 years and 60, were trained and drilled; the national fleet of ships (in number only 34 at first) was enlarged by public contributions and by private ships, filled out by noblemen; the City of London, of its own accord, furnished double the number of ships and men that it was required to provide; and if ever the national spirit was up in England, it was up all through the country to resist the Spaniards. Some of the Queen's advisers were for seizing the principal English Catholics, and putting them to death; but the Queen rejected the advice, and only confined a few of those who were the most suspected among them, in the fens in Lincolnshire. The great body of Catholics deserved this confidence; for they behaved most loyally, nobly, and bravely.

So, with all England firing up like one strong angry man, and with both sides of the Thames fortified, and with the soldiers under arms, and the sailors in their ships, the country waited for the coming of the proud Spanish fleet which was called the *Invincible Armada*. The Queen herself, riding on a white horse, with armour on her back, and the Earl of Essex and the Earl of Leicester holding her bridle rein, made a brave speech to the troops at Tilbury Fort opposite Gravesend, which was received with such enthusiasm as is seldom known. Then came the Spanish Armada into the English Channel sailing along in the form of a half moon, of such great size, that it was seven miles broad. But the English were quick upon it, and woe then to all the Spanish ships that dropped a little out of the half moon, for the English took them instantly. And it soon appeared that the great Armada was anything but invincible, for, on a summer night, bold Drake sent eight blazing fire-ships right into the midst of it. In terrible consternation the Spaniards tried to get out to sea, and so became dispersed; the English pursued them at a great advantage; a storm came on, and drove the Spaniards among rocks and shoals; and the swift end of the invincible fleet was that it lost thirty great ships and 10,000 men, and, defeated and disgraced, sailed home again. Being afraid to go by the English Channel, it sailed all round Scotland and Ireland; and some of the ships getting cast away on the latter coast in bad weather, the Irish, who were a kind of savages, plundered those vessels, and killed their crews. So ended this great attempt to invade and conquer England.   (Charles Dickens).

20. The Gunpowder Plot.

The Roman catholics had expected great favour and indulgence on the accession of James, both as he was descended from Mary, whose life they believed to have been sacrificed to their cause, and as he himself, in his early youth, was imagined to have shown some partiality towards them, which nothing, they thought, but interest and necessity had since restrained. It is pretended, that he had even entered into positive engage‐ ments to tolerate their religion, as soon as he should mount the throne of England; whether their credulity had interpreted in this sense some obliging expressions of the king's, or that he had employed such an artifice, in order to render them favourable to his title. Very soon they discovered their mistake, and were at once surprised and enraged to find James, on all occasions, express his intention of strictly executing the laws enacted against them, and of persevering in all the rigorous measures of Elizabeth. Catesby, a gentleman of good parts and of an ancient family, first thought of a most extraordinary method of revenge; and he opened his intention to Piercy, a descendant of the illustrious house of Northum‐ berland. In one of their conversations with regard to the distressed con‐ dition of the catholics, Piercy having broken into a sally of passion, and mentioned assassinating the king; Catesby took the opportunity of revealing to him a nobler and more extensive plan of treason, which not only included a sure execution of vengeance, but afforded some hopes of restoring the catholic religion in England. In vain, said he, would you put an end to the king's life: he has children, who would succeed both to his crown and maxims of government. In vain would you extinguish the whole royal family: the nobility, the gentry, the parliament, are all infected with the same heresy, and could raise to the throne another prince and another family, who, besides their hatred to our religion, would be an‐ imated with revenge for the tragical death of their predecessors. To serve any good purpose, we must destroy, at one blow, the King, the royal family, the lords, the commons, and bury all our enemies in one common ruin. Happily, they are all assembled on the first meeting of the parliament, and afford us the opportunity of glorious and useful vengeance. Great pre‐ parations will not be requisite. A few of us, combining, may run a mine below the hall, in which they meet; and choosing the very moment when the king harangues both houses, consign over to destruction these determined foes to all piety and religion. Meanwhile, we ourselves standing aloof, safe and unsuspected, shall triumph in being the instruments of divine wrath, and shall behold with pleasure those sacrilegious walls, in which were passed the edicts for proscribing our church and butcher-ing her children, tossed into a thousand fragments; while their impious inhabitants, meditating, perhaps, still new persecutions against us, pass from flames above to flames below, there for ever to endure the torments due to their offences.

Piercy was charmed with this project of Catesby; and they agreed to communicate the matter to a few more, and among the rest to Thomas Winter, whom they sent over to Flanders, in quest of Fawkes, an officer in the Spanish service, with whose zeal and courage they were all tho-roughly acquainted. When they inlisted any new conspirator, in order to bind him to secrecy, they always, together with an oath, employed the Communion, the most sacred right of their religion. And it is remark-able, that no one of these pious devotees ever entertained the least com-punction with regard to the cruel massacre which they projected, of what-ever was great and eminent in the nation. Some of them only were start-led by the reflection, that of necessity many catholics must be present, as spectators or attendants to the king, or as having seats in the house of peers: but Tesmond, a Jesuit, and Garnet, superior of that order in England, removed these scruples, and showed them how the interests of religion required that the innocent should here be sacrificed with the guilty.

All this passed in the spring and summer of the year 1604; when the conspirators also hired a house in Piercy's name, adjoining to that in which the parliament was to assemble. Towards the end of that year they began their operations. That they might be less interrupted, and give less suspicions to the neighbourhood, they carried in store of pro-visions with them, and never desisted from their labour. Obstinate in their purpose, and confirmed by passion, by principle, and by mutual exhortation, they little feared death in comparison of a disappointment; and having provided arms, together with the instruments of their labour, they resolved there to perish in case of discovery (1605). Their perse-verance advanced the work; and they soon pierced the wall, though three yards in thickness; but on approaching the other side, they were some-what startled at hearing a noise, which they knew not how to account for. Upon inquiry, they found that it came from the vault below the house of Lords; that a magazine of coals had been kept there; and that, as the coals were selling off, the vault would be let to the highest bidder. The opportunity was immediately seized: the place hired by Piercy; thirty-six barrels of powder lodged in it; the whole covered up with fagots and billets; the doors of the cellar boldly flung open; and every body admitted, as if it contained nothing dangerous.

Confident of success, they now began to look forward, and to plan the remaining part of their project. The king, the queen, prince Henry, were all expected to be present at the opening of parliament. The duke, by reason of his tender age, would be absent; and it was resolved, that Piercy should seize him, or assassinate him. The princess Elizabeth, a child likewise, was kept at lord Harrington's house at Warwickshire; and Sir Everard Digby, Rockwood, Grant, being let into the conspiracy, engaged to assemble their friends on pretence of a hunting-match, and seizing that . princess, immediately to proclaim her queen. So transported were they with rage against their adversaries, and so charmed with the prospect of revenge, that they forgot all care of their own safety; and trusting to the general confusion, which must result from so unexpected a blow, they foresaw not, that the fury of the people, now unrestrained by any authority, must have turned against them, and would probably have satiated itself by a universal massacre of the catholics.

The day, so long wished for, now approached, on which the parliament was appointed to assemble. The dreadful secret, though communicated to above twenty persons, had been religiously kept, during the space of near a year and a half. No remorse, no pity, no fear of puishment, no hope of reward, had as yet induced any one conspirator, either to abandon the enterprise, or make a discovery of it. The holy fury had extinguished in their breast every other motive; and it was an indiscretion at last, proceeding chiefly from these very bigoted prejudices and partialities, which saved the nation.

Ten days before the meeting of parliament, lord Monteagle, a catholic, son to lord Morley, received the following letter, which had been delivered to his servant by an unknown hand: «My lord, Out of the love I bear to some of your friends, I have a care of your preservation. Therefore I would advise you, as you tender your life, to devise some excuse to shift off your attendance at this parliament. For God and man have concurred to punish the wickedness of this time. Aud think not slightly of this advertisement; but retire yourself into your country, where you may expect the event in safety. For, though there be no appearance of any stir, yet, I say, they will receive a terrible blow this parliament, and yet they shall not see who hurts them. This counsel is not to be condemned, because it may do you good, and can do you no harm: for the danger is past, as soon as you have burned the letter. And I hope God will give you the grace to make good use of it, unto whose holy protection I commend you».

Monteagle knew not what to make of this letter; and though inclined to think it a foolish attempt to frighten and ridicule him, he judged it safest to carry it to lord Salisbury, secretary of state. Though Salisbury too was inclined to pay little attention to it, he thought proper to lay it before the king, who came to town a few days after. To the king it appeared not so light a matter; and from the serious earnest style of the letter, he conjectured that it implied something dangerous and important. A terrible blow, and yet the authors concealed; a danger so sudden, and yet so great; these circumstances seemed all to denote some contrivance by gunpowder; and it was thought advisable to inspect all the vaults below the houses of parliament. This care belonged to the earl of Suffolk, lord chamberlain, who purposely delayed the search, till the day before the meeting of parliament. He remarked those great piles of wood and faggots, which lay in the vault under the upper house; and he cast his eye upon Fawkes, who stood in a dark corner, and passed himself for Piercy's servant. That daring and determined courage, which so much distinguished this conspirator, even among those heroes in villany, was fully painted in his countenance, and was not passed unnoticed by the chamberlain. Such a quantity also of fuel for the use of one who lived so little in town as Piercy, appeared a little extraordinary, and upon camparing all circumstances, it was resolved that a more thorough inspection should be made. About midnight, sir Thomas Knevet, a justice of peace, was sent with proper attendants; and before the door of the vault finding Fawkes, who had just finished all his preparations, he immediately seized him, and turning over the faggots, discovered the powder. The matches and every thing proper for setting fire to the train were taken in Fawkes's pocket; who finding his guilt now apparent, and seeing no refuge but in boldness and despair, expressed the utmost regret, that he had lost the opportunity of firing the powder at once and of sweetening his own death by that of his enemies. Before the council, he displayed the same intrepid firmness, mixed even with scorn and disdain; refusing to discover his accomplices, and showing no concern but for the failure of the enterprise. This obstinacy lasted two or three days: but being confined to the Tower, left to reflect on his guilt and danger, and the rack being just shown to him; his courage, fatigued with so long an effort, and unsupported by hope or society, at last failed him; and he made a full discovery of all the conspirators.

Catesby, Piercy, and the other criminals, who were in London, though they had heard of the alarm taken at a letter sent so Monteagle; though they had heard of the chamberlain's search; yet were resolved to persist to the utmost, and never abandon their hopes of success. But at last, hearing that Fawkes was arrested, they hurried down to Warwickshire; where Sir Everard Digby, thinking himself assured that success had attended his confederates, was already in arms, in order to seize the princess Elizabeth. She had escaped into Coventry; and they were obliged to put themselves on their defence against the country, who were raised from all quarters, and armed, by the sheriff. The conspirators with all their attendants, never exceeded the number of eighty persons; and being surrounded on every side, could no longer entertain hopes, either of prevailing or escaping. Having therefore confessed themselves, and received absolution, they boldly prepared for death, and resolved to sell their lives as dear as possible to the assailants. But even this miserable consolation was denied them. Some of their powder took fire, and disabled them for defence. The people rushed in upon them. Piercy and Catesby were killed by one shot. Digby, Rockwood, Winter, and others, being taken prisoners, were tried, confessed their guilt, and died, as well as Garnet, by the hands of the executioner. Notwithstanding this horrid crime, the bigoted catholics were so devoted to Garnet that they fancied miracles to be wrought by his blood; and in Spain he was regarded as a martyr.

Neither had the desperate fortune of the conspirators urged them to this enterprise, nor had the former profligacy of their lives prepared them for so great a crime. Before that audacious attempt, their conduct seems, in general, to be liable to no reproach. Catesby's character had entitled him to such regard, that Rockwood and Digby were seduced by their implicit trust in his judgment; and they declared that, from the motive alone of friendship to him, they were ready, on any occasion, to have sacrificed their lives. Digby himself was as highly esteemed and beloved as any man in England; and he had been particularly honoured with the good opinion of queen Elizabeth. It was bigoted zeal alone, the most absurd of all prejudices masqued with reason, the most criminal of passions covered with the appearance of duty, which seduced them into measures, that were fatal to themselves, and had so nearly proved fatal to their country.

The lords Mordaunt and Stourton, two catholics, were fined, the former ten thousand pounds, the latter four thousand, by the Star-Chamber; because their absence from parliament had begotten a suspicion of their being acquainted with the conspiracy. The earl of Northumberland was fined thirty thousand pounds, and detained several years prisoner in the Tower; because, not to mention other grounds of suspicion, he had admitted Piercy into the number of gentlemen pensioners, without his taking the requisite oaths.

The king, in his speech to the parliament, observed, that though religion had engaged the conspirators in so criminal an attempt, yet ought we not to involve all the Roman catholics in the same guilt, or suppose them equally disposed to commit such enormous barbarities. Many holy men, he said, and our ancestors among the rest, had been seduced to concur with that church in her scholastic doctrines; who yet had never admitted her seditious principles, concerning the pope's power of dethroning kings, or sanctifiyng assassination. The wrath of Heaven is denounced against crimes, but innocent error may obtain its favour; and nothing can be more hateful than the uncharitableness of the puritans, who condemn alike to eternal torments, even the most inoffensive partisans of popery. For his part, he added, that conspiracy, however atrocious, should never alter, in the least, his plan of government; while with one hand he punished guilt, with the other he would still support and protect innocence.   (Hume).

---

21. The Petition of Right (1628).

Some of the stipulations of Magna Charta were as suitable to the necessities of after ages as to the circumstances of that period to which it owes its origin, but this was the case in a remarkable degree in the reigns of James I and Charles I. The latter monarch especially had grossly violated its claims in manifold instances. He had, in the exercise of his own will, unlawfully committed persons to prison . . . Instead of having offenders tried by a jury, they were brought before tribunals, over which he exercised unlimited control: these were the Courts of High Commission and the Star Chamber — the former for the examination of religious offenders . . . . And to raise the money necessary to carry on his wars on the continent, when he found the Commons unwilling to vote him the supplies, he extorted money from the people in so many unlawful ways that they would endure it no longer. The commons therefore drew up a petition, which asked for nothing but what the Magna Charta conceded to them as a right, and then requested Charles to give it the force of law by adding to it his signature. The King tried various mean shifts to avoid signing the paper, but the sturdy Commons were determined, and Charles was at length compelled to sign. It was passed in 1628.

This famous document has always been known as the Petition of Right, and has very properly been prized by the English people as a safeguard to their liberties in no way inferior to the great Charter itself. Its most important provisions, stated in plain, every day language, are the following:

First. It was declared unlawful to molest or punish any person for not lending money to the King, unless required to do so by Act of Parliament.

Secondly. No magistrate, judge, or peace-officer, was allowed to put any one into prison, unless some clear charge could be made against him.

Thirdly. No prisoner should be refused the right of trial by jury.

Fourthly. Martial law was declared illegal, in the case of all offences which properly ought to come before the courts of common law.

So long as the Courts of High Commission and Star Chamber existed, however, Charles managed to make all these obligations of none effect.

---

22. The Puritans.

We would first speak of the Puritans, the most remarkable body of men, perhaps, which the world has ever produced. The odious and ridiculous parts of the character lie on the surface. He that runs, may read them; nor have there been wanting attentive and malicious observers to point them out. For many years after the Restoration, they were the theme of unmeasured invective and derision. They were exposed to the utmost licentiousness of the press and of the stage, at the time when the press and the stage were most licentious. They were not men of letters; they were, as a body, unpopular; they could not defend themselves; and the public would not take them under its protection. They were, therefore, abandoned, without reserve, to the tender mercies of the satirists and dramatists. The ostentatious simplicity of their dress, their sour aspect, their nasal twang, their stiff posture, their long graces, their Hebrew names, the scriptual phrases which they introduced on every occasion, their contempt of human learning, their detestation of polite amusements, were indeed fair game for the laughers. But it is not from the laughers alone that the philosophy of history is to be learnt. And he who approaches this subject should carefully guard against the influence of that potent ridicule which has already misled so many excellent writers.

Those who roused the people to resistance — who directed their measures through a long series of eventful years — who formed, out of the most unpromising materials, the finest army that Europe had ever seen — who trampled down king, church, and aristocracy—who, in the short intervals of domestic sedition and rebellion, made the name of England terrible to every nation on the face of the earth, were no vulgar fanatics. Most of their absurdities were mere external badges, like the signs of freemasonry, or the dresses of friars. We regret that these badges were not more attractive; we regret that a body, to whose courage and talents mankind has owed inestimable obligations, had not the lofty elegance which distinguished some of the adherents of Charles I., or the easy good breeding for which the court of Charles II. was celebrated. But, if we must make our choice, we shall, like Bassanio in the play, turn from the specious caskets which contain only the Death's head and the Fool's head, and fix our choice on the plain leaden chest which conceals the treasure.

The Puritans were men whose minds had derived a peculiar character from the daily contemplation of superior beings and eternal interests. Not content with acknowledging, in general terms, an overruling Providence, they habitually ascribed every event to the will of the Great Being, for whose power nothing was too vast, for whose inspection nothing was too minute. To know him, to serve him, to enjoy him, was with them the great end of existence. They rejected with contempt the ceremonious homage which other sects substituted for the pure worship of the soul. Instead of catching occasional glimpses of the Deity through an obscuring vail, they aspired to gaze full on the intolerable brightness, and to commune with him face to face. Hence originated their contempt for terrestrial distinctions. The difference between the greatest and meanest of mankind seemed to vanish, when compared with the boundless interval which separated the whole race from him on whom their own eyes were constantly fixed. They recognized no title to superiority but his favour; and, confident of that favour, they despised all the accomplishments and all the dignities of the world. If they were unacquainted with the works of philosophers and poets, they were deeply read in the oracles of God; if their names were not found in the registers of heralds, they felt assured that they were recorded in the Book of Life; if their steps were not accompanied by a splendid train of menials, legions of ministering angels had charge over them. Their palaces were houses not made with hands; their diadems, crowns of glory, which should never fade away! On the rich and the eloquent, on nobles and priests, they looked down with contempt; for they esteemed themselves rich in a more precious treasure, and eloquent in a more sublime language — nobles by the right of an earlier creation, and priests by the imposition of a mightier hand. The very meanest of them was a being to whose fate a mysterious and terrible importance belonged — on whose slightest actions the spirits of light and darkness looked with anxious interest — who had been destined, before heaven and earth were created, to enjoy a felicity which should continue when heaven and earth should have passed away. Events which short-sighted politicians ascribed to earthly causes, had been ordained on his account. For his sake, empires had risen, and flourished, and decayed; for his sake, the Almighty had proclaimed his will by the pen of the evangelist, and the harp of the prophet. He had been rescued by no common deliverer from the grasp of no common foe; he had been ransomed by the sweat of no vulgar agony, by the blood of no earthly sacrifice. It was for him that the sun had been darkened, that the rocks had been rent, that the dead had arisen, that all nature had shuddered at the sufferings of her expiring God! (Macaulay).

23. Habeas Corpus Act (1679).

The object of this Act of Parliament was to prevent any one from being kept in prison unlawfully, and unless the crime with which he was charged could be fully proved against him.

The great importance of such an act can be understood even by a child, if he will consider for a moment what could be the effect of his own father's imprisonment for several weeks or months together. Of course, his business would be neglected, his wife and family would be left to starve, and very likely his own health would be seriously impaired.

And yet, in the days of the Tudors and Stuarts, many persons of all ranks were imprisoned, merely because they gave some slight offence to the King or some of his favorites, although they were guilty of no crime whatever. Moreover, they were kept in prison and not brought to trial, as the Magna Charta and Petition of Right demanded. On this account, the parliament resolved upon obtaining a distinct law to prevent such abuses of authority for the future; and a new act was worded in such a way as to give every prisoner a right to what is called a writ of *habeas corpus* — Latin words, which mean: «Thou mayst have the body». When this writ was presented to the jailor, he was bound to give up the prisoner, that he might appear before the judge and take his trial.

Now let us suppose a man to be charged with some offence, for which it is considered he ought to be punished according to law. He is taken before a magistrate, and if the magistrate thinks there are good grounds for sending him to prison, he signs a warrant, which is handed to the jailor, and which authorises the jailor to keep the man in prison till another notice to the contrary is received . . . The prisoner so situated now applies to his jailor for a copy of the warrant, by authority of which he is detained. This is sent to a judge who, on examining the warrant, will at once set him at liberty, if there is not proper cause shown why he should be detained... Or, secondly, he bails him, that is, allows him to go at large, if certain persons of good character will give security for his appearance, at the quarter sessions, assizes or other court . . . Or, thirdly, he will remand him, that is, send him to prison again till the assizes, etc., take place, when he would be tried before a jury of his own countrymen and equals. By gradual instalments like these have Englishmen obtained their liberties and privileges.

---

24. Earl of Nithsdale.

Among the persons, who were condemned to suffer, for their share in attempting to place the pretender on the British throne, in 1715, was the Earl of Nithsdale: and there is no doubt but that he would have shared the fate of the Earl of Derwentwater and the others, who had suffered, had not his amiable wife. effected his escape. This circumstance, exhibiting so strong an instance of courage and conjugal affection, cannot be better related, than in the following · extract of a letter from the countess of Nithsdale to her sister, the countess of Traquair, in 1716.

«The next morning I could not go to the Tower, having so many things in my hands to put in readiness; but in the evening, when all was ready, I sent for Mrs. Mills, with whom I lodged, and acquainted her with my design of attempting my lord's escape, as there was no prospect of his being pardoned, and this was the last night before the execution. I told her that I had every thing in readiness, and that I trusted she would not refuse to accompany me, that my lord might pass for her. I pressed her to come immediately, as we had no time to lose. At the same time I sent for a Mrs. Morgan, then usually known by the name of Hilton, to whose acqnaintance my dear Evans had introduced me, and to whom I immediately communicated my resolution. She was of a tall and slender make; so I begged her to put under her own ridinghood one I had prepared for Mrs. Mills, as she was to lend hers to my lord. Mrs. Mills was then corpulent, so that she was not only of the same height, but nearly the same size as my lord. When we were in the coach I never ceased talking, that they might have no leisure to reflect. Their surprise and astonishment, when I first opened my design to them, had made them consent, without ever thinking of the consequences. On our arrival at the tower, the first I introduced, was Mrs. Morgan, for I was only allowed to take one in at a time. She brought in the clothes, that were to serve Mrs. Mills, when she left her own behind her. When Mrs. Morgan had taken off, what she had brought for my purpose, I conducted her back to the staircase, and, in going, I begged her to send me in my maid to dress me: that I was afraid of being too late to present my last petition, that night, and went partly down stairs to meet Mrs. Mills, who had the precaution to hold her handkerchief to her face, as was very natural for a woman to do, who was going to bid her last farewell to a friend, on the eve of his execution. I had indeed desired her to do it, that my lord might go out in the same manner. Her eyebrows were rather inclined to be sandy, and my lord's were dark and very thick; however, I had prepared some paint of the colour of hers to disguise them; I also brought an artifical head dress of the same coloured hair as hers, and painted his face with white, and his cheeks with rouge, to hide his long beard, which he had not had time to shave. All this provision I had before left in the tower. The poor guards, whom my slight liberality the day before, had endeared me to, let me go quietly with my company, and were not so strictly on the watch as they usually had been, and the more so. as from what I had told them, the day before, they were persuaded that the prisoners would obtain their pardon. I made Mrs. Mills take off her own hood, and put on that, which I had brought for her; I then took her by the hand, and led her out of my lord's chamber; in passing through the next room, in which there were several people, with all the concern imaginable, I said: My dear Mrs. Catherine, go in all haste, and send me my waiting maid; she certainly cannot reflect how late it is; she forgets, that I am to present a petition to night, and if I let slip this opportunity I am undone; for to-morrow will be too late. Hasten her as much as possible; for I shall be on thorns till she comes. Every person in the room, chiefly the guards' wives and daughters, seemed to compassionate me exceedingly, and the sentinel officiously opened the door. When I had seen her out, I returned back to my lord, and finished dressing him. I had taken care that Mrs. Mills did not go out crying, as she came in, that my lord might the better pass for the lady, who came in crying and afflicted; and the more so, because he had the same dress on, which she wore. When I had almost finished dressing my lord in all my petticoats excepting one, I perceived that it was growing dark, and was afraid that the light of the candles might betray us, so I resolved to set out. I went out leading him by the hand; and he held his handkerchief to his eyes. I spoke to him in the most piteous and afflicted tone of voice, bewailing bitterly the negligence of Evans, who had ruined me by her delay. Then, said I, my dear Mrs.

Betty, for the love of God, run quickly and bring her with you. You know my lodging, and if ever you made despatch in your life, do it at present, for I am almost distracted with this dasappointment. The guards opened the doors; and I went down stairs with him, still conjuring him to make all possible despatch. As soon as he had cleared the door, I made him walk before me, for fear the sentinel should take notice of his gait; but I still continued to press him to make all the haste he possibly could. At the bottom of the stairs I met my dear Evans, into whose hands I confided him. I had before engaged Mr. Mills to be in readiness, before the Tower, to conduct him to some place of safety, in case we succeeded. He looked upon the affair as so very improbable to succeed, that his astonishment, when he saw us, threw him into such consternaion, that he was almost beside himself, which Evans perceiving, without telling him any thing, lest he should mistrust them, conducted my Lord to some of her own friends, on whom she could rely, and so secured him, without which we should have been undone. When she had conducted him, and left him with them, she returned to find Mr. Mills, who by this time had recovered himself from his astonishment. They went home together, and having found a place of security, they conducted him to it».

After being concealed a few days in London, the Earl passed with the retinue, and in the livery of the Venetian ambassador, to Dover, where, hiring a small vessel, he escaped to Calais, and thence travelled to Rome, where he died in the year 1744.

---

25. Stratagem Signally Defeated.

A few days after the battle of Falkirk so disastrous to the English army, Lord Loudon made a dashing attempt to seize the Pretender at Moy, the account of which is thus narrated by the Chevalier Johnstone.

On the 16-th of February the prince slept at Moy, a castle belonging to the chief of the clan of Mackintosh, about two leagues from Inverness. Lord Loudon, lieutenant general in the service of King George, and a colonel of a regiment of Highlanders, being at Inverness, with about two thousand regular troops, the prince intended to wait the arrival of the other column, before approaching nearer to that town. In the meantime, Lord Loudon formed the project of seizing by surprise the person of the prince, who could have no suspicion of any attempt of the kind, conceiving himself in perfect security at Moy; and His Lordship would have succeeded in his design, but for the intervention of that invisible being, who frequently chooses to manifest his power, in overturning the best contrived means of feeble mortals. His Lordship, at three o'clock in the afternoon, posted guards, and a chain of sentinels, all round Inverness, both within and without the town, with positive orders not to suffer any person to leave it, on any pretext whatever, of whatever rank the person might be. He ordered, at the same time, fifteen hundred men to hold themselves in readiness to march at a moment's warning; and having assembled this body of troops without noise, he put himself at their head, and instantly set off, planning his march so as to arrive at the castle of Moy about eleven o'clock at night.

Whilst some English officers were drinking in the house of Mrs. Baily, an innkeeper of Inverness, and passing the time till the hour of their departure, her daughter, a girl of about thirteen or fourteen years of age, who happened to wait on them, paid great attention to their conversation, and, from certain expressions dropped from them, she discovered their designs. As soon as this generous girl was certain as to their intentions, she immediately left the house, escaped from the town notwithstanding the vigilance of the sentinels, and took the road to Moy, running as fast as she was able, without shoes or stockings, which, to accelerate her progress, she had taken off, in order to inform the prince of the danger that menaced him. She reached Moy, quite out of breath, before Lord Loudon; and the prince, with difficulty, escaped in his robe de chambre, nightcap and slippers, to the neighbouring mountains, where he passed the night in concealment. The dear girl, to whom the prince owed his life, was in great danger of losing her own, from her excessive fatigue on this occasion; but by the care and attentions she experienced, her health was re-established. The prince having no suspicion af such a daring attempt, had very few people with him in the castle of Moy.

As soon as the girl had spread the alarm, the blacksmith of the village of Moy presented himself to the prince, and assured his Royal Highness, that he had no occasion to leave the castle, as he would answer for it with his head, that Lord Loudon and his troops should be obliged to return faster than they came. The prince had not sufficient confidence in his assurances, to neglect seeking safety by flight to the neighbouring mountains. However, the blacksmith, for his own satisfaction, put his project into execution. He instantly assembled a dozen of his companions, and advanced with them about a quarter of a mile from the castle, on the road to Inverness. There he laid an ambuscade, placing six of his companions on each side of the highway, to wait the arrival of the detachment of Lord Loudon, enjoining them not to fire, till he should tell them; and then not to fire together, but one after another. When the head of the detachment of Lord Loudon was opposite the twelve men, about eleven o'clock in the evening, the blacksmith called out, with a loud voice: «Here come the villains, who intend carrying off our prince; fire, my lads, do not spare them, give no quarter». In an instant, muskets were discharged from each side of the road; and the detachment seeing their project had taken wind, began to fly in the greatest disorder; imagining, that the whole army was lying in wait for them. Such was their terror and consternation, that they did not stop till they had reached Inverness. In this moment did a common blacksmith and twelve of his companions put Lord Loudon and fifteen hundred of his regular troops to flight. The fifer of His Lordship, who happened to be at the head of the detachment, was killed at the first discharge; and the detachment did not wait for a second.

---

26. The Country Gentlemen, Clergy, and Yeomanry.

We should be much mistaken, if we pictured to ourselves the squires of the seventeenth century as men bearing a close resemblance to their descendants, the country members and chairmen of quarter sessions, with whom we are familiar. The modern country gentleman generally receives a liberal education, passes from a distinguished school to a distinguished college, and has every opportunity to become an excellent scholar. He has generally seen something of foreign countries. A considerable part of his life has generally been passed in the capital; and the refinements of the capital follow him into the country. There is perhaps no class of dwellings so pleasing as the rural seats of the English gentry. In the parks and pleasure grounds, nature, dressed but not disguised, by art, wears her most alluring form. In the buildings, good sense and good taste combine to produce a happy union of the comfortable and the graceful. The pictures, the musical instruments, the library, would in any other country be considered as proving the owner to be an eminently polished and accomplished man. A country genleman who witnessed the Revolution, was probably in receipt of about a fourth part of the rent which his acres now yield to his posterity. He was, therefore, as compared with his posterity, a poor man, and was generally under the necessity of residing, with little interruption, on his estate. To travel on the Continent, to maintain an establishment in London, or even to visit London frequently, were pleasures in which only the great proprietors could indulge. It may be confidently affirmed that of the squires, whose names were then in the Commissions of Peace and Lieutenancy, not one in twenty went to town once in five years, or had ever in his life wandered so far as Paris. Many lords of manors had received an education differing little from that of their menial servants. The heir of an estate often passed his boyhood and youth at the seat of his family with no better tutors than grooms and gamekeepers, and scarce attained learning enough to sign his name to a Mittimus. If he went to school and to college, he generally returned before he was twenty to the seclusion of the old hall, and there, unless his mind were very happily constituted by nature, soon forgot his academical pursuits in rural business and pleasure. His chief serious employment was the care of his property. He examined samples of grain, handled pigs, and, on market days, made bargains, over a tankard, with drovers and hop merchants. His chief pleasures were commonly derived from field sports and from an unrefined sensuality. His language and pronunciation were such as we should now expect to hear only from the most ignorant clowns. His oaths, coarse jests, and scurrilous terms of abuse, were uttered with the broadest accent of his province. It was easy to discern, from the first words which he spoke, whether he came from Somersetshire or Yorkshire. He troubled himself little about decorating his abode, and if he attempted decoration, seldom produced anything but deformity. The litter of a farm-yard gathered under the windows of his bed-chamber, and the cabbages and gooseberry bushes grew close to his hall door. His table was loaded with coarse plenty; and guests were cordially welcomed to it. But, as the habit of drinking to excess was general in the class to which he belonged, and

27

as his fortune did not enable him to intoxicate large assemblies daily with claret or canary, strong beer was the ordinary beverage. The quantity of beer consumed in those days was indeed enormous. For beer then was to the middle and lower classes, not only all that it now is; but all that wine, tea, and ardent spirits now are. It was only at great houses, or on great occasions, that foreign drink was placed on the board. The ladies of the house, whose business it had commonly been to cook the repast, retired as soon as the dishes had been devoured, and left the gentlemen to their ale and tobacco. The coarse jollity of the afternoon was often prolonged till the revellers were laid under the table.

It was very seldom that the country gentleman caught glimpses of the great world; and what he saw of it tended rather to confuse than to enlighten his understanding. His opinions respecting religion, government, foreign countries, and former times, having been derived, not from study, from observation, or from conversation with enlightened companions, but from such traditions as were current in his own small circle, were the opinions of a child. He adhered to them, however, with the obstinacy which is generally found in ignorant men accustomed to be fed with flattery. His animosities were numerous and bitter. He hated Frenchmen and Italians, Scotchmen and Irishmen, Papists and Presbyterians, Independents and Baptists, Quakers and Jews. Towards London and Londoners he felt an aversion which more than once produced important political effects. His wife and daughter were in tastes and acquirements below a housekeeper or a still-room maid of the present day. They stitched and spun, brewed gooseberry wine, cured marigolds, and made the crust for the venison pasty.

From this description it might be supposed that the English esquire of the seventeenth century did not materially differ from a rustic miller or alehouse keeper of our time. There are, however, some important parts of his character still to be noted, which will greatly modify his estimate. Unlettered as he was, he was still in some most important points a gentleman. He was a member of a proud and powerful aristocracy, and was distinguished by many both of the good and of the bad qualities which belong to aristocrats. His family pride was beyond that of a Talbot or a Howard. He knew the genealogies and coats of arms of all his neighbours, and could tell which of them had assumed supporters without any right, and which of them were so unfortunate as to be great grandsons of aldermen. He was a magistrate, and, as such, administered gratuitously to those who dwelt around him a rude patriarchal justice which, in spite of innumerable blunders and of occasional acts of tyranny, was yet better than no acts at all. He was an officer of the trainbands; and his military dignity, though it might move the mirth of gallants who had served a compaign in Flanders, raised his character in his own eyes and in the eyes of his neighbours. Nor indeed was his soldiership justly a subject of derision. In every county there were elderly gentlemen who had seen service which was no child's play. One had been knighted by Charles the First, after the battle of Edgehill. Another still wore a patch over the scar which he had received at Naseby. A third had defended his old house till Fairfax had blown in the door with a petard. The pre-sence of these old cavaliers, with their old swords and holsters, and with their old stories about Goring and Lunsford, gave to the musters of militia an earnest and warlike aspect which would otherwise have been wanting. Even those country gentlemen who were too young to have themselves exchanged blows with the cuirassiers of the Parliament had, from childhood, been surrounded by the traces of recent war, and fed with stories of the martial exploits of their fathers and uncles. Thus the character of the English esquire of the seventeenth century was compound-ed of two elements which we are not accustomed to find united. His ignorance and uncouthness, his low tastes and gross phrases, would, in our time, be considered as indicating a nature and a breeding thoroughly plebeian. Yet he was essentially a patrician, and had, in large measure, both the virtues and the vices which flourish among men set from their birth in high place, and accustomed to authority, to observance, and to self-respect. It is not easy for a generation, which is accustomed to find chivalrous sentiments only in company with liberal studies and polished manners, to imagine to itself a man with the deportment, the vocabulary, and the accent of a carter, yet punctilious on matters of genealogy and prece-dence, and ready to risk his life rather than see a stain cast on the honour of his house. It was however only by thus joining together things seldom or never found together in our own experience, that we can form a just idea of that rustic aristocracy which constituted the main strength of the armies of Charles the First, and which long supported, with strange fidelity, the interest of his descendants.

The gross, uneducated, untravelled country gentleman was commonly a Tory: but, though devotedly attached to hereditary monarchy, he had no partiality for courtiers and ministers. He thought, not without reason, that Whitehall was filled with the most currupt of mankind; that of the great sums which the House of Commons had voted to the crown since the Restoration, part had been embezzled by cunning politicians, and part squandered on buffoons and foreign courtesans. His stout English heart swelled with indignation at the thought that the government of his country should be subject to French dictation. Being himself generally an old Cavalier, or the son of an old Cavalier, he reflected with bitter resentment on the ingratitude with which the Stuarts had requited their bests friends. Those who heard him grumble at the neglect with which he was treated, and at the profusion with which wealth was lavished on the bastards of Nell Gwynn and Madam Carwell, would have supposed him ripe for rebellion. But all this humour lasted only till the throne was really in danger. It was precisely when those whom the sovereign had loaded with wealth and honours shrank from his side that the country gentlemen, so surly and mutinous in the season of his prosperity, rallied round him in a body. Thus, after murmuring twenty years at the misgovernment of Charles the Second, they, came to his rescue in his extremity, when his own Secretaries of State and Lords of the Treasury had deserted him, and enabled him to gain a complete victory over the opposition; nor can there be any doubt that they would have shown equal loyalty to his brother James, if James would, even at the last moment, have refrained from outraging their strongest feeling. For there was one institution, and one only, which they prized even more than hereditary monarchy; and that institution was the Church of England. Their love of the Church was not, indeed, the effect of study and meditation. Few among them could have given any reason, drawn from Scripture or Ecclesiastical history, for adhering to her doctrines, her ritual, and her polity; nor were they, as a class, by any means strict observers of that code of morality, which is common to all Christian sects. But the experience of many ages proves that men may be ready to fight to the death, and to persecute without pity, for a religion whose creed they do not understand, and whose precepts they habitually disobey.

The rural clergy were even more vehement in Toryism than the rural gentry, and were a class scarcely less important. It is to be observed, however, that the individual clergyman, as compared with the individual gentleman, then ranked much lower than in our days. The main support of the Church was derived from the tithe; and the tithe bore to the rent a much smaller ratio than at present. King estimated the whole income of the parochial and collegiate clergy at only four hundred and eighty thousand pounds a year; Davenant at only five hundred and forty-four thousand a year. It is certainly now more than seven times as great as the larger of these two sums. The average rent of the land has not, according to any estimate, increased proportionally. It follows that rectors and vicars must have been, as compared with the neighbouring knights and squires, much poorer in the seventeenth than in the nineteenth century.

The place of the clergyman in society had been completely changed by the Reformation. Before that event, ecclesiastics had formed the majority of the House of Lords, had, in wealth and splendour, equalled and sometimes outshone, the greatest of the temporal barons, and had generally held the highest offices. The Lord Treasurer was often a Bishop. The Lord Chancellor was almost always so. The Lord Keeper of the Privy Seal and the Master of the Rolls were ordinarily churchmen. Churchmen transacted the most important diplomatic business. Indeed, almost all that large portion of the administration, which rude and warlike nobles were incompetent to conduct, was considered as especially belonging to divines. Men, therefore, who were averse to the life of camps, and who were, at the same time, desirous to rise in the state, ordinarily received the tonsure. Among them were sons of all the most illustrious families, and near kinsmen of the throne, Scroops and Nevilles, Bourchiers, Staffords, and Poles. To the religious houses belonged the rents of immense domains, and all that large portion of the tithe, which is now in the hands of laymen. Down to the middle of the reign of Henry the Eighth, therefore, no line of life bore so inviting an aspect to ambitious and covetous natures as the priesthood. Then came a violent revolution. The abolition of the monasteries deprived the Church at once of the greater part of her wealth, and of her predominance in the Upper House of Parliament. There was no longer an abbot of Glastonburg or an Abbot of Reading seated among the peers, and possessed of revenues equal to those of a powerful Earl. The princely splendour of William of Wykeham and of William of Waynflete had disappeared. The scarlet hat of the Cardinal, the silver cross of the Legate, were no more. The clergy had also lost the ascendancy which is the natural reward of superior mental culti- vation. Once the circumstance that a man could read had raised a pre- sumption that he was in orders. But, in an age which produced such laymen as William Cecil and Nicholas Bacon, Roger Ascham and Thomas Smith, Walter Mildmay and Francis Walsingham, there was no reason for calling away prelates from their dioceses to negotiate treaties, to superintend the finances, or to administer justice. The spiritual character not only ceased to be a qualification for high civil office, but began to be regarded as a disqualification. Those worldly motives, therefore, which had formerly induced so many able, aspiring and high born youths to assume the ecclesiastical habit, ceased to operate. Not one parish in two hundred then afforded what a man of family considered as a mainte- nance. There were still indeed prizes in the Church: but they were few; and even the highest were mean, when compared with the glory which had once surrounded the princes of the hierarchy. The state kept by Par- ker and Grindal seemed beggarly to those who remembered the imperial pomp of Wolsey, his palaces, which had become the favourite abodes of royalty, Whitehall and Hampton Court, the three sumptuous tables daily spread in his refectory, the forty-four gorgeous copes in his chapel, his running footmen in rich liveries, and his body guards with gilded pole- axes. Thus the sacerdotal office lost its attraction for the higher classes. During the century which followed the accession of Elizabeth, scarce a single person of noble descent took orders. At the close of the reign of Charles the Second, two sons of peers were Bishops; four or five sons of peers were priests, and held valuable preferment : but these rare ex- ceptions did not take away the reproach which lay on the body. The clergy were regarded as, on the whole, a plebeian class. And, indeed, for one who made the figure of a gentleman, ten were mere menial ser- vants. A large proportion of those divines, who had no benefices, or whose benefices were too small to afford a comfortable revenue, lived in the houses of laymen. It had long been evident that this practice tended to degrade the priestly character. Laud had exerted himself to effect a change; and Charles the First had repeatedly issued positive orders that none but men of high rank should presume to keep domestic chaplains. But these injunctions had become obsolete. Indeed, during the domina- tion of the Puritans, many of the ejected ministers of the Church of England could obtain bread and shelter only by attaching themselves to the households of royalist gentlemen; and the habits, which had been formed in those times of trouble, continued long after the reestablishment of monarchy and episcopacy. In the mansions of men of liberal sentiments and cultivated understandings, the chaplain was doubtless treated with urbanity and kindness. His conversation, his literary assistance, his spiritual advice, were considered as an ample return for his food, his lodging, and his stipend. But this was not the general feeling of the country gentlemen. The coarse and ignorant squire, who thought that it belonged to his dignity to have grace said every day at his table by an ecclesiastic in full canonicals, found means to reconcile dignity with economy. A young Levite — such was the phrase then in use — might be had for his board, a small garret, and ten pounds a year, and might not only perform his own professional functions, might not only be the most patient of butts and of listeners, might not only be always ready in fine weather for bowls, and in rainy weather for shovel-board, but might also save the expense of a gardener, or of a groom. Sometimes the reverend man nailed up the apricots, and sometimes he curried the coach horses. He cast up the farrier's bills. He walked ten miles with a message or a parcel. He was permitted to dine with the family; but he was expected to content himself with the plainest fare. He might fill himself with the corned beef and the carrots: but, as soon as the tarts and cheese cakes made their appearance, he quitted his seat, and stood aloof till he was summoned to return thanks for the repast, from a great part of which he had been excluded.

Perhaps, after some years of service, he was presented to a living sufficient to support him: but he often found it necessary to purchase his preferment by a species of Simony, which furnished an inexhaustible subject of pleasantry to three or four generations of scoffers. With his cure he was expected to take a wife. The wife had ordinarily been in the patron's service; and it was well if she was not suspected of standing too high in the patron's favour. Indeed, the nature of the matrimonial connections, which the clergymen of that age were in the habit of forming, is the most certain indication of the place which the order held in the social system. An Oxonian, writing a few months after the death of Charles the Second, complained bitterly, not only that the country attorney and the country apothecary looked down with disdain on the country clergyman, but that one of the lessons most earnestly inculcated on every girl of honourable family was to give no encouragement to a lover in orders, and that, if any young lady forgot this precept, she was almost as much disgraced as by an illicit amour. Clarendon, who assuredly bore no ill will to the Church, mentions it as a sign of the confusion of ranks, which the great rebellion had produced, that some damsels of noble families had bestowed themselves on divines. A waiting woman was generally considered as the most suitable helpmate for a parson. Queen Elizabeth, as head of the Church, had given what seemed to be a formal sanction to this prejudice, by issuing special orders that no clergyman should presume to marry a servant girl, without the consent of the master or mistress. During several generations accordingly the relation between priests and handmaidens was a theme for endless jest; nor would it be easy to find, in the comedy of the seventeenth century, a single instance of a clergyman who wins a spouse above the rank of a cook. Even so late as the time of George the Second, the keenest of all observers of life and manners, himself a priest, remarked that, in a great household, the chaplain was the resource of a lady's maid whose character had been bown upon, and who was therefore forced to give up hopes of catching the steward.

In general the divine, who quitted his chaplainship for a benefice and a wife, found that he had only exchanged one class of vexations for another. Not one living in fifty enabled the incumbent to bring up a family comfortably. As children multiplied and grew, the household of the priest became more and more beggarly. Holes appeared more and more plainly in the thatch of his parsonage and in his single cassock. Often it was only by toiling on his glebe, by feeding swine, and by loading dung-carts, that he could obtain daily bread; nor did his utmost exertions always prevent the bailiffs from taking his concordance and his inkstand in execution. It was a white day on which he was admitted into the kitchen of a great house, and regaled by the servants with cold meat and ale. His children were brought up like the children of the neighbouring peasantry. His boys followed the plough; and his girls went out to service. Study he found impossible: for the advowson of his living would hardly have sold for a sum sufficient to purchase a good theological library; and he might be considered as unusually lucky, if he had ten or twelve dog-eared volumes among the pots and pans on his shelves.

Even a keen and strong intellect might be expected to rust in so unfavourable a situation.

Assuredly there was at that time no lack in the English Church of ministers distinguished by abilities and learning. But it is to be observed that these ministers were not scattered among the rural population. They were brought together at a few places where the means of acquiring knowledge were abundant, and where the opportunities of vigorous intellectual exercise were frequent. At such places were to be found divines qualified by parts, by eloquence, by wide knowledge of literature, of science, and of life, to defeud their Church victoriously against heretics and sceptics, to command the attention of frivolous and worldly congregations, to guide the deliberations of senates, and to make religion respectable, even in the most dissolute of courts. Some laboured to fathom the abysses of metaphysical theology; some were deeply versed in biblical criticism; and some threw light on the darkest parts of ecclesiastical history. Some proved themselves consummate masters of logic. Some cultivated rhetoric with such assiduity and success that their discourses are still justly valued as models of style. These eminent men were to be found, with scarce a single exception, at the Universities, at the great Cathedrals, or in the capital. Barrow had lately died at Cambridge; and Pearson had gone thence to the episcopal bench. Cudworth and Henry More were still living there. South and Pococke, Jane and Aldrich, were at Oxford. Prideaux was in the close of Norwich, and Whitby in the close of Salisbury. But it was chiefly by the London clergy, who were always spoken of as a class apart, that the fame of their profession for learning and eloquence was upheld. The principal pulpits of the metropolis were occupied about this time by a crowd of distinguished men, from among whom was selected a large proportion of the rulers of the Church. Sherlock preached at the Temple, Tillotson at Lincoln's Inn, Wake and Jeremy Collier at Gray's Inn, Burnet at the Rolls, Stillingfleet at St. Paul's Cathedral, Patrick at St. Paul's, Covent Garden, Fowler at St. Giles's, Cripplegate, Sharp at St. Giles's in the Fields, Tenison at St. Martin's, Sprat at St. Margaret's, Beveridge at St. Peter's in Cornhill. Of these twelve men, all of high note in ecclesiastical history, ten became Bishops, and four Archbishops. Meanwhile almost the only important theological works, which came forth from a rural parsonage, were those of George Bull, afterwards Bishop of St. David's; and Bull never would have produced those works, had he not inherited an estate, by the sale of which he was enabled to collect a library, such as probably no other country clergyman in England possessed.

Thus the Anglican priesthood was divided into two sections which, in acquirements, in manners, and in social position, differed widely from each other. One section, trained for cities and courts, comprised men familiar with all ancient and modern learning; men able to encounter Hobbes or Bossuet at all the weapons of controversy; men who could, in their sermons, set forth the majesty and beauty of Christianity with such justness of thought, and such energy of language, that the indolent Charles roused himself to listen, and the fastidious Buckingham forgot to sneer; men whose address, politeness, and knowledge of the world qualified them to manage the consciences of the wealthy and noble; men with whom Halifax loved to discuss the interests of empires, and from whom Dryden was not ashamed to own that he had learned to write. The other section was destined to ruder and humbler service. It was dispersed over the country, and consisted chiefly of persons not at all wealthier, and not much more refined, than small farmers or upper servants. Yet it was in these rustic priests, who derived but a scanty subsistence from their tithe sheaves and tithe pigs, and who had not the smallest chance of ever attaining high professional honours, that the professional spirit was strongest. Among those divines who were the boast of the Universities and the delight of the capital, and who had attained, or might reasonably expect to attain, opulence and lordly rank, a party, respectable in numbers and more respectable in character, leaned towards constitutional principles of government, lived on friendly terms with Presbyterians, Independents, and Baptists, would gladly have seen a full toleration granted to all protestant sects, and would even have consented to make alterations in the Liturgy, for the purpose of conciliating honest and candid Nonconformits. But such latitudinarianism was held in horror by the country parson. He was, indeed, prouder of his native gown than his superiors of their lawn and their scarlet hoods. The very consciousness that there was little in his worldly circumstances to distinguish him from the villagers to whom he preached led him to hold immoderately high the dignity of that sacerdotal office which was his single title to reverence. Having lived in seclusion, and having had little opportunity of correcting his opinions by reading or conversation, he held and taught the doctrines of indefeasible hereditary right, of passive obedience, and of nonresistance in all their crude absurdity. Having been long engaged in a petty war against the neighbouring dissenters, he too often hated them for the wrongs which he had done them, and found no fault with the Five Mile Act and the Conventicle Act, except that those odious laws had no sharper edge. Whatever influence his office gave him was exerted with passionate zeal on the Tory side; and that influence was immense. It would be a great error to imagine, because the country rector was in general not regarded as a gentleman, because he could not dare to aspire to the hand of one of the young ladies of the manor house, because he was not asked into the parlours of the great, but was left to drink and smoke with grooms and butlers, that the power of the clerical body was smaller than at present. The influence of a class is by no means proportioned to the consideration which the members of that class enjoy in their individual capacity. A Cardinal is a much more exalted personage than a begging friar: but it would be a grievous mistake to suppose that the College of Cardinals has exercised a greater dominion over the public mind of Europe than the Order of Saint Francis. In Ireland, at present, a peer holds a far higher station in society than a Roman Catholic priest: yet there are in Munster and Cannaught few counties where a combination of priests would not carry an election against a combination of peers. In the seventeenth century the pulpit was to a large portion of the population what the periodical press now is. Scarce any of the clowns who came to the parish church ever saw a Gazette or a political pamphlet. Ill informed as their spiritual pastor might be, he was yet better informed than themselves: he had every week an opportunity of haranguing them; and his harangues were never answered. At every important conjuncture, invectives against the Whigs and exhortations to obey the Lord's anointed resounded at once from many thousands of pulpits; and the effect was formidable indeed. Of all the causes which, after the dissolution of the Oxford Parliament, produced the violent reaction against the Exclusionists, the most potent seems to have been the oratory of the country clergy.

The power, which the country gentlemen and the country clergymen exercised in the rural districts, was in some measure counterbalanced by the power of the yeomanry, an eminently manly and truehearted race. The petty proprietors who cultivated their own fields with their own hands, and enjoyed a modest competence, without affecting to have scutcheons and crests, or aspiring to sit on the bench of justice, then formed a much more important part of the nation than at present. If we may trust the best statistical writers of that age, not less than a hundred and sixty thousand proprietors, who with their families must have made up more than a seventh of the whole population, derived their subsistence from little freehold estates. The average income of these small landholders, an income made up of rent, profit, and wages, was estimated at between sixty and seventy pounds a year. It was computed that the number of persons who tilled their own land was greater than the number of those who farmed the land of others. A large portion of the yeomanry had, from the time of the Reformation, leaned towards Puritanismn, had, in the civil war, taken the side of the Parliament, had, after the Restoration, persisted in hearing Presbyterian and Independed preachers, had, at elections, strenuously supported the Exclusionists, and had continued, even after the discovery of the Rye House plot *) and the proscription of the Whig leaders, to regard Popery and arbitrary power with unmitigated hostility.   (Macaulay.)

27. Difficulty of Travelling.

It was by the highways that both travellers and goods generally passed from place to place. And those highways appear to have been far worse than might have been expected from the degree of wealth and civilisation, which the nation had even then attained. On the best lines of communication the ruts were deep, the descents precipitous, and the way often such as it was hardly possible to distinguish, in the dusk, from the uninclosed heath and fen which lay on both sides. Ralph Thoresby, the antiquary, was in danger of losing his way on the great North road, between Barnby Moor and Tuxford, and actually lost his way between Doncaster and York. Pepys and his wife, travelling in their own coach, lost their way between Newbury and Reading. In the course of the same tour they lost their way near Sa-

---

*) The Rye House plot, заговоръ, составленный для убіенія Карла II и его брата, герцога Іоркскаго, названный такъ по находящейся на улицѣ, ведущей въ Ньюмаркетъ, фермѣ, назначенной для совершенія убійства. Но такъ какъ домъ, въ которомъ Карлъ обыкновенно имѣлъ пребываніе въ Ньюмаркетѣ, случайно загорѣлся, то король оставилъ городъ восемью днями раньше чѣмъ былъ намѣренъ сперва, и этому обстоятельству обязанъ былъ своимъ спасеніемъ.

lisbury, and were in danger of having to pass the night on the plain. It was only in fine weather that the whole breadth of the road was available for wheeled vehicles. Often the mud lay deep on the right and the left; and only a narrow track of firm ground rose above the quagmire. At such times obstructions and quarrels were frequent, and the path was sometimes blocked up during a long time by carriers, neither of whom would break the way. It happened, almost every day, that coaches stuck fast, until a team of cattle could be procured from some neighbouring farm, to tug them out of the slough. But in bad seasons the traveller had to encounter inconveniences still more serious. Thoresby, who was in the habit of travelling between Leeds and the capital, has recorded, in his Diary, such a series of perils and disasters as might suffice for a journey to the Frozen Ocean or to the Desert of Sahara. On one occasion he learned that the floods were out between Ware and London, that passengers had to swim for their lives, and that a higgler had perished in the attempt to cross. In consequence of these tidings he turned out of the high road, and was conducted across some meadows, where it was necessary for him to ride to the saddle skirts in water. In the course of another journey he narrowly escaped being swept away by an inundation of the Trent. He was afterwards detained at Stamford four days, on account of the state of the roads, and then ventured to proceed only because fourteen members of the House of Commons, who were going up in a body to Parliament with guides and numerous attendants, took him into their company. On the roads of Derbyshire travellers were in constant fear for their necks, and were frequently compelled to alight and lead their beasts. The great route through Wales to Holyhead was in such a state that, in 1685, a viceroy, going to Ireland, was. five hours in travelling fourteen miles, from Saint Asaph to Conway. Between Conway and Beaumaris he was forced to walk great part of the way; and his lady was carried in a litter. His coach was, with great difficulty, and by the help of many hands, brought after him entire. In general, carriages were taken to pieces at Conway, and borne, on the shoulders of stout Welsh peasants, to the Menai Straits. In some parts of Kent and Sussex none but the strongest horses could, in winter, get through the bog, in which, at every step, they sank deep. The markets were often inaccessible during several months. It is said that the fruits of the earth were sometimes suffered to rot in one place, while in another place, distant only a few miles, the supply fell far short of the demand. The wheeled carriages were, in this district, generally pulled by oxen. When Prince George of Denmark visited the stately mansion of Petworth in wet weather, he was six hours in going nine miles; and it was necessary that a body of sturdy hinds should be on each side of his coach, in order to prop it. Of the carriages which conveyed his retinue several were upset and injured. A letter from one of his gentlemen in waiting has been preserved, in which the unfortunate courtier complains that, during fourteen hours, he never once alighted, except when his coach was overturned or stuck fast in the mud.

One chief cause of the badness of the roads seems to have been the defective state of the law. Every parish was bound to repair the highways which passed through it. The peasantry were forced to give their gratuitous labour six days in the year. If this was not sufficient, hired labour was employed, and the expense was met by a parochial rate. That a route connecting two great towns, which have a large and thriving trade with each other, should be maintained at the cost of the rural population scattered between them is obviously unjust; and this injustice was peculiarly glaring in the case of the great North road, which traversed very poor and thinly inhabited districts, and joined very rich and populous districts. Indeed it was not in the power of the parishes of Huntingdonshire to mend a highway worn by the constant traffic between the West Riding of Yorkshire and London. Soon after the Restoration this grievance attracted the notice of Parliament; and an act, the first of our many turnpike acts, was passed, imposing a small toll on travellers and goods, for the purpose of keeping some parts of this important line of communication in good repair. This innovation, however, excited many murmurs; and the other great avenues to the capital were long left under the old system. A change was at length effected, but not without much difficulty. For unjust and absurd taxation to which men are accustomed is often borne far more willingly than the most reasonable impost which is new. It was not till many toll bars had been violently pulled down, till the troops had in many districts been forced to act against the people, and till much blood had been shed, that a good system was introduced. By slow degrees reason triumphed over prejudice; and our island is now crossed in every direction by near thirty thousand miles of turnpike road.

On the best highways heavy articles were, in the time of Charles the Second, generally conveyed from place to place by stage waggons. In the straw of these vehicles nestled a crowd of passengers, who could not afford to travel by coach or on horseback, and who were prevented by infirmity, or by the weight of their luggage, from going on foot. The expense of transmitting heavy goods in this way was enormous. From London to Birmingham the charge was seven pounds a ton; from London to Exeter twelve pounds a ton. This was about fifteen pence a ton for every mile, more by a third than was afterwards charged on turnpike roads, and fifteen times what is now demanded by railway companies. The cost of conveyance amounted to a prohibitory tax on many useful articles. Coal in particular was never seen except in the districts where it was produced, or in the districts to which it could be carried by sea, and was indeed always known in the south of England by the name of sea coal.

On byroads, and generally throughout the country north of York and west of Exeter, goods were carried by long trains of packhorses. These strong and patient beasts, the breed of which is now extinct, were attended by a class of men who seem to have borne much resemblance to the Spanish muleteers. A traveller of humble condition often found it convenient to perform a journey mounted on a pack-saddle between two baskets, under the care of these hardy guides. The expence of this mode of conveyance was small. But the caravan moved at a foot's pace; and in winter the cold was often insupportable.

The rich commonly travelled in their own carriages, with at least four horses. Cotton, the facetious poet, attempted to go from London to the Peak with a single pair, but found at Saint Albans that the journey would be insupportably tedious, and altered his plan. A coach and six is in our time never seen, except as part of some pageant. The frequent mention therefore of such equipages in old books is likely to mislead us. We attribute to magnificence what was really the effect of a very disagreeable necessity. People, in the time of Charles the Second, travelled with six horses, because with a smaller number there was great danger of sticking fast in the mire. Nor were even six horses always sufficient. Vanbrough, in the succeeding generation, described with great humour the way in which a country gentleman, newly chosen a member of Parliament, went up to London. On that occasion all the exertions of six beasts, two of which had been taken from the plough, could not save the family coach from being imbedded in a quagmire.

Public carriages had recently been much improved. During the years which immediately followed the Restoration, a diligence ran between London and Oxford in two days. The passengers slept at Beaconsfield. At length, in the spring of 1669, a great and daring innovation was attempted. It was announced that a vehicle, described as the Flying Coach, would perform the whole. journey between sunrise and sunset. This spirited undertaking was solemnly considered and sanctioned by the Heads of the University, and appears to have excited the same sort of interest which is excited in our own time by the opening of a new railway. The Vicechancellor, by a notice affixed in all public places, prescribed the hour and place of departure. The success of the experiment was complete. At six in the morning the carriage began to move from before the ancient front of All Souls College: and at seven in the evening the adventurous gentlemen who had run the first risk were safely deposited at their inn in London. The emulation of the sister University was moved; and soon a diligence was set up which in one day carried passengers from Cambridge to the capital. At the close of the reign of Charles the Second, flying carriages ran thrice a week from London to the chief towns. But no stage coach, indeed no stage waggon, appears to have proceeded further north than York, or further west than Exeter. The ordinary day's journey of a flying coach was about fifty miles in the summer; but in winter, when the ways were bad and the nights long, little more than thirty. The Chester coach, the York coach, and the Exeter coach generally reached London in four days during the fine season, but at Christmas not till the sixth day. The passengers, six in number, were all seated in the carriage. For accidents were so frequent that it would have been most perilous to mount the roof. The ordinary fare was about twopence halfpenny a mile in summer, and somewhat more in winter.

This mode of travelling, which by Englishmen of the present day would be regarded as insufferably slow, seemed to our ancestors wonderfully and indeed alarmingly rapid. In a work published a few months before the death of Charles the Second, the flying coaches are extolled as far superior to any similar vehicles ever known in the world. Their velocity is the subject of special commendation, and is triumphantly contrasted with the sluggish pace of the continental posts. But with boasts like these was mingled the sound of complaint and invective. The interests of large classes had been unfavourably affected by the establishment of the new diligences; and, as usual, many persons were, from mere stupidity and obstinacy, disposed to clamour against the innovation, simply because it was an innovation. It was vehemently argued that this mode of conveyance would be fatal to the breed of horses and to the noble art of horsemanship; that the Thames, which had long been an important nursery of seamen, would cease to be the chief thoroughfare from London up to Windsor and down to Gravesend; that saddlers and spurriers would be ruined by hundreds; that numerous inns, at which mounted travellers had been in the habit of stopping, would be deserted, and would no longer pay any rent; that the new carriages were too cold in winter; that the passengers were grievously annoyed by invalids and crying children; that the coach sometimes reached the inn so late that it was impossible to get supper, and sometimes started so early that it was impossible to get breakfast. On these grounds it was gravely recommended that no public carriage should be permitted to have more than four horses, to start oftener than once a week, or to go more than thirty miles a day. It was hoped that, if this regulation were adopted, all except the sick and the lame would return to the old mode of travelling. Petitions embodying such opinions as these were presented to the King in council from several companies of the City of London, from several provincial towns, and from the justices of several counties. We smile at these things. It is not impossible that our descendants, when they read the history of the opposition offered by cupidity and prejudice to the improvements of the nineteneth century, may smile in their turn.

In spite of the attractions of the flying coaches, it was still usual for men who enjoyed health and vigour, and who were not encumbered by much baggage, to perform long journeys on horseback. If the traveller wished to move expeditiously he rode post. Fresh saddle horses and guides were to be procured at convenient distances along all the great lines of road. The charge was threepence a mile for each horse, and fourpence a stage for the guide. In this manner, when the ways were good, it was possible to travel, for a considerable time, as rapidly as by any conveyance known in England, till vehicles were propelled by steam. There were as yet no post chaises; nor' could those who rode in their own coaches ordinarily procure a change of horses. The King, however, and the great officers of state were able to command relays. Thus Charles commonly went in one day from Whitehall to Newmarket, a distance of about fifty-five miles through a level country; and this was thought by his subjects a proof of great activity. Evelyn performed the same journey in company with the Lord Treasurer Clifford. The coach was drawn by six horses, which were changed at Bishop Stortford and again at Chesterford. The travellers reached Newmarket at night. Such a mode of conveyance seems to have been considered as a rare luxury confined to princes and ministers.

Whatever might be the way in which a journey was performed, the travellers, unless they were numerous and well armed, ran considerable risk of being stopped and plundered. The mounted highwayman, a marauder known to our generation only from books, was to be found on every main road. The waste tracts which lay on the great routes near London were especially haunted by plunderers of this class. Hounslow Heath, on the great Western Road, and Finchley Common, on the great Northern Road, were perhaps the most celebrated of these spots. The Cambridge scholars trembled when they approached Epping Forest, even in broad daylight. Seamen who had just been paid off at Chatham were often compelled to deliver their purses on Gadshill, celebrated near a hundred years earlier by the greatest of poets as the scene of the depredations of Poins and Falstaff. The public authorities seem to have been often at a loss how to deal with the plunderers. At one time it was announced in the Gazette that several persons, who were strongly suspected of being highwaymen, but against whom there was sufficient evidence, would be paraded at Newgate in riding dresses: their horses would also be shown; and all gentlemen who had been robbed were invited to inspect this singular exhibition. On another occasion a pardon was publicly offered to a robber, if he would give up some rough diamonds, of immense value, which he had taken when he stopped the Harwich mail. A short time after appeared another proclamation, warning the innkeepers that the eye of the government was upon them. Their criminal connivance, it was affirmed, enabled banditti to infest the roads with impunity. That these suspicions were not without fundation, is proved by the dying speeches of some penitent robbers of that age, who appear to have received from the innkeepers services much resembling those which Farquhar's Boniface rendered to Gibbet.

It was necessary to the success and even to the safety of the highwayman that he should be a bold and skilful rider, and that his manners and appearance should be such as suited the master of a fine horse. He therefore held an aristocratical position in the community of thieves, appeared at fashionable coffee-houses and gaming-houses, and betted with men of quality on the race ground. Sometimes, indeed, he was a man of good family and education. A romantic interest therefore attached, and perhaps still attaches, to the names of freebooters of this class. The vulgar eagerly drank in tales of their ferocity and audacity, of their occasional acts of generosity and good nature, of their amours, of their miraculous escapes, of their desperate struggles, and of their manly bearing at the bar and in the cart. Thus it was related of William Nevison, the great robber of Yorkshire, that he levied a quarterly tribute on all the northern drovers, and, in return, not only spared them himself, but protected them against all other thieves; that he demanded purses in the most courteous manner; that he gave largely to the poor what he had taken from the rich; that his life was once spared by the royal clemency, but that he again tempted his fate, and at length died, in 1685, on the gallows of York. It was related how Claude Duval, the French page of the Duke of Richmond, took to the road, became captain of a formidable gang, and had the honour to be named first in a royal proclamation against notorious offenders; how at the head of his troop he stopped a lady's coach, in which there was a booty of four hundred pounds; how he took only one hundred, and suffered the fair owner to ransom the rest by dancing a coranto with him on the heath; how his vivacious gallantry stole away the hearts of all women; how his dexterity at sword and pistol made him a terror to all men; how, at length, in the year 1670, he was seized when overcome by wine; how dames of high rank visited him in prison, and with tears interceded for his life; how the King would have granted a pardon, but for the interference of Judge Morton, the terror of highwaymen, who threatened to resign his office unles the law were carried into full effect; and how, after the execution, the corpse lay in state with all the pomp of scutcheons, wax lights, black hangings, and mutes, till the same cruel Judge, who had intercepted the mercy of the crown, sent officers to disturb the obsequies. In these anecdotes there is doubtless a large mixture of fable; but they are not on that account unworthy of being recorded; for it is both an authentic and an important fact that such tales, whether false or true, were heard by our ancestors with eagerness and faith.

All the various dangers by which the traveller was beset were greatly increased by darkness. He was therefore commonly desirous of having the shelter of a roof during the night; and such shelter it was not difficult to obtain. From a very early period the inns of England had been renowned. Our first great poet had described the excellent accommodation which they afforded to the pilgrims of the fourteenth century. Nine and twenty persons, with their horses, found room in the wide chambers and stables of the Tabard in Southwark. The food was of the best, and the wines such as drew the company on to drink largely. Two hundred years later, under the reign of Elizabeth, William Harrison gave a lively description of the plenty and comfort of the great hostelries. The Continent of Europe, he said, could show nothing like them. There were some in which two or three hundred people, with their horses, could without difficulty be lodged and fed. The bidding, the tapestry, above all, the abundance of clean and fine linen was matter of wonder. Valuable plate was often set on the tables. Nay, there were signs which had cost thirty or forty pounds. In the seventeenth century England abounded with excellent inns of every rank. The traveller sometimes, in a small village, lighted on a public house such as Walton has described, where the brick floor was swept clean, where the walls were stuck round with ballads, where the sheets smelt of lavender, and where a blazing fire, a cup of good ale, and a dish of trouts fresh from the neighbouring brook, were to be procured at small charge. At the larger houses of entertainment were to be found beds hung with silk, choice cookery, and claret equal to the best which was drunk in London. The innkeepers too, it was said, were not like other innkeepers. On the Continent the landlord was the tyrant of those who crossed the threshold. In England he was a servant. Never was an Englishman more at home than when he took his ease in his inn. Even men of fortune, who might in their own mansions have enjoyed every luxury, were often in the habit of passing their evenings in the parlour of some neighbouring house of public entertainment. They seem to have thought that comfort and freedom could in no other place be enjoyed in equal perfection. This feeling continued during many generations to be a national peculiarity. The liberty and jollity of inns long furnished matter to our novelists and dramatists. Johnson declared that a tavern chair was the throne of human felicity; and Shenstone gently complained that no private roof, however friendly, gave the wanderer so warm a welcome as that which was to be found at an inn.

Many conveniences, which were unknown at Hampton Court and Whitehall in the seventeenth century, are to be found in our modern hotels. Yet on the whole it is certain that the improvement of our houses of public entertainment has by no means kept pace with the improvement of our roads and of our conveyances. Nor is this strange; for it is evident that, all other circumstances being supposed equal, the inns will be best where the means of locomotion are worst. The quicker the rate of travelling, the less important is it that there should be numerous agreeable resting places for the traveller. A hundred and sixty years ago a person who came up to the capital from a remote county generally required twelve or fifteen meals, and lodging for five or six nights by the way. If he were a great man, he expected the meals and lodging to be comfortable, and even luxurious. At present we fly from York or Exeter to London by the light of a single winter's day. At present, therefore, a traveller seldom interrupts his journey merely for the sake of rest and refreshment. The consequence is that hundreds of excellent inns have fallen into utter decay. In a short time no good houses of that description will be found, except at places where strangers are likely to be detained by business or pleasure.

The mode in which correspondence was carried on between distant places may excite the scorn of the present generation; yet it was such as might have moved the admiration and envy of the polished nations of antiquity, or of the comtemporaries of Raleigh and Cecil. A rude and imperfect establishment of posts for the conveyance of letters had been set up by Charles the First, and had been swept away by the civil war. Under the Commonwealth the design was resumed. At the Restoration the proceeds of the Post Office, after all expenses had been paid, were settled on the Duke of York. On most lines of road the mails went out and came in only on the alternate days. In Cornwall, in the fens of Lincolnshire, and among the hills and lakes of Cumberland, letters were received only once a week. During a royal progress a daily post was despatched from the capital to the place where the court sojourned. There was also daily communication between London and the Downs; and the same privilege was sometimes extended to Tunbridge Wells and Bath at the seasons when those places were crowded by the great. The bags were carried on horseback day and night at the rate of about five miles an hour.

The revenue of this etablishment was not derived solely from the charge for the transmission of letters. The Post office alone was entitled to furnish post horses; and, from the care with which this monopoly was guarded, we may infer that it was found profitable. If, indeed, a traveller had waited half an hour without being supplied, he might hire a horse wherever he could.

To facilitate correspondence between one part of London and another was not originally one of the objects of the Post Office. But, in the reign of Charles the Second, an enterprising citizen of London, William Dockwray, set up, at great expense, a penny post, which delivered letters and parcels six or eight times a day in the busy and crowded streets near the Exchange, and four times a day in the outskirts of the capital. This improvement was, as usual, strenuously resisted. The porters complained that their interests were attacked, and tore down the placards in which the scheme was announced to the public. The excitement caused by Godfrey's death, and by the discovery of Coleman's papers, was then at the height. A cry was therefore raised that the penny post was a Popish contrivance. The great Doctor Oates, it was affirmed, had hinted a suspicion that the Jesuits were at the bottom of the scheme, and that the bags, if examined, would be found full of treason. The utility of the enterprise was, however, so great and obvious that all opposition proved fruitless. As soon as it became clear that the speculation would be lucrative, the Duke of York complained of it as infraction of his monopoly, and the courts of law decided in his favour.

The revenue of the Post Office was from the first constantly increasing. In the year of the Restoration a committee of the House of Commons, after strict inquiry, had estimated the net receipt at about twenty thousands pounds. At the close of the reign of Charles the Second, the net receipt was little short of fifty thousand pounds; and this was then thought a stupendous sum. The gross receipt was about seventy thousand pounds. The charge for conveying a single letter was twopence for eighty miles, and threepence for a longer distance. The postage increased in proportion to the weight of the packet. At present a single letter is carried to the extremity of Scotland or of Ireland for a penny; and the monopoly of post horses has long ceased to exist. Yet the gross annual receipts of the department amount to more than eighteen hundred thousands pounds, and the net receipts to more than seven hundred thousand pounds. It is, therefore, scarcely possible to doubt that the number of letters now conveyed by mail is seventy times the number which was so conveyed at the time of the accession of James the Second.

No part of the load which the old mails carried out was more important than the newsletters. In 1685 nothing like the London daily paper of our time existed, or could exist. Neither the necessary capital nor the necessary skill was to be found. Freedom too was wanting, a want as fatal of either capital or skill. The press was not indeed at that moment under a general censorship. The licensing act, which had been passed soon after the Restoration, had expired in 1679. Any person might therefore print, at his own risk, a history, a sermon, or a poem, without the previous approbation of any public officer; but the Judges were unanimously of opinion that this liberty did not extend to Gazettes, and that, by the common law of England, no man, not authorised by the crown, had a right to publish political news. While the Whig party was still formidable, the government thought it expedient occasionally to connive at the violation of this rule. During the great battle of the Exclusion Bill, many newspapers were suffered to appear, the Protestant Intelligence, the Current Intelligence, the Domestic Intelligence, the True News, the London Mercury. None of these was published oftener than twice a week. None exceeded in size a single small leaf. The quantity of matter, which one of them contained in a year, was not more than is often found in two numbers of the Times. After the defeat of the Whigs it was no longer necessary for the King to be sparing in the use of that which all his Judges had pronounced to be his undoubted prerogative. At the close of his reign no newspaper was suffered to appear without his allowance: and his allowance was given exclusively to the London Gazette. The London Gazette came out only on Mondays and Thursdays. The contents generally were a royal proclamation, two or three Tory addresses, notices of two or three promotions, an account of a skirmish between the imperial troops and the Janissaries on the Danube, a description of a highwayman, an announcement of a grand cockfight between two persons of honour, and an advertisement offering a reward for a strayed dog. The whole made up two pages of moderate size. Whatever was communicated respecting matters of the highest moment was communicated in the most meagre and formal style. Sometimes, indeed, when the government was disposed to gratify the public curiosity respecting an important transaction, a broadside was put forth giving fuller details than could be found in the Gazette: but neither the Gazette nor any supplementary broadside printed by authority ever contained any intelligence which it did not suit the purposes of the court to publish. The most important parliamentary debates, the most important state trials, recorded in our history, were passed over in profound silence. In the capital the coffee-houses supplied in some measure the place of a journal. Thither the Londoners flocked, as the Athenians of old flocked to the market place, to hear whether there was any news. There men might learn how brutally a Whig had been treated the day before in Westminster Hall, what horrible accounts the letters from Edinburgh gave of the torturing of Covenanters, how grossly the Navy Board had cheated the crown in the victualling of the fleet, and what grave charges the Lord Privy Seal had brought against the Treasury in the matter of the hearth money. But people who lived at a distance from the great theatre of political contention could be kept regularly informed of what was passing there only by means of newsletters. To prepare such letters became a calling in London, as it now is among the natives of India. The newswriter rambled from coffee-room to coffee-room, collecting reports, squeezed himself into the Sessions House at the Old Bailey if there was an interesting trial, nay, perhaps obtained admission to the gallery of Whitehall, and noticed how the King and Duke looked. In this way he gathered materials for weekly epistles destined to enlighten some county town or some bench of rustic magistrates. Such were the sources from which the inhabitants of the largest provincial cities, and the great body of the gentry and clergy, learned almost all that they knew of the history of their own time. We must suppose that at Cambridge there were as many persons curious to know what was passing in the world as at almost any place in the kingdom, out of London. Yet at Cambridge, during a great part of the reign of Charles the Second, the Doctors of Laws and the Masters of Arts had no regular supply of news except through the London Gazette.

At length the services of one of the collectors of intelligence in the capital were employed. That was a memorable day on which the newsletter from London was laid on the table of the only coffee-room in Cambridge. At the seat of a man of fortune in the country the newsletter was impatiently expected. Within a week after it had arrived it had been thumbed by twenty families. It furnished the neighbouring squires with matter for talk over their October, and the neighbouring rectors with topics for sharp sermons against Whiggery or Popery.   (Macaulay).

28. England in 1685, and England in 1857.

It is time that the description of the higher classes of the English whom Charles the Second governed should draw to a close*). Yet one subject of the greatest moment still remains untouched. Nothing has as yet been said of the great body of the people, of those who held the ploughs, who tended the oxen, who toiled at the looms of Norwich, and squared the Portland stone for Saint Paul's. Nor can very much be said. The most numerous class is precisely the class respecting which we have the most meagre information. In those times philanthropists did not yet regard it as a sacred duty, nor had demagogues yet found it a lucrative trade, to expatiate on the distress of the labourer. History was too much occupied with courts and camps to spare a line for the hut of the peasant or for the garret of the mechanic. The press now often sends forth in a day a greater quantity of discussion and declamation about the condition of the working man than was published during the twenty-eight years which elapsed between the Restoration and the Revolution. But it would be a great error to infer from the increase of complaint that there has been any increase of misery.

The great criterion of the state of the common people is the amount of their wages; and, as four fifths of the common people were, in the seventeenth century, employed in agriculture, it is especially important to ascertain what were the wages of agricultural industry. On this subject

---

*) In the preceding part of his History of England, Macaulay proves beyond doubt, that the higher classes, of the present day, are in every respect much more moral, much more humane, much more intellectual and honourable than they ever were in former times.

we have the means of arriving at conclusious sufficiently exact for our purpose.

It is evident that, in a country where no man can be compelled to become a soldier, the ranks of an army cannot be filled, if the government offers much less than the wages of common rustic labour. At present the pay and beer money of a private in a regiment of the line amount to seven shillings and seven pence a week. This stipend, coupled with the hope of a pension, does not attract the English youth in sufficient numbers; and it is found necessary to supply the deficiency by enlisting largely from among the poorer population of Munster and Connaught. The pay of the private foot soldier in 1685 was only four shillings and eightpence a week, yet it is certain that the government in that year found no difficulty in obtaining many thousands of English recruits at very short notice. On the whole, therefore, it seems reasonable to conclude that, in the reign of Charles the Second, the ordinary wages of the peasant did not exceed four shillings a week; but that, in some parts of the kingdom, five shillings, six shillings, and during the summer months, even seven shillings were paid. At present a district where a labouring man earns only seven shillings a week is thought to be in a state shocking to humanity. The average is very much higher; and, in prosperous counties, the weekly wages of husbandmen amount to twelve, fourteen, and even sixteen shillings.

The remuneration of workmen employed in manufactures has always been higher than that of the tillers of the soil. In the year 1680, a member of the House of Commons remarked that the high wages paid in this country made it impossible to maintain a competition with the produce of the Indian looms. An English mechanic, he said, instead of slaving like a native of Bengal for a piece of copper, exacted a shilling a day. Other evidence is extant, which proves that a shilling a day was the pay to which the English manufacturer then thought himself entitled, but that he was often forced to work for less. A ballad of that epoch describes the good old times when every artisan employed in the woolen manufacture lived as well as a farmer. But those times were past. Sixpence a day was now all that could be earned by hard labour at the loom. If the poor complained that they could not live on such a pittance, they were told that they were free to take it or leave it. Whereas in our days the average rate of wages for weavers is from two shillings and sixpence to three shillings a day.

It may here be noticed that the practice of setting children prematurely to work, a practice which the state, the legitimate protector of those
who cannot protect themselves, has, in our time, wisely and humanely
interdicted, prevailed in the seventeenth century to an extent which,
when compared with the manufacturing system, seems almost incredible.
At Norwich, the chief seat of the clothing trade, a little creature of six
years old was thought fit for labour. Several writers of that time, and
among them some who were considered as eminently benevolent, mention,
with exultation, the fact that in that single city boys and girls of very
tender age created wealth exceeding what was necessary for their own
subsistence by twelve thousand pounds a year. The more carefully we
examine the history of the past, the more reason shall we find to dissent
from those who imagine that our age has been fruitful of new social
evils. The truth is that the evils are, with scarcely an exception, old.
That which is new is the intelligence which discerns and the humanity
which remedies them.

When we pass from the weavers of cloth to a different class of arti-
sans, our inquiries will still lead us to nearly the same conclusions. During
several generations, the Commissioners of Greenwich Hospital have kept a
register of the wages paid to different classes of workmen who have been
employed in the repairs of the building. From this valuable record it appears that, in the course of a hundred and twenty years, the daily earnings
of the bricklayer have risen from half a crown to four and tenpence, those
of the mason from half a crown to five and three pence, those of the
carpenter from half a crown to five and fivepence and those of the
plumber from three shillings to five and tenpence.

It seems clear, therefore, that the wages of labour, estimated in
money, were, in 1685, not more than half of what they now are; and
there were few articles important to the working man of which the price
was not, in 1685, more than half of what it is now. Beer was undoubtedly much cheaper in that age than at present. Meat was also cheaper,
but was still so dear that hundreds of thousands of families scarcely
knew the taste of it. In the cost of wheat there has been very little
change. The average price of the quarter, during the last twelve years
of Charles the second, was fifty shillings. Bread, therefore, such as is
now given to the inmates of a workhouse, was then seldom seen, even
on the trencher of a yeoman or of a shopkeeper. The great majority of

the nation lived almost entirely on rye, barley, and oats. All other com·
modities were positively dearer than at present.

Of the blessings which civilization and philosophy bring with them a
large proportion is common to all ranks, and would, if withdrawn, be
missed as painfully by the labourer as by the peer. The market place
which the rustic can now reach with his cart in an hour was, a hundred
and sixty years ago, a day's journey from him. The streets which now
afford to the artisan, during the whole night, a secure, a convenient, and
a brilliantly lighted walk was, a hundred and sixty years ago, so dark after
sunset that he would not have been able to see his hand, so ill paved
that he would have run constant risk of breaking his neck, and so ill
watched that he would have been in imminent danger of being knocked
down and plundered of his small earnings. Every bricklayer who falls
from a scaffold, every sweeper of a crossing who is run over by a carriage, may now have·his wounds dressed and his limbs set with a skill
such as, a hundred·and sixty years ago, all the wealth of a great lord
like Ormond, or of a merchant prince like Clayton could not have purchased. Some frightful disceases have been extirpated by science; and
some have been banished by the police. The term of life has been length-
ened over the whole kingdom, and· especially in the towns. The year
1685 was not accounted sickly; yet in the year 1685 more than one in
twenty-three of the inhabitants of the capital died. At present only one
inhabitant of the capital in forty-two dies annually. The difference in
salubrity between London of the nineteenth century and the London of
the seventeenth century is very far greater than the difference between
London in an ordinary season and London in the cholera.

The prisons in those times were hells on earth, seminaries of every
crime and of every disease. At the assizes the lean and yellow culprits
brought with them from their cells to the dock an atmosphere of pestilence, which sometimes avenged them signally on bench, bar, and jury.
But on all this misery society looked with profound indifference. Nowhere
could be found that sensitive and restless compassion which has, in our
time, extended a powerful protection to the factory child, to the Hindoo
widow, to the Negro slave, which pries into the stores and water-casks
of every emigrant ship, which winces at every lash laid on the back of
the drunken soldier, which will not suffer the thief in the hulks to be
ill fed or overworked, and which has repeatedly endeavoured to save the

life of the murderer. It is true that compassion ought, like every other feeling, to be under the government of reason, and has, for want of such government, produced some ridiculous and some deplorable effects. But the more we study the annals of the past, the more shall we rejoice that we live in a merciful age, in an age in which cruelty is abhorred, and in which pain, even when deserved, is. inflicted reluctantly and from a sense of duty. Every class doubtless has gained largely by this great moral change: but the class which has gained most is the poorest, the most dependent, and the most defenceless.

It is pleasing to reflect that the public mind of England has softened while it has ripened, and that we have, in the course of ages, become not only a wiser, but also a kinder people. There is scarcely a page of the history or lighter literature of the seventeenth century which does not contain some proof that our ancestors were less humane than their post-- erity. The discipline of workshops, of schools, of private families, though not more efficient than at present, was infinitely harsher. Mas- ters, well born and bred, were in the habit of beating their servants. Pedagogues knew no way of imparting knowledge but by beating their pupils. Husbands, of decent station, were not ashamed to beat their wives.

The general effect of the evidence which has been submitted to the reader seems hardly to admit of doubt. Yet, in spite of evidence, many will still imagine to themselves the England of the Stuarts as a more pleasant country than the England in which we live. It may at first seem strange that society, while constantly moving forward with eager speed, should be constantly looking backward with tender regret. But these two propensities, inconsistent as they may appear, can easily be resolved into the same principle. That impatience, while it stimulates us to sur- pass preceding generations, disposes us to overrate their happiness. It is, in some sense unreasonable and ungrateful in us to be constantly dis- contented with a condition which is constantly improving. But, in truth, there is constant improvement, because there is constant discontent. If we were perfectly satisfied with the present, we should cease to contrive, to labour, and to save for the future. And it is natural that, being dis- satisfied with the present, we should form a too favourable estimate of the past.

In truth we are under a deception similar to that which misleads the traveller in the Arabian desert. Beneath the caravan all is dry and

bare: but far in advance, and far in the rear, is the semblance of refresh-
ing waters. The Pilgrims hasten forward and find nothing but sand
where, an hour before, they had seen a lake. They turn their eyes and
see a lake where, an hour before, they were toiling through sand. A similar illusion seems to haunt nations through every stage of the long progress from poverty and barbarism to the highest degrees of opulence and
civilization. But, if we resolutely chase the mirage backward, we shall
find it recede before us into the regions of fabulous antiquity. It is now
the fashion to place the golden age of England in times when noblemen
were destitute of comforts the want of which would be intolerable to a
modern footman, when farmers and shopkeepers breakfasted on loaves,
the very sight of which would raise a riot in a modern workhouse, when
men died faster in the purest country air than they now die in the most
pestilential lanes of our large towns, and when men died faster in the
lanes of our towns than they now die on the coast of Guinea We too
shall, in our turn, be outstripped, and in our turn be envied. It may well
be, in the twentieth century, that the peasant of Dorsetshire may think
himself miserably paid with fifteen shillings a week ; that the carpenter
at Greenwich may receive ten shillings a day; that labouring men may
be as little used to dine without meat as they are now to eat rye bread;
that sanitary police and medical discoveries may have added several more
years to the average length of human life; that numerous comforts and
luxuries which are now unknown, or confined to a few, may be within
the reach of every diligent and thrifty working man. And yet it may
then be the mode to assert that the increase of wealth and the progress
of science have benefitted the few at the expense of the many, and to
talk of the reign of Queen Victoria as the time when England was truly
merry England, when all classes were bound together by brotherly sympathy, when the rich did not grind the faces of the poor, and when the
poor did not envy the splendour of the rich.

Macaulay. Hist. of England.

Sketches from the British Empire.

I. General Physical Features of England.

The British Empire is one of the most important, powerful, and the largest empires of the globe. It includes a larger population than any other empire, except that of China. Among the countries subject to British rule are territories situated in every quarter of the globe; some of them in either division of the old world, others within the limits of the western hemisphere. While some of them, again, border upon the north polar circle, and touch the shores of the Frozen Ocean; others lie within the warm belt of the torrid zone, and display the brilliant vegetation of the tropics. The centre of the British empire is the United Kingdom of *Great Britain* and *Ireland*. Of the principal island (Great Britain), England is the southern and larger portion, the remaining or nothern part being Scotland.

England is bounded on the east by the German Ocean; on the south, by the English Channel, separating it from France; and on the west, by St. George's Channel and the Irish Sea, separating it from Ireland. Scotland adjoins it on the north. The shape of England and Wales bears some resemblance to that of a triangle, of which the longest side is to the westward.

At the straits of Dover the breadth of the English Channel is little more than twenty miles. In clear weather the opposite shores are distinctly visible. It has been supposed that this narrow passage was once closed by an isthmus. The correspondence between the rocks, with the fact of the same noxious animals, the bear and the wolf, having existed on both sides of the straits, are the chief reasons, assigned for the supposition.

The general aspect of England is varied and delightful. In some parts verdant plains extend as far as the eye can reach, watered by copious streams, and covered by innumerable castles. In others, the pleasing vicissitudes of gently rising hills and bending vales, fertile in corn, waving with wood, and interspersed with meadows, offer delightful landscapes of opulence and beauty. Some tracts abound with prospects of the more romantic kind, — lofty mountains, craggy rocks, deep narrow dells, and tumbling torrents; nor are there wanting, as a contrast, the gloomy features of black moors, and wide uncultivated heaths.— The general aspect of Wales, as distinguished from England, is bold, romantic, and mountainous. It consists of continued ranges of lofty mountains, and impending crags, intersected by numerous and deep ravines and extensive valleys.

The eastern, central, and southern parts of England are generally level, presenting only a few chalk ranges and picturesque eminences, which do not reach any considerable elevation, but serve to diversify agreeably the surface of the country. But around the estuary of the Wash, there is an extensive tract of low, flat land, extremely monotonous, owing to the large amount of water brought down by the rivers, their very slight fall, and the lowness of the district, it is naturally exposed to floods from heavy rains, and to inundations of the sea, requiring a net-work of artificial channels, with hydraulic machinery, to promote drainage, and embankments, in order to keep the waters in check. By works of this kind, constructed at an immense expense, a region once nearly useless to man, consisting of stagnant pools and spongy earth, has been converted into rich meadows and corn-bearing lands.

From the Scottish border, a range of mountains, *the Cheviot hills*, extends southward. The loftiest point is *Cross Fell*, 2901 feet above the sea. Grander highlands are clustered on the west of this range, connected with it. The most prominent elevation is the *Sea Fell*, 3166 feet, the highest point of England.

The Snowdon «the snow-clad hil» in Wales, forty miles in circuit, attains the height of 3571 feet, and is the most elevated point of Wales.

Owing to the westerly position of the higher elevations, the general slope of the entire country is towards the east; and hence most of the important Rivers are formed in that direction, flowing to the North Sea. These, proceeding from north to south, are the Tyne, Wear, Tees, Humber, including Trent and Ouse, Yare, Orwell, and Thames, with Medway. On the western side of the kingdom, proceeding from south to north, there are the Parret, Severn and Wye, entering the

Bristol Channel; the Dee, Mersey, Ribble, Lune, and Eden, discharging
into the Irish sea. On the south, and connected with the English Channel,
passing from west to east, there are the Tamar, the Exe, and Salisbury
Avon, with several of minor note. The three largest examples of the
whole, are the Humber, Severn and Thames.

The *Humber* is the name of an estuary, formed by the junction of
the Trent and Ouse. They geographically constitute a single river system,
the most important in the British Isles as to the magnitude of its basin,
which is very nearly equal to one-sixth of the total area of England and
Wales. The Trent is the longest and largest tributary. Its name is said
to be derived from its containing thirty varieties of fish. Where it is
joined by the Ouse, the estuary of the Humber commences, varying in
breadth from two to four miles. Though much encumbered with shoals,
there is a main channel available for ships of the largest size up to Hull,
on the north bank.

The *Severn* with the tributary of the Bristol Avon is the longest
river, owing to its circuitous route, for its actual length of 240 miles,
is twice the distance from source to mouth. Few of the English rivers
are charged with such an amount of sediment, owing to its own course,
and that of its tributaries, being for considerable distance through tracts
of marl and soft sandstone.

The *Thames*, though only the third in point of magnitude, ranks
the first as a tidal river, and is commercially the most important stream
on the face of the globe.

Many of the second class rivers are of the highest commercial value,
as the Tyne, Wear, and Tees, for the shipment of coal; and the *Mersey*
for its noble expansion, before reaching the sea, facilitating the foreign
trade of Liverpool. It flows through the cotton manufacturing district;
and one of its affluents, the Irwell, on which Manchester stands, has
been aptly styled, «the hardest-worked river in the world», from the
number of mills and factories on its banks.

The upper courses of most of the northern streams, the banks of
the Dove and Derwent, in Derbyshire, those of the Dee, Wye and Towy,
in Wales, and of the Tamar, in Cornwall, are renowned for their fine
scenery.

The Thames, the Mersey, the Severn, and the Humber are connected
by Canals and thus a water communication is maintained between Lon-

don, Liverpool, Bristol and Hull, the four great commercial ports of Great Britain.

The subordinate isles of any important extent are western and southern. They consist of the *Isle of Man* in the Irish sea, nearly midway between England and Ireland, with judicial institutions and revenue laws peculiar to itself; *Anglesea*, on the north-west coast of Wales, and one of its counties, separated from the mainland by the Menai Straits, but now connected with it by a suspension, and a tubular bridge; the *Scilly Isles,* to the west of the Land's End, a compact group of from one to two hundred granitic masses, only forty of which have herbage, and six are inhabited; and the beautiful Isle of Wight, divided from the mainland of Hampshire by the Channel of the Solent, and the great naval road-stead of Spithead. Besides these, there are the *Channel Islands*, consisting of Jersey, Guernsey, Alderney and others, geographically belonging to France, but subject to the English crown since the eleventh century; and the Isle of Thanet, off the coast of Kent.

The Lakes are few, and of unimportant size, chiefly confined to the Cumbrian mountains, where they occupy deep hollows and glens between them. But they are very celebrated for natural beauty, heightened by cultivation and charming residences on the banks. *Windermere*, the largest, is ten miles long, by from one to two broad.

The climate of the kingdom is remarkable for its dense fogs, frequent rains and perpetual change; but it is also noted for its mildness, compared with that of continental districts. Not only is the mean annual temperature higher from ten to twenty degrees (Fahrenheit), and even more in some instances, but the seasons are never in such violent contrast. This arises from the vast surrounding expanse of ocean, for water every where preserves a more uniform temperature than land, from the warm current of the Gulf Stream; and the prevailing south west winds which blow up from the direction of the tropics. The western sides, both of Great Britain and Ireland, are warmer than the eastern, being more exposed to the influences which contribute to raise the temperature. On the south coast, the climate is remarkably genial, and the rich, lasting verdure there, vies with that of any other country in Europe.

The snow rarely lies upon the ground more than two or three days, the sea-ports of England are never known to suffer the inconvenience of being blocked up with ice during winter time.

The soil is either naturally good, or, being rendered so by culture, is capable of producing all the valuable kinds of grain, in abundance, and of excellent quality. Owing to the nature of the climate, the western districts are better adapted to pasturage, and the eastern to tillage. In the north, there are still extensive moors, which have hitherto resisted all the improvements of agriculture. Particular attention has been paid in England to the improving of the breed of horses, oxen, and sheep, which are perhaps not to be surpassed by those of any other country. In strength, spirit, swiftness, docility, and beauty, the English horses yield to none in the world; possessing, as they do, all the qualities of the best foreign breeds. Race horses have been brought to the highest perfection.

England is remarkably rich in its mineral productions, and to this it is indebted in a great measure for its unparalleled and growing prosperity. The most important are coal, iron, tin, copper, lead, salt, zinc, slate, lime and clay.

The principal coal district of England is in the North; another stretching for about a hundred miles along the Bristol Channel.

The south coast, including that of the Isle of Wight, generally consists of chalky cliffs, constantly mouldering away from the action of the sea.

On account of the general deficiency of hard stone near the surface, the houses throughout the greater part of England are built of brick.

II. Civil and Ecclesiastical State.

The *government* of the United Kingdom of Great Britain and Ireland is constitutional, or possesses a regular form, in which the civil rights of all classes are acknowledged and guaranteed. It is a limited monarchy, consisting of King or Queen, Lords, and Commons.

In early times, the king possessed the chief influence, while the Parliament, in general, was rather an obsequious council of the sovereign than an independent body. At the Revolution of 1688, the strength of the monarchy was diminished by a breach of the hereditary line, and the Parliament became the predominant power. As the nobility and superior gentry had then the chief influence in both Houses of Parliament, it might be said that the aristocratic principle had become ascendant. It continued to be so till the passing of the Reform Bill in 1832, when the power of electing the majority of the House of Commons being extended to the middle-classes of the people, the democratic principle was, for the first time, brought into any considerable degree of force.

The *sovereign* has power to make war or peace; to assemble or dissolve parliament, and to ratify all its acts by his assent. He appoints all civil and military authorities, as well as dignitaries of the Church, and can increase the number of peers at pleasure by creating new ones. He is held to be incapable of doing wrong; and if an unlawful act be done, the minister instrumental in that act is alone liable to punishment. The succession to the throne is hereditary; but, by the coronation oath, the sovereign is bound to govern according to the laws of the realm, and to maintain inviolate the Protestant religion, with all the rights and privileges of the Church.

The *House of Lords* is composed of the lords spiritual and temporal; the former of whom are the archbishops and bishops; the latter, the dukes, marquises, earls, viscounts, and barons of the United Kingdom. Peers cannot be arrested except for treason and some other high offences, and they must be tried by a jury of themselves, who give their verdict merely upon their honour. The peers may vote by proxy.

The *House of Commons* is composed of knights, citizens, and burgesses, respectively chosen by counties, cities, and boroughs. Its members cannot be arrested in civil causes during their attendance on parliament, nor can they be called to account out of the House for anything said within it. They posses the sole right of regulating the collection and distribution of the public money — it being recognised as a principle, that the people shall not be taxed but by their own consent through their representatives. The Commons cannot vote by proxy.

A bill — that is, any proposed measure — before it can become the law of the land, must be first read three times in the House of Commons, and then thrice in the House of Lords, obtaining a majority of votes on each reading; and, finally, it must receive the royal assent. A *rejected bill* cannot be introduced again during the same session.

The peculiar boast of the criminal law of the British empire is Trial by Jury. In England and Ireland, where the principle of the criminal law requires the injured party or his representative to prosecute, he can only do so by permission of a jury of accusation, called the Grand Jury; another jury sits for the purpose of deciding whether the evidence against the accused has established the guilt. These juries consist in England of twelve men whose verdict must be unanimous. In Scotland, there is no grand jury, and there the jury upon the charge consists of fifteen men, who decide by a majority of votes. The jury is an institution justly considered as a most officient protection of the subject from the vindictiveness of power. Civil cases, turning upon matters of fact, are also decided by juries in all parts of the United Kingdom.

The established religion in England and Wales is the Protestant, and the English Church is under the government of two archbishops and twenty six bishops, the sovereign being its supreme head.

In Scotland, the established form of worship is that called Presbyterian; the ministers of the Scotch church are under the government of a body called the General Assembly. There is likewise in Scotland a branch of the English Episcopal Church, which is presided over by seven bishops.

In Ireland, the Established Church is a branch of the English (forming, with it, the United Church of England and Ireland), and is governed by two archbishops and ten bishops. But the majority of the people of Ireland are members of the Roman Catholic religion.

There are numerous dissenters from the established form of worship. in all parts of the United Kingdom, and full toleration is allowed to all persuasions.

Branches of the English Church exist in all the colonies of the empire, and are under the government of bishops of the Colonial Church, all the principal settlements abroad having been arranged into dioceses for the purpose.

III. National Character — Language, Literature, Arts, and Sciences.

The predominant feature in the *Character of the English* is an ardent love of liberty, which renders them extremely tenacious of their civil rights, stern advocates of justice, and patriotic in the highest degree. In their manners, they are grave rather than gay, blunt rather than ceremonious; in their habits, they are enterprising, industrious, and provident; in their feelings, humane; in mercantile transactions generally the greatest integrity exists, and promises are faithfully performed; in the middle and upper classes, the highest civilisation prevails, and all the social virtues and comforts of domestic life are sedulously cultivated. There are some fovourite field-sports and boisterous amusements; but the enjoyments of the English are chiefly within doors in their own well-regulated homes. A love of home is a marked peculiarity in the affections of the English.

The *Welsh*, the descendants of the ancient Britons, are said to be choleric, but brave, kind-hearted, and hospitable. Their minds are also said to be tinged with superstitious notions, supposed to be in some measure owing to the wild mountain scenery of their country.

The English language is, radically, of a twofold origin, being derived from the *Teutonic* through the Anglo-Saxons and the Danes, and from the *Latin* through the Norman-French. But although principally based upon the Anglo-Saxon, it may be said in its present state to be compounded, more or less, of many European tongues. Its construction is simple, but its pronunciation, on account of the variety of sounds to the same letters, is perhaps the most difficult, especially to foreigners, of all modern languages.

The language spoken by the original inhabitants of Britain was nearly related to that now spoken by the Welsh.

England has long borne a distinguished part in the *literary and scientific* world. In the various departments of philosophy, poetry, and history, it can number many illustrious authors; some of matchless excellence. A similar distinction marks the cultivation of those arts and sciences which refine and embellish the social state, as well as add to its comforts and conveniences. Institutions for the encouragement of every description of knowledge, are established throughout the country on the most liberal principles. Literature flourishes in England not only from the intelligence of the people, but because the press is free.

The *dawn of English literature* may be dated about the middle of the fourteenth century; in the reign of Elizabeth it was in a flourishing state; and from that period a numerous train of literary and scientific men swell the page of biography.

The chief institutions for education in England are — the ancient national universities of Oxford and Cambridge; the more recent colleges of London, Durham, and Lampeter in Wales; the classical schools of Eton, Westminster, Winchester, Harrow, Charterhouse, and Rugby; the military college of Sandhurst; the colleges of various dissenting denominations; and the elementary schools of the National and British and Foreign Societies. There are numerous schools for elementary instruction, which are conducted by private exertion, and supported by fees, along with, in some instances, aid from the state. After all that is done, however, there is still a great and lamentable deficiency in educational establishments.

IV. The City of London.

London, the capital of the British empire, and the most important commercial city on the globe, is situated on both sides of the river Thames, in the counties of Middlesex and Surrey. It extends nearly ten miles in length, from east to west, and covers more than sixty square miles of country. The number of inhabitants amounts to more than 3 millions. Its general form is oval. There are from twelve thousand to thirteen thousand squares, streets, lanes, and courts, and about a quarter of a million of houses. The river Thames is crossed by several handsome bridges. These are seven in number, connecting the Middlesex portion of the metropolis with that on the Surrey side; of these, three are toll free, and four are subject to a small impost. The free bridges are Southwark, Waterloo, and Westminster; the others are Southwark, Waterloo, Hungerford, and Vauxhall.

London still retains the character, not of one compact city, but of a conglomeration of different towns, connected by long streets. It has in various parts of it all the features of a large town. Thus, in one district of it one finds a busy, bustling street, every house of which has its lower floor opened as a shop. Behind this street one finds handsome streets and squares, where there are few or no shops, the houses being occupied by persons of property. At a little distance one finds narrow streets, with mean houses occupied by the poor. One passes away to another district, several miles off, and one finds the same features of a large town repeated, the great shop streets, the streets and squares for the aristocracy, and the narrow streets and lanes for the poor. One moves off several miles in other directions, and the same features are repeated again and again.

The streets are crowded, not only with people, but with carriages, omnibuses, and vehicles of every description; and one would at first imagine that some great occasion had drawn everybody out of their houses; but day after day one would observe the same busy multitude passing and repassing like so many bees.

It is also greatly diversified in the occupations and manners of the inhabitants. To the east upon the river, is a great seaport, with all the sounds, sights, and smells connected with the arriving, sailing, loading, and unloading of vessels. Another quarter of it is a manufacturing town, the streets generally silent, the people being in their houses at work, with the sound of the shuttle heard from house to house, and the master manufacturers residing in well built handsome streets and squares in the vicinity. Another district is manisfestly the seat of the Court, everything wearing the air of splendour and fashion, the manners of the shopkeepers as different from those of their brethren in other quarters as if they were not natives of the same country.

In ancient times, London was not nearly so large as it now is. The houses were, in general, badly built, and constructed of wood and plaster; and the streets were mean and narrow. There were not wanting, however, several very handsome buildings, both public and private; among the former, the old cathedral of St. Paul held the preeminence; its steeple is said to have been five hundred and twenty feet high. But in the reign of Charles II., a dreadful plague, which swept away one hundred thousand persons, was followed by a fire which destroyed almost all the city, consuming four hundred streets, thirteen thousand houses, eighty-nine churches, including St. Paul's Cathedral, the Guildhall, the Royal Exchange, and many other buildings. In rebuilding, the city was much improved; the streets were widened, and the houses constructed with brick instead of wood and plaster.

London has many fine buildings, but most of them are unfavourably situated for being seen to advantage. The general character of London is not splendour, but comfort, cleanliness, and convenience. A person arriving there will soon see that its inhabitants are not bent on show or pleasure, but on business, and every facility is provided for aiding them. The abundance of water conveyed into every house, the thorough and perfect illumination with gas, the excellent repair in which the streets and roads are kept, the facility with which persons of all ranks can be conveyed from one part of the town to another, or to any part of the world, form the most remarkable features of this extraordinary city.

One of the finest buildings is St. Paul's Cathedral, which was rebuilt by Sir Christopher Wren after the great fire; the first stone was laid on the 21st of June, 1675, by the architect himself, who lived to see it completed, although it took thirty-five years in building; the top stone being laid by the architect's son, in 1710. It is a magnificent structure, and, with the exception of St. Peter's at Rome, the grandest cathedral in the world. Within it, are several fine statues in commemoration of generals, statesmen, and other celebrated persons who are buried there. Inside the dome is a curious gallery, called the whispering gallery. If a person at one end of this gallery puts his mouth against the wall and whispers ever so faintly, any one at the other end will hear him distinctly. The highest part of the building is about three hundred and seventy feet from the ground; and a fine view of London may be obtained from it; but the people, houses, carriages, and other objects, being seen from such a height, look exceedingly small, and have a curious effect.

Another building is Westminster Abbey, a very ancient building. On its side originally stood a Christian church, built by Sebert, king of Essex, in 610, A. D., but afterwards destroyed by the Danes. The Abbey, as such, was founded by Edward the Confessor, who, in 1041, restored the Saxon line of the kings of England; it was afterwards rebuilt by Henry III. and enlarged by his successors. It was also repaired, and two of its towers were built by Sir Christopher Wren. One part of the abbey is called the Poets' Corner; and there are buried some of the most celebrated poets that England has reproduced. There one may find the names of Chaucer, Spenser, Shakspeare, Milton, and many others; and there are many beautiful monuments in marble erected to their memory.

The chief curiosities of Westminster Abbey are the chapels at the eastern end of the church, with their tombs. One of these, which stands behind the altar, is dedicated to Edward the Confessor. Here is to be seen his tomb, which was built by Henry III., and which contains the ashes of the Confessor. In this chapel, also, are the tombs of several kings and queens of England. The helmet of Henry V. is preserved, with the saddle on which he rode at the battle of Agincourt; stripped of everything, however, but the wood and iron. At the eastern extremity of the church, and opening up to it, is the famous chapel of Henry VII., one of the finest specimens of Gothic architecture in the world. It was built at an enormous expense, and Henry's tomb alone costs ten thousand pounds, a sum equal to two hundred thousand pounds of the English money. The mosaic pavement of the choir is an object of great beauty. It was made by Archbishop Ware, and is formed of a great many pieces of jasper, alabaster, porphyry, lapis lazuli, serpentine marble, and touchstone, varying in size from half an inch to four inches.

Most of the English kings lie buried here, even down to the time of George III. At his decease, in 1820, St. George's Chapel, Windsor, was used for the last resting place of royalty.

In going to Westminster Abbey one passes through the old gateway called Temple Bar, where the heads of state malefactors used to be exposed The gate at Temple Bar is always closed when it is known that the reigning sovereign designs to visit the city: the ceremony on this occasion is very imposing on account of the grandeur of the procession, and the crowds of people which assemble to behold the spectacle. Before the present gate was built, there was a bar or barrier of posts and chains, which separated the Strand from Fleet Street, and which, from its vicinity to the Temple, received the name of Temple Bar.

There is another very interesting building near Westminster Abbey, called Westminster Hall. It was built by William II. in 1097, and is part of a palace which he erected on the side of one occupied by Edward the Confessor. The ceiling is said to be the largest in Europe unsupported by pillars. The Parliament used formerly to meet in this hall, and it is now used for state trials, and on some other occasions. Close to this structure, and communicating with it by a passage, were the buildings in which the parliament used to meet: these contained a variety of apartments connected by passages. In 1834, a terrible fire burnt down a great part of these buildings, and new Houses of Parliament have been erected. The vault, called Guy Fawkes's cellar, situated under the House of Lords, was the old kitchen of Edward the Confessor's palace. Within it the gunpowder and other combustibles, intended to blow up the king and parliament, were deposited by the conspirators, in the reign of James I. in 1605; and at the entrance of the vault Guy Fawkes was seized the night before the intended execution of his plot.

The new Houses of Parliament are much handsomer and more commodious than the old. This very handsome pile of buildings was erected under the superintendence of Sir C. Barry; the first stone was laid on the 27. of April 18'10. The style is of richly decorated gothic, and will be memorable for ages, as the largest building of this kind in the world. It covers an area of eight acres, and has four fronts and three principal towers. The north part of the building is devoted to the House of Commons and the various Committee rooms and other offices. The House of Lords is decorated in a most gorgeous style with richly gilt mouldings, emblazonings of arms, stained glass, and fine pictures of historical subjects. There is also a stranger's gallery, to which persons having orders signed by members are admitted.

In this neighbourhood the Queen has an extensive old palace called St. James's, and another much more splendid, and far more costly, called Buckingham Palace. This palace, with its triumphal arch, magnificent gates of mosaic gold, quadrangles, columns, capitals, pediments, entablatures, and internal magnificence, is a wondrous pile. King George said it was not «a King's Palace, but a Palace for Kings».

The Bank of England, in Threadneedle Street, is the first place in the whole world with respect to money matters. What heaps of gold! what piles of bank notes does one see there! It is said to contain generally eighteen millions of gold sovereigns.

It is very large, and of different kinds of architecture, and looks as though it would be no easy matter to get out any of the gold it contains against the will of the owners. The present building was opened for business in May 1817. Its length is four hundred and ninety feet, and breadth one hundred and eight feet.

Over the hall is a very curious clock; it has in the different rooms of the Bank sixteen clock faces, and the hands are all moved by brass rods fixed to this one clock.

The tower, a renowned fortress, is situated on the N. bank of the Thames, at the E. extremity of the city. The White tower appears to have been built by William the Conqueror, and it then formed the principal nucleus, as it still presents the most prominent feature, of the present imposing aggregate of towers and fortifications. It was used in former times for a state-prison; is was here that the unfortunate Lady Jane Grey was confined and executed. The tower as it now exists, is a great irregular pile of buildings, surrounded by a ditch, now dry, and separated fram the Thames by a platform. The exterior circuit of the ditch is 3156 feet. The tower is capable of accommodating upwards of 900-soldiers; but the force usually occupying it does not exceed 500 or 600. The new jewel-office, erected in 1840, is of the Elizabethan style of architecture, and of a very massive construction, the walls being upwards of 3 feet in thickness, and the whole bomb proof in every part. The regalia are placed in the centre of the apartment in a case of plate glass mounted in polished brass, and surrounded by an octagonal enclosure of iron-railing. The room is lit by windows so constructed as to direct a full blaze of light upon the jewels which are raised upon pedestals covered with rich velvet.

V. The Streets of London.

The appearance presented by the streets of London an hour before sun rise, on a summer's morning, is most striking. There is an air of cold, solitary desolation about the noiseless streets, which we are accustomed to see thronged at other times by a busy, eager crowd, and over the quiet closely shut buildings, which throughout the day are swarming with life and bustle, that is very impressive. The last houseless vagrant, whom penury and police have left in the streets, has coiled up his chilly limbs in some paved corner, to dream of food and warmth. The drunkard, the dissipated and the wretched have dissappeared: the more sober and orderly part of the population have not yet awakened to the labour of the day, and the stillness of death is over the streets. The coachstands in the larger thoroughfares are deserted: the night-houses are closed; and the chosen promenades of misery are empty.

An occasional policeman may alone be seen at the street-corners; and now and then a cat runs across the road. A partially opened bedroom window here and there bespeaks the heat of the weather and the uneasy slumbers of its occupant; and the dim scanty light, through the window blind denotes the chamber of watching or sickness. With these exceptions the streets present no signs of life, nor the houses of habitation.

An hour wears away; the spires of the churches and roofs of the principal buildings are faintly tinged with the light of the rising sun, and the streets begin to resume their bustle and animation. Market-carts roll slowly along; the sleepy waggoner impatiently urging on his tired horses, or vainly endeavouring to awaken the boy who, stretched on the top of the fruit-baskets, forgets his long cherished curiosity to behold the wonders of London.

Sleepy-looking men begin to take down the shutters of early public houses; and little deal tables, with their ordinary preparation for a street-breakfast, make their appearance at the customary stations. Numbers of men and women, carrying upon their heads heavy baskets of fruit, toil down their way to Covent garden, and following each other in rapid succession, form a long straggling line.

Here and there a bricklayer's labourer, with the day's dinner tied up in a handkerchief, walks briskly to his work, and occasionally a little knot of three or four schoolboys on a stolen bathing expedition, rattle merrily over the pavement, their mirth constrasting forcibly with the demeanour of the little sweep who, having knocked and rung till his arm aches, and being interdicted by a merciful legislature from endangering his lungs by calling out, sits patiently down on the door-step until the house-maid may happen to awake.

Covent garden-market, and the avenues leading to it, are thronged with carts of all sorts, sizes, and descriptions. The pavement is already strewed with decayed cabbage-leaves, broken haybands, and all the indescribable litter of a vegetable market, men are shouting, horses neighing, boys fighting, basket-women talking. These and a hundred other sounds form a compound discordant enough to a Londoner's ears, and remarkably disagreeable to those of country gentlemen, who are sleeping for the first time at an inn near it.

Another hour passes away, and the day begins in good earnest. The servant of all work lights the fire and opens the street-door to take in the milk. The mail goes to the coach office in due course, and the passengers, who are going out by the early coach, stare with astonishment at the passengers, who are coming in by the early coach, who look blue and dismal, and are evidently under the influence of that odd feeling produced by travelling. The coach-office is all alive, and the coaches, which are just going out, are surrounded by the usual crowd of Jews, who seem to consider, that it is quite impossible any man can mount a coach without requiring at least six penny worth of oranges, a pen-knife, a pocket book, a last year's almanack, a pencil case, a piece of sponge and a small series of caricatures.

Half an hour more, and the sun darts his bright rays cheerfully down the still half empty streets, and shines with sufficient force to rouse the dismal laziness of the apprentice, who pauses every other minute from his task of sweeping out the shop and watering the pavement in front of it, to tell another apprentice how hot it will be to-day; he is gazing at the «Wonder» or the «Tally ho» or the «Nimrod» or some other fast coach, till it is out of sight, when he reenters the shop. Cabs with trunks and band-boxes between the driver's legs and outside the apron, rattle briskly up and down the streets on their way to the coach-offices or steam-packet wharfs; and the cab-drivers and hackney-coachmen polish up the ornamental part of their vehicles. The shops are now completely opened, and apprentices and shopmen are busily engaged in cleaning and decking the windows for the day. The bakers' shops in town are filled with servants and children waiting for the drawing of the first batch of rolls.

Seven o' clock, and a new set of people fill the streets. The goods in the shop-window are invitingly arranged; the carts have dissappeared from Coventgarden; the waggoners have returned, and the costermongers repaired to their ordinary «beats» in the suburbs, clerks are at their offices, and gigs, cabs, omnibusses, and saddle horses are conveying their masters to the same destination. The streets are thronged with a vast concourse of people gay and shabby, rich and poor, idle and industrious, and we come to the heat, bustle and activity of noon.

VI. The river Thames.

The Thames traverses some of the richest districts of England; but it is one of those rivers which rather derive their peculiar character from the countries through which they flow, than impose distinctive features on the landscape by the boldness and rapidity of their course. Even in the most hilly districts, where its current is naturally strongest, the Thames can at no point be properly called a rapid stream; but it is by no means a sluggish river, and is throughout distinguishable for the majestic progress of its pure and silvery stream which generally fills its verdant banks, and is rarely discoloured with mud except after great floods. To these, independently of its tidal floods, it is also occasionably liable; and their influence has been very extensive, as well as of long continuance in the level parts of its tract, making the whole country appear like a sea, and many of the towns and villages on its banks like islands, when viewed from the several eminences commanding the plain.

Its course is most distinguished by romantic scenery and natural beauty leading through valleys bounded by hills richly clothed with beech woods, and finely embellished by the magnificent seats of many of the highest nobility and gentry.

For many miles above the metropolitan vicinity, the river is enlivened with a multitude of small commercial craft, and latterly with river steamers running to and from the metropolis; but here it becomes a great and noble tide river, full of vessels of all description. The tides affect it for 15 or 16 miles above the city; but the salt water comes no farther than 30 m. below it. Such, however, is the volume and depth of water, that vessels of 700 or 800 tons reach the city on its E. quarter.

There is nothing finer in London, than the view from Waterloo-bridge on a July evening, whether coloured by the gorgeous hues of the setting sun, reflected on the water in tenfold glory, or illuminated by a thousand twinkling lights, from lamps, and boats, and houses, mingling with the mild beams of the rising moon. The calm and glassy river, gay with unnumbered vessels; the magnificent buildings which line its shores, produce a picture gratifying alike to the eye and to the heart. The whole voyage down the river presents a series of villages, magnificent seats, splendid villas, beautiful pleasure grounds, and highly cultivated gardens.

It is worthy of remark, that notwithstanding the very existence of London depends on the navigation of the Thames, insomuch that if this river were rendered unnavigable, London would soon become a heap of ruins, like Nineveh and Babylon, yet some of the passages of this important River are suffered to become half choked up and almost impassable from the increase and shifting of sandbanks.

There has been formed in 1824 a ground thoroughfare for carriages and passengers across the Thames, at a point, below all the bridges, where, from the constant passage of shipping of all descriptions, the erection of a bridge would have been highly inconvenient, if not practi= cally impossible. Entering the ground by an easy spiral staircase for passengers, and an entrance leading to a spiral roadway for carriges, the tunnel crosses about 75 feet below the surface of the river at high water, by two distinct avenues cr arched vaults connected with each other by openings, and comprising each a carriage-way and footpath. The ground is arched, so that the tunnel, as a whole, may be said to consist of two cylinders, with a central portion common to both. It issues, on the S. side of the river, also by an inclined spiral plane and staircase similar to those on the N. side. The engineer who had the high merit of accomplishing this great work is Sir J. Brunel.

VII. Life and Manners of the Inhabitants of Scotland.

The Scots are commonly divided into two classes: the Highlanders and Lowlanders, — the former occupying the northern and mountainous provinces, and the latter the southern districts. These classes differ from each other in language, manners, and dress. In their persons, the Scots have an athletic bony frame, a hard weatherbeaten countenance, in- dicating cool prudence and cautious circumspection, and broad and high cheek-bones. Nor are the sources of this peculiarity of character and conformation difficult to be discovered. Exposure to a climate rather severe, with modes of living that may be styled spare rather than mo- derate, give health and vigour to the body; while an early moral and religious education imparts to the mental powers shrewdness, solidity, and strength. In the case of the Highland and pastoral Scot, daily and severe toil, the perpetual presence of scenery calculated to make a deep and permanent impression on the feelings, — the broad expanse of ocean, indented by rocky promontories, or studded with islands, the gloomy glen for ever re-echoing the roar of innumerable streams pour- ed from the craggy mountains, whose towering heads hide themselves for a great part of the year amid the clouds, the rapid descent of thick vapours, and the darkness of conflicting tempests, — give existence to that daring and sublime, though. sombre and romantic cast of thought which so remarkably distinguishes Scotsmen in every quarter of the world.

The Scots have been celebrated for their taste in music; and in song, particularly of the pastoral and plaintive kind, they are unrivalled. The origin of their national airs is still involved in much obscurity.

Attachment to his native soil has been considered, and perhaps not without reason, as peculiarly characteristic of a Scotsman; although, considering the extent of her population, perhaps no country sends forth a greater number of emigrants than Scotland. Many of these, however, it may be observed, emigrate purely from the strength of this principle: a few years of separation are endured to purchase the delight of closing life happily and independently amid the scenes of infancy and youth. Even the poor emigrants who have been forced to exile themselves from their native Scotland, still carry with them their national feelings and customs, and preserve the remembrance of their native woods and streams and mountains in the names which they bestow upon the scenery of their new abodes beyond the wide rolling Atlantic.

The chief distinction of the Scots from the people of England originates in the difference of religion; that of Scotland being Presbyterianism, that of England Episcopacy. This occasions a difference in the mode of conducting baptisms, marriages, and funerals.

The Highlanders have a language, a dress, and many customs peculiar to themselves. The Highland dress consists of a short coat, a vest, a short kind of petticoat reaching scarcely so low as the knee, and known by the name of a philabeg or kilt, with short hose, leaving the knees entirely uncovered. The head is covered with a bonnet totally different in its appearance from the broad flat lowland bonnet; it is stiffened so as to stand upright on the head, and has no slight resemblance to a hat without a brim. The coat, the vest, the kilt, and the hose, are usually of tartan, — a kind of chequered stuff of various colours, often not inelegant. Instead of the kilt, is sometimes substituted the belted plaid, which is a large piece of tartan, part of it fastened round the body in the form of a philabeg, a part tucked up to one of the shoulders, having on the whole, a graceful appearance, and exhibiting a strong resemblance to the dress of the ancient Romans. The Sprochan or pouch, formed generally of some kind of fur, decorated with tassels and various other ornaments, and fastened round the middle of the body, so as to hang down before, is esteemed an essential part of the Highland garb.

To this, before the Highlanders were disarmed, were added a broad sword, with a large basket handle, a dirk, or short dagger, a knife and fork in the same sheath with the dirk, and in the girdle a pistol, often much ornamented. The music of the Highlanders is in a great measure peculiar; their favourite instrument, the bagpipe, though enthusiastically admired by the Highlanders, is not, unless in very skilful hands, agreeable to the natives of other countries. Dancing is a favourite Highland amusement; but it is generally performed with more agility than grace. The houses or huts of the Highlanders are mean structures of loose stones, generally without either chimney or grate. The fire is made upon the hearth, in the middle of the house, the smoke finding its way out by an aperture in the roof. The ordinary food of the Highland peasantry is coarse and spare, consisting chiefly of oatmeal variously prepared, and milk, in the neighbourhood of the sea, of fish. It may be here remarked that the Scottish Highlanders are daily losing that exclusive attachment to their ancient dress and manners by which they were formerly distinguished. They are rapidly adopting the dress and the customs of the low country; and in a short time, it is probable the customs of the Highlands will be described rather as manners which existed, than as manners still existing in any part of the island.

VIII. Colonies and Dependencies of Great Britain.

Britain possesses upwards of thirty dependencies in different parts of the world, which it acquired by virtue of discovery or conquest. The dependencies are of two kinds — military establishments, useful for the concentration of naval forces, such as Gibraltar, Helgoland, Bermuda, and St. Helena; and colonial possessions, valuable for trade and the reception of emigrant settlers, but still more important as the means of extending the English language, arts, and civilised usages. The chief colonies are geographically connected with America and the West Indies, and with Australasia.

The Spaniards and Portuguese were the first European nations that colonised the New World, and, when the native Indians perished before them, imported negroes from Africa to perform the agricultural labour as slaves. The English were not slow to follow in their steps. Sir Walter Raleigh formed a settlement in North America about the year 1607, and called it Virginia, in honour of Queen Elizabeth. Two companies of merchants enlarged the British territory, part of which received the name of New England; and, subsequently, numerous bands of religious and political refugees sought a home on its shores; but, when these colonies rose in wealth and strength, they found themselves in a position to maintain their independence of the mother-country, and before the close of the last century, achieved that independence; so that they are now no longer known as colonies, but as the independent republic of the United States of America.

The settlements in the West Indian Islands began to flourish in the half of the seventeenth century, when factories were established by private companies in Barbadoes and St. Christopher's, and the culture of the sugar-cane, transplanted from Brazil, was found to succeed. During the Protectorate of Cromwell, Jamaica was conquered from Spain, and opened a new source of wealth. Trinidad, the smaller islands, the district of Honduras or Belize, on the adjacent coast of North America, and Guiana, in South America, have been acquired at various periods since, and chiefly by conquest from Spain, Holland, and France. All these territories are together denominated the British West Indies. They are the oldest British colonies, and are rich in every tropical product, yielding sugar, coffee, tobacco, cotton, cabinet timber, spices, fruits, drugs, and dye-stuffs. Jamaica, the largest and most important of the islands, has an area of more than five thousand square miles, with a population of more than four hundred thousand, of which only about thirty-eight thousand are whites, the majority being negroes, most of whom were originally slave labourers. Trinidad, St. Lucia, Dominica, Barbadoes, and the other islands belonging to Britain, may contain an aggregate area of eighty-three thousand square miles, with a population of about four hundred and sixty thousand, of which the greater portion are negroes and creoles. Belize is comparatively a small territory; but Guiana has an area of sixty-seven thousand square miles, with a population of more than one hundred thousand.

Since the abolition of slavery by the British government, the want of labourers has been severely felt, the coloured population being generally disinclined to hired labour, and the work to be done being unsuitable to European constitutions. These colonies are, therefore, somewhat on the decline.

Since the independence of the North American states in 1776, the British possessions in that continent have been wholly in the northern section, embracing the province of Canada, the colonies of Nova Scotia, Cape Breton, Prince Edward's Island, New Brunswick, and Newfoundland; and the vast region stretching to the Arctic Ocean, at present occupied by savage tribes and the trappers of the Hudson's Bay Company. The whole population amounts to about three millions.

The rise of the British power in India is reckoned one of the most surprising things in history. It originated in a charter granted in 1600 by Queen Elizabeth to a body of English merchants, since known as the East India Company. In 1611, they received permission from the native government at Delhi to establish factories at Surat, and other spots in Eastern Hindostan. About the middle of the seventeenth century, a settlement was formed at Madras; and by the marriage of Charles II. with a princess of Portugal, the valuable position of Bombay was also obtained. At the beginning of the eighteenth century, the French influence in India was considerable, and their settlements superior to the English; but from about the year 1750, when the forces of the two nations came into collision, the French gradually gave way, while the British territories rapidly extended; and a succession of conquests, almost forced upon, placed one district of India after another in the power of Great Britain.

In 1773, it was deemed proper to place a check on the rapidly increasing power of the Company, by the appointment of a governor-general on behalf of the Crown. At a later period, a council and a Board of Control were added. In 1780, Hyder Ali, the sultan of Mysore, suddenly burst into the Carnatic with an overwhelming force, and ravaged all before him. The war, which was continued with various success under his son, Tippoo Saib, terminated at length in the capture of Seringapatam and the death of Tippoo, whose kingdom became the spoil of the English. Early in the present century, the jealousy of some of the Mahratta rulers led to another war of conquest, which gave the victor extensive territories in Central India, including Delhi, the Mogul capital, and Agra, with the custody of the Mogul emperor. A war provoked by the Burmese government in 1826, added Assam and other provinces east of the Bay of Bengal to British India. During the war with Affghanistan, which lasted from 1839 till 1842, it was felt to be very desirable for the British to command the navigation of the Indus; and Lord Ellenborough was induced to attempt the acquisition of territory in Scindia. Here, also, the natives were forced to yield before the superior prowess of Britain. In the adjacent kingdom of the Punjaub, events were still more remarkable. A number of chiefs among the Sikhs contending for the vacant throne, provoked a collision with the English forces in 1845. The war terminated in 1849, by their unconditional surrender, and the Punjaub was by proclamation annexed to British India.

All territories lying in or near Hindostan, are known by the common appellation of East Indies; and from their geographical position, yield every species of tropical produce, as sugar, coffee, tea, rice, silk, cotton, hardwoods, ivory, spices, fruits, drugs, dye-stuffs, and other similar commodities. Goods to the value of more than eight millions sterling are annually exported from Britain to the East Indies; while goods to the value of more than fourteen millions are imported from the east Indies to Britain.

In 1857 a most formidable insurrection broke out in the Indian army. For many years the East India Company had maintained a large force of native troops under British officers and armed and disciplined in the European manner. These Sepoys, as they were called, were a fine body of men, and had done excellent service in many wars; and notwithstanding several instances of insubordination, very great confidence was placed in them generally.

The cause of the outbreak is even now scarcely certain. Some strange, unfounded suspicion of an attempt about to be made by the British authorities for their forcible conversion to Christianity seems to have found its way to the minds of the Sepoys, both Mohamedan and Hindoo. This alarm was founded, or pretended to be founded, on the issue, of new cartridges, adapted to the improved fire-arms now used by all the infantry, and which it was supposed were greased with the fat either of the cow, which is a sacred animal with the Brahmins, the highest caste of Hindoos, or of swine, which are an abomination to the Mahomedans, as to the Jews.

The first very serious outbreak of this mutiny took place early in May, at Meerut, a military station about thirty miles to the north of Delhi. The insurgents murdered their officers and their families, and marched to Delhi, where they were joined by the garrison, consisting entirely of native regiments, and the atrocities committed at Meerut were here repeated. They also took the nominal king of Delhi, the lineal descendant of the Mogul sovereigns, a feeble old man, who was then living in that magnificent capital a pensioner of the East India company, and proclaimed him Emperor of India.

By the firm attitude assumed by the British in India, surprised and outnumbered as they were, and placed in a position of unexampled peril, by the prompt and powerful support sent out from home, and by the distinguished talent and valour of their commanders, and of many other most able men in every rank and of all conditions, the most formidable military revolt that has ever been known was crushed into mere fragments in less than a year. It is likewise to be observed that throughout the whole of this critical period, neither the mass of the population of India nor the princes of the country have shown any sympathy with the mutineers. The insurrection was moreover confined to the Bengal Presidency, the Madras and Bombay troops having, with few exceptions, proved trustworthy.

A most important change in the government of India, of which the necessity had long been foreseen, has been accelerated by the events which have been now related. The great East India Company was abolished, and its vast empire transferred to the direct dominion of the Crown, Sept. 1, 1858.

In Australasia, the British settlements are those of New South Wales, of which that of Sydney, on the south shore of Port Jackson, was established in 1788; Western Australia or Swan River, of which the capital in Perth, in 1829; South Australia, of which Adelaide is the capital; and Port Philip, or Victoria, of which Melbourne is the capital, established in 1837. North Australia was colonised in 1838, and Australia, and the western coast, about eighty miles south of Swan River, was settled in 1841. The Colonisation of this part of the world began by the practice of depositing criminals on the coast of Australia, after the American war of independence put a stop to their being transported to the plantations of the New World. One spot, from the profusion of flowers found on it, was called Botany Bay, long used as a penal settlement; and thus the town of Port Jackson or Sydney had its origin. But the advantages of the place tempted free emigrants to settle in it, and Van Diemen's Land became the penal settlement instead of New South Wales. Many of the inhabitants of Sydney removed to other parts of the coast, and were joined by new emigrants. Thus arose the settlement of Port Philip, at the southern extremity; of Swan River, far to the west; and Adelaide, with many smaller ones between them. Still more recently, Port Essington became the nucleus of settlements in the north, but they have not succeeded like the rest. The staple productions have hitherto been the wool, tallow, and hides of the numerous flocks of sheep fed on the natural pasture. But the recent discovery of gold is likely to change the aspect of affairs. The adjacent island of Van Diemen's Land (which contains 24,000 square miles, or some what less than Ireland) is the seat of another British colony, planted in 1824, and is altogether a thriving settlement being more hilly and better watered than Australia. Its principal towns are Hobart-Town, the capital, and Launceston. New Zealand, composed of three contiguous islands, ranging from 1100 miles in length, with a breadth varying from 5 to 200, is also the seat of a British colony; and if its internal management would be fairly adjusted, it would probably rise to firstrate importance. Two centuries have passed since these islands were first discovered by the Dutch; but little was known of the natives till the voyages of Captain Cook. They were fierce, warlike, cannibal tribes, whom Europeans cared not to meddle with. In 1837, however, a New Zealand Company was formed, and land bought from the chiefs. The mother-country has since provided means of protection and government for the colonists.

At the Cape of Good Hope, Sierra Leone, Cape Coast, and other parts of Africa, Britain possesses upwards of' 200,000 square miles, with a population of 400,000. Cape Colony, taken from the Dutch in 1806, has been a thriving settlement, and the recent colony at Port Natal gave high promise; but a recent war with the Caffres has been productive of much injury. The Mauritius, and some minor islands in the Indian Ocean; the rocky islets of St. Helena and Ascension, in the Atlantic; and Fernando Po, in the Gulf of Guinea, complete the sum of British possessions connected with Africa. Their principal products are ivory, gold, hides, horns, sugar, coffee, palmoil, teakwood, aloes, and articles of minor importance.

The laws and judicial usages- of England are extended to the chief colonial possessions, along with all the rights and privileges which are common to British subjets. Hence the inhabitants of the most distant part of the empire, whatever be their origin, rank, or colour, are entitled by the constitution to enjoy the same degree of civil and religious liberty, and the same careful protection of life and property as their fellow-subjects in the mother-country. This is - an invaluable boon, for in no nation do the people practically enjoy greater rational liberty of speech ar action, and in none is the press more free. In India, the natives are subject to their own laws, and in this privilege they are carefully protected by the British authorities. Uninterrupted, likewise, in the exercise of their own peculiar religious usages, sheltered from the oppression of native chiefs, and instructed at schools which have been recently planted amongst them, the inhabitants of India are really more happy and prosperous under a foreign rule than they were under the dominion of the former sovereigns of the country.

According to the constitution, wherever Britain established her civil authority, there also is established the Protestant Episcopalian form of church government and worship, except in cases where provision to the contrary has been made by terms of capitulation. Practically, however, there is perfect freedom in the exercise of religious belief and worship in all parts of the empire. In Lower Canada and Malta, Roman Catholicism; in Hindostan, Brahminism and Muhammedanism; and in Ceylon, the religion of Buddha, prevails. The Protestant Presbyterian form of church government and worship, similar to that of Scotland, predominates in the Cape of Good Hope, according to agreement with the former Dutch occupants. In all the colonial possessions, much is done by means of missionaries, to introduce a knowledge of Christianity among the natives.

The English language now predominates over the whole United Kingdom, with the exception of a portion of the Highlands of Scotland, part of Ireland, part of the Isle of Man, and Wales; but in all these places it is gradually superseding the native Celtic dialects. It has been extended, by means of numerous dependencies abroad, over nearly the whole of North American and the West India Islands; also the Australian continent and islands, the Cape of Good Hope, part of Hindostan and Ceylon and various other places, including several islands in the Pacific. This diffusion of the English tongue, and with it the Christian religion, as well as English literature and habits of thought, over so large a portion of the earth's surface, is perhaps the most extraordinary fact, connected with the ·history of modern civilisation.

XI. Commerce and Manufactures of Great-Britain.

The eminent importance attained by the British in the scale of nations appears to depend mainly upon two features of the common character — the high moral and intellectual character of the people at large, and their extraordinary skill in producing articles of necesity · and luxury, as well as their dexterity in the commerce by which these are diffused over the world.

In manufactures and commerce Britain has long enjoyed a supe- iority over all other countries. For this the nation has been indebted, not only to their naturally industrious dispositions and the enlightened men, who have in the course of time invented machinery for increas- ing and cheapening the products of labour, but to the extraordinary abun- dance of mineral substances requisite for manufactures, and to the in- sular nature of the country, which admits of ready maritime commu- nication with other regions. In consequence of these advantages com- bined, Britain has for a long time furnished articles of clothing and household conveniency to many parts of the world, receiving in ex- change either money or acticles of value. The cotton manufacture, not- withstanding that the raw material can be obtained only in distant parts of the earth, has risen in Great Britain, during seventy years from about 200,000 pound of annual import to the enormous sum of 965 millions, of which more than one half is exported again. Cotton

34

goods are manufactured chiefly by means of machinery, in large factories, the chief seats of the manufacture being Manchester, Glasgow, Paisley. Cotton goods are also manufactured by hand-loom weavers, of whom a considerable number continue to strive against the overpowering competition of machinery.

The Woolen Manufacture is the oldest in Britain. The west of England is the chief seat of this manufacture. The silk Manufacture, introduced by French Emigrants in the sixteenth century, is carried on to a great extent at Spitalfields, Coventry, Manchester, Paisley, and Glasgow. The Hardware Manufacture is one in which the skill of British workmen has long given them a high reputation. Iron to the amount of nearly 2 millions of tons was, in 1866 prepared from British mines for the purpose of being manufactured into articles of conveniency. The manufacture of the finer class of hardware is chiefly seated at Birmingham and Sheffield, while canon and machinery are produced on an extensive scale at Carron in Scotland. The manufacture of earthenware, china and glass is also carried on to a great extent.

The commerce of Britain is conducted by vessels belonging to private parties within the realm, or in other countries. In 1865 the mercantile navy of the home country and its colonies consisted of nearly thirty thousand vessels, of nearly five millions of aggregate tonnage, and navigated by a three hundred and eighty-five thousand men. We obtain, however, a more distinct idea of the extent of the national commerce from a calculation of the number of vessels, British and foreign, which in 1865, entered and departed from British harbours. These were — of British, twenty-one thousand nine hundred; of foreign twelve thousand eight hundred; comprehending an aggregate of about ten millions of tonnage. The chief mercantile port of Britain is London, after which Liverpool, Dublin, Hull and Greenock, rank in succession. Duties exceeding twenty millions are annually paid to Government for goods imported into London; and harbour dues to the amount of two hundred and fifty thousand pounds were collected in 1860, for vessels in the docks at Liverpool, which have a waterroom of a hundred and eleven acres and a quay-space of eight miles.

Besides tea, wine, and sugar the imports of Britain consist chiefly of raw materials for manufactures, while the exports, are almost exclusive by manufactured goods. The greatest quantity of imports is from

America; the greatest quantity of exports, to the same part of the world. Tea is obtained from China; wine chiefly from Portugal and Spain. Sugar, is exclusively imported from the West Indies. Cotton in its raw state is obtained chiefly from the United States and in lesser quantities from Brazil and Egypt. Of wool the coarser sort is obtained at home, while the finer kinds are imported from Germany and the colonies of Australia. Tallow, hemp and timber, are imported from Russia.

Poetry.

1. The Busy Bee.

«Little bee, come here and say
What you're doing all the day»?
«Oh, every day, and all day long,
Among the flowers you hear my
song.
I creep in every bud I see,
And all the honey is for me;
I take it to the hive with care,
And give it to my brothers there:
That when the winter time com-
es on,
And all the flowers are dead and
gone,
And when the wind is cold and
rough,
The busy bee may have enough».

2. The Lazy Fly.

«Little fly, come here and say
What you're doing all the day?
«Oh, I'm a gay and merry fly,
I never do anything — no, not I —
I go where I like, and I stay where I please,
In the heat of the sun, or the shade of the trees,
On the window-pane, or the cup-board shelf;
And I care for nothing except myself.

I cannot tell, it is very true,
When the winter comes, what I mean to do:
And I very much fear, when I'm getting old,
I shall starve with hunger, or die of cold».

3. The Field Daisy.

I'm a little pretty thing,
Always coming with the spring;
In the meadows green I'm found,
Peeping just above the ground;
And my stalk is covered flat
With a white and yellow hat.

Little lady, when you pass
Lightly o'er the tender grass,
Skip about, but do not tread
On my meek and healthy head,
For I always seem to say:
«Surely, Winter's gone away».

4. The Little Coward.

Why, here's a foolish little man,
Laugh at him, donkey, if you can;
And cat, and dog, and cow, and calf,
Come every one of you and laugh:

For only think, he runs away,
If honest donkey does but bray!
And when the bull begins to bellow,
He's like a crazy little fellow.

Poor Brindle cow can hardly pass
Along the edge to nip the grass,
Or wag her tail to lash the flies,
But off he runs and out he cries.

And when old Tray comes jumping too,
With bow, wow, wow, for how d'ye do,
And means it all for civil play,
'Tis sure to make him run away.

5. The Evening Bells.

Those evenings-bells, those evenings-bells,
How many a tale their music tells
Of youth, and home, and that sweet time,
When last I heard their soothing chime.

Those joyous hours are passed away
And many a heart that then was gay,
Within the tomb now darkly dwells,
And hears no more those evening-bells.

And so't will be when I am gone:
That tuneful peal will still ring on,
While other bards shall walk these dells,
And sing our praise, sweet evening-bells!

Th. Moore.

---

6. The Disobedient Little Fish.

«Dear Mother», said a little fish,
  «Pray is not that a fly?
I'm very hungry, and I wish
  You'd let me go and try».

«Sweet innocent», the mother cried
  And started from her nook,
«That horrid fly is put to hide
  The sharpness of the hook».

Now, as I've heard, this little trout
  Was young and foolish too,
And so he thought he'd venture out
  To see if it were true.

And round about the hook he play'd
  With many a longing look,
And — «Dear me», to himself he said,
  «I'm sure that's not a hook».

I can but give a little pluck:
  Let's see, and so I will».
So, on he went, and lo! it struck
  Quite through his little gill.

And as he faint and fainter grew
  With hollow voice he cried:
«Dear Mother, had I minded you,
  I need not now have died».

---

7. The Idle Boy.

Young Thomas was an idle lad,
  And lounged about all day;
And though he many a lesson had,
  He minded nought but play.

He only car'd for tops and ball,
  Or marbles, hoop, and kite;
But as for learning, that was all
  Neglected by him quite.

In vain his mother's kind advice,
In vain his master's care;
He followed ev'ry idle vice,
And learned to curse and swear.

And think you, when he grew a
      man,
He prospered in his ways?
No — wicked courses never can
Bring good and happy days.

Without a shilling in his purse,
Or cot to call his own,
Poor Thomas grew from bad to
       worse,
And hardened as a stone.

And oh! it grieves me much to
       write
His melancholy end;
Then let us leave the dreadful
       sight,
And thoughts of pity send.

But may we this important truth
  Observe and ever hold,
«That most who're idle in their youth,
  Are wicked, when they're old».

---

8. The Monkey.

Monkey, little merry fellow,
Thou art Nature's Punchinello;
Full of fun as Puck could be —
Harlequin might learn of thee!

In the very ark, no doubt,
You went frolicking about,
Never keeping in your mind
Drowned monkeys left behind.

Have you no traditions? — none
Of the court of Solomon?
No memorial how you went
With Prince Hiram's armament?

Look at him now! — slily peep;
He pretends he is asleep;
Fast asleep upon his bed,
With his arm beneath his head.

Now that posture is not right,
And he is not settled quite;
There! that's better than before —
And the knave pretends to snore.

Ha! he is not half asleep;
See, he slily takes a peep.
Monkey, though your eyes were
      shut,
You could see this little nut.

You shall have it, pigmy brother!
What! another! and another!
Nay, your cheeks are like a sack, —
Sit down, and begin to crack.

There the little ancient man
Cracks as fast as crack he can!
Now good-bye, my merry fellow,
Nature's primest Puuchinello.
      Mary Howitt.

---

9. Questions and Answers.

Who'showed the little ant the way
  Her narrow hole to bore,
And spend the pleasant summer day
  In laying up her store?

The sparrow builds her clever nest
  Of wool, and hay, and moss:
Who told her how to weave it best,
  And lay the twigs across?

Who taught the busy bee to fly
  Among the sweetest flowers,
And lay his feast of honey by,
  To eat in winter hours?

'T was God who showed them all
          the way,
  And gave their little skill,
And teaches children, if they pray,
  To do his holy will.

10. A Morning Hymn.

My father, I thank thee for sleep,
  For quiet and peceable rest;
I thank thee for stooping to keep,
  An infant from being distrest.
O, how can a poor little creature repay
Thy fatherly kindness by night and by day!

My voice would be lisping thy praise,
  My heart would repay thee with love;
O teach me to walk in thy ways,
  And fit me to see thee above:
For Jesus said: «Let little children come nigh!»
And he will not despise such an infant as I.

As long as thou seest it right,
  That here upon earth I should stay,
I pray thee to guard me by night,
  And help me to serve thee by day;
That when all the days of my life shall have past,
I may worship thee better in heaven at last.

11. An Evening Hymn.

Lord, I have passed another day,
  And come to thank thee for thy care,
Forgive my faults in work and play,
  And listen to my evening prayer.

Thy favour gives me daily bread,
  And friends who all my wants supply;
And safely now I rest my head,
  Preserved and guarded by thine eye.

Look down in pity and forgive,
  Whate'er I've said or done amiss;
And help me every day I live
  To serve thee better than in this.

Now while I speak, be pleased to take
  A helpless child beneath thy care:
And condescend, for Jesus' sake
  To listen to my evening prayer.

---

12. The Great Shepherd.

Knowest thou how many stars
There are shining in the sky?
Knowest thou how many clouds
Every day go floating by?
God, the Lord, has counted all;
He would miss one should it fall.

Knowest thou how many flies
Flicker in the noon-day sun?
Or of fishes in the water?
God has counted every one.
Every one he called by name,
When into the world it came.

Knowest thou how many babes
Go to little beds at night?
That without a care or trouble
Wake up with the morning light?
God in heaven each name can tell;
Knows thee too, and loves thee well.

---

13. The Glow Worm.

Beneath the hedge, or near the
stream,
A worm is known to stray,
That shows by night a lucid beam,
Which disappears by day.

Disputes have been and still pre-
vail,
From whence his rays proceed;
Some give that honuor to his tail,
And others to his head.

But this is sure, the hand of night,
That kindless up the skies,
Gives him a modicum of light,
Proportion'd to his size.

Perhaps indulgent nature meant,
By such a lamp bestow'd,
To bid the traveller as he went,
Be careful where he trod.

Nor crush a worm, whose useful
light
Might serve, however small,
To show a stumbling stone by night,
And save him from a fall

Whate'er she meant, this truth
divine
Is legible and plain,
'Tis power almighty bids him
shine,
Nor bids him shine in vain.

Ye proud and wealthy, let this then
Teach humbler thoughts to you,
Since such a reptile has its gem,
And boasts its splendour too.

Cowper.

----

14. God Provideth for the Morrow.

Lo, the lilies of the field,
How their leaves instruction yield!
Hark to Nature's lesson, given
By the blessed birds of heaven!
Every bush and tufted tree
Warbles sweet philosophy:
Mortal, fly from doubt and sorrow,
God provideth for the morrow!

Say, with richer crimson glows
The kingly mantle than the rose?
Say, have kings more wholesome fare
Than we poor citizens of air?
Barns nor hoarded grains have we,
Yet we carol merrily.
Mortal, fly from doubt and sorrow,
God provideth for the morrow!

One there lives, whose guardian eye
Guides our humble destiny;
One there lives, who Lord of all,
Keeps our feathers lest they fall.
Pass we blithely then the time,
Fearless of the snare and lime,
Free from doubt and faithless sorrow:
God provideth for the morrow!

(Reginald Heber).

---

15. Paraphrase on Psalm XXIII.

The Lord my pasture shall prepare,
And feed me with a shepherd's care;
His presence shall my wants supply,
And guard me with a watchful eye:
My noon-day walks he shall attend,
And all my midnight hours defend.

When in the sultry glebe I faint,
Or on the thirsty mountain pant;
To fertile vales and dewy meads
My weary wandering steps he leads:
Where peaceful rivers, soft and slow,
Amid the verdant landscape flow.

Though in the paths of death I tread,
With gloomy horrors overspread,
My steadfast heart shall fear no ill,
For thou, 0 Lord, art with me still;
Thy friendly crook shall give me aid,
And guide me through the dreadful shade.

Though in a bare and rugged way,
Through devious lonely wilds I stray,
Thy bounty shall my wants beguile:
The barren wilderness shall smile,
With sudden greens and herbage crown'd,
And streams shall murmur all around.

(Addison).

16. We Are Seven.

. . . . A simple child
That lightly draws its breath,
And feels its life in every limb,
What should it know of death?

I met a little cottage girl;
She was eight years old, she
said;
Her hair was thick with many a
curl
That clustered round her head.

She had a rustic woodland air,
And she was wildly clad;
Her eyes were fair, and very fair—
Her beauty made me glad.

«Sisters and brothers, little maid,
How many may you be?»
«How many? Seven in all», she
said,
And wondering looked at me.

«And where are they? I pray you,
tell».

She answered: «Seven are we;
And two of us at Conway dwell,
And two are gone to sea.

«Two of us in the churchyard lie,
My sister and my brother;
And in the churchyard-cottage, I
Dwell near them with my mo-
ther».

«You say that two at Conway
dwell,
And two are gone to sea,
Yet ye are seven! — I pray you,
tell,
Sweet maid, how this may be?»

Then did the little maid reply,
«Seven boys and girls are we;
Two of us in the churchyard lie,
Beneath the churchyard tree.

›You run about, my little maid,
Your limbs they are·alive;
If two are in the churchyard laid,
Then ye are only five.»

«Their graves are green, they may
be seen,»
The little maid replied,
«Twelve steps or more from my
mother's door,
And they are side by side.

«My stockings there I often knit,
My kerchief there I hem,
And there upon the ground I sit —
I sit and sing to them.

«And often after sunset, sir,
When it is light and fair,
I take my little porringer,
And eat my supper there.

«The first that died was little Jane;
In bed she moaning lay,
Till God released her of her pain,
And then she went away.

«So in the churchyard she was
laid;
And all the summer dry,
Together round her grave we
play'd —
My brother John and I.

«And when the ground was white
with snow,
And I could run and slide,
My brother John was forced to
go —
And he lies by her side.›

«How many are you then,» said I,
If they two are in heaven?›
The little maiden did reply:
«O master! we are seven.»

«But they are dead; those two are dead!
· Their spirits are in heaven!»
'Twas throwing words away; for still
The little maid would have her will,
And said: «Náy, we are seven!»

Wordsworth.

----

17. The Bundle of Sticks.

A good old man, — no matter where
Whether in York or Lancashire,
Or on a hill, or in a dale,
It cannot much concern our tale, —
Had children very much like others,

Composed of sisters and of brothers;
In life he had not much to give,
Save his example how to live;
His luck was what his neighbours had;
For some were good, and some were bad;
When of their father death bereft 'em,
His good advice was all he left 'em.

This good old man who long had lain
Afflicted with disease and pain,
With difficulty drew his breath,
And felt the sure approach of death.
He still had lived an honest life,
Kind to his neighbour and his wife;
His practice good. his faith was sound,
He built his hopes on Scripture ground;
And knowing life hangs on a breath,
He always lived prepared for death;
He trusted God, nor feared to die —
May it be thus with you and I!
Nor let us hope to die content,
Unless our lives be wisely spent.

He called his children round his bed,
And with a feeble voice he said:
«Alas! Alas! my children dear,
l well perceive my end is near :
I suffer much, but kiss the rod,
And bow me to the will of God.
Yet ere from you I'm quite removed,
From you whom always I have loved,
I wish to give you all my blessing,
And leave you with a useful lesson;
That when I've left this world of care,
Each may his testimony bear,
How much my latest thoughts inclined
To prove me tender, good, and kind!
Observe that fagot on the ground,
With twisted hazel firmly bound».

The children turned their eyes that way,
And viewed the fagot as it lay?
But wondered what their father meant,
Who thus expounded his intent:
«I wish that all of you would take it,
And try if any one can break it».
Obedient to the good old man,
They all to try their strength began:
Now boy, now girl, now he, now she,
Applied the fagot to their knee;
They tugg'd and strain'd, and tried again,
But still they tugg'd and tried in vain!
In vain their skill and strength exerted;
The fagot every effort thwarted;
And when their labour vain they found,
They threw the fagot on the ground.

Again the good old man proceeded
To give the instructions which they needed:
«Untwist», says he, «the hazel bind,
And let the fagot be disjoined».
Then stick by stick, and twig by twig,
The little children and the big,
Following the words their father spoke,
Each sprig and spray they quickly broke:
«There, father!» all began to cry,
«I've broken mine! — and I! — and I!»
Replied the sire: «'Twas my intent
My family to represent:
While you are join'd in friendship's throng,
My dearest children, you'll be strong!
But if by quarrel and dispute,
You undermine affection's root,
And thus the strengthening cord divide,
Then will my children ill betide:
E'en beasts of prey in bands unite,
And kindly for each other fight;

And shall not Christian children be
Join'd in sweet links of amity?
If separate, you will each be weak;
Each like a single stick will break:
But if you're firm, and true and hearty,
The world, and all its spite, can't part ye».
The father having closed his lesson,
Proceeded to pronounce his blessing:
Embraced them all, then pray'd and sigh'd,
Look'd up and dropp'd his head — and died.

Application.

And thus, my countrymen, should you,
And I, and all, be firm and true;
If Christian faith and love combine us,
And sweet affection's cord entwine us,
We need encourage no dejection,
Secure in the Divine protection;
In prosperous days we'll bless our God,
And when He smites, we'll kiss the rod.

18. The Hare and the Tortoise.

In days of yore, when Time was young,
When birds conversed as well as sung,
When power of speech was not confined
To animals of human kind, —
A forward Hare, of swiftness vain,
The genius of the neighbouring plain,
Would oft deride the trudging crowd;
For geniuses are ever proud.
He'd boast his flight 'twere vain to follow,
For dog and horse, he'd beat them hollow: —
Nay, if he put forth all his strength,
Outstrip his brethren half a length.

A Tortoise heard his vain oration,
And vented thus his indignation:

«Oh Puss! it bodes thee dire disgrace,
When I defy thee to the race.
Come, 'tis a match; — nay, no denial;
I'll lay my shell upon the trial».
'Twas done and done — all fair — a bet —
Judges prepared, and distance set.
The scampering Hare outsripped the wind;
The creeping Tortoise lagged behind,
And scarce had passed a single pole,
When Puss had almost reached the goal.

«Friend Tortoise», quoth the jeering Hare,
«Your burden's more than you can bear;
To help your speed, it were as well
That I should ease you of your shell:
Jog on a little faster pr'ythee;
I'll take a nap, and then be with thee».
The Tortoise heard his taunting jeer,
But still resolved to presevere;
Still drawled along, as one might say,
Winning, like Fabius, by delay;
On to the goal securely crept,
While Puss, unknowing, soundly slept.

The bets were won; — the Hare awoke,
And thus the victor Tortoise spoke:
«Puss, though I own thy quicker parts,
Things are not always done by starts;
You may deride my awkward pace, —
But *slow* and *steady* wins the race».

                              Lloyd.

———————

19. Destruction of Sennacherib.

The Assyrian came down like the wolf on the fold,
And his cohorts were gleaming in purple and gold;
And the sheen of their spears was like stars on the sea,
When the blue wave rolls nightly on deep Galilee.

Like the leaves of the forest when summer is green,
That host with their banners at sunset were seen;
Like the leaves of the forest when autumn hath blown,
That host on the morrow lay withered and strown.

For the Angel of Death spread his wings on the blast,
And breathed on the face of the foe as he pass'd;
And the eyes of the sleepers wax'd deadly and chill,
And their hearts but once heaved, and for ever grew still!

And there lay the steed with his nostril all wide,
But through it there roll d not the breath of his pride;
And the foam of his gasping lay white on the turf,
And cold as the spray of the rock-beating surf.

And there lay the rider distorted and pale,
With the dew on his brow and the rust on his mail;
And the tents were all silent, the banners alone,
The lances unlifted, the trumpet unblown.

And the widows of Ashur are loud in their wail,
And the idols are broke in the temple of Baal;
And the might of the gentile, unsmote by the sword,
Hath melted like snow in the glance of the Lord. •

Byron.

---

20. Pity for Poor Africans.

I own I am shocked at the purchase of slaves,
And fear those who buy them and sell them are knaves;
What I hear of their hardships, their tortures and groans,
Is almost enough to draw pity from stones.

I pity them greatly, but I must be mum,
For how could we do without sugar and rum?
Especially sugar, so needful we see!
What! give up our desserts, our coffee, and tea!

Besides, if we do, the French, Dutch, and Danes
Will heartily thank us, no doubt, for our pains;
If we do not buy the poor creatures, they will,
And tortures and groans will be multiplied still.

If foreigners likewise would give up the trade,
Much more in behalf of your wish might be said:
But while they get riches by purchasing blacks,
Pray tell me why we may not also go snacks?

Your scruples and arguments bring to my mind
A story so pat, you may think it is coin'd,
On purpose to answer you, out of my mint;
But I can assure you, I saw it in-print.

A youngster at school, more sedate than the rest,
Had once his integrity put to the test;
His comrades had plotted an orchard to rob,
And asked him to go and assist in the job.

He was shock'd, Sir, like you, and answer'd «Oh no:
What! rob our good neighbour! I pray you don't go;
Besides, the man's poor, his orchard's his bread,
Then think of his children, for they must be fed».

«You speak very fine, and you look very grave,
But aples we want, and apples we'll have;
If you will go with us, you shall have a share,
If not, you shall have neither apple nor pear».

They spoke and Tom ponder'd — «I see they will go:
Poor Man! what a pity to injure him so! —
Poor Man! I would save him his fruit if I could,
But staying behind will do him no good.

If the matter depended alone upon me,
His apples might hang till they dropp'd from the tree;
But since they will take them, I think I'll go too,
He will lose none by me, though I get a few».

His scruples thus silenc'd, Tom felt more at ease,
And went with his comrades, the apples to seize;
He blam'd and protested, but join'd in the plan;
He shar'd in the plunder, but pitied the man,

Cowper.

21. My Heart's in the Highlands.

My heart's in the Highlands, my heart is not here;
My heart's in the Highlands, a chasing the deer,
Chasing the wild deer, and following the roe —
My heart's in the Highlands, wherever I go.
Farewell to the Highlands, farewell to the North,
The birthplace of valour, the country of worth!
Wherever I wander, wherever I rove,
The hills of the Highlands for ever I love.

Farewell to the mountains high covered with snow;
Farewell to the straths and green valleys below;
Farewell to the forests and wild-hanging woods;
Farewell to the torrents and wild-pouring floods!
My heart's in the Highlands, my heart is not here,
My heart's in the Highlands, a chasing the deer,
Chasing the wild deer, and following the roe —
My heart's in the Highlands, wherever I go.

(Robert Burns).

22. Rule Britannia.

When Britain first at Heaven's Command
Arose from out the azure main,
This was the charter of her land,
And guardian angels sang the strain:

Rule Britannia! Britannia rule the waves!
Britons never shall be slaves!

The nations not so blest as thee
Must in their turn to tyrants fall,

Whilst thou shalt flourish great
and free,
The dread and envy of them all.
Rule Britannia! etc.

Still more majestic shalt thou rise.
More dreadful from each foreign
stroke;
As the loud blast that tears the
skies
Serves but to root thy native oak.
Rule Britannia! etc.

Thee haughty tyrants ne'er shall
tame;
All their attempts to bend thee
down
Will but arouse thy generous flame
And work their woe and thy re-
nown.
Rule Britannia! etc.

To thee belongs the rural reign;
Thy cities shall with commerce
shine,
All thine shall be the subject main,
And every shore it circles thine!
Rule Britannia! etc.

The Muses, still with Freedom
found,
Shall to thy happy coast repair:
Blest Isle, with matchless beauty
crown'd,
And manly hearts to guard the
fair: —
Rule Britannia! Britannia rule the
waves!
Britons never shall be slaves!

(Thomson).

23. The Inchcape Rock.

No stir in the air, no stir in the sea,
The ship was still as she could be,
Her sails from heaven received no motion,
Her keel was steady in the ocean.

Without either sign or sound of their shock
The waves flow'd over the Inchcape Rock;
So little they rose, so little they fell,
They did not move the Inchcape Bell.

The Abbot of Aberbrothok
Had placed that bell on the Inchcape Rock;
On a buoy in the storm it floated and swung,
And over the waves its warning run.

When the Rock was hit by the surge's swell,
The mariners heard the warning bell;
And then they knew the perilous Rock,
And blest the Abbot of Aberbrothok.

The Sun in heaven was shining gay,
All things were joyful on that day;
The sea-birds scream'd as they wheel'd round,
And there was joyance in their sound.

The buoy of the Inchcape Bell was seen
A darker speck on the ocean green;
Sir Ralph the Rover walk'd his deck,
And he fixed his eye on the darker speck.

He felt the cheering power of spring,
It made him whistle, it made him sing;
His heart was mirthful to excess,
But the Rover's mirth was wickedness.

His eye was on the Inchcape float;
Quoth he, «My men. put out the boat,
And row me to the Inchcape Rock,
And I'll plague the Abbot of Aberbrothok».

The boat is lower'd, the boatmen row,
And to the Inchcape Rock they go;
Sir Ralph bent over from the boat,
And he cut the Bell from the Inchcape float.

Down sunk the Bell with a gurgling sound,
The bubles rose and burst around;
Quoth Sir Ralph, «The next who comes to the Rock
Wo'n't bless the Abbot of Aberbrothok».

Sir Ralph the Rover sail'd away,
He scour'd the seas for many a day;
And now grown rich with plunder'd store,
He steers his course for Scotland's shore.

So thick a haze o'erspreads the sky
They cannot see the Sun on high;
The wind hath blown a gale all day,
At evening it hath died away.

On the deck the Rover takes his stand,
So dark it is they see no land.
Quoth Sir Ralph, «It will be lighter soon,
For there is the dawn of the rising Moon».

«Canst hear», said one, «the breakers roar?
For methinks we should be near the shore».
«Now where we are I cannot tell,
But I wish I could hear the Inchcape Bell!

They hear no sound, the swell is strong;
Though the wind hath fallen they drift along,
Till the vessel strikes with a shivering shock, —
«Oh Christ! it is the Inchcape Rock!»

Sir Ralph the Rover tore his hair;
He curst himself in his despair;
The waves rush in on every side,
The ship is sinking beneath the tide.

But even in his dying fear
One dreadful sound could the Rover hear,
A sound as if with the Inchcape Bell,
The Devil below was ringing his knell.

                              (Robert Southey).

---

24. Sir Lancelot du Lake.

When Arthur first in court began,
And was approved king,
By force of arms great victories
                              wan,
And conquest home did bring.

Then into England straight he
                              came,
Where fifty good and able
Knights then resorted unto him,
And were of his Round table:

And he had justs and turnaments,
Whereto were many prest,
Wherein these knights did far
excell
And eke surmount the rest.

But one Sir Lancelot du Lake,
Who was approved well,
He for his deeds and feats of arms
All others did excell.

When he had rested him a while,
In play, and game, and sport,
He said he would go prove himself
In some adventurous sort.

He armed rode in a forest wide,
And.met a damsel fair,
Who told him of adventures great,
Whereto he gave great care.

Such would I find, quoth Lancelot,
For that cause came I hither.
Thou seemst, quoth she, a knight
full good,
And I will bring thee thither.

Whereas a mighty knight doth
dwell,
That now is of great fame :
Therefore tell me what wight thou
art,
And what may be thy name.

« My name is Lancelot du Lake. »
Quoth she, it likes me then :
Here dwells a knight who never
was
Yet matched with any man:

Who has in prison threescore
knights
And four, that he did wound;
Knights of King Arthur's court
they be,
And of his Table Round.

She brought him to a river side,
And also to a tree,
Whereon a copper bason hung,
And many shields to see.

He struck so hard, the bason broke;
And Tarquin soon he spied :
Who drove a horse before him fast,
Whereon a knight lay tied.

Sir knight, then said Sir Lancelot,
Bring me that horse-load hi-
ther,
And lay him down, and let him
rest ;
We'll try our force together:

For, as I understand, thou hast,
So far as thou art able,
Done great despite and shame unto
The knights of the Round Table.

If thou be of the Table Round,
Quoth Tarquin speedily,
Both thee and all thy fellowship
I utterly defy.

That's over much, quoth Lancelot
though,
Defend thee by and by.
They set their spurs unto their
steeds,
And each at other fly.

They couched their spears, (their
    horses ran,
As though there had been
    thunder)
And struck them each immidst
    their shields,
Wherewith they broke in sun-
    der.

Their horses' backs brake under
    them,
The knights were both astound:
To avoid their horses they made
    haste
And light upon the ground.

They took them to their shields
    full fast,
Their swords they drew out
    then,
With mighty strokes most eagerly
Each at the other ran.

They wounded were, and bled full
    sore,
They both for breath did stand,
And leaning on their swords awhile,
Quoth Tarquin, Hold thy hand,

And tell to me what I shall ask.
Say on, quoth Lancelot though.
Thou art, quoth Tarquin, the best
    knight
That ever I did know;

And like a knight that I did hate:
So that thou be not he,
I will deliver all the rest,
And eke accord with thee.

That is well said, quoth Lancelot:
But sith it must be so,
What knight is that thou hatest
    thus?
I pray thee to me show.

His name is Lancelot du Lake
He slew my brother dear;
Him I suspect of all the rest:
I would I had him here.

Thy wish thou hast, but yet un-
    known,
I am Lancelot du Lake,
Now knight of Arthur's Table
    Round,
King Hand's son of Benwake;

And I desire thee do thy worst.
Ho, ho, quoth Tarquin though,
One of us two shall end our lives
Before that we do go.

If thou be Lancelot du Lake,
Then welcome shalt thou be:
Wherefore see thou thyself defend,
For now defy I thee.

They buckled then together so,
Like unto wild boars rashing
And with their swords and shields
    they ran
At one another slashing:

The ground besprinkled was with
    blood:
Tarquin began to yield;
For he gave back for weariness,
And low did bear his shield.

This soon Sir Lancelot espied,
  He leapt upon him then,
He pull'd him down upon his
              knee,
And, rushing off his helm,

Forthwith he struck his neck in two,
  And, when be had so done,
From prison threescore knights
             and four
Delivered every one.

25. King Leir and His Three Daughters.

King Leir once ruled in this land
  With princely power and peace;
And had all things with heart's content,
  That might his joys increase.
Amongst those things that nature gave,
  Three daughters fair had he,
So princely seeming beautiful,
  As fairer could not be.

So on a time it pleased the king
  A question thus to move,
Which of his daughters to his grace
  Could show the dearest love:
For to my age you bring content,
  Quoth he, then let me hear,
Which of you three in plighted troth
  The kindest will appear.

To whom the eldest thus began:
  Dear father, mind, quoth she,
Before your face, to do you good,
  My blood shall render'd be:
And for your sake my bleeding heart
  Shall here be cut in twain,
Ere that I see your reverend age
  The smallest grief sustain.

And so will I, the second said,
  Dear father, for your sake;

The worst of all extremities
   I'll gently undertake:
And serve your highness night and day
   With diligence and love;
That sweet content and quietness
   Discomforts may remove.

In doing so, you glad my soul,
   The aged king reply'd:
But what sayst thou, my youngest girl,
   How is thy love ally'd?
My love, quoth young Cordelia then,
   Which to your grace I owe,
Shall be the duty of a child,
   And that is all I'll show.

And wilt thou show no more, quoth he,
   Than doth thy duty bind?
I well perceive thy love is small,
   When as no more I find.
Henceforth I banish thee my court,
   Thou art no child of mine;
Nor any part of this my realm
   By favour shall be thine.

Thy elder sisters' loves are more
   Than well I can demand,
To whom I equally bestow
   My kingdom and my land,
My pompal state and all my goods,
   That lovingly I may
With those thy sisters be maintained
   Until my dying day.

Thus flattering speeches won renown,
   By these two sisters here;
The third had causeless banishment,
   Yet was her love more dear:

For poor Cordelia patiently
   Went wandering up and down,
Unhelp'd, unpity'd, gentle maid,
   Through many an English town.

Until at last in famous France
   She gentler fortunes found;
Though poor and bare, yet she was deem'd
   The fairest on the ground:
Where when the king her virtues heard,
   And this fair lady seen,
With full consent of all his court.
   He made his wife and queen.

Her father King Leir this while
   With his two daughters staid:
Forgetful of their promised loves,
   Full soon the same decay'd;
And living in Queen Ragan's court,
   The eldest of the twain,
She took from him his chiefest means,
   And most of all his train.

For whereas twenty men were wont
   To wait with bended knee:
She gave allowance but to ten,
   And after scarce to three;
Nay, one she thought too much for him;
   So took she all away;
In hope that in her court, good king,
   He would no longer stay.

Am I rewarded thus, quoth he,
   In giving all I have
Unto my children, and to beg
   For what I lately gave?
I'll go unto my Gonorell:
   My second child, I know,

Will be more kind and pitiful,
And will relieve my woe.

Full fast he hies then to her court;
Where when she heard his moan
Return'd him answer, That she griev'd,
That all his means were gone:
But no way could relieve his wants;
Yet if that he would stay
Within her kitchen, he should have
What scullions gave away.

When he had heard, with bitter tears,
He made his answer then;
In what I did let me be made
Example to all men.
I will return again, quoth he,
Unto my Ragan's court;
She will not use me thus, I hope,
But in a kinder sort.

Where when he came, she gave command
To drive him thence away:
When he was well within her court,
She said, he would not stay.
Then back again to Gonorell
The woeful king did hie,
That in her kitchen he might have
What scullion boys set by.

But there of that he was deny'd
Which she had promised late:
For once refusing, he should not
Come after to her gate.
Thus twixt his daughters, for relief
He wander'd up and down;
Being glad to feed on beggars' food,
That lately wore a crown.

And calling to remembrance then
  His youngest daughter's words,
That said the duty of a child
  Was all that love affords:
But doubting to repair to her
  Whom he had banish'd so,
Grew frantic mad; for in his mind
  He bore the wounds of woe:

Which made him rend his milk white locks,
  And tresses from his head,
And all with blood bestain his cheeks,
  With age and honour spread.
To hills and woods and watry founts
  He made his hourly moan,
Till hills and woods and senseless things
  Did seem to sigh and groan.

Even thus possest with discontents,
  He passed o'er to France,
In hopes from fair Cordelia there,
  To find some gentler chance;
Most virtuous dame! which when she heard
  Of this her father's grief,
As duty bound, she quickly sent
  Him comfort and relief:

And by a train of noble peers,
  In brave and gallant sort,
She gave in charge he should be brought
  To Aganippus' court;
Whose royal king, with noble mind
  So freely gave consent,
To muster up his knights at arms,
  To fame and courage bent.

And so to England came with speed,
  To repossess King Leir,

And drive his daughters from their thrones
  By his Cordelia dear.
Where she, true-hearted noble queen,
  Was in the battle slain;
Yet he good King, in his old days,
  Possest his crown again.

But when he heard Cordelia's death,
  Who died indeed for love
Of her dear father, in whose cause
  She did this·battle move,
He swooning fell upon her breast,
  From whence he never parted;
But on her bosom left his life,
  That was so truly hearted.

The lords and nobles when they saw
  The end of these events,
The other sisters nnto death
  They doomed by consents;
And being dead their crowns they left
  Unto the next of kin:
Thus have you seen the fall of pride,
  And disobedient sin.

---

26. King John and the Abbot of Canterbury.

An ancient story I'll tell you anon
Of a notable prince that was called King John;
And he ruled England with main and with might,
For he did great wrong, and maintain'd little right.

And I'll tell you a story, a story so merry,
Concerning the Abbot at Canterbury;
How for his house-keeping and high renown
They rode post for him to fair London town.

A hundred men, the king did hear say,   .
The abbot kept in his house every day;
And fifty gold chains *), without any doubt,
In velvet coats waited the abbot about.

How now, father abbot, I hear it of thee,
Thou keepest a far better house than me,
And for thy house-keeping and great renown,
I fear thou workst treason against my crown.

My liege, quo' the abbot, I would it were known,
I never spend nothing but what is my own;
And I trust, your Grace will do me no dear
For spending of my own true gotten gear.

Yes, yes, father abbot, thy fault is so high,
And now for the same thou needs must die;
For except thou canst answer me questions three,
Thy head shall be smitten from thy body.

And first, quo' the king, when I'm in this stead,
With my crown of gold so fair on my head,
Among all my liege-men so noble of birth,
Thou must tell me to one penny what I am worth.

Secondly tell me, without any doubt,
How soon I may ride the whole world about.
And at the third question thou must not shrink,
But tell me here truly what I do think.

O, these are hard questions for my shallow wit,
Nor I cannot answer your Grace as yet:
But if you will give me but three weeks' space,
I'll do my endeavour to answer your Grace.

---

*) Gold chains=vassals decorated with gold chains.

Now three weeks' space to thee will I give,
And that is the longest time thou hast to live;
For if thou dost not answer my questions three,
Thy lands and thy livings are forfeit to me.

Away rode the abbot all sad at that word,
And he rode to Cambridge and Oxenford;
But never a doctor there was so wise,
That could with his learning an answer devise..

Then home rode the abbot of comfort so cold,
And he met his shepherd a going to fold :
How now, my lord abbot, you are welcome home;
What news do you bring us from good King John?

Sad news, sad news, shepherd, I must give,
That I have but three days more to live.
For if I do not answer him questions three,
My head will be smitten from my body.

The first is to tell him there in his stead,
With his crown of gold so fair on his head,
Among all his liege-men, so noble of birth,
To within one penny of what he is worth.

The second, to tell him without any doubt,
How soon he may ride this world about;
And at the third question I must not shrink,
But tell him there truly what he does think.

Now cheer up, sir abbot ; did you never hear yet,
That a fool he may learn a wise man wit?
Lend me horse, and serving men, and your apparel,
And I'll ride to London to answer your quarrel.

Nay, frown not, if it hath been told unto me,
I am like your lordship, as ever may be;
And if you will but lend me your gown,
There is none shall know us at fair London town.

Now horses and serving-men thou shalt have,
With sumptuous array most gallant and brave;
With crosier, and mitre, and rochet, and cope,
Fit to appear 'fore our father the pope.

Now welcome, sir abbot, the king he did say,
'Tis well thou'rt come back to keep thy day;
For if thou canst answer my questions three,
Thy life and thy living both saved shall be.

And first, when thou seest me here in this stead,
With my crown of gold so fair on my head,
Among all my liege-men so noble of birth,
Tell me to one penny what I am worth.

For thirty pence our Saviour was sold
Among the false Jews, as I have been told;
And twenty-nine is the worth of thee,
For I think thou art one penny worser than he.

The king he laughed, and swore by St. Bittel,
I did not think I had been worth so little! —
Now secondly tell me, without any doubt,
How soon I may ride this whole world about.

You must rise with the sun, and ride with the same,
Until the next morning he riseth again;
And then your Grace need not make any doubt,
But in twenty-four hours you'll ride it about.

The king he laughed, and swore by St. John,
I did not think, it could be gone *) so soon! —
Now from the third question thou must not shrink,
But tell me here truly what I do think.

Yea, that shall I do, and make your Grace merry:
You think I'm the abbot of Canterbury; ·

---

*) Gone = gone about.

But I'm his poor shepherd, as plain you may see,
That am come to beg pardon for him and for me.

The king he laughed, and swore by the mass:
I'll make thee lord abbot this day in his place! —
Now nay, my liege, be not in such speed,
For alack! I can neither write nor read.

Four nobles a week then I will give thee,
For this merry jest thou hast shown unto me;
And tell the old abbot, when thou comest home,
Thou hast brought him a pardon from good King John.

(Percy's Reliques)

---

27. Chevy-Chase.

God prosper long our noble king,
Our lives and safeties all;
A woful hunting once there did
In Chevy-Chase befall.

To drive the deer with hound and
horn,
Earl Percy took his way;
The child may rue that is unborn,
The hunting of that day.

The stout Earl of Northumberland
A vow to God did make,
His pleasure in the Scottish woods
Three summer's day to take;

The chiefest harts in Chevy-Chase
To kill and bear away.
These tidings to Earl Douglas came,
In Scotland where he lay:

Who sent Earl Percy present word,
He would prevent his sport.

The English Earl, not fearing that,
Did to the woods resort.

With fifteen hundred bow-men
bold,
All chosen men of might,
Who knew full well in time of need
To aim their shafts aright.

The gallant grey hounds swiftly ran,
To chase the fallow deer :
On Monday they began to hunt,
Ere daylight did appear;

And long before high noon they had
An hundred fat bucks slain;
Then having dined the drovers went
To rouse the deer again.

The bow-men muster'd on the hills,
Well able to endure;
Their backsides all, with special
care
That day were guarded sure.

The hounds ran swiftly through
the woods
The nimble deer to take,
That with their cries the hills and
dales
An echo shrill did make.

Lord Percy to the quarry went,
To view the slaughter'd deer;
Quoth he, Earl Douglas promised
This day to meet me here:

But if I thought he would not come,
No longer would I stay.
With that a brave young gentleman
Thus to the Earl did say:

Lo, yonder doeth Earl Douglas come.
His men in armour bright;
Full twenty hundred Scottish spears
All marching in our sight;

All men of pleasant Tivydale,
Fast by the river Tweed:
O cease your sports, Earl Percy
said,
And take your bows with speed:

And now with me, my countrymen,
Your courage forth advance;
For there was never champion yet,
In Scotland or in France,

That ever did on horseback come,
But if my hap it were,
I durst encounter man for man,
With him to break a spear.

Earl Douglas on his milk-white
steed,

Most like a baron bold,
Rode foremost of his company,
Whose armour shone like gold.

Show me, said he, whose men
you be
That hunt so boldly here,
That, without my consent, do chase,
And kill my fallow deer.

The first man that did answer
make,
Was noble Percy he;
Who said, We list not to declare,
Nor show whose men we be:

Yet we will spend our dearest blood
Thy chiefest harts to slay.
Then Douglas swore a solem oath,
And thus in rage did say,

Ere thus I will outbraved be,
One of us two shall die:
I know thee well, an earl thou art;
Lord Percy, so am I.

But trust me, Percy, pity it were,
And great offence to kill
Any of these our guiltless men,
For they have done no ill.

Let thou and I the battle try,
And set our men aside.
Accurst be he, Earl Percy said,
By whom this is denied.

Then stepped a gallant squire forth,
Witherington was his name,
Who said, I would not have it told
To Henry our king for shame,

That e'er my captain fought on
foot,
And I stood looking on ;
You bo two earls, said Wither-
ington,
And I a squire alone:

I'll do the best that do I may,
While I have power to stand:
While I have power to wield my
sword,
I'll fight with heart and hand.

Our English archers bent their bows
Their hearts were good and true;
At the first flight of arrows sent,
Full fourscore Scots they slew.

They closed full fast on every side,
No slackness there was found;
And many a gallant gentleman
Lay gasping on the ground.

O dear! it was a grief to see,
And likewise for to hear,
The cries of men lying in their gore,
And scatter'd here and there.

This fight did last from break of
day
Till setting of the sun ;
For when they rang the evening-
bell,
The battle scarce was done.

With stout Earl Percy there was
slain
Sir John of Egerton,
Sir Robert Ratcliff, and Sir John,
Sir James that bold baron:

And with Sir George and stout Sir
James,
Both knights of good account,
Good Sir Ralph Raby there was
slain
Whose prowess did surmount.

For Witherington needs must I
wail,
As one in doleful dumps;
For when his legs were smitten off,
He fought upon his stumps.

Of fifteen hundred Englishmen,
Went home but fifty three;
The rest was slain in Chevy-Chase,
Under the greenwood tree.

Next day did many widows come,
Their husbands to bewail;
They washed their wounds in
brinish tears,
But all would not prevail.

Their bodies bathed in purple gore,
They bare with them away:
They kissed them dead a thousand
times,
Ere they were clad in clay.

God save our king, and bless this
land
With plenty, joy, and peace ;

And grant henceforth, that foul
debate
'Twixt noblemen may cease.

---

28. The diverting History of John Gilpin,

showing that he went farther than he intended, and came safe home again.

John Gilpin was a citizen
Of credit and renown,
A train-band captain eke was he
Of famous London town.

John Gilpin's spouse said to her
dear,
Though wedded we have been
These twice ten tedious years, yet
we
No holiday have seen.

To-morrow is our wedding-day,
And we will then repair
Unto the Bell at Edmonton
All in a chaise and pair.

My sister and my sister's child,
Myself and children three,
Will fill the chaise: so you must
ride
On horseback after we.

He soon replied, I do admire
Of womankind but one,
And you are she, my dearest dear,
Therefore it shall be done.

I am a linen-draper bold,
As all the world doth know,

And my good friend, the calendrer,
Will lend his horse to go.

Quoth Mrs. Gilpin, That's well
said;
And for that wine is dear,
We will be furnished with our own,
Which is both bright and clear.

John Gilpin kissed his loving wife,
O'erjoyed was he to find
That, though on pleasure she was
bent,
She had a frugal mind.

The morning came, the chaise was
brought,
But yet was not allowed
To drive up to the door, lest all
Should say that he was proud.

So three doors off the chaise was
stayed,
Where they did all get in;
Six precious souls, and all agog
To dash through thick and thin.

Smack went the whip, round went
the wheels,
Were never folk so glad ;

The stones did rattle underneath,
　As if Cheapside were mad.

John Gilpin at his horse's side
　Seized fast the flowing mane,
And up he got, in haste to ride,
　But soon came down again;

For saddle-tree scarce reached
　　　　had he,
　His journey to begin,
When, turning round his head,
　　　　he saw
　Three customers come in.

So down he came; for loss of time,
　Although it grieved him sore,
Yet loss of pence, full well he
　　　　knew,
　Would trouble him much more.

'Twas long before the customers
　Were suited to their mind,
When Betty screaming came down
　　　　stairs,
　«The wine is left behind!»

Good lack! quoth he — yet bring
　　　　it me,
　My leathern belt likewise,
In which I bear my trusty sword,
　When I do exercise.

Now Mrs. Gilpin (careful soul!)
　Had two stone-bottles found,
To hold the liquor that she loved,
　And keep it safe and sound.

Each bottle had a curling ear,
　Through which the belt he drew,

And hung a bottle on each side
　To make his balance true.

Then over all that he might be
　Equipped from top to toe,
His long red cloak, well brush-
　　　　ed and neat,
He manfully did throw.

Now see him mounted once again
　Upon his nimble steed,
Full slowly pacing o'er the stones,
　With caution and good heed.

But finding soon a smoother road
　Beneath his well-shod feet,
The snorting beast began to trot,
　Which galled him in his seat.

So, fair and softly, John, he cried,
　But John he cried in vain;
That trot became a gallop soon,
　In spite of curb and rein.

So stooping down, as needs he must
　Who cannot sit upright,
He grasped the mane with both his
　　　　hands,
　And eke with all his might.

His horse, who never in that sort
　Had handled been before,
What thing upon his back had got
　Did wonder more and more.

Away went Gilpin, neck or nought;
　Away went hat and wig;
He little dreamt, when he set out,
　Of running such a rig.

The wind did blow, the cloak did
                    fly,
Like streamer long and gay,
Till, loop and button failing both,
At last it flew away.

Then might all people well discern
The bottles he had slung;
A bottle swinging at each side,
As hath been said or sung.

The dogs did bark, the children
                    screamed,
Up flew the windows all;
And every soul cried out, Well
                    done!
As loud as he could bawl.

Away went Gilpin — who but he?
His fame soon spread around,
He carries weight! he rides a race!
'Tis for a thousand pound!

And still, as fast as he drew near,
'Twas wonderful to view
How in a trice the turnpike-men
Their gates wide open threw.

And now, as he went bowing down
His reeking head full low,
The bottles twain behind his back
Were shattered at a blow.

Down ran the wine into the road,
Most piteous to be seen,
Which made his horse's flanks to
                    smoke,
As they had basted been.   ●

But still he seemed to carry weight,
With leathern girdle braced;
For all might see the bottle-necks
Still dangling at his waist.

Thus all through merry Islington
These gambols he did play,
Until he came unto the Wash
At Edmonton so gay.

And there he threw the Wash about
On both sides of the way,
Just like unto a trundling mop,
Or a wild goose at play.

At Edmonton his loving wife
From the balcony spied
Her tender husband, wondering
                    much
To see how he did ride.

Stop, stop, John Gilpin!—Here's
                    the house —
They all aloud did cry;
The dinner waits, and we are
                    tired:
Said Gilpin — So am I!

But yet his horse was not a whit
Inclined to tarry there;
For why? — his owner had a house
Full ten miles off at Ware.

So like an arrow swift he flew.
Shot by an archer strong;
So did he fly — which brings me to
The middle of my song.

Away went Gilpin out of breath,
And sore against his will,

Till at his friend the calendrer's
His horse at last stood still.

The calendrer, amazed to see
His neighbour in such trim,
Laid down his pipe, flew to the gate,
And thus accosted him:

What news? what news? your
tidings tell;
Tell me you must and shall —
Say, why bare-headed you are
come?
Or why you come at all?

Now Gilpin had a pleasant wit,
And loved a timely joke;
And thus unto the calendrer
In merry guise he spoke:

I came because your horse would
come;
And if I well forebode,
My hat and wig will soon be here,
They are upon the road.

The calendrer, right glad to find
His friend in merry pin,
Returned him not a single word,
But to the house went in;

When straight he came with hat
and wig;
A wig that flowed behind,
A hat not much the worse for wear,
Each comely in its kind.

He held them up, and in his turn
Thus showed his ready wit,

My head is twice as big as yours,
They therefore needs must fit.

But let me scrape the dirt away,
That hangs upon your face;
And stop and eat, for well you may
Be in a hungry case.

Said John—it is my wedding-day,
And all the world would stare,
If wife should dine at Edmonton,
And I should dine at Ware.

So turning to his horse, he said,
I am in haste to dine;
'Twas for your pleasure I came
here,
You shall go back for mine.

Ah luckless speech, and bootless
boast!
For which he paid full dear;
For, while he spake, a braying ass
Did sing most loud and clear;

Whereat his horse did snort, as he
Had heard a lion roar,
And galloped off with all his might,
As he had done before.

Away went Gilpin, and away
Went Gilpin's hat and wig:
He lost them sooner than at first,
For why? — They were too big.

Now Mrs. Gilpin, when she saw
Her husband posting down
Into the country far away,
She pulled out half a crown;

And thus unto the youth she said,
That drove them to the Bell,
This shall be yours, when you
bring back
My husband safe and well.

The youth did ride, and soon did
meet
John coming back amain;
Whom in a trice he tried to stop,
By catching at his rein:

But not performing what he meant,
And gladly would have done,
The frighted steed he frighted more,
And made him faster run.

Away went Gilpin, and away
Went post-boy at his heels,
The post-boy's horse right glad to
miss
The lumbering of the wheels.

Six gentlemen upon the road
Thus seeing Gilpin fly,

With post-boy scampering in the
rear,
They raised the hue and cry: —

Stop thief! Stop thief! — a high-
wayman!
Not one of them was mute;
And all and each that passed that way
Did join in the pursuit.

And now the turnpike-gates again
Flew open in short space;
The toll men thinking as before
That Gilpin rode a race.

And so he did, and won it too,
For he got first to town;
Nor stopped till where he had
got up
. He did again get down.

Now let us sing, long live the king,
And Gilpin, long live he;
And when he next doth ride abroad,
May I be there to see!

---

29. The Cataract of Lodore.

Described in rhymes for the nursery.

«How does the Water
Come down at Lodore?»
My little boy ask'd me
Thus, once on a time;
And moreover he task'd me
To tell him in rhyme.
Anon at the word,

There first came one daughter,
And then came another,
To second and third
The request of their brother,
And to hear how the water
Comes down at Lodore,
With its rush and its roar,
As many a time
They had seen it before.
So I told them in rhyme,
For of rhymes I had store:
And 'twas in my vocation
For their recreation
That so I should sing;
Because I was Laureate
To them and the King.

From its sources which well
In the Tarn on the fell;
From its fountains
In the mountains,
Its rills and its gills;
Through moss and through brake,
It runs and it creeps
For a while, till it sleeps
In its own little Lake.
And thence at departing,
Awakening and starting,
It runs through the reeds
And away it proceeds,
Through meadow and glade,
In sun and in shade,
And through the wood-shelter,
Among crags in its flurry,
Helter-skelter,
Hurry-skurry.
Here it comes sparkling,
And there it lies darkling;

Now smoaking and frothing
It's tumult and wrath in,
  Till in this rapid race
  On which it is bent,
  ¯ It reaches the place
  Of its steep descent.

  The Cataract strong
  Then plunges along,
   Striking and raging ˉ
   As if a war waging
  Its caverns and rocks among:
    Rising and leaping,
   Sinking and creeping,
   Swelling and sweeping,
  Showering and springing,
    Flying and flinging,
 Writhing and ringing,
 Eddying and whisking,
 Spouting and frisking,
 Turning and twisting,
   Around and around
 With endless rebound!
 Smiting and fighting,
 A sight to delight in;
 Confounding, astounding,
Dizzying and deafening the ear with its sound.

Collecting, projecting,
Receding and speeding,
And shocking and rocking,
And darting and parting,
And threading and spreading,
And whizzing and hissing,
And dripping and skipping,
And hitting and splitting,
And shining and twining,
And rattling, and battling,

And shaking and quaking,
And pouring and roaring,
And waving and raving,
And tossing and crossing,
And flowing and going,
And running and stunning,
And foaming and roaming,
And dinning and spinning,
And dropping and hopping,
And working and jerking,
And guggling and struggling,
And heaving and cleaving,
And moaning and groaning;

And glittering and frittering,
And gathering and feathering,
And whitening and brightening,
And quivering and shivering,
And hurrying and skurrying,
And thundering and floundering;

Dividing and gliding and sliding,
And falling and brawling and sprawling,
And driving and riving and striving,
And sprinkling and twinkling and wrinkling,
And sounding and bounding and rounding,
And bubbling and troubling and doubling,
And grumbling and rumbling and tumbling,
And clattering and battering and shattering,

Retreating and beating and meeting and sheeting,
Delaying and straying and playing and spraying,
Advancing and prancing and glancing and dancing,
Recoiling, turmoiling and toiling and boiling,
And gleaming and streaming and steaming and beaming,
And rushing and flushing and brushing and gushing,
And flapping and rapping and clapping and slapping,
And curling and whirling and purling and twirling,

And thumping and plumping and bumping and jumping,
And dashing and flashing and splashing and clashing;

And so never ending, but always descending,
Sounds and motions for ever and ever are blending,
All at once and all o'er, with a mighty uproar,
And this way the Water comes down at Lodore.

(Southey).

СЛОВАРЬ.

СЛОВАРЬ

КЪ ПЕРВЫМЪ 10 СТРАНИЦАМЪ.

Elementary Sentences.
Легкія Предложенія.

I.

There is a knock, стучатся.
at the door, въ дверь.
somebody, нѣкто.
Knocks, стучится.
go, пойдите.
and, и.
see, посмотрите.
who it is, кто это.
open, отворите.
the door, дверь.
It is Mr. B., это г. Б.
Good morning to you, желаю Вамъ добраго утра.
I am very glad, я очень радъ.
to see you, Васъ видѣть.
I am very happy, я очень счастливъ.
I have not seen you this age, уже цѣлый вѣкъ какъ я Васъ не видалъ.
You are quite a stranger, Вы точно чужой человѣкъ.

pray, пожалуйста.
be seated, садитесь.
do, pray, пожалуйста прошу Васъ.
sit down, садитесь.
Please to sit down, пожалуйста садитесь.
give, подайте.
a chair, стулъ.
to Mr. B., г-ну Б.
fetch, принесите.
a seat, стулъ.
will you stay, не угодно ли Вамъ остаться.
and take dinner with us, и пообѣдать съ нами.
I cannot stay, я не могу остаться.
I only came in to ask how you did, я зашелъ только для того чтобъ спросить какъ Вы поживаете.
I must go, я долженъ

отправиться.
You are in a great hurry, Вы очень торопитесь.
I have a good many things to do, у меня очень много дѣлъ.
Surely you can stay a little longer, Вы конечно можете остаться подольше.
I have many places to call at, еще много мѣстъ, куда я долженъ зайти.
I will stay, я останусь.
longer, долѣе.
another time, другой разъ.
I thank you, благодарю Васъ.
for your visit, за Вашъ визитъ.
I hope, я надѣюсь.
I shall see you soon again, что я вскорѣ опять увижу Васъ.

II.

Have you breakfasted? позавтракали ли Вы?
not yet, нѣтъ еще.

you come just in time, Вы пришли совершенно во время.

You will breakfast, Вы позавтракаете.
breakfast, завтракъ (ут-

40

рекій кофе или чай).
is ready, (есть) готовъ.
come, придите.
to breakfast, завтракать.
Do you drink tea or coffee?
чего Вы желаете, чаю
или кофе?
Would you prefer choco-
late?, нехотите ли луч-
ше шеколаду?
I prefer, я предпочитаю.
coffee, кофе.
What shall I offer you?,
что я могу предложить
Вамъ.

here are, вотъ.
rolls, булки.
toast, поджареный хлѣбъ.
Which do you like best?,
что Вы больше любите?
I will take, я возьму.
some toast, (нѣсколько)
поджаренаго хлѣба.
How do you like?, какъ
Вамъ нравится?
is as you like it?, Вамъ
по вкусу.
strong, крѣпкій.
enough, довольно.

it is rather, онъ (есть)
скорѣе.
too, слишкомъ.
excellent, превосходный.
sweet, сладкій.
not, не.
clear, чистый.
if, если.
I beg you will say so, то
прошу мнѣ сказать
объ этомъ.

III.

What time do we dine?,
въ какое время будемъ
мы обѣдать?
to-day, сегодня.
we are to dine, мы дол-
жны обѣдать.
at four o'clock, въ че-
тыре часа.
dinner, обѣдъ.
will not be, не будетъ.
before five o'clock, ранѣе
пяти часовъ.
Is any one coming, бу-
детъ ли кто нибудь.
to, къ.
besides, сверхъ, кромѣ.
our, нашъ.

own, собственный.
family, семейство.
Do you expect?, ожидае-
те ли Вы?
company, гости.
the weather, погода.
fine, прекрасный.
has promised, обѣщался.
Have you given orders
for?, заказали ли Вы?
What have you ordered
for dinner?, что Вы за-
казали къ обѣду?
What have we got?, что
у насъ будетъ?
Have you sent?, послали
ли Вы?

for any fish, за рыбой.
Shall we have?, будетъ
ли у насъ?
I could not, я не могъ.
to get, достать.
there was not, не было.
in the market, на рынкѣ.
I fear, я боюсь.
we shall have, что у насъ
будетъ.
plain, простой.
We must manage as well
as we can, намъ на-
добно устроиться по
возможности.

IV.

What shall I help you to?,
что я могу Вамъ пред-
ложить?
would you like?, не угод-
но ли Вамъ?
to taste, попробовать.
the soup, супъ.
some soup, супу.
I will trouble you for, я
попрошу у Васъ.
a little, немного.
beef, говядина.
It looks very nice, на
видъ она очень хоро-
ша.

What part, какая часть.
well done, довольно жа-
реный.
under done, не дожаре-
ный.
rather, скорѣе; немного.
if you please, если Вамъ
угодно; пожалуйста.
Have I helped you as you
like?, довольны ли Вы
тѣмъ что я Вамъ по-
далъ?
It, оно это.
Will you let me?, не по-
зволите ли Вы мнѣ?

send you?, послать Вамъ?
a piece, кусокъ.
of this pie, этого пирож-
наго.
of that pudding, того пу-
динга.
Try them both, попро-
буйте того и другаго.
you had better, Вы бы
лучше.
some of both, (немного)
того и другаго.
a slice, (тоненькій) ку-
сокъ.
mutton, баранина.

Do you choose?, желаете ли Вы?
any of the fat, (немного) жиру.

I am not very fond of fat, я не большой охотникъ до жиру.
of the lean, любовины.

this, этотъ.
will suit your taste, будетъ Вамъ по вкусу.

V.

You have no gravy, у Васъ нѣтъ подливки.
sauce, соусъ.
on, на.
plate, тарелка.
I have plenty, у меня вдоволь.
as much as I wish for, столько сколько я желаю.
boiled, вареный.
veal, телятина.
delightful, отличный.
remarkably, замѣчательно, особенно.

fine, прекрасный.
remarkably fine, преотличный, славный.
meat, мясо.
vegetables, зелень.
here is, вотъ.
spinage, шпинатъ.
brocoli, броколь.
these are new potatoes, это свѣжая картофель.
peas, горохъ.
cauliflower, цвѣтная капуста.
asparagus, спаржа.
extremely, чрезвычайно.

tender, нѣжный.
sweet, сладкій.
do you eat?, ѣдите ли Вы, охотникъ ли Вы до?
salad, салатъ.
both — and, и—и.
carrots, морковь.
turnips, рѣпы.
have you, есть ли у Васъ.
bread, хлѣбъ.
brown bread, черный хлѣбъ.
white, бѣлый.
home-made, домашняго печенія.

VI.

Allow me, позвольте мнѣ.
leg of mutton, задняя четверть баранины.
full, полный.
tart, тортъ.
ham, ветчина, окорокъ.
delicious, превкусный.
I will thank you for, я . попрошу у Васъ.
small, малый.
just, только чтобъ.
Give me, дайте мнѣ.
but, только.
bit, кусочекъ.

appetite, апетитъ.
nothing, ничего.
I beg your pardon, извините.
I have eaten very heartily, я порядкомъ поѣлъ.
partridge, куропатка.
cannot, не можетъ.
hurt you, повредить Вамъ.
plum, сливный.
give, давать.
wing, крыло.
leg, нога.

you have helped me, Вы наложили мнѣ.
too, слишкомъ.
plentifully, достаточно, много.
Will you please to cut it in two, пожалуйста, разрѣжьте это пополамъ.
half, половина.
sufficient, достаточный.
for me, для меня.

VII.

Have you carried in?, принесли ли Вы?
the tea things, чайный приборъ.
every thing, все.
the table, столъ.
Does the water boil?, кипитъ ли вода?
tea, чай.
quite, совершенно.
They are waiting for you,

Васъ ждутъ.
I am coming, я сейчасъ буду.
I will follow you, я пойду за Вами.
You have not put, Вы не поставили.
a basin, полоскательная чашка.
cup, чашка.
we want, намъ нужны.

two cups more, еще двѣ чашки.
bring, принесите.
another, другой, еще одинъ.
spoon, ложка.
a saucer, блюдечко.
you have not brought in, Вы не принесли.
sugar tongs, щипцы для сахару.

Do you take sugar?, пье-
те ли Вы съ сахаромъ?
cream, сливки.
milk, молоко.
will you fill up, долейте
пожалуйста.
my, мой.
water, вода.
black, черный.
or, или.

green, зеленый.
here, здѣсь.
What will you take to
eat?, что Вы желаете
кушать?
cakes, кэксъ.
muffins, лепешки.
bread and butter, хлѣбъ
съ масломъ.

get some more, прине-
сите еще.
not any more, болѣе не
надобно.
had you rather not?, Вы
болѣе не желаете?
much rather not, вовсе
не желаю.
I assure you, увѣряю
Васъ.

VIII.

Will you be so kind as,
не будете ли Вы такъ
добры.
to pull the bell, позво-
нить въ колокольчикъ.
ring the bell, позвоните
въ колокольчикъ.
Make more toast, под-
жарьте еще нѣсколько
кусковъ хлѣба
as soon as possible, какъ
можно скорѣе.
along with you, съ собой.
have I put?, положилъ
ли я?

do you find?, находите ли
Вы?
so, такъ.
most excellent, преотлич-
ный.
Where do you get it?, от-
куда Вы его получае-
те?
a friend, другъ, пріятель.
has procured me, досталъ
мнѣ.
chest (of tea), цыбикъ.
only, единственный.
way, способъ.

good, хорошій.
cheap, дешевый.
I will pour you out, я
налью Вамъ.
only, только.
I never take, я никогда
не пью.
more than three cups,
болѣе трехъ чашекъ.
call, позовите.
the servant, слуга, слу-
жанка.
to take away, убрать.

IX.

To sup, ужинать.
cheese, сыръ.
take your bread and cheese
with us, откушайте
съ нами.
much obliged, очень обя-
занъ.
but, но.
I am afraid, я боюсь.

late, поздно.
we shall, мы будемъ.
directly, сейчасъ.
cold, холодный.
a few, нѣсколько.
oysters, устрицы.
very much, очень (много).
which, что, чего.
first, сперва.

they are quite fresh, они
(суть) совершенно
свѣжи.
no, нѣтъ.
apple, яблочный.
I have done extremely
well, я поѣлъ чрезвы-
чайно хорошо.

X.

Glass, рюмка, стаканъ.
wine, вино.
with much pleasure, съ
большимъ удоволь-
ствіемъ.
claret, Бордоское.
port wine, портвейнъ.
sherry, хересъ.

what do you drink? что
Вы пьете?
table beer, столовое пиво.
porter, портеръ.
Scotch, Шотландскій.
ale, эль.
fine, хорошій.
ripe, поспѣлый.

how long has it been?,
сколько времени онъ
былъ?
bottle, бутылка.
I think I never drank
better, мнѣ кажется,
что я никогда не пилъ
лучшаго.

XI.

Have you written?, написали ли Вы?

exercise, упражненіе, урокъ.

where, гдѣ.

translation, переводъ.

I am very sorry, мнѣ очень жаль.

I have forgot, я забылъ.

to make, сдѣлать.

I was prevented from making it, я не могъ его сдѣлать.

I had a very bad tooth ache, у меня была ужасная зубная боль.

copy, переписанное на чисто.

badly written, дурно написано.

It is scarcely legible, это съ трудомъ можно прочесть.

You must write it better, Вамъ надобно написать это лучше.

or I shall expect you to make it over again, иначе Вамъ придется переписать все снова.

Have you learnt your vocabulary?, учили лы Вы слова?

repeat, повторите.

dialogues, разговоры.

let me hear, скажите мнѣ.

irregular, неправильный.

verb, глаголъ.

the rules, правила.

lesson, урокъ.

You hardly know a single word, Вы не знаете почти ни одного слова.

after school, послѣ класса.

I will have it said perfectly, чтобъ Вы его знали вполнѣ удовлетворительно!

without missing a single word, не ошибаясь ни въ одномъ словѣ.

XII.

Where shall I sit?, гдѣ я долженъ сидѣть?

Take your seat, садитесь.

form, скамейка.

higher up, повыше.

Do not make such a noise, не шумите такъ.

spell, складывайте.

word, слово.

again, опять, снова.

do not shake, не трясите.

I cannot write, я не могу писать.

unless you sit still, когда Вы не сидите смирно.

lend, одолжите.

knife, ножикъ.

I have lost, я потерялъ.

my, мой.

pen, перо.

one, одинъ.

I have none to spare, у меня нѣтъ лишняго.

I want, я хочу.

to use mine, употреблять свое.

myself, (я) самъ.

I can't find, я не могу найти.

copybook, тетрадь.

where did you leave it, гдѣ Вы ее оставили?

upon, на.

desk, конторка.

under, подъ.

other, другой.

book, книга.

I put it, я положилъ ее.

into, въ (съ винит. падежемъ).

I laid it, я положилъ ее.

shelf, полка.

just by my seat, подлѣ самаго моего мѣста.

Have you got your slate?, у Васъ ли Ваша (аспидная) доска?

Look for it, ищите ее.

I have found, я нашелъ.

was, былъ.

XIII.

To know, знать.

what o'clock?, который часъ?

I don't know, я не знаю.

exactly, точно.

tell you, сказать Вамъ.

to a quarter of an hour, (съ вѣрностью) до четверти часа.

Look at your watch, посмотрите который часъ по Вашимъ (карманнымъ) часамъ.

It is not wound up, они не заведены.

I forgot, я позабылъ.

to wind up, заводить.

It does not go, они не

ходятъ.

It has stopped, они остановились.

well, хорошо.

it loses, они отстаютъ.

every day, каждый день.

Mine gains as much, мои уходятъ столько же.

main, главный,

spring, пружина.
is broken, сломана.
it must be sent, надобно
их послать.
watchmaker, часовой
мастеръ.
are you up? Вы вставши?
already, уже.
I have been up this hour,
я уже цѣлый часъ
вставши.
you got up, Вы встали.
early, рано.
generally, обыкновенно.
to rise, вставать.

have you slept?, спали
ли Вы?
I never woke, л ни разу
не просыпался.
all night, всю ночь.
I could not sleep a wink,
л не могъ спать ни од-
ной мпнуты.
I never closed my eyes,
я глазъ не смыкалъ.
the whole night, цѣлую
ночь.
what, какой.
What do you think of
taking a short walk?,

как Вы думаете, не
сдѣлать ли намъ малень-
кую прогулку?
time, время.
They won't breakfast this
hour, завтракать бу-
дутъ не ранѣе какъ
черезъ часъ.
We have full an hour
before us, у насъ еще
цѣлый часъ впереди.
the walk, прогулка.
us, намъ.

XIV.

It begins to grow very
late, становится очень
поздно.
almost, почти.
to go to bed, идти спать.
is not yet come, еще не
пришелъ.
home, домой.
to hear, слышать.
a knock, стукъ.
very likely, очень вѣ-
роятно.
there he is, вотъ онъ.
I have not kept you up,
я не задержалъ Васъ
ложиться спать.
not at all, нисколько.
ten, десять.
Have you had a pleasant
walk, сдѣлали ли Вы
пріятную прогулку?

very much so, (очень
много такъ) очень
пріятную.
charming, прелестный.
evening, вечеръ.
Are you not tired?, не
устали ли Вы?
sopha, софа.
rest yourself, отдохните.
a little, не много.
hot, жаркій.
summer, лѣто.
we have had no, у насъ
не было.
this year, нынѣшній годъ.
we have had a fire, мы
топили.
even, даже.
month, мѣсяцъ.
July, іюль.
a great deal, много.

hay, сѣно.
they have begun, начали.
the harvest, жатва.
The crop will be good,
урожай будетъ хо-
рошъ.
There is wheat cut down
already, уже пожнали
пшеницу.
the corn will all be hou-
sed, весь хлѣбъ бу-
детъ убранъ подъ
крышку.
next week, на будущей
недѣлѣ.
no wonder, не удиви-
тельно.
warm, теплый.
the dog days, каникулы.

XV.

Is over, прошло.
to expect, ожидать.
many more, еще мно-
гихъ.
the leaves, листья.
to begin, начинать.
to fall, падать.
we have begun fires, мы
начали топить.
a fire, каминный огонь.
begins, начинаетъ.

comfortable, пріятный,
комфортабельный.
The days are very much
shortened, дни стали
гораздо короче.
long, долгій.
we cannot see, ничего не
видать.
it is hardly day light,
едва свѣтло.

in the afternoon, попо-
лудни.
It is soon dark, рано
темнѣетъ.
winter, зима.
draws near, приближ-
ается.
the shortest, кратчайшій.
in three weeks, черезъ
три недѣли.
christmas, рождество.

I wish it were, я бы же-
лалъ чтобъ оно было.
to lengthen, становиться
дольше.
is very low, едва го-
ритъ.
poor, плохой.
put, кладите.
turf, торфъ.
wood, дрова.

stove, печка.
you have not kept up,
Вы не поддержали.
you have let go out, Вы
дали гаснуть.
it must be lighted, на-
добно зажечь его.
What are you looking
for?, чего Вы ищите?
I am looking for, я ищу.

tongs, щипцы.
now, теперь.
..put on, положите.
two, два.
three, три.
a piece of wood, полѣно.
It will soon draw up,
скоро разгорится.

XVI.

New, новый.
What is it about?, о чемъ
она?
A little of every thing,
обо всемъ по немно-
жку.
entertaining, занима-
тельный.
yes, да.
for, для.
young, молодой.
people, люди.
full of anecdotes, напол-
нена анекдотами.
serious, серіозный.
sad, печальный.
lively, веселый.
laughable, смѣшной.
I am sure, я увѣренъ.
I shall like it, она мнѣ
понравится.
shall we read?, не про-
честь ли намъ?
a page or two, нѣсколько
страницъ.
to spare, лишній.
before I go out, передъ
моимъ уходомъ.
Are you going, собирае-
тесь ли Вы?
to walk, гулять.
this evening, сегодня
вечеромъ.

if the weather continues
fine, если будетъ про-
должаться хорошая
погода.
but, но.
I think, я думаю.
it will rain, пойдетъ
дождь.
dark, темный.
cloudy, облачный.
the wind is too high,
вѣтеръ слишкомъ си-
ленъ.
which way?, съ которой
стороны, какъ?
east, восточный.
west, западный.
I have taken exercise,
я сдѣлалъ моціонъ.
strong, крѣпкій, сильный.
well, здоровый.
I was just wishing, я
только что желалъ.
to meet, встрѣтиться.
which way are you go-
ing?, въ которую сто-
рону Вы идете?
something, кое-что, нѣ-
что.
beautiful, прекрасный.
to show, показать.
come, пойдемте.
for a long time, давно.

where have you been?,
гдѣ Вы были?
I thought, я думалъ, по-
лагалъ.
you had left town, что
Вы оставили городъ.
you never go out, Вы
никогда не выходите.
why, почему.
oftener, чаще.
to visit, навѣщать, по-
сѣщать.
to walk, ходить пѣшкомъ.
to ride, ѣздить.
into the country, въ де-
ревню, за городъ.
to sail, идти подъ па-
русами.
to row, идти на греблѣ.
up the river, вверхъ по
рѣкѣ.
we went out shooting,
мы отправились на
охоту.
yesterday, вчера.
we are going to the
races, мы отправимся
на скачку.
on Wednesday, въ среду.
on Thursday, въ четвергъ.
balloon, воздушный
шаръ.
to ascend, подыматься.

Connected Phrases.
Связныя Фразы.

General Remarks on the World.
Общія понятія о мірѣ.

The coldest, самая хо- лодная.

country, страна.

world, міръ, свѣтъ.

Greenland, Гренландія.

the hottest, самая жаркая.

the Burmese empire, Бирманская имперія.

the largest, величайшая.

Europe, Европа.

Russia, Россія.

the smallest, наименьшее.

kingdom, королевство.

Saxony, Саксонія.

the tallest, самый высо- корослый.

people, народъ.

the Patagonians, Пата- гонцы.

the shortest, самый ма- лорослый.

the Laplanders, Лап- ландцы.

the most polished, самый образованный.

the most savage, самый дикій.

Africa, Афрпка.

the most numerous, са- мый многочисленный.

Asia, Азія.

the thinnest, самое скуд- ное.

population, народонасе- леніе.

America, Америка.

the Chinese, Китайцы.

the freest, самая сво- бодная.

England, Англія.

the most enslaved, са- мая порабощенная.

Turkey, Турція.

the oldest, древнѣйшая.

China, Китай.

the newest, новѣйшая.

Brazil, the Brazils, Бра- зилія.

the most mountainous, самая гористая.

Norway, Норвегія.

the flattest, самая плоская.

the highest, высочайшая.

mountain, гора.

Mount Blanc, Монбланъ.

Savoy, Савоія.

France, Франція.

one of the Himalaya mountains, одна изъ Пмалайскихъ горъ.

the Maranon, Мараньонъ.

Amazon, Амазонская.

South America, Южная Америка.

Great Britain, Велико- британія.

has, имѣетъ.

the largest, самый боль- шой.

fleet of ships, корабель- ный флотъ.

Austria, Австрія.

armies, арміи.

the most trading, самая торговая.

the United States, Сое- дпненные Штаты.

next to it, слѣдующая послѣ нея.

remarkable, замѣчатель- ный.

for its mines, своими рудниками.

gold, золото, золотой.

silver, серебро, сере- бряный.

Arabia, Аравія.

is famed, славится.

for horses, лошадьми.

Egypt, Египетъ.

Palestine, Палестина.

were civilized, были просвѣщенны.

when, когда.

was all barbarous, была вся необразована.

now, нынѣ.

rude, грубый.

state, состояніе.

Greece, Греція.

once, однажды.

the mightiest, самая мо- гущественная.

nation, нація, народъ.

the weakest, слабѣйшая.

the Italians, Италіянцы.

the Germans, Нѣмцы.

the most musical, самый музыкальный.

the least so, всѣхъ меньше.

he who speaks, тотъ кто говоритъ.

French, французскій.

language, языкъ.

can, можетъ.

to travel, путешество- вать.

all over, по всей.

English, англійскій.

to trade, торговать про- мышлять.

all over the world, по всему свѣту.

Productions of various countries.
Произведенія разныхъ странъ.

Anchovy, анчоусъ, сардель.
from, изъ.
the Mediterranean, Средиземное море.
the best, самая лучшая.
brandy, водка.
is distilled, дистилируется.
butter, масло (коровье).
is carried(to),возится(въ).
Ireland, Ирландія.
Holland, Голландія.
Holstein, Голштинія.
carpet, коверъ.
of the best sort, самаго лучшаго сорта.
are manufactured, выдѣлываются.
Persia, Персія.
cheese, сыръ.
one, одинъ.
kind, родъ, сортъ.
called, называемый.
Dutch, голландскій.
cocoa, кокосъ.
grows, растетъ.
the East Indies, Восточная Индія.
the West Indies, Западная Индія.
Polynesia, Полинезія.
cork, пробочная кора.
Spain, Испанія.
Italy, Италія.
cotton, хлопчатая бумага.
is brought, привозится.
tree, дерево.
also, также.
Cyprus, Кипръ.
Smyrna, Смирна.
etc. (et caetera) и прочее, и такъ далѣе.
deal wood, еловое дерево.
Sweden, Швеція.
diamond, алмазъ.
are found, находятъ.
India, Восточная Индія.
fig, винная ягода.

chiefly, преимущественно.
codfish, треска.
Newfoundland, Нью-Фаундлендъ.
gin, джинъ, можжевеловая водка.
gloves, перчатки.
are made, дѣлаются.
Siberia, Сибирь.
for the most part, по большой части.
California, Калифорнія.
Australia, Австралія.
ivory, слоновая кость.
made of, выдѣлываемая изъ.
elephants' teeth, слоновые клыки.
is sent, присылается.
island, островъ.
Ceylon, Цейлонъ.
lace, кружево.
Belgium, Бельгія.
muslin, муслинъ; кисея.
Bengal, Бенгалія.
oil, масло (деревянное).
for eating, для употребленія въ пищу.
is imported, привозится.
orange, апельсинъ.
Portugal, Португалія.
the Cape Verd islands, острова Зеленаго Мыса.
Madeira, Мадера.
the Azores, Азорскіе острова.
pearls, жемчугъ.
by diving, посредствомъ ныранія, водолазами.
plum, слива.
raisins, изюмъ.
are dried, сушатся.
rice, рисъ.
is cultivated, разводится.

rum, ромъ.
Jamaica, Ямайка.
silk worm, шелковичный червь.
are bred, воспитываются.
the Caucasus, Кавказъ.
Mexico, Мексика.
spices, пряности.
such as, таковыя какъ.
cinnamon, корица.
clove, гвоздика.
pepper, перецъ.
the Moluccas, Молуккскіе острова.
sponge, губка.
sea, море.
near, близь.
the Archipelago, Архипелагъ, -скій.
tallow, сало.
timber, строевой лѣсъ.
tobacco, табакъ.
cigar, сигара.
Manilla, Манилла.
Cuba, Куба.
Virginia, Виргинія.
toy, игрушка.
mostly, по большой части.
Germany, Германія.
whalebone, китовый усъ.
out of, изъ.
bone, кость.
whale, китъ.
huge, огромный.
caught, ловимый.
off, противъ, на высотѣ.
whisky, уиски (родъ водки).
Scotland, Шотландія.
Sicily, Сицилія.
Cape of Good Hope, мысъ Доброй Надежды.
wool, шерсть.
Saxony, Саксонія.

41

Of the difference and distance of a mile in different countries.
О различіи и величинѣ мили въ различныхъ странахъ.

Length, длина.
mile, миля.
the same, тотъ самый, одинакій.
different, различный.
for, ибо, потому что.
much less, гораздо меньше.
than, нежели.
Indian, индейскій.
Spanish, испанскій.
German, нѣмецкій.
statute, узаконенный.

consists of, состоитъ изъ.
feet, Футы.
yard, ярдъ, англійскій аршинъ.
to agree, согласоваться.
nearly, почти.
measure, мѣра.
Turkish, турецкій.
Italian, итальянскій.
old, древній.
Roman, римскій.
Russian, русскій,
more, больше.

three quarters, три четверти.
Polish, польскій.
about, около.
half, половина.
Irish, ирландскій.
Arabian, аравійскій.
Swedish, шведскій.
Danish, датскій.
Hungarian, венгерскій.
six, шесть.

Varieties of the human species.
О различныхъ породахъ рода человѣческаго.

There are, есть, имѣются.
grand, великій, главный.
variety, различіе, порода.
the human race, человѣческій родъ.
imperceptibly, непримѣтно.
to approach, сближаться.
are lost, теряются.
in each other, одно въ другомъ.
first, во первыхъ.
brownish, смугловатый.
western, западный.
coast, морской берегъ.
who, который.
according to our notions, по нашимъ понятіямъ.
of beauty, о красотѣ.
the handsomest, самый красивый.
best formed, самый стройный.
next, потомъ.
yellow, желтый.
olive coloured, оливковаго цвѣта.
Monguls, Монголы.
Calmucs, Калмыки.

eastern, восточный.
with whom, съ которыми, въ числѣ которыхъ.
may be reckoned, можно считать.
the most northerly, самый сѣверный.
American, американскій.
tribe, племя.
having, имѣющій.
flat, плоскій.
forehead, лобъ.
little, малый, маленькій.
eye, глазъ.
wide, широкій.
mouth, ротъ.
thirdly, въ третьихъ.
copper coloured, мѣдноцвѣтный.
Indian, Индѣецъ.
dispersed over, разсѣянный по
entire, весь.
continent, материкъ.
broad, широкій.
face, лице.
bristly, щетиноватый.
hair, волосы.

stout, дюжій.
masculine, мужественный.
limb, членъ.
fourthly, въ четвертыхъ.
jet black, черный какъ смоль.
negro, Негръ.
African, Африканецъ.
various, разный.
shade, оттѣнокъ.
woolly, шерстистый.
thick, толстый.
lip, губа.
nose, носъ.
prominent, выдающійся.
chin, подбородокъ.
downy, пушистый.
skin, кожа.
fifthly, въ пятыхъ.
dark brown, темнобурый.
Australian, Австралецъ.
the Pacific ocean, Тихій океанъ.
large, большой.
feature, черта (лица).
strong, крѣпкій, твердый.
nostrils, ноздри.

great, большой.
men, люди.
offspring, потомки.
common, общій.
parent, родитель.

among, между.
swarthy, смуглый.
delicate, нѣжный.
European, Европеецъ.
brethren, братья.

descended, происходящіе.
from, отъ.
ancestor, праотецъ.

Useful knowledge.
Полезныя свѣдѣнія.

One is often surprised, часто удивляешься.
when talking, разговаривая.
boy, мальчикъ.
them, ихъ.
ignorant, невѣдущій.
thing, вещь.
which, который.
ought to have known, должны былибъ знать.
as — as, также — какъ.
their own, собственныя свои.
name, имя.
I was questioning, я спрашивалъ.
at least, по крайней мѣрѣ.
eight years old, восемь лѣтъ отъ роду.
the other day, недавно.
who, который.
neither — nor, ни — ни.
knew, зналъ.
number, число.
there are in the year, (сколько имѣется) въ году.
he could not tell, онъ не могъ сказать.
whether the sun rose, восходитъ ли солнце.
west, западъ.
equally, равно.
whether his pocket was made, сдѣланъ ли его карманъ.
of hemp, изъ конопли.
flax, лёнъ.

certainly, конечно.
more important, важнѣе.
he should make himself better acquainted, онъ бы долженъ былъ ознакомиться лучше.
of this nature, такого рода.
that, что.
sense, чувство.
seeing, зрѣніе.
hearing, слухъ.
smelling, обоняніе.
feeling, осязаніе.
tasting, вкусъ.
season, время года.
spring, весна.
autumn, осень.
winter, зима.
the earth, земля.
turns round, вращается (около оси).
travels round the sun, обращается около солнца.
is composed of, состоитъ изъ.
land, земля.
is divided into, раздѣляется на.
six, шесть.
Oceania, Океанія или Австралазія.
cardinal points, страны свѣта.
north, сѣверъ.
south, югъ.
metal, металлъ.
coal, уголь.
are dug out, выкапываются.

indeed, дѣйствительно, въ самомъ дѣлѣ.
does not know, не знаетъ.
flour of wheat, пшеничная мука.
is mingled, мѣшаютъ.
yeast, дрожди.
it makes, то сдѣлается.
leavened, квашеный.
light, легкій.
is used, употребляютъ.
heavy, тяжелый.
unleavened, безквасный.
the passover cakes, пасхальныя пирожныя.
the Jews, Жиды.
biscuit, сухарь.
eaten, употребляемыя въ пищу.
sailor, матросъ.
barley bread of Scotland, Шотландскій ячменный хлѣбъ.
at an early age, въ раннемъ возрастѣ.
to be acquainted, быть знакомымъ, знать.
such — as, такія — которыя.
use, употребленіе.
I have found, я нашелъ.
frequently, часто.
necessary, необходимый.
to explain, объяснять.
juice, сокъ.
sugar cane, сахарный тростникъ.
the Indies, Индія.
dried, сушеный.

shrub, кустъ
size, величина.
currant bush, смородин-
    ный кустъ.
berry, ягода.
growing, растущій.
cacao, какао.
vanilla, ваниль.
malt, солодъ.
hop, хмѣль.
cider, яблоновка.
apple, яблоко.
perry, грушёвка.
pear, груша.
grape, виноградъ.
juniper berry, можжеве-
    ловая ягода.
they have been, они были.
citron, цитронъ.
lemon, лимонъ.
cloves, гвоздика.
nutmeg, мушкатный
    орѣхъ.
kernel, зерно.
fruit, плодъ.
peach, персикъ.
bark, кора.
ginger, инбирь.
rhubarb, ревень.

root, корень.
plant, растѣніе.
knowledge, познаніе.
may be obtained можетъ
    быть пріобрѣтаемо.
if they keep their ears
    and eyes open, если
    будутъ смотрѣть и
    слушать внимательно.
now and then, иногда.
to ask a question, дѣлать
    вопросъ.
those who, тѣ которые.
wiser than themselves,
    умнѣе самихъ.
father, отецъ.
who is very anxious, ко-
    торый очень заботится
    (о томъ).
that his children should
    obtain, чтобъ его дѣти
    пріобрѣтали.
I heard him explain to
    them, я слышалъ какъ
    онъ объяснялъ имъ.
salt, соль.
sea water, морская вода.
salt water, соленая вода.
glue, клей.

sinew, сухая жила.
feet, ноги.
animal, животное.
boiled down, выварен-
    ный.
fibre, волокно.
stalk, стебель.
resembling, похожій на.
nettle, крапива.
tow, пакля.
refuse, отрёпки, бракъ.
he told them, онъ гово-
    рилъ имъ.
paper, бумага.
principally, преимуще-
    ственно.
linen, полотняный.
rags, тряпьё, ветошь.
torn to pieces, разорван-
    ный въ куски.
formed into a pulp, пре-
    вращенный въ мякоть.
lastly, наконецъ.
glass, стекло.
sand, песокъ.
flint, кремень.
alkaline, щелочный.

Languages of the World.
О числѣ языковъ въ мірѣ.

Enumeration, исчисленіе.
professor, профессоръ.
thousand, тысяча.
sixty-four, шестьдесятъ
    четыре.
of which, изъ коихъ, изъ
    числа которыхъ.
hundred, сто.

eighty-seven, восемьде-
    сятъ семь.
are spoken, говорятъ
    (на).
nine, девять.
thirty-seven, тридцать
    семь.
two hundred, двѣстѣ.

seventy-six, семьдесятъ
    шесть.
probably, вѣроятно.
includes, включаетъ.
provincial corruption,
    провинціализмъ (мѣст-
    ное выраженіе).
general, общій, главный.

АЛФАВИТНЫЙ СЛОВАРЬ.

А.

a, an, членъ неопред.; одинъ, нѣкоторый; 12 hours—day, по двѣнадцати часовъ въ день; — day or two, нѣсколько дней, дня два; — chasing, — going, см. *in chasing, in going.*

abaft, позади.

abandon, оставлять, покидать.

abbey, аббатство, игуменство, монастырь.

abbot, аббатъ, игуменъ, настоятель въ монастырѣ.

abhor, гнушаться чѣмъ.

ability, способность, дарованіе.

able, способный, искусный; to be — быть въ состояніи.

aboard, на суднѣ, на судно;—the sloop, на шлюпѣ.

abode, жилище, мѣстопребываніе.

abolish, уничтожать, отмѣнять.

abolition, уничтоженіе.

abominable, мерзкій, гнусный.

abomination, отвращеніе, омерзеніе.

aboriginal, первобытный.

abound, изобиловать чѣмъ.

about, вокругъ, о, объ, около, касательно, по, въ; those immediately—the person, приближённые; — the house, по всему дому;—to entangle, готовый запутывать; to be—быть готову, собираться; an attempt—to be made, попытка, которую хотѣли сдѣлать; to have —one's self, имѣть съ собою.

above, надъ, на верху, на небесахъ, болѣе, выше, вышеписанный; — all, но что важнѣе всего.

abroad, на дворѣ, въ чужихъ краяхъ.

abruptly, быстро, вдругъ.

absence, отсутствіе.

absent, отсутствующій; to be—отсутствовать, быть въ отсутствіи.

absolute, абсолютный, совершенный, неограниченный;—ly, совершенно.

absolution, отпущеніе грѣховъ, разрѣшеніе отъ грѣховъ.

abstraction, разсѣянность.

absurd, нелѣпый; — ity, нелѣпость;—ly, нелѣпо.

abundance, изобиліе.

abundant, изобильный.

abuse, злоупотребленіе, ругательство; term of — ругательное или бранное слово.

abyss, бездна, пропасть, пучина.

academical, академическій.

academy, академія.

accede, соглашаться; to— to a request, исполнять просьбу.

accelerate, ускорять.

accent, удареніе, произношеніе.

accept, принимать;—able, пріятный, выгодный; — ance, принятіе.

access, доступъ, приступъ;—ion, восшествie, вступленіе (на престолъ).

accident, случай, несчастіе; I had an, — со мной случилось несчастіе; — ally, случайно.

acclamation, восклицаніе, радостное восклицаніе.

accolade, обрядъ посвященія въ рыцари.

accommodate, приноравливать, снабжать (всѣмъ нужнымъ).

accommodation, удобство, устройство, помѣщеніе..

accompany, провожать, сопровождать, аккомпанировать.

accomplice, соучастникъ.

accomplish, совершать, исполнять; — ed, благовоспитанный, образованный; — ment, совершеніе, исполненіе, познаніе, образованность.

accord, согласіе; to — соглашаться; of its own — добровольно, по собственной волѣ, по собственному побужденію; — ance, согласіе; in — ance with, согласно съ.

according to, согласно съ, по; — ly, согласно, слѣдовательно, въ слѣдствіе сего; which he — ly did, что онъ и сдѣлалъ.

accost, заговорить съ, вступать въ разговоръ съ.

account, счетъ, отчетъ, разсказъ, причина; to, — считать, почитать; to — for, изъяснять что, давать отчетъ о чемъ;

give a further —, разскажите дальше; on his —, ради него; not on any — , on no — , ни подъ какимъ видомъ; of good — , знатный; on — of, по причинѣ, по случаю; on that —, по этому.

accumulate, накоплять.

accumulation, накопленіе

accuracy, точность.

accurately, вѣрно, точно, аккуратно.

accurst, проклятый.

accusation, обвиненіе.

accuse, обвинять.

accustomed, привычный; to be —, имѣть обыкновеніе; to which men are — , къ которому люди привыкли.

ache, болѣть.

achieve, совершать, оканчивать, исполнять, одерживать, пріобрѣтать; — ment, подвигъ.

acknowledge, признавать, признаваться; — ment, признаваніе, признательность; after making suitable — ments, изъявивъ приличнымъ образомъ свою признательность.

acknowledging, признаваніе.

acorn, желудь.

acquaint, знакомить, увѣдомлять, извѣщать; to — one's self, узнавать; — ed, свѣдущій, знакомый; to become — ed with, узнавать о чемъ, ознакомливаться съ; to make — ed, знакомить; — ance, знаком-

ство, знакомый, знакомецъ.

acquiescent, уступчивый.

acquire, пріобрѣтать, снискивать; — ments, познанія.

acquisition, пріобрѣтеніе, снисканіе.

acquit, оправдать; to — one's self, держать себя, вести себя, исполнять свою обязанность; to — one's self in a trial, выдерживать испытаніе.

acre, акръ, полдесятины.

across, поперегъ, чрезъ.

act, дѣйствіе, дѣяніе, поступокъ, дѣло, указъ; to —, дѣйствовать, поступать, играть; with nothing for their legs and feet to — upon, не имѣя никакой опоры для ногъ; — of parliament, законъ изданный парламентомъ; the Five Mile —, указъ воспрещающій всякому священнику, не принадлежащему англиканской церкви, находиться ближе пяти миль отъ нѣкоторыхъ городовъ; the licensing —, цензурное правило; the turnpike —, таможенное постановленіе; — of tyranny, тиранское, произвольное дѣйствіе; he was in the — of handing him, онъ уже сталъ ему подавать.

action, дѣйствіе, жалоба, искъ, сраженіе, битва; to bring an — , начинать процессъ.

active, дѣятельный, расторопный.

activity, дѣятельность.

actual, дѣйствительный, настоящій;—ly, дѣйствительно, въ самомъ дѣлѣ.

actuate, побуждать.

acuteness, проницательность, остроуміе.

A. D. (Anno Domini), въ лѣто отъ Рождества Христова.

adapt, примѣнять, приспособлять;—ed, способный къ чему.

add, прибавлять, присовокуплять, прилагать, придавать, увеличивать; to — to, чтобъ увеличить; — ed, въ совокупности съ; — itional, прибавочный.

address, адресъ, обращеніе, ловкость, искуство; to—, адрессоваться, обращаться, обращать.

Adelaide, Адельгейдъ, Аделанда.

adhere, держаться, придерживаться;—nt;приверженецъ, послѣдователь.

adjacent, прилежащій, смежный.

adjoin, присоединять; —ing, смежный.

adjust, приводить въ порядокъ, слаживать, рѣшать.

admeasurement, мѣра, измѣреніе.

administer, пріобщать, давать; to — to, способствовать, споспѣшествовать чему, отправлять (правосудіе); to — justice, чинить судъ и расправу.

administration, управлсніе, правленіе;—of justice, отправлсніе правосудія.

admirable, удивительный, удивленія достойный.

admiral, адмиралъ;—ty, адмиралтейство.

admiration, удивлсніе.

admire, уважать, почитать, удивляться, любоваться.

admission, впускъ,входъ.

admit, допускать, впускать, принимать.

ado, хлопоты.

adopt, принимать, усвоивать;to — the contrary plan, избирать противоположный путь.

adorn, украшать.

Adrian, Адріанъ.

adrift, на волю.

adulation, лесть.

advance, двигаться, подвигаться, идти впередъ,двигать впередъ, ускорять, поспѣшать, представлять,ссужать, производить въ чинъ, прибавляться (о днѣ, лунѣ);to — in years, старѣть; to — towards any one, подходить къ кому; your courage forth—, покажите свою храбрость; in— впреди.

advantage, выгода, польза, преимущество; to be seen to—, представляться съ выгодной стороны;to take —, см. take.

adventure, приключеніе, похожденіе, — r, искатель приключеній, удалецъ.

adventurous, отважный, удалой.

adversary, противникъ.

advertisement, объявленіе.

advice, совѣтъ.

advisable, благоразумной полезный.

advise, совѣтовать, присовѣтовать;—r, совѣтователь.

advocate, адвокатъ, заступникъ.

advowson, право, попечителя.

affect, трогать, затрогивать, смущать, имѣть вліяніе на что, притворяться чѣмъ; —ion, склонность,привязанность, любовь, чувство, движеніе душевное;—ionate, нѣжный, любящій.

affirm, подтверждать.

affix, прибивать.

afflict, опечаливать, сокрушать, мучить; — ion, огорченіе, скорбь.

affluent, притокъ.

afford, доставлять, давать, быть въ состояніи.

affright, испугъ.

affront, оскорблять, обижать.

afloat,плывущій на водѣ, находящійся на вольной водѣ.

aforesaid, вышесказанный, вышеупомянутый.

afraid. To be—, бояться; to become—, начинать бояться.

afresh, снова, съизнова.

Africa, Африка;—n, африканскій.

after, послѣ, послѣ того, послѣ того какъ, по прошествіи, за, спустя, по; they are—us, они гонятся за нами; who was—a frolick, которому хотѣлось напроказить; —all, наконецъ, сверхъ того; —ages, будущія времена; —circumstances, послѣдующія обстоятельства;—life, остатокъ жизни; — noon, пополуденное время; —noon or in the—noon, пополудни; — wards, въ послѣдствіи, послѣ, послѣ того, потомъ, спустя.

again, опять, снова; never —, больше никогда.

against, противъ, о, объ, на, къ.

age, вѣкъ, возрастъ, лѣта, старость; four years of —, четыре года отъ роду; — d, пожилой, старый, престарѣлый.

agent, агентъ.

aggregate, соединеніе, совокупность, скопленіе, сцѣпленіе; совокупный, соединенный.

aggrieve, огорчать.

agility, ловкость.

agitate, волновать.

agitation, внутреннее волненіе, смущеніе.

ago, тому назадъ; long—, давно.

agog, жаждущій чего.

agonizing, истерзающій.

agony, агонія, предсмертная борьба.

agree, соглашаться, быть

согласнымъ, согласоваться; —able, пріятный; —ably, пріятно; —ment, соглашеніе, согласіе.

agricultural, земледѣльческій.

agriculture, земледѣліе.

ah, ахъ! а!

ahead, впередъ, впереди.

ahoy, гей! слушай! sail—, судно видно! boat—, на шлюпкѣ, Алло!

aid, помощь; to—, помогать, пособлять; to — the success, содѣйствовать успѣху.

aim, прицѣливать, мѣтить, домогаться чего.

air, воздухъ, арія, мелодія.

ajar, полуотпертый.

alabaster, алебастръ.

alack, увы!

alacrity, радость, живость.

alarm, тревога, суматоха, смута, испуга; to—, тревожить, испугать, обезпокоить; the — of fire, пожарная тревога; — ing, тревожный, обезпокоивающій; — ingly rapid, страшно быстрый.

alas, увы!

alderman, альдерманъ.

ale, эль, англійское пиво;—house, пивная лавка, шинокъ; — house keeper, содержатель питейнаго дома, шинкарь.

Alexander, Александръ.

alienate, отчуждать, продавать, переводить, передавать.

alight, слѣзать, садиться.

alike, равнымъ образомъ, равномѣрно.

alive, живой, въ живыхъ, оживлённый.

alkaline, щелочный.

all, всё, весь, всякій; весьма, очень, крайне, —along, все время; —round, вокругъ всего или всей;—through, по всему, по всей; seven in — , всѣхъ (насъ) сѣмеро.

allege, показывать, приводить, представлять, ссылаться на что.

alleviate, облегчать.

alliance, союзъ.

alligator, кайманъ, американскій крокодилъ, аллигаторъ.

allot, назначать.

allow, жаловать, назначать, позволять, допускать; —ance, дозволеніе, позволеніе, согласіе, порція, паекъ.

allure, манить, приманивать.

alluring, приманчивый.

allusion, намеканіе, намекъ.

ally, союзникъ; to —, соединять, быть въ свойствѣ.

almanac, almanack, мѣсяцословъ, календарь; —maker, сочинитель календаря; —weather wisdom, предсказываніе погоды по календарю.

Almighty, всемогущій.

almost, почти.

alms, милостыня.

aloes, алоевое или райское дерево.

alone, одинъ; толко, единственно; to let—, оставлять, не трогать.

along, вдоль по; as they went—,во время пути; had come—, присталъ къ борту; —side, подлѣ, бортъ съ бортомъ; —with, вмѣстѣ съ.

aloof, въ отдаленіи.

aloud, громко.

already, уже.

also, также.

altar, престолъ, алтарь, жертвенникъ (у древнихъ).

alter, перемѣнять; —ation, перемѣна, измѣненіе.

alternate, поперемѣнный; on the—days, черезъ день;—ly, поперемѣнно.

although, хотя.

altina, алтынникъ.

altogether, совсѣмъ.

always, всегда.

A. M., утра, до полудня.

am, см. be; how — I to know .... from, какъ мнѣ отличить.... отъ?

amain, во всю силу.

amass, скоплять, накоплять.

amaze, изумлять;—ment, изумленіе.

Amazon, Амазонская рѣка.

ambassador, посолъ.

ambition, честолюбіе.

ambitious, честолюбивый; —of, жадный къ.

ambuscade, засада.

amends, замѣна, удовлетвореніе; to make—, вознаграждать.

America, Америка; —n, Американецъ, американскій.

amiable, любезный, милый.

amid, amidst, среди, посреди, между.

amiss, несчастіе, бѣда; худо, не такъ.

amity, дружество.

ammunition, боевые припасы.

among, amongst, между, въ числѣ; from—, изъ среды, изъ числа.

amount, сумма, количество, число; to—to, составлять, доходить до.

amour, любовная связь.

ample, полный достаточный.

amply, обширно, пространно, вполнѣ.

amuse, забавлять;—ment, забава, увеселеніе.

analogy, аналогія, подобіе.

analyze, разбирать, разлагать.

anathematize, предавать анаѳемѣ.

ancestor, праотецъ, предокъ.

anchor, якорь; the best bower —, плехтъ; —ed, стоящій на якорѣ; to be — ed, стоять на якорѣ.

ancient, древній, старинный, бывшій, прежній; —ly, въ старину, издревле.

anchovy, анчоусъ, сардель.

and, и.

anecdote, анекдотъ.

anew, снова, опять.

angel, ангелъ.

anger, гнѣвъ; in—, въ сердцахъ.

Anglican, англиканскій.

Anglo-Saxon, Англо-Саксонецъ, англо-саксонскій языкъ; англо-саксонскій.

angry, гнѣвный, сердитый; to be — with, сердиться на.

animal, животное.

animate, одушевлять.

animation, одушевленіе, движеніе.

animosity, вражда, враждебность, раздоръ.

annalist, лѣтописецъ.

annals, лѣтописи.

Anne, Анна.

annex, присоединять, прилагать. ·

announce, возвѣщать, объявлять;—ment,объявленіе, повѣстка.

annoy, обезпокоивать, надоѣдать.

annual, годовой, годичный, ежегодный; —ly, ежегодно, въ годъ.

annul, уничтожать, отмѣнять.

anoint, мазать, помазывать; the Lord's —ed, помазанникъ.

anon, тотчасъ.

another, другой, еще одинъ; one —, другъ друга, одинъ другаго.

answer, отвѣтъ; to make —, отвѣчать; to—, отвѣчать, отвѣчать на, соотвѣтствовать; to — prayer, услышать молитву; to — the purpose, служить чѣмъ; to — a quarrel, кончить ссору.

ant, муравей.

we a'n't = we are not.

antagonist, противникъ.

Anthony, Антонъ, Антоній.

antichrist, антихристъ.

anticipate, предварять, предполагать, предупреждать,опережвать.

antiquary, антикварій, знатокъ древностей.

antiquity,древность,старина.

anxiety, нетерпѣніе, любопытство, опасеніе, забота,озабоченіе; she was in the greatest —, она была весьма озабочена.

anxious,заботливый,безпокойный, любопытный; to· be —, опасаться, заботиться, домогаться чего; the — fears, опасенія.

any, какой нибудь, какой либо, любой, всякій, кто нибудь, что нибудь, нѣсколько; — воду, — man, — one, —person, кто нибудь, всякій, который нибудь; — how, какъ нибудь; — thing, что нибудь, все; — thing but, вовсе не; for — thing I know, сколько я знаю, сколько мнѣ извѣстно; not — thing, ничего; not to allow — person, не позволять никому; — where, гдѣ бы то ни было, гдѣ нибудь.

apart, особо, отдѣльно, въ сторонѣ; — ment, компата, покой; sleeping — ment, спальня.

aperture, отверстіе.

apologize, извиняться, оправдываться.

apology, извиненіе; to make an —, извиняться.

apothecary, аптекарь.

appalling, устрашительный, страшный.

apparel, платье, одежда, нарядъ.

apparent, очевидный, явный, притворный; по видимому, на взглядъ; —ly, по видимому.

appear, являться, казаться,явствовать, выходить, показываться, представлять; it — s, видно. .

appearance, видъ,наружность,наружный видъ, признакъ, примѣта, появленіе, явка въ судъ; made his —, появился; to all —, по видимому; with much —, со всѣми признаками.

appellation, прозваніе, наименованіе.

appendage,придача,прибавленіе, дополненіе.

appetite, апетитъ.

applaud, хвалить, одобрять.

apple,яблоко; яблочный.

application,примѣненіе, просьба.

apply,прикладывать,обращаться, ·употреблять, назначать; to — for, испрашивать; to — one's self, прилагать стараніе.

appoint, назначать; — ment, назначеніе, мѣсто, должность.

appreciate, цѣнить.

apprehend, опасаться, бояться.

apprehension, опасеніе, боязнь.

to be **apprehensive** of, опасаться, страшиться чего.

apprentice, ученикъ, — ship, ученіе (у мастера).

approach, приближеніе; to —, сближаться, приближаться, подходить, приступать къ чему.

approbation, одобреніе.

appropriate,употреблять, опредѣлять,назначать.

approve, одобрять.

apricot, абрикосъ.

April, Апрѣль.

apron, передникъ, фартукъ, запонъ.

apt, склонный, способный, готовый; — ly, прилично, кстати.

Apulius, Апулій.

Arabia, Аравія; —n, аравійскій.

arbitrary,самовластный, произвольный.

Arcadian, аркадскій.

arch, сводъ, арка; —ed, со сводомъ, дугообразный.

archbishop,архіепископъ; —ric,архіепископство.

archer, стрѣлецъ (изъ лука), лучникъ; — y meeting, состязательная стрѣльба (изъ луковъ).

Archipelago,Архипелагъ; архипелагскій.

architect, архитекъ; —ure, зодчество, архитектура.

Arctic, арктическій, сѣверный.

ardent, пылкій, горячій, усердный.

ardour, пылкость, усердіе; in the — of joy, въ пылу радости.

are, есми, есте суть; см. **be.**

area, поверхность, площадь.

argue, доказывать, спорить.

argument, доводъ.

aright, хорошо; do I understand you—, хорошенько ли я Васъ понялъ?

arise, подниматься, вставать, воскресать, возставать (изъ мертвыхъ), происходить.

aristocracy, аристократія.

aristocrat, аристократъ; —ic, —ical, аристократическій.

ark, ковчегъ (Ноевъ).

arm, рука, мышца; - s, оружіе, ружья, гербъ; at—s, in—s, вооруженный; to—, вооружать; — ada, армада, флотъ; — ament, морская сила; — ed to the teeth, heavy — ed, вооруженный съ головы до ногъ; — istice, перемиріе; — oreal, гербовый;—our, броня, латы;—у, войско, армія.

around, вокругъ; — and —, кругомъ, those—, окружающіе.

arose, см. **arise**.

arouse, разбуждать, возбуждать.

arrange, устроивать, учреждать, выстраивать, • приводить въ порядокъ, убирать, распредѣлять по.

array, строй, боевой порядокъ,одежда,нарядъ.

arrest,задерживать, оста-

навливать,арестовать.

arrival, прибытіе, приходъ, пріѣздъ.

arrive, прибывать, приходить, пріѣзжать, наставать,наступать,доходить, достигать; to —at conclusions, доходить до заключеній.

arriving, прибытіе, приплытіе.

arrow, стрѣла.

art, художество, искуство; — of war, военное искуство.

Arthur, Артуръ

article,товаръ,вещь;—s of value, цѣнныя вещи.

artifice, хитрость.

artificial, искуственный.

artillery, артиллерія.

artisan, ремесленникъ.

artist, художникъ, артистъ.

artlessness, простодушіе.

as, какъ, такъ какъ, по мѣрѣ того какъ, что, когда, какой; —...—, также... какъ; — for, —to, что касается до; — if, какъ будто бы; — it were, какъ бы, такъ сказать;—much, столько; — much —, столько сколько;—soon — possible, какъ можно скорѣе; — well—, также какъ, также хорошо какъ, сколько; so — to, такъ чтобы; so kind—, такъ добръ; so much—, на столько чтобы; a thousand times —high, въ тысячу разъ выше; it might be—well to return, не

дурно бы было возвратиться.

ascend, подыматься, восходить, вступать (на престолъ); — ancy, —ant, превосходство; —ant, превосходящій, сильнѣе.

Ascension, Островъ Вознесенія.

ascent,восходъ (на гору), возвышеніе.

ascertain, опредѣлять, вывѣдывать, узнавать, удостовѣряться.

ascribe, приписывать.

to be ashamed of, стыдиться чего.

ashes, зола, пепелъ.

ashore, на берегъ, на берегу.

Asia, Азія.

aside, въ сторону.

ask, спрашивать, просить; to—(in church), провозглашать; to—a question, дѣлать вопросъ, спрашивать; to—for, просить, требовать, потребовать.

asleep, спящій; to be—, спать; to fall—, засыпать.

asparagus, спаржа.

aspect, видъ; the — of affairs,положеніе дѣла.

aspen, осиновый.

aspiration, стремленіе.

aspire, домогаться, добиваться чего, стремиться къ чему.

ass, оселъ.

assail, наступать на кого, захватывать, застигать; —ant, нападающій.

assassin, убійца; to — ate, убивать, умерщ-

влять; —ation, убій-
ство, смертоубійство.

assault, прпступъ, нападеніе; to—, штур-
мовать, идти прпсту-
помъ на что, напа-
дать на кого.

assemble, собпрать, созывать, собпраться.

assembly, собраніе, съ-
ѣздъ.

assent, согласіе, сопз-
воленіе, to—, согла-
шаться.

assert, утверждать;—ion,
увѣреніе.

assiduity, прилежаніе.

assign, назначать; to—a,
reason, приводить прп-
чпну.

assimilate, уподоблять.

assist, помогать;—ance,
помощь; — ant, по-
мощнпкъ.

assize, уголовный судъ,
засѣданіе, палата прп-
сяжныхъ.

associate, сообщнпкъ,
товарпщъ; to—, сое-
дпнять, присоедпнять.

associations, подробно-
сти, обстоятельства.

assume, прпнпмать, прп-
свопвать.

assurance, увѣреніе, об-
надежпваніе.

assure, увѣрять; — dly,
навѣрно.

astonish, удпвлять, пзумлять; — ing, удпвп-
тельный ; — ment,
удивленіе, пзумленіе.

astound, пзумлять, оглушать.

asunder, пополамъ.

asylum, убѣжпще, пріютъ.

at, въ, у, прп, по, на,

за, съ; not — all, нп-
сколько.

ate, см. **eat.**

Athenian, Аѳинянпнъ.

athletic, атлетпческій,
богатырскій.

Atlantic, Атлантпческій
океанъ.

atmosphere, воздухъ, ат-
мосфера; — of pesti-
lence , зачумленный
воздухъ.

atmospheric, атмосфери-
ческій.

atrocious, жестокій, гнусный.

atrocity, гнусность, жестокость.

attach, привязывать, сое-
дпняться; to — an im-
portance to, высоко
цѣнить; —ed, привя-
занный, преданный; —
ment, привязанность.

attack, аттака, нападеніе; to— аттаковать,
нападать ; to — any
one's interests, дѣй-
ствовать въ ущербъ
пнтереса кого.

attain, достпгать;—ment,
достпженіе, знаніе, по-
знаніе.

attempt, попытка, поку-
шеніе; to—, пытаться,
покушаться, старать-
ся, пробовать.

attend, прпсутствовать,
бывать у, бывать прп,
провожать, сопровож-
дать, служпть у; to—
to, внимать чему, пе-
щися о чемъ, соблю-
дать, псполнять;—an-
се, присутствіе, посѣ-
щеніе; —ant, сопро-
вождающій, спутнпкъ,
служитель ; — ants,

прпслуга, свпта; — ed
with сопряженный съ.

attention, внпманіе; to
pay—, обратпть внп-
маніе, внпмать, слушать.

attentive, внимательный.

attitude, положеніе тѣла,
осанка; firm —, твер-
дость.

attorney, адвокатъ,
стряпчій, повѣренный.

attract, привлекать; —
ion, прптяженіе, прп-
влекательность; — ive,
прпвлекательный.

attribute, приписывать.

audacious, отважный,
смѣлый.

audacity, отважность,
смѣлость.

audience, слушатели.

auditor, слушатель.

augment, умножать, уве-
лпчпвать, увелпчп-
ваться.

August, Августъ.

aunt, тетка.

Australasia, Австразія.

Australia, Австралія;
—n, Австралецъ, ав-
стральскій.

Austria, Австрія.

authentic, достовѣрный;
to — ate, утверждать,
засвпдѣтельствовать.

author, сочпнитель, —нп-
ца, авторъ, вп новъ-
нпкъ; to—ise, уполно-
мочпвать; — ity, на-
чальство, власть, сп-
ла, мнѣніе, авторп-
тетъ.

autobiography, автобіо-
графія.

autumn, осень.

auxiliary, вспомогатель-
ное войско.

avail, польза; to be of

no —, не приносить пользы, ничего не помогать; to —, пользоваться чѣмъ; — able, полезный, годный, способный.

avarice, скупость.

avenge, отмщать; —r, мститель.

avenue, поѣздъ, дорога.

aver, утверждать.

average, среднее число; средній.

averse, несклонный, неохотный.

aversion, отвращеніе.

avidity, алчность, жадность.

avoid, избѣгать, миновать, удалять.

avow, признавать, обнаруживать; —al, признаніе; to make an—al, признаваться; —ed, признанный, общепризнанный, извѣстный.

await, ждать, выжидать, предстоять.

awake, разбуждать, пробуждать, пробуждаться, просыпаться; to be —, не спать.

awaken, см. awake

award, рѣшеніе, приговоръ.

aware, осмотрительный, осторожный; to be —, предвидѣть, остерегаться, знать; to make —, давать знать, указывать на.

away, прочь; — went Gilpin, улетѣлъ нашъ Гильпинъ; — went hat and wig, слетѣли шляпа и парикъ.

awe, страхъ; to —, устрашать.

awful, страшный; —ly, страшно.

awhile, нѣсколько времени, не долго.

awkward, неловкій, неуклюжій, неудобный.

awoke, см. awake.

ay, ахъ!

aye, увы!

the Azores, Азорскіе острова.

azure, лазуревый, голубой.

B.

babe, baby, ребенокъ, малютка.

Babel, Babylon, Вавилонъ.

back, спина; задній; назадъ, обратно; at the —, сзади; with armour on her —, одѣтая въ латы; —side, задъ; —ward, —wards, назадъ.

bad, худой, дурной; a — tooth ache, сильная зубная боль; —ly, дурно; — ness, худое состояніе.

bade, см. bid.

badge, знакъ, примѣта.

bag, мѣшокъ, сумка, волынка; a — full of, мѣшокъ съ; — gage, поклажа, багажъ; — pipe, волынка; — piper, волыночникъ.

bail, освобождать порукою.

bailiff, судейскій приставъ, экзекуторъ.

bait, блевка.

bake, печь; —r, пекарь,

булочникъ; —r's shop, булочная.

balance, равновѣсіе; to —, to keep —d, держать въ равновѣсіи.

balcony, балконъ.

bale, bale out, отливать (воду).

ball, мячикъ, балъ.

ballad, баллада.

balloon, воздушный шаръ.

ban, церковное оглашеніе.

band, толпа, шайка, дружина; — box, коробочка, картонъ.

bandage, перевязывать.

bandit, banditto, разбойникъ, бандитъ.

banish, изгонять, удалять; —ment, изгнаніе, удаленіе.

bank, берегъ, банка, мель, пригорокъ, банкъ; — bill, — note, банковый билетъ.

banner, знамя.

banter, издѣваться, насмѣхаться.

baptism, крещеніе.

baptist, креститель, перекрещенецъ, баптистъ.

baptize, крестить.

bar, брусокъ, полоса, запоръ, поперечина, перила, загородка, завалъ, преграда, баррикада, рогатка, судъ, судейская, судебная палата, присутствіе; toll —, шлагбаумъ.

Barbadoes, Барбадосъ.

barbarian, варваръ.

barbarism, barbarity, варварство, дикое состояніе.

barbarous, варварскій.

, необразованный.

Barbary, Варварія.

barber, брадобрей.

bard, бардъ, пѣвецъ.

bare, см. **bear.**

bare, голый, непокры-
тый, скудный, про-
стой, единственный;
— headed, непокры-
тою головою.

bargain, покупка; into
the —, въ добавокъ.

barge, баржа, катеръ;
— man, гребецъ на
шлюпкѣ.

bark, кора, лай; to —,
лаять.

barley, ячмень; — bread,
ячменный хлѣбъ.

barn, житница, рига.

baron, баронъ.

barrack-square, казар-
менная площадь.

barrel, бочка, стволъ
(ружейный).

barren, безплодный.

barricado, загораживать
рогатками, ставить
баррикады.

barrier, барьеръ, загородка, перила, рѣ-
шетка, рогатка, шлаг-
баумъ.

base, основаніе; низкій,
подлый; to —, осно-
вывать.

basin, bason, полоскательная чашка, чаша,
тазикъ, водоемъ, бас-
сейнъ.

basket, корзина, корзи-
ночный; — handle,
дужка (у шпаги); —
hilted, съ дужкою; —
woman, разнощица;
—work, корзинщичьи
издѣлія.

bastard, побочное дитя.

baste, обливать масломъ.

batch, печь.

bathe, купать, прима-
чивать, купаться.

bathing expedition, экспедиція для купанія.

battalion, баталіонъ.

batter, колотить.

battery, батарея.

battle, сраженіе, битва;
to fight a —, давать
сраженіе; to —, биться,
сражаться; — field,
поле сраженія.

bawl out, кричать во все
горло, орать.

bay, губа, бухта; to—,
лаять, выть.

be, быть. находиться;
conceiving to — chan-
ged, полагая, что слѣ-
довало размѣнять; he
will not — long, онъ
долго не останется; if
any one — to tell me,
еслибъ кто нибудь мнѣ
сказалъ; it was to —
found, его можно бы-
ло найти; nothing is
to — hoped, ничего не-
льзя ожидать; no time
was to — lost, нельзя
было терять времени;
the work to — done,
работа, которую слѣ-
довало заниматься;
there is no describing
it but, описать это
можно только; there
was nothing to—seen,
ничего не было видно;
they were to tell, онѣ
должны были сказать;
to — off, убираться
уйти; we are to dine,
мы должны обѣдать;
who was sitting, кто
сидѣлъ?

beach, морской берегъ.

beam, брусъ, бревно,
бимсъ, лучъ; on her
—ends, стойкомъ на
бимсѣ, на боку; to—,
испускать лучи.

bear, медвѣдь.

bear, носить, приносить,
выдерживать, пытать;
to—an aspect, имѣть
видъ; to—a distinguish-
ed part, играть важ-
ную роль; to — an ill
will, желать кому зла;
to — a likeness, to—re-
semblance, походить
на; to — a ratio to,
имѣть размѣръ отно-
сительно; to—regard,
оказывать уваженіе;
to — away, уносить,
выигрывать, получать.
пріобрѣтать; to —
down, нестись, спу-
скаться; to—over, пе-
реносить, переводить

beard, борода.

bearer, носильщикъ; см.
также **sedar-bearer.**

bearing, поведеніе, мѣстоположеніе, направ-
леніе, пеленгъ, фигу-
ра въ щитѣ; armoreal
—s, гербовыя фигуры.

beast, звѣрь, животное.

beat, извѣстное про-
странство, опредѣлен-
ное надзору дежурнаго
полисмена; to—, бить,
биться, побѣждать, об-
бѣжать; to—about, ла-
вировать.

beaten, см. **beat.**

beating, побои; was sure
of a—, могъ быть увѣ-
ренъ, что его по-
бьютъ; him that you talk
of —, тотъ, котораго

Вы собираетесь по-
бить;—of the surf, при-
бои буруна.
beautiful, прекрасный,
красивый, изящный;
—girl, красавица,
красотка.
beauty, красота.
beaver, бобровая шляпа.
became, см. **become**.
because, потому что;—of,
ради.
become, сделаться; what
became of him,' что съ
нимъ сделалось?
bed, постель, кровать;
to go to—, ложиться
спать; — chamber, —
room, спальня; — clo-
thes, одеяло, просты-
ни; — ding, постель-
ный приборъ;—room
window, окно спальни.
bee, пчела.
beech, букъ, буковый.
beef, говядина.
been, см. **be**.
beer, пиво; table—, столовое пиво; —money,
деньги на пиво.
befall, случаться.
before, прежде, ранее, до,
прежде нежели, передъ,
передъ темъ, впередъ;
from—, отъ места впе-
реди;—hand, впереди;
to be—hand with any
one, опередить кого.
beg, просить, просить
милостыню; I — your
pardon, извините; to—
assistance, просить по-
мощи.
began, см. **begin**.
beget, порождать, причинять.
beggar, нищій; —ly, ни-
щенскій.

begging friar, нищенствующій монахъ.
begin, начинать;—ning,
начало.
begotten, см. **beget**.
beguile, обольщать, проводить, облегчать, со-
кращать.
begun, см. **begin**.
behalf, польза; in — of,
on — of, въ пользу
чего.
behave, вести себя.
behaviour, поведеніе.
behead, обезглавливать,
отсекать голову.
beheld, см. **behold**.
behind, позади, за; to leave
—, оставлять.
behold, смотреть, уви-
деть, видеть; — er, зри-
тель.
being, существо.
Belgian, Бельгіецъ.
Belgium, Бельгія.
belief, вера, верованіе.
believe, верить, веро-
вать, полагать, ду-
мать; —г, верующій.
bell, колоколъ, коло-
кольчикъ.
bellow, мычать, реветь
bellows, мехъ.
belong, принадлежать.
beloved, любимый, воз-
любленный.
below, подъ, ниже, внизу, to go —, идти
внизъ.
belt, поясъ; to—, опоя-
сывать, перепоясы-
вать.
bench, скамейка, засе-
датели; — of justice,
судилище, судъ, су-
дебное место.
bend, нагибать, натяги-
гивать (лукъ), накло-

няться, приклонять
(колени); to — down,
сокрушать, поражать;
to—over, перегибаться.
beneath, подъ.
benefactor, благодетель.
benefice, духовное место.
beneficial, благотворный,
полезный.
benefit, благодеяніе, выгода, польза, прибыль;
to—, приносить пользу.
benevolence, благоде-
тельность, благотво-
рительность.
benevolent, благодетель-
ный, благотворитель-
ный.
Bengal, Бенгалія; Бен-
гальскій.
bent, склонный, расположенный; см. **bend**;
to be—on, настоять,
хотеть непременно.
bequeath, отказать, за-
вещать.
bereave, лишать чего.
bereft, см. **bereave**.
berry, ягода.
beset, осаждать, окружать, безпокоивать,
смущать.
beside, подле; — him-
self, вне себя.
besides, сверхъ, кроме,
сверхъ того.
besiege, осаждать.
bespeak, предвещать, показывать.
besprinkle, окроплять.
best, самый лучшій, на-
илучшій; лучше, наи-
лучшимъ образомъ;
at—, по лучшему; I will
do the—I can, я сде-
лаю все что могу; to
make the — of one's
way поспешать.

bestain, запятывать, замарывать.

bestow, давать, дарить; to—on, жаловать кому, подавать; to — one's self on, выходить за мужъ за.

bet, закладъ; to—, биться объ закладъ, держать пари.

betide, случаться, приключаться.

betray, передавать, измѣнять, открывать, обнаруживать, показывать.

better, лучшій, лучше.

Betty, Елисавета.

between, betwixt, между, промежду.

beverage, питье, напитокъ.

bewail, сѣтовать о чемъ, оплакивать, вопіять.

beyond, по ту сторону, за, сверхъ, выше.

Bible, Библія.

biblical, библейскій.

bid, велѣть, приказывать; to—farewell прощаться съ кѣмъ; to— any one a good-morrow, пожелать кому добраго утра; the highest — der, сулящій больше всѣхъ за что либо, предлагающій высшую цѣну за что.

big, большой, обширный.

bight, бухта (у каната).

bigoted, изувѣрный, пустосвятый, лицемѣрный.

bill, объявленіе, вексель, счетъ, проэктъ, предложеніе, законъ, билль; Exclusion —, Предложеніе объ Исключеніи.

billet, полѣно.

billow, волна.

bind, вѣтка; to—, вязать, обвязывать, обязывать; to — together, связывать, соединять.

biography, жизнеописаніе, біографія.

bird, птица.

birth, рожденіе, рождество, происхожденіе, положеніе;—day, день рожденія;— place, мѣсто рожденія, родина;— right, право рожденія.

biscuit, сухарь.

bishop, епископъ; — ric, епископство.

bit, кусочекъ, мундштукъ; a—of a breeze, легкій вѣтерокъ.

bitter, горькій, жестокій, непримиримый (о враждѣ);—ly, горько.

black, черный цвѣтъ, Негръ; черный;—bearded, съ черною бородой;—smith, кузнецъ.

blade, клинокъ.

blame, порицать, винить.

blanket, одѣяло покрывало.

blast, вѣтеръ, порывъ, звукъ, тонъ.

blaze, пыл, пламя, сіяніе, блескъ; to—, пылать, пламенѣть; to—forth, воспламеняться, воспаляться.

bleak, блѣдный, холодный, открытый.

bled, см. bleed.

bleed, крови течь, обливаться кровію; to—to death, изойти кровію, умереть отъ сильнаго

кровотеченія; — ing, изливающійся кровію.

blend, сливаться, смѣшиваться.

bless, благословлять; — ed, благословенный, блаженный;—ing, благословеніе, благодать.

blest, см. bless.

blew, см. blow.

blind, штора; слѣпой.

blithely, весело, радостно.

block, кусокъ необдѣланный;—head, болванъ; — house, крѣпосца, блокгаузъ; to—up, задѣлывать, запирать, загораживать, преграждать.

blockade, блокировать, обложить блокадою.

blood, кровь, храбрецъ, щеголь;—shed, кровопролитіе;—y, окровавленный, кровопролитный.

blow, ударъ, толчекъ; at one—, однимъ ударомъ; to—, дуть, раздувать, играть на, трубить, давать (сигналъ); to — in, выламывать, вышибать; to—off, сдувать; to — out, задувать; to — up, взрывать, поднимать на воздухъ; to—upon, чернить.

blue, голубой цвѣтъ, синій цвѣтъ, синій, голубой.

blunder, ошибка.

blunderbuss, мушкетонъ.

blunt, суровый, грубый, неучтивый, неуклюжій.

blush, краска на лицѣ.

boar, боровъ, кабанъ,

board, бортъ столъ; on—, on—the ship,на суднѣ, на судно; over —, за бортъ, за бортомъ;Navy—, Адмиралтействъ-Совѣтъ; —of Control, контрольная палата.

boast, хвастаніе, хвастовство, слава, гордость; to —, хвастать, хвастаться, хвалить, выхвалять.

boat, лодка, шлюпка, судно; лодочный;—action, сраженіе на лодкахъ; — man, лодочникъ,гребецъ,матросъ.

Bob, см. Robert.

bode, предвѣщать, предзнаменовать.

Bodleian, Бодлейскій.

body, тѣло, туловище, трупъ, особа, множество, масса, куча, толпа, общество, сословіе;—guard, тѣлохранитель;in a—,вмѣстѣ, всѣ вмѣстѣ; — of troops, отрядъ войска.

bog, болото.

Bohemia, Богемія.

boil, варить, кипѣть, кипятить,бить вверхъ ключемъ;to—up, вскипать;—ed down, вывареный; — er, котелъ; — ing, кипѣніе.

boisterous, буйный.

bold, смѣлый, отважный, крутой; — ly, смѣло; —ness, смѣлость, отважность.

bomb proof, непроницаемый бомбами.

bombard,бомбардировать.

Bombay, Бомбей; Бомбейскій.

bandage, неволя, рабство.

bondsman, крѣпостной.

bone, кость.

bonnet, шапка.

bony,костяной;костистый.

book, книга.

boom, лисель - спиртъ, гикъ.

boon, благодѣяніе, милость, подарокъ.

boot, сапогъ.

bootless, безполезный.

booty, добыча.

border,пограничная земля, граница; to—upon, граничить, быть смежнымъ съ чѣмъ.

bore, сверлить дыру; см. также bear.

born, рожденный; to be—, родиться; high —, знатнаго происхожденія; well—,благородный.

borne, см. bear.

borough,мѣстечко,посадъ.

borrow, занимать, брать въ займы.

bosom, грудь, сердце.

Botany-Bay, Ботани-бей.

both, оба, обѣ, то и другое; — and, и ... и, какъ . . . такъ и.

bother, оглушать, надоѣдать.

bottle, бутылка;—neck, горло (у бутылки).

bottom, дно, глубина, низъ, исподъ; to be at the—of any thing,быть побудительною причиной чему.

bough, сукъ, сучекъ.

bought, см. buy.

bound, см. bind; скокъ, скачекъ;to—,прыгать, скакать, ограничить, граничить; to be — , быть обязаннымъ; —

for, назначенный, отправляющійся въ; to—along, поскакать; — ary, предѣлъ; — less, безпредѣльный; — s, предѣлы.

bounty, щедрость, щедрота, благотворительность.

bouse out, выдвигать (пушку).

bow, поклонъ, лукъ, арчакъ (у сѣдла), корабельный носъ, скула; long—, лукъ; the best—er anchor, якорь плехтъ;—man, стрѣлецъ; — sprit, бушпритъ.

bowl, чаша.

bowls, игра въ кегли, кегельная игра.

box, ящикъ, ларчикъ, кружка, мѣсто, козлы.

boy, мальчикъ,ребенокъ; —hood, отрочество.

boyar, бояринъ.

brace, подтяжка; to —, стягивать;—let, браслетъ, зарукавье, напястье, наручень.

Brahminism, Браминское исповѣданіе.

brain, мозгъ.

brake, кустарникъ; см. также break.

branch, сукъ, вѣтвь, отрасль.

brandy, водка.

brass, желтая мѣдь, латунь, красная мѣдь; мѣдный.

bravado, хвастовство, чванство.

brave, храбрый, бодрый, славный; to—, презирать, не страшиться;

— ly, храбро; — гу, храбрость.

brawl, горланить, журчать.

brawny, мышковатый, дюжій.

bray, ревѣть.

Brazil, the Brazils, Бразилія.

breach, проломъ, прерываніе, нарушеніе; — of faith, вѣроломство.

bread, хлѣбъ, пропитаніе , ‘ прокормленіе ; brown —, черный хлѣбъ; — and butter, хлѣбъ съ масломъ.

breadth, ширина.

break, ломать, переламывать, ломаться, бить или ударять (о волнахъ), прорывать, сокрушать, сокрушаться; to — a spear, биться съ кѣмъ на копьяхъ; to—down, сламывать; to — fast, завтракать; to—in, врываться; to —in a horse, выѣзживать лошадь; to—loose, освобождаться ; to — off, отламывать, прекращать, прерывать; to — out, начинаться, вспыхивать, загораться; to— out in, выражать, разсыпаться въ чемъ о комъ; to—the way, давать или уступать дорогу, сворачивать; to—upon, прерывать, врываться; to be broken in the spirit, сокрушаться о чемъ, быть приведеннымъ въ уныніе;—ers, бурунъ, прибой; — fast, завтракъ (утренній чай или кофе);—of day, разсвѣтъ.

breast, грудь, сердце, упорная подушка (у орудія); —high, вышиною до груди.

breath, дыханіе; to be out of—, запыхаться, уставать; to hang on a—, висѣть на волоскѣ; to—e, дышать чѣмъ.

bred, см. **breed,** well—, благовоспитанный.

breed, порода, разведеніе (животныхъ); to —, порождать, производить, воспитывать; — of horses, разведеніе лошадей, конозаводство;—ing, воспитаніе, поведеніе; good —ing, вѣжливость.

breeze, вѣтерокъ.

brethren, см. **brother.**

brew, варить (пиво).

brick, кирпичъ; кирпичный;—layer, каменщикъ.

bride, невѣста;—groom, женихъ.

bridge, мостъ.

bridle, узда; to hold her — rein, держать за ея повода; to — , взнуздывать.

brigade, бригада.

bright, яркій, свѣтлый, сіяющій, лоснистый; to — en, свѣтлѣть ; — ness, блескъ, сіяніе.

brilliant, блистательный, блестящій; —ly, великолѣпно.

brim, край, поле (у шляпы).

brindle, пестрина, рябь.

bring, приносить, приводить, привозить; to — back, возвращать; to — down, сносить, ловить, поймать; to—in, вносить; to—intelligence,

увѣдомлять, извѣщать; to — into, вводить; to —into force, возъимѣть силу или дѣйствіе; to —into judgment, производить судъ надъ кѣмъ; to — into one's power, завладѣть кѣмъ; to—on or upon, наводить, причинять; to—out, выносить, выводить; to—over, переносить, перевозить, приносить съ собою, переваливать; to—succour, подавать помощь; to — to, доводить до, перевозить, отвозить въ; to—to do, заставить дѣлать; to—together, собирать; to — to pass, совершать; to — up, воспитывать; to — up the rear, быть аріергардомъ; to—upon, навлекать; he succeded in —ing up the watch, ему удалось достать часы.

brinish, солоноватый.

brink, край.

briskly, бодро, живо, проворно; when the glass had gone—about, когда они порядочно напились вина.

bristly, щетиноватый.

Bristol, Бристоль; Бристольскій.

Britain, Бритапія; Great —, Великобританія.

Britany, Brittany, Бретань (во Франціи).

British, британскій; the —, Британцы.

Briton, Британецъ.

broach, брошка; to —, початать (бочку).

broad, широкій, обшир-

ный, грубый, нескром-
ный; шириною; in —
day light, среди бѣ-
лаго дня; — side, пла-
кардъ.

brocoli, броколь.

broiling of the sun, солнечный жаръ.

broke, см. **break**.

broken, см. **break**.

brook, ручей ручеёкъ.

brother, братъ, това-
рищъ; we had been —
officers, мы вмѣстѣ
служили офицерами; —
ly, братскій.

brought, см. **bring**.

brow, бровь, лобъ; with
the sweat of one's—,
въ потѣ лица своего.

brown, бурый;—ish, смугловатый;—red, буро-
красный, темнокрас-
ный.

bruise, ушибать.

Brunswick, Брауншвейгъ.

brush, чистить щеткою,
помчаться, проби-
раться.

brutal, звѣрскій, скот-
скій;—ly, весьма гру-
бо, жестоко.

brute, звѣрь, скотъ, ско-
тина.

bubble, пузырь; to blow
— s out of soap, пу-
скать мыльные пузы
ри; to —, вскипать,
журчать.

buck, косуля.

bucket, ведро.

buckle, пряжка; to —,
драться, биться.

bud, почка.

buffoon, шутъ.

bugle, **bugle-horn**, ро-
жекъ съ клапанами.

build, строить, основы-

вать;— er, строитель;
—ing, постройка, строе-
ніе, зданіе.

built, см. **build**.

bull, быкъ, булла, пап-
ская грамота.

bullet, пуля.

bully, храбрецъ, буянъ.

bulwark, оплотъ, ограда.

bump, колотить, уда-
рять, бухать.

bundle, связка, пучекъ.

bungalow, соломою кры-
тый домъ (въ Индіи).

buoy, бакенъ, 'томбуй,
буй.

burden, грузъ, тяжесть,
вмѣстимость, ноша,
бремя.

burgess, мѣщанинъ, также депутатъ мѣстечка
(въ Англіи).

Burgundy, Бургундія.

burial-place, мѣсто по-
гребенія.

burly, дюжій, дородный.

Burmese, Бирманскій.

burn, сжигать, горѣть,
сгорать; to — down,
сжигать, сгорать;—ing,
палящій, знойный.

burnt, см. **burn**; a hole
—in the floor, отвер-
стіе, прогорѣвшее въ
полу.

burst, разрываться, пере-
ламываться; to—forth,
прорываться, выхо-
дить; to—into, вры-
ваться, вторгаться; to
—into tears, заплакать;
to—out, вырываться,
трескаться, лопаться.

bury, зарывать, похо-
ронять, погребать.

bush, кустъ.

busily, заботливо, дѣя-
тельно.

business, занятіе, торговля, ремесло, мас-
терство, дѣло, дѣла,
обязанность; I went
to my—, я сталъ за-
ниматься дѣлами; to
make a good — of it,
хорошо обдѣлывать
свои дѣла.

bust, бюстъ.

bustle, хлопоты, суматоха, волненіе; to—,
хлопотать, заботиться.

busy, дѣятельный, трудолюбивый, шумливый.

but, но, только, кромѣ,
если 'бы не; nothing
—, только;—for, еслибъ
не было; —just, толь-
ко что; —that he was
very glad to accept,
чтобы не принять съ
радостію; not knowing
— that there might
be ... ashore, не зная
не будетъ ли на бе-
регу; there was not
a soul—felt, не было
ни одной души, кото-
рая бы не почувство-
вала.

butcher, мясникъ; to—,
убивать, зарѣзывать.

butler, кельнеръ, по-
гребщикъ.

butt, цѣль, предметъ
(насмѣшки);—end, то-
рецъ, конецъ.

butter, масло (коровье).

button, пуговица.

buy, купить, покупать.

buz, жужжать.

by, съ, со, подлѣ, у,
посредствомъ, мимо,
къ, черезъ, по, подъ,
за, (означаетъ также
твор. падежъ); — all
means, непремѣнно;

—and by, ужё, скоро;
— one's self, одинъ,
самъ; —the light, при
свѣтѣ; —the road, на
дорогѣ;—this time, къ
этому времени;— what,
—which, чѣмъ.

byroad, bye-road, просе-
лочная дорога.

byword, пословица, по-
говорка.

C.

cab, извощичій кабріо-
летъ; — driver, изво-
щикъ.

cabaret, шинокъ, кабакъ

cabbage, капуста;—leaf,
капустный листъ.

cabin, хижина, шалашъ,
каюта; — door, дверь
каюты;—et,кабинетъ;
—et timber,дерево для
столярной работы.

cable, канатъ.

cacao, какао.

Cadiz, Кадиксъ.

Caesar, Цесарь.

Caffre, Кафръ.

cage, клѣтка.

cake, пэксъ, пирожное.

calculate,исчислять,раз-
считывать; he was bet-
ter—d,онъ былъ болѣе
способенъ;—d to, слу-
жащій къ тому,чтобы...

calculation, вычисленіе,
разсчетъ.

Caledonian, Каледоня-
нинъ.

calendrer, катальщикъ,
лощильщикъ.

calf, теленокъ.

call, призывъ; to —,звать,
называть, кричать,при-

зывать, созывать, за-
ходить, заѣзжать; to —
away, отзывать; to —
fire, звать на пожаръ;
to — for, спрашивать,
требовать; to — for
help, звать на помощь;
to — forth, вызывать;
to —from, to—off, от-
зывать; to — on, вы-
зывать, заходить; to
—out, закричать, вос-
клицать;to —over.при-
зывать; to — to, кли-
кать, закричать, to—
to account, требовать
отъ кого отчета; to —
together, созывать;—
ing,должность ремесло.

calm, тишина, спокой-
ствіе, штиль; спо-
койный, тихій; to —,
успокоивать; — ly,спо-
койно; — ness, спо
койность; a man of
great—ness, человѣкъ
съ большимъ спокой-
ствіемъ духа.

Calmuc, Калмыкъ.

came, см. come.

camp, лагерь; life of—s,
лагерная или походная
жизнь; — aign, походъ,
кампанія.

can, кружка.

can, могу; I cannot(сокр.
can't), я не могу;прош.
время I could, я могъ.

Canada, Канада.

Canadian, Канадецъ.

canal, каналъ.

canary, канарское вино.

candid, чистосердечный,
откровенный, искрен-
ній.

candidate, кандидатъ.

candle, свѣча, свѣчка;
—stick, подсвѣчникъ.

cane, камышъ, трость;
sugar —, сахарный
тростникъ.

canine, собачій.

cannibal,каннибалъ, лю-
доѣдъ; лютый, жесто-
кій, безчеловѣчный.

cannon, пушка, - орудіе,
пушки.

canoe, лодка.

canonicals, облаченіе
(церковное).

can't, см **can**

cantonments,кантонир-
квортиры.

canvass, паруспна, парусъ.

canzonet, пѣсенька.

cap, шапка, фуражка.

capable, способный, въ
состояніи; nothing was
—, ничего не могло.

capacity, способность,
качество.

caparison, покрывать ча-
пракомъ, наряжать.

cape, мысъ.

the **Cape Coast,** Капъ.
Костъ; —Colony, Кап
ская Земля; the—Verd
Islands, острова Зе-
ленаго мыса.

capital, столица, капиталъ, капитель; слав-
ный, отличный.

capitulation,капитуляція.

caplin, каплинъ.

capricious,своенравный,
причудливый, каприз-
ный.

capsize опрокидыватъ.

captain,начальникъ, пол-
ководецъ, капитанъ,
шкиперъ, комендоръ
(у орудія); —of a gang
of robbers, предводи-
тель разбойничьей шай-

ки, разбойничій атаманъ.

captive, плѣнникъ; плѣнный.

captivity, плѣнъ.

capture, взятіе; to —, брать, перехватывать.

car, повозка, колесница.

Carausius, Каравзій.

caravan, караванъ.

carbine, карабинъ.

carbonate, углекислый.

carcass, оставъ, трупъ.

card, карта.

cardinal, кардиналъ; главный.

care, забота, попеченіе, стараніе, вниманіе, тщаніе; to be in the—, находиться подъ присмотромъ; to — about, to — for, пещись, заботиться о чемъ; I—not for, мнѣ дѣла нѣтъ; learning was little—d for, объ ученіи мало заботились; whom Europeans—d not to meddle with, съ которыми Европейцы не хотѣли имѣть дѣла; he would not—to sell them for less than, что онъ не можетъ взять за нихъ менѣе; —ful, тщательный, бережливый, осторожный; to be — ful of, заботиться, печься о чемъ; —fully, тщательно; —less, беззаботный, неосторожный; —lessly, небрежно, неосторожно; for myself I am—less, о самомъ себѣ я не хлопочу, не забочусь.

career, поприще, карьера.

caress, ласка; to—, ласкать.

cargo, грузъ, кладь.

caricature, карикатура.

carnival, карнавалъ, масляница.

carol, пѣть, воспѣвать.

carouse, пировать.

carpenter, плотникъ, тимерманъ.

carpet, коверъ.

carriage, повозка, карета, экипажъ; — way, проѣзжая дорога.

carrier, извощикъ.

carrot, морковь.

carry, носить, водить, возить, переносить, перевозить, перемогать, преодолѣвать, вовлекать; a cry calculated to — a distance, крикъ который можнобъ было слышать на большомъ разстояніи; to—about one, носить на себѣ; to — against, отстаивать противъ; to—along, уносить; to —away, сносить; to—in, вносить, приносить; to —into effect, приводить въ исполненіе; to — devastation into, предавать опустошенію; to — off, снести, увозить, убивать; to—on, производить, продолжать; to—on correspondence, вести переписку; to — one's point, достигать своей цѣли; to—out, вывозить; to — over, перевозить; to — any one to one's side, склонять кого на свою сторону; to—to the high-

est pitch, доводить до высшей степени.

cart, телѣга, возъ; —er, извощикъ.

cartridge, патронъ, картузъ.

cascade, водопадъ, каскада.

case, случай, положеніе, обстоятельство, колчанъ, футляръ, ящикъ; to be the—, случаться, быть такъ; which was the common —, что обыкновенно случалось или бывало; his own—, что бываетъ съ нимъ самимъ.

cash, наличныя деньги.

cask, бочка, боченокъ.

casket, шкатулка, ларчикъ.

cassock, ряса.

cast of thought, образъ мыслей; to —, кидать, бросать; to — a stain, запятнывать; to—away, выбрасывать (на берегъ), претерпѣвать крушеніе; to — down, потуплять (глаза); to — off, сбрасывать, скидывать; to—one's eyes on, взглядывать на; to—up, считать, выкладывать.

castaway, извергъ, покинутый.

caste, каста.

castle, замокъ; — wall, замковая стѣна.

casual, случайный; —ly случайно.

cat, кошка.

cataract, водопадъ, падунъ.

catastrophe, необыкновенное приключение.

catch, ловить, поймать, захватывать, задѣвать; to—at, хвататься за что; to—hold of, схватывать что, хвататься за что; to—the breeze, войти въ полосу вѣтра.

Cateran, разбойникъ въ горахъ Высокой Шотландіи.

cathedral, соборъ, соборная церковь.

Catherine, Екатерина.

catholic, католикъ; католическій; — ism or Roman—ism, римско-католическая вѣра.

cattle, скотъ.

Catus, Катъ.

the Caucasus, Кавказъ.

caught, см. catch.

cauliflower, цвѣтная капуста.

cause, причина, дѣло, партія, тяжба, процессъ; to—, причинять, заставлять, велѣть;—less, безпричинный.

caution, осторожность; to take—, брать мѣры предосторожности.

cautious, осторожный, разсудительный; —ly, осторожно.

cavalier, кавалеръ, роялистъ.

cavalry, конница, кавалерія.

cavern, пещера.

cease, переставать.

cedar, кедръ; кедровый.

ceiling, потолокъ.

celebrate, праздновать; —d, знаменитый, извѣстный.

celerity, поспѣшность, быстрота.

cell, келья.

cellar, погребъ.

Celtic, кольтскій.

censorship, цензура.

censure, порицать, осуждать,

central, средоточный, центральный.

centre, центръ.

century, столѣтіе, вѣкъ.

ceremonial, церемоніялъ.

ceremonies, обряды; master of the —, церемоній-мейстеръ.

ceremonious, церемонный, чинный.

ceremony, обрядъ, церемонія.

certain, вѣрный, нѣкоторый, извѣстный; are—to rise, непремѣнно явятся, she was —, она была увѣрена; —ly, конечно; — ty вѣрность, увѣренность.

Cesar, Цесарь, Кесарь.

Ceylon, Цейлонъ.

chagrin, огорченіе, досада.

chain, цѣпь, цѣпочка.

chair, стулъ; easy —, кресла; — man, предсѣдатель; chairmen of quarter sessions, предсѣдатели засѣданій, бывающихъ каждые три мѣсяца по назначенію окружныхъ начальниковъ.

chaise, коляска.

chalk, мѣлъ, мѣловой; —у, мѣловой.

challenge, вызовъ; to —, вызывать; —r, вызыватель, вызывающій

(на поединокъ или дуэль).

chamber, покой;— lain, каммергеръ.

chambre, см. robe.

champ, жевать.

champion, боецъ.

chance, случай, возможность, удача, судьба; to take one's —, рисковать; to —, случаться, происходить.

chancellor, канцлеръ; Lord —, государственный канцлеръ.

change, перемѣна, измѣненіе, мелкія деньги, сдача; to —, перемѣнять, измѣнять, размѣнять, перемѣняться; to — situations, перемѣняться мѣстами.

channel, каналъ, проливъ; канальный; the —, Британскій каналъ.

chap, человѣкъ, молодчина.

chapel, часовня, капелла, молитвенный домъ, церковь.

chaplain, капелянъ, капланъ;— ship, капелянство.

chapter, глава.

character, буква, литера, нравъ, свойство, качество, характеръ, слава, доброе имя, честное имя; he bore a respectable —, онъ слылъ честнымъ человѣкомъ;—istic, характеристика, отличительное свойство, характеристическій.

charge, бремя, грузъ, расходъ, издержки, плата, присмотръ, попеченіе , порученіе , должность, жалоба, обвиненіе, приступъ, нападеніе, атака; at small —, за незначительную плату, не дорого; in — of several boats , имѣющій въ своемъ распоряженіи нѣсколько лодокъ; to make a —, представлять обвиненіе ; to —, обременять , отягощать, нагружать, ставить въ счетъ, возлагать, требовать, просить; with which he was — d, что ему было поручено; —r, боевой конь, ратный конь.

chariot, колесница.

charitably, ласково.

charity, милостыня.

Charlemagne, Карлъ Великій.

Charles, Карлъ

charm, прелесть, привлекательность; to —, очаровать, прельщать; —ing, прелестный.

charter, граммата, хартія.

chase, охота; to —, гоняться за, преслѣдовать, охотиться, травить.

chasm, отверстіе, пучина, пропасть.

chasteness, чистота

chattering of teeth, щелканіе зубами.

chawed up, сухой, вялый.

cheap, дешевый; to —en, сдѣлать дешевле, сбавлять цѣну.

cheat, обманывать.

check, уронъ, задержка,

препона, узда; to —, препятствовать.

checkered, пестрый.

cheek, щека, лице; — bone, скуловая или скульная кость.

cheer, восклицаніе, ура; to give three hearty—s, трижды усердно кричать ура; to —, веселить, развеселять; to— up, скрѣпиться духомъ; — fully, весело ; — fulness, веселость ; —ing, утѣшительный, отрадный.

cheese, сыръ ; — cake, сырникъ, ватрушка.

cherish, питать (надежду).

cherry, вишня; — tree, вишенное дерево.

Chersonesus, полуостровъ, Херсонесъ.

chest, сундукъ, ящикъ, грудь; — of tea, цыбикъ.

chevalier, кавалеръ.

chew, жевать.

chief, глава, начальникъ; главный; — ly, преимущественно; — tain, начальникъ, глава племени.

child, дитя, ребенокъ; from a —, съ дѣтства ; — hood, дѣтство ; — like, дѣтскій; —'s play, дѣтская игра, дѣтская забава, игрушка, бездѣлица.

Chili, Чили; of —, —an, Чилейскій.

chill, знобъ; холодный; to strike a—, бросать въ дрожь; —y, знобкій, зябкій.

chime, звонъ, трезвонъ, куранты.

chimney, труба; — corner, уголъ камина; — sweep,—sweeper, трубочистъ.

chin, подбородокъ.

China, Китай, Фарфоръ; Фарфоровый.

Chinese, Китаецъ.

chip-box, коробочка.

chivalrous, рыцарскій, богатырскій.

chivalry, рыцарство.

choice, выборъ; выборный, отборный, драгоцѣнный.

cholera, холера.

choleric, холерическій, желчный.

choir, клиросъ , хоръ, хоры.

choke up , заваливать, засаривать.

choose, выбирать, избирать, хотѣть.

chopping knife, сѣчка, поварской ножикъ.

chose, см. choose.

chosen, см. choose.

Christ, Христосъ; in the year of —, (въ такомъто) году послѣ Рождества Христова; — endom , христіанство, христіанскіе народы; — ian, Христіанинъ, христіанскій; —ianity, христіанство, христіанская вѣра; — mas, — mas time, Рождество Христово.

Christopher, Христофоръ.

church, церковь; церковный; doctor of the —, докторъ богословія; the—of England, англиканская церковь; — man, духовная особа; —yard, кладбище, цер-

ковный погостъ;—yard
cottage,кладбищенскій
домикъ.

cider, яблоновка.

cigar, сигара.

Cimbrian, кимврійскій.

cinnamon, корица.

circle, кругъ; to —, окружать, обнимать.

circuit, окружность, объемъ;—ous, околичный.

circumference, окружность.

circumspection,осмотрительность.

circumstance, обстоятельство.

circumstancial, обстоятельный, подробный.

cistern, цистерна, водоемъ.

citizen, гражданинъ.

citron, цитронъ.

city, городъ (имѣющій соборъ), также названіе древнѣйшей, коммерческой части Лондона (древній городъ, торговый кварталъ).

civil, гражданскій, междоусобный, вѣжливый, учтивый; — isation, цивилизація, просвѣщеніе; — ized, просвѣщенный; —ly, учтиво, вѣжливо.

clad, см. **clothe.**

claim, притязаніе,право; to—, требовать чего, имѣть притязаніе на что, объявлять претензію на что.

clamour, кричать, вопіять, шумѣть.

clan, племя.

clap, хлопать (руками).

claret, Бордоское вино.

clash, брякаться, сталкиваться.

clasp, застежка,зацѣпка.

class, классъ, сословіе, родъ,разрядъ; second, — river,второклассная рѣка;—ical, классическій.

clatter, брякать,стучать, хлопать.

Claudius, Клавдій.

clause, клаузула, оговорка, прибавочная условная статья.

clay, глина, земля.

clean, чистый; чисто;to—, чистить;—ing, чищеніе, чистка; — liness, опрятность,чистоплотность.

cleanse away, отчищать.

clear, чистый, ясный, явный, внятный; ясно; to—, прочищать, очищать; to — one's self of any one, освобождаться, избавляться, отдѣлываться отъ кого; to—the door, выходить изъ дверей;—ly, ясно, явно.

cleave, раскалывать,раскалываться, колоться.

cleft, см. **cleave.**

clemency, милость, милосердіе.

Clement, Климентъ,Климентій.

clergy, духовенство; — man, священникъ, пасторъ.

clerical, духовный.

clerk, секретарь, писарь, прикащикъ.

clever, искусный, свѣдущій.

cliff, утесъ, крутояръ.

climate, климатъ, страна.

climb, лазить; to— up, взлѣзать.

cling, прицѣпляться.

cloak, плащъ, шинель.

clock, (стѣнные или столовые) часы; часовой; four o'clock, четыре часа; what o'clock, который часъ? — face, циферблатъ,цыфирная доска.

clog, деревянный башмакъ.

close, огородка, загороженное мѣсто, заключеніе, окончаніе, конецъ, исходъ; сомкнутый, затворенный, внимательный,точный, близкій, плотно, тѣсно, близко; to keep in — custody, строго держать въ заперти; to—, смыкать, закрывать, затворять, кончать, оканчивать, прекращать, кончаться; — by, —to, возлѣ, подлѣ;—ly, плотно, близко;—ness, духота, спертый воздухъ.

cloth, сукно, скатерть; to—e, одѣвать, покрывать;—es,—ing, одежда,платье; —ing trade, торгъ сукномъ.

cloud, облако; —y, облачный.

clove, гвоздика.

clown, мужикъ.

clumsy, грубый, топорный.

clung, см. **cling.**

cluster, группировать, расти гроздиами.

coach, карета, дилижансъ; a—and six, шестерка; by —, въ каретѣ; —

horse , каретная ло-
шадь; — man, кучеръ;
— office, контора дилп-
жансовъ; — stand, пз-
вощичья биржа.

coal, уголь; угольный; — pit,
каменноугольная копь.

coarse, грубый.

coast, морской берегъ;
to—, плавать вдоль бе-
реговъ.

coat, кафтанъ, сюртукъ;
— of arms; гербовый
щитъ; — of mail, коль-
чуга.

cock, пѣтухъ, кранъ; —
fight, пѣтушій бой.

cockle, гребенка (рако-
вина).

cocoa, кокосъ; кокосовый.

code, сводъ законовъ,
уложеніе.

codfish, треска.

coffee, кофе; кофейный;
— house, кофейня, кофей-
ный домъ; — room, кофей-
ная зала (въ гостин-
ницѣ).

coffin-like, похожій на
гробъ, подобный гробу.

cohort, когорта, толпа,
шайка.

coil, складывать (бух-
тами), свертывать.

coin, монета, деньги; to
—, чеканить, выду-
мывать.

cold, холодъ, простуда;
холодный; I am—, мнѣ
холодно, я зябну; — of
comfort, безутѣшный,
безотрадный.

collar, ошейникъ.

collect, собирать; — ed,
спокойный; she in-
stantly became calm
and — ed, она тотчасъ
успокоилась и собра-

лась мыслями; — ion,
собраніе, собираніе;
— or, собиратель, сбор-
щикъ.

college, университетъ,
факультетъ, коллегія,
высшее учебное заве-
деніе, академія; mili-
tary —, военно-учебное
заведеніе.

collegiate, соборный,
коллегіяльный.

collision, столкновеніе.

colonel, полковникъ.

colonial, колоніальный.

colonisation, колониза-
ція, поселеніе, водво-
реніе, учрежденіе ко-
лоніи.

colonise, поселять.

colonist, поселенецъ, ко-
лонистъ.

colony, колонія, поселе-
ніе.

colour, цвѣтъ, краска;
to—, красить, окраши-
вать; — ed, цвѣтной;
copper — ed, мѣдно-
цвѣтный; olive — ed,
оливковаго цвѣта; the
water was — ed with
the blood, вода обагря-
лась кровію

column, колонна.

combat, битва, сраженіе,
бой; to — сражаться,
бороться, биться; — ant,
борецъ, боецъ, рат-
никъ.

combination, соединеніе,
совокупленіе.

combine, соединять, сое-
диняться , сговари-
ваться.

combustible, горючій ма-
теріалъ.

come, приходить, пріѣз-
жать, идти, воспослѣ-

довать, случаться, на-
ставать; (пов. накл)
пойдемъ! — on, man!
давайте! to — along,
идти; to — back, воз-
вращаться; to — down,
сходить , спускаться,
слѣзать, опускаться,
нагрянуть; to — forth,
выходить изъ печати,
быть изданнымъ; to—
in, входить, прихо-
дить, пріѣзжать, захо-
дить; to — leaping, пры-
скакать; to — near, под-
ходить, приближаться;
to — on, наступать; to—
out, выходить, выхо-
дить въ свѣтъ; to —
over, переходить, пе-
реправляться; to —
round, поправляться,
перемѣняться; to — to
be true, осуществлять-
ся; to — to hand, быть
подъ рукою; to — to
pass, случаться; to —
to possess, вступать
во владѣніе (чѣмъ); to—
up, всходить на, под-
ниматься на, выхо-
дить на верхъ, подхо-
дить; to — up to the
capital, пріѣхать въ
столицу; to — up with,
догонять; I am coming,
я сейчасъ буду; is any
one coming, будетъ ли
кто нибудь? let little
children — nigh, пус-
тите дѣтей ко мнѣ!
the tide was coming
in, вода стала прибы-
вать; which ought to
— before the courts of
common law, которыя
подходятъ подъ общіе
законы.

44

comedy, комедія.

comely, приличный, достойный.

comer, см. new comer.

comfort, удобство, уютность, комфортъ, утѣшеніе; a house of —, домъ снабженный всѣми удобствами; — able, пріятный, комфортабельный; — ably, пріятно, комфортабельно, прилично; — less, безутѣшный.

command, повелѣніе, приказаніе, заповѣдь, начальство, командованіе, предводительство; — of one's temper, власть надъ собою; at his word of—, по приказанію его; to —, начальствовать, командовать, велѣть, приказывать, владѣть (чѣмъ), имѣть въ распоряженіи, обнимать (взоромъ); — er, начальникъ, командиръ, командующій; — er in chief, главнокомандующій; — ing, повелительный.

commemoration, воспоминаніе.

commence, начинать, начинаться; —ment, начинаніе, начало.

commend, поручать, препоручать; — ation, одобреніе, похвала.

comment, замѣчаніе, толкованіе, пересужденіе.

commerce, торговля, торгъ.

commercial, торговый, коммерческій; —ly, въ коммерческомъ или торговомъ отношеніи.

commission, коммиссія, порученіе; in the —, въ должности; high—, надворный судъ, Высшая Коммиссія; to be —ed, имѣть порученіе; — er, коммиссіонеръ, уполномоченный, чиновникъ.

commit, препоручать, ввѣрять, сажать въ тюрьму, учинять, совершать; to — an error, дѣлать ошибку, впадать въ ошибку; — tee, комитетъ, коммиссія, комитетскій, коммиссіонный.

commodious, удобный, уютный, покойный, просторный.

commodity, товаръ.

commodore, командоръ, начальникъ отряда.

common, общій выгонъ, общая паства; общій, простой, обыкновенный; —s, нижняя палата, нижній парламентъ; — ly; обыкновенно; —ness, всеобщность; — wealth, республика.

commune, имѣть общеніе.

communicate, соединяться, сообщать, сообщаться, имѣть сообщеніе·

communication, сообщеніе; a line of—, коммуникаціонная линія.

communion, причащеніе.

community, общество·

compact, плотный, сплошный, сжатый.

companion, товарищъ, собесѣдникъ, спутникъ, подруга; — way входъ

въ капитанскую каюту (на купеческомъ суднѣ).

company, общество, гости, провожатые, рота, кампанія, бесѣда; in—with, вмѣстѣ съ; to join—with, присоединяться къ.

comparatively, сравнительно.

compare, сравнивать, сличать; to—notes, перешептываться; — d with, въ сравненіи съ.

comparison, сравненіе.

compass, компасъ.

compassion, состраданіе; —ate, сострадательный; to—ate, сожалѣть.

compel, понуждать, принуждать, заставлять.

compensate, вознаграждать.

competence, пропитаніе, достаточное содержаніе.

competition, соперничество, состязаніе, конкуренція.

competitor, соискатель, соперникъ.

compile, составлять, сочинять.

complain, жаловаться, сѣтовать; —t, жалоба, сѣтованіе.

complement, комплектъ.

complete, полный, совершенный, комплектный; to—, довершать, доканчивать, совершать; — ly, совершенно.

compliant, сговорчивый, угодливый.

compliment, поклонъ, привѣтствіе, поздравленіе.

comply, соглашаться.

compose, составлять, сочинять, успокоивать; —d, составленный; to be—d of, состоять изъ.

compound, составъ,смѣсь; to—, составлять.

comprehend, понимать, заключать, содержать въ себѣ.

comprise, вмѣщать, заключать.

compunction, раскаяніе.

computation, счисленіе, вычисленіе.

compute, счислять, вычислять.

comrade, товарищъ.

conceal,скрывать;—ment, скрытое мѣсто, убѣжище.

concede, уступать.

conceive, понимать, думать,воображать; to—hopes, возымѣть надежду, питать надежду; he — d the idea, ему пришло на умъ.

concentration, сосредоточиваніе,

concern, дѣло, забота, безпокойство, скорбь; to—, касаться; —ing, касательно, о, объ.

conciliate, соглашать, примирять.

conclude, заключать, кончать, рѣшать, оканчивать; to—a bargain, сторговаться.

conclusion, заключеніе.

concordance, указатель изреченій библейскихъ.

concourse, стеченіе.

concur, споспѣшествовать, содѣйствовать, сходиться, соглашать-

ся; — rence, стеченіе, соединеніе.

condemn, осуждать, присуждать, приговаривать; — ation, осужденіе, приговоръ.

condescend, снисходить.

condition, условіе, положеніе, состояніе; on —, съ условіемъ, съ уговоромъ, съ тѣмъ чтобы.

conduct, поведеніе, поступокъ, веденіе (дѣлъ); to —, вести, провожать, устроивать, руководить, управлять, отправлять (церковныя требы); —or, проводникъ.

confederate, союзникъ.

confer on, жаловать кому; — ence, совѣщаніе.

confess, исповѣдывать, признаваться; — or, исповѣдникъ; исповѣдающій, вѣрующій въ.

confide, ввѣрять, ввѣряться, полагаться;—nce, довѣренность, довѣріе; — nt, увѣренный; in—nce, — ntly, съ увѣренностью.

confine, ограничивать, заключать, запирать, посадить въ тюрьму; to be —d to one's bed, лежать въ постелѣ; —ment, заключеніе, роды, арестъ,

confirm, утверждать, укрѣплять.

conflict, стычка, состязаніе; to—, бороться.

conformation, составъ, строеніе, сложеніе.

confound, разстроить, разрушать, смущать.

confuse, сбивать, запутывать; —d, смущенный, смѣшанный, безпорядочный; to become —d, смущаться, сбиваться.

confusion, замѣшательство, смущеніе, запутанность, путанница.

congenial, согласный, единодушный; — minds, люди одинаково мыслящіе, люди того же (умственнаго или духовнаго) направленія.

conglomeration, накопленіе, совокупленіе.

congratulate, поздравлять.

congregation, собраніе, сходка, конгрегація.

conjecture, догадка, предположеніе; to —, догадываться,

conjugal, супружескій.

conjunction, соединеніе, союзъ.

conjuncture, стеченіе(обстоятельствъ), случай.

conjure, заклинать; —r, колдунъ.

connect, соединять, связывать; — ed, связный, въ соотношеніи; — ion, связь, союзъ, сообщеніе, сношеніе.

connivance, потворство, допущеніе.

connive, потакать, потворствовать.

conquer, завоевывать, покорять, обуздывать, побѣждать; — or, побѣдитель, завоеватель·

conquest, завоеваніе.

conscience, совѣсть.

conscientiously, добросовѣстно.

conscious, увѣренный, знающій; — ness, сознаніе, чувство.

consent, согласіе; to—, соглашаться.

consequence, слѣдствіе, послѣдствіе, важность; by —, in —, въ слѣдствіе сего.

consequently, слѣдовательно.

consider, разсуждать, обдумывать, принимать въ соображеніе, считать, разсматривать; they will—twice, они хорошенько подумаютъ; —able, значительный, многозначущій, важный; —able time, продолжительное время; —ably, значительно;—ation, обдумываніе, разсужденіе, уваженіе.

consign over, предавать.

consist, состоять; —ent, совмѣстный.

consolation, утѣшеніе.

consonant, согласная буква.

conspiracy, заговоръ.

conspirator, заговорщикъ.

conspire, составлять заговоръ.

constable, коннетабль.

constancy, твердость, постоянство.

constant, постоянный; — ly, постоянно, безпрестанно.

Constantius, Констанцій.

consternation, смятеніе, изумленіе.

constitute, составлять; to be happdily —d

имѣть счастливое направленіе.

constitution, государственное учрежденіе, конституція, тѣлосложеніе;—al, конституціонный.

construct, строить, созидать; —ion, постройка, порядокъ, размѣщеніе или расположеніе словъ, конструкція.

construe, дѣлать конструкцію.

consult, спрашивать совѣта у кого, совѣтоваться съ кѣмъ.

consume, съѣдать, пожирать, потреблять.

consummate, совершенный.

consumption, потребленіе, истрата, чахотка.

contagion, зараза.

contain, содержать, содержать въ себѣ.

contaminate, осквернять.

contemn, презирать что, пренебрегать чѣмъ.

contemplation, созерцаніе, размышленіе.

contemporary, современникъ; современный.

contempt, презрѣніе.

contend, спорить, состязаться; to—for, состязаться за, подвизаться за.

content, довольство, удовольствіе; довольный, безропотный; to—one's self, удовольствоваться; — s, содержаніе; —ion, споръ, преніе, состязаніе.

contest, состязаніе, споръ.

contiguous, смежный.

continent, матсрикъ; — al, континентальный.

continual, безпрестанный; — ly, безпрестанно, безпрерывно.

continuance, продолженіе, продолжительность.

continue, продолжать, продолжаться;—d, безпрерывный; the impression — ing on my mind, такъ какъ это произвело глубокое впечатлѣніе на меня.

contract, получать, договариваться; вести переговоры; to—debts, входить въ долги.

contrary, противное; противный; — to my expectation, противъ моего ожиданія; a notice to the—, отмѣнительное предписаніе; on the—, to the — , напротивъ.

contrast, противоположность; to—, противуполагать, сличать, сравнивать, составлять контрастъ или противоположность, отличаться, различествовать между собою.

contribute, споспѣшествовать, способствовать, содѣйствовать.

contribution, контрибуція, сборъ, складчина, вносъ, споспѣшествованіе, содѣйствіе.

contrivance, выдумка, намѣреніе, умыселъ.

contrive, ухитряться, придумывать.

control, контроль, вліяніе, власть, повѣрка.

controversy, состязаніе, споръ, полемика.

convenience, conveniency, удобство, огнивница, трутъ.

convenient, удобный.

convent, монастырь, обитель;—icle, сходбище, сборище;—ion, собраніе, конвентъ.

conversation, разговоръ, бесѣда.

converse, разговаривать, бесѣдовать.

conversion, обращеніе.

convert, превращать, пре творять, обращать (въ истинную вѣру).

convey, отвозить, перевозить,пересылать,доставлять,сообщать,носить; —ance, везеніе, возка, провозъ, переѣздъ,повозка,экипажъ; —ance of letters, пересылка писемъ.

convict, изобличать; — ion, убѣжденіе.

convince, убѣждать.

convincing, убѣдительный.

convulsed, схваченъ судорогою.

cook, поваръ, кухарка; to—, стряпать, готовить; —ery, поваренное искуство; choice —ery, отличный столъ.

cool, прохладный, хладнокровный;—ly, хладнокровно.

cope, балдахинъ, каминлавка (у бѣлаго духовенства), клобукъ (у монаховъ).

copeek, копейка.

Copenhagen, Копенгагенъ.

copious, обильный, изобильный.

copper, мѣдь, мѣдныя деньги; мѣдный.

copse, кустарникъ.

copy, копія, переписанное на чисто; to —, подражать; — book, тетрадь.

coranto, курантъ (танецъ).

cord, веревка, союзъ, связь;—ially, радушно.

cork, пробочная кора.

corn, жито, хлѣбъ; — bearing, хлѣбородный; —ed beef, солонина.

corner, уголъ, уголокъ.

Cornwall, Корнваллисъ.

coronation, коронація.

corporal, капралъ.

corporeal, тѣлесный.

corpse, трупъ, мертвое тѣло.

corpulent, дородный, дебелый.

correct, исправлять;—ly, правильно.

correspondence, соотвѣтственность, сходство, переписка, корреспонденція.

correspondent, корреспондентъ.

corridor, корридоръ.

corrupt, испорченный, развратный;—ion, порча, испорченность, развратъ.

cost, цѣна, цѣнность, издержки, расходъ; at the—of, на счетъ; to —, стоить; —ly, цѣнный,драгоцѣнный, дорогой.

costermonger, яблочникъ.

cot, хижина;—tage, хижина, сельскій до-

микъ; a — tage girl, деревенская дѣвушка.

cotemporary, современникъ.

cotton, хлопчатая бумага; бумажный, хлопчатобумажный.

couch, постель, кушетка; to —, направлять (копье).

could, см. can.

council, совѣтъ.

counsel, совѣтъ; — lor, совѣтователь.

count, графъ; to—, считать; to—out, to — to any one, отсчитывать кому.

countenance, лицо, выраженіе лица; to —, благопріятствовать, покровительствовать.

counter, прилавокъ; to— balance, сохранять равновѣсіе, равняться, уравновѣшивать, приводить въ равновѣсіе; —part, двойникъ.

countess, графиня.

country, отечество, деревня, поле, страна, земля; деревенскій; to go into the—, ѣхать за городъ; — gentleman, сельскій дворянинъ;—man, землякъ, соотечественникъ, единоземецъ, деревенскій житель, селянинъ; a—seat, помѣстье, деревня; a — village, деревня.

county, графство;—town, уѣздный городъ.

couple, пара; a—of minutes, минуты двѣ; to —, соединять.

courage, мужество, хра-

брость, духъ, бодрость;
— gious, смѣлый.

course, ходъ, бѣгъ, те-
ченіе, курсъ, поприще,
время, порядокъ, оче-
редь, способъ дѣй-
ствія, обращеніе (солн-
ца), образъ жизни; of
—, конечно, натураль-
но, разумѣется; a mat-
ter of —, дѣло очень
обыкновенное.

court, дворъ, судъ; —
of justice, — of law,
судъ, приказъ, пала-
та; to —, домогаться,
добиваться, искать че-
го, свататься за; —
eous, вѣжливый; —
esan, распутная жен-
щина; —esy, учтивость,
вѣжливость; —favour,
царская милость; —ier,
придворный.

cousin, двоюродный
братъ, двоюродная се-
стра.

cove, небольшой заливъ,
бухта.

Covenanter, участникъ
въ конвентѣ.

cover, cover up, покры-
вать; —ed, съ покры-
тою головою; — ing,
покрышка, покрыва-
ло; —t, уголокъ.

covetous, алчный, жад-
ный, любостяжатель-
ный.

cow, корова; —herd, ко-
ровникъ, пастухъ.

coward, трусъ; —ice, тру-
сость; —ly, трусливый.

cower, сидѣть на корточ-
кахъ, прижиматься,
скорчиваться; to —
down, присѣсть под-
жавъ ноги.

crack, трескъ, хлопаніе,
трещина, разсѣлина;
to—, хлопать, грызть
(орѣхи).

cradle, люлька, колыбель.

craft, мелкое судно.

crafty, коварный, хит-
рый.

crag, утесъ; —gy, уте-
систый.

cram, набивать, напол-
нять, втискиваться.

cramp, судорога, спазма.

crash, трескъ.

crave, молить (о чемъ).

craven, трусъ.

craving, алканіе, желаніе.

crawl, ползать.

crazy, сумасшедшій.

cream, сливки.

create, сотворять, про-
изводить въ, назна-
чать, опредѣлять.

creation, твореніе, со-
твореніе.

creator, творецъ.

creature, тварь, суще-
ство, твореніе, созда-
ніе.

credibility, достовѣрность.

credit, кредитъ, довѣріе,
уваженіе; of—, поль-
зующійся уваженіемъ,
—or, заимодавецъ, кре-
диторъ.

credulity, легковѣріе.

creed, исповѣданіе вѣры,
символъ вѣры.

creek, бухта.

creep, ползать, таскать-
ся; to—in, вползывать.

Creole, Креолъ.

crept, см. creep.

crest, нашлемникъ, шлемъ,

crew, экипажъ корабля,
матросы.

crime, преступленіе.

criminal, преступникъ;
преступный, уголов-
ный.

crimson, кармазинный
цвѣтъ.

cripple, калѣка.

crisis, кризисъ, крити-
ческое обстоятельство.

criterion, отличительный
признакъ.

critical, критическій.

criticism, критика.

crook, пастушій посохъ;
—ed, кривой, горбатый.

crop, урожай.

crosier, посохъ архіе-
рейскій, жезлъ, пате-
рица.

cross, крестъ; кресто-
вый, крестообразный,
поперечный; to—, пе-
ресѣкать, переступать,
перешагивать, пере-
правляться; — bow,
арбалетъ, самострѣлъ;
— ing, перекрестокъ;
— man, арбалетникъ.

crowd, толпа; to—, тол-
питься, тѣсниться, на-
бивать, наполнять.

crown, корона, казна, правительство, кроунъ (1
руб. 56 коп. сер.); to
—, вѣнчать, короно-
вать, увѣнчивать.

crucify, распинать.

crude, незрѣлый.

cruel, жестокій; —ly, же-
стоко; —ty, жестокость.

cruise, кружка, крейсер-
ство.

crumble, крошить.

crusade, крестовый по-
ходъ; — r, крестоно-
сецъ.

crush, раздавливать.

crust, корка.

cry, крикъ, лай; to —, плакать, кричать, восклицать; to—after any one, кричать кому вслѣдъ; to—out, вскрикивать, восклицать.

Cuba, Куба.

cuff, тузъ, ударъ.

cuirass, броня, латы, кирасъ; — ier, латникъ, кирасиръ.

culprit, обвиненный, преступникъ.

cultivate, обработывать, разводить, упражняться въ чемъ, образовать.

cultivation, culture, обработываніе, воздѣлываніе, разведеніе, упражненіе, образованность.

cunning, хитрый.

cup, чаша, чашка; — board, шкапъ.

cupidity, жадность, алчность.

curate, викарный священникъ.

curb, цѣпочка (у мундштука); to—, обуздывать.

cure, приходъ (церковный), священническая должность; to —, варить въ сахарѣ.

curiosity, любопытство, рѣдкость.

curious, любопытный, искусный, странный.

curl, букля, локонъ; to —, виться, извиваться, волноваться; a- ing еаг, согнутое ушко.

currant, смородинный.

current, теченіе; текущій, ходячій, вообще принятый.

curry, чистить гребницею (лошадь).

curse, проклятіе; to —, клясть, проклинать.

curst, см. curse.

curved, согнутый.

custody, смотрѣніе за чѣмъ, сохраненіе, заключеніе, арестъ, тюрьма.

custom, обычай, обыкновеніе;—агу, обыкновенный, употребительный; as is—агу, какъ водится; — er, заказчикъ, плательщикъ, знакомый, покупатель.

cut, разрѣзывать; to — any one's throat, зарѣзать кого, перерѣзать кому горло; to— down, срубать, сжинать; to—from, отрѣзывать отъ; to — off, отрѣзывать, отсѣкать, отрубать, лишать чего; to—out, вырѣзывать; to—to pieces, разрѣзывать на куски, изрѣзывать на кусочки, разбивать въ дребезги.

cylinder, цилиндръ, валъ.

cypress, кипарисъ.

Cyprus, Кипръ.

czar, царь.

D.

d-ye (damn ye), убирайтесь къ черту.

dagger, кинжалъ, короткій мечъ.

daily, каждый день, всякій день, со дня на день, изо-дня въ день, день—ото—дня, ежедневный,

ежедневно; the—bread, насущный хлѣбъ.

daisy, маргаритка.

dale, долина, долъ.

dame, барыня, госпожа, дама, хозяйка.

damp, испарина; fire —, рудничный газъ.

damsel, дѣвица, барышня.

dance, пляска, танецъ; to—, плясать, танцовать.

dancing, танцованіе, плясаніе.

Dane, Датчанинъ.

danger, опасность, —ous, опасный.

dangle, качаться, болтаться.

Daniel, Даніилъ.

Danish, датскій.

Danube, Дунай.

dare, смѣть, дерзать, осмѣливаться; I—say, мнѣ кажется.

daring, дерзновенный, отважный.

dark, темнота, потемки; темный; after —, по наступленіи темноты; —brown, темнобурый; to—en, затмѣвать, помрачать;—ling, въ потемкахъ;—ly, мрачно; —ness, темнота, тьма, мракъ.

darling, любимый.

dart, испускать (лучи), кидаться, пускаться; to—off, ускакать, умчаться.

dash, хлынуть, бросаться, раздавливать, разбивать;--ing, щегольской, великолѣпный; the — ing, удареніе, ударъ; the water kept —ing in, вода не пе-

реставала вливаться;
to—against, удариться
объ; to — down, топ-
тать, растаптывать;
to—out, высовывать;
to — out any one's
brains, раздроблять
кому черепъ; to — to
pieces, разбивать въ
дребезги.
date, число; to—, напи-
сать число, считать,
считаться.
daub, мазать, пачкать;
to—over, обмазывать.
daughter, дочь.
dawn, разсвѣтъ, заря;
начало, начинаніе.
day, день, время, битва,
побѣда; — break, раз-
свѣтъ;—light, дневной
свѣтъ; one—, однаж-
ды; to—, сегодня.
dazzle, ослѣплять, пре-
льщать.
dead, мертвый, умершій;
he was—, онъ умеръ;
in the — of the night,
въ глубокую ночь; to
kiss—, зацѣловать; to
shoot—, застрѣливать;
—ly, смертельный, по-
мертвѣлый.
deafen, оглушать, заглу-
шать.
deal, множество; еловый,
дощатый; a great or
good —, много, пре-
много; to—, поступать
съ кѣмъ, раздавать;
to—a blow, наносить
ударъ.
dean, деканъ.
dear, другъ; дорогой, цѣнный, любезный, милый;
дорого; to do—, оби-
жать кого; —me, о—,
ай! ей!

death, смерть; —'s head,
мертвая голова.
debate, распря, ссора,
пренie.
debt, долгъ; I am in your—,
я у Васъ въ долгу;
—or, должникъ.
decay, тлѣніе, гніеніе,
упадокъ; to —, увя-
дать, уменьшаться, при-
ходить въ упадокъ.
decease, кончина смерть;
—d, покойникъ, умер-
шій.
deceive, обманывать.
decent, приличный, при-
стойный, благопристой-
ный, скромный.
deception, заблужденіе,
обманъ.
deceptive, обманчивый.
decide, рѣшать.
decipher, разбирать, тол-
ковать.
decision, рѣшеніе.
decisive, рѣшительный.
deck, палуба, декъ;—ing,
украшеніе, убираніе.
declaim, декламировать.
declamation, декламація.
declare, объявлять, увѣ-
рять, объясняться.
decline, упадокъ; to—,
упадать, склоняться,
отказываться.
decorate, украшать, уби-
рать.
decoration, украшеніе.
dedicate, посвящать, под-
носить.
deed, дѣяніе; —of blood,
кровавое злодѣяніе.
deem, почитать; to —
proper, благоразсудить.
deep, глубина, глубь; глубокій, низкій, густой;
—, —ly, глубоко.

deer, олень, красный
звѣрь.
defeat, пораженіе; to—,
поражать, разбивать,
уничтожать, воспрепят-
ствовать.
defect, недостатокъ, по-
рокъ;—ion, отпаденіе,
отложеніе; — ive, не-
достаточный, неудовле-
творительный, неспо-
собный.
defence, защита, оборона;
to make a valiant—,
храбро обороняться;
—less, беззащитный.
defend, защищать;—ant,
отвѣтчикъ; — er, за-
щитникъ.
defensive, оборонитель-
ный; to stand upon
the—, см. stand.
defer, отсрочивать, от-
лагать.
deficiency, недостатокъ.
deform, изуродовать; —
ity, безобразіе, урод-
ливость.
defy, вызывать, прези-
рать.
degenerate, развращен-
ный, развратный; to—,
развращаться, выраж-
даться, измѣняться,
портиться.
degrade, унижать; — d
from the station, пав-
шій съ того мѣста.
degree, степень, градусъ;
by — s, постепенно;
with a —of strength,
съ силою.
deity, божество.
dejected, унылый, упав-
шій духомъ.
dejection, уныніе.
delay, проволочка, оста-
новка, медлительность;

to—, замедлять, отлагать.

deliberate, обдуманный; to—, разсуждать, обдумывать; —ly, обдуманно, медленно.

deliberation, разсужденіе.

delicate, нѣжный, щекотливый, сомнительный, опасный.

delicious, сладостный, превкусный.

delight, восхищеніе, восторгъ, to—, услаждать, восхищать, услаждаться, восхищаться; — ful, отличный, прелестный.

delinquent, виновный въ проступкѣ.

deliver, избавлять, освобождать, отдавать, вручить, передавать, выражать; to — up, выдавать; — ance, освобожденіе, избавленіе; —er, освободитель, избавитель.

dell, долъ, долина.

demagogue, демагогъ.

demand, требованіе, спросъ; to —, требовать; to — in marriage, свататься за.

demeanour, поведеніе.

democratic, демократическій.

demonstration, доказательство, изъявленіе.

denial, отказъ.

Denmark, Данія,

denominate, называть, именовать.

denomination, наименованіе, секта.

denote, означать, показывать.

denounce, объявлять.

dense, густой.

deny, отрицать, отказывать, отпираться; who would not be denied, который не принималъ никакихъ отказовъ.

depart, отправляться, оставлять; —ment, вѣдомство, отрасль (науки); — ure, отправленіе.

depend upon, зависѣть отъ чего, надѣяться на что; —ence, —ency, зависимость, подчиненность, отдаленное владѣніе; — ent, зависимый, зависящій.

deplorable, плачевный.

deportment, пріёмы (въ обращеніи), поведеніе.

depose, свергать, отрѣшать.

deposit, ссаживать, высаживать, низлагать, класть, ставить.

depredation, грабёжъ, грабительство.

depress, отягощать, опечаливать.

deprive, лишать.

depth, глубина, глубокомысліе.

depute, посылать, отправлять.

deputy, депутатъ, посолъ, посланникъ, посланный, посланецъ, избранный, выборный.

derange, разстроивать.

deride, осмѣивать.

derision, осмѣяніе, насмѣшка.

derive, извлекать, выводить, получать, производить.

descend, сходить, спускаться, происходить,

вести свой родъ отъ; —ant, потомокъ.

descent, нисхожденіе, происхожденіе, сходъ, спускъ, спусканіе.

describe, описывать; not to be —d, невыразимый.

description, описаніе, родъ.

descry, усмотрѣть, завидѣть.

desert, пустыня, необитаемый; to —, покидать, оставлять, бѣжать.

deserve, заслуживать; — d, заслуженный; —dly, достойно.

design, предпріятіе, намѣреніе, умыселъ, начертаніе, проектъ; to —, намѣреваться.

desirable, желательный.

desire, желаніе; to —, желать, просить, приказывать; to — one's best compliments to any one, засвидѣтельствовать кому свое почтеніе.

desirous, желающій; as if —, какъ бы желая; to be—of, желать чего.

desist, отставать, переставать.

desk, конторка.

desolate, пустой, необитаемый.

desolation, опустошеніе.

despair, отчаяніе; to — of, отчаяваться въ.

despatch, отправлять.

desperate, отчаянный; —ly, отчаянно.

despise, презирать.

despite, досада, злоба; to do — , досаждать

кому, оказывать кому зло.

dessert, дессертъ.

destination, назначеніе.

destine, назначать, опредѣлять.

destiny, судьба, участь.

destitute, лишенный.

destroy, разрушать, убивать, истреблять, уничтожать.

destruction, истребленіе, гибель.

destructive, разрушительный, губительный.

detach, отдѣлять, отряжать; —ment, отрядъ.

detail, подробность; to —, подробно разсказывать.

detain, задерживать.

deter, удерживать.

determine, рѣшать, рѣшаться, намѣреваться, — d, рѣшительный, смѣлый; to be —d, имѣть намѣреніе, рѣшиться.

detestation, отвращеніе, ненависть.

dethrone, свергать съ престола.

devastation, опустошеніе.

devil, чёртъ, дьяволъ; he was in a — of a fright, онъ ужасно перепугался, онъ былъ въ ужасномъ страхѣ.

devious, уклоняющій, совращающій.

devise, придумывать.

devote, посвящать; —d, переданный; —dly, съ преданностью; —e, ханжа, изувѣръ.

devotion, благоговѣніе, преданность; to perform one's —s, молиться.

devour, пожирать, поглощать.

dew, роса; —y, росистый.

dexterity, ловкость; — at sword and pistol, искусство обращаться шпагой и пистолетомъ.

dexterously, ловко.

diadem, діадема, царскій вѣнецъ.

dialect, нарѣчіе, діалектъ.

dialogue, разговоръ.

diameter, діаметръ.

diamond, алмазъ; бриліантовый.

diary, дневникъ, поденникъ.

dice, см. die.

dictation, приказаніе, указаніе, диктовка.

dictionary, словарь, лексиконъ.

did, didst, см. do.

die, игральная кость; to —, умирать, издыхать, околѣвать, засыхать, вянуть; to — a martyr, умирать мученикомъ; to—away, утихать.

differ, разнствовать, различаться, не соглашаться; — ence, различіе; — ent, различный, другой, несогласный; to take a —ent turn, принимать другой оборотъ.

difficult, трудный, затруднительный, мудрёный; — of access, малодоступный, малоприступный; —y, трудность, затрудненіе, затруднительное положеніе; with — y,

съ трудомъ, насилу.

diffuse, распространять, разбраживаться.

diffusion, распространеніе.

dig, копать, to — out, to — up, выкапывать.

dignified, почтенный, достойный уваженія.

dignity, достоинство, санъ.

dilate, расширяться.

diligence, прилежаніе, дилижансъ.

diligent, прилежный; —ly, прилежно.

dim, тусклый, тёмный; —ly, тёмно.

diminish, уменьшать, убавлять.

diminution, уменьшеніе.

din, шумъ, стукъ, стукотня, гулъ; to —, оглушать.

dine, обѣдать.

dinner, обѣдъ.

diocese, епархія.

dip, погружать, окунуть.

diplomatic, дипломатическій.

dire, ужасный.

direct, прямой, непосредственный; to —, направлять, указывать, руководствовать, обращать, приказывать; to — a punishment, распоряжаться наказаніемъ; — ion, направленіе, наставленіе, адресъ; from all — ions, со всѣхъ сторонъ; —ly, сейчасъ, тотчасъ.

dirk, кинжалъ (у Шотландцевъ).

dirt, грязь; — y, грязный; to — y, загрязнять, запачкать; he had his boots — ied, ему сапоги были запачканы.

disable, дѣлать неспособнымъ.

disagreeable, непріятный.

disappear, исчезать.

disappoint, обманывать въ ожиданіи; —ment, обманутое ожиданіе, разочарованіе. неудача.

disarm, обезоруживать; they —ed him of his knife, они отняли у него ножъ.

disaster, несчастіе, злополучіе.

disastrous, бѣдственный, несчастный.

disbelieve, не вѣрить.

discern, различать, распознавать.

discharge, выстрѣлъ, залпъ, квитанція; a full —, квитанція въ полученіи всего сполна; to —, выстрѣливать, выплачивать, изливаться, вливаться, впадать.

disciple, ученикъ.

discipline, дисциплина; to —, обучать.

disclosure, открытіе.

discolour, лишать краски.

discomfit, разбивать, разстроивать; —ure, разбитіе, пораженіе.

discomfort, безпокойность, печаль.

disconcert, разстроивать, смущать.

disconsolate, безутѣшный; with a — air, нахмурившись.

discontent, неудовольствіе; —ed, недовольный.

discord, несогласіе, раздоръ; —ant, разногласный, неблагозвучный.

discourage, лишать бодрости или мужества, приводить въ уныніе; —ment, лишеніе охоты, стращаніе.

discourse, разговоръ, рѣчь, статья.

discover, открывать, обнаруживать, узнавать, усматривать; —y, открытіе.

discretion, благоусмотрѣніе, произволъ.

discuss, разбирать, обсуждать; —ion, ученый споръ, преніе, изслѣдованіе, обсужденіе.

disdain, пренебреженіе, презрѣніе.

disease, болѣзнь.

disengage, отвязывать, освобождать, освобождаться.

disgrace, безчестіе; to —, лишать милости, попадать въ немилость, осрамлять себя, безчестить, обезчещивать, унижать.

disguise, переодѣваніе, маскированіе, личина; to —, прикрывать, маскировать.

disgusting, отвратительный, противный.

dish, блюдо, кушанье.

dishearten, приводить въ отчаяніе; to be —ed, упасть духомъ.

dishevelled, простоволосый, растрёпанный.

dishonour, безчестіе, позоръ.

disinclined, нерасположенный.

disjoin, равнимать, разрывать.

dislodge, переселяться, выступать.

dismal, угрюмый, скучный, печальный, ужасный.

dismay, смущеніе, страхъ; to —, смущать, устрашать.

dismiss, отпускать.

dismount, слѣзать съ, сходить съ (лошади), сбивать съ коня, ссаживать съ лошади.

disobedience, непослушаніе, неповиновеніе.

disobedient, ослушный, непокорный.

disobey, не повиноваться, ослушиваться.

disorder, безпорядокъ; —ed, въ безпорядкѣ; —ly, безпорядочный.

dispatch, поспѣшность; to make —, поспѣшать.

disperse, разсѣвать, разсыпать, расходиться; —d, разсѣянный.

display, выказаніе, показъ; to —, выказывать, отказывать, выставлять.

displease, не нравиться; —d, недовольный.

disposal, распоряженіе.

dispose, располагать; —r, распорядитель, властитель (вселенной).

disposition, распоряженіе, расположеніе, нравъ.

disputant, диспутантъ, спорщикъ.

disputation, состязаніе, преніе.

dispute, споръ; to —, оспаривать; спорить, состязаться (о чёмъ).

disqualification, неспособность.

disregard, пренебрегать
чѣмъ.

dissatisfied, недовольный.

dissension, раздоръ, распря.

dissent, несогласіе; to—,
не соглашаться; —er,
диссентеръ , иновѣ-
репъ; —ing, диссен-
терскій, иновѣрный,
иновѣрческій.

dissipated, расточительный, распутный.

dissipation, расточеніе,
расточительность. мо-
товство.

dissolute, развратный.

dissolution, уничтоженіе,
прекращеніе.

dissolve, прерывать, прекращать, распускать.

dissuade, отсовѣтовать,
отговаривать.

distance, разстояніе, от-
даленность, отдаленіе.

distant, отдаленный, на
разстояніи.

distil, дистилировать.

distinct, внятный, ясный,
различный; - ion. раз-
личіе, отличіе, отлич-
ность; — ive, отличи-
тельный; —ly, внятно,
ясно.

distinguish , отличать,
различать; —able, раз-
личаемый, отличаемый;
—ed, отличный, зна-
менитый.

distort, обезображивать.

distract, отвлекать; - ed,
сумасшедшій.

distress, бѣда, нужда,
бѣдствіе, несчастіе, со-
крушеніе, крайность;
to - , сокрушать, стѣс-

нять; —ed, несчастный.

distribute, раздавать, раздѣлять.

distribution, раздача, рас-
предѣленіе.

district, округъ, страна,
область.

disturb, тревожить, безпокоить, мѣшать; —er,
нарушитель спокой-
ствія.

disuse, отучаться, от-
выкать.

ditch, ровъ, канава.

dive, — down, нырять.

diversify, разнообразить.

divert, отвлекать; —ing,
забавный.

divide, раздѣлять (into,
на), раздѣляться; to be
— d, расходиться; to—
from, отдѣлять отъ.

dividend, дивидендъ.

divine, духовная, божест-
венный; the — Spirit,
Духъ Святый.

diving, ныряніе, водо-
лазничаніе.

divinity, божественность.

division, раздѣленіе, ди-
визія.

divorce, разводъ; to —,
разводить, удалять.

dizzy, оглушать.

do, дѣлать, учинять, дѣйствовать, поступать,
совершать, исполнять,
оказывать, поживать,
годиться; — I,— you,
да? въ самомъ дѣлѣ?
— pray, пожалуйста,
прошу Васъ ; — you
like, любите ли Вы,
нравится ли Вамъ? and
— unto others as they
would be done by, и
поступать съ другими,
какъ они хотѣли, что-

бы поступали съ ними;
how can we —without,
какъ намъ жить безъ;
how little that would—,
какъ мало въ этомъ
пользы; I — not (сокр.
don't) know, я не знаю;
this counsel may —
you good, этотъ со-
вѣтъ можетъ быть
Вамъ полезнымъ; phi-
lanthropists did not
regard, филантропы не
считали; to —a service,
оказать услугу; to —
dear, обижать кого;
to — harm, причинять
вредъ; to — one's end-
eavour, стараться.

docility, переимчивость.

dock, докъ, также мѣсто,
гдѣ стоятъ подсудимые
во время допроса,
«скамья обвиненныхъ».

doctor, врачъ, докторъ;
— of Law, Докторъ
Правовѣдѣнія; to —,
врачевать, лечить.

doctrine, ученіе.

document, документъ.

does, см. do.

dog, собака; the — days,
каникулы; — eared, съ
загибами (о книгѣ);
—sleep, просонки; —
wolf, собака-волкъ.

doleful, унылый, зау-
нывный.

dollar, талеръ.

domain, имѣніе, недвижимое имѣніе.

dome, куполъ.

domestic, домашній.

domination, владычество.

domineering, повелительный, властолюбивый.

dominion, владѣніе, господство, владычество.

done, см. **do**; сдѣланный, готовый, конченный; бьюсь, держу, согласенъ! I have—extremely well, я поѣлъ чрезвычайно хорошо; the story is not yet —, разсказъ ещё не конченъ; to have —, переставать, кончить, быть готовымъ.

donkey, осёлъ.

don't, см. **do not**.

doom, осуждать.

door, дверь; in —s, within —s, въ домѣ, дома; to go in —s, приходить домой; out of —s, изъ дома, со двора; —step, верхняя ступень.

dose, давать лекарство.

dot, точка.

doth, см. **do**.

double, двойной; to —, обгибать, обходить; to — on the enemy's ships, поставить часть непріятельскихъ кораблей между двухъ огней; —barreled, двуствольный.

doubt, сомнѣніе; to —, сомнѣваться; no—, — less, безъ сомнѣнія; —ful, сомнѣвающійся, сомнительный; to be —ful of, сомнѣваться на счетъ чего.

down, внизъ, внизу; — right, прямой, явный; Dows, Дюны; — stairs, внизъ по лѣстницѣ, внизу; — to, до; —у, пушистый.

dozen, дюжина.

Dr., сокр. **Doctor**, Докторъ.

draft out, выходить, вырываться (о воздухѣ).

drag, тащить; to — out, вытаскивать; to—up, встаскивать.

drainage, дренажъ, подпочвенная осушка водотягами.

dramatist, драматикъ, сочинитель драмъ, драматическій писатель.

drank, см. **drink**.

draught, тащеніе, везеніе; — animals, рабочій скотъ.

draw, тянуть, тащить, везти, придвигать, вынимать, обнажать (шпагу), проводить (траншеи); to — any one's attention to, обращать чье вниманіе на; to — ashore, вытаскивать на берегъ; to — breath, дышать; to — close to any one, прижиматься къ тому; to — from, извлекать, стаскивать съ, исторгать (у кого слёзы); to — near, приближаться; to — on, навлекать, заманивать, приближаться, подходить; to — one's cloak around one, завернуться въ свою шинель; to — out, вытаскивать, вынимать, извлекать, выманивать, выходить; to — through, продѣвать, протаскивать, проволакивать; to — to a close, to — towards a period, кончаться, приходить къ концу; to — up, поднимать, извлекать, черпать, на-

чертывать, писать, разгораться; to — up an army, строить, выстраивать, построить войско; to — up the beach, встаскивать на берегъ; it drew from him this acknowledgment, это заставило его сдѣлать слѣдующій отзывъ; —bridge, подъемный мостъ; —er, выдвижной ящикъ; —ing, рисованіе, рисунокъ.

drawl, плестись нога за ногу.

drawn, см. **draw**.

dread, страхъ, боязнь; to —, страшиться; —ed, — ful, страшный; — fully, страшно.

dream, сновидѣніе, сонъ; to —, видѣть во снѣ, мечтать.

dreamt, см. **dream**.

dreary, пустый, скучный, дремучій.

drench, промачивать; he was well —ed, его порядкомъ промочило.

dress, одежда, уборъ, нарядъ; riding —, одежда для верховой ѣзды; to —, одѣвать, наряжать; to—a wound перевязывать рану; to — one's self up, наряжаться чѣмъ; — ing, box, туалетный ящикъ; —ing room, уборная.

drew, см. **draw**.

drift along, дрейфовать, нестись;

drill, выучивать, обучать (ружью и пр.)

drink, питье, напитокъ;

to —, пить; to — any one's health, пить за чье здоровье; the vulgar eagerly drank in tales, простой народъ съ напряженнымъ вниманіемъ выслушивалъ разсказы.

drip, капать, накапывать.

drive, гнать, везти, править, гоняться, охотиться, травить, доводить, дрейфовать, нестись, сносить; to — a good bargain, выгодно сторговаться; to — away, отгонять, прогонять, уѣзжать, to — back, прогонять, отбивать, отражать; to — from, сгонять съ; to — on, погонять, поѣхать; to—on shore, дрейфовать на берегъ; to — out, выгонять, изгонять; to — up, подъѣзжать; drove it entirely from his mind, заставило его совершенно забыть объ этомъ; the snow was —n about by whirlwinds, вихрями снѣгъ несло; they were —n, ихъ снесло; —r, кучеръ, извощикъ.

driven, см. **drive.**

droop, повѣсить голову.

drop, капля; to —, ронять, уронить, опускать, выпускать, поваливаться, спадать, нечаянно вымолвить (словечко); to — out of any thing, отставать отъ чего.

drove, см. **drive**; —r,

подгонщикъ, скотникъ, пастухъ.

drown, тонуть; —ed, утопленный, to be—ed, утонуть.

drug, зеліе, аптекарское снадобье, москотильный товаръ.

Druid, друидъ (жрецъ); —, —ical, друидскій.

drum, барабанъ; —mer, барабанщикъ.

drunk, —en, см. **drink;** пьяный; — ard, пьяница; —enness, пьянство.

dry, сухой; to —, сушить, высушивать; to rub —, вытирать на сухо; — footed, съ сухими ногами.

ducat, червонецъ.

duchess, герцогиня.

duck, утка; to —, окунывать.

due, должное; должный, достодолжный, надлежащій; is justly —, надобно по справедливости отнести къ.

dug, см. **dig.**

duke, герцогъ.

dull, глухой, безтолковый.

dump, печаль, задумчивость.

dung-cart, навозная телѣга.

durable, прочный.

duration, продолжительность.

during, во время, въ продолженіе.

durst, см. **dare.**

dusk, сумерки.

dust, пыль.

Dutch, голландскій; the —, Голландцы.

duty, долгъ, обязанность, должность, пошлина; to be at one's post of —, быть при своемъ мѣстѣ.

dwell, обитать, жить; —ing, жилище.

dwindle, истощаться; to — away, чахнуть.

d'ye, см. **do you.**

dye-stuff, красильное вещество.

dying day, день смерти, день кончины;—speech, предсмертныя слова.

Е.

each, каждый; on—side, съ той и другой стороны; — other, другъ друга.

eager, ревностный, пылкій, горячій, падкій, любопытный;— ly, со рвеніемъ, усердно, съ жадностью; he listened — ly, онъ со вниманіемъ слушалъ; — ly to request, убѣдительно просить;—ness, ревность, рвеніе, усердіе, жадность; to hear with — ness, выслушивать со вниманіемъ.

ear, ухо, ушко, ручка; reached his —s, дошло до него.

earl, графъ (англійскій).

early, ранній, благовременный, прежній, древній; рано, рановременно.

earn, вырабатывать, зарабатывать, наживать; — ings, выработка.

earnest, серьёзный, важный, усердный, усильный; in —, серьёзно, усердно; in good—, in right—, серьёзно, въ самомъ дѣлѣ, не шутя, безъ шутокъ;—ly, усильно,настоятельно.

earth, земля, глина; — enware, глиняная посуда; —ly, земной.

ease, спокойствіе, облегченіе, покой, отдыхъ; to —, облегчать, избавлять; he felt more at—, ему стало легче.

easily, легко.

east, востокъ, восточный, къ востоку; East India Company, Остъ-Индская Компанія; —ern, восточный; —ward, въ востоку.

easy, легкій, удобный, спокойный, ловкій, развязный; to make one's mind —, успокоиваться.

eat, ѣсть, кушать; to— — one's supper, ужинать.

eaten, см. eat.

eccentricity, странность, причудливость.

Ecclesiast, Эклезіастъ.

ecclesiastic, духовное лице, духовный; —al, церковный, духовный.

echo, отголосокъ, эхо.

economical, хозяйственный.

economist, экономъ, сберегатель.

economize, беречь; to—time, выигрывать время.

economy, экономія, хозяйство,бережливость.

eddy, крутиться.

edge, острее, лезвее, край, опушки (у лѣса).

edict, указъ, повелѣніе.

edifice, зданіе, строеніе.

edition, изданіе.

editor, издатель, редакторъ.

educate, воспитывать.

education, воспитаніе; a man of —, человѣкъ образованный; — al, воспитательный.

educe, выводить, извлекать.

Edward, Эдуардъ.

e'en, см. even.

e'er, см. ever.

effect, дѣйствіе, слѣдствіе; to have an—, производить дѣйствіе, имѣть вліяніе; with what —, какое дѣйствіе было произведено; — s, пожитки; to —, производить, приводить въ дѣйство, совершать, содѣлывать, исполнять, причинять;—ual, дѣйствительный; would be —ual in, будуть имѣть слѣдствіемъ; — ually, дѣйствительно, сильно.

effeminate, разнѣживать, разслаблять.

effervescence, вспыльчивость.

efficacious, полезный.

efficacy, дѣйствіе.

efficient, дѣйствующій, дѣйствительный, полезный.

effort, усиліе, напряженіе.

egg, яйцо.

Egypt, Египетъ.

eight, восемъ; —een, восемнадцать; — eenth,

восемнадцатый; — h, осьмой; an— h, одна осьмая; —у, восемьдесять;

either, либо, или, тотъ или другой, каждый; —ог, либо..либо, или.. или, и..и; not — ..ог, ни..ни.

eject, извергать, выгонять.

eke, также, тоже.

elapse, истекать, проходить.

elastic, упругій, эластическій; — ity, упругость, эластичность.

elbow, локоть.

elder, старшій; — ly, пожилой.

eldest, старшій.

Eleanor, Элеонора.

elect, избирать, выбирать;—ion, избираніе, выборъ.

elegance, изящность, пріятность.

elegant, красивый.

element, начало, элементъ, стихія; — ary, первоначальный, элементарный, легкій.

elephant, слонъ.

elevate, возвышать.

elevation, возвышеніе.

eleven, одиннадцать;—th, одиннадцатый.

Elijah, Илья.

Elizabeth, Елисавета;— an, Елисаветинскій.

elocution, краснорѣчіе.

eloquence, краснорѣчіе.

eloquent, краснорѣчивый.

else, другое, иначе, а то.

'em, см. them.

embankment,насыпь,плотина.

embark, посажать на корабль, нагружать (товары), сѣсть на корабль, ввязываться во что; in which his whole property was — ed, въ которомъ онъ участвовалъ всѣмъ своимъ имуществомъ; to—for, отправляться на кораблѣ въ.

embarrass, затруднять.

embassy, посольство.

embellish, украшать.

embezzle, утаивать.

emblazoning, гербовая фигура.

emblem, эмблема, символъ.

embody, включать.

embrace, обнимать, пользоваться, принимать.

emigrant, выходецъ, переселенецъ, эмигрантъ, переселяющійся; — ship, судно служащее для перевозки переселенцевъ (эмигрантовъ).

emigrate, переселяться.

eminence, высота, возвышеніе.

eminent, высокій, возвышенный, отличный, превосходный; —ly, превосходно, отмѣнно, чрезвычайно, въ высокой степени.

emperor, императоръ.

emphasis, напряженіе голоса.

empire, имперія, царство, государство, власть.

employ, употреблять, занимать; —ment, употребленіе, занятіе.

empower, уполномочивать.

empress, императрица.

empty, пустой.

emulation, соревнованіе.

enable, давать возможность; to be—d, быть въ состояніи, мочь.

enact, узаконять, предписывать закономъ.

encamp, располагаться станомъ или лагеремъ.

enchant, обворажвать, очаровывать; — er, волшебникъ; — er's wand, магическій или волшебный жезлъ.

enclose, окружать.

enclosure, огороженное мѣсто, ограда.

encomium, похвала, похвальное слово.

encounter, встрѣчать, приступать, нападать на кого, преодолѣвать, претерпѣвать, схватываться, сражаться; the ship — ed a severe gale of wind, корабль былъ настигнутъ жестокимъ вѣтромъ.

encourage, ободрять, поощрять; we need— no dejection, намъ не для чего унывать; — ment, ободреніе, поощреніе.

encumber, загромазживать, заваливать, обременять.

encumbrance, обремененіе, препятствіе, препона.

end, конецъ, кончина, послѣдокъ, цѣль, предметъ; in the —, наконецъ, напослѣдокъ; to.—, кончать, кончаться, окан-

чиваться; —less, безконечный.

endanger, подвергать опасности.

endear, дѣлать милымъ, привязывать.

endeavour, стараніе; to —, стараться, покушаться.

endow, одарять; — ment, дарованіе.

endurance, претерпѣніе, перенесеніе.

endure, выдерживать, терпѣть, потерѣть, претерпѣвать, переносить, испытывать, держаться.

enemy, непріятель, врагъ.

energy, энергія, сила, твердость, выразительность.

engage, уговаривать, зазывать, снискивать, занимать, пускаться, вступать, вступать въ сраженіе, нападать на, обязываться; to be —d in, быть занятымъ чѣмъ; to be —d in a battle, участвовать, находиться въ сраженіи; —ment, обязательство, сраженіе, битва.

engaging, привлекательный.

engine, машина, инструментъ; —er, инженеръ, инженеръ-механикъ.

England, Англія.

English, англійскій языкъ; англійскій; the —, Англичане; the —Church, англиканская церковь; —man, Англичанинъ; —Saxon, англійско-саксонскій.

engraving, гравированіе, изображеніе.

enjoin, строго предписы- вать.

enjoy, наслаждаться, поль- зоваться чѣмъ, потѣ- шаться, имѣть;—ment, наслажденіе, удоволь- ствіе. -

enlarge, увеличивать, расширять; — ment, расширеніе, распро- страненіе, развитіе.

enlighten, просвѣщать.

enlist, вербовать.

enliven, оживлять.

enormous, огромный, без- мѣрный; —ly, безмѣр- но, огромно.

enough, довольно; kind —, столь добрый.

enquire, см. inquire.

enrage, раздражать, взбѣсить.

enrich, обогащать.

ensign, кормовой флагъ, знакъ, признакъ; — staff флагштокъ.

enslave, порабощать.

ensue, воспослѣдовать, слѣдовать.

entablature, антабле- ментъ; карнизъ съ ар- хитравомъ и фризомъ.

entangle, запутывать; to be — d, запуты- ваться.

enter, входить, вступать; to — the lists, высту- пать на бой, подви- заться на поприщѣ to—into engagements, обязываться къ чему; to — upon business, принимать за дѣло.

enterprise, предпріятіе.

enterprising, предпріим- . чивый.

entertain, угощать, пи- тать, забавлять; to — compunction, чувство- вать раскаяніе; to —to a different tone, за- пѣть другимъ тономъ; —ing, занимательный; — ment, угощеніе, пиръ.

enthusiasm, энтузіазмъ, восторгъ.

enthusiastic, восторжен- ный; —ally, съ восхи- щеніемъ, съ энтузіаз- момъ. ·

entire, цѣльный, весь — ly, совершенно, со- всѣмъ.

entitle, давать право на что; to be —d, имѣть право на что.

entrance, входъ.

entreat, умолять, про- сить; — y, просьба, упрашиваніе.

entrust, ввѣрять.

entwine, обвивать.

enumeration, исчисленіе.

environs, окружности.

envoy, посолъ, послан- никъ.

envy, зависть; to—, за- видовать чему.

epic, эпическій.

episcopacy, епископ- ство.

episcopal, — ian, епи- копскій; the English— church, Англиканская церковь.

epistle, посланіе, письмо.

epoch, эпоха; of that—, того времени.

equability, равность.

equable, равный, одно- образный.

equal, равный, одинакій; to —, равняться съ

кѣмъ; — ly, равно, равнамѣрно.

equip, снаряжать;—age, экипажъ.

equity, справедливость.

'ere, см. your.

ere, прежде нежели.

erect, воздвигать, соору- жать, ставить, учреж- дать, основывать; пря- мо; —ion, сооруженіе.

errand, посылка.

erroneous, ошибочный, ложный.

error, погрѣшность, о- шибка.

erudition, ученость.

escape, побѣгъ, спасеніе; см. также narrow и fire-escape; to make one's —, убѣгать; to —, спасаться, убѣгать, уходить, избѣгать, миновать; he narrow- ly —d, онъ съ тру- домъ спасся.

escort, прикрытіе, конвой.

especially, особенно.

espouse, обручать, же- ниться на комъ; to — any one's cause, при- нимать чью сторону.

espy, усматривать.

esquire, щитоносецъ, ору- женосецъ, помѣщикъ.

essential, существен- ный;—ly, существенно.

establish, учреждать, основывать, назначать, опредѣлять, установ- лять, утверждать, до- казывать, заводить; to be—d, укрѣпляться (на престолѣ);—ment, учрежденіе, заведеніе, постоянная квартира.

estate имѣніе, помѣстье.

esteem уваженіе; to —,

уважать, почитать, считать.

estimate, оцѣнка; to—, оцѣнивать.

estuary, лиманъ.

etc. (et caetera), и прочее, и такъ далѣе.

eternal, вѣчный.

Euripides, Еврипидъ.

Europe, Европа; — an, Европеецъ, Европейскій.

Eva, Евва.

evangelist, евангелистъ.

eve, вечеръ, капунъ; on the — of becoming, готовый сдѣлаться; — ning, вечеръ, вечерній.

even, гладкій, равный; даже.

event, событіе, происшествіе, развязка, успѣхъ, результатъ; I waited with horror the —, я съ ужасомъ выжидалъ чѣмъ дѣло кончится; at all —s, во всякомъ случаѣ; — ful, замѣчательный по важнымъ событіямъ.

ever, всегда, когда нибудь, когда либо; as — may be, какъ нельзя болѣе; for — and —, безпрестанно, безпрерывно, вѣчно; —since, съ тѣхъ поръ; — so, сколько бы ни, какъ бы ни; without—thinking, нисколько не подумая; — lasting, вѣчный.

Everard, Эбергардъ.

every, всякій, — body, —one, всякій; — other minute, каждыя двѣ минуты, черезъ мину-

ту; on — side, со всѣхъ сторонъ; — thing, все; — where, вездѣ, повсюду, повсемѣстно.

evidence, свидѣтельство, показаніе, доказательство.

evident, очевидный; —ly, очевидно.

evil, зло.

ev'ry, см **every.**

ewer, кружка, кувшинъ, рукомойникъ.

exact, точный; to —, взыскивать, требовать; — ion, лихоимство, грабительство; — ly, точно, точь въ точь; — ness, точность.

exalt, возвышать, превозносить; — ation, возвышеніе.

examination, разсмотрѣніе, допросъ.

examine, экзаменовать, разсматривать, испытывать; — r, экзаменаторъ, испытатель.

example, примѣръ, образецъ.

exasperate, раздражать.

exceed, превосходить, преступать, превышать; — ingly, чрезмѣрно, крайне.

excell, превосходить, отличаться; — ence, превосходство, достоинство; — ent, превосходный, отличный.

except, —ing, исключая, кромѣ, если не; —ion, исключеніе.

excess, чрезмѣрность, невоздержность; —ive, чрезмѣрный; — ively, чрезмѣрно.

exchange, обмѣнъ, раз-

мѣнъ, биржа; to —, обмѣниваться чѣмъ; to — for, промѣнять, на, замѣнять чѣмъ.

excite, возбуждать; — ment, внутреннее волненіе, встревоживаніе, раздраженіе.

exclaim, восклицать.

exclamation, восклицаніе; to make an —, восклицать.

exclude, выключать, исключать.

exclusion, выключеніе, исключеніе; —bill, см. **bill;** — ist, приверженецъ выключки Герцога Іоркскаго (какъ католика) отъ престолонаслѣдія.

exclusive, исключительный; — ly, исключительно.

excommunicate, отлучать отъ церкви.

excommunication, отлученіе отъ церкви; bill of —, булла изрекающая проклятіе.

excuse, извиненіе, предлогъ; to make —s, извиняться, приводить въ оправданіе; to —, извинять.

execute, исполнять, совершать, казнить.

execution, исполненіе, совершеніе, казнь, взысканіе долговъ; to issue —, предписать привести въ дѣйствіе; —er, палачъ.

executor, душеприкащикъ.

exercise, упражненіе, урокъ, тѣлодвиженіе, приведеніе въ дѣйство, исполненіе, исправленіе; a holy —, святое дѣло; to —, упражняться, быть на ученіи, употреблять, пользоваться; to — a power, имѣть сильное вліяніе; to—dominion, владычествовать; to—oppression, притѣснять, угнетать; to — outrage, учинять насиліе; to — pasture, выгонять въ поле, пасти (скотъ).

exert, напрягать, употреблять; to—courage выказывать храбрость; to — one's self, силиться, стараться; — ion, усиліе, напряженіе.

exhaust, истощать.

exhibit, показывать, выказывать, выставлять, представлять; — ion, выставленіе, представленіе.

exhort, увѣщевать, — ation, увѣщеваніе, ободреніе.

exigence, надобность, нужда, случай нужды, крайнее состояніе.

exile, изгонять, ссылать.

exist, существовать, быть; — ence, существованіе; in — ence, существующій.

expanse, протяженіе, пространство.

expansion, растяженіе, расширеніе.

expatiate, распространяться о чемъ.

expect, ожидать, надѣяться; or I shall — you to make it over again,

иначе Вамъ придется переписать все снова; — ation, ожиданіе

expediency, полезность, удобность.

expedient, средство; приличный, удобный, полезный.

expedite, отправлять (въ экспедицію).

expedition, военное предпріятіе, экспедиція, отправленіе.

expeditiously, поспѣшно.

expel, выгонять, изгонять.

expend, издерживать, истрачивать.

expense, издержка, расходъ; at the — of, на счетъ кого.

experience, опытность, опытъ, испытаніе; to —, испытывать; —d, опытный.

experiment, опытъ.

expiate, заглаживать.

expiration, истеченіе (срока).

expire, умирать, скончаться, кончаться, миновать.

explain, объяснять.

explanation, объясненіе.

explode, взрываться.

exploit, подвигъ.

explore, изслѣдовать, развѣдывать.

explosive взрывающійся.

export, вывозъ, вывозный товаръ; to—, вывозить, отпускать за границу.

expose, подвергать, выставлять.

exposure, выставленіе, подверженіе.

expound, излагать, изъяснять.

express, нарочный, именной; to —, выражать, изъявлять; — ion, выраженіе.

exquisite, отмѣнный.

extant, существующій въ наличности; is —, имѣется.

extemporal, не приготовленный.

extempore, безъ приготовленія.

extend, растягивать, расширять, распространять, расширяться, распространяться, простираться.

extensive, пространный, обширный.

extent, протяженіе, объемъ, степень.

extenuation, смягченіе.

exterior, наружный, внѣшній.

exterminate, истреблять, искоренять.

external, внѣшній, наружный.

extinct, погасшій, вымерлый.

extinguish, потушать, погашать, пресѣкать.

extirpate, искоренять, истреблять.

extol, превозносить, выхвалять.

extort, вынуждать, исторгать.

extract, извлеченіе, выписка; to—, вытаскивать, вынимать.

extraordinary, чрезвычайный, необыкновенный.

extravagance, расточительность.

extravagant, расточительный, мотовской.

extreme, крайній; — ly, чрезвычайно, крайне, въ высшей степени.

extremity, край, конецъ, граница, крайніе предѣлы, крайность, крайняя нужда.

extricate, выпутывать, освобождать.

exultation, восторгъ.

eye, глазъ, око, взоръ; the — of the government is upon them, глазъ правительства устремленъ на нихъ; — brow, бровь.

F.

Fabius, Фабій.

fable, басня, вымыселъ, баснословіе.

fabricate, вымышлять.

fabulous, баснословный.

face, лице, поверхность, наличная сторона;— to —лицемъ къ лицу; to know any one's —, знать кого съ лица; to — about, оборачиваться лицемъ.

facetious, шутливый.

facilitate, облегчать, способствовать.

facility, легкость, облегчительное средство, пособіе.

fact, истинное происшествіе, фактъ; in —, въ самомъ дѣлѣ.

faction, партія.

factious, мятежный.

factory, факторія, ману-

фактура, мастерская; —child ребенокъ принадлежащій факторіп.

fade away, увядать.

fagot,faggot,пукъ прутьевъ, связка хворосту.

fail, не доходить, не доставать, не достигать цѣли, не успѣвать, не соотвѣтствовать, преминовать, слабѣть, ослабѣвать, пустѣть ; could not — of, не могъ не; till loop and button — ing both. пока не разстегнулась пуговица; —ing, погрѣшность, слабость; —ure, неуспѣхъ, неудача.

fain, охотно, съ охотою.

faint, истощенный, слабый; to —, томиться, упадать въ обморокъ; — ly, слабо.

fair, ярмарка; прекрасный, ясный, справедливый ; the secret was in a — way of dying along with him, надежда открыть тайну, со смертію его, казалось, исчезла на всегда; — and softly, John, легонько, Ванька, тихонько! —ly, справедливо, выгодно, благопріятно, совершенно.

faith, вѣра, вѣрность, честность; — ful,вѣрный; — fully, вѣрно; —less, невѣрующій.

fall, паденіе, водопадъ; to —, падать, упадать, опускаться, стихать, попадаться ; to — asleep, заснуть; to —

back, подаваться назадъ, отступать; to — behind,отступать,удаляться ; to — calm, стихать; to — down, падать, упадать, падать на колѣни; to — from, опускать, терять, to — iu into a row, становиться въ рядъ; to — into any one's way, заступить кому дорогу; to —into decay, to — into ruin, приходить въ упадокъ; to — into a quarrel, начинать спорить;to — in with, встрѣчаться, соглашаться съ; to — off, отпадать; to —on, выдумывать; to —out, выпадать,вываливаться; to — short, недостигать; to — to, to — to any one's share, доставаться кому; to —upon, нападать на.

fallen, см. **fall**.

fallow-deer,красные звѣри, олень.

false, ложный, невѣрный, неправильный, вѣроломный, фальшивый, поддѣльный, накладной (о волосахъ).

fame, слава; to be —d for, славиться чѣмъ.

familiar, знакомый; to make one's self—,ознакомлпваться.

family, семейство фамилія; семейный, родовой; a man of —, семянинъ.

famine, голодъ

famous, знаменитый, славный.

fan, опахивать.

fanatic, фанатикъ.

fanciful, мечтательный, фантастическій.

fancy, воображеніе, мечта; расположеніе, пристрастіе; to —, воображать, мечтать.

far, далёкій; далёко, гораздо, очень, много; —and wide, повсюду; —away, вдали; as—as, сколько; how —, сколько; so —as, до; thus —, до сего мѣста.

fare, пища, пропитаніе, кушанье, угощеніе, плата за провозъ; — well, прощаніе, прощайте!

farm, хуторъ, ферма; to —, брать на откупъ, обработывать; — er, арендаторъ; —yard, хуторный дворъ.

farrier, кузнецъ.

farther, далѣе, сверхъ того.

farthing, фардингъ (1½ денежки).

fashion, обыкновеніе, мода; to be in the —, слѣдовать модѣ; —able, модный.

fast, крѣпкій, скорый, шибкій; скоро, шибко, крѣпко; to —, поститься; to make —, to —en, закрѣплять, прикрѣплять; —ing, постничанье; —ness, крѣпость, укрепленное мѣсто.

fastidious, брезгливый, разборчивый.

fat, жиръ; жирный.

fatal, злополучный, пагубный.

fate, судьба, участь.

father, отецъ; —ly, отцовскій, отеческій.

fathom, сажень; in five —s of water, на глубинѣ пяти сажень; to —, измѣрять глубину, вывѣдывать, испытывать, проницать.

fatigue, утомленіе, усталость; to —, утомлять.

fault, погрѣшность, ошибка, вина.

favour, милость, одолженіе; in the — of, въ чью пользу; to —, одолжать, удостоивать, покровительствовать, благопріятствовать;—able, благосклонный, выгодный, удобный; —ite, любимецъ, любимый.

fear, боязнь, опасеніе; to be in —, бояться, опасаться; dying —, смертельный страхъ; for —, боясь, дабы не; to —, бояться, страшиться чего; — ful, боязливый; they were — ful that, они опасались чтобы; —fully, страшно; — less, безбоязненный, не боясь; lessness, безбоязненность.

feast, пиръ.

feat, подвигъ, дѣло; — of arms, геройскій подвигъ.

feather, перо; to —, покрывать перьями, периться; — bed, перина.

feature, черта.

February, Февраль.

fed, см. feed.

fee, плата.

feeble, слабый, немощный.

feed, кормить, питать, кормиться, питаться; at —ing time, во время кормленія.

feel, чувствовать; to — assured, быть увѣреннымъ въ чемъ; —ing, чувство, осязаніе, чувствованіе.

feet, см. foot.

feign, притворяться.

felicity, счастіе.

fell, каменный холмъ; см. также fall.

fellow, товарищъ, сотоварищъ, человѣкъ, парень; — citizen, согражданинъ; — passenger, ѣдущій вмѣстѣ съ кѣмъ, сопутникъ; — ship, товарищество, братство; — traveller, сопутникъ.

felon, преступникъ.

felt, см. feel.

female, женщина; женскій.

fen, болото.

fencing, фехтованіе.

ferocious, лютый.

ferocity, лютость, свирѣпость.

ferry, перевозъ, переправа (чрезъ рѣку).

fertile, плодоносный, плодовитый; —in corn, хлѣбородный.

fertility, плодовитость.

festive, торжественный.

fetch, позвать, привести, ходить за, приносить; let him be —ed, сходите за нимъ; to — over, перевозить, привозить.

fever, горячка.

few, немногіе; немного,

мало; в —, нѣкоторые, нѣсколько.

fibre, волокно.

fickle, непостоянный, перемѣнчивый.

fidelity, вѣрность.

field, поле; полевой; — sports, забавы на открытомъ полѣ.

fiend, злой духъ.

fierce, свирѣпый, лютый; —ness, свирѣпость, лютость.

fiery, горячій, пылкій.

fifer, флейщикъ.

fifteen, пятнадцать; —hundred, тысяча пятьсотъ.

fifth, пятый; four —s, четыре пятыхъ; —ly, въ пятыхъ.

fifty, пятьдесять.

fig, винная ягода.

fight, сраженіе; the —is fought, сраженіе дано; to —, сражаться, драться; to — a battle, дать сраженіе; to — it out, рѣшать дѣло (оружіемъ, единоборствомъ и пр.); to — one's — way, пробиваться; —ing, бой, борьба, сраженіе.

figure, видъ, фигура, станъ.

fill, наполнять, исполнять, пополнять, комплектовать, наливаться; to — up, дополнять, доливать, занимать (мѣсто).

finally, наконецъ, напослѣдокъ.

finances, финансы.

find, находить; to — for any one, отыскивать кому; to — one's self, находиться, чувство-

вать себя; to — out, отыскивать, . открывать, узнавать.

fine, прекрасный, красивый, изящный, тонкій, хорошій; remarkably —, преотличный, славный; to —, штрафовать; —ly, прекрасно, изящно; —ry, убранство, нарядъ.

finger, палецъ.

finish, оканчивать, доканчивать, отдѣлывать.

fire, огонь, каминный огонь, пожаръ; пожарный; on —, въ огнѣ, горящій; to take —, загораться, зажигаться, вспыхивать; we had a —, мы топили; we have begun —s, мы начали топить; to —, стрѣлять, палить, зажигать, зажигаться; to — for distress, дѣлать сигнальные выстрѣлы для означенія опасности; to — up, воспламеняться; we —d two shot, мы сдѣлали два выстрѣла; —arms, огнестрѣльное оружіе; —damp, рудничный газъ; —escape, пожарная спасительная машина; —escape dog, собака при пожарной спасительной машинѣ;—fly, свѣтлякъ; — place, очагъ; —ship, брандеръ; — side, каминъ.

firm, твёрдый, крѣпкій, непоколебимый; —ly, твёрдо, крѣпко; —ness, твёрдость, непоколебимость.

first, первый; сперва, во первыхъ, въ первый разъ, впервые, прежде, напередъ; at —, . сперва; from the —, съ самаго начала; —rate, первостепенный, первоклассный.

fish, рыба; —erman, рыбакъ, рыболовъ; —ing, рыбная ловля; —ing boat, рыбацкая лодка.

fissure, разсѣлина, щель.

fit, годный, способный къ чему, удобный, приличный; to think —, считать нужнымъ; to —, дѣлать способнымъ, быть въ пору; to — out, вооружать, оснащивать.

five, пять.

fix, прикрѣплять, опредѣлять, назначать, обращать, устремлять; to — one's choice, выбирать; he —ed him to the spot, онъ не спустилъ его съ мѣста; he —ed his eyes eagerly upon it, онъ съ жадностію устремилъ свои глаза на нея.

flag, флагъ; —ship, флагманскій корабль.

flail, цѣпъ.

flame, пламя, огонь, пылъ.

Flanders, Фландрія.

flank, бокъ, флангъ; to —, прикрывать съ боку.

flap, ударять, бить, хлопать.

flash, блескъ; to —, блистать, сверкать.

flat, плоская сторона клинка; плоскій; —bottomed, плоскодонный.

flatter, льстить, ласкать; —ег, льстецъ; —у, лесть, ласкательство.

flaw, порывъ вѣтра.

flax, лёнъ.

flay, сдпрать кожу.

fled, см. **flee**.

flee, бѣжать, убѣгать, убѣжать.

fleet, флотъ; флотскій; — of ships, корабельный флотъ.

flesh, мясо, плоть.

flew, см. **fly**.

flicker, порхать.

flight, полётъ, бѣгъ, бѣгство, теченіе; to take to —, см. **take**.

fling, — down, бросать, швырять; to — open, насильно растворять.

flint, кремень.

float, буй, поплавокъ; to —, плавать, носиться; to — off, уплывать.

flock, стадо; а — of sheep, стадо овецъ, овечье стадо; to —, толпиться, собираться, стекаться.

flood, потокъ, изліяніе, наводненіе, приливъ, рѣки, струя.

floor, полъ, ярусъ, этажъ.

florin, флоринъ, гульденъ.

flounder, барахтаться, биться.

flour, мукá.

flourish, процвѣтать, успѣвать; —ing, цвѣтущій.

flow, течь; to — behind, (о парикѣ) разлетаться; to — through, протекать; —ing, взвѣвающійся.

flower, цвѣтъ, цвѣтокъ, мука; — of wheat, пшеничная мука.

fluency, свободность, бѣглость.

flung, см. **fling**.

flurry, смущеніе.

flush, стремиться.

fly, муха; to —, летать, бѣжать, бросаться, распускаться; to — away, улетать; to — into the arms, броситься въ объятія; to — off, отлетать, слетать; to — open, растворяться, распахиваться; to — up, взлетать.

foam, пѣна; to —, пѣниться.

foe, врагъ, непріятель.

fog, туманъ; —gy, туманный.

fold, стадо; to —, загонять въ загородку (овецъ).

folk, люди, народъ.

follow, слѣдовать, по-слѣдовать, идти за; to — in any one's steps, идти по чьимъ слѣдамъ; to — any one's way, ѣхать дальше по той же дорогѣ; —ег, провожатый, послѣдователь.

folly, глупость, безраз-судность.

fond, нѣжный; I am — of, я охотникъ до; to — le, ласкать; —ly, нѣжно, безумно.

food, пища.

fool, дуракъ, шутъ; to —, дурачить; —ish, дурацкій, глупый.

foot, нога, футъ; on —, пѣшкомъ; at a —'s

pace, шагомъ; —man, лакей; running—man, лакей для посылокъ, разсыльный; — path, пѣшеходная дорога; — runner, бѣгунъ; — soldier, пѣхотинецъ; —step, стопа, слѣдъ.

fop, щёголь, франтъ.

for, за, для, ради, по, къ, на, въ продолженіе, отъ; ибо, потому что; — myself, что касается до меня самаго; man — man, одинъ противъ одного; now — it, ну не ро-бѣй! — the third time, въ третій разъ.

forbid, запрещать; God —, сохрани Богъ!

force, сила, войско; —of numbers, численное превосходство; to —, принуждать, брать силою, форсировать; to — forward, понукать, погонять впередъ; to — one's way, проби-ваться; to — out, вы-тѣснять, выгонять; to — up and down, тол-кать то вверхъ то внизъ; to — upon, на-вязывать кому; —cing itself from below, про-рываясь снизу.

forcible, насильственный, понудительный.

forcibly, сильно, насиль-ственно.

ford, бродъ.

'fore, см. **before**.

fore, передній; to—bode предвѣщать; — by, возлѣ, подлѣ; —going, предъидущій; — head, лобъ; — mast, фокмачта; — most, передній, передовой, первый, первѣйшій; —tell, предсказывать; — top, форъ-марсъ.

foreign, заграничный, иностранный, чужой; a—land, чужой край; — travel, путешествіе за границу;—er, иностранецъ.

foresail, Фокъ; down—, ставь Фокъ; up—,Фокъ на гитовы!

foresaw, см. foresee.

foresee, предвидѣть.

forest, лѣсъ; лѣсной; —er, лѣсникъ, лѣсничій, лѣсной житель.

forfeit, конфискованный; to —, конфисковать.

forge, ковальня, кузница; to—, ковать.

forget, забывать; —ful, забывчивый.

forgive, прощать, отпускать; — ness, прощеніе, отпущеніе.

forgot, forgotten, см. forget.

fork, вилка, развилина.

forlorn, отчаянный

form, форма, видъ,станъ, стать, скамейка; to—, образовать, составлять, формировать, строить; to — a design, to — a resolution, принимать или возъимѣть намѣреніе; to — a habit, усвоивать привычку; well — ed, стройный; —al, формальный.

former, первый, прежній;— ly, прежде, нѣкогда

formidable, грозный, страшный.

fort, фортъ, укрепленное мѣсто, укрѣпленіе, замокъ; — ification, у-крѣпленіе.

forth, вонъ, прочь, впередъ; to send —, см.

send; — with, тотчасъ, немедленно.

fortify, укрѣплять.

fortitude, сила души, твердость.

fortnight, двѣ недѣли.

fortress, крѣпость.

fortunate, счастливый, удачный; — ly, къ счастію.

fortune, счастіе, Фортуна, судьба, имѣніе, состояніе; desperate—, отчаянное положеніе; a gentleman of —, человѣкъ съ состояніемъ.

forty, сорокъ.

forward, тщеславный; — or — s, впередъ.

fought, см. fight.

foul, скверный, гнусный.

found, см. find; to —, основывать; — ation, основаніе; — ation fund, основный капиталъ; — er, основатель, учредитель; to — er, потонуть, пойти на дно.

fount, fountain, ключъ, фонтанъ, источникъ.

four, четыре; — score, восемьдесять; — teen, четырнадцать;—teenth, четырнадцатый;— th, четвертый; —thly, въ четвертыхъ.

fowl, птица.

fox, лисица.

fragment, отломокъ, обломокъ.

frail, бренный, слабый.

frame, тѣлосложеніе, станъ; to —, составлять, устраивать.

France, Франція.

Francis, Францискъ.

frank, откровенный; —ly, откровенно, охотно.

frantic, бѣшеный, неистовый.

fraud, обманъ.

free, свободный; to —, освобождать, избавлять отъ чего; —boot er, разбойникъ; — dom, свобода; — hold estate,бѣлое помѣстье; — ly, свободно, вольно, добровольно, откровенно; — masonry, масонство, масонское общество.

freeze, мёрзнуть, замерзать.

freight, грузъ, кладь.

French, Французскій языкъ; Французскій; to speak —, говорить по Французски;—man. Французъ;the—,Французы.

frequent, частый, многократный; to —, часто посѣщать; — ly, часто.

fresh, свѣжій, новый; — from college,прямо изъ университета; — ly, свѣжо; are — ly re-membered, въ свѣжей памяти; — man, новичекъ.

friar, монахъ; — or begging —, нищенствующій монахъ.

friend, другъ, пріятель, подруга; —ly, дружественный, дорогой; — ship, дружба.

frigate, фрегатъ.

fright,—en,пугать, испугать; they were half—ened out of their wits, они почти съ ума сходили отъ испуга; — ful, страшный, ужасный; —fully, страшно, ужасно.

frisk, рѣзвиться, попрыгивать.

Frith of Forth, Фортскій заливъ.

fritter, крошить, искрошивать.

frivolous, суетный, легкомысленный.

frock, кафтанъ, армякъ.

frog, лягушка.

frolic, frolick, проказа, шутка; to—, шалить, рѣзвиться.

from, отъ изъ, съ, по, судя по

front, фасадъ, передъ, передняя сторона, лицѣ, фронтъ; in — спереди; in — of, передъ; in his—, передъ фронтомъ.

frost, морозъ; —у, морозный, холодный.

froth, пѣниться.

frown, нахмуриваться, показывать сердитый видъ.

frozen, см. freeze.

the **Frozen** Ocean, Ледовитое море.

frugal, бережливый.

fruit, плодъ, плоды, фрукты; — basket, корзина съ фруктами, корзина для плодовъ; — ful, плодовитый, плодородный, плодонос-

ный; — less, безполезный, тщетный.

frustrate, разрушать, дѣлать тщетнымъ.

fry, жарить на рашпрѣ.

fuel, топливо, дрова на топку.

fulfil, исполнять, выполнять.

full, полный, наполненный, совершенный, цѣлый; совсѣмъ, вполнѣ, совершенно, весьма; — an hour, цѣлый часъ; — of popularity, имѣющій большую популярность; — length, во весь ростъ, — у, вполнѣ.

fumble, ощупывать.

fun, забава, шутка.

function, отправленіе.

fund, капиталъ.

funeral, похороны, погребеніе; похоронный, погребальный.

fur, мѣхъ.

furious, свирѣпый, яростный; — ly, свирѣпо.

furnish, доставлять, снабжать, меблировать.

furniture, мебель.

further, дальнѣйшій; далѣе, болѣе, сверхъ того.

fury, свирѣпость, ярость.

fusee, трубка (бомбовая или гранатная), ружье.

future, будущее время; будущій; in —, впредь, впередъ.

G.

gaff, гафель.

gain, выигрывать, добывать, пріобрѣтать, достигать одерживать (побѣду); to — admis-

sion, быть впущеннымъ; to—possession, овладѣть чѣмъ; my watch — s, мои часы уходятъ.

gait, походка.

gale, a — of wind, свѣжій, сильный, крѣпкій вѣтеръ, штормъ.

Galilee, Галилейское море.

Galileo, Галилей.

gall, сдирать кожу, саднѣть, безпокоить; — ing, непріятный, оскорбительный.

gallant, храбрецъ; храбрый, доблестный, хорошій, знатный, великолѣпный, красивый; —ly, храбро, доблестно; — гу, учтивость, любезничанье; —s, брамсели; the ship had her — s up, у корабля брамсели были привязаны.

gallery, галерея.

galley, кухня, камбузъ.

gallon, галёнокъ (вина — 2,46 штофа).

gallop, скачь, галопъ; to — away, ускакать.

gallows, висѣлица.

gambol, рѣзвость, шалость; to play —s, проказить.

game, игра, забава, охота, травля, дичь; — keeper, лѣсничій, смотритель за дичью.

gaming, играніе за деньги, игра,—house, игорный домъ, картёжный домъ;—table, карточный столъ.

gang, шайка.

gangrene, гангрена, антоновъ огонь.

47

gangway, шкафутъ.

garb, одежда, платье.

garden, садъ; — er, садовникъ.

garret, чердакъ.

garrison, гарнизонъ.

gas, газъ.

gasp, съ трудомъ дышать, задыхаться; the foam of his — ing, пѣна послѣдняго его издыханія.

gate, ворота; — way, проѣзжія ворота.

gather, собирать, собираться.

Gaul, Галлія, Галлъ.

gave, см. give.

gay, весёлый, живой, блистательный.

gaze, (пристально) глядѣть на что, лицезрѣть (Бога).

gazette, газета, вѣдомость; I'll have a — of my own, у меня будетъ газета своя.

gear, утварь.

gem, драгоцѣнный камень.

genealogy, родословіе, генеалогія.

general, генералъ; генеральный, главный, общій, общественный, обыкновенный; — in chief, главнокомандующій; in —, —ly, вообще, обыкновенно, — ity, большая часть.

generation, родъ, поколѣніе.

generosity, великодушіе, благородство, щедрость.

generous, великодушный, благородный, щедрый; — ly, великодушно.

genial, плодоносный.

genius, геній, творческій умъ.

Genoa, Генуя.

Genoese, Генуэзецъ; генуэзскій.

gentile, язычникъ; языческій.

gentle, кроткій, милый, нѣжный, мягкій, покатый, отлогій; a — stroke, лёгкій ударъ; —tly, тихо, кротко, постепенно.

gentleman, человѣкъ благороднаго происхожденія, господинъ, жентльменъ; country — , сельскій дворянинъ; — in waiting, камердинеръ; gentlemen pensioners, тѣлохранители, учрежденные Генрихомъ VII для охраненія англійскихъ королей. Каждый изъ этихъ гвардейцевъ получалъ по 100 фунт. ст. годоваго содержанія.

gentry, земское дворянство.

geographical, географическій; — ly, географически.

George, Георгій, Егоръ.

German, Нѣмецъ, Германецъ; нѣмецкій, германскій; —y, Германія.

gesticulation, тѣлодвиженіе, жестикуляція, пантомима.

gesture, жестъ, тѣлодвиженіе.

get, пріобрѣтать, доставать, получать, дѣлаться, доходить; to — aboard, садиться на

(судно); to — alongside, добраться до борта; to — back, придти назадъ; to—cast away, быть выброшеннымъ на (мель, берегъ); to — down, сходить; to — hold of, схватывать, ухватываться за; to — in, садиться (въ колиску и пр.); to — into, входить, сажать во что; to — off, отвязывать; to — on, успѣвать; to — on any thing, взбираться на что; to—on board, садиться на корабль, отправляться на корабль, вытаскивать на судно; to—out, вынимать, выманивать, выходить, to—out of bed, вставать съ постели; to — possession, завладѣвать чѣмъ; to—ready, приготовлять; to—rid of, избавляться, освобождаться отъ; to—through, проходить, пробираться; to—to, добираться до; to — together, собираться; to—up, подниматься, взлѣзать, вставать; to — upon one's knees, стать на колѣни; to—upon the bottom, взлѣзть на дно; —some more, принесите еще; what have we got for dinner, что у насъ будетъ къ обѣду?

ghost, духъ, привидѣніе.

giant, великанъ, исполинъ.

Gibraltar, Гибралтаръ.

gift, дарованіе, даръ.

gig, одноколка.

gild, золотить, позлащать, украшать.

gill, жабры (у рыбы), ручей, горный потокъ.

gilt, позолоченный; см. также **gild.**

gin, джинъ, можжевеловая водка.

ginger, инбирь.

gipsy, цыганъ, цыганка; — woman, цыганка.

gird on the sword, перепоясать или надѣть мечъ.

girdle, поясъ, кушакъ.

girl, дѣвушка, дѣвочка.

give, давать, передавать, подавать, отдавать, доставлять; to—a blow, наносить ударъ; to—a groan, испускать стонъ; to — a letter, употреблять букву; to—any one a beating, побить кого; to — a passage from a book, прочитать мѣсто изъ книги; to—a song, спѣть пѣсню; to — attention, обращать вниманіе; to — a verdict, произносить приговоръ; to — away, отдавать; to — back, отступать; to — encouragement, поощрять; to — great care to, обращать на что большое вниманіе; to — ground, отступать; to - high promise,обѣщать много хорошаго, подавать большія надежды; to — in charge, поручать, приказывать; to—offence, обижать, сердить; to — orders for, зака-

зать; to — suspicion, возбуждать подозрѣніе; to—thanks, приносить благодареніе; to—up,уступать,оставлять, отказываться отъ, выдавать; to—up to, посвящать; to — way, поддаваться, уступать.

given, см. **give.**

glad, радъ; to make —, to —, радовать; — ly, охотно; — some, радостный.

glade, прогалина, просѣка.

glance, сіяніе, взоръ, взглядъ; giving a single —,взглянувъ разъ; to —, блистать, сверкать.

glaring,очевидный,странный, поразительный.

glass, стекло, стаканъ, рюмка; — y, стеклянный, стекловидный, чистый.

gleam, мелькать, сіять, блистать.

glebe, земля, почва.

gleeman,музыкантъ, пѣвецъ.

glen, долъ, долина.

glide, скользить, течь, катиться; to — along upon, кататься по.

glimpse, сіяніе, лучъ; to catch a—of, видѣть мелькомъ.

glitter, блистать, сверкать.

globe, земной шаръ.

gloom, темнота, мракъ; —y, мрачный.

glorious, славный.

glory, слава.

glove, перчатка.

glow, пылъ, жаръ; to—, пылать, горѣть;—ing, пылкій, пламенный;—worm, свѣтлякъ.

glue, клей.

go, ходить, идти, ступать, ѣхать, отправляться; not to — far in, далеко не хватать; to — about, обходить, ходить по, прохаживаться по; to—away, уходить, уѣзжать; to — down, спускаться, тонуть, идти ко дну; to —into, входить; to — into the fashions of others, подражать модамъ другихъ; to — near, подходить, приближаться; to — on, продолжать, продолжать путь, происходить, совершаться; to — out, выходить, отправляться, гаснуть; to—out to service, наниматься къ кому въ услуженіе; to — over, переходить, переправляться; to — overboard, бросаться за бортъ; to — round, пить круговую; to — through, проходить; to—to bed, идти спать; ложиться спать; to — to see a person, отправляться къ кому нибудь въ гости; to—up, идти, ѣхать, подходить.

goal, цѣль.

goblet, кубокъ, бокалъ.

God, Богъ; — dess, богиня; — father, крестный отецъ.

going, хожденіе, ходъ;

to be —, собираться, готовиться, хотѣть.

gold, золото; —, — en, золотой.

gone, ушелъ, уѣхалъ, см. **go**; all his means were —, онъ лишился всѣхъ средствъ; if life so soon is —, если жизнь такъ скоро проходитъ; when I am — когда меня не будетъ.

good, добро, польза; добрый, хорошій; — s, пожитки, вещи, товары; — bye, прощай! прощайте! —humouredly, въ веселомъ расположеніи духа; a — ly number, порядочное число; — man, хозяинъ, домохозяинъ; — natured, добродушный; — sized, статный; but staying behind will do him no —, но если я отстану отъ прочихъ, то отъ этого ему пользы не будетъ.

goose, гусь; —berry bush, крыжовникъ; — berry wine, крыжовниковка.

gore, кровь, запёкшаяся кровь.

gorgeous, пышный, великолѣпный, роскошный.

gospel, евангеліе.

got, см. **get**.

Gothic, готескій.

gouty, подагрическій; a — man, подагрикъ, страждущій подагрою.

govern, управлять; — ment, правленіе, управленіе, владѣніе, власть, правительство, губернія;—ment house,

домъ гдѣ помѣщается правительство; — or, правитель, губернаторъ;— or-general, генералъ-губернаторъ; they belong to the — or-general for the time being, они принадлежатъ ген.-губернатору за время его правленія.

gown, женское платье, мантія; a bishop's —, епископская риза.

grace, пріятность, грація, милость, благодать, застольная молитва; His Grace, Его Свѣтлость (старинный титулъ королей); to say —, прочитать молитву за столомъ; to —, удостоивать;—ful,граціозный, милый;—fulness, пріятность, миловидность, прелесть.

gradation, постепенность.

gradual, постепенный;— ly, постепенно.

grain, зерно, зёрна, хлѣбъ, зерновой хлѣбъ.

grand, величественный, великолѣпный, великій, главный; the — fleet, большая эскадра; — eur, величіе; — father, дѣдъ; — mother, бабка, бабушка; — son, внукъ; great — son, правнукъ.

granitic, гранитный.

grant, жаловать, пожаловать, давать, соглашаться.

grape, виноградъ.

graphic, графическій, живописный.

grapple, сцѣпляться.

grasp, хватка, власть; he kept his dying —, онъ умирая не выпускалъ изъ рукъ; to —, хватать, схватывать, ухватываться за.

grass, трава; — green, травяной цвѣтъ.

grate, каминъ; to —, хрустѣть, скрипѣть, трещать.

grateful, признательный, благородный.

gratify, удовлетворять, угождать, награждать; to be gratified with a sight of it, имѣть удовольствіе видѣть её; — ing, удовлетворительный, пріятный.

gratitude, благодарность.

gratuitous, даровой, безденежный; — ly, даромъ, безплатно.

grave, могила; важный, серьёзный; — ly, серьёзно.

gravitation, тяготѣніе.

gravity, важность, степенность.

gravy, подливка.

gray, сѣрый; — friar, капуцинецъ;— hound, борзая собака.

graze, слегка задѣвать.

grease, смазывать.

greasy, сальный, засаленный, грязный.

great, великій, большой, высокій; — coat (длинный) сертукъ;—grandson, правнукъ; — ly, очень;— ness, величина; the — ness of his strength, великую свою силу.

Grecian, Грекъ, Эллинистъ.

Greece, Греція.

greedily, съ жадностью.

Greek, греческій языкъ; греческій; to quote—, приводить мѣста изъ греческихъ писателей.

green, зеленый цвѣтъ, зелень; зелёный; —wood, покрытый листьями лѣсъ, зелёный лѣсъ.

Greenland, Гренландія.

Greenwich, Гриничъ; Гриничскій.

grew, см. grow.

grey, greyhound, см. gray.

grief, горесть, печаль, грусть.

grievance, жалоба, тягость, тягостное положеніе.

grieve, огорчать, горевать, грустить.

grievous, тяжкій, огорчительный, горестный, опасный; — ly, тяжко, крайне.

grimly, угрюмо, отвратительно, ужасно.

grin, зубоскальство, смѣяніе.

grind, раздробляться, угнетать, притѣснять; to — the teeth, скрежетать зубами; — ing of teeth, скрежетаніе зубами, скрежетъ зубовъ.

gripe, когти, пасть.

groan, стонъ; to —, стонать, брюзжать; —ing, стонаніе, стонъ.

grog, грогъ.

grogram, грогранъ; грограновый (изъ верблюжьей шерсти).

groom, конюхъ, стремянной.

grope, ходить ощупью.

gross, цѣльный, гуртовый, грубый, нескромный, неучтивый; —ly, грубо, весьма, очень.

ground, см. grind.

ground, земля, мѣсто, мѣстность, основаніе, причина; rising—, возвышеніе, возвышенное мѣсто; — floor, нижній этажъ; — swell, прибываніе воды подъ льдомъ; — thoroughfare, подземный проходъ или проѣздъ.

group, группа.

grove, роща.

grow, расти, возрастать, увеличиваться, становиться, дѣлаться; to—up, подрастать, выростать; he grew tired, ему наскучило.

grown, см. grow.

grumble, ворчать, брюзжать.

guarantee, гарантировать, ручаться, отвѣчать за что.

guard, стража, защита, охраненіе, караулъ, часовой, сторожъ, гвардія, осторожность; the officer of the —, караульный офицеръ; to put any one on his—, предостерегать кого; to —, хранить, охранять, остерегаться, беречься;—house, гауптвахта; — ian, хранитель, охранительный; — ian angel, ангелъ хранитель.

guess, угадывать, догадываться.

guest, гость.

guggle, см. gurgle.

Guiana, Гвіана или Гіана.

guidance, руководство; God's —, промыселъ Божій.

guide, проводникъ; to—, руководствовать, указывать путь, провожать, править, управлять.

guildhall, ратуша.

guilt, вина; — less, безвинный; — y, виновный, виноватый.

guinea, гинея (21 шиллингъ, около 7 руб.)

Guinea, Гвинея; — man, купеческое судно служащее къ перевозу товаровъ въ Гвинею.

guise, образъ.

guitar, гитара.

Gulf of Guinea, Гвинейскій заливъ;—Stream, заливное теченіе.

gun, пушка, артиллерійское орудіе, ружьё;—deck, гондекъ, нижній декъ; — powder, порохъ; — powder plot, пороховой заговоръ; — wale, шкафутъ.

gurgle, клокотать, журчать.

gush, брызгать, стремиться.

gust, сильный внезапный порывъ вѣтра.

Guy, Витъ.

H.

ha, а! ахъ!

Habeas Corpus Act, актъ о личной свободѣ.

habit, одѣяніе, одежда, обыкновеніе, обычай,

привычка; to be in the —, имѣть привычку; — ation, обитаніе, жилище; — ually, привычно, по привычкѣ.

hackney-coachman, извощикъ, наёмный кучеръ.

had, см. **have**.

Hadrian, Адріанъ.

hail, градъ, привѣтствіе; all —, хвала тебѣ! to —, привѣтствовать, окликать;—stone, градина.

hair, волосы.

half, половина, въ половину, полу, полъ; — an hour, полчаса; — moon, полумѣсяцъ; — penny, полупенни; — way, половина дороги, половина; who was not for doing things by halves, который не любилъ недовершать начатаго.

hall, зала, передняя зала, палата, галлерея, портикъ, мыза; servants' —, лакейская, дѣвичья.

halt, останавливаться.

ham, ветчина, окорокъ.

hammer, молотокъ.

hand, рука, ладонь, стрѣлка (у часовъ), сторона; —to—, рукопашнымъ боемъ; at —, близко, вблизи; to have a—in, участвовать въ; to—, вручать, подавать; to—in, вводить за руку; to—over, передавать;—ful, горсть; — kerchief, платокъ, косынка;—loom, ручной ткацкій станокъ;

— maiden, служанка, услужница; — some, красивый, приличный (о вознагражденіи); — somely, щедро.

handle, поступать съ кѣмъ, заниматься чѣмъ.

hang, висѣть, вѣшать, повѣсить, обвѣшивать, убирать; to — against, anything, повѣсить на что; to — round any one, прицѣпляться къ кому; to—up, вѣшать; to upon, быть въ тягость, обременять; — ing, висячій, повислый, повисшій;—ings, драпировка.

hanimal, см. **animal**.

Hanover, Гановеръ.

hap, удача, случай;—less, несчастный.

happen, случаться; to—to awaken, случайно пробудиться; I do not — to recollect, я что-то не помню; —ed to take place, когда-то случился; who — ed to wait on them, которой случилось прислуживать имъ.

happily, счастливо, благополучно, къ счастію.

happiness, счастіе.

happy, счастливый, удачный.

harangue, рѣчь; to —, говорить рѣчь, привѣтствовать.

harass, терзать, тревожить.

harbour, гавань, пристань;—dues, пристанная пошлина.

hard, твердый, крѣпкій, трудный; очень, весь-

ма, сильно; to — en, твердѣть, окрѣплять, ожесточать, ожесточаться; the—est-worked river, рѣка работающая больше всѣхъ; —ly, съ трудомъ, едва; —ship, трудность, неудобство, превратность, тягость; — ware, желѣзныя или стальныя издѣлія; — wood, твёрдое дерево; — у, дюжій, крѣпкій, смѣлый, отважный.

hare, заяцъ.

hark, слушай! слушайте!

harlequin, арлекинъ.

harm, вредъ.

harp, арфа;—er, арфистъ.

harpoon, гарпунъ, копьё, острога, которыми бьютъ китовъ и другихъ рыбъ.

harsh, жесткій, суровый, строгій.

hart, олень (шестигодовой).

harvest, жатва.

has, см. **have**.

haste, поспѣшность; in — спѣша; I am in—, я тороплюсь; to make—, спѣшить; to—n, торопить, спѣшить, поспѣшать.

hastily, спѣшно, поспѣшно.

hasty, поспѣшный, торопливый, безразсудный, необдуманный.

hat, шляпа.

hatch, hatchway, люкъ.

hate, ненавидѣть; — ful ненавистный.

hath=has, см. **have**.

hatred, ненависть.

haughty, спесивый, надменный.

haul, тащить; to—forth, вытаскивать; to — in, тянуть, выбирать слабину; to — on board, вытащить на судно.

haunt, осаждать, преслѣдовать, обезпокоивать.

have, имѣть, хотѣть, надлежать; I —, я имѣю, у меня есть; I — many places to call at, ещё много мѣстъ, куда я долженъ зайти; he has had his reward, ему по дѣламъ и награда; he had his boots cleaned, онъ велѣлъ вычистить свои сапоги; Bill has not to bark in vain, Билю лаять напрасно не приходится; he has to be very wakeful, онъ долженъ много бодрствовать; we had to wait long, намъ пришлось долго ждать; had you rather not, Вы больше не желаете? you had better take, Вы бы лучше взяли; that they had better try and learn, что имъ лучше надобно постараться узнать; to—breakfast, завтракать; to—made, заказывать; to—on, имѣть на себѣ, быть въ чёмъ; to — one's will, оставаться при своёмъ мнѣніи; to let—, давать.

hawk, соколъ; to—, спускать соколовъ;—ing, соколиная охота.

hay, сѣно; — band, пукъ сѣна, связка сѣна.

hazard, рискъ, опасность; at all —s, во что бы то ни стало; to—, рисковать, отваживаться; — ous, опасный, рискованный.

haze, туманъ.

hazel, орѣшина, орѣшникъ; орѣховый.

head, голова, глава, начальникъ, вершина, верховье, источникъ, передовое войско, носъ (у корабля); fool's —, дурацкій колпакъ;to—, начальствовать, предводительствовать; — dress, головной уборъ; — land, мысъ; а —, см. **ahead**.

health, здоровье; — у, здоровый.

heap, куча, груда, толпа.

hear, слышать, слушать, выслушивать , услыхать; to — from, получать письмо отъ; — ing, слухъ; — say, наслышка, слухъ.

heard, см. **hear**.

heart, сердце; by —, наизусть; to be of good —, собраться съ духомъ, крѣпиться духомъ; — ily, сердечно, усердно; I have eaten very — ily, я порядкомъ поѣлъ; —у, сердечный, усердный, крѣпкій.

hearth, очагъ; — money, подымный сборъ.

heat, жаръ; the — of the weather, жаркая погода; to —, воспламенять.

heath, степь.

heathen, язычникъ; языческій.

heave, подниматься; to — in sight, показываться.

heaven, небо, рай; for Heaven's sake, ради Бога.

heavily, тяжело.

heavy, тяжёлый, сильный (о дождѣ); а — sea, бурное море; she gave a — sigh, она глубоко вздохнула; — armed, см. **arm**.

Hebrew, еврейскій.

he'd, см. **he would**.

hedge, живой заборъ.

heed, вниманіе, осторожность; — lessness, невнимательность , неосторожность.

heel, пятка; to go at any one's —s, по пятамъ преслѣдовать; to —, крениться; to make—, накренить.

height, вышина, высота, возвышеніе, наибольшая высота, высшая степень; to — en, возвышать, увеличивать, украшать.

heir, наслѣдникъ; —ess, наслѣдница.

held, см. **hold**.

hell, адъ, преисподняя.

helm, руль.

helm, helmet, шлемъ,шишакъ.

help, помощь; to—, помогать, пособлять, услуживать, подавать, накладывать (на тарелку), удерживаться; to — to, подавать, доставлять; — less, безсильный; — mate, супругъ, супруга.

helter-skelter , стрем-

главъ, опрометью, кое-
какъ.

hem, обрубать; to—round,
окружать.

hemisphere, полушаріе.

hemp, конопель.

hence, отсюда, отъ этого; — forth, — forward,
отнынѣ, съ этого вре-
мени, впредь.

Henry, Генрихъ.

her, ея, ей.

herald, герольдъ.

herbage, травы, пажить.

herd, стадо, табунъ (лошадей).

here, здѣсь, сюда; - and
there, тутъ и тамъ,
тамъ и сямъ, мѣстами,
въ иныхъ мѣстахъ;
—is, —age, вотъ; —in,
въ этомъ; from—, от-
сюда.

hereditary, наслѣдствен-
ный.

here's, см. here is.

heresy, ересь, расколъ.

heretic, еретикъ, расколь-
никъ.

hero, герой; —ic, геройскій, еройческій.

herself, сама, она сама,
себя.

he's, см. he is.

hesitate, колебаться, за-
пинаться.

hesitation, мѣшканіе, за-
пиваніе.

heyda, гей! эй!

hid, hidden, см. hide.

hide, шкура, кожа; to -,
скрывать.

hiding, прятаніе; —place,
тайникъ.

hie, спѣшить, поспѣшать.

hierarchy, іерархія, свя-
щенноначаліе.

higgler, разнощикъ.

high, высокій, великій,
важный, сильный; вы
шиною, въ вышину,
ростомъ; высоко, спль-
но; with — pretensions
to, съ большими пре-
тензіями на; on —, на
верху, на небѣ; —land,
горная страна, гор-
ный; Highland amuse-
ment, увеселеніе гор-
цевъ; the Highland
mountains, the High-
lands, горы Высокой
Шотландіи; — lander,
горный житель, го-
рецъ; — ly, высоко,
весьма, очень, сильно,
въ высокой степени;
— minded, велиходуш-
ный; — ness, Высоче-
ство; — road, — way,
большая дорога; - spi-
rited, пылкій, горячій,
гордый; — wayman,
разбойникъ (на боль-
шой дорогѣ).

hill, холмъ, гора ; — у,
холмистый, бугристый.

him, его, ему, см. he.

Himalaya, Пмалайскій.

himself, онъ самъ, самъ,
себя; by—, одинъ.

hind, мужикъ.

Hindoo, Индостанецъ; the
— widow, вдова Ин-
достанца; —stanee, Ин-
достанскій языкъ.

Hindostan, Индостанъ.

hint, намёкъ, предостереженіе; to —, наме-
кать.

hire, нанимать; —d, наёмный.

his, его, свой.

hiss, шипѣть.

historian, историкъ.

historic, historical, исто-
рическій.

history, исторія, повѣствованіе.

hit, попадать; to — on,
попадать въ.

hitch, зацѣпляться.

hither, сюда; — to, до
сихъ поръ.

hive, улей.

ho, о! гей!

hoard, скапливать.

hobble, храмота, бѣда;
to get into a—, попа-
дать въ бѣду; to —,
хромать.

hobgoblin, домовой.

hog, свинья, боровъ.

hogshead, оксгофтъ, бочка.

hoist, поднимать; to—out,
спускать.

hold, задержка, удержа-
ніе. трюмъ, интрюмъ;
to have—, держаться;
to let go one's—, опус-
кать; to —, держать,
имѣть, владѣть, почи-
тать, удерживать, дер-
жаться; hold! держи!
стой! постой! to — a
conversation, перего-
варивать; to—a feast,
задать пиръ; to—a po-
sition, to — a station,
занимать мѣсто; to —
in, удерживать; to—in
horror, приводить въ
ужасъ; to — on, дер-
жаться; to — out, про-
тягивать, держаться;
to - to, подавать; to—
up, поднимать; to—va-
luable preferment; за-
нимать высокую долж-
ность.

hole, дыра, отверстіе,
яма.

holiday, праздникъ.

Holland, Голландія.

holloa, гей! слушай!

hollow, впадина, пустота, бездна, пучина; глухой; вполнѣ, совсѣмъ; to — out, выдалбливать.

Holstein, Голштинія.

holster, чушки (для пистолета).

holy, святой, священный.

homage, поклоненіе, благоговѣніе, присяга въ вѣрности; to pay — to any one, оказывать кому глубочайшее почтеніе.

home, домъ, отчизна, родина, родная страна; домой; — country, родная сторона; at —, дома; — made, домашняго печенія.

honest, честный; — y, честность; a life of—y, честная жизнь.

honey, мёдъ.

honor, honour, честь, почесть; person of —, честный человѣкъ, благородный ч.;Your—, Ваша Милость; to —, почитать, чтить, удостоивать чѣмъ;—able, почётный, славный, почтенный.

Honorius, Гонорій.

hood, чепчикъ, капоръ, клобукъ монашескій.

hoof, копыто.

hook, крюкъ.

hoop, кольцё.

hop, хмѣль; — merchant, хмѣлеводъ.

hop, прыгать, подпрыгивать.

hope, надежда; in—s, въ надеждѣ; to —, надѣяться, ожидать; — less, безнадёжный; escape was now — less, на спасеніе теперь уже не было надежды.

Horace, Горацій.

horizon, горизонтъ.

horn, рогъ, рожёкъ;—ed, рогатый.

horrible, ужасный.

horrid, ужасный, гнусный.

horror, ужасъ.

horse, лошадь, конница; лошадиный, конный; on—back, верхомъ;—man, всадникъ;—manship, верховая ѣзда, искуство ѣздить верхомъ; — pistol, карманный пистолетъ; — pond, купальня для лошадей; — soldier, конный солдатъ, кавалеристъ.

hose, штаны.

hospitable, гостепріимный.

hospitably, гостепріимно.

hospital, гошпиталь, больница;—ity, гостепріимство, хлѣбосольство.

host, хозяинъ, трактирщикъ, войско, рать; — age, заложникъ;—elry, отель, гостинница; — ile, непріятельскій, враждебный; — ility, непріязненность, вражда, враждебность, непріятельское (военное) дѣйствіе; — ler, конюхъ въ гостиннцѣ, дворникъ.

hot, жаркій, горячій.

hotel, гостинница, отель.

hound, гончая собака.

hour, часъ; — ly, ежечасно.

house, домъ; — of Commons, нижній парламентъ; — of entertainment гостинница, отель; — of parliament, палата, парламентъ, домъ парламента; — of Lords — of peers, upper —, upper — of Parliament, верхній парламентъ; religious —, монастырь; the — of God, домъ Божій, храмъ Господень;—hold, домъ, хозяйство, семейство, управленіе семействомъ, домашній; — keeper, дворецкій, ключница; — keeping, хозяйство, управленіе хозяйствомъ, домоводство; — less, бездомный, безкровный; — maid, горничная, to—, убирать подъ крышку.

hove, см. **heave**.

hover, носиться.

how, какъ; — ever, однако же, сколько бы, сколько ни, какъ ни; — is this, какъ это такъ? — long, долго ли, давно ли? — many, — much, сколько?—now, ну что же?

howl, выть; — ing, вой.

Hudson's Bay, Гудсоновъ Заливъ.

hue, цвѣтъ, оттѣнка; — and cgy, крикъ на что.

huge, огромный.

Hugh, Гугонъ.

hulks, блокшпфъ.

hum, напѣвать.

human, человѣческій;—e,

человѣколюбивый; — ely, человѣколюбиво; — ity, человѣчество, человѣколюбіе.

humble, скромный, низкаго состоянія; to —, усмирять.

humbly, смиренно.

humour, нравъ, прихоть, расположеніе духа, юморъ.

hump-backed, горбатый.

Hun, Гуннъ.

hundred, сто, сотня; four —, четыреста; three—, триста; two—, двѣсти.

hung, см. hang.

Hungarian, венгерскій.

hunger, голодъ.

hungry, голодный.

hunt, —ing, охота, травля; to—, травить, ходить на охоту, гнаться за чѣмъ; — ing match, выѣздъ обществомъ на охоту.

hurry, торопливость; to be in a—, торопиться, спѣшить;—skurry, въ торопяхъ, въ суматохѣ; to—, торопиться; to — away to prison, со всею поспѣшностію отводить въ тюрьму; to — down, спѣшить; to—into the cascades, ввергнуть въ водопады; to—on, торопиться, спѣшить, подстрекать, поджигать.

hurt, вредъ; without—, невредимъ; to —, повреждать, причинять вредъ; I'll not —a hair of your head, я вашего ни волоска не трону.

husband, мужъ, супругъ; —man, хлѣбопашецъ, земледѣлецъ.

hut, хижина, шалашъ.

hydraulic, гидравлическій.

hydrogen, водородный, водотворный.

hymn, гимнъ, пѣсня.

I.

I, я.

ice, лёдъ.

idea, идея, мысль.

identity, тождество.

idle, праздный, лѣнивый.

idol, идолъ, кумиръ; — atrous, идолопоклоннический; to — ize, обожать.

if, если, ли; as—, какъ будто.

ignominious, позорный, безчестный.

ignorance, невѣжество, невѣдѣніе.

ignorant, невѣдущій, безграмотный.

I'll, см. I will.

ill, зло, несчастіе; худой, дурной, больной; худо, дурно, плохо, скверно; — nature, сердитость, угрюмость; —natured, злой, брюзгливый; — ness, болѣзнь; — timed, неумѣстный; — will, недоброжелательство.

illegal, незаконный.

illegitimacy, незаконное рожденіе.

illicit, недозволительный, запрещенный, незаконный.

illiterate, неучёный, некнижный, неграмотный.

illuminate, освѣщать, раскрашивать; to — one's pipe, закуривать трубку.

illumination, освященіе.

illumine, озарять, просвѣщать.

illusion, обольщеніе, призракъ.

illustrate, изъяснять, пояснять.

illustration, изъясненіе, пясненіе, приведеніе въ примѣръ.

illustrious, славный, знаменитый, знатный.

I'm, см. I am.

image, воображать, воображать себѣ.

imaginable, вообразимый.

imaginary, воображаемый, мнимый.

imagination, воображеніе.

imagine, воображать.

to be imbedded in a quagmire, засѣсть въ болотѣ.

imitate, подражать.

immediate, немедленный, непосредственный; — ly, тотчасъ, непосредственно.

immense, безмѣрный, несмѣтный, преогромный.

immersion, погруженіе.

immidst, среди, посреди, въ серединѣ.

imminent, предстоящій, угрожающій.

immoderately, неумѣренно.

immovable, неподвижный, непоколебимый.

impair, разстроивать.

impart, сообщать.

impassable, непроходимый.

impatience, нетерпѣніе, нетерпѣливость.

impatient, нетерпѣливый; to be — to do anything, жаждать чего, домагаться чего;— ly, нетерпѣливо.

impeach, взводить обвиненіе на кого, обвинять.

impede, препятствовать, мѣшать.

impel, понуждать, побуждать, возбуждать.

impending, надвислый, навѣсный.

imperceptibly, непримѣтно.

imperfect, несовершенный, недостаточный; — ly, несовершенно, недостаточно.

imperial, императорскій.

impervious, непроницаемый.

impetuous, буйный, пылкій.

impious, нечестивый.

implacable, неумолимый.

implement, орудіе, снарядъ.

implicit, безусловный.

implore, умолять.

imply, значить.

import, привозъ; to —, привозить; — ance, важность, значительность; — ant, важный.

importunate, безотвязчивый, неотступный.

importunity, докучливость, навязчивость, неотступность.

impose, налагать, возла-гать; to—upon, обманывать.

imposing, величественный.

imposition, наложеніе, возложеніе.

impossibility, невозможность.

impossible, невозможный.

impost, налогъ, подать, пошлина.

impotent, немощный, безсильный.

impracticable, непсполнимый, невозможный.

impress, дѣлать впечатлѣніе, I felt — ed, мною обладѣла мысль; — ion, впечатлѣніе; to be very — ive, производить глубокое впечатлѣніе, сильно дѣйствовать.

imprison, сажать въ тюрьму; — ment, заточеніе, заключеніе.

improbable, невѣроятный.

improve, улучшать, совершенствовать, улучшаться, совершенствоваться, поправляться; — ment, улучшеніе, усовершенствованіе, успѣхъ; with so improving a voracity, съ такою увеличивающеюся жадностью.

improvisation, импровизація.

imprudence, неблагоразуміе, безразсудство.

imprudent, неблагоразумный, неосторожный, безразсудный.

impudent, нахальный.

impulse, побужденіе.

impunity, безнаказанность, ненаказанность; with —, безнаказанно.

impure, нечистый.

impute, вмѣнять, приписывать.

in, въ, во (съ предложн пад.), черезъ, на; — copper, мѣдью, мѣдными деньгами; — summer, лѣтомъ; — the footsteps, по слѣдамъ; — time, со временемъ.

inability, неспособность.

inaccessible, неприступный, недоступный.

inadequate, недостаточный.

inadvertently, по оплошности.

incalculable, неисчислимый.

incantation, магическое изреченіе.

incapable, неспособный къ чему.

incapacitate, приводить въ несостояніе, лишать возможности.

incapacity, неспособность.

incense, раздражать.

inch, дюймъ.

incident, случай, приключеніе; — to, свойственный кому.

incline, клониться; — d, склонный, расположенный, наклонный; to be — d, клониться.

include, включать, заключать въ себѣ.

income, доходъ, ежегодный доходъ.

incompetent, недостаточный, неспособный, неимѣющій права на что, невластный.

inconsistent, несовмѣстный, несообразный.

inconvenience, неудоб-
ство.

inconvenient, неудобный.

incorrect, неправильный,
неверный.

incorruptibly , непод-
купно.

increase, увеличеніе; to—,
увеличивать, увеличи-
ваться, возрастать, у-
силиваться.

incredible, невимоверный,
невероятный.

inculcate, впѣрять, под-
тверждать.

incumbent, имѣющій при-
ходъ, бенеФиціарій.

incursion, набѣгъ, наше-
ствіе.

indebt, одолжать; —ed,
одолжённый чѣмъ.

indecorum , неприлич-
ность, непристойность.

indeed, въ самомъ дѣлѣ,
дѣйствительно.

indefatigable, неутоми-
мый.

indefeasible, неотчуждае-
мый, неразрушимый.

indent, зубрить, зазу-
бривать.

independence, независи-
мость.

independent , Индепен-
дентъ ; индепендент-
скій, независимый; —
ly, независимо.

indescribable, неописы-
ваемый.

India, восточная Индія;
—n, Индѣецъ, Индѣй-
скій.

indicate, означать, по-
казывать.

indication, указаніе, признакъ.

Indies, Индія; the East—,
Восточная Индія; the

West—, Западная Ин-
дія.

indifference, равнодушіе.

indignantly, съ негодо-
ваніемъ.

indignation, негодованіе.

indignity, оскорбленіе,
обида.

indigo, индиго, кубовая
краска.

indiscretion, неразсуди-
тельность, опрометчи-
вость, нескромность,
болтливость.

indiscriminate , безраз-
борчивый.

indistinctness, неясность.

individual, лицо, особа;
личный, частный, от-
дѣльный.

indolent, лѣнивый, без-
печный.

indoors, см. door.

induce, побуждать, при-
чинять, производить.

indulge, угождать, ле-
лѣять, потворствовать,
предаваться чему; —
nce, снисхожденіе; —
nt, снисходительный.

Indus, Индъ.

industrious, трудолюби-
вый, старательный,
рачительный

industry, радѣніе, ста-
раніе, прилежаніе, тру-
долюбіе, промышлен-
ность.

inelegant , неизящный,
некрасивый.

inestimable, неоцѣнен-
ный, безцѣнный.

inevitable, неминуемый.

inevitably, неминуемо.

inexhaustible, неисто-
щимый.

inexorable, неумолимый.

inexperience, неопыт-
ность; — d, неопытный.

infamous , безчестный,
позорный.

infancy, дѣтство.

infant, младенецъ, дитя.

infantry, пѣхота, инфан-
терія.

infatuate, ослѣплять, о-
больщать.

infect, заражать.

infer, выводить, заклю-
чать.

inferior, меньшій, худ-
шій, нижній, низшій,
подначальный, подчи-
ненный; to be —, у-
ступать.

infest , обезпокоивать,
опустошать.

infidel, невѣрный.

infinitely, безконечно.

infirmity, дряхлость, слабость.

inflame, воспламенять.

inflict, налагать.

influence, вліяніе; to —,
имѣть вліяніе на.

inform, увѣдомлять, из-
вѣщать, наставлять; —
ation, извѣщеніе, на-
ставленіе, извѣстіе,
свѣдѣнія.

infraction, нарушеніе.

ingenious, замысловатый;
— ly, остроумно.

ingratitude, неблагодар-
ность.

inhabit, обитать; a thin-
ly —ed district, мало-
людная страна; — ant,
обитатель, житель.

inherit, наслѣдовать; —
ance, наслѣдство.

inhuman, безчеловѣчный;
— ity, безчеловѣчіе,
жестокость; —ly, без-
человѣчно.

injunction, повелѣніе, подтвержденіе.

injure, вредить, повреждать, оскорблять.

injury, вредъ, повреж-деніе, несправедли-вость, обида.

injustice, несправедли-вость.

inkstand, чернильница.

inlist, вербовать.

inmate, житель.

inn, гостинница;—keeper, er, содержатель или содержательница го-стинницы.

innocence, невинность, безвинность.

innocent, младенецъ; не-винный, невинный, безвинный,простодуш-ный.

innovation,нововведеніе.

innumerable, безчислен-ный.

inoffensive, безвредный.

inoperative,бездѣйствен-ный, недѣйствующій.

inquire, навѣдываться, справляться, спраши-вать, изслѣдовать.

inquiry, распросъ, за-просъ, вопросъ, справ-ка, изслѣдованіе.

inroad, набѣгъ.

insatiable, ненасытный.

inscription, надпись.

insect, насѣкомое.

insensibly, неprimѣтно.

insert, вмѣщать.

inside, внутри.

insist upon, настоять на чёмъ.

insolence, заносчивость, надменность.

insomuch that, такъ что, въ такой степени что.

inspect, осматривать,

смотрѣть, свидѣтель-ствовать; — ion, о-смотръ, надзоръ.

inspire, вдыхать, вну-шать.

inspirit, одушевлять, о-бодрять.

instalment, опредѣленіе.

instance, примѣръ, слу-чай.

instant,мгновеніе, мигъ; немедленный; for an—, на минуту; in an — вмигъ; on the —, тот-часъ; — ly, тотчасъ, сейчасъ, сію минуту.

instead, вмѣсто ; — of, вмѣсто того чтобъ.

instigate, подущать,под-стрекать.

instinctive, инстиктив-ный.

institution, учрежденіе; — for education, вос-питательное или учеб-ное заведеніе.

instruct,учить, обучать, наставлять; — ion, о-бученіе, наставленіе, наказъ, инструкція, — ive, поучительный; — or, наставникъ, учи-тель.

instrument, орудіе, ин-струментъ; —al, слу-жащій орудіемъ, ин-струментальный ; to be — al, служить ору-діемъ.

insubordination, непо-виновеніе, непослу-шаніе.

insufferably,нестерпимо, несносно.

insular, островской.

insult, обида, оскорбле-ніе; to—, обижать, о-

скорблять ; — ing, о-скорбительный.

insupportable, несное-ный, нестерпимый.

insupportably, несносно, нестерпимо.

insure, обезпечивать.

insurgent, инсургентъ, бунтовщикъ.

insurrection, возстаніе, бунтъ.

integrity, непорочность, искренность,честность, правосудіе.

intellect, разумъ, умъ; —ual, умственный.

intelligence, разумѣніе, смышленіе, умствен-ныя способности, спо-собность мыслить,свѣ-дѣніе, извѣстіе, ново-сти, вѣдомость.

intelligent,понятливый, умный.

intelligible, вразуми-тельный, понятный.

intemperate, неумѣрен-ный, невоздержный.

intend, означать, намѣ-реваться, имѣть на-мѣреніе, имѣть что въ виду, вознамѣри-ваться, предназна-чать; — ed, преднамѣ-ренный, умышляемый

intense, сильный, на-пряженный.

intent, намѣреніе; вни-мательный ; to be — on a thing, обратить большое вниманіе на что,заботиться очёмъ; to be — on the inter-est of anything, инте-ресоваться чѣмъ ни-нибудь; — ion, намѣ-реніе;—ionally,умыш-

ленно, нарочно, съ на-
мѣреніемъ.

intercede, ходатайство-
вать, просить о чёмъ.

intercept, мѣшать, пре-
крашать, останавли-
вать, перехватывать.

interdict, запрещать,
возбранять.

interest, интересъ, поль-
за, проценты, вліяніе;
to—, интересовать; to
be—ed, интересовать-
ся; —ing, занматель-
ный, любопытный, ин-
ресный.

interfere, вмѣшиваться;
— nce, вмѣшиваніе,
вмѣшательство, по-
средничество.

interior, нутръ, внутрен-
няя часть; внутренній.

interment, погребеніе,
хороненіе.

internal, внутренній.

interpret, толковать,
объяснять;—er, пере-
водчикъ.

interrogation, спраши-
ваніе, вопрошеніе;
note of —, вопроси-
тельный знакъ.

interrupt, перерывъ, о-
становка; to —, мѣ-
шать, прерывать.

intersect, пересѣкать.

intersperse, усыпать, пе-
ремѣшивать.

interval, промежутокъ.

intervene, проходить
между тѣмъ; — ning,
промежуточный.

intervention, посредни-
чество, заступничество.

interweave with, впле-
тать въ.

intimate, намѣкать;—ly,
коротко.

intimation, намекъ, ука-
заніе.

into, въ, во (съ винит.
пад.).

intolerable, несносный,
нестерпимый.

intolerably, нестерпимо.

intoxicate, напоить до
пьяна, упоить; — d,
нетрезвый, пьяный.

intrenchment, окопъ,
ретраншаментъ.

intrepid, неустрашимый;
—ity, неустрашимость.

intricate, запутанный.

introduce, вводить, пред-
ставлять, to—to any
one's aquaintance, зна-
комить съ кѣмъ.

introductory, служащій
введеніемъ.

intruder, незванный
гость.

intrusion, неумѣстный
входъ, входъ безъ
позволенія.

intrust, ввѣрять.

inundation, наводненіе.

invade, насильно овла-
дѣть, нападать, втор-
гаться; —r, завладѣ-
тель, нападатель.

invalid, инвалидъ.

invaluable, неоцѣненный.

invariable, неизмѣнный;
—bly, неизмѣнно.

invasion, набѣгъ, втор-
женіе.

invective, поношеніе,
брань.

invent, изобрѣтать, вы-
думывать; —ion, изо-
брѣтеніе; —ive, изо-
брѣтательный.

Inverness-shire, графство
Инвернесъ.

investigation, изслѣдо-
ваніе.

invincible, непобѣдимый,
непреодолимый.

inviolable, ненарушимый.

inviolate, неприкосно-
венный, ненарушимый.

invisible, невидимый.

invitation, приглашеніе.

invite, приглашать, при-
влекать.

inviting, привлекатель-
ный; —ly, привлека-
тельно.

involuntary, невольный.

involve, вовлекать, за-
путывать.

Ireland, Ирландія.

Irish, Ирландскій, the—,
Ирландцы; — man,
Ирландецъ.

iron, желѣзо; желѣзный.

irregular, неправиль-
ный, безпорядочный,
безчинный.

irremediable, неисправи-
мый.

irresistible, неодолимый,
непреодолимый, непо-
бѣдимый.

irresolute, нерѣшитель-
но; as if—, какъ буд-
то колебаясь.

irritable, раздражитель-
ный.

irritation, раздраженіе;
in a tone of—, раз-
дражённымъ голосомъ.

is, есть; см. be.

Isaac, Исаакъ.

island, островъ; — er,
островитянинъ.

isle, островъ; — t, ос-
тровокъ.

issue, потомство, ис-
ходъ, конецъ, послѣд-
ствіе, результатъ, раз-
дача; to—, издавать,
выходить, (отдавать
приказъ).

isthmus, перешеекъ.

it, оно, это, —was, бы-ло; of—, его.

Italian, Италіянецъ; италіянскій.

Italy, Италія.

its, онаго, его.

it's см. it is.

itself, оно само, само, себя, самаго себя; in —, само по себѣ.

I've, см. I have.

ivory, слоновая кость.

J.

Jack, Иванъ.

jacket, куртка; to get a wet —, промокать; — pocket, карманъ куртки.

jaguar, ягуаръ, амери-канскій тигръ.

jail, тюрьма; —or, тю-ремщикъ.

Jamaica, Ямайка.

James, Яковъ.

Jane, Іоанна, Анна.

Janissary, янычаръ.

jasper, яшма.

jaw, пасть, зѣвъ.

jealous, ревнивый; to be—of the success of, завидовать кому въ удачѣ; —y, ревность, ревнивость, ревно-ваніе.

jeer, насмѣшка, издѣв-ка; to—, насмѣхаться надъ кѣмъ.

jeopardy, опасность.

Jeremy, Іеремія.

jerk, дёргать, потрясать.

jest, жутка.

Jesuit, іезуитъ.

Jesus, Іисусъ.

jet black, чёрный какъ смоль.

Jew, Жидъ.

jewel, драгоцѣнный ка-мень; —office, храни-лище государствен-ныхъ драгоцѣнностей.

jib, кливеръ; down —, кливеръ долой! up—, кливеръ поднимай!

Joan, Іоанна.

job, дѣло, работа.

jog, толкать, пихать; to—on, подвигаться.

John, Иванъ.

join, соединять, присое-динять, соединяться, присоединяться къ; to — company, присое-диняться къ кому; to —in, участвовать въ; the procession was—ed, къ процессіи при-соединился.

joke, шутка.

jollity, веселость, за-бавность, веселье, по-тѣха.

jolt, переваливаться; to —on, бѣжать перевали-ваясь.

Jonathan, Богданъ.

Joseph, Іосифъ, Осипъ.

Josiah, Іосія.

journal, дневникъ, жур-налъ.

journey, путешествіе (бе-регомъ), путь; a day's —, день ѣзды.

joust, just, бой на копьяхъ, турниръ.

joy, радость; — aunce, веселость, веселіе; —ful, —ous, радостный; —fully, радостно.

jubilee, юбилей.

judge, судья, знатокъ; to —, судить, почи-

тать; to — safest, за-благоразсудить.

judgment, судъ, сужде-ніе, наказаніе, приго-воръ, рѣшеніе.

judicial, судебный.

juice, сокъ.

Julius, Юлій.

July, Іюль; іюльскій.

jump, прыжёкъ, ска-чёкъ; to give a —, скакнуть; to—, пры-гать, скакать; to — down, соскакивать; to — out, выскакивать; to — overboard, бро-саться за бортъ.

junction, соединеніе.

June, Іюнь.

juniper, можжевеловый.

jurisdiction, судебное вѣдомство.

jury, судъ присяжныхъ, присяжные; —of accu-sation, grand —, об-винительная палата.

just, см. joust.

just, справедливый, пра-ведный, вѣрный, точ-ный; совершенно, точ-но, лишь только, толь-ко что, только для того чтобы; —as, when, въ то самое время когда; —by my seat, подлѣ самаго моего мѣста; — ice, правосудіе, справед-ливость, судья; to do — ice, отдавать спра-ведливость; — ice of the peace, мировой судья; — ly, справед-ливо, — ness, точ-ность, справедливость.

Jutland, Ютландія.

K.

keel, киль.

keen, острый, проницательный.

keep, держать, содержать, продерживать, удерживать, соблюдать, сохранять, продолжать, держаться, оставаться; to—a day, соблюсти срокъ, явиться въ срокъ; to — a good look-out, хорошенько караулить; to — any one out of sight, устранять кого; to —from, защищать; to — in check, останавливать, препятствовать; to — informed of what was passing, доставлять извѣстія о всемъ что происходило; to — in good repair, содержать въ хорошемъ состояніи; to — out, не впускать; to — pace, идти наравнѣ съ чѣмъ, не отставать отъ кого; to—secret, сохранять въ тайнѣ; to—sheep, пасти овецъ; to — up, поддерживать; to — upon one's guard, остерегаться; I have kept you up, я задержалъ Васъ ложиться спать; never — ing in mind, мало думая; — er, хранитель, сторожъ, смотритель.

kelson, кильсонъ.

Kentish, кентскій.

kept, см. **keep.**

kerchief, головной уборъ, платокъ.

kernel, зерно.

key, ключь, клавишъ.

kick, пинокъ, ударъ ногою; to—off, сшибать, сталкивать.

kidmudgar, слуга (въ Индіи).

kill, убивать.

kilt, короткая юбка (у Шотландцевъ).

kin, родство, свойство.

kind, родъ, сортъ; добрый, ласковый; — hearted, добродушный, добросердечный, радушный; — ly, благосклонный, ласковый, кроткій, добрый, благосклонно, ласково;— ness, доброта.

kindle, возжигать, воспалять, разгораться; to — up, зажигать.

king, король; — dom, королевство; — ly, королевскій; — maker, дѣлатель королей.

kinsman, родственникъ.

kiss, цѣловать.

kitchen, кухня.

kite, бумажный змѣй.

knave, плутъ.

knavish, плутоватый.

knee, колѣно.

kneel down, становиться на колѣни.

knell, колокольный звонъ по умершемъ.

knew, см. **know.**

knife, ножъ, ножикъ.

knight, рыцарь, кавалеръ; to—, посвящать въ рыцари; — hood, рыцарство.

knit, вязать.

knock, стукъ; to—, стучаться; to — backwards, сшибать на-

задъ; to — down, повалить кого наземь; — ing, стучаніе, стукотня.

knot, узёлъ, куча, толпа.

know, знать, узнавать; to — any one from, различать, отличать отъ; — ledge, знаніе, познаніе, свѣдѣніе; without his — ledge, безъ его вѣдома; — ledge of the world, знаніе свѣта, умѣніе жить въ свѣтѣ.

known, извѣстный; см. также **know.**

L.

label, ерлыкъ; to—, писать или привязывать ерлыкъ.

labor, см. **labour;**—ious, трудолюбивый, многотрудный; — iously, тщательно.

labour, трудъ, работа; to —; работать, трудиться; — er, работникъ, поденщикъ.

lace, кружево.

lacerate, изрывать, раздирать.

lack, недостатокъ; —, good —, увы!

laconic, лаконическій.

lad, молодой человѣкъ, парень, молодчикъ,

ladder, лѣстница; — machine, лѣстничная машина.

lade, нагружать.

laden, см. **lade.**

lady, дама, госпожа, леди (титулъ супругъ

лицъ высшаго дворянства), супруга.

lag, отставать, мѣшкать.

laid, см. **lay; to be — on a bed of sickness**, слечь на одръ болѣзни, занемочь.

lain, см. **lie**.

lake, озеро.

lamb, ягнёнокъ, агнецъ.

lame, увѣчный, хромой; **to —**, дѣлать хромымъ.

lament, оплакивать, сожалѣть о чёмъ; **— able**, плачевный, жалкій, сожалѣнія достойный.

lamp, лампа, лампада.

lampoon, ругательное сочиненіе, пасквиль.

Lancastrian, приверженецъ дома Ланкастерскаго; Ланкастерскій.

lance, копьё, пика.

land, земля, почва, страна, помѣстье, берегъ; береговой; **to —**, приставать къ берегу, выходить на берегъ, высаживать на берегъ; **— ed property**, помѣстье, недвижимое имѣніе; **— holder**, помѣщикъ; **— ing**, приставаніе къ берегу; **— lord**, хозяинъ, содержатель гостинницы; **— scape**, ландшафтъ, пейзажъ.

lane, переулокъ.

language, языкъ, рѣчь, слогъ; **every day —**, обыкновенный языкъ.

languid, слабый; **to make —**, изнурять.

lantern, фонарь.

lap, колѣни.

lapis lazuli, лазуревый камень.

Laplander, Лапландецъ.

lapse, истеченіе, происествіе.

larboad, лѣвая сторона (корабля).

large, большой, великій; **at —**, на волѣ, на свободѣ, вообще, въ совокупности; **— ly**, значительно, щедро, въ избыткѣ, въ изобиліи; **to enlist — ly**, вербовать въ большомъ числѣ.

lash, ударъ; **to —**, хлестать, принайтовить.

lass, дѣвка, дѣвица.

last, послѣдній разъ; **— night**, вчера вечеромъ; послѣдній; **at —**, наконецъ; **to the —**, до крайности; **the — instance**, крайній случай; **to —**, продолжаться, держаться; **— ing**, продолжительный, постоянный; **— ly**, наконецъ, въ заключеніе; **— named**, послѣднеупомянутый, послѣднепоименованный.

late, поздній, недавній, покойный, бывшій; поздно, недавно; **to be —**, опаздывать; **— ly, of —** недавно.

Latin, латинскій языкъ; латинскій.

latitudinarianism, вольнодумство.

latter, послѣдній; **— ly**, въ послѣднее время.

laudable, похвальный.

laugh, смѣхъ; **to —**, смѣяться; **to — at**, смѣяться надъ, насмѣхаться;

— able, смѣшной; **— er**, насмѣшникъ; **— ter** смѣхъ.

launch, баркасъ; **to —**, спускать судно на воду.

laureate, увѣнчанный стихотворецъ, придворный стихотворецъ.

laurels, лавры.

lavender, лавенда.

lavish, расточать, проматывать.

law, законъ, правовѣдѣніе; **— ful**, законный; **— less**, беззаконный, необузданный; **— yer**, законовѣдецъ, адвокатъ.

lawn, лино, покрывало.

lay, класть, положить, ставить; см. также **lie; to — an ambuscade**, сдѣлать засаду; **to — at the feet**, повергать къ стопамъ; **to — before any one**, представлять кому; **to — before the king**, представлять королю, повергать на воззрѣніе короля; **to — by**, сохранять; **to — down**, полагать, ложиться, слагать съ себя; **to — down one's arms**, класть, положить оружіе, сдаваться; **to — down one's head**, ложиться спать; **to — down one's life**, положить животъ; **to — hold of**, захватывать; **to — in the churchyard**, предавать тѣло землѣ; **to — off**, держать отъ берега прочь; **to — on the back**, ввалить въ спину; **to — up**, накоплять; to — upon, налагать; to — waste, опустошать.

layman, мірянинъ, свѣтскій человѣкъ.

laziness, лѣнь.

lazy, лѣнивый.

lead, — ership, предводительство; to —, водить, вести, путеводить, руководить, предводительствовать, побуждать; to—out, выводить; to — through, проходить по; to—to, доводить до чего, повести къ чему, приводить, наводить на что; — er, передовой, предводитель, вождь, начальникъ.

lead, свинецъ; — en, свинцовый.

leaf, листъ.

league, лига (5,208 вёрстъ), союзъ.

leak, — age, течь; —у, съ течью.

lean, любовина; худой, худощавый; to—, прислоняться, склоняться.

leap, скочёкъ, прыжёкъ; to —, скакать, прыгать; to — in, впрыгивать; to — on, вскакивать на; to — out, выскакивать; to — over, перескакивать.

leapt, см. **leap**.

learn, учить, учиться, слышать о чемъ, узнавать, научаться; — ed, учёный; —ing, ученіе, изученіе, учёность.

least, малѣйшій; меньше; at—, по крайней мѣрѣ; in the —, ни

мало; not the —, нисколько.

leather, кожа; — n, кожаный.

leave, позволеніе; — of absence, отпускъ; to—, оставлять, покидать, завѣщать, отказывать по духовной; to — behind, оставлять дома; to — off, переставать; to — out, пропускать; to—to, предоставлять; he had just left, онъ только что вышелъ отъ него.

leavened, квашеный.

lecture, лекція, выговоръ; to read any one a—, дѣлать кому выговоръ.

led, см. **lead**.

lee, подвѣтренная сторона; подвѣтренный.

left, лѣвая сторона; —, — hand, лѣвый; to the —, налѣво; см. также **leave**.

leg. нога, голень, задняя часть (ноги); — of mutton, задняя четверть баранины.

legal, законный, узаконенный; — ity, законность.

legate, легатъ, папскій посолъ.

legatee, участникъ въ завѣщаніи.

legible, чёткій; it is scarcely—, это съ трудомъ можно прочесть.

legion, легіонъ.

legislation, законодательство.

legislature, законодательная власть.

legitimate, законный.

leisure, досугъ, свободное время; —ly, исподоволь, потихоньку.

lemon, лимонъ.

lend, одолжать, ссужать чѣмъ, давать.

length, длина, разстояніе, продолжительность; in the course of a great — of time, въ теченіе весьма продолжительнаго времени; at—, наконецъ; to — en, становиться дольше, прибавлять, увеличивать.

Lent, постъ.

lent, см. **lend**.

Leo, Лёвъ.

leopard, леопардъ; леопардовый.

less, меньше, менѣе, меньшій; — er, меньшій.

lesson, урокъ, поученіе.

lest, дабы не, чтобы не.

let, пускать, позволять, давать, отдавать въ наймы; — me hear the irregular verbs, скажите мнѣ неправильные глаголы; —us see, посмотримъ; —us suppose, предположимъ; to — any one go, отпустить кого; to—fly, пускать, бросать; to —go, выпускать (изъ рукъ), отдавать; to — into, впускать, сообщать; to — out, выпускать.

lethargy, сонная немочь, летаргія.

let's, см. **let us**.

letter, письмо, буква; a man of — s, ученый; — s patent, жалованная грамота, патентъ.

levee, выходъ.

level, уровень; ровный, гладкій; to —, разорять до основанія.

levite, левитъ, ветхозавѣтный священнослужитель.

levy, набирать, взимать (подать).

Lewis, Людовикъ.

to be liable, подлежать, быть подвергнутымъ.

liar, лгунъ, лжецъ.

liberal, свободно мыслящій, либеральный; — ity, великодушіе, щедрость, благородство; —ly, щедро.

liberate, овобождать.

liberty, свобода; — ties, права, преимущества.

library, библіотека.

license, свобода, позволеніе.

licensing, act, см. act.

licentious, распутный, развратный; — ness, своевольство, распутство.

lick, лизать, локать.

lie, лежать, ложиться, стоять, находиться, жительствовать; to — down, ложиться; to — in jail, сидѣть въ тюрьмѣ; to — in state, лежать на парадномъ одрѣ; to — in wait, быть или держаться въ засадѣ; to — over, ложиться на бокъ; it lay heavy on his heart, ему было тяжело на сердцѣ.

liege, верховный; —or lord, государь;—man, вассалъ, голдовникъ, ленникъ.

lieutenancy, намѣстничество (графства).

lieutenant, лейтенантъ, заряжатель (у орудія); — general, генералълейтенантъ.

life, жизнь, жизнеописаніе; the book of —, книга живота; — less, безжизненный, мёртвый.

lift, поднимать, приподнимать; to — up one's voice, возвышать голосъ.

light, свѣтъ, свѣча, свѣчка; свѣтлый, лёгкій, незначительный, неважный, маловажный; the father of — s, отецъ всякаго просвѣщенія; to—, зажигать, засвѣчать, освѣщать, закуривать, слѣзать, сходить; to — on, натыкаться на что; to — up, вспыхивать; — blue, голубой цвѣтъ; — green, свѣтлозелёный цвѣтъ; — ly, легко, слегка; — ning, молнія;

lighter, плашкоутъ, лихтеръ.

like, подобный, похожій; подобно; to—, любить, нравиться; he would —to, ему бы хотѣлось, онъ охотно бы; how do you —, какъ Вамъ нравится? — ness, сходство, подобіе, изображеніе, портретъ; — wise, также.

likely, вѣроятный; вѣроятно; if he is — to be late, если вѣроятно, что онъ опоздаетъ; is — to mislead, легко

можетъ ввести въ заблужденіе; the work most — to prove, сочиненіе, которое по всей вѣроятности окажется.

liking, охота; to take а—, полюбить, захотѣть, понравиться.

lily, лилія.

limb, членъ.

lime, известь, извёстка, птичій клей.

limit, граница, предѣлъ; to—, ограничивать.

line, строка, строчка, линія, линія родства, поколѣніе; to —, застанавливать;—of life, родъ жизни, званіе;— of road, трактъ; — al, родовой, поколѣнный.

linen, полотно; полотняный; — draper, холщечникъ, торгующій полотномъ.

linger, медлить, мѣшкать.

link, звено, связь.

lion, левъ; — hearted, львиное сердце.

lip, губа.

liquor, жидкость, напитокъ.

lisp, лепетать.

list, списокъ, поприще, арена; to enter the — s, см. enter; to —, хотѣть.

listen, внимать, слушать, прислушиваться; — er, слушатель.

lit, см. light.

literally, буквально.

literary, словесный, литературный, учёный; а — man, литераторъ.

literati, литераторы.

literature, словесность, литература.

litter, носилки, безпорядокъ, помётъ.

little, малый, маленькій; мало, немного; a —, немного, немножко, нѣсколько; by — and —, мало по малу; not a —, не мало; after a — reflection, послѣ нѣкотораго соображенія дѣла.

liturgy, литургія, церковная или божественная служба, порядокъ богослуженія.

live, жить, доживать; to — on any thing, питаться чѣмъ; long —, да здравствуетъ! — lihood, пропитаніе; — ly, весёлый, живой.

Liverpool, Ливерпуль; Ливерпульскій.

livery, ливрея.

living, жизнь, пропитаніе, духовное мѣсто; живой; to be —, жить; more than any person —, больше всѣхъ людей на свѣтѣ.

'llwill.

lo, вотъ! смотри!

load, возъ, кладь, тяжесть; to —, накладывать, нагружать, заряжать, одарять чѣмъ; — ed, обремененный свинцёмъ; the — ing, нагрузка.

loaf, цѣлый хлѣбъ.

lobster, морской ракъ.

local, мѣстный.

lock, локонъ; to — up, замыкать, запирать.

locomotion, движеніе съ мѣста на мѣсто.

lodge, жить, стоять, помѣщать.

lodging, помѣщеніе, пристанище, квартира; a night's —, ночлегъ.

lofty, высокій, возвышенный.

log, чурбанъ, пень, бревно; — house, бревенчатое строеніе.

logic, логика.

London, Лондонъ; Лондонскій; — er, житель Лондона.

lone, уединенный, одинокій; — ly, уединённый, глухой.

long, долгій, продолжительный, длинный, дальній; длиною, долго, долгое время, давно; въ продолженіе; as — as, so — as, пока, доколѣ, даже до; before —, вскорѣ послѣ того; — drawn, протяжный; no — er, не долѣе, не болѣе.

longing, страстное желаніе чего-либо; желающій, прихотливый.

Longshanks, длинноногій, долгоногій.

look, взоръ, взглядъ, видъ; — out, высматриваніе; to be on the — out, впередъ смотрѣть; to keep a good — out, хорошенько караулить; to —, глядѣть, смотрѣть, имѣть видъ, казаться; to — about, to — around, оглядываться, осматриваться; to — at, смотрѣть на, въ; to — down, смотрѣть или глядѣть внизъ, низ-

зрѣть; to — for, искать; to — into, заглядывать; to — on, смотрѣть, глядѣть; to — round, оглядываться; to — to, глядѣть на; to — up to, взглядывать на.

loom, ткальный станокъ, просны.

loop, петля.

loose, слабкій, слабый, отвязанный, свободный, шаткій, несвязный, распутный; to — n, развязывать; to let —, отвязывать; to run —, бѣгать на свободѣ.

Lord, Господь, владыка, владѣтель, Лордъ (титулъ лицъ высшаго дворянства); — Chamberlain, оберъ-гофмейстеръ; — Keeper of the Privy Seal, — Privy Seal, Хранитель государственной печати; — ly rank, высокій санъ; — ship, Сіятельство.

lose, потерять, теряться; to — one's way, заблудиться, сбиться съ дороги; to — sight of, потерять изъ виду; my watch — s, мои часы отстаютъ.

loss, потеря, погибель; to be at a —, быть въ недоумѣніи, не знать.

lost, см. **lose**; to be —, погибать.

loud, громкій, громко; — ly, громко; — pouring, бушующій.

Louis, Людовикъ.

lounge about, праздно шататься, шляться.

love, любовь; — of pleasure, жажда удоволь-

ствій; - of power, вла-
столюбіе, любонача-
ліе; to —, любить; —
ly, милый; —r, любов-
ннкъ.

loving, ласковый; — ly,
ласково, умильно.

low, низкій, низменный,
тихій; низко; the fire
is very —, огонь едва
горитъ; —er, нижній,
низшій, ниже; to — er,
понижать, спускать,
снимать; — land, низ-
менное мѣсто; — land
bonnet, шапка упо-
требляемая обитателя-
ми ннзм. мѣстъ; —
lander, житель или о-
битатель низменныхъ
мѣстъ; — ness, низ-
кость.

loyal, вѣрный, постоянный; — ly, вѣрно; —
ty, вѣрность.

lucid, свѣтлый.

luck, удача, счастіе; ill—,
неудача, несчастіе; —
less, неудачный, не-
счастный , несчастли-
вый; — y, счастливый,
удачный.

lucrative, прибыльный,
доходный.

luggage, поклажа, ба-
гажъ.

lull, штиль, затишье.

lumbering, тасканіе.

lung, лёгкое.

lustre, блескъ.

Luther, Лютеръ.

luxurious, роскошный,
пышный; — ly, рос-
кошно, пышно.

luxury, роскошь.

lying, ложь.

M.

machine, машина; — гу,
машины, механизмъ,
устройство.

mad, сумасшедшій, бѣ-
шеный; — man, сума-
сшедшій, безумецъ.

Madam, Мадамъ, госпожа,
Сударыня.

made, см. to **make**.

Madeira, Мадера.

magazine, анбаръ, магазинъ.

magic, магія, волшеб-
ство; — ian, магикъ,
чародѣй;—ian's wand,
магическій или вол-
шебный жезлъ.

magistrate, начальсвен-
ное лицё, судья.

Magna Charta, великая
хартія (англійская).

magnanimity, великодушіе.

magnificence, пышность
великолѣпіе, роскошь.

magnificent, великолѣпный.

magnitude, величина.

Mahomedan, Магомета-
нинъ.

maid, дѣвка, дѣвушка,
дѣвственница, служан-
ка; — en, дѣвица, дѣв-
ка; — servant, слу-
жанка.

mail, броня, панцырь,
латы, почта, почтовая
карета.

main, сила, власть, от-
крытое море, океанъ;
главный, важный, боль-
шой; — land, мате-
рикъ, твёрдая земля;
— ly, преимуществен-
но, особливо; — mast,

гротъ-мачта; — stay,
грота-штагъ ; — top,
гротъ-марсъ ; — top-
mast, гротъ-стеньга;
—topsail-halyard-block,
гротъ - марсафальный
блокъ; — yard, грота-
рей.

maintain, поддерживать,
содерживать , сохра-
нять выдерживать, у-
держивать (мѣсто сра-
женія), удерживаться
на.

maintenance, содержаніе,
пропитаніе.

majestic , величественный.

Majesty, Величество, величіе.

major, маіоръ; — ity, боль-
шинство, совершенно-
лѣтіе.

make, станъ; to —, дѣлать, сдѣлать, заста-
влять, достигать, до-
ходить до чего; to — а
camp, располагаться
лагеремъ; to — a com-
plaint, приносить жа-
лобу, жаловаться; to
— a deep impression,
производить глубокое
впечатлѣніе , сильно
подѣйствовать; to — a
discovery, открывать;
to — a doubt, допу-
стить сомнѣніе; to — a
figure, имѣть впдъ; to
— a fire, разводить о-
гонь ; to — a fool of
one's self, притворять-
ся дурачкомъ, корчить
изъ себя дурапа; to —
a good use, употре-
блять въ пользу; to —
a league, вступать въ
союзъ; to — an answer,

давать отвѣтъ; to—an apology, извиняться; to — an attempt, пытаться; to — an effort, прилагать стараніе; to — an end of, положить конецъ чему; to — an exertion, употребить усиліе; to — any one merry, веселить, забавлять кого; to — a retreat, отступать; to — a speech, говорить или сказать рѣчь; to — a vigorous resistance, храбро защищаться, оказывать упорное сопротивленіе; to — a vow, дать обѣтъ; to — excuses, извиняться, приводить въ оправданіе; to — fast, закрѣплять, прикрѣплять; to — for, направляться; to — good, приводить въ дѣйствіе, совершать; to — good one's right, защищать свое право; to — haste, торопиться, спѣшить; to — head against any one, воспротивляться кому, не уступать; to — it a rule, ставить себѣ въ правило; to — one's appearance, являться, показываться; to — one's moan, испускать вопль; to — one's self familiar, ознакомливаться; to — peace, заключать миръ; to — prisoner, взять въ плѣнъ; to—ready, приготовляться; to—room, давать мѣсто; to—the most of, извлекать все-

возможную пользу; to — towards any one, бросаться или кидаться на кого; to — up, составлять; to — up one's mind, рѣшаться, рѣшать; to — use of, пользоваться чѣмъ; to — war, воевать, вести войну, объявить войну; to — way, дать дорогу, прокладывать себѣ дорогу; he knew not what to — of this letter, онъ не зналъ, что это письмо значило; — more toast, поджарьте еще нѣсколько кусковъ хлѣба; that was making the best of its way under the bed, которая такъ и покатилась подъ кровать.

malefactor, преступникъ.
malice, злоба.
malicious, злобный.
malt, солодъ.
Malta, Мальта.
mamma, маменька.
man, человѣкъ, мущина, молодецъ; he's the — for you to trust, на него-то Вы можете положиться; fellow —, товарищъ; — fully, мужественно; — kind, человѣческій родъ; — ly, мужескій, мужественный; — of war, военное судно.
manage, хозяйствовать, устроиваться, управлять, дѣйствовать, обходиться съ кѣмъ, владѣть чѣмъ, успѣвать, (кому) удаваться; — able, послуш-

ный, послушливый, уклончивый, уклонивый; — ment, управленіе, владѣніе, исполненіе.
mane, грива.
manger, ясли.
manifest, изъявлять, обнаруживать; — ly, явно, очевидно.
manifold, многочисленный.
manner, образъ, манеръ, пріёмы; in a —, нѣкоторымъ образомъ; in what —, какимъ образомъ? — s, нравы, обычаи.
manor, помѣстье, маетность; — house, усадьба, барскій домъ.
mansion, барскій домъ.
mantle, плащъ.
manufactory, фабрика, заводъ.
manufacture, фабрика, заводъ; фабрикація, мануфактурная промышленность, мануфактурное издѣліе; to —, выдѣлывать, изготовлять, производить; cotton —, бумагопрядильная мануфактура; hardware —, фабрикація желѣзныхъ или стальныхъ издѣлій; silk —, шёлкодѣліе; — r, мануфактуристъ, фабричный работникъ, фабричникъ.
manufacturing, мануфактурный, фабричный.
manuscript, рукопись.
many, многій, многіе, множество; a good —, очень много; how —, сколько; so —, столь-

ко; — a time, много разъ.

map, ландкарта, географическая к.; — of the world, к. земнаго шара.

Maranon, Мараньонъ.

marauder, грабитель, мародёръ.

marble, мраморъ, мраморный шарикъ; мраморный.

march, походъ, маршъ; to —, идти, маршировать, выступать.

March, Мартъ.

Margaret, Маргарита.

marigold, ноготки.

marine, морской солдатъ; —г, морякъ.

maritime, морской.

mark, знакъ, марка; to — мѣтить, отмѣчать, замѣчать, примѣчать, означать, обозначать, усматривать, указывать.

market, рынокъ; рыночный; — day, торговой, рыночный или базарный день; — place, рынокъ, площадь.

marl, мергель, рухлякъ.

marquis, маркизъ.

marriage, бракосочетаніе, бракъ.

marry, жениться (на), выходить замужъ (за).

marshy, болотистый.

martial, военный, воинскій, воинственный.

martyr, мученикъ.

Mary, Марія, Марья.

masculine, мужественный.

mask, личина, маска; to —, маскировать, переряжать, прикрывать.

masque, см. **mask.**

mason, каменщикъ, мурникъ.

mass, масса, обѣднл; — ive, массивный.

massacre, рѣзня, сѣча; to —, избивать, рѣзать.

mast, мачта; — head, топъ мачты.

master, баринъ, хозяинъ, господинъ, шкиперъ (командиръ купеческаго судна), мастеръ, учитель, преподаватель, владѣтель, государь; to be — of, обладать чѣмъ; — or — of Arts, магистръ; — manufacturer, владѣтель или содержатель фабрики; — of the Rolls, начальникъ парламентскаго архива.

masticate, разжёвывать.

mastiff, бульдогъ, цѣпная собака.

match, партія, бракъ, состязаніе, сѣрная спичка, фитиль; равный; 't is a —, побьёмся объ закладъ; we are their —, мы съ ними сладимъ; to —, сравнивать; — less, несравненный, безподобный.

mate, метъ, помощникъ (на купеческомъ суднѣ).

material, матеріалъ; — ly, существенно, значительно.

maternal, материнскій; — uncle, дядя по матери.

matrimonial, супружескій.

matter, вещество, матерія, предметъ, дѣло;

по —, нужды нѣтъ; no — for that, это ничего; there was something the —, тутъ что-то было не такъ; — of fact, истинное происшествіе, фактъ.

mattress, матрацъ, тюфякъ.

maturity, зрѣлость.

Maurice, Маврикій, Морицъ.

The Mauritius, островъ Маврикія.

maxim, правило, положеніе.

Maximus, Максимъ.

may, могу, имѣю позволеніе, пусть; — he make you happy, да сдѣлаетъ онъ Васъ счастливымъ! прош. вр. might, могъ.

May, Май.

me, меня, мнѣ.

mead, meadow, лугъ.

meagre, скудный, плохой.

meal, мука, ѣда, обѣдъ, ужинъ, чай, вообще столъ.

mean, посредственный, средній, промежуточный, низкій, маловажный; in the — time, — while, между тѣмъ.

mean, подразумѣвать, значить, хотѣть, намѣреваться; —ing, значеніе, намѣреніе; what is the — ing, что значитъ?

means, средство; by — of посредствомъ; by this —, такимъ образомъ; by no —, нисколько.

meant, см. **mean.**

measure, мѣра, распоряженіе; beyond —, чрезмѣрно; in a great—, въ высокой степени; in some —, нѣкоторымъ образомъ; to—, имѣть (въ протяженіе); —d, мѣрный; long —d, долгомѣрный.

meat, мясо.

mechanic, ремесленникъ; —al, механическій; —ally, механически.

medal, медаль.

meddle, with any one, связываться, имѣть дѣло съ кѣмъ.

medical, медицинскій.

meditate, размышлять о чемъ, обдумывать, умышлять.

meditation, размышленіе.

mediterranean, средиземный; the—, Средиземное море.

meek, кроткій, покорный.

meet, встрѣчать, находить, встрѣчаться, собираться, съѣзжаться, сходиться; to—the expense, покрывать издержки; he had met with an accident, съ нимъ случилось несчастіе; — ing, собраніе, богослужебное собраніе.

melancholy, грустный, жалкій.

melt, таять, растаивать, умилять, смягчать.

member, членъ; county —, выбранный графствомъ членъ парламента.

memorable, достопамятный.

memorial, воспоминаніе, память, памятникъ, (древнія) рукописп.

memory, память.

menace, угроза; to —, грозить, угрожать;

men-at-arms, вооружённые люди.

mend, починивать, исправлять, поправлять.

menial, служитель, слуга; домашній, дворовый.

mental, умственный.

mention, упоминаніе; to—, упоминать, называть; not to—, не упоминать о чемъ, не говоря о.

mercantile, купеческій, торговый.

merchant, купецъ.

merciful, милосердый, сострадательный.

mercilessness, немилосердіе, безжалостность.

Mercury, Меркурій.

mercy, милосердіе, милость, помилованіе; in —, по милости Божіей.

mere, одинъ только, ни что иное какъ только; — ly, единственно, только.

merit, достоинство, заслуга; to—, заслуживать.

merrily, весело.

merriment, веселіе, весёлость.

merry, весёлый; весело; — man, весёлый малый, весельчакъ.

mesh, петля (у сѣти).

message, вѣсть, сообщеніе, порученіе; to be going on a — from, имѣть порученіе отъ;

to deliver a—, исполнить порученіе; he sent him a — enjoining him sobriety, онъ послалъ ему наставленіе быть трезвымъ.

messenger, посланный, вѣстникъ.

met, см. meet.

metal, металлъ; металлическій.

metaphysical, метафизическій.

metaphysics, метафизика.

methinks, мнѣ кажется.

method, метода, способъ.

Methodist, Методистъ; a — meeting, богослужебное собраніе Методистовъ.

metropolis, столица.

metropolitan, столичный.

Mexico, Мексика.

mezzotinto, эстампъ чёрнымъ манеромъ.

mid-day, полдень;

middle, средина; средній.

midnight, полночь; полуночный.

midship, средина корабля; to draw in a —, вдвигать въ корабль.

midst, средина; среди, посреди; in the —, среди.

midway, на половинѣ дороги или пути.

might, могущество, сила; men of—, сильные люди; см. также may; — ily, сильно, весьма; —y, могущественный, могучій, сильный.

mild, кроткій, нѣжный, пріятный, умѣренный; — ness, умѣренность (климата).

mile, миля.

military, воинскій, военный.

militia, милиція, ополченіе.

milk, молоко; — white, бѣлый какъ молоко.

mill, мельница, заводъ; — er, мельникъ

million, милліонъ.

mind, умъ, духъ, душа, память; to put in —, to bring, to any one's —, напоминать кому; to —, внимать чему, радѣть о чёмъ, смотрѣть, заботиться о чёмъ; never —, ничего! — ful of, помнящій что.

mine, рудникъ, рудокопня, подкопъ, мина; мой; —r, рудокопъ.

mineral, минеральный.

mingle, мѣшать, перемѣшивать.

miniature, миніатюра.

minister, министръ, священникъ, пасторъ; — of state, государственный министръ; to —, служить, прислуживать.

minor, меньшій, маловажный.

minstrel, миннезенгеръ, пѣвецъ любви.

mint, монетный дворъ или заводъ.

minute, минута; мелкій, подробный.

miracle, чудо.

miraculous, дивный, чудесный.

mirage, миражъ, марево.

mire, грязь, тина, илъ.

mirth, весёлость; — ful, весёлый.

miry, илистый, тинистый.

mischief, зло, вредъ.

mischievous, зловредный.

miseltoe, омела (растеніе).

miser, скупецъ, скряга; — able, бѣдственный, бѣдный, жалкій, жалостный, злосчастный; — ably, дурно, плохо; — у, бѣдствіе, бѣда, бѣдность, нищета.

misfortune, несчастіе.

misgive, предчувствовать; my heart misgave me, мнѣ что-то предчувствовалось.

misgovernment, дурное управленіе.

misguide, сбивать съ пути; this —d father, этотъ заблудившійся отецъ.

mislead, вводить въ заблужденіе.

Miss, Дѣвица, Барышня, Сударыня.

miss, пропускать, не имѣть, не видѣть, не находить, съ сожалѣніемъ вспоминать о комъ, чувствовать потерю кого; without — ing a single word, не ошибаясь ни въ одномъ словѣ.

missile, метательный.

missionary, миссіонеръ; касающійся до миссіи; — money-box, кружка въ пользу миссіи.

mist, туманъ, мгла; —у, туманный.

mistake, ошибка; по —, положительно такъ! to —, ошибкою принимать, не понимать, ошибаться, обсчитываться.

mistaken, см. mistake; ошибочный; — man, обманывающій самаго себя человѣкъ; to be — ошибаться.

mistook, см. mistake.

mistress, владѣтельница, барыня, хозяйка.

mistrust, не довѣрять.

mitre, митра, епископская шапка.

mittimus, письменное предписаніе мироваго судьи арестовать и содержать въ тюрьмѣ подсудимаго.

mix, мѣшать, смѣшивать; to — up, перемѣшивать; —ture, смѣшеніе, примѣсь.

mizen, бизань, бизань-мачта; — mast, бизань-мачта; —shrouds, бизань-ванты; — top, крюйсъ-марсъ; — topmast, крюйсъ-стеньга.

moan, стонъ, стенаніе; to —, стонать; — ing, стонаніе.

mode, образъ, способъ, обычай, мода.

model, модель, образецъ.

moderate, умѣренный, средній, посредственный.

modern, новый, новѣйшій, нынѣшній.

modest, скромный.

modicum, доля, крошечка.

modify, измѣнять, опредѣлять.

Mohammedan, магометанскій.

moisten, намачивать.

molest, безпокоить.

The Moluccas, Молуккскіе острова.

moment, моментъ, мгно.

веніе, мигъ, минута, время, важность; for a few—s, на нѣсколько минутъ; — ary, мгновенный, временный.

monarch, монархъ; — y, единодержавіе, монархія.

monastery, монастырь.

Monday, понедѣльникъ.

money, деньги; денежный; a piece of —, монета.

Mongul, Монголъ.

monk, монахъ.

monkey, обезьяна.

monopoly, монополія.

monotonous, единообразный, монотонный.

monotony, однообразіе.

monster, чудовище.

month, мѣсяцъ.

monument, памятникъ, монументъ.

moon, мѣсяцъ, луна.

moor, степь, болото; to — укрѣплять, швартовить.

mop, швабра.

moral, нравственный; — ity, нравоученіе, нравственность; — s, нравоученіе, мораль.

more, большій, болѣе, больше; ещё; — important, важнѣе; — over, сверхъ того; — than one, не одинъ; not any —, болѣе не надобно; two —, еще два.

morning, утро; утренній; — light, утренняя заря; in the — утромъ, по утру.

morrow, завтрашній день, утро.

mortal, смертный.

mortgage, закладывать, давать въ закладъ.

mortify, огорчать; — ing, огорчительный.

mosaic, мозаическій.

Moscow, Москва.

moss, мохъ.

most, большая часть, самый; весьма, болѣе всего, наиболѣе; — excellent, преотличный; for the — part, — ly, по большой части; — of all, болѣе всего.

mother, мать; — country, отечество, родина.

motion, движеніе; — less, безъ движенія, неподвижный.

motive, побудительная причина, поводъ.

motto, девизъ, надпись.

moulder away, разсыпаться, распадать.

moulding, гзымсъ, карнизъ.

mound, плотина.

mount, восходить на что, садиться (на лошадь, въ карету), обдѣлывать, оправлять; — ain, гора, горный; — ainous, гористый; — ed, верховой; — ed on horseback, верхомъ.

Mount Blanc, Монъ-Бланъ.

mourner, скорбящій, — щая, оставшійся послѣ умершаго.

mournful, плачевный, печальный, заунывный.

mourning, трауръ, траурный.

mouse, мышь.

mouth, ротъ, морда, устье; — ful, глотокъ, кусокъ.

movable, подвижной.

move, двигать, приводить въ движеніе, возбуждать, предлагать, трогать, двигаться, трогаться, ходить; to — aside, отодвигать; to — off, уходить, идти далѣе; to — one's fingers about, шевелить пальцами; to — to, переходить на (другое мѣсто); — ment, движеніе.

Mr. (сокр. Mister), господинъ.

Mrs. (сокр. Mistress), госпожа.

much, многое, многій, большой; много, очень, гораздо; as — as to say выражая этимъ; four times as —, въ четыре раза больше; in — distress, сильно сокрушаясь; so —, столько, такъ; so — the more, тѣмъ больше; to be too — for one, пересиливать кого; with — pleasure, съ большимъ удовольствіемъ.

mud, грязь, илъ, тина, глина.

muffin, лепёшка.

muffle, окутывать, завертывать.

Muhammedanism, магометанская вѣра.

muleteer, подгонщикъ лошаковъ.

multiply, умножать, размножать.

multitude, множество, толпа.

mum, безмолвный, нѣмой; I must be —, я долженъ молчать.

murder, смертоубійство;
to —, убивать; — er,
смертоубійца.

murmur, ворчаніе, ро-
потъ, роптаніе; to —,
журчать, роптать.

muse, муза; to —, ду-
мать о чёмъ.

museum. музеумъ, музей.

music, музыка; — al, му-
зыкальный; — ian, му-
зыкантъ.

musket, мушкетъ, ружье;
— гу, ружья; — shot,
ружейный выстрѣлъ.

muslin, муслинъ, кисея.

must, долженъ, долженъ
былъ; they — all have
perished, должно быть
они всѣ погибли.

muster, смотръ (вой-
скамъ); to —, соби-
рать, собираться.

mute, нѣмой, безмолв-
ный; not one of them
was —, ни одинъ изъ
нихъ не молчалъ;—s,
люди, которыхъ рас-
порядители похоронъ
ставятъ у дверей до-
ма покойника до вы-
носа тѣла.

mutilate, искажать, изу-
вѣчивать. ·

mutineer, бунтовщикъ,
мятежникъ.

mutinous, бунтовской,
мятежный.

mutiny, мятежъ.

mutter, бормотать.

mutton, баранина.

mutual, взаимный; — ly,
взаимно, обоюдно.

my, мой; — self, я самъ.

Mysore, Мизоръ; of —,
Мизорскій.

mysterious, таинствен-
ный, непонятный.

mystery, тайна.

mythology, миѳологія.

N.

nag, лошадка.

nail up, прибивать, гвоз-
дями.

naked, нагой, голый.

name, имя, фамилія, на-
званіе; my — is, меня
зовутъ; to —, имено-
вать, называть, до-
ставлять свѣдѣнія о
чёмъ; — ly, именно;
— sake, тёзка, одно-
фамилецъ.

nap, короткій сонъ, дре-
мота; to take a—, со-
снуть.

Naples, Неаполь.

narrate, разсказывать,
повѣствовать.

narrative, разсказъ; по-
вѣствовательный.

narrator, разсказщикъ.

narrow, узкій, тѣсный;
he had a—escape, онъ
съ трудомъ спасся;
in — circumstances,
въ стѣснённыхъ об-
стоятельствахъ; to—,
съуживаться; — ly,
чуть, чуть чуть;—ness,
ограниченность.

nasal, гнусливый.

nation, нація, народъ;
—al, народный, націо-
нальный; the—al debt,
государственныйдолгъ.

native, уроженецъ, ту-
земецъ, природный жи-
тель; отечественный;
туземный, родной.

natural, естественный,
природный, натураль-

ный,свойственный; —
ly, естественно, нату-
рально.

nature, природа, родъ,
свойство, натура,
нравъ; good—, добро-
душіе.

naval, морской, флот-
скій, приморскій.

navigate, плавать; to —
a ship, управлять,
править судномъ, вести
судно.

navigation, судоходство,
судоплаваніе, корабле-
плаваніе, навигація.

navigator, мореплава-
тель, мореходецъ, на-
вигаторъ.

navy, флотъ, морскія си-
лы;—board, см. board.

nay, нѣтъ, но, даже.

near, близкій; близко,
близь, почти, вблизи;
—by, подлѣ, возлѣ;
— ly, близко, почти;
not — ly so, совсѣмъ
не такъ.

neat, опрятный; — ly,
чисто, опрятно, кра-
сиво.

necessaries, потребности.

necessary, необходимый.

necessitate, принуждать.

necessitous, нуждающійся.

necessity, нужда, необ-
ходимость, потреб-
ность.

neck, шея; —or nought,
на смерть, а не на
животъ.

Ned, см. Edward.

need, нужда, надобность;
in time of—, въ слу-
чаѣ необходимости; to
be in great—of, очень
нуждаться въ чемъ;
to —, нуждаться въ

чемъ, имѣть надобность; —ful, нужный, потребный; — s, необходимо, непремѣнно.

ne'er, см. never.

nefarious, гнусный, подлый.

negative, отрицаніе, отказъ; to answer in the —, отвѣчать на что отрицательно.

neglect, пренебреженіе, запущеніе; to—, пренебрегать, запускать, упускать.

negligence, нерадивость, оплошность.

negociate, negotiate, договариваться, вести переговоры.

Negro, Негръ.

neigh, ржать.

neighbour, сосѣдъ, ближній; — hood, сосѣдство, страна; — ing, сосѣдственный.

neither, ни тотъ ни другой, ни одинъ, также не; —...nor, ни...ни.

nephew, племянникъ.

nest, гнѣздо.

nestle, вселяться во что.

net, network, сѣть.

net, чистый, нетто.

nettle, крапива.

never, никогда; не, ни; — the less, при всемъ томъ, тѣмъ не менѣе; —once, ни одного раза, ни разу.

new, новый, свѣжій; — comer, пришелецъ; — ly, вновь, недавно.

Newcastle, Нью-кастель.

Newfoundland, Нью-Фаундлендъ; Нью-Фаундлендскій.

New-Orleans, Новый-Орлеанъ.

news, новости, вѣсть, извѣстіе; — letter, газетное письмо; — paper, вѣдомость, газета; — writer, газетчикъ.

New South Wales, Новый Южный Валлисъ.

New Zealand, Новая Зеландія.

next, слѣдующій, будущій, ближайшій; потомъ, послѣ этого; — week, на будущей недѣлѣ.

nice, хорошій, вкусный, славный, точный, разборчивый, опасный, затруднительный; — ty, разборчивость, точность.

Nicholas, Николай.

nickname, прозвище, данное въ насмѣшку; to —, прозывать въ насмѣшку.

nigh, близко.

night, ночь, вечеръ; ночной; — cap, ночной или спальный колпакъ; — dress, спальное платье; — ly, ночью; — quarters, ночлегъ; at —, ночью, вечеромъ; at — fall, при наступленіи ночи; to —, сегодня вечеромъ.

Nile, Нилъ; of the —, Нильскій.

nimble, быстрый.

nine, девять; — and twenty, двадцать девять; — teenth, девятнадцатый; — tieth, девяностый; — ty, девяносто.

Nineveh, Ниневія.

ninth, девятый.

nip, отщипывать, кусать.

no, никакой, нѣтъ, не; you have — gravy, у Васъ нѣтъ подливки; — body, — man, — one, никто; — doubt, безъ сомнѣнія; — where, нигдѣ.

nobility, дворянство, благородство.

noble, дворянинъ; нобль (старинная монета, на наши деньги около 2 руб. 10 коп. с.); благородный, славный, превосходный; — man, дворянинъ.

nobly, благородно.

nod, знакъ.

noise, шумъ; — less, безшумный.

nominal, мнимой, почетный; — ly, по имени; the complement of the ship was — ly, штатный комплектъ корабля былъ.

nonconformist, нонконформистъ.

none, ни одинъ, никто, ничто, ничего; — the less, при всемъ томъ, тѣмъ не менѣе; that they were — the better for the blessings of the Druids, and — the worse for the curses of the Druids, что благословенія Друидовъ имъ не приносили никакой пользы и что ихъ проклятія не причиняли имъ никакого вреда.

nonresistance, несопротивленіе.

nonsense, пустяки.

nook, уголъ.

noon, полдень; — day, полдень, полуденный.

nor, ни, не, и не;— do I believe, и я не думаю.

Norman, Норманнъ; нор-манскій;—dy, Норман-дія; the —French, Нор-манно-Французы.

north, сѣверъ; сѣверный, къ сѣверу; — erly, — ern, сѣверный;—west, сѣверо-западъ, сѣве-ро-западный.

North American, сѣверо-американскій; the — Sea, Нѣмецкое море.

Norway, Норвегія.

Norwegian, Норвежецъ.

nose, носъ.

nostril, ноздря.

not, не, ни;—yet, нѣтъ еще.

notable, заботливый, хло-потливый, знатный.

notch, зарубка, зазу-брина; to —, зару-бать, зазубривать.

note, знакъ, записка, билетъ, замѣчаніе, примѣчаніе, нота, важ-ность, извѣстность; she did not make a single false—, она ни разу не сфальшивила; to—, примѣчать; —d, извѣстный.

nothing, ничто, ничего.

notice, замѣчаніе, вни-маніе, извѣстіе, увѣ-домленіе, объявленіе; at very short —, въ весьма скоромъ вре-мени по заявленіи; without his —, безъ его вѣдома; to —, замѣ-чать, примѣчать.

notion, понятіе, мнѣніе.

notorious, извѣстный, общественный.

notwithstanding, не смотря на, не взирая на.

nought, ничто.

Nova Scotia, Новая Шот-ландія.

novel, романъ; —ist, но-велистъ, сочинитель романовъ; — ty, но-вость, новизна.

November, Ноябрь.

now, теперь, нынѣ; но, а, же; ну! — a-days, въ нынѣшнія времена; — and then, иногда; till —, до сихъ поръ, по сіе время.

noxious, вредный.

nucleus, ядро, зерно, су-щественное, сущность, начало.

nuisance, безпокойство, зараза.

number, число, множе-ство; to —, считать; — s, численная сила (войска), множество.

Numbers, Числа.

numerous, многочислен-ный.

nunnery, женскій мона-стырь.

nurse, нянька, кормили-ца; to —, ходить за кѣмъ; — гу, дѣтская, разсадникъ, питомникъ.

nut, орѣхъ; —meg, му-шкатный орѣхъ.

0.

o, oh, о! ахъ!

oak, дубъ, дубовое де-рево; —, — en, дубо-вый.

oar, весло.

oath, клятва, присяга, божба; to utter an —, божиться.

oatmeal, овсяная мука.

oats, овёсъ.

obedience, послушность, послушаніе.

obedient, послушный, покорный.

obey, слушаться, пови-новаться.

object, предметъ, цѣль, намѣреніе; —ion, воз-раженіе.

obligation, одолженіе, о-бязательство.

oblige, обязывать, одол-жать, принуждать; much —d, очень обя-занъ.

obliging, обязательный, одолжительный.

oblivion, забвеніе, все-прощеніе.

obscure, мрачный, тем-ный; to —, помрачать, затмѣвать.

obscurity, мрачность, не-ясность.

obsequies, похороны, по-гребеніе.

obsequious, подслужли-вый.

observance, почтеніе, по-чтительность.

observant, наблюдатель-ный.

observation, наблюденіе, созерцаніе, замѣчаніе.

observe, наблюдать, со-блюдать, замѣчать; he —d as follows, онъ сдѣлалъ слѣдующія за-мѣчанія; —r, наблю-датель, примѣчатель.

obsolete,обветшалый,не-
употребительный.

obstinacy, упрямство.

obstinate, упрямый, у-
порный; —ly, упрямо,
упорно.

obstruction, препятствіе.

obtain, доставать, пріо-
брѣтать, получать, до-
бывать; to — a victory,
одержать побѣду.

obviate,отвращать,пред-
упреждать.

obvious, очевидный; —
ly, очевидно.

occasion, случай, надоб-
ность, поводъ, причи-
на; to take —, поль-
зоваться случаемъ; to
—, причинять, пода-
вать поводъ къ чему;
— al, случайный; —
ally, случайно, при
случаѣ.

occupant, занимающій,
обладатель.

occupation,занятіе,упраж-
неніе.

occupy, занимать, зани-
маться.

occur,приключаться,слу-
чаться, происходить;
—rence, приключеніе,
происшествіе, встрѣча.

ocean, океанъ.

Oceania, Океанія или Ав-
стралія.

o'clock, см. clock.

octagonal,осьмиугольный.

October, Октябрь, также
крѣпкое пиво, варимое
въ Октябрѣ.

odd, странный.

ode, ода.

odious, ненавистный.

o'er, см. over.

o'erjoyed, см. overjoy.

of, знакъ родит. падежа;
изъ, отъ, у, о, объ;
— themselves, сами
собою.

off, далеко, далѣе, на
разстояніи,отъ,прочь,
долой, противъ, на
высотѣ; three doors
—, противъ третьяго
дома оттуда; the better
— the people would
be, тѣмъ народу было
бы лучше.

offence, обида, преступ-
леніе; to give —, оби-
жать, сердить.

offend, обижать, оскорб-
лять, провиняться; —
er, преступникъ; —er
against discipline, на
рушитель дисциплины.

offer, предложеніе; to —,
предлагать, представ-
лять, приносить; to —
opposition, оказывать
сопротивленіе; to — up
prayers, возсылать мо-
литвы.

office, должность, мѣсто,
служба, контора, кан-
целярія, присутствен-
ное мѣсто, услуга;
—r, офицеръ, чинов-
никъ; —r of state, го-
сударственный санов-
никъ.

officious, услужливый,
слишкомъ услужливый;
—ly, услужливо.

offspring, потомки.

oft, often, часто.

oh, о! ахъ!

oil, масло (деревянное).

old, старый, древній;
eight years —, восемь
лѣтъ отъ роду; of —,
искони,издревле,древ-
ній; —age, старость;

— man, старикъ; —
woman, старуха.

Old Bailey, названіе од-
ной тюрьмы въ Лон-
донѣ.

olive, оливковый.

omission, опущеніе.

omit, упускать.

omnibus, омнибусъ, об-
щественная карета.

on, впередъ, далѣе; на,
надъ, къ, о, объ, при,
по, въ, съ; когда; —
all sides, со всѣхъ
сторонъ; — which,
послѣ чего.

once, одинъ разъ, разъ,
однажды; all at —,
вдругъ; at — вдругъ,
тотчасъ ;—more, ещё
разъ.

one, одинъ, нѣкто; —
by —, одинъ по од-
ному; every —, каж-
дый, всякій; — horse,
одноконный; —is oft-
en surprised, часто
удивляешься.

only, единственный;
только.

onwards, впередъ, далѣе.

ooze, тихо вѣять, ше-
лестить.

open, открытый, отво-
ренный; to —, откры-
вать, отворять, отпи-
рать, распечатывать,
развёртывать, откры-
ваться; to — up to,
выходить на, быть
обращеннымъ къ; —
ing, отверстіе, откры-
тіе, начало.

operate, дѣйствовать.

operation, дѣйствіе, опе-
рація.

opinion, мнѣніе; in my
—, по моему мнѣнію.

opponent, противникъ.

opportunity, случай.

oppose, противополагать, противопоставлять, сопротивляться, противостоять, противоборствовать.

opposite, противоположный, противный; супротивъ.

opposition, противоположность, сопротивленіе, противная партія, оппозиція; in — to, противъ кого.

oppress, угнетать;—ion, притѣсненіе, угнетеніе; —ive, притѣснительный; — or, притѣснитель, гонитель.

optical, зрительный, оптическій.

opulence, благосостояніе, достатокъ, богатство.

or, или, иначе, а не то.

oracle, оракулъ, прорицаніе.

orange, апельсинъ, померанецъ, оранжевый цвѣтъ; померанцовый.

oration, рѣчь, слово.

oratory, витійство, краснорѣчіе, риторика.

orb, шаръ, небесное тѣло.

orbit, орбита.

orchard, фруктовый садъ.

ordain, повелѣвать, опредѣлять.

order, приказъ, приказаніе, предписаніе, заказъ, ордеръ, порядокъ, устройство, чинъ, сословіе, орденъ; in — that, in — to, чтобы; to give —, отдавать приказъ; to be in .— s, принадле-

жать духовному званію; to —, приказывать, заказывать; to — out, командировать, наряжать, приказать подавать; she — ed from the table, она велѣла убрать со стола; — ly, порядочный, скромный, благоправный.

ordinarily, обыкновенно.

ordinary, простой, обыкновенный.

organ-player, органистъ.

origin, начало, происхожденіе; — al, подлинникъ, оригиналъ; оригинальный, первоначальный, первобытный; — ally, первоначально; to — ate in, происходить, проистекать изъ.

ornament, украшеніе; to —, украшать, убирать; —al, служащій украшеніемъ,

orse, см. horse.

oscillation, качаніе, маханіе.

osse, см. horse.

ostentatious, тщеславный, хвастливый.

ostler, см. hostler.

Ostorious, Осторій.

ostrich, строусъ; строусовый.

other, другой; the—day, недавно; — wise, иначе.

ought, долженъ, долженъ былъ; they — to know, они должны знать; they— to have known, они должны былибъ знать.

our, намъ; come to —

aid, прійдите намъ на помощь! —selves, мы сами.

out, вонъ, внѣ, на дворѣ; the floods are —, рѣки выступили изъ береговъ; the wolves are—, волки ходятъ; — at sea, въ открытомъ морѣ; —of, изъ, изъ числа, внѣ; — of proportion, не въ пропорціи, несоразмѣрно; —of sight, изъ виду; she was—of the way, ея тутъ не было.

outbrave, превышать въ храбрости, презирать.

outbreak, начало, начатіе.

outcast, извергъ, изгнанникъ.

outdo, превосходить.

outer, внѣшній.

outlaw, изгнанникъ.

outline, очеркъ, абрисъ.

outnumber, превосходить числомъ.

outrage, поруганіе, оскорбленіе, насильствованіе; to—, поругать, оскорблять.

outshine, превосходить въ блескѣ, помрачать.

outshone, см. outshine.

outside, наружная сторона; снаружи; на дворѣ.

outskirt, край, предмѣстіе.

outstrip, обгонять, опереживать.

oval, овальный.

over, черезъ, надъ, сверхъ, по, за; слишкомъ; —again, снова; —and again, снова и снова; all —, по всему; to

be —, кончаться, про-
ходить.

overboard, за бортъ.

overcome, одолѣвать, пре-
одолѣвать.

overflowing, превзбы-
точный, чрезмѣрный.

overgrown, оброслый,
непомѣрный.

overhead, надъ головою,
на верху.

overjoy, обрадовать, вос-
хитить.

overleap, перескакивать,
перепрыгивать.

overlook, просматривать,
пропускать.

overmatch, пересиливать,
преодолѣвать.

overpower, перемогать,
пересиливать.

overrate, слишкомъ вы-
соко цѣнить, преуве-
личивать.

overruling, всѣмъ управ-
ляющій или распола-
гающій.

overrun, покрывать, на-
воднять, опустошать.

over-scrupulous, слиш-
комъ мнительный.

overset, опрокидывать.

overspread, покрывать,
распространяться по.

overtake, догонять, на-
стигать.

overtaken, см. overtake.

overthrow, пораженіе,
разореніе, погибсль;
to —, поражать, раз-
бивать.

overturn, опрокидывать,
разрушать.

overwhelm, одолѣвать.
преодолѣвать, осили-
вать, побѣждать, по-
корять, обуздывать,
затоплять.

overwork, надорваться
работою.

Ovid, Овидій.

owe, быть должнымъ,
быть обязаннымъ чѣмъ.

owing, должный; — to,
по причинѣ; to be —
to, происходить отъ,
проистекать изъ.

own, собственный; to —,
признавать; —er, вла-
дѣлецъ, хозяинъ.

ox, быкъ, волъ.

Oxford, Оксфордъ; Окс-
фордскій.

Oxonian, Оксфордскій сту-
дентъ.

oyster, устрица.

P.

pace, шагъ; to —, ходить
шагомъ; to — up and
down the room, рас-
хаживать по комнать.

the Pacific, the — océan,
Тихій океанъ.

pack, стадо.

packet, пакетъ, связка.

packhorse, ломовая или
вьючная лошадь.

packsaddle, вьючное сѣ-
дло.

paddle, лопасть, гребокъ,
родъ весла употребля-
емаго у дикихъ наро-
довъ на лодкахъ.

pagan, языческій; —
looking, языческій на
видъ.

page, страница, пажъ.

pageant, позорище.

paid, см. pay.

pain, боль, огорченіе,
мука; —s, трудъ, тру-
ды; — ful, причиняю-
щій боль, прискорб-
ный, огорчительный;

a — ful death, ужас-
ная смерть; — fully,
съ прискорбіемъ.

paint, краска, румяны;
to —, красить, писать
красками, румянить,
изображать, описывать;
— ing, живопись.

pair, пара, чета.

palace, дворецъ.

palanquin, паланкинъ,
носилки.

pale, блѣдный; — blue,
голубой, свѣтлосиній.

Palestine, Палестина.

palfrey, парадная или
дамская лошадь.

pallet, нары, кроватка.

palm, ладонь; — oil, паль-
мовое масло.

pamphlet, памфлетъ,
брошюра.

pan, противень, сково-
рода.

pane, оконное стекло.

panel, панель, филенка.

pant, задыхаться.

paper, бумага, вѣдомость,
газета, бумажка; to
put in — s, класть въ
бумажки, завивать.

papist, папистъ.

parade, выставлять на
показъ.

parallel, параллельный.

paraphrase, перифраза,
перифразис.

parcel, связка, узелъ,
пакетъ.

parched, истомленный,
пасохшій.

pardon, прощеніе; to —,
прощать, помиловать.

parent, родитель.

Paris, Парижъ

parish, приходъ; при-
ходскій; — ioner, при-
хожанка.

park, паркъ.

parliament, парламентъ;
—ary, парламентскій.

parlor, parlour, гостиная.

parochial, приходскій.

parson, приходскій свя‑
щенникъ, пасторъ; —
age, домъ священника.

part, часть, роль, сто‑
рона; for my —, что
до меня касается; in
the early—of winter,
въ началѣ зимы; on
the — of, со стороны;
—’s, способности, да‑
рованія; though I own
thy quicker — s, хотя
я не отвергаю твоей
большей быстроты; to
—, разлучать, раздѣ‑
лять, разставаться; to
—with, разставаться
съ; — ing, разстава‑
ніе; at—ing, прощаясь;
—ly, частію, отчасти.

partake, участвовать,
быть участникомъ въ
чемъ.

partial, частный, при‑
страстный; —ity, при‑
страстіе, склонность;
—ly, пристрастно, от‑
части, частію.

particular, подробность;
особенный, особли‑
вый; in —, — ly, въ
особенности, особен‑
но, особливо.

partisan, приверженецъ,
послѣдователь.

partner, компаніонъ,
участникъ въ торго‑
влѣ; to admit any
one—, принимать ко‑
го въ товарищество.

partook, см. partake.

partridge, куропатка.

party, отрядъ, обще‑

ство, партія, сторона,
особа, лицё.

pass, проходъ, ущеліе,
ударъ (рапирою);to —,
миновать, проходить,
проѣзжать, переходить,
переѣзжать, переправ‑
ляться, происходить,
проводить (время), из‑
давать (законъ), to—
away, проходить, пре‑
ходить; to—for, слыть,
почитаться; to — on,
проходить; to — one’s
self for, выдавать се‑
бя за; to—out, выхо‑
дить; to — over, про‑
пускать, переправлять,
переправляться.

passage, переходъ, пе‑
реѣздъ, переправа,
перевозъ, проходъ,
корридоръ, мѣсто (въ
книгѣ).

passenger, пассажиръ.

passion, страсть; — ate,
страстный, горячій;—
ately, горячо, страстно.

passive, пассивный, не‑
дѣйствующій.

passover, пасха.

passport, паспортъ, видъ.

past, прошедшее время,
прошедшее; прошедшій,
прошлый, минувшій;
мимо; см. также pass.

pastime, забава, увесе‑
леніе.

pastor, пасторъ, па‑
стырь; — al, пасто‑
ральный, пастушескій.

pasturage, пастбище.

pasture, паства.

pasty, паштетъ.

pat, удобный, умѣстный;to
—, поглаживать рукою.

Patagonian, Патагонъ.

patch, заплатка, муш‑
ка (на лицѣ).

patent, патентъ; приви‑
легія.

paternal, отцовскій, оте‑
ческій.

path, стезя, путь.

patience, терпѣніе.

patient, больной; тер‑
пѣливый; — ly, тер‑
пѣливо.

patriarchal, патріархаль‑
ный.

patrician, патрицій.

patriot, патріотъ; — ic,
патріотическій; —ism,
патріотизмъ, любовь
къ отечеству.

patron, покровитель, па‑
тронъ; to—ize, покро‑
вительствовать.

Paul, Павелъ; for Saint
— ’s, для собора Св.
Павла.

pause, остановка; to—,
пріостанавливаться,
помолчать.

pave, мостить; — ment,
мостовая.

pavillion, палатка, па‑
вильонъ.

paw, лапа.

pawn, закладывать, от‑
давать въ закладъ.

pay, плата, жалованіе;
to—, платить, запла‑
тить, оказывать (ува‑
женіе); to —a compli‑
ment, свидѣтельство‑
вать своё почтеніе;
to — attention, обра‑
щать вниманіе, вни‑
мать, слушать; to—a
visit, дѣлать визитъ,
навѣщать; to — full
dear, дорого попла‑
титься; to — off, вы‑
дать слѣдуемое жало‑

ваніе; to — one's respects, свидѣтельствовать свое почтеніе; to pay the penalty, претерпѣвать наказаніе, поплатиться.

pea, горохъ.

peace, миръ, спокой, спокойствіе, полиція, управа благочинія; in —, въ мирное время; — able, мирный, тихій; —ably, спокойно; —ful, мирный, тихій, спокойный; — officer, полицейскій чиновникъ.

peach, персикъ.

peak, верхушка, вершина, пикъ.

Peak, Пикъ, гористая страна въ Дербишпрѣ, изобилующая металлами, мраморомъ, алебастромъ, кристаллами и замѣчательными пещерами.

peal, звукъ, звонъ.

pear, груша.

pearls, жемчугъ.

peasant, крестьянинъ, мужикъ;—ry, крестьяне.

pebble, голышъ, кремень.

peculiar, свойственный, собственный, особенный; —ity, свойство, особенное свойство, особенность; — ly, особенно.

pedagogue, педагогъ, наставникъ.

pedestal, подножіе, піедесталъ.

pediment, фронтонъ, щипецъ.

peep, проглядываніе, взглядъ; to take a—,

to —, выглядывать, глядѣть украдкою; to —through, проглядывать.

peer, ровня, товарищъ, перъ; равный, подобный.

pelting. проливной.

pen, перо; —knife, перочинный ножикъ.

penal, карательный, уголовный; —ty, наказаніе; —settlement, ссыльное поселеніе.

pence, см. **penny.**

pencil, кисть, кисточка, карандашъ; — case, карандашникъ.

pendulum, маятникъ.

penetrate, проницать, проходить.

penitent, кающійся.

penny, пенни (2¼ коп.), деньги; loss of pence, потеря денегъ.

pension, пенсія; — er, получающій пенсію, пенсіонеръ; gentlemen—ers, см. **gentleman.**

penthouse, навѣсъ.

penury, бѣдность, скудность, скудость, нужда.

people, народъ, люди; to—, населять.

pepper, перецъ.

per, за; — annum, въ годъ.

perceive, усматривать, примѣчать.

perceptible, примѣтный.

peremptorily, рѣшительно.

perfect. совершенный; —ion, совершенство; — ly, совершенно; I will have it said—ly, чтобъ

Вы его знали вполнѣ удовлетворительно.

perfidious, вѣроломный.

perform, совершать, исполнять; to — a part, играть роль; — ance, выполненіе, дѣйствіе, сочиненіе, представленіе; —er, исполнитель, совершитель; to be an excellent—er, отлично играть.

perhaps, можетъ быть.

peril, опасность; —ous, опасный.

period, періодъ, время, конецъ; —ical, періодическій.

perish, погибать.

perjured, клятвопреступный.

permanent, постоянный.

permission, позволеніе.

permit, дозволять, допускать.

pernicious, вредный, пагубный.

perpetual, безпрерывный.

perplexity, смущеніе, затрудненіе.

perry, грушёвка.

persecute, притѣснять, преслѣдовать.

persecution, гоненіе, притѣсненіе.

perseverance, неослабность, прилежаніе, стойкость, твёрдость, настойчивость.

persevere, быть постоянно, не измѣняться, быть устойчивымъ въ чёмъ, устоять въ чёмъ.

persevering, настойчивый, стойкій.

Persia, Персія.

persist, настаивать, устоять въ чёмъ.

person, лицо, особа, человѣкъ, ли чность; — age, особа, лицо; — al, личный; — ally, in —, лично.

persuade, убѣждать, уговаривать; to — any one to the contrary, отговаривать кого отъ чего.

persuasion, убѣжденіе, вѣра, религія.

peruse, прочитывать.

pestilence, чума, моръ, моровая язва, зараза.

pestilential, заразительный, чумный.

petard, петарда.

Peter, Петръ.

petition, прошеніе.

petrified; окаменѣлый.

petticoat, юбка.

petty, малый, мелкій.

phenomenon, явленіе.

philanthropist, филантропъ.

Philip, Филиппъ.

philosopher, философъ.

philosophic, —al, философическій.

philosophy, философія.

Phoenician, Финикілнинъ.

phrase, фраза.

physic, лекарство; —al, физическій; — ian, врачъ.

piano, piano-forte, фортопіаны.

Picardy, Пикардія.

pick, собрать; to —up, подбирать, поднимать; to — one's self up, вскакивать.

Pict, Пиктъ.

picture, картина, портретъ; to —, изобра-

жать, представлять;— sque, живописный.

pie, пирожное.

piece, кусокъ, часть, монета, ружьё, пушка, орудіе, піеса, сочиненіе, статья; a — of artillery, пушка, орудіе; a — of copper, мѣдная монета; a — of wood, кусокъ дерева, полѣно; —s of indecorum, неприличности.

pierce, пронзать, проницать, просверливать, прокалывать.

piercing, пронзительный.

piety, благочестіе, набожность.

pig, поросёнокъ.

pigmy, пигмейный, малорослый.

pile, строеніе, куча,груда, громада, масса; to —up, складывать въ кучу.

pilgrim, пилигримъ, богомолъ, богомолецъ.

pill, пилюля; — box, коробочка для пилюль.

pillage, грабёжъ, расхищеніе; to —, расхищать, грабить.

pillar, столбъ, стойка, подпора.

pillow, подушка.

pilot, лоцманъ.

pin, булавка, шпилька; in merry —, въ веселомъ духѣ; to —, пригвазживать; —cushion, булавочная подушка.

pinion,связывать крылья.

pink, розовый цвѣтъ.

pious, благочестивый.

pipe, трубка; to —, свистать; —r, волынщикъ.

piqued at, въ досадѣ на.

piracy, морской разбой, морское разбойничество.

pirate-ship,разбойничье судно.

Pisa, Пиза.

pistol, пистолетъ.

pistole,пистоля (монета, 5 руб. сер.).

pit, яма.

pitch, степень, высота, вышина; to —, бросать, кидать; — ed battle,правильный бой.

piteous, жалостный; — ly, жалостно.

pitiful, сострадательный.

pitiless, безжалостный.

pittance, доля, малость.

pity, жалость, сожалѣніе; to take — , сжалиться; what a — it is, какъ жаль! to—, жалѣть.

Pius, Пій.

placard, (прибитое) объявленіе.

place, мѣсто;— of landing, пристань; to take —, происходить, случаться; to — , помѣщать, класть, ставить; to—a check, полагать предѣлы; to — around the neck, надѣвать на шею; to — at any one's disposal, предоставлять въ чьё либо распоряженіе; to —confidence in any one довѣрять кому, оказывать кому довѣріе; to —in the power, покорять; to—on any one's head,надѣвать на голову; to—one-s,self, становиться,стать; to—on the throne —,возводить на престолъ; she — d herself at their head, она стала въ головѣ ихъ.

placid, тихій.

plague, чума, моръ, зараза; to —, мучить, досаждать, надоѣдать.

plaid, шотландскій плащъ.

plain, равнина; простой, ясный; —, —ly. ясно.

plaintive, жалобный, плачевный.

plan, планъ, начертаніе, устройство, предпріятіе, намѣреніе; to —, замышлять, размышлять, располагать, начертывать.

plane, плоскость.

planet, планета.

plank, доска.

plant, растѣніе; to —, сажать, учреждать; — er, плантаторъ.

plaster, цементъ, замазка, гипсъ.

plate, тарелка, серебряная посуда, мѣдная доска; — glass, зеркальное или шлифованное стекло.

platform, платформа, помостъ.

plausible, правдоподобный.

Plautius, Плавтій.

play, игра, забава, комедія, піеса; to —, играть, представлять; to — a trick, съиграть штуку; to — off a joke, съ играть шутку; — mate, подруга.

plead, отзываться.

pleasant, пріятный, забавный; — ly, шутя,

въ шутку; — гу, шутки, насмѣшка.

please, правиться, быть угоднымъ, изволить, хотѣть; — to sit down, пожалуйста садитесь; if you — если Вамъ угодно, пожалуйста; will you — to cut it in two, пожалуйста разрѣжьте это пополамъ.

pleased, довольный; to be —, благоволить.

pleasing, пріятный; a — anecdote, интересный анекдотъ.

pleasure, удовольствіе, произволъ; a man of —, человѣкъ жаждущій удовольствій; at —, по благоусмотрѣнію; — grounds, паркъ, гульбище, мѣсто прогулки.

plebeian, плебейскій, простонародный.

pledge, залогъ, закладъ, порука, заложникъ.

plentiful, изобильный; — ly, изобильно, много, достаточно.

plenty, изобиліе, вдоволь; — of, довольно.

plight, обрекать.

plot, заговоръ; to —, сговариваться.

plough, плугъ; to —, пахать, разсѣкать (волны).

pluck, дёрганіе; to give a little, —, подернуть; to —, дёргать, рвать, драть.

plum, слива; сливный, изюмный, кориночный.

plumber, свинцовыхъ дѣлъ мастеръ.

plump, бухнуться, шлёпнуться, шмякнуться.

plunder, грабёжъ, добыча; to —, грабить, ограбить; — er, грабитель; — ing, грабёжъ, похищеніе; — ing incursion, разбойническій набѣгъ.

plunge, бросаться, погружаться, барахтаться.

Plymouth, Плимутъ.

pocket, карманъ; карманный; — book, бумажникъ.

poem, поэма, стихотвореніе.

poet, стихотворецъ, поэтъ; — ical, поэтическій; — гу, стихотворство, поэзія, стихотвореніе.

point, точка, острокопечіе, кончикъ, пунктъ, коса, низкій мысъ, румбъ, предметъ, цѣль, свойство; the cardinal — s, страны свѣта; to reduce to the — of despair, доводить почти до отчаянія; in — of, въ разсужденіи, въ отношеніи чего; in some — s, въ нѣкоторыхъ отношеніяхъ; to — out, показывать, указывать на; to — to, указывать на; — ed, остроконечный.

poison, ядъ; to —, отравлять.

poker, кочерга.

polar, полярный.

pole, полюсъ, колъ, шестъ, вѣха; — ax, бердышъ, аллебарда.

polemic, полемическій.

police, полиція; — man, полицейскій чиновникъ.

policy, политика, благоразуміе.

Polish, польскій.

polish, лощить, полировать, чистить, просвѣщать, образовать; to — up, выполировать.

polite, вѣжливый, учтивый, тонкій, утонченный; —ness,учтивость, вѣжливость.

political, политическій.

politician, политикъ.

politics, политика.

polity, правленіе,устройство.

Polynesia, Полинезія.

pommel, сѣдельная шишка, ефесная головка.

pomp, пышность, великолѣпіе; — al, пышный.

pond, прудъ.

ponder, обдумывать.

pontiff, первосвященникъ, Папа Римскій.

pood, пудъ.

poodle, пудель.

pool, лужа.

poor, бѣдный, плохой.

pop up, выскакивать, вдругъ,высовываться.

pope, папа; — ry, Римско-католическая вѣра.

popish, папистскій.

popular, популярный; — ity, популярность.

population, народонаселеніе.

populous, многолюдный.

pore over, сидѣть надъ, рыться въ.

pork, свинина.

porphyry, порфиръ.

porringer, чашка, миска.

port, портъ; — al, порталъ, главный входъ; — hole, пушечный портъ;—wine, портвейнъ.

porter, портеръ, носильщикъ.

portion, часть, доля, порція, надѣлъ.

portrait, портретъ.

Portugal, Португалія.

Portuguese, Португалецъ.

position, положеніе, мѣсто, позиція, состояніе.

positive,положительный; — ly, положительно, настоятельно; most — ly, рѣшительно.

possess, имѣть, владѣть, обладать; to be—ed of, владѣть чѣмъ; to be — ed with, бѣсноваться; — ion, владѣніе; to take — ion, завладѣвать; —or, владѣтель, владѣлецъ.

possest, см. possess.

possibility,возможность.

possible, возможный; as dear as —, какъ можно дороже; — bly, по возможности, можетъ быть.

post, столбъ, столбикъ, тумба, мѣсто, почта; почтовый; to ride —, см. ride; to —, ставить, разставлять; to — down, умчаться; — age, вѣсовыя или портовыя деньги; — boy, ямщикъ; — house, почтовой дворъ; — illion, почталіонъ,ямщикъ;—office, почтовое вѣдом-

ство, почтамтъ, почтовая контора.

posterity, потомство, потомки.

postern, задняя дверь; задній.

posture, осанка, положеніе тѣла, позитура.

pot, горшокъ.

potato, картофель, картофельный.

potent,могущественный, сильный; — ate, потентатъ, властитель, властелинъ..

pouch,карманъ, мѣшокъ, сумка.

pounce, трескъ, ударъ.

pound, фунтъ, фунтъ стерлингъ; 24 and 31 —ers, 24-хъ и 31 фунтовыхъ.

pour, лить, изливать, разливать, литься; to — in upon, бросаться, кидаться, нахлынуть на кого, пускать на кого что; to—out, наливать.

poverty, бѣдность.

powder, порохъ; —, plot, пороховой заговоръ.

power, могущество, власть, сила, мочь, способность; the — s, боги; the — of music, сила дѣйствія музыки; — ful, могущественный, сильный, здоровый, плотный.

practicable,исполнимый, возможный.

practical, практическій; — ly, практически.

practice, практика, навыкъ, употребленіе, обыкновеніе, образъ дѣйствія, поступокъ;

as is their general —, какъ это у нихъ обшеупотребительно; to be in the —, имѣть обыкновеніе.

practise, практиковать, упражняться въ чемъ, дѣлать, содѣлывать, употреблять.

prairie, степь.

praise, хвала; to —, хвалить.

prance, стать на дыбы, чваниться.

prank, проказа.

pray, пожалуйста, прошу Васъ; to —, молиться, просить, молить; to—on, продолжать молиться; — er, молитва; to say one's — ers, молиться; — ing, моленіе.

preach, проповѣдывать; — er, проповѣдникъ.

precaution, предосторожность.

precede, предшествовать; a few minutes preceding, нѣсколько минутъ передъ тѣмъ; — nce, преимущество, первенство.

precept, наставленіе, правило; — or, наставникъ.

precious, драгоцѣнный.

precipice, стремнина, пропасть.

precipitate, сбрасывать, низвергать, ускорять; —ly, опрометчиво.

precipitation, торопливость, поспѣшность, скорость, стремительность.

precipitous, крутой, стремнистый.

precisely, точно, именно.

precision, точность.

predecessor, предшественникъ, предмѣстникъ.

predetermination, предположеніе.

predict, предсказывать; —ion, предсказаніе.

predominance, перевѣсъ, превосходство, преобладаніе.

predominant, первенствующій, преобладающій.

predominate, первенствовать, преобладать.

preeminence, превосходство, преимущество.

prefect, префектъ.

prefer, предпочитать; — ence, предпочтеніе; in — ence, предпочтительно; — ment, производство.

prejudice, предразсудокъ.

prematurely, преждевременно.

preparation, приготовленіе.

prepare, приготовлять, — ся; —d, готовый.

preponderance, перевѣсъ.

prepossessing, привлекательный, пріятный.

prerogative, право преимущества, преимущественное право.

Presbyterian, пресвитеріанинъ; пресвитеріанскій, консисторіяльный; —ism, пресвитеріанисмъ.

prescribe, предписывать.

prescription, рецептъ.

presence, присутствіе, собраніе, общество;

бытность; entering his—, входя къ нему.

present, подарокъ, настоящее время; присутствующій, настоящій, нынѣшный, теперешній; as a—, въ подарокъ; at —, теперь; for the—. въ ту минуту; to be—, присутствовать; to—, представлять, дарить, подносить, подавать; to — one's compliments, кланяться; to— one's self, являться; to — prayers, возсылать молитвы;—ation, представленіе; he gave him the — ation to a living, онъ поднесъ ему назначеніе на духовное мѣсто;—ly, тотчасъ, сейчасъ, теперь.

preservation, сохраненіе.

preserve, охранять, оберегать, сохранять;—r, хранитель, сохранитель.

preside, предсѣдательствовать; Presidency, президентство, предсѣдательство, судебный округъ пресѣдателя въ Восточной Индіи; — nt, предсѣдатель, президентъ.

press, печать, печатаніе, книгопечатаніе; to issue from the—, выходить изъ печати; to—, прижимать, тѣснить, принуждать, уговаривать, упрашивать; to—hard on, сильно устремляйся на; she —ed the inquiry, она упрашивала отвѣчать на вопросъ; — иге, давка, тѣснота.

prest, см. **press.**

presume, осмѣливаться, дерзать.

presumption, предположеніе.

pretence, предлогъ; on — of, подъ видомъ, подъ предлогомъ.

pretend, имѣть притязаніе на что, представлять, говорить, притворяться; — er, претендентъ.

pretension, притязаніе, претензія.

pretext, предлогъ.

pretty, красивый, милый; довольно.

prevail, одерживать верхъ, господствовать, преобладать; but all would not —, но это ничего не помогло; disputes have been and still —, были споры и дѣло ещё не рѣшено.

prevalence, господствованіе.

prevalent, господствующій; to be —, господствовать, преобладать.

prevent, препятствовать, мѣшать, задерживать, предупреждать, отвращать.

previous, предшествующій, предварительный; —to, прежде; — ly, прежде, передъ тѣмъ.

prey, добыча; beast of—, хищный звѣрь.

price, цѣна; —less, безцѣнный, неоцѣненный.

prick up, навастривать (уши).

pride, гордость, честолюбіе.

priest, жрецъ, священникъ; — hood, священническое званіе, духовенство; — ly, священническій.

prime, цвѣтъ, цвѣтущее состояніе; первый, лучшій.

prince, государь, принцъ, князь; — ly, царскій, княжескій; — ss, принцесса, княгиня; — ss royal, королевна.

principal, главный; —ly, преимущественно.

principle, начало, принципъ, правило, побудительная причина.

print, печать; to —, печатать.

prioress, настоятельница.

prison, тюрьма, темница; — er, плѣнникъ, заключённый въ тюрьмѣ, подсудимый; — er of war, военноплѣнный; to take—er, взять въ плѣнъ.

prithee, (сокр. I pray thee), прошу тебя, пожалуйста.

private, рядовой; уединенный, частный; — ly, тайно, на единѣ, частно, приватно; — er, каперъ, приватиръ, каперское судно.

privilege, привилегія.

privy, тайный, частный; to be — to, знать о чёмъ; Lord Privy Seal, см. **Lord.**

prize, призъ, добыча, премія, награда, вы-

пгрышъ; to —, оцѣнивать, уважать; — fighter, кулачный боецъ (на премію).

probable, вѣроятный.

probably, вѣроятно.

procedure, производство; legal —, судопроизводство.

proceed, происходить отъ чего, проистекать изъ чего, приниматься за, приступать къ, продолжать, идти, идти дальше, ѣхать дальше, переходить; to — through, проѣхать; he — ed to examine, онъ началъ разсматривать; — ing, судебное производство; this mode of — ing, этого рода путешествованіе; — s, доходъ, доходы.

process, операція, способъ, производство, процесъ; — ion, процессія, торжественное шестіе.

proclaim, провозглашать, объявлять.

proclamation, обнародованіе, объявленіе, прокламація.

procure, доставать, добывать, доставлять; to — the notice, удостоиваться вниманія.

prodigy, диво, чудо.

produce, произведеніе; to —, производить, раждать, производить, причинять, представлять, производить на свѣтъ, предъявлять.

product, произведеніе, продуктъ; — ion, произведеніе; — ive, про-

изводящій, плодород-
ный; to be — ive of,
производить, пораж-
дать.

profess, являть объявлять, выказывать, ис-
поведывать, призна-
вать; — ion, званіе,
признаніе, профессія,
ремесло; — ional func-
tion, занятіе по долж-
ности;—ional honours,
отличія или почести,
присвоенныя долж-
ностнымъ лицамъ; —
ional spirit, сослов-
ный духъ, сословное
чувство; — or, про-
фессоръ.

profit, барышъ,прибыль;
to —, успѣвать, поль-
зоваться чѣмъ, полу-
чать выгоду отъ чего;
— able, выгодный.

profligacy, развратъ,рас-
путство.

profound, глубокій.

profuse,расточительный;
—ly, въ избыткѣ.

profusion, изобиліе, то-
роватость.

prognosticate, предвѣщать, предсказывать.

progress, ходъ, шествіе,
переходъ,путешествіе,
поѣздка, успѣхъ, те-
ченіе; the — of the
creature was by no
means impeded, это
нисколько не остано-
вило эту тварь; to
arrest their — оста-
новить ихъ.

prohibit, запрещать; —
ion, запрещеніе; —
ory, запретительный.

project, намѣреніе, про-

ектъ, предпріятіе; to
—, умышлять.

prolong,продолжать,про-
тягивать,отсрочивать.

promenade, гулянье,про-
гулка.

prominent, выдающійся,
бросающійся въ глаза,
отличный.

promise,обѣщаніе; to —,
обѣщать, — ся; to —
well, обѣщать много
хорошаго.

promontory, мысъ, носъ.

promote, споспѣшествовать, производить (въ
чинъ).

promotion,производство,
повышеніе.

prompt, проворный, скорый,поспѣшный; to —,
побуждать, поощрять,
внушать; — ly, скоро.

pronounce, произносить,
объявлять; to — one's
blessing, благослов-
лять.

pronunciation,выговоръ,
произношеніе.

proof, доказательство.

prop, подпирать, поддерживать.

propel, двигать.

propensity, наклонность,
склонность.

proper, приличный, удобный, надлежащій;—ly,
собственно, надлежа-
щимъ образомъ, при-
лично; —ty, собствен-
ность, имущество; a
person of—ty, чело-
вѣкъ съ состояніемъ.

prophecy, пророчество,
предвѣщаніе.

prophesy, прорицать,
предвѣщать.

prophet, пророкъ; — ess,
пророчица.

proportion, часть, со-
размѣрность; in—of,
соразмѣрно чему; to—,
соразмѣрять; — ably,
соразмѣрно, пропор-
ціально;—ate, сораз-
мѣрный;—ately, сораз-
мѣрно.

proposal, предложеніе.

propose, предлагать.

proprietor, владѣлецъ,
хозяинъ.

propriety, приличность
соотвѣтственность.

proscribe, осуждать на
изгнаніе, принуждать
къ изгнанію, подвер-
гать кого опалѣ.

proscription, изгнаніе.

prose, проза.

prosecute, продолжать
(начатое), просить въ
судѣ на кого, обви-
нять.

prospect, видъ, надежда.

prosper, споспѣшествовать, успѣвать, бла-
годенствовать; — ity,
преуспѣяніе, благо-
денствіе;—ous, успѣш-
ный, благоуспѣшный,
благоденственный; —
ously, благоуспѣшно.

protect, охранять, защищать; —ion, охра-
неніе, защита, покро-
вительство; — or, за-
щитникъ, покровитель,
протекторъ — orate,
покровительство, прав-
леніе протектора.

protest, протестовать;
— ant, протестантъ,
протестантскій.

proud, гордый; to be—of,
гордиться чѣмъ

Prov. (Proverbs), притчи Соломоновы.

prove, повѣрять, доказывать, оказываться.

provide, снабжать, запасать, припасать, готовить, приготавливать, пристроивать, заводить, доставлять; to—for, пристроивать, пещись; — d, если только, съ тѣмъ чтобы;—nt, бережливый, предусмотрительный.

Providence, Провидѣніе, промыслъ Божій.

providential, отъ Божія промысла; — impulse, побужденіе внушенное промысломъ Божіимъ; — ly, промысломъ Божіимъ.

province, область, провинція.

provincial, провинціальный.

provision, запасъ, провизія, съѣстной припасъ, узаконеніе.

provoke, раздражать, вызывать.

prowess, храбрость, доблесть.

proxy, полномочіе, повѣренный, уполномоченный.

prudence, благоразуміе, осторожность.

prudent, благоразумный; —ly, благоразумно.

Prussian, прусскій; — blue, Берлинская лазурь.

pry into, вывѣдывать.

prythee (сокр. I pray thee), прошу тебя, пожалуйста.

psalm, псаломъ.

public, публика; публичный, всенародный, общественный; a—house, гостинница, трактиръ; —ation, изданіе;—ly, публичный, публично.

publish, обнародовать, публиковать, издавать.

puck, домовой.

pudding, пудингъ.

puff, —of wind, порывъ, вѣтра; to—, дуть; to — away, пускать дымъ.

pull, тянуть, тащить, дёргать, грести; to — aboard, вытаскивать на шлюпку; to — down, стаскивать, сламывать, повалить; to—from, вынимать; to—out, вытаскивать, вынимать, выгребать; to — the bell звонить въ колокольчикъ; to — to pieces, растерзать.

pulp, мякоть.

pulpit, каѳедра.

pump, помпа; to—, качать.

punchinello, полишинель, шутъ.

punctilious, мелочной.

punish, наказывать; — ment, наказаніе.

puny, крошечный.

pupil, питомецъ, воспитанникъ.

puppet, кукла, маріонетка.

purchase, покупка; to—, покупать, пріобрѣтать.

pure, чистый;—ly, чисто, единственно, только.

puritan, пуританецъ; — ism, пуританское ученіе.

purl, журчать, течь съ журчаніемъ.

purple, багряница, порфира; багряный.

purpose, намѣреніе, предметъ, цѣль; for the — of, съ цѣлію; on —, нарочно; to such —, съ такимъ успѣхомъ; to —, намѣреваться, имѣть намѣреніе; —ly,съ намѣреніемъ, нарочно.

purse, кошелёкъ; a— of gold, кошелёкъ съ золотомъ.

pursue, преслѣдовать, гнаться за, продолжать; to—the advantage, воспользоваться выгодой; —r, преслѣдователь.

pursuit, преслѣдованіе, занятія, труды; to be in—of, преслѣдовать, гнаться, искать; they were in full—, они гнались за нимъ во весь опоръ.

push, толкать; to—forward, погонять; to — off, отваливать; to—open, толкая отворять; to—out, выталкивать; to—to the utmost one's advantage against, извлекать всю возможную пользу изъ своего превосходства надъ.

pusillanimity, малодушіе, робкость.

puss, киса, кошка, заяцъ.

put, ставить, становить, полагать, класть; to —an end, to —a stop to, положить конецъ чему, прекратить что; to — any one out of the way, сбивать кого съ толку; to — a question to any one, спрашивать у кого; to — aside, откладывать; to—back, возвращаться; to—down, поставлять, выставлять, спускать; to — forth выказывать, издавать, печатать; to —in, вставлять; to — in any one's mind, напоминать кому; to —in arms, вооружать; to—in readiness, приготовлять; to—in the news-papers, напечатать въ газетахъ; to —into any one's hand, подавать кому, выдавать; to — into any one's mind, внушать кому; to — in or into execution, приводить въ исполненіе; to—off, откладывать, отлагать, отваливать; to —on, надѣвать; to — one's hand to one's heart, прикладывать руку къ сердцу; to — one's self at the head of the troops, принять предводительство войскомъ; to — one's self in motion, трогаться съ мѣста; to — one's self on one's defence, становиться въ оборонительное положеніе; to —out a boat, спустить шлюпку; to — out of question, дѣлать невозможнымъ; to—to, прикладывать, запрягать; to—to death, умерщвлять, казнить смертію; to—to flight, обращать въ бѣгство; to—to the rout, раз-

бивать, поражать; to —to the sword, заколоть, убить, умерщвлять, (всѣхъ) перерубить, переколоть; to—up, останавливаться; to — up a horse, поставить лошадь (въ постояломъ дворѣ); to —upon, наносить (оскорбленія); to —up prayers, возсылать молитвы.

puzzle, загадка; it is a —, это непонятно; to — спутывать, сбивать съ толку.

Q.

quadrangle, четыреугольникъ.

quagmire, болотная почва, болотина.

quake, трепетать, трястись.

Quaker, квакеръ.

qualification, потребное качество, способность.

qualify, дѣлать, способнымъ къ чему, давать право.

quality, качество, знать; a man of —, знатная особа.

quarrel, ссора, споръ; to—, ссориться, спорить.

quarry, дичь, добыча.

quarter, четверть, кварталъ, часть, сторона, квартира, пощада, помилованіе; — boat, барказъ (на купеческихъ судахъ),

—deck, шканцы; — sessions, трёхмѣсячныя засѣданія;—staff, короткая палка, дубина.

quay, набережная, пристань; — space, пространство, занимаемое набережною.

queen, королева.

quell, останавливать, подавлять, превозмогать, преодолѣвать, укрощать.

quench, тушить, гасить.

in quest of, чтобы отыскать.

question, вопросъ; the passage in—, мѣсто о коёмъ идетъ рѣчь; to address a —, обращаться съ вопросомъ; to—, спрашивать.

quick, живой, быстрый; быстро, скоро; be — now, потороппсь пожалуйста! проворнѣе! поскорѣй! —ly, живо, быстро, скоро.

quiet, спокойный, тихій; to —, успокоивать; —ly, спокойно;—ness; спокойствіе.

quit, оставлять.

quite, совершенно, совсѣмъ, точно.

quiver, колчанъ; to —, трепетать, дрожать.

quo', см. quoth.

quotation, ссылка на что, цитатъ.

quote, приводить (мѣста изъ писателей).

quoth, сказалъ.

R.

race, порода, поколѣніе, бѣганіе въ запуски, скачка; the human —, человѣческій родъ; — ground, .расталище, бѣгъ; — horse, бѣгунъ, скаковал .лошадь.

rack, пыточная скамья.

radiant, лучезарный, сіяющій.

radically, первоначально.

rage, прость, свирѣпость; to—, свирѣпствовать.

ragged,.оборванный, ободранный.

raging, свирѣпствованіе.

rags, тряпьё, ветошь.

railing, рѣшётка, перила.

railway, желѣзная дорога; —company, общество желѣзныхъ дорогъ.

rain, дождь, дождикъ; it will — дождь пойдетъ.

raise, поднимать, воздвигать, возвышать, возбуждать, производить, доставать (деньги), набирать (войско, деньги, сумму); to — to the throne, возводить на престолъ; to —up, поднимать, возвышать.

raisins, изюмъ.

rally, собирать или соединять снова, собираться.

Ralph, Рауль, Рудольфъ.

ram, баранъ.

ramble, поѣздка, прогул-

ка; to -, бродить, шататься.

rampart, валъ.

ran, см. run.

rung, см. ring.

range, рядъ, цѣпь (горъ); to—, строить, стоять въ ряду, бродить.

rank, рядъ, шеренга, разрядъ, чинъ, классъ, званіе, мѣсто; to—, стоять на ряду, причислаться къ чему, занимать мѣсто.

rankle, раздражать.

ransom, выкупъ; to — , выкупать.

rap, стучать.

rapacity, хищничество, жадность къ грабежу.

rapid, быстротокъ, порогъ; быстрый; – ity, быстрота; -- ly, быстро, шибко.

rapier, рапира.

rare, рѣдкій, славный; —ly, рѣдко.

rascal, бездѣльникъ, мошенникъ.

rash, опрометчивый, безразсудный; to—, раздирать клыками;—ly, опрометчиво, безразсудно;—ness, опрометчивость

rat, крыса;—hole крысья нора.

rate, мѣра, степень, соразмѣрная часть, доля, цѣна, скорость, подать, налогъ; at any —, по крайней мѣрѣ; at the — of six miles, по шести миль.

rather, нѣсколько, скорѣе, лучше.

ratify, подтверждать, у-

тверждать, ратификовать.

ratio, отношеніе, пропорція; —nal, разумный, раціональный.

ratlins, выблинки (верёвочныл ступеньки).

rattle, трещётка, стукотня, шумъ; to —, стучать, звучать, гремѣть, бренчать.

ravage, разореніе, опустошеніе; to—, разорить, опустошать;— r, разоритель, опустошитель.

rave at any one, разсердиться, вознегодовать на кого.

raven, воронъ; — ous, обжорливый, ненасытный.

ravine, оврагъ.

ravish, похищать, изнасиловать;— er, похититель.

raw, сырой, неспѣлый, неопытный, несвѣдущій.

ray, лучъ.

reach, область, предѣлъ, кругъ, дѣйствія, достиженіе; above the —of man, сверхъ силъ человѣческихъ; to be within the —, быть доступнымъ; to—, достигать, доѣзжать, доходить, простираться; to—out, протягивать.

reaction, противодѣйствіе, реакція.

read, начитанный; to—, читать; —er, читатель; —ing, чтеніе, начитанность.

readily, охотно, тотчасъ.

readiness, готовность,

бѣглость, свободность; to put in—, приготовлять.

ready, готовый, скорый; he showed his — wit, онъ показалъ что за острымъ словцёмъ у него дѣло не стаиетъ.

real, настоящій, истинный, дѣйствительный; — ity, дѣйствительность; —ly, дѣйствительно; —ize, осуществлять, исполнять, пріобрѣтать, выручать.

realm, царство, королевство.

reap, жать.

reappear, опять являться; to — upon deck, что могъ выходить на палубу; — ance, вторичное появленіе; on his—ance upon deck, когда онъ опять вышелъ на палубу.

rear,—guard, аріергардъ. заднее войско; in the —, назади, позади; to scamper in the —, гоняться за.

reason, разумъ, разсудокъ, причина; by — of, по причинѣ; in —, по справедливости; — able, благоразумный; — ableness, справедливость; —ably, справедливо.

rebel, мятежникъ, бунтовщикъ; to —, бунтоваться;—lion, бунтъ, мятёжъ, возмущеніе.

rebound, отскокъ.

rebuild, вновь строить, перестраивать.

recantation, отреченіе.

recede, отступать.

receipt, приходъ, доходъ; to be in — of, получать, имѣть доходъ.

receive, получать, принимать; to—the sacrament, пріобщаться Святыхъ Таинъ.

recent, недавній, новый; —ly, недавно.

reception, принятіе, пріёмъ.

recess, ниша, уединеніе, одиночество.

re-christen, перекрестить.

recital, повѣствованіе, повтореніе.

recite, повторять; to—prayers, читать молитвы.

reckless, беззаботливый.

reckon, считать; — ing, счётъ.

recognise, узнавать, признавать.

recoil, подаваться назадъ, пятиться.

recollect, помнить, вспоминать.

recollection, воспоминаніе; from —, на память; to bring to one's —, напоминать кому о чёмъ.

recommend, рекомендовать, присовѣтовать.

recompense, вознаграждать, награждать.

reconcile, примирять.

reconnoitring, рекогносцировка.

record, протоколъ; to—, записывать или вносить въ книгу, разсказывать.

recourse, прибѣжище; to have—, прибѣгать.

recover, получать, обратно, отыскивать, воротить, поправлять, изцѣлять, поправляться, опомниться; — у, возвращеніе, выздоравливаніе.

recreation, увеселеніе, отдохновеніе.

recruit, рекрутъ.

rector, приходскій священникъ.

red, красный цвѣтъ; красный;—coat, красный кафтанъ, солдатъ; — hot, раскалённый.

redouble, удвоивать, усугублять.

redress, удовлетвореніе.

reduce, приводить, доводить, превращать, покорять, укрощать, разстроивать.

re-echo, отдавать, отдаваться.

reed, тростникъ, камышъ.

reek, дымиться, испаряться.

reenter, опять входить.

reestablish, возстановлять, поправлять; — ment, возстановленіе.

refectory, трапеза, столовая.

refer, относить, передавать, предоставлять.

refine, утончать, облагороживать; — ment, утонченіе, утонченность, прикраса.

reflect, отражать, отсвѣчивать, размышлять, разсуждать, подумать, о чёмъ; —ion, размышленіе, разсужденіе, обсужденіе.

reform, преобразованіе; to—, преобразовывать; —ation, преобразованіе, реформація;—ed, реформатскій; — er, преобразователь, реформаторъ.

refrain, удерживаться.

refresh, освѣжать, прохлаждать;—ment, отдохновеніе, отдыхъ.

refuge, убѣжище; — e, выходецъ, убѣжникъ.

refusal, отказъ.

refuse, отрепки, бракъ; to—, отказывать, отказываться.

refute, опровергать.

regain, вновь достигать.

regaler, угощать, подчивать.

regalia, регалій, знаки царскаго достоинства.

regard, уваженіе, почтеніе; in—to, with — to, касательно; to—, почитать, принимать въ соображеніе, обращать вниманіе, смотрѣть на; to—as, принимать за, считать чѣмъ.

regent, регентъ, —тша, правитель, —ница.

regiment, полкъ; — of the line, линейный полкъ.

region, страна, область.

register, реестръ, списовъ.

regret, сожалѣніе; to—, жалѣть о чёмъ.

regular, правильный, регулярный, настоящій, безпрерывный, постоянный;—ity, правильность;—ly,правильно, постоянно,каждыйразъ.

regulate, приводить въ порядокъ, устроивать; well—d, благоустроенный.

regulation, постановленіе, узаконеніе.

reign, царство, царствованіе; to—, царствовать.

rein, поводъ, узда; to—up, удерживать.

reinforce, подкрѣплять; —ment, подкрѣпленіе.

reinstate, возстановлять.

reject, отвергать, не принимать.

rejoice, радоваться, веселиться.

rejoicing, пзъявленіе радости.

rejoin, возражать.

relate, разсказывать, касаться, относиться; — d, родственный.

relation, отношеніе, родственникъ,—ица.

relative, родственникъ, —ица.

relax, ослаблять, сбавлять.

relay, подстава, перемѣна.

release, освобожденіе; to —, освобождать, выпускать.

relic, остатокъ.

relief, облегченіе, помощь, вспоможеніе, поданіе помощи.

relieve, облегчать, помогать кому, смѣнять.

religion, религія; the Roman Catholic —, Римско-Католическое исповѣданіе.

religious, религіозный; — offender, преступникъ противъ вѣры;

— refugee, убѣжникъ за религію; —ly, религіозно; to keep a secret — ly, свято сохранить тайну.

relique, см. **relic**.

reluctance, нерасположеніе, неохота.

reluctantly, неохотно.

rely, полагаться.

remain, оставаться; — der, остатокъ, остальное; —ing, остающійся, остальной; — s, остатки, останки.

remand, отсылать.

remark, примѣчаніе, замѣчаніе; to —, замѣчать; —able, замѣчательный, достопримѣчательный; — able for its mines, з. своими рудниками; — ably, замѣчательно, особенно.

remedy,лекарство,противодѣйствующее средство; to—, помогать, исправлять, устранять.

remember, воспоминать, припоминать, помнить.

remembrance, воспоминаніе, память.

remind, напоминать.

remit, ослаблять, убавлять, уменьшать, ослабѣвать (въ чёмъ).

remnant, остатокъ, кусокъ.

remonstrance, представленіе, увѣщаніе.

remorse, угрызеніе совѣсти.

remote,отдаленный, дальній.

remount, вновь садиться (на лошадь); to be—

—ed, снова быть верхомъ или на лошади.

remove, отдвигать, удалять, устранять, снимать, переносить, переѣзжать.

remuneration, вознаграждение, плата.

rend, раздирать, растерзать.

render, отдавать, оказывать, дѣлатъ чѣмъ.

renew, возобновлять; — al, возобновление.

renown, слава; to be — ed, быть славнымъ, знаменитымъ, извѣстнымъ, славиться.

rent, аревда, плата за аренду, доходъ; см. также to rend.

repair, исправление, починка; to keep in good —, см. keep; to —, чинить, поправлять, отправляться.

repass, опять проходить.

repast, кушанье, обѣдъ, столъ.

repay, отплачивать.

repeat, повторять, читать, приводить (мѣмѣсто изъ книги); — ed, повторительный; —edly, повторительно.

repel, отражать, отбрасывать, отталкивать.

repent, раскаиваться; — ance, раскаяние.

repetition, повторение.

reply, ответъ; to —, отвѣчать.

report, трескъ, слухъ, молва, отголосокъ, выстрѣлъ; to —, разсказывать, извѣщать, доносить, докладывать.

repose, спокойствие; to — trust in any one, довѣрять кому.

repossess a king, возвращать королю престолъ.

reprehension, порицание, выговоръ.

represent, представлять; — ation, представление; — ative, представитель.

reprimand, выговоръ.

reproach, упрёкъ, нарекание, поношение, позоръ; to—with, упрекать въ.

reproduce, вновь производить.

reproof, попрёкъ.

reptile, пресмыкающееся животное.

republic, республика.

repudiate, отрекаться отъ, разводиться съ.

repulse, отбивать, отталкивать, отражать.

reputable, почтенный.

reputation, репутация, слава, честное имя.

repute, слава; to bring into —, сделать извѣстнымъ; to —, почитать кого чѣмъ.

request, просьба; to —, просить.

require, требовать; he was — d, онъ былъ принужденъ.

requisite, потребный, нужный.

requite, воздавать, отплачивать.

rescue, освобождение, избавление; to —, спасать.

reseat, вторично посадить (на престолъ).

resemblance, сходство, подобие.

resemble, походить на.

resembling, похожий на.

resent, чувствовать; — ment, мстительность, злопамятство, памятозлобие.

reserve, воздержание; to —, сберегать, сохранять, предоставлять.

reside, пребывать, жить; — nce, мѣстопребывание, пребывание, мѣсто пребывания, жилище, жительство; — nt, пребывающий, живущий.

resign, отказываться отъ чего, слагать съ себя.

resist, противиться, сопротивляться; — ance, сопротивление; — less, непреодолимый.

resolute, рѣшительный, смѣлый, отважный; — ly, рѣшительно, смѣло.

resolution, рѣшительность, смѣлость, намѣрение.

resolve, to be — d, рѣшаться, намѣреваться; рѣшать.

resort, прибѣгать къ чему, отправляться.

resound, отдаваться, раздаваться.

resource, прибѣжище, средство; — в, деньги.

respect, почтение, уважение, отношение; with — to, въ отношении къ, въ разсуждении чего, относительно чего; to —, почитать, уважать; — ability, почтенность; —able, достойный уважения, благопристойный; — able looking, приличный на видъ; —ful, почтительный; —ing, относительно, касательно; — ive, относительный; they retired to their — ive chambers, они удалились каждый въ свой покой; — ively, относительно, особенно.

rest, остатокъ, остальное, остальная часть, другіе, прочіе, отдыхъ, отдохновеніе; the — of the money, остальныя деньги; to —, подпирать, основываться, отдыхать, давать отдохнуть; — ing place, мѣсто отдохновенія, м. упокоенія; —less, безпокойный, неутомимый, неусыпный.

Restoration, возстановленіе, реставрація.

restore, возвращать, возстановлять.

restrain, удерживать, воздерживать, обуздывать, укрощать.

result, результатъ, послѣдствіе; to —, происходить, проистекать.

resume, повторять, снова начинать, возобновлять, продолжать (прежній разсказъ).

retain, удерживать, держать.

retake, взять назадъ, вновь завладѣть.

retinue, свита.

retire, отступать, удаляться, уединяться.

retook, см. **retake**.

retreat, отступленіе, ретирада; to—, ретироваться, отступать.

return, возвращеніе, возвратъ, отплата; to—, возвращать, отдавать, отвѣчать, возвращаться; to—an answer, давать отвѣтъ; to — thanks, благодарить; to—to one's task, снова приниматься за дѣло.

Rev., Reverend, почтенный, преподобный.

reveal, открывать, обнаруживать; — ed, откровенный.

reveller, пирователь.

revenge, месть, мщеніе; —ful, мстительный.

revenue, доходъ; —law, таможенный уставъ.

revere, чтить, почитать; — nce, благоговѣніе, почитаніе, почтеніе; your—nce, Ваше Преподобіе.

reverie, задумчивость.

reverse, выворачивать.

revisit, вновь посѣщать.

revival, возобновленіе, возстановленіе.

revive, оживлять, возстановлять, возобновлять.

revoke, отмѣнять.

revolt, возмущеніе, бунтъ, возстаніе.

Revolution, революція, переворотъ.

revolve, обращаться; — r, револьверъ; a — r affair, дѣло рѣшимое лишь только револьверами.

reward, награда, награж-

деніе; to — , награждать.

rhetoric, риторика, краснорѣчіе.

Rhine, Рейнъ.

rhubarb, ревень.

rhyme, риѳма, стихи.

ribbon, лента.

rice, рисъ.

rich, богатый, драгоцѣнный, тучный, дородный; —es, богатство; —ly, богато; — ly does he deserve, онъ вполнѣ заслуживаетъ.

Richard, Рихардъ, Ричардъ.

rid, избавлять; to—get of, избавляться.

riddle, загадка.

ride, ѣзда, катаніе; to — , ѣздить, ѣздить верхомъ; — for your life, пустите лошадь во весь опоръ, что есть духу! to—about, объѣхать вокругъ; to — abroad, разъѣзжать верхомъ; to — a race, скакать въ запуски; to—away, уѣзжать; to—by, проѣхать мимо; to — off, уѣзжать; to — out, выѣзжать; to — over, переѣзжать; to—post, ѣхать на почтовыхъ; — r, всадникъ.

ridicule, насмѣшка; to — any one, насмѣхаться надъ кѣмъ, осмѣять кого.

ridiculous, смѣшной.

riding, верховая ѣзда; —dress, см. **dress**; — hood, дорожный капоръ; — whip, хлыстъ.

rifle, ограбить; — man, стрѣлокъ, егерь.

rig, шутка, проказы; to run a — , проказничать, куролесить; — ging, оснастка, такелажъ.

right, правая сторона, правая рука, правота, справедливость, правда, право; правый, справедливый, настоящій, исправный; вѣрно, справедливо, прямо, очень; we are all —, у насъ все въ исправности; to — ship, ставить корабль прямо; to put to—s, поправлять;—ly, справедливо.

rigid, строгій.

rigorous, суровый, жестокій.

rill, ручей, ручеёкъ.

ring, кольцо, перстень; to—, звонить, звучать, раздаваться;to—again, отдаваться ; to — the bell, звонить въ колокольчикъ; — bolt, рымъ-болтъ.

riot, возмущеніе, бунтъ, мятежъ, пиршество, распутство.

ripe, зрѣлый, поспѣлый, готовый; to—n, созрѣвать.

ripple, струя, рябь; to —, струиться, подбираться рябью.

rise, повышеніе, возвышеніе, увеличеніе, благоуспѣшность; to —, вставать, восходить, возвышаться, подниматься, увеличиваться, усиливаться, рас-

пространяться, расширяться, возникать, возставать, бунтоваться; to—against, to — upon, возставать, бунтоваться противъ; the wind rose to a storm, вѣтеръ усилился до бури.

risen, см. rise.

rising, прибываніе, возвышеніе; — ground, см. ground.

risk, рискъ, опасность, подверганіе опасности; at any—, не смотря ни на какую опасность; to run the —, to—, рисковать, подвергать опасности.

rite, обрядъ, уставъ (церковный).

ritual, церковный уставъ, служебникъ.

rival, соперникъ.

rive, раздирать.

river, рѣка рѣчной; up the—,вверхъ по рѣкѣ.

rivet, заклёпывать; his eyes were — ed, его глаза были устремлены на.

rivulet, рѣчка.

road, дорога, путь;—side, сторона дороги; — stead, рейдъ; — way, большая дорога.

roam, бродить, странствовать по.

roar, ревъ;—of laughter, громкій смѣхъ, хохотъ; to — , реветь; to—out, заревѣть; the — ing of the wind, бушеваніе вѣтра.

roast, жарить.

rob, ограбить; — ber,

разбойникъ; — bery, разбой, покража.

robe, парадное или нарядное платье; — de chambre, халатъ.

Robert, Робертъ.

Robin, Робертъ.

rochet, стихарь.

rock, скала, утёсъ, камень; to — , качать, колыхать, качаться, колыхаться;—beating, ударяющій объ скалу; —bound, окруженный скалами; — y, утѐсистый, каменистый.

rod, прутъ, лоза, стержень, штокъ, тяга.

rode, см. ride.

roe, козуля, дикая коза.

Roger, Рожеръ.

rogue, плутъ, мошенникъ.

roll, булка; to — , валять, катать, катиться; to — along, кататься, катиться; to—on, покатиться; to—up, подъѣхать; —er, катокъ, валъ; — ing, волнистый; a high — ing sea, сильно волнующееся море; she came —ing by, она покатилась мимо насъ; she went— ing over and over, она такъ и покатилась; — s, лѣтописи, архивъ, канцелярія.

Roman, Римлянинъ; Римскій; —catholic, римско-католическій.

romantic, романтическій.

Rome, Римъ.

Romish, римско-католическій.

roof, крыша, кровля.

room, мѣсто, комната, поводъ.

root, корень; to -, вкоренять, укоренять.

rope, верёвка, снасть.

rose, роза; см. также **rise**.

rot, гнить, портиться.

rouge, румяны.

rough, негладкій, шероховатый, грубый, невыдѣланный, суровый, бурный; a—beard, растрёпанная борода; — ness, шероховатость.

round, круглый; вокругъ, около; to —, ходить кругомъ; all —, кругомъ; all the country —, по всей странѣ; all — the house, вокругъ всего дома; — about, кругомъ, около; — about way, обходъ, кругъ; —shouldered, сутулый; — went the wheels, покатились колёса.

rouse, будить, разбуждать, возбуждать, изгонять (звѣря); to — to arms, призывать къ оружію,

rout, разбитіе, пораженіе; to —, разбивать, поражать.

route, дорога, путь, трактъ.

rove, скитаться, бродить; —r, морской разбойникъ, корсеръ.

row, рядъ; to —, грести, идти на греблѣ; — galley, гребная галера; — ing, гребля.

royal, королевскій, царскій; — ist, роялистъ, приверженецъ короля;

— ty, королевское достоинство.

'rt, = art, см. **be.**

rub, тереть, тереться; to — away, to — off, стирать, оттирать; to — down, обтирать.

rubbish, мусоръ, соръ, щебель.

rude, грубый, безъискусственный, простой; — ly, грубо, неучтиво.

rue, каяться, раскаиваться, жалѣть, сожалѣть о ч.

ruffian, злодѣй, разбойникъ.

rugged, шероховатый, шерошенный, неровный, грубый, суровый.

ruin, развалина, погибель, пагуба, разореніе; to —, разстроивать, разорять, погублять.

rule, правило, господство, владычество, власть, правленіе; to — править, управлять, опредѣлять, господствовать; —r, правитель, владѣтель, власитель.

rum, ромъ; —cask, бочка съ ромомъ; — lighter, лихтеръ съ ромомъ.

rumble, гремѣть, ворчать, раздаваться.

rumbling, стукъ.

rummage, шарить.

rumour, молва, слухъ.

run, бѣжаніе, бѣгъ, ходъ; to —, бѣгать, ходить; to—about, бѣгать по, бѣгать взадъ и впередъ; to—a mine, подводить подкопъ; to — away, убѣгать; to —

back, катиться назадъ (о пушкѣ); to — cold, охладѣвать; to — down, течь внизъ, ловить, поймать; to—off, убѣгать; to — out, выдвигать; to — risk, рисковать, подвергать опасности; to — round, обѣгать; to — straight in, направиться прямо къ берегу; to — upon a rock, сѣсть на камень; to — with violence after, стремительно бросаться за; he — s before his master, онъ бѣжитъ впереди своего хозяина; she ran her fingers, over the keys, она пробѣжала польцами по клавишамъ; the waves — very high, волны очень высоки.

runaway, бѣглецъ, дезертиръ.

rung, см. **ring**.

rupture, разрывъ.

rural, сельскій, деревенскій.

rush, стремленіе, порывъ; to —, бросаться, стремиться; to — in, врываться, нахлынуть; to — off, сшибать; to — up, вбѣжать.

Russia, Россія; — n, русскій.

rust, ржавчина; to —, ржавѣть, притупляться; — y, ржавый, заржавѣлый.

rustic, крестьянинъ, мужикъ; деревенскій, сельскій.

rut, колея.

rye, рожь; ржаной.

53

S.

's — is.
sable, чёрный.
sacerdotal, священниче-
ский.
sack, мѣшокъ.
sacrament, таинство,
тайна.
sacred, священный.
sacrifice, жертва; to —,
жертвовать.
sacrilegious, святотат-
ственный.
sad, печальный; — ly,
печально, очень.
saddle, сѣдло, сѣдель-
ный; — horse, верхо-
вая лошадь; — r, сѣ-
дельникъ, сѣдельный
мастеръ; — tree, лу-
ка, арчакъ.
safe, невредимый, безо-
пасный, надёжный,
въ безопасности; to
make —, обезопасить;
— guard, защита;
— ly, надёжно, спо-
койно, безвредно, не-
вредимо, въ сохран-
ности, благополучно;
— ty, безопасность; a
place of —, безопасное
мѣсто; in —ty, невре-
димо, въ сохранности,
благополучно; — ty
lamp, предохранитель-
ная лампа
sagacious, остроумный,
умный.
sagacity, остроуміе, умъ,
смѣтливость.
Sahara, Сахара.
said, см. say; упомяну-
тый; it is —, говорятъ;
he is —, говорятъ что
онъ.

sail, парусъ, судно; —
ahoy, судно видно! to
— идти подъ паруса-
ми, плыть, отплывать,
подпимать паруса; to
— away, to — from,
отплыть, уйти въ мо-
ре; to — over, пере-
плывать; — ing, пла-
ваніе, отплытіе, от-
плываніе; — or, ма-
тросъ, мореходецъ,
морякъ.
Saint, святой.
sake, ради, для; for the
— of, для.
salad, салатъ.
sale, продажа.
salient, выдающійся.
sally, порывъ, пылъ; to
— out, дѣлать вылазку.
salmon, лосось, сёмга.
salt, соль; солёный, со-
ляной; to — солить.
salubrity, здоровость.
salutation, привѣтствіе.
salute, привѣтствовать.
same, тотъ самый, оди-
накій.
sample, образчикъ, проба.
Samuel, Самуилъ.
sanctify, святить, освя-
щать.
sanction, утвержденіе,
подтвержденіе; to —,
утверждать, устано-
влять.
sanctuary, святилище.
sand, песокъ; — bank,
песчаная банка; — stone,
песчаникъ; — y, ры-
жій.
sandwich, сандвичъ (лом-
тикъ холоднаго мяса
между двумя кусками
хлѣба съ масломъ).
sang, см. sing.
sanguinary, кровожад-

ный, лютый, кровопро-
литный.
sanguine, горячій, пыл-
кій, увѣренный.
sanitary, санитарный,
медицинскій.
sank, см. sink.
Saracen, Саррацинъ.
sercastically, извитольно.
sat, см. sit.
satiate, насыщать.
satirist, сатирикъ, пи-
сатель сатиръ.
satisfaction, удовольствіе,
угода, удовлетвореніе.
satisfied, довольный.
satisfy, удовлетворять,
угождать.
sauce, саусъ; — pan, ка-
стрюля; — r, блюдечко.
savage, дикарь; дикій,
лютый, свирѣпый.
save, спасать, беречь,
сохранять; кромѣ, ис-
ключая; to — farther
trouble, чтобъ изба-
виться отъ дальнѣй-
шихъ хлопотъ.
savings, сбереженныя
деньги.
Saviour, Спаситель.
Sovoy, Савоія; of —, Са-
войскій.
saw, см. see.
Saxon, Саксонецъ; сак-
сонскій; — y, Саксо-
нія.
say, сказывать, говорить;
— on, говори!
scaffold, подмостки, лѣса,
эшафотъ.
scald, обваривать; — ing
water, кипятокъ.
scale, масштабъ, мѣрило,
мѣра.
scaly, чешуйчатый, че-
шуистый.
scamper, бѣжать, уби-

раться , навострить лыжи.

scanty, скудный, недостаточный.

scarce, рѣдкій; — или — ly, едва, только что, насилу, врядъ ли; with —ly an exception, съ весьма рѣдкими развѣ исключеніями.

scare away, отпугивать.

scarf, шарфъ.

scarlet, шарлаховый, яркокрасный.

scatter, разсѣвать, разбрасывать, распространять.

scene, сцена, зрѣлище, мѣсто дѣйствія; — гу, мѣстоположеніе.

scent, чутьё, слѣдъ; to get — of, отыскивать по чутью.

sceptic, скептикъ.

sceptre, скипетръ.

scheme, намѣреніе, планъ.

scholar, ученикъ, учёный.

scholastic, школьный, схоластическій.

school, училище, школа; after —, послѣ классовъ; — boy, ученикъ; — fellow, соученикъ, школьный товарищъ; — master, наставникъ.

science, наука.

scientific, учёный.

scoffer, насмѣшникъ, поноситель.

scold, бранить.

scorch, опалять.

score, счётъ, двадцать; on this, —, на счётъ этого, относительно сего.

scorn, презрѣніе.

Scot, —chman, —sman,

Шотландецъ ; — ch , — tish, шотландскій; the — ch, Шотландцы; — land, Шотландія.

scoundrel, подлецъ, бездѣльникъ.

scour, обходить, обѣгать, бродить по.

scourge, сѣчь, бичевать.

scrape, скоблить; to — away, отскоблить; to — down, соскребать, соскабливать.

scratch, царапать, чесать.

scream, кричать, визжать; to — out, закричать.

scriptural, библейскій.

Scripture , Священное Писаніе; he built his hopes on — ground, онъ основывалъ свои надежды на ученіиСвященнаго Писанія.

scruple, совѣстность, сомнѣніе, недоумѣніе , мнительность; — of conscience, угрызеніе совѣсти; without —, безъ зазрѣнія совѣсти.

scrupulous, совѣстный, мнительный.

scrutiny, разсматриваніе, взвѣшиваніе, преслѣдованіе.

scuffle, хватка, драка.

scullion, — boy, поварёнокъ.

sculptor, ваятель, скульпторъ.

scurrilous , шутливый, непристойный, неприличный.

scutcheon, гербовый щитъ.

scythe, коса.

sea, море, волненіе; морской; by —, моремъ;

— faring, морской,мореходный; — horse, моржъ,рѣчная лошадь; — man, морякъ, матросъ; — shore, — side, морской берегъ.

seal, печать; to —, печатать; to – any one's fate, рѣшать чью судьбу.

search, изслѣдованіе; to go in—of, идти искать; to —, обыскивать; искать; to—for, искать.

season, время года, время, пора; — able, своевременный; — ably, благовременно.

seat, стулъ, мѣсто, сидѣніе, намѣстье, дача, мѣстоположеніе, мѣстопребываніе; to have a —, засѣдать; to take a —, садиться; to —, сажать; to be — ed, сидѣть , находиться, засѣдать; be—ed, садитесь; firmly — ed, укрѣпленный, утвержденный.

seclusion, уединеніе.

second, секунда; второй, другой;upon—thought, по болѣе зрѣлому обсужденію; to —, помогать, поддерживать;— ly, во вторыхъ.

secrecy,тайность,сохраненіе въ тайнѣ.

secret, тайна, секретъ; —ly,тайно,внутренно.

secretary of state,статсъ секретарь.

secrete, таить,скрывать.

sect, секта, расколъ; — ion отдѣленіе, часть.

secure, увѣренный, безопасный; to —, обез-

опасить, охранять, о-
безпечивать, упрочи-
вать, закрѣплять, у-
тверждать; —ly, безо-
пасно, надёжно, увѣ-
ренно.

security, безопасность,
порука, обезпеченіе.

sedar, — bearer, сидаръ
(родъ камердинера въ
Индіи).

sedate, степенный, тихій.

sediment, осадка, оса-
докъ, отстой, подонки.

sedition, возмущеніе,
мятежъ, бунтъ.

seditious, возмутитель-
ный, мятежный.

seduce, обольщать, раз-
вращать.

sedulously, прилежно,
радиво, рачительно.

see, епархія; holy —,
папскій престолъ.

see, видѣть, увидѣть,
смотрѣть, посмотрѣть,
усматривать; to come
to —, навѣщать, про-
вѣдывать; to — after a
thing, смотрѣть за
чѣмъ, заботиться о
чёмъ; to—it right, за-
благоразсуждать; to —
out, выводить, прово-
жать; to — to, смо-
трѣть за, присматри-
вать; —ing that, при-
нимая во вниманіе что;
the dog saw the whole
affair in an instant,
собака тотчасъ смек-
нула всё дѣло; — ing,
зрѣніе.

seek, искать; to — out,
прискивать.

seem, казаться; he did

not — hear, онъ, ка-
залось, не слыхалъ.

seen, см. **see**.

Seine, Сена.

seize, схватывать, завладѣть чѣмъ, аресто-
вать, воспользоваться
(случаемъ, выгодой);
to — hold of, схваты-
вать; to — on, to —
upon, схватывать, за-
владѣть.

seldom, рѣдко.

select, отборный, вы-
борный; to —, выби-
рать, избирать; — ion,
выбираніе.

self, самъ, себя; — possession, самоувѣрен-
ность; — respect, ува-
женіе самаго себя.

sell, продавать; to — off,
распродавать.

semblance, видъ, подобіе.

seminary, семинарія.

senate, сенатъ.

send, посылать; to —
about, разсылать; to
— adrift, пускать на
волю; to — for, посы-
лать за; to — forth,
высылать, издавать,
выпускать; to — in,
всылать, присылать;
to — in arrows among,
пускать стрѣлы въ
кого; to — out, высы-
лать, отправлять; to
— over, пересылать.

seneschal, сенешалъ мар-
шалъ.

Sennacherib, Санхерибъ
(Сеннахеримъ).

sensation, ощущеніе, чувствованіе.

sense, чувство, умъ,
смыслъ; good —, здра-

вый разсудокъ; a man
of — умный человѣкъ;
— less, безъ чувствъ,
неразумный.

sensible, ощутительный,
умный, разумный; to
be — чувствовать.

sensitive, чувствительный.

sensuality, чувствен-
ность, сластолюбіе.

sent, см. **send**.

sentence, предложеніе,
фраза, приговоръ.

sentiment, чувство, мнѣніе, мысль.

sentinel, часовой; to
stand —, стоять на
часахъ.

separate, отдѣльный, о-
собенный; to —, раз-
лучать, отдѣлять, раз-
дѣлять.

separation, разлученіе,
разлука.

Sepoy, сипой (индейскій
солдатъ).

September, сентябрь.

serf, крѣпостной человѣкъ.

series, рядъ, коллекція.

serious, серіозный; — ly,
серіозно; — ness, се-
ріозность.

sermon, проповѣдь.

serpent, змѣя; — ine,
серпентинный (о мра-
морѣ).

servant, слуга, человѣкъ,
служанка; — girl, слу-
жанка; — s, прислуга.

serve, служить, годиться,
благопріятствовать об-
ходиться съ кѣмъ.

service, служба, служеніе, услуженіе, бого-
служеніе, заслуга, у-
слуга; to be of —, по-

служить, быть полезнымъ.

serving-man, слуга, человѣкъ.

servitude, рабство, подданство.

session, засѣданіе, время засѣданій; Sessions House, домъ для засѣданій, присутствіе.

set, приборъ, сервизъ, родъ, разрядъ, рядъ, шайка; to —, ставить, садиться или заходить (о солнцѣ); to — a distance, обозначать разстоянiе; to — an example, являть, подавать примѣръ; to — any one down for, записывать за кѣмъ; to — any one's limbs, вправлять члены; to — aside, устранять; to — at liberty, освобождать; to — at work, приводить въ дѣйствіе; to — by, устранить; to — eyes upon, устремлять глаза на что; to — fire to, зажигать; to — foot on, ступать на, ставить ногу на; to — forth, отправляться въ дорогу, выставлять, показывать; to be — home upon any one's heart, глубоко трогать чьё сердце; to — in, наставать, наступать; to — off, to — out, отправляться; to — on, напускать, подтравливать; to — spurs, пришпоривать; to — to, приниматься за дѣло; to — to work, сажать за работу, заставлять

работать; to — up, поднимать, учреждать, заводить, возстановлять; — ting of the sun, захожденіе или закатъ солнца.

settle, устроивать, поселять, устроиваться, поселяться, успокоиваться; to — an account, покончить счётъ, расчитываться; to — on any one, назначать кому; — d, постоянный; — ment, поселеніе; — r, поселенецъ, колонистъ.

seven, семь; — teen, семнадцать; — teenth, семнадцатый; — th, седьмой; — ty, семьдесятъ.

sever, отдѣлять, разлучать.

several, нѣкоторые, многіе, разный, отдѣльный; — ly, отдѣльно, особенно.

severe, строгій, жестокій, суровый, тяжелый; — ly, тяжело, сильно, строго.

severity, строгость.

Severn, Севернъ

Severus, Северъ.

sex, полъ.

shabby, ободранный.

shade, тѣнь, оттѣнокъ.

shaft, стрѣла.

shaggy, косматый, мохнатый.

shake, трясти, трястись, потрясаться, полоскать (о парусѣ); to — one's head, покачать головой; — of hand, пожатіе руки; to give a — потрясти.

shall, долженъ; означ. буд. вр. I — see, я увижу; прош. врем. **should**, долженъ былъ.

shallow, мелкій, неглубокій, пустой, поверхностный.

shame, стыдъ, срамъ; — ful, постыдный, срамный; — fully, постыдно, срамно.

shan't, см. shall not.

shape, видъ, образъ, форма, фигура; — less, безобразный.

share, доля, участіе; to — раздѣлять, дѣлиться, участвовать.

shark, окула.

sharp, рѣзкій, острый, пронзительный, строгій; — ness, остроконечность; — pointed, остроконечный.

shatter, разбивать въ дребезги, разбиваться.

shave, брить, стричь.

she, она.

sheaf, снопъ.

sheath, ножны.

shed, навѣсъ, сарай; to — изливать, проливать (кровь), испускать (лучи).

sheen, сіяніе, блескъ.

sheep, овца.

sheet, листъ, простыня, шкотъ; to —, покрывать; — iron, листовое желѣзо, жесть.

shelf, полка.

shell, черепъ.

shelter, прикрытіе, пріютъ, прибѣжище, убѣжище, пристанище; to —, прикрывать, защищать.

shepherd, пастухъ; пастушій.

sheriff, шерифъ, исправникъ, земскій судья.

sherry, хересъ.

shew, см. show.

shield, щитъ, защита.

shift, увёртка; to make —, успѣвать; to — избавляться, отдѣлываться отъ; to — to each other, передавать другъ другу; — ing, перемѣна мѣста.

shilling, шиллингъ.

shine, сіять, свѣтить, блестѣть; to — out, свѣтить сквозь, просвѣчивать.

ship, корабль, судно; — ment, перевозка (товаровъ) на суднѣ; — of war, военное судно; — ping, корабли, суда; — wrecked, претерпѣвшій крушеніе.

shire, графство (въ Англіи).

shirt, рубаха (мужская).

shiver, разбивать, разшибать, дрожать.

shoal, мелкое, неглубокое мѣсто, банка.

shock, столкновеніе, ударъ, потрясеніе, испугъ; gave her a sudden —, причинило ей внезапное сотрясеніе; to —, поражать, сталкиваться, ужасать, ужасаться.

shod, см. shoe.

shoe, башмакъ, подкова; to —, подковывать; — black, чистильщикъ сапоговъ; — ing, подковка; — maker, башмачникъ.

shone, см. shine.

shook, см. shake.

shoot, стрѣлять, застрѣливать; to go a — ing, отправляться на охоту.

shop, лавка, магазинъ; лавочный; — keeper, лавочникъ; — man, сидѣлецъ.

shore, берегъ.

short, короткій, краткій, близкій, малорослый, недостаточный; a — distance, въ небольшомъ разстояніи; a — walk, маленькая прогулка; to be little — of, не много не доходить; to fall —, см. fall; in —, однимъ словомъ; — ly, чрезъ короткое время, скоро; to — en, коротить; — sighted, близорукій, недальновидный.

shot, см. shoot; выстрѣлъ ядро, пуля, зарядъ (пушечный), снаряды.

should. прош. вр. всп. глаг. shall; означаетъ также условное накл. и переводится прошедш. временемъ главнаго глагола, предшествуемымъ частицею бы; I — see, я бы видѣлъ; we — not have gained, мы не выиграли бы; how we — act, какъ намъ надобно было дѣйствовать.

shoulder, плече.

shout, восклицаніе, крикъ; to —, кричать, восклицать.

shove, пихать, отталкивать.

shovel-board, игра въ камышки.

show, показъ, нарядъ, пышность, великолѣпіе; to —, показывать, указывать, являть, предъявлять, провожать, показываться; — ing, показаніе.

shower, ливень, дождь, дождичекъ; a heavy — of rain, проливной дождь; to —, лить, изливать, обливать, переливать дождемъ.

shown, см. show.

shred, лоскутокъ.

shrewdness, догадливость, острота, хитрость.

shriek, пронзительный крикъ; she uttered a faint —, она слабымъ голосомъ вскрикнула.

shrill, пронзительный.

shrink, отступать, уклоняться, бояться, страшиться; to — back, отскакивать.

shrouds, ванты.

shrub, кустъ.

shrunk, см. shrink.

shudder, содроганіе; with a — содрогаясь.

shut, затворять, запирать, смыкать, закрывать; to — up, затворять, запирать; — ter, ставень.

shuttle, ткацкій челнокъ.

Siberia, Сибирь.

Sicily, Сицилія.

sick, больной; — ly, хворый, болѣзненный; a — ly year, годъ, порождающій болѣзни; — ness, болѣзнь, тошнота.

side, бокъ, сторона, бортъ, берегъ, партія; — by —, другъ подлѣ друга, рядомъ; a river —, берегъ одной рѣки; at the — of the body, подлѣ тѣла; by any one's —, подлѣ кого.

siege, осада.

sigh, вздохъ; to give a —, вздохнуть; to —, вздыхать, стонать.

sight, видъ, зрѣніе, зрѣлище; in the — of, предъ лицёмъ; second — двойное зрѣніе, предчувствіе; the — of thine eyes, отрада очей твоихъ; to get — of, терять изъ виду.

sign, знакъ, признакъ, вывѣска; to —, подписывать.

signal, извѣстительный знакъ, сигналъ; — ly, чрезвычайно, славно, значительно.

signature, подпись.

signify, значить, означать.

silence, молчаніе; to —, заставлять молчать.

silent, безмолвный; — ly, молча.

silk, шёлкъ, шёлковый; — worm, шёлковичный червь.

silver, серебро; серебряный; — y, серебряный, серебристый.

similar, подобный.

simony, симонія, святокупство.

simple, простой, простодушный, одинъ только.

simplicity, простота, простодушіе.

simply, просто.

sin, грѣхъ;—ner, грѣшникъ.

since, тому назадъ, послѣ этого, съ тѣхъ поръ, съ тѣхъ поръ какъ, съ, послѣ, такъ какъ; not long —, недавно.

sincere, искренній.

sinew, сухая жила.

sing, пѣть.

singe, опалять.

single, единственный, единый, одинъ, одинъ только; you hardly know a — word, Вы не знаете почти ни одного слова; — horse, одноконный; to — out, выбирать.

singular, особенный, единственный, странный, причудливый.

sink, погружаться, опускаться, тонуть, потоплять, копать, изнемогать; to — with, изнемогать, быть удрученнымъ.

sip, попивать.

Sir, сударь, Милостивый Государь, Сэръ (титулъ баронета и кавалера). Какъ вопросъ Sir? значитъ: какъ? что Вы сказали? что Вамъ угодно?

Sire, Государь, Ваше Величество, отецъ.

sister, сестра; — in law, свояченица.

sit, сидѣть, садиться; to — down, садиться.

sith, см. **since**.

situate, — d, лежащій, находящійся, расположенный, состоящій; to

be — d, находиться; being so — d, находясь въ такомъ положеніи; she felt herself fearfully—d, она чувствовала, что положеніе ея было ужасное.

situation, положеніе, мѣсто, ситуація.

six, шесть; — pence, полушиллингъ; — teen, шестнадцать; — teen hundred, тысяча шесть сотъ; — teenth, шестнадцатый; — th, шестой; — ty, шестьдесять.

size, величина, размѣръ, ростъ.

skeleton, оставъ, скелетъ.

sketch, очеркъ, эскизъ, начертаніе, to —, начерчивать.

skilful, искусный, ловкій; — ly, искусно, ловко.

skill, искуство, ловкость, способность.

skin, кожа, кожица.

skip, прядать, скакать, прыгать.

skirmish, стычка; a — ing party, партія отправляющаяся на стычку.

skirt, край, конецъ, опушка.

skurry, (мѣстное выраженіе), см. **hurry**.

sky, небо; open to the —, подъ открытымъ небомъ; — blue, голубой цвѣтъ.

slacken, ослаблять, убавлять, замедлять.

slackness, медленность, нерадивость.

slain, см. slay.

slap, тузить, шлёпать.

slash, рубить.

slate, аспидъ, шиферъ, аспидная доска.

slaughter, кровопролитіе; to —, бить, убивать.

slave, невольникъ, рабъ; to —, утомляться работая; — гу, невольничество, рабство.

slay, убивать, умерщвлять.

sledge, сани.

sleep, сонъ; to —, спать, почивать; — er, спящій; —y, сонный; сонливый.

slender, стройный.

slept, см. sleep.

slew, см. slay.

slice, (тоненькій) кусокъ.

slide, кататься (польду), скользить.

slight, незначительный, малый; — ly, легко, слегка, немного.

slily, хитростію, исподтишка.

sling, подвязка; to —, подвязывать, подвѣшивать, поднимать, поднимать на стропахъ, положить стропы на что нибудь.

slip, пропускать; if I let — если я дамъ ускользнуть; — per, туфель.

sloop, шлюпъ (одномачтовое судно); — of war, военный шлюпъ.

slope, откосъ, наклонъ, скатъ, покать, покатость.

slough, топь, лужа.

slow, медленный; to be —, медлить, мѣшкать;

by — degrees, мало по малу; — ly, медленно, тихо.

sluggish, лѣнивый, вялый.

slumber, дремота, сонъ; to —, дремать, спать, почивать.

slung, см. sling.

smack, хлопать; — went the whip, захлопалъ кнутъ.

small, малый, маленькій, мелкій, маловажный; — beer, полпиво.

smell, запахъ; to—, пахнуть, нюхать; — ing, обоняніе; —ing bottle, душница, флакончикъ.

smelt, см. smell.

smile, улыбаться; to — upon, благопріятствовать.

smite, ударять, поражать, толкать, карать, наказывать, сталкиваться; to — from, to — off, срѣзывать, смахнуть.

smock frock, балахонъ, армякъ, блузъ.

smoke, дымъ; to—, курить, дымиться; — г, куритель табаку, курильщикъ.

smooth, гладкій; — ly, плавно.

smuggle into, тайно вводить.

Smyrna, Смирна.

smack, доля; to go — s, дѣлиться.

snare, сѣть, силокъ, западня.

snatch, хватать; to — away, to—out, выхватывать, вырывать; to — up, подхватывать.

sneer, зубоскалить, насмѣхаться надъ кѣмъ.

snipe, куликъ, бекасъ.

snore, храпѣть.

snort, фыркать (о лошади).

snow, снѣгъ; — clad, покрытый снѣгомъ.

snuff-box, табакерка.

snug, уютный.

so, такъ, такимъ образомъ, и такъ, столь; — many, — much, столько; — am I, и я также; by a few feet or —, нѣсколькими футами или около того; in an hour or —, чрезъ часъ времени или около того; to do —, сдѣлать это.

soap, мыло.

sob, рыдать.

sober, трезвый, воздержный, степенный; to—, протрезвлять.

sobriety, трезвость, воздержность.

social, общественный.

society, общество.

soft, мягкій, тихій, спокойный; — ly, тихо; to — en, умягчать, смягчать, смягчаться.

soil, почва, земля; to—, марать, замарывать.

sojourn, пребывать.

solar, солнечный.

sold, см. sell.

soldier, солдатъ, воинъ; — ship, солдатское званіе.

sole, единственный, единый; — ly, единственно.

solemn, торжественный; — ly, торжественно.

solicit, просить, убѣдительно просить; — ude, попеченіе, опасеніе; with painful — ude, съ прискорбіемъ и опасеніемъ.

solid, основательный; — ity, твёрдость, основательность, надёжность.

solitary, уединенный.

solitude, уединеніе.

Solomon, Соломонъ.

solve, рѣшать, изъяснять.

sombre, мрачный.

some, нѣкоторый, какой нибудь; нѣсколько, немного; —soup, супу; at - distance, въ небольшомъ разстояніи; — body, — one, нѣкто, кто-нибудь; — thing, нѣчто, что-то, кое-что, что нибудь; thing like, нѣсколько походящій на; — times, иногда; — what, нѣчто, что нибудь, нѣсколько.

son, сынъ; — in law, зять; great grand —, правнукъ.

sonata, соната.

song, пѣсня, пѣніе.

sonnet, сонетъ.

soon, скоро, рано, вскорѣ; as — as, лишь только, какъ только, коль скоро; —er, скорѣе; no — er than, лишь только . . . какъ уже.

soothe, ласкать, утѣшать.

sopha, софа.

Sophocles, Софоклъ.

Sorbonne, прежній ду-

ховный факультетъ въ Парижѣ.

sore, больно, крайне, весьма.

sorrow, печаль, горесть, скорбь.

sorry, печальный; I am very —, мнѣ очень жаль.

sort, родъ, сортъ, образъ; all — s of, всякаго рода.

so't, см. so it.

sought, см. seek.

soul, душа.

sound, звукъ; здоровый, крѣпкій, твердый, основательный; a—believer, твёрдо вѣрующій; to —, трубить (въ трубу), звучать, отзываться, отдаваться; — ly, крѣпко, сильно·

soup, супъ.

sour, кислый, угрюмый.

source, источникъ.

south, югъ, южный, къ югу;—east, юго-восточ. ный, къ югу-востоку; — ern, южный; — ward, къ югу.

sovereign, царствующая особа, владѣтель, государь, царь, соверень (ок. 7 руб. с.); верховный, высшій.

sow, сѣять.

space, пространство, промежутокъ, продолженіе (времени).

spade, заступъ, лопата.

Spain, Испанія.

spake, см. speak.

Spaniard, Испанецъ.

spaniel, лягавая собака.

Spanish, испанскій.

spare, бережливый, эко-

номный, умѣренный, скудный; to —, щадить, беречь, избавлять, сохранять; лишній.

sparing, бережливый, экономный, умѣренный.

sparkle, блистать, сверкать.

sparrow, воробей.

speak, говорить, произносить; to — for any one, вступаться за кого; —er, говорящій, ораторъ.

spear, копье, пика; — head, остріе копья.

special, особенный, чрезвычайный.

specie, монета, наличныя деньги.

species, родъ.

specimen, образчикъ, образецъ.

specious, благовидный.

speck, пятно.

spectacle, зрѣлище.

spectator, зритель.

spectrum, изображеніе.

speculation, размышленіе, спекуляція.

speculator, умозритель, созерцатель.

sped, см. speed.

speech, слово, языкъ, рѣчь.

speed, поспѣшность, быстрота, прыткость; at full —, во всю прыть, во весь опоръ; to be in—, спѣшить, торопиться; to —, спѣшить, —ily, поспѣшно, скоро, быстро;—у, спѣшный, поспѣшный, скорый.

spell, складывать.

54

spend, издержвать, истрачвать, истощать, проводить.

spent, см. **spend.**

spice, пряный;—s, пряность.

spider, паукъ.

spin, прясть, вертѣться, струиться; . — ning, пряденіе.

spinage, шпинатъ.

spiral, винтовой, спиральный.

spire, шпицъ (у башни).

spirit, духъ, душа, бодрость, спиртъ; a woman of—, женщина съ характеромъ; —s, крѣпкіе напитки; in—s, въ духѣ; in high —s. къ весьма хорошемъ расположеніи духа; —ed, смѣлый, отважный; high -- ed, пылкій, горячій, гордый; — ual, духовный.

spit out, выплёвывать.

spite, злоба, досада; in —of, вопреки, на зло, не смотря на.

splash, забрызгвать.

splendid, великолѣпный.

splendour, блескъ, великолѣпіе.

split, раскалывать, треснуть, разбивать.

spoil, добыча, грабёжъ; to—, портпть.

spoke, см. **speak.**

spoken, см. **speak.**

sponge, губка.

spongy, губчатый, ноздреватый.

spoon, ложка.

sport, игра, забава, увеселеніе, потѣха, псовал охота

spot, пятно, мѣсто.

spouse, супруга, жена.

spout, разбрызгвать.

sprang, см. **spring.**

sprawl, барахтаться, валяться.

spray, вѣтка, хворостъ, брызги волнъ; to —, брызгать, пѣниться.

spread, растягивать разсыпать, распростра- нять, разглашать, покрывать, накрывать (столъ), распространяться, разсыпаться; to — a cloth, постилать скатерть; to — around, повсемѣстно, распространяться.

sprig, вѣточка.

sprightly, живой, рѣзвый, весёлый.

spring, весна, пружина; to—, скакать, прыгать, показывать (течь), происходить; to — back, скакать назадъ; to —one's rattle, вертѣть свою трещётку; to—out, выскакивать; to — towards any one, кидаться на кого; to—up, возрастать, подниматься.

sprinkle, окроплять, опрыскивать.

sprung, см. **spring.** •

spun, см. **spin.**

spunging house, временная тюрьма для несостоятельныхъ должниковъ.

spur, шпора; to set — s, пришпоривать; — rier, шпорникъ, шпорный мастеръ.

spurn, пинать ногою, презирать.

spy, усматривать.

squander, расточать.

square, скверъ, огороженный садикъ на площади, квадратный; to - , отсыпать квадратно.

squeeze, жать, сжимать; to—into, втискиваться, втираться.

squire, щитоносецъ, оруженосецъ, вассалъ, помѣщикъ.

St., сокр. **saint,** святой, святая; — Andrew, Св. Андрей; at —Andrew's, въ университетѣ Св. Андрея; — Bittel. вѣроятно сокр. St. Botolph, Св. Ботольфъ; —Christopher, островъ Св. Христофора; — David, Св. Давидъ;—Frances, Св. Францискъ;— George, Св. Георгій; — Giles, Св. Эгидій; — Helena, островъ Св. Елены; —John, Св. Іоаннъ; —Lawrence, Св. Лаврентій; — Louis, Св. Людовикъ; — Lucia, островъ Св. Люціи; —Margaret, Св. Маргарита; — Mary, Св. Марія; — Paul, Св. Павелъ;— Peter, Св. Петръ.

stab, закалывать, произать, прокалывать.

stability, твердость, прочность, постоянность.

stable, конюшня.

stage, ступень, степень, сцена, театръ, поприще, станція; —

coach, дилижансъ; — waggon, почтовая телега, обозная повозка.

stagger, колебать, изюмлять.

stagnant, застойный, стоячій.

stain, пятно; to —, пятнать, красить, крапать, заплтнывать; — ed glass, расписанное стекло; — ed with vices, погрязнувшій въ порокахъ.

staircase, лѣсница, крыльцѣ.

stairs, лѣстница, крыльцѣ; down —, въ низъ; up—, на верхъ.

stake, ставить (ставку).

stalk, стебель; to —, шагать.

stall, мясная лавка.

stamp, топаніе; with a — of the foot, топая ногой.

stand, стоянie, стойка, мѣсто; to —, стоять, останавливаться; to — any one's friend, быть чьимъ другомъ, оказать кому дружескую услугу; to — on end, стоять дыбомъ (о волосахъ); to— over any one, наклоняться надъ кѣмъ; to—still, останавливаться; to—upon the defensive, обороняться, держать себя въ оборонительномъ положеніи, дѣйствовать оборонительно; —ing, постоянный, неизмѣнный; —ing up, стоя.

standard, знамя, штандартъ.

staple, складочное мѣсто; главный.

star, звѣзда; —chamber, звѣздная палата.

starboard, правая сторона (корабля).

stare, таращить глаза, пристально смотрѣть на кого.

start, вспыхъ, отрывка; by—s, отрывками; to —, вскакивать, встрепенуться, отправляться; to — back, отскочить назадъ; to —off, отправляться, пускаться въ дорогу; to—up, вскапщать; we could not—it, мы не могли сдвинуть ее съ мѣста; —ing, отправленіе.

startle, смущать, устрашать, озадачивать.

starvation, голодная смерть, изнеможеніе; to expire from —, умереть отъ голоду или голодною смертію.

starve, голодать, уписъ голоду; — d, изморённый, голодный.

state, состояніе, положеніе, государство, чинъ, сословіе, званіе, штатъ, великолѣпіе, пышность, величіе; an affair of—, государственное дѣло; to —, утверждать, предлагать, сказывать, свидѣтельствовать; — ly, великолѣпный, пышный; — ment, изложеніе, представленіе; — prison, тюрьма для государственныхъ преступниковъ; — man,

мужъ государственный, политикъ.

station, станція, мѣсто, постъ, положеніе (въ свѣтѣ); to —, ставить; — ary, постоянный, неподвижный.

statistical; статистическій.

statue, статуя.

stature, станъ, ростъ.

statute, узаконенный.

staunch, постоянный, вѣрный.

stave, расшибаться.

stay, подпора, штагъ; to —, оставаться, пробывать, останавливать; to — behind, отставать отъ другихъ, не приходить.

stead, мѣсто; — fast, стойкій, твердый, постоянный; — y, постоянный, въ одномъ положеніи (о килѣ); to keep the ship's head—y, держать корабль носомъ противъ вѣтра.

steal, красть; to — away, похищать; to — into, вкрадываться.

steam, паръ; to —, дымиться, испускать пары; — boat, — er, пароходъ; — packet, паровой пакетботъ.

steed, конь.

steel, сталь; стальной.

steep, крутой.

steeple, колокольня.

steer, править, управлять; — age, передняя каюта.

stem, стволъ.

step, шагъ, ступень, ступенька, слѣдъ, поступокъ; to make this —, поступпть такпмъ образомъ; to —, ступать, ходпть; to—before, подступать; to —forth, to —forward, выступать впередъ; to—in, входить; to—into the boat, сѣсть въ лодку; to — out, ходить, выступать; — mother, мачиха.

Stephen, Стефанъ, Стефанъ.

sterile, неплодоносный.

sterling, стерлпнгъ, стерлинговая монета.

stern, корма; суровый, непреклонный, серьёзный, строгій.

steward, дворецкій, каютъ-юнга.

stick, палка, трость; to —fast, увязнуть; to—round, оклеивать, облепливать; to — up, прилѣплять, прибивать.

stiff, окоченѣлый, прпнужденный, натянутый; to—en, дѣлать тугпмъ плп жёсткимъ.

stifle, задушать.

still, тихій, смирный, спокойный; ещё, всё ещё, при всёмъ томъ, до сихъ поръ, всегда; но, однако; to be —, молчать; to grow —, утихать; to sit —, сидѣть смирно, не трогаться съ мѣста; —ness, молчаливость; — room maid, горничная.

stimulate, возбуждать, поощрять.

stipend, жалованіе, окладъ.

stipulation, постановленіе.

stir, движеніе, шевеленіе, волненіе, возмущеніе, мятежъ; to—, мѣшать (уголья).

stirrup, стремя.

stitch, стёжка; to —, стегать, шпть.

stock, запасъ.

stocking, чулокъ.

stolen, тайный; см. также to steal.

stomach, желудокъ, гнѣвъ, сердце.

stone, камень; каменный; — dead, совершенно мёртвый.

stony, каменный, каменистый.

stood, см. stand.

stool, скамейка, подножіе.

stoop, нагибаться, снпсходить.

stop, остановка, препятствіе, помѣха, точка; to —, останавливать, — ся, оставаться; stop! стой! to — one's ears, затыкать уши.

store, запасъ.

storm, буря; a — of thunder and lightning, гроза; to —, штормовать, брать приступомъ; — ish, — y, бурный.

story, повѣсть, разказъ, сказка, этажъ; there is a courious — told, разказываютъ любопытный анекдотъ.

stout, мужественный, дюжій.

stove, печка.

stow, укладывать, нагружать.

a **straggling** line, растянутая линія.

straight, прямой; прямо.

strain, голосъ, пѣсня, тонъ; to—, напрягать силы, напрягаться.

strait, узкій; —s, проливъ.

strand, берегъ (морской), набережная.

strange, странный, удивительный; — г, чужой, незнакомый, незнакомецъ; — 's gallery, галерея для чужихъ или гостей.

stratagem, военная хитрость.

strath, долина.

straw, солома; — coloured, палевый; — covered, соломою покрытый.

stray, бродпть; a — ed dog, забѣжавшая собака.

streak, полоса.

stream, потокъ, рѣка; to—, струпться, течь, развѣваться; — er, вымпелъ.

street, улица, уличный; —corner, уголъ улицы; —door, дверь въ улицу, парадная дверь.

strength, сила; from the—, въ сплу; to—en, укрѣплять, успливать.

strenuously, горячо, сильно.

stretch, растягивать, распростирать, растопыривать, простираться; to — out, распростираться; to lie — ed

out, лежать растянув-
шись.

strew, сыпать, разсы-
пать; to—about, раз-
сыпать; to—with, усы-
пать.

strewn, см. strew.

strict, строгій, точный;
—ly, строго; — ness,
строгость.

strike, поражать, уда-
рять, бить, попадать,
ударяться, набѣжать,
наткнуться на мель;
to — any one a blow,
наносить кому ударъ;
to—a fire, высѣкать
огонь; to—away, от-
биваться; to--through,
прошибать.

striking, поразительный.

string, тетива (у лука).

strip, полоска, лоску-
токъ; to—, обнажать,
лишать чего, раздѣ-
ваться; to— off, ски-
дывать.

strive, силиться, усили-
ваться, стараться, бо-
роться, состязаться.

stroke, ударь; to—, гла-
дить, поглаживать; I
could not swim a —,
я не могъ подаваться
впередъ ни на одинъ
размахъ.

strong. крѣпкій, силь-
ный, твёрдый; a —
resemblance, большое
сходство; —box, же-
лѣзный сундукъ; —
ly, сильно.

strove, см. strive.

strewed, см. strew.

strown, см. storw.

struck, пораженный, см.
strike.

structure, зданіе.

struggle, борьба; to —,
бороться.

stud, украшать, усы-
пать.

study, ученіе, изученіе,
наука, кабинетъ; to
—, заниматься (нау-
ками), учиться, об-
учаться въ универси-
тетѣ, изучать, разби-
рать, обдумывать.

stuff, матеріл, ткань,
матеріалъ.

stumble, спотыкаться;
to—on, наткнуться.

stumbling-stone, камень
преткновенія.

stump, культя.

stun, оглушать.

stupendous, огромный,
изумительный.

stupidity, глупость, без-
толковость.

sturdy, здоровый, дю-
жій, упорный.

style, слогъ (архитек-
турный), стиль; to—,
называть, наименовы-
вать.

subdue, преодолѣвать,
побѣждать, покорять,
укрощать.

subject, подданный, пред-
метъ, тема; под-
властный, подверженный,
подлежащій; to—, под-
вергать; —ion, поко-
реніе.

subjugation, покореніе.

sublime, возвышенный,
выспренный, величе-
ственный.

submerge, затоплять.

submission, покорность,
послушаніе.

submissive, покорный,
покор ивый.

submit, предавать, пред-
лагать, покоряться,
подвергаться.

subordinate, подчинен-
ный, низшаго достоин-
ства.

subsequently, потомъ,
послѣ.

subsidies, субсидіи, де-
нежное пособіе.

subsistence, пропитаніе.

substance, вещество,
сущность, содержаніе.

substitute, замѣнять,
подмѣнивать, подло-
жить.

suburb, предмѣстіе.

succeed, послѣдовать,
наслѣдовать, быть
преемникомъ, успѣ-
вать, удаваться, имѣть
успѣхъ.

success, успѣхъ, удача;
—ful, успѣшный; —
fully, успѣшно, удач-
но; —ion, рядъ, чере-
довой порядокъ, на-
слѣдіе, наслѣдованіе
(престола); — ion to
the throne, престоло-
наслѣдіе; in — ion,
сряду; —ive, послѣдо-
вательный; — ively,
послѣдовательно;—or.
преемникъ, наслѣд-
никъ.

succour, помощь, под-
крѣпленіе.

such, такой, таковъ, та-
ковой; as —, самъ по
себѣ; — as, такой ка-
кой, такой который,
тѣ которые.

sudden, внезапный, не-
ожиданный; on a —,
all of a—, —ly, вне-
запно, вдругъ.

Suetonius, Светоній.

suffer, страдать, претерпѣвать, дозволить; —
er, страдалецъ; —ing,
страданіе.
suffice, быть достаточ-
нымъ, стать на что.
sufficient, достаточный;
— ly, достаточно.
suffocate, задушать, задыхаться.
suffrage, голосъ (при из-
бираніи).
sugar, сахаръ; —. basin,
сахарница; — cane, са-
харный тростникъ; —
tongs, щипцы для са-
хару.
suggest, надоумѣвать,
внушать.
suit, приборъ, полное
число; a — of clothes,
полное платье, нарядъ;
to—, приноравливать,
годиться, соотвѣтство-
вать, согласоваться;
to—to any one's mind,
угодить кому; this piece
will — your taste,
этотъ кусокъ будетъ
Вамъ по вкусу;—able,
приличный, сообраз-
ный, соотвѣтствен-
ный; — ably, соотвѣт-
ственно.
suite, свита.
sultan, султанъ.
sultry, жаркій, знойный,
душный.
sum, сумма; to—up the
evidence, сличить всѣ
показанія.
summer, лѣто; лѣтній;
in the — , лѣтомъ; a
—'s morning, лѣтнее
утро.
summon, звать, приглашать, созывать, тре-

бовать (сдачи); — s,
требованіе.
sumptuous, пышный.
sun, солнце; — dial, сол-
нечные часы;—down,
—set, захожденіе солн-
ца; — rise, восхожде-
ніе солнца.
Sunday, воскресеніе.
in **sunder**, на двое, пополамъ.
sung, см sing.
sunk, см. sink.
sup, ужинать; — per,
ужинъ.
superb, великолѣпный,
величавый.
superintend, надзирать,
наблюдать за, присма-
тривать за; — ence,
главный надзоръ.
superior, начальникъ, настоятель; верхній, выс-
шій, большій; —, —
to, превосходящій; to
be — то, превышать,
превосходить; — ity,
превосходство.
supersede, замѣнять.
superstition, суевѣріе.
superstitious, суевѣрный.
supplant, вытѣснять, вы-
живать.
supplementary, приба-
вочный.
supply, доставка, доста-
вленіе, запасъ, посо-
біе, средства, подкрѣ-
пленіе; to —, снаб-
жать, доставлять, за-
пасать, дополнять, по-
могать, устранять; to
— the place, замѣ-
нять
support, подпора, опора,
помощь; for —, чтобъ
не упасть; to —, под-
пирать, поддерживать,

содержать, пропиты-
вать; — er, щитодер-
жатель.
suppose, полагать, предполагать.
supposition, предположеніе.
supremacy, верховная
власть, первенство.
supreme, верховный.
suppress, утушать, у-
крощать, удерживать,
останавливать, умал-
чивать.
sure, вѣрный, надёжный,
непогрѣшительный; на-
дёжно; — enough, въ
самомъ дѣлѣ; I am —,
я увѣренъ; be — not
to forget, смотрите не
забудьте! he is — to
wake him, онъ не-
премѣнно его разбу-
дитъ; to be —, конеч-
но; — ly, навѣрно,
конечно.
surf, бурунъ по берегу
или по камню.
surface, поверхность.
surge, зыбь, толчея, (водяной) валъ.
surgeon, хирургъ.
surly, угрюмый, огрыз-
ливый.
surmount, преодолѣвать,
превышать.
surname, прозывать.
surpass, превосходить,
превышать.
surprise, surprize, удивленіе, изумленіе, не-
чаянное нападеніе; to
— нечаянно напасть
на кого; —d удивлён-
ный; to be — d, уди-
вляться.
surprising, удивительный, изумительный.

surrender, сдача; to —, сдавать, сдаваться, покоряться; he summoncd to —, онъ требовалъ сдачи.

surround, окружать.

survey, обозрѣвать, осматривать.

survive, переживать; — r, переживающій, остающійся въ живыхъ.

suspect, подозрѣвать, опасаться, бояться.

suspend, вѣшать, прекращать.

suspension bridge, висячій или цѣпной мостъ.

suspicion, подозрѣніе; having no —, не подозрѣвая.

sustain, поддерживать, претерпѣвать, понести (потерю).

swallow, проглатывать.

swam, см. swim.

swamp, болото.

swan, лебедь; лебединый, лебяжій.

swarm, роиться, кишѣть, копышиться, толпиться.

swarthy, смуглый.

sway, владѣніе, правленіе, власть, вліяніе.

swear, присягать, приводить къ прясягѣ, клясться-божиться; to —upon, клясться чѣмъ; to be sworn, присягать.

sweat, потъ.

Sweden, Швеція.

Swedish, шведскій.

sweep, трубочистъ; to — мести выметать, мчаться; to — away, уносить, похищать: to — down, сносить;

to — out, выметать; — er, метальщикъ.

sweet, сладкій, пріятный, милый; to — en; услаждать; — tempered, кроткій

swell, прибываніе, зыбь, волненіе; to —, пухнуть, надуваться, надмеваться, пыщиться, увеличиваться, увеличивать.

swept, см. sweep.

swift, шибкій, быстрый, скорый; — ly, шибко, быстро; — ness, быстрота, скорость.

swim, плавать; to — for one's life, спастись вплавь; — mer, пловецъ.

swine, свинья.

swing, махать, качать, качаться.

swoon, впадать въ обморокъ.

sword, мечъ, шпага; — in hand, съ мечемъ въ рукѣ; to put to the — см. put.

swore, см. swear.

sworn, см. swear.

swum, см. swim.

swung, см. swing.

sympathize, соболѣзновать, сочувствовать.

sympathy, сочувствіе, симпатія.

symptom, признакъ.

system, система; —building, приведеніе въ систему.

T.

table, столъ.

tackle, тали.

taffrail, гакабортъ.

tail, хвостъ.

tailor, портной.

take, взять, брать, принимать, носить, возить, вести, завладѣвать; — your bread and cheese with us, откушайте съ нами; — your seat, садитесь; do you — sugar, пьёте ли Вы (чай, кофе) съ сахаромъ? it would—, потребность было; I was — n off the barge, я былъ взятъ съ баржи; their project had — n wind, замыслъ ихъ пронюхали; the alarm —n, тревога произведенная или причиненная; what will you — to eat, что Вы желаете кушать? to — across, перевозить, переправлять; to — advantage of, пользоваться чѣмъ; to — aim, прицѣливаться; to — a nap, соснуть; to — an oath, давать или учинять присягу, присягать; to — any one's life, лишить кого жизни; to—any one's part, приставать къ чьей сторонѣ; to — any one's place, занимать чье мѣсто; to— any one's picture, снимать портретъ съ кого; to — a peep, глядѣть украдкою; to —arms, поднять, браться за оружіе; to — a run over the island, перебѣжать чрезъ островъ; to — a seat, садиться; to — a step, принять мѣру; to — a view, осматривать; to

— a walk, прогули-
ваться; to — away, у-
бирать, отнимать; to
— away the reproach,
избавлять отъ наре-
канія; to—by surprise,
настигнуть въ рас-
плохъ; to — care, бе-
речься; to — care of,
пещись, заботиться;
to — dinner, обѣдать;
to — down, снимать,
сталкивать; to— exer-
cise, дѣлать моціонъ;
to — fire, загораться;
to—from, снимать съ,
отнимать что у кого;
to—hold of, завладѣть
чѣмъ; to — in, прини-
мать, впускать, вби-
рать; to — in execu-
tion, конфисковать; to
— notice, замѣчать;
обращать вниманіе; to
— occasion, пользо-
ваться случаемъ; to—
off, снимать; to — off
any one's likeness,
снимать портретъ съ
кого; to — on, тоско-
вать; to—one's advice,
слушать чей либо со-
вѣтъ, слушать кого;
to — one's ease, отды-
хать; to — one's re-
venge on, отмщать
кому (за); to — one's
stand, стать, занять
мѣсто; to — orders,
вступать въ духовное
званіе; to—out, выни-
мать; to—pains, тру-
диться, стараться,брать
на себя трудъ; to —
pity, сжалиться; to —
place, происходить,
случаться, бывать; to
pleasure, находить у-

довольствіе; to — poi-
son, отравляться; to
— possession, завла-
дѣвать; to — prisoner,
взять въ плѣнъ; to—
refuge, искать убѣжи-
ще, пріютиться; to —
rest, отдыхать; to —
revenge, мстить, от-
мщать; to — shelter,
искать убѣжище, скры-
ваться; to — tea, чай
пить; to — the lead,
быть предводителемъ
или вождемъ; to — the
opportunity, пользо-
ваться случаемъ; to —
the place of any one,
занимать чьё мѣсто;
to — the shortest way,
избирать ближайшую
дорогу, ѣхать по бли-
жайшей дорогѣ; to —
time, требовать вре-
мени; to — to, браться
за, убираться; to — to
another trade, взяться
за другое ремесло; to
— to flight, обращать-
ся въ бѣгство; to—to
jail, сажать въ тюрь-
му; to — to one's heels
пуститься бѣжать, на-
вострить лыжи; to —
to pieces, разбирать,
разнимать; to—to the
road, сдѣлаться раз-
бойникомъ; to — to
wife, жениться на
комъ; to — up, подни-
мать, заводить, начи-
нать; to — up one's
night's lodging, посе-
литься на ночь; to —
up one's residence,
поселиться.

taken, см. take.

tale, повѣсть, разсказъ,
сказка.
talent, дарованіе, даръ,
талантъ.
talisman, талисманъ.
talk, разговоръ; to —,
говорить, разговари-
вать.
tall, высокій, высоко-
рослый.
tallow, сало.
Tally-ho, охотничій
кликъ, которымъ бу-
дятъ собакъ.
tame, ручной, смирный;
to—, укрощать, усми-
рять, обуздывать; —
ness, ручное состоя-
ніе.
tankard, кружка (имѣю-
щая крышку).
tap, кранъ (у бочки);
to—, трепать, тюкать;
to — on the shoulder,
трепать по плечу.
taper, восковая свѣча.
tapestry, обои, шпале-
ры.
tar, смола, тиръ, ма-
тросъ; — pawling,
брезентъ.
Tarquin, Тарквиній.
tarry, пробывать, оста-
ваться.
tart, тортъ.
tartan, тартанъ (ма-
терія).
task, заданная робота,
урокъ, занятіе, обя-
занность; to —, зада-
вать урокъ или ра-
боту.
tassel, кисть, кисточка.
taste, вкусъ, вкушеніе,
склонность; to—, по-
пробовать.
tasting, вкусъ.
taught, см. teach.

taunting, попрекатель-
ный.

tavern, трактиръ; —
chair, стулъ въ трак-
тирѣ.

tax, дань, подать, так-
са; to—any one with,
обвинять кого въ чёмъ;
—ation, наложеніе по-
датей, обложеніе по-
датью, налогъ.

tea, чай; чайный; —
things, чайный прп-
боръ.

teach, учить, научать; —
—ableness, переимчи-
вость.

teakwood, желѣзное де-
рево, тикъ.

team, упряжь; a — of
cattle, пара воловъ.

tear, слеза.

tear, рвать, раздирать;
to — at full gallop,
скакать во всю прыть;
to — away, понести;
to — down, сдрать,
повалить; to — from,
срывать; to — off,
оторвать; to — one's
self away, вырывать-
ся; to—out, вырывать;
to — to pieces, разор-
вать въ куски.

tedious, скучный, тя-
гостный.

tell, сказывать, гово-
рить, разсказывать; to
—fortunes, гадать.

temper, нравъ.

temperature, темпера-
тура.

tempest, буря, штормъ.

temple, храмъ, високъ.

temporal, временной,
свѣтскій.

tempt, соблазнять, ис-
кушать, побуждать,

пробовать, пытаться;
— ation, искушеніе,
соблазнъ.

ten, десять; — fold, де-
сятеричный; —th, де-
сятый.

tenacious of, упорно
стоящій за.

tend, смотрѣть за кѣмъ
или чѣмъ, клониться,
стремиться, служить;
— ency, клоненіе,
стремленіе.

tender, чувствительный,
нѣжный, заботливый;
to — one's life, до-
рожить жизнію; — hear-
tedness, мягкосердечіе.

tennis, игра въ мячики.

tenor, tenour, продолже-
ніе; —of life, жизнь,
образъ жизни.

tent, палатка, тентъ.

term, слово, терминъ,
выраженіе, условіе,
договоръ, срокъ, вре-
мя; friendly — s, дру-
жественныя сношенія;
the — of life, продол-
жительность жизни;
to—, нарекать, назы-
вать; to—inate, окан-
чивать, прекращаться;
— ination, оканчива-
ніе, край, конецъ.

terrestrial, земной.

terrible, terrific, ужас-
ный, страшный.

terrify, устрашать.

territory, область, вла-
дѣніе, земля.

terror, ужасъ, страхъ.

test, испытаніе; to put
to the —, испробовать,
испытывать; to—, пс-
пытывать.

thriving, успѣшный.

throne, престолъ, тронъ;

testify, свидѣтельство-
вать, показывать.

testimony, свидѣтельство;
to bear one's —, сви-
дѣтельствовать.

Teutonic, Тевтонскій
языкъ.

text, текстъ.

Thames, Темза.

than, нежели, чѣмъ;
more — three, болѣе
трёхъ; without any
other reward—, безъ
всякаго другаго на-
гражденія кромѣ.

thane, (англосаксонскій)
баронъ; — dom, ба-
ронія, правленіе.

thank, благодарить; —
heaven, —God, слава
Богу, благодаря Бога;
I will — you for, я
попрошу у Васъ; —s,
благодарность.

that, тотъ, этотъ; ко-
торый; что; мн. those,
тѣ.

thatch, кровельная со-
лома.

that's, см. that is.

the, членъ опред.; тотъ,
этотъ; —.. — чѣмъ..
тѣмъ.

theatre, театръ, попри-
ще, сцена.

thee, тебя, тебѣ.

theft, кража, воровство.

their, ихъ, — s, ихъ,
свой.

them, ихъ, имъ; with—,
съ собой; — selves,
сами, они сами, себя.

theme, тема, задача,
тезисъ.

then, тогда, въ то время,
потомъ, послѣ, въ та-
комъ случаѣ, и такъ;
till —, до того вре-

мени; —се, оттуда —;
ceforth, съ тѣхъ поръ,
впредь.
theological, богословскій.
theology, богословіе.
theory, теорія.
there, тамъ; —, — is,
вотъ! на! —is, — are,
есть, имѣется, имѣют-
ся; — was not, не
было; —fore, слѣдова-
тельно, по этому.
these, см. **this**.
Theseus, см. Тезей.
they, они, онѣ; —who,
—that, тѣ которые.
they're, см. **they are**.
thick, толщина, сре-
дина; толстый, толщи-
ною, густой; — and
thin, что бы ни по-
пало; — ness, тол-
щина.
thief, воръ.
thigh, ляшка, бедро.
thin, тонкій, скудный,
тощій, худощавый,—
ly, скудно.
thine, твой.
thing, вещь, дѣло, соз-
даніе, тварь.
think, думать, подумать,
полагать, казаться,
считать, помышлять,
намѣреваться; to —
lightly of, принимать
слегка; — ing, мыш-
леніе.
third, третій; a—, треть;
to — a request, усп-
лнть просьбу; — ly,
въ третьихъ.
thirst, жажда; —у, жаждущій, алчущій; to be
—у for, жаждать, ал-
кать чего.
thirteen, тринадцать.
thirtieth, тридцатый.

thirty, тридцать.
this, этотъ, сей; мн.
these, эти; in—manner,
такимъ образомъ,
— day, сегодняшній
день; — year, нынѣш-
ній годъ.
thither, туда.
Thomas, Ѳома.
thorn, колючка, игла;
to be on—s, быть на
шильяхъ.
thorough, совершенный,
полный; —fare, про-
ходъ, проѣздъ; — ly,
совершенно.
those, см. **that**.
thou, ты.
though, хотя; однако,
однако же; as —, будто,
будто бы.
thought, мысль, вниманіе, разсужденіе; см.
также **think**.
thousand, тысяча.
thrash, молотить, бить,
колотить.
thread, нить; to —, пробираться.
threat, угроза; to — en,
грозить, угрожать.
three, три; —and twenty,
двадцать три; —decker,
трёхъ-дечный корабль,
—pence, три пенса;—
score, шестьдесятъ.
threshold, порогъ.
threw, см. **throw**.
thrice, три раза, трижды.
thrifty, экономный,
успѣвающій.
thrilling, наводящій
страхъ, бросающій въ
дрожь, страшный.
thrive, успѣвать, преу-
спѣвать.
thriving, успѣшный.
throne, престолъ, тронъ;

the—of human felicity,
верхъ человѣческаго
счастія.
throng, толпа, тѣснота;
friendship's—, друже-
ственная связь; to —,
тѣснить, стѣснять,
тѣсниться, толпиться;
are — ed with, бит-
комъ набиты.
through, черезъ, сквозь,
отъ; — out, во весь,
по всему, по всей,
вездѣ.
throw, бросать, кидать,
сваливать; to—about,
разбрасывать; to —
away, отбрасывать; to
—from, сбрасывать;
to—into any one's way,
подбрасывать, подки-
дывать кому; to—into
confusion, to — into
perplexity, приводить
въ смущеніе, озада-
чивать; to — into dis-
order, приводить въ
безпорядокъ; to— off,
сбрасывать, отбрасы-
вать; to — one's arm
around any one, об-
нимать кого; to —
out a hint, намекать
на что; to — up, на-
сыпать, копать, дѣ-
лать; to— wide open,
растворять настежь;
to —words away, те-
рять слова.
thrown, см. **throw**.
thrust, толкать; to —
into, втыкать; to —
through, прокалывать,
протыкать.
thumb, марать пальцами,
перелпстывать.
thump, тузить, толкать,
колотить.

thunder, громъ; to — греметь, раздаваться; — shower, дождь съ грозою; — storm, гроза.

Thursday, четвергъ.

thus, такъ, этакъ, такимъ образомъ.

thwart, банка гребецкая; to—, поперечить, противостоять.

thy, твой; — self, ты самъ, себя, себѣ.

tidal, имѣющій приливъ и отливъ, приливный.

tide, приливъ, теченіе;— river, рѣка имѣющая приливъ и отливъ.

tidings, извѣстія, новости.

tie, привязывать; —up, привязывать, связывать.

tiger, тигръ.

tile, крыть черепицами.

till, until, до, до того, пока, до тѣхъ поръ пока.

till, воздѣлывать, пахать; —age, обработываніе, воздѣлываніе, паханіе;—er, воздѣлыватель.

tilt, сражаться въ турнирѣ; — ing, бой въ турнирѣ; match of — ing, турниръ.

timber, строевой лѣсъ.

time, время, пора, разъ, мѣра, тактъ; at a—, вдругъ, въ одно и тоже время; once upon a—, однажды, когда-то; —ly, умѣстный.

tin, олово; оловянный.

tinge, красить, оттѣнивать, напитывать; every well bred cheek

was— d with confusion, у всѣхъ благовоспитанныхъ лицъ загорѣлись щёки отъ стыда.

tingle, шумѣть (въ ушахъ).

tiny, крошечный.

tire, уставать; — d, усталый; they were— d of, имъ наскучилъ.

't is, 'tis, см. it is,

tissue, ткань, связь, сцѣпленіе.

tithe, десятая доля, десятина; десятинный.

title, заглавіе, титулъ, претензія, право.

titter, хикать, лукаво смѣяться.

titular, почётный, титулярный, по титулу.

to, къ, до, въ, на, для, по; чтобы; означаетъ дат. падежъ: — you, Вамъ; знакъ неок. накл.: —ask, спросить.

toast, поджаренный хлѣбъ.

tobacco, табакъ.

to-day, сегодня.

toe, палецъ на ногѣ.

together, вмѣстѣ, сряду.

toil, трудъ, многотрудіе; to — , трудиться, мучиться; to — down, тащиться внизъ; to—through, съ трудомъ пробираться сквозь; by hard and long —ing, тяжкою и продолжительною борьбою.

toilet, туалетъ.

token, знакъ.

told, см. tell.

tolerate, терпѣть.

toleration, терпимость.

toll, пошлина, дорожная

пошлина; to —, звонить въ похоронный колоколъ;—bar, шлагбаумъ;—free, безпошлинный, не платящій пошлины; — man, пошлинникъ, сборщикъ пошлинъ.

Tom, Ѳомка.

tomb, могила гробъ.

to-morrow, завтра.

ton, тонна (62 пуда);—nage, грузъ (судна).

tone, тонъ, голосъ.

tongs, щипцы.

tongue, языкъ, нарѣчіе.

tonsure, тонсура, пострижение.

too, слишкомъ, также, притомъ.

took, см. take.

tooth, зубъ; —ache, зубная боль; множ. teeth, зубы и зубья (у пилы); elephants' teeth, слоновые клыки.

top, верхъ, вершина, поверхность, кубарь, волчёкъ, марсъ; верхній; from—to toe, съ головы до ногъ; who stood at the—, который былъ первымъ; —mast, стеньга.

topic, предметъ, тема.

torch, факелъ.

tore, см. tear.

torment, мука, мученіе.

torn, см. tear.

torrent, потокъ.

torrid, знойный, жаркій; the—zone, жаркій поясъ.

tortoise, черепаха.

torture, пытка, мука, мученіе; to—, пытать.

Tory, тори, приверженецъ королевской парtіп; — iꙧm, система торіевъ.

toss, кидать, бросать, бросаться, качаться, колебаться.

total, весь, цѣлый, полный; — ly, вовсе, совершенно.

totter, шататься.

touch, тронуть, растрогать, дотрогиваться, касаться; to—glasses, чокаться рюмками; — ing, трогательный; — stone, пробирный камень.

tough, жесткій, крутой.

tour, поѣздка, путешествіе.

tow, накля; to—, буксировать.

toward, — s, къ, противъ; —ness, переимчивость.

towel, полотенце; oaken —, дубина.

tower. башня, крѣпость, тюрьма, цитадель; to —, возноситься;—ing. возвышенный, высокій.

town, городъ; городскій; —sman, горожанинъ.

toy. игрушка; — s for children, дѣтскія игрушки.

trace, слѣдъ; to—, слѣдить, идти по слѣдамъ, начертывать.

track, слѣдъ, стезя, путь; to—, слѣдить за, открыть чьи слѣды, найти слѣдъ, набѣжать на слѣдъ.

tract, страна, полоса.

trade, торгъ, торговля, промыселъ, ремесло; to—, торговать, про-

мышлять; —sman, лавочникъ.

trading. торговый; a — vessel, купеческое судно.

tradition, преданіе; —al, на преданіи основанный.

traffic, торгъ, торговля, сообщеніе.

tragical, трагическій.

train. рядъ, свита, приводъ (пороху); to —, учить, воспитывать, пріучать, дрессировать; — band, городская милиція.

trait, черта.

traitor, измѣнникъ.

trample down, топтать, попирать.

trampling, топтаніе, топотъ.

tranquil, спокойный; — lity, спокойствіе.

transact, производить, учинять, отправлять, исправлять; — ion, отправленіе (дѣлъ), дѣло; — ions, записки, труды.

transfer, переносить, переводить, передавать.

transfix, прокалывать, пронзать.

transient, преходящій; the chill was but —, но ужасъ этотъ продолжался не долго.

translate, переводить.

translation, переводъ.

transmission, пересылка, передача.

transmit, передавать, пересылать.

transplant, пересаживать, переселять.

transport, восторгъ; to

— перевозить, увлекать.

trapper, бобролов, бобровникъ.

travel, путешествіе, поѣздка; to —, путешествовать, ѣздить; to — up, пройти, проѣхать; the earth — s round the sun, земля обращается около солнца; — ler, путешественникъ, пассажиръ; — ling, путешествованіе, ѣзда.

traverse, переходить, пересѣкать, проходить.

treacherous, измѣнническій, вѣроломный.

tread, шагъ, топотъ; to — ступать; to — on, наступать на.

treason, измѣна; high—, Государственная измѣна.

treasure, сокровище, кладъ; Lord — r, государственный казначей.

treasury, казначейство.

treat, угощеніе, пиршество; an acceptable—, пріятный гостинецъ; to—, обходиться, обращаться, поступать съ кѣмъ, трактовать, разсуждать; — ment, обращеніе; — y, трактатъ, договоръ.

tree, дерево.

tremble, дрожать; trembling all over, весь дрожащій.

tremendous, ужасный.

trench, окопъ, траншея.

trencher, столъ, обѣденный столъ.

tress, коса, локонъ.

trial, испытаніе, попытка, искушеніе, сужденіе, допросъ, судебное слѣдствіе; to bring to a —, доводить до суда, судить; to take one's — судиться.

triangle, треугольникъ.

tribe, племя.

tribunal, судилище, судъ.

tributary, побочная рѣка, притокъ.

tribute, дань, подать; to pay any one the last —, отдать кому послѣдній долгъ.

trice, мигъ; in a —, мигомъ.

trick, шутка, штука, проказа, шалость.

trifle, шутить.

trifling, пустыя занятія; незначительный, маловажный, неважный.

trim, нарядъ; to —, чистить, упрашать; to — a boat, уравновѣсить лодку.

triumph, торжество; to — торжествовать, преодолѣвать, побѣждать; — al, тріумфальный;— antly, торжественно.

trod, см. **tread**.

troop, толпа; — s, войско, войска.

tropic, поворотный кругъ, тропикъ; — al, тропическій.

trot, рысь; to —, бѣжать рысью, бѣгать.

troth, вѣра, вѣрность.

trouble, хлопоты, безпокойство, трудъ, забота, смущеніе, печаль, горесть; to —, мутить, безпокоить, смущать, озабочивать; a — d sea, взволнованное море; I will — you for, я попрошу у Васъ; — some, тягостный, безпокойный, докучливый.

trout, пеструшка, форель.

trudge, таскаться, много трудиться, мучиться.

true, вѣрный, истинный, правдивый; it is —, правда; — gotten, благопріобрѣтенный; — hearted, чистосердечный, прямодушный.

truly, вѣрно, истинно; — hearted, прямодушный.

trumpet, труба.

trundle, катиться.

trunk, пень, стволъ, сундукъ, ящикъ.

trust, довѣріе; to —, полагаться на что, уповать, надѣяться; to — one's self to, довѣряться чему; — worthy, надёжный, благонадёжный; — y, вѣрный, надёжный.

truth, правда, истина; the — is, правду сказать; in —, по истинѣ.

try, пробовать, испытывать, судить, стараться, пытаться; to — experiments, дѣлать опыты; let thou and I the battle —, рѣшимъ дѣло единоборствомъ.

tub, кадка.

tube, труба.

tubular, трубчатый.

tuck up, подбирать, подвязывать.

tufted, въ пучкахъ, клочковатый.

tug, силиться, трудиться; to — out, вытаскивать.

tumble, поваливаться, падать.

tumult, шумъ, суматоха.

tuneful, благозвучный, стройный.

tunnel, туннель, тоннель, подземный ходъ.

turban, тюрбанъ.

turbot, палтусъ, торбегъ, морская камбала.

turbulent, шумный, буйный, безчинный, безпокойный.

turf, дёрнъ, торфъ.

Turkey, Турція.

Turkish, турецкій.

turmoil, безпокоить, мучить.

turn, очередь, услуга; to —, вертѣть, вертѣться, поворачивать, превращать, направлять, дѣлаться; to — about, поворачивать; to — any one aside, совращать, отклонять кого; to — away, отворачивать, отсылать, увольнять, прогнать; to — back, отгибать, отворачивать; to — from, отворачиваться; to — in, входить; to — on, обращаться на; to — out, выгонять, выпускать, выходить, показываться, являться; to — out of the high road, сворачивать съ большой дороги; to — over, переворачивать; to—round, вращать, оборачивать, оборачиваться; to — to, обращаться къ; to — upon, относиться къ, касаться чего, зависѣть отъ.

turnament. турниръ.

turnip, рѣпа.

turnkey, тюремщикъ.

turnpike, пошлинная застава; — act, таможенное постановленіе; — man, сборщикъ шоссейной пошлины; — road, шоссе, насыпанная дорога.

tut, тфу!

tutor, наставникъ, гувернёръ.

twain, двое, два.

twang, гнусливое произношеніе.

't was, см. **it was**.

twelve, двѣнадцать.

twentieth, двадцатый.

twenty, двадцать; the — first, двадцать первый.

twere, см. **it were**.

twice, дважды.

twig, вѣтка, лоза.

twine, обвивать, вертѣться.

twinkle, сверкать, блистать.

twirl, вертѣться, крутиться.

twist, сучить, крутить, плесть, обвивать; to — any one's neck, свернуть кому шею.

twixt, см. **betwixt**.

two, два, двое; in —, на двѣ части, пополамъ; in a moment or —, чрезъ нѣсколько минутъ; — bedded, имѣющій двѣ постели; —

fold, двойной, двоякій; — hundred, двѣсти.

tyranny, тиранство, мучительство.

tyrant, тиранъ, мучитель.

tyro, новичекъ.

U.

ultimate, послѣдній, крайній.

umpire, посредникъ, третейскій судья.

unable, не въ состояніи.

unacquainted, незнакомый, несвѣдущій.

unanimous, единодушный, единогласный; — ly, единодушно.

unavailing, безполезный.

unaware, невнимательный, незнающій.

unblown, неигранный.

unborn, нерожденный.

unbounded, неограниченный, безпредѣльный, ненасытный.

uncertain, невѣрный, неизвѣстный, ненадежный; — ty, неизвѣстность, недоумѣніе.

unchanged, неизмѣнившійся, неизмѣнный.

uncharitableness, немилосердіе, безжалостность.

unchewed, неразжёванный.

uncivilized, непросвѣщенный, грубый.

uncle, дядя.

uncomfortable, непокойный, неуютный.

uncommon, необыкновенный; very — with, весьма рѣдко встрѣчаемомъ въ.

unconditional, безусловный.

unconquerable, непобѣдимый.

unconsciously, безотчётно.

uncouthness, неловкость, неуклюжесть.

uncover, обнажать, раскрывать; — ed, съ непокрытою или обнаженною головой.

uncrushed, нераздавленный.

uncultivated, необработанный.

undaunted, неустрашимый.

undecided, нерѣшённый.

under, подъ, при; — done, недожареный; — neath, подъ низомъ; — standing, разумѣніе, понятіе, разумъ; — taking, предпріятіе; to — go, претерпѣвать; to — take, предпринимать, брать на себя, ручаться; to — mine, подкапывать, подрывать; to — stand, понимать, умѣть, знать, быть свѣдущимъ въ, слышать.

understood, см. **understand**.

underwent, см. **undergo**.

undeviating, неизмѣнный.

undisturbed, невстревоженный.

undo, развязывать.

undone, погубленный.

undoubted, несомнѣнный; — ly, несомнѣнно.

undrawn, невытащенный.

undress, раздѣваться.

undulatory, волнообразный.

uneasy, безпокойный, неудобный.

unexampled, безпримѣрный.

unexpected, неожиданный; — ly, неожиданно, нечаянно.

unexperienced, неопытный.

unfavourable, неблагопріятный.

unfavourably, неблагопріятно.

unfit, непригодный, неприличный, неспособный.

unfold, развёртывать.

unfortunate, несчастный; — ly, къ несчастію, на бѣду.

unfounded, неосновательный.

ungrateful, непризнательный, неблагодарный.

unguardedly, неосторожно.

unhappy, несчастный.

unhelped, безпомощный.

uniform, мундиръ; однообразный.

unimportant, маловажный, неважный.

uninclosed, не окруженный, не обнесенный (заборомъ), не огороженный.

uninhabited, необитаемый.

uninjured, неповрежденный.

uninterrupted, непрерванный, непріостанавливаемый, непомѣшаемый.

union, соединеніе, сочетаніе, союзъ.

unite, соединять, сочета-

вать, соединяться;—d, соединенный; —d States, Соединенное Штаты.

universal, всеобщій, повсемѣстный; — ly, повсемѣстно.

universe, вселенная.

university, университетъ.

unjust, несправедливый.

unknowing, незнающій, невѣдущій.

unknown, незнакомый, неизвѣстный, невѣдомый; — to him, безъ его вѣдома.

unlawful, незаконный; — ly, незаконно.

unleavened, безквасный.

unless, если не, развѣ, иначе какъ.

unlettered, некнижный, неучёный.

unlifted, неподнятый.

unlike, непохожій.

unlimited, неограниченный.

the unloading, выгрузка.

unlucky, несчастливый, несчастный.

unmanageable, неуправимый; the ship was —, кораблемъ не возможно было управлять.

unmeasured, неограниченный, неизмѣримый, безмѣрный.

unmitigated, несмягченный, неумолкный.

unmixed, несмѣшанный.

unmolested, невредимый.

unmoved, нетронутый, безъ умиленія.

unnaturally, ненатурально.

unnavigable, несудоходный.

unnecessary, ненужный.

unnoticed, незамѣченный.

unnumbered, несмѣтный.

unparalleled, несравненный, безподобный.

unpardonable, непростительный.

unpitied, неудостоенный соболѣзнованія.

unpleasing, непріятный.

unplundered, неограбленный.

unpopular, непопулярный, нелюбимый.

unpremeditated, не приготовясь, безъ приготовленія.

unprincipled, безъ правилъ.

unpromising, мало обѣщающій.

unreasonable, безразсудный.

unrefined, необлагороженный.

unrestrained, неудержанный.

unrivalled, безподобный.

unshaken, непоколебимый.

unskilfulness, неловкость, неумѣнье.

unsmote, непораженный.

unsubdued, непокорённый.

unsuccessful, безуспѣшный, неудачный.

unsuitable, несогласный, несоотвѣтственный, несообразный.

unsupported, неподдержанный.

unsuspected, неподозрѣваемый.

untameable, неукротимый.

until, см. till.

unto, см. to.

untouched, нетронутый; one subject still remains —, до одного предмета мы еще не коснулись.

untrue, ложный.

untwist, разсучивать, расплетать.

unusual, необыкновенный; — ly, необыкновенно.

unused, непривыкший.

unwarlike, невоинственный.

unwearying, неутомимый.

unwelcome, непріятный.

unwell, нездоровый.

unwholesome, нездоровый.

unwilling, неохотный.

unwisely, неблагоразумно.

unworthy, недостойный.

up, вверхъ, на верхъ; — and down, туда и сюда; —to, до; he is —, онъ всталъ; to get —, вставать; the national spirit was—, духъ народа былъ пробужденъ; the ship would be well —with the land, судно подойдетъ поближе къ берегу.

upheld, см. uphold.

uphold, поддерживать.

upon, на, при, по, о, объ, въ; —a journey, въ дорогѣ; — which, послѣ чего; the English were quick — it, Англичане были тотчасъ готовы, тотчасъ подоспѣли.

upper, верхній, высшій.

upright, отвѣсный; прямо.

uproar, волненіе, бушеваніе, тревога.

upset, опрокидывать.

upward, upwards, вверхъ, болѣе.

urbanity, вѣжливость, учтивость.

urge, побуждать, понукать, настоятельно просить; to — an objection, представлять возраженіе; to — on, погонять, понукать; ntly, настоятельно.

us, насъ намъ; with—, съ нами.

usage, обычай, обыкновеніе, обрядъ.

use, употребленіе, польза, пользованіе чѣмъ, пользованіе доходами съ чего; no— talking to —, какая польза, что толку, къ чему разговаривать съ? of —, пригодный полезный; of no—, безполезный; to make—of, употреблять, пользоваться; to—, употреблять, имѣть обыкновеніе, дѣлать что обыкновенно, обходиться съ кѣмъ; to — the sword, владѣть шпагою; they — d to be exposed, они обыкновенно выставлялись; they—d to meet, они собирались; —d, привычный; he is — d, онъ привыкъ; — ful, полезный; —less, безполезный.

usual, употребительный, обыкновенный, обычный; it is—here, здѣсь

принято; —ly, обыкновенно.

usurper, самозванецъ.

utility, полезность.

utmost, крайній, величайшій; to the —, до крайности.

utter, крайній, совершенный, положительный; to --, произносить, говорить; to — prayers, читать молитвы; — ance, произношеніе языкъ;—ly, крайне, совершенно.

V.

vacant, упраздненный.

vagabond, бродяга.

vagrant, бродяга, скитаецъ.

vail, покрывало, вуаль.

vain, тщетный, суетный, гордый, тщеславный; in —, — ly, тщетно, напрасно.

vale, долъ, долина.

valet, слуга, камердинеръ.

valiant, доблестный, храбрый; —ly, доблестно, храбро.

valley, долина.

valour, доблесть, храбрость.

valuable, цѣнный, драгоцѣнный.

value, цѣна, цѣнность, важность; to —, цѣнить.

van, vanguard, авангардъ, передовое войско.

Van Diemen's Land, Ванъ-Дименова Земля.

vanilla, ваниль.

vanish, изчезать.

vanity, суета, тщета.

vanquish, побѣждать.

vapour, паръ.

varied, многоразличный.

variety, разнообразіе, различіе, порода; a — of talk, разные разговоры.

various, разный, разнообразный, разли чный, многоразличный; —ly, различно, разно, разнообразно.

varlet, человѣкъ, плутъ.

vary, разнообразить, разнствовать, измѣнятьсл, перемѣнятьсл.

vassal, вассалъ, голдовникъ, ленникъ.

vast, обширный, огромный; —lý, чрезмѣрно; — ness, обширность, безмѣрность.

vault, сводъ, подвалъ;— ed, со сводомъ; the— ed sky, небесный сводъ.

veal, телятина.

vegetable market, овощный или зеленной рынокъ; —s, зелень.

vegetation, произрастеніе, прозябаніе.

vehement, пылкій, горячій, запальчивый; — ly, сильно, горячо, жарко.

vehicle, повозка.

velocity, быстрота, скорость.

velvet, бархатъ; бархатный.

venerable, почетный.

veneration, почптаніе, благоговѣніе, чествованіе.

Venetian, венеціанскій.

vengeance, мщеніе, месть.

venison, дичина; — dinner, обѣдъ (состоящій) изъ дичины; —pasty, паштетъ съ дичиной.

vent, испускать, изливать.

venture, осмѣливаться, отваживаться, пускаться; to — out, осмѣливаться выдти.

verandah, веранда (лёгкая галерея вокругъ дома).

verb, глаголъ; —al, словесный; — al alteration, измѣненіе словъ.

verdant, зеленѣющій, зелёный.

verdict, приговоръ или отвѣтъ присяжныхъ.

verdure, зелень.

verify, свѣрять.

verse, стихъ, стихи.

versed, свѣдущій.

versification, стихосложеніе, версификація.

verst, верста.

very, самый, настоящій; очень, весьма; —mnch, гораздо.

vessel, сосудъ, сосудина, судно.

vest, камзолъ, жилетъ.

veteran, заслужённый, опытный.

vexation, досада, огорченіе.

viand, кушанье.

vibrate, махаться, размахиваться.

vicar, викарій, сельскій священникъ.

vice, порокъ.

vice chancellor, вице-канцлеръ, —roy, вице-король, вицерой.

vicinity, сосѣдство.

vicissitude, перемѣна.

victim, жертва.

victor, побѣдитель, побѣдоносецъ; — ions, побѣдоносный;— iously, побѣдоносно; —y, побѣда.

victual, снабжать, съѣстными припасами.

vie, соперничать, соревновать.

view, видъ, взглядъ, обозрѣніе, цѣль, намѣреніе; to —, видѣть, смотрѣть, разсматривать.

vigilance, бдительность.

vigorous, сильный, мощный.

vigour, энергія, сила, крѣпость, здоровье.

vile, низкій, подлый.

villa, загородный домъ, дача.

village, деревня; — r, деревенскій житель, поселянинъ.

villain, подлецъ, злодѣй, мошенникъ; —y, злодѣйство.

villany, мошенничество.

vindictive, мстительный; — ness, мстительность.

vinegar, уксусъ.

violate, нарушать; to — any one's purse, опоражнивать у кого кошелёкъ.

violation, нарушеніе.

violence, насиліе, сила, свирѣпость, стремительность.

violent, сильный, насильный, насильственный; — ly, сильно, стремительно, насильственно.

Virgil, Виргилій.

56

Virginia, Виргинія; —n, Вергиніецъ.

virtue, добродѣтель, превосходное качество; by —, въ силу, по силѣ.

viscount, винонтъ.

visible, видимый, очевидный.

visit, визитъ, посѣщеніе, навѣщаніе; to be on a —, гостить; to —, навѣщать, посѣщать.

visual, зрительный; — knowledge, нагляддое распознаваніе.

vivacious, живой, веселый.

vivid, живой, яркій.

vocabulary, словарь.

vocal, вокальный, голосовой.

vocation, призваніе, должность, обязанность, склонность, расположеніе.

vociferate, кричать изо всей мочи.

voice, голосъ.

volatile, летучій.

volume, объёмъ, книга, томъ.

voluntarily, добровольно, охотно.

voracious, прожорливый, жадный.

voracity, прожорливость жадность.

vote, голосъ, мнѣніе; to —, подавать голосъ, п. мнѣніе, согласиться дать.

vouch, ручаться.

vow, обѣтъ.

vowel, гласная буква.

voyage, путешествіе, вояжъ; — of discovery, путешествіе, (пред-принимаемое) для открытій); — r, путешественникъ.

vulgar, простой народъ, простой людъ, чернь; простонародный, простой, обыкновенный.

W.

wade, ходить въ бродъ.

wag, маханіе (хвостомъ); to —, махать.

wage, вести (войну).

wager, закладъ; for a —, на пари.

wages, жалованье, плата.

waggoner, извозчикъ.

wail, вопль; are loud in their —, громко вопіютъ; to —, плакать, сѣтовать.

waist, поясница, талія, также мѣсто на открытомъ декѣ судна между шканцами и бакомъ (шкафутъ и ростры); — coat, жилетъ.

wait, засада; to —, ждать, выжидать, служить, прислуживать; to — for, дожидать, дожидаться; to —on, to —upon, прислуживать, навѣщать, поспѣшать, заѣзжать; — er, прислужникъ, половой; — ing-maid, —ing-woman, горничная; gentleman in — ing, см. **gentleman.**

wake, будить, разбуждать, просыпаться; to —up, пробуждаться;— ful, бодрый, бдительный.

Wales, Валлисъ.

walk, ходъ, ходьба, хож-деніе, прогулка; to —, ходить, ходить пѣшкомъ, гулять, прогуливаться; to — about, прохаживаться; to — out, выходить; to — over, переходить; to —up to, подходить къ.

wall, стѣна.

wallet, сумка.

Walter, Вальтеръ.

wan, см. **win.**

wand, прутъ, жезлъ.

wander, блуждать, бродить, скитаться, странствовать; —er, странникъ, бродяга; —ing, странствованіе, странствующій.

want, недостатокъ, неимѣніе, бѣдность, нужда, надобность; for — of, за отсутствіемъ, по неимѣнію; in — of repair, требующій исправленія; who all my — s supply, которые доставляютъ мнѣ всё нужное; to —, недоставать, имѣть недостатокъ, имѣть надобность, нуждаться въ, хотѣть, желать, —ed, нужный.

war, война; — of conquest, война для завоеваній; in —, въ военное время; to make —, вести войну, воевать; — chariot, боевая колесница; —like, воинственный; — rior, воинъ.

warble, чирикать; журчать, пѣть съ трелями, распѣвать.

ward, отдѣленіе, комната; to —, отражать.

warm, тёплый; — th, теплота.

warn, предостерегать, отдалять; to--off, отгонять; — ing, предостереженіе, предувѣдомленіе;at a moment's, —, тотчасъ послѣ приказанія.

warrant, полномочіе, повелѣніе.

was, былъ; см. **be**.

wash, болото, помои; to —, мыть, обмывать; to—off, смывать; the sea — ed over him, его заплёскивало волнами.

waste, трата; пустой, пустынный;to—,истощать, истрачивать.

watch, караулъ, часы, вахта, карманные часы; lieutenant on the —, вахтенный лейтенантъ; officer of the —, вахтенный начальникъ; to —, бдѣть, стеречь, караулить, подкарауливать, поджидать, наблюдать за; to — for, подкарауливать; — ful, бдительный, попечительный; to be—fnl of, примѣчать что, наблюдать за чѣмъ; — ing, бдѣніе, безсонница; — maker, часовой мастеръ; — man, часовой.

water, вода; водяной; to—, поливать, орошать; —cask, водяная бочка; — man, лодочникъ, перевозчикъ;—room, пространство занимаемое водою; —у, водяной.

wave, волна; to—, махать, волноваться.

wax, воскъ, восковой; to—, становиться, дѣлаться.

way, путь, дорога, разстояніе, сторона, способъ, образъ, манеръ, обращеніе, привычка; —out, выходъ; —side, сторона, дороги; by the — side, подлѣ дороги; by—of, въ видѣ, какъ; by the—, дорогою, на дорогѣ; in по —, ни чуть не; round about—, обходъ, кругъ; that —, туда, такимъ образомъ; the right -- of the fur, по шерсти; which—, куда? to give — , поддаваться, уступать; to make—, давать, уступать дорогу; to make one's — пробираться.

waylaid, см. **waylay**.

waylay, подстерегать, подкарауливать.

we, мы;—are seven, насъ семеро.

weak, слабый; to — en, ослаблять, обезсиливать; —ness, слабость, хилость.

wealth, добро, имущество, богатство; —у, зажиточный, богатый.

weapon, оружіе.

wear, носка; to —, носить, истощать, испортить; to — away, протекать, проходить; to — out, истомлять; to — the air, имѣть видъ.

weariness, усталость.

weary, утомленный, усталый, скучный.

weather, погода, навѣтренная сторона, навѣтренный; to —, обогнать, объѣзжать; — beaten, загорѣвшій.

weave, ткать, плесть; to — together, сплетать; — r. ткачъ; — r of cloth, суконщикъ.

we'ave, см. **we have**.

web, паутина.

wed, жениться на комъ, выйти за мужъ за кого;—ded, въ супружествѣ;—ding, свадьба.

Wednesday, середа.

weed, платье, плевелы, трава; mourning —, траурное платье, трауръ.

week, недѣля;—ly, еженедѣльный, за недѣлю.

weep, плакать.

weigh, поднимать.

weight, вѣсъ, вѣсы, тяжесть.

welcome, ласковый пріемъ, пріятный; to—,to make —, привѣтствовать; he is—, you are—, милости просимъ, добро пожаловать.

welfare, благосостояніе.

well, колодезь, льяло; здоровый; хорошо, хорошенько, пань слѣдуетъ; ну что! to —, течь, бить ключёмъ; —a-day, увы! —bred, благовоспитанный; — done, довольно жареный; — you may be in a hungry case, я думаю, Вы проголодались; it were as —, не друно бы было;

when he became so
—, когда онъ на столь-
ко поправился.

we'll, см. **We will.**

Welsh, Валлискій; · the
—, Валлисцы; --man,
Валлисецъ.

welter, валяться, плавать.

went, см, **go.**

wept, см. **weep.**

were, были; см. **be.**

west, западъ, западный,
къ западу; —erly, —
ern, западный;—ward,
къ западу.

West Indian, вестъ-ин-
дейскій; — minster,
Вестминстеръ, Вест-
минстерскій.

wet, мокрый; to – to the
skin, промачивать до
костей или на сквозь.

whale, китъ; — boat,
вельботъ, также шлюп-
ка китоловнаго судна;
— bone, китовый усъ;
—man, китоловъ.

wharf, пристань.

what, то что, что; какой, который; какъ!
—ever, какой бы ни
былъ, что бы ни;
nothing—ever, реши-
тельно ничего; — time,
въ какое время? —
with not having, ча-
стію отъ того что не
имѣлъ.

wheat, пшеница; flour
of—, пшеничная мука.

wheel, колесо; to—, катать, вертѣться, обра-
щаться; to—out, вы-
катывать; — ed, ко-
лесный, на колёсахъ.

when, когда; — ever,
всегда когда, всякій

разъ когда; he had
scarcely...—, онъ толь-
ко что успѣлъ...какъ.

whence, from whence,
откуда. ·

where, гдѣ, куда; every
—, вездѣ, повсюду,
повсемѣстно; — as,
между тѣмъ какъ, по-
тому что; — at, на
что; —ver, гдѣ бы ни,
куда бы ни; —fore, по-
чему,для чего;—from,
откуда; —in, въ чёмъ;
— on, на чёмъ, на
которомъ; — soever,
куда бы ни; — to, къ
чему, къ которому;
— upon, послѣ чего;
—with, чѣмъ.

whether, ли; —..or, ли..
или

which, который, что,
какой; of—, котораго,
которыхъ ; — way
куда.

Whig, вигъ, привержа-
нецъ оппозиціи; the
—party, партія ви-
говъ; —gery, систе-
ма виговъ.

while, время; а —, нѣсколько времени, нѣ-
которое время; after,
a little—, немного по-
годя.

while, whilst, между
тѣмъ какъ, тогда какъ,
пока.

whip, кнутъ, бичъ, хлы-
стикъ; to —, сѣчь

whirl, быстро обращаться,вертѣться,кружить-
ся; — wind, вихрь.

whisk, мчаться, летать.

whiskers, бакенбарды.

whisky, уиски (родъ водки).

whisper, шёпотъ; in —s,
шёпотомъ; to—, шеп-
тать.

whist, вистъ (карточная
игра).

whist, стъ, цыцъ!

whistle, дудка, свистокъ;
to —, свистать.

whit, крошечка, малость;
not a —, ни мало.

white, бѣлый цвѣтъ; бѣлый; — bottomed, съ
бѣлымъ дномъ; a —
day, счастливый день;
to — n, бѣлѣть, бѣ-
литься.

whither, куда.

whiz, свистѣть, шипѣть.

who, кто, который; —
ever, кто бы ни, тотъ
кто.

whole, цѣлое, всё; цѣлый, весь; the — of the
Bible, всю библію; the
— of the guns, всѣ
орудія; on the —, во-
обще; — some, цѣлеб-
ный, здоровый.

wholly, совсѣмъ, совершенно.

whom, кого, котораго;
by —, кѣмъ; with —,
съ кѣмъ.

who're, см. **who are.**

whose, чей, коего.

whosoever, кто бы ни
былъ.

why, почему, зачѣмъ;
какъ! вѣдь! ну! ну
чтожъ! извольте ви-
дѣть!

wicked, нечестивый, без-
божный, злодѣйскій;—
ness, злоба, нечести-
вость.

wicker, ивовый.

wide, широкій, обшир-
ный, просторный, ши-

рпною; — open, на-
стежь; with his nostrils
all —, съ отверстыми
ноздрями; to—n, рас-
ширять; — ly, далёко,
вдали, значительно,
очень.

widow, вдова.

wield, владѣть, управлять чѣмъ, держать.

wife, жена, супруга.

wig, парикъ.

wight, человѣкъ.

wild, пустыня; дикій,
свирѣпый, распутный,
бурный; — erness, пу-
стыня; — hanging
woods, повисшія де-
ревья, т. е. деревья
съ повислыми вѣтвя-
ми, какъ то берёзы,
ивы плакучія, и т. д;
— ly, дико.

will, воля, произволъ,
духовная, завѣщаніе;
to—, хотѣть, желать,
имѣть обыкновеніе;
какъ вспом. глаг. о-
значаетъ будущее вре-
мя; — you fill up, до-
лейте пожалуйста; when
circumstances would
permit, когда позво-
ляли обстоятельства;
— ing, охотный; to
be—ing, соглашаться,
быть готову, хотѣть;
— ingly, охотно.

Will, William, Виль-
гельмъ.

win, выигрывать, пріобрѣтать, доставать,
побѣждать, одержать
(побѣду); to — the
race, получать награ-
ду; slow and steady—
s the race, « тише
ѣдешь дальше бу-

дешь»; — ning, при-
влекательный.

wince, содрогаться.

wind, вѣтеръ; a good
prize was in the —,
достанется хорошая
добыча; which way is
the —, съ которой
стороны, какъ вѣтеръ?

wind, вертѣть; to — up
a watch or clock, за-
водить часы; — ing,
извилина, излучина.

window, окно; оконный.

wine, вино.

wing, крыло, флангъ;
on the —, на лету.

wink, мигъ; to give a —,
мигать.

winter, зима; зимній; in
the —, зимою; — 's
gone away, зима про-
шла; a - 's day, зим-
ній день.

wire, проволока.

wisdom, мудрость, умъ,
благоразуміе.

wise, мудрый, умный; —
ly, благоразумно; —
man, мудрецъ.

wish, желаніе; to —, желать; I — myself far
from hence, я желаю
быть далёко отсюда;
to — for, желать чего;
it is to be — ed, жела-
тельно; — ful, сильно
желающій.

wit, остроуміе, острота
умъ, разумъ, остроу-
мецъ; G. had a pleas-
ant —, Г. былъ боль-
шой остракъ; — ty, о-
строумный.

witch, колдунья, вѣдьма.

with, съ, отъ, у; знакъ
твор. падежа; — all
England firing up, меж-

ду тѣмъ какъ вся Анг-
лія воспламенялась.

withdraw, отнимать, у-
далять.

wither, wither away, вянуть, увядать.

withhold, удерживать.

within, внутри, въ, во,
болѣе какъ черезъ
(часъ и пр); — a very
short distance, на очень
близкое розстояніе;
to be—the reach, быть
доступнымъ; to — one
penny, до одного пенни.

without, внѣ, за, безъ;
не; — waiting, не до-
жидаясь.

witness, быть свидѣте-
лемъ.

woe, горе.

woful, горестный, бѣдственный.

woke, см. **wake**.

wolf, волкъ.

woman, женщина; —kind,
женскій полъ, женщи-
ны.

won, см. **win**.

wonder, диво, чудо, удивленіе, изумленіе; no
— не удивительно; to
— удивляться, хотѣть
знать; — ful, чудес-
ный, удивительный,
дивный; — fully, див-
но, удивительно.

wondrous, дивный, удивительный, чудесный.

wont, обыкновеніе; to
be—, имѣть привычку
или обыкновеніе; —ed,
привычный, обыкно-
венный.

won't, wo'n't, см. **will
not**.

woo, свататься за кого,
искать.

wood, дерево, дрова, лѣсъ; лѣсной; — ashes, древесняя зола, древесный пепелъ; — en, деревянный; — land, лѣсистое мѣсто, лѣсъ; she had a rustic — land air, съ виду она была обитательница лѣсовъ и полей.

wool, шерсть; — en, шерстяной; — ly, шерстистый.

word, слово; — for —, слово въ слово, отъ слова до слова; — of command, командное слово, команда; upon my—, право; to send present —, тотчасъ давать знать; to —, выражать словами, сочинять.

wore, см. wear.

work, работа, дѣло, сочиненіе; of all —, на всѣ руки; to be at — upon, быть занятымъ работою надъ чѣмъ, быть занятымъ чѣмъ; to—, работать, дѣлать, производить, причинять, бродить; to — miracles, творить чудеса; to — treason, затѣвать измѣну; he —ed hard to masticate it, онъ всячески старался разжевать его; —house, рабочій домъ; —' man, работникъ; — shop, мастерская, рабочая.

world, свѣтъ, міръ; a man of the —, человѣкъ свѣтскій; (that) I have in the —, какой только у меня есть; he looked for all the — like, онъ походилъ точь въ точь на; — ly, свѣтскій, мірской.

worm, червь.

worn, см. wear.

worry, мучить, терзать.

worse, хуже, худшій.

worser, см. worse.

worship, поклоненіе, богослуженіе; to —, поклоняться.

worst, самый худой, худшій; to have the — of it, оставаться въ накладѣ, понесть убытокъ.

worth, цѣна, цѣнность, достоинство; стоющій, достойный; to be —, стоить; it is — while, стоитъ того чтобы; six penny —, на шесть пенсовъ; —less, негодный, недостойный, низкій; — y, достойный.

would, см. will; когда would вспом. глаголъ, то см. его главн. глаг.

wound, рана; to —, ранить.

woven, см. weave.

wrap, закутывать, погружать во что.

wrath, гнѣвъ.

wreck, крушеніе, обломки; to —, разрушать.

wrest, вывертывать, вырывать, исторгать, отнимать.

wretch, несчастный, злодѣй; —ed, несчастный, злополучный, жалкій, бѣдный, негодный, скверный; — edness, злополучіе, бѣда.

wrinkle, морщиться.

writ, вызовъ, требованіе.

write, писать, написать; to - down, записывать; — r, сочинитель, писатель, писавшій (письмо).

writhe, крутиться, корчиться.

writing, писаніе.

written, см. write.

wrong, несправедливость; невѣрный, ненастоящій; несправедливо.

wrote, см. write.

wrought, см. work.

Würtemberg, Виртембергъ.

Y.

yard, ярдъ, англійскій аршинъ (1,286 арш.), дворъ.

ye, см. you.

year, годъ, лѣто.

yeast, дрожди.

yellow, жёлтой цвѣтъ; жёлтый.

yeoman, однодворецъ; — ry, однодворцы.

yes, да.

yesterday, вчера.

yet, еще, до сихъ поръ, однако, всё-таки; as —, ещё, все ещё; there were as — no, тогда ещё не было.

yield, производить, приносить, давать, поддаваться, уступать; to — up, уступать.

yoke, яремъ, иго; to put into the —, запрягать подъ яремъ.

yon, тотъ.

yonder, тамъ.

yore, давно; of —, въ старину.

York, Іоркъ; — ist, Іоркистъ (приверженецъ герцога Іоркскаго).

you, Вы, вы, ты, Васъ, Вамъ, тебѣ; how many may — be, сколько васъ можетъ быть?

you'd, см. you would.

you'll, см. you will.

young, молодой; — ster, молодой человѣкъ, юноша.

your, Вашъ, вашъ, твой; — s, вашъ; — self, Вы сами, себя.

you're, см. you are.

youth, юноша, молодость, юность, молодёжь; — ful, юношескій, молодой, моложавый; of a very — ful appearance, очень моложавъ на видъ.

Z.

zeal, ревность; — ous, ревностный.

zest, вкусъ.

zinc, цинкъ, шпіаутеръ.

zone, поясъ, зона.

zoological, зологическій.

ОПЕЧАТКИ.

Стран.	Строк.	Напеч.	Слѣд. напеч.	Стран.	Строк.	Напеч.	Слѣд. напеч.
7	4	ibe world	the world	176	15	briks	bricks
11	26	solider	soldier	181	8	excmple	example
—	30	solider	soldier	—	16	auswer	answer
23	2	enterning	entering	182	7	neight	night
26	30	hin	him	188	32	np	up
30	25	o sleep	to sleep	189	9	cautions	cautious
45	31	at onco	at once	190	35	Garman	German
57	2	cango	can go	192	2	is should	it should
70	24	abjoining	adjoining	201	12	scriptual	scriptural
71	24	de Scotch- man	the Scotch- man	227	1	fundation	foundation
74	11	rosolutely	resolutely	—	35	unles	unless
83	34	from of	from off	236	18	diseases	diseases
85	12	Espuimaux	Esquimaux	237	27	stimnlates	stimulates
89	11	his novelty	its novelty	244	26	posses	possess
—	32	happend	happened	256	6	carriges	carriages
92	1	fell with	fell in with	257	20	Scotsf rom	Scots from
93	34	soom	soon	262	32	in Perth	is Perth
96	31	relived	relieved	265	19—20	supeiority	superiority
107	17	hast lost	had lost	269	8	our praise	your praise
110	13	appeard	appeared	273	10	honnor	honour
141	10	are said	were said	282	22	aples	apples
171	32—33	when inten- tions	when his in- tentions	314	47	оно это	оно, это
				317	15	лы	лп
				—	31	skake	shake
173	33	Bnt	But	319	12	yon	you

Словарь.

Стран.	Строк.	Напеч.	Слѣд. напеч.	Стран.	Строк.	Напеч.	Слѣд. напеч.
327 advance	14	впреди	впереди	388 'llwill			'll, см. will
332 attack	5	ущебъ	ущербъ	399 our	1	намъ	нашъ
342 Celtic	1	кольтскій	кельтскій	400 pace	4	по комнать	по комнатѣ
350 creed	2	спмволъ	спмволъ	— parish	3	—ioner прп- хожанка	—ioner, прп- хожанин, прихожанка
352 dedicate	1	посвящать	посвящать.				
357 draw	12	къ тому	къ кому	402 perfect	1	соршпсн- ный	совершенный
358 drop	3—4	повали- ватьсь	повалпваться	405 pontiff	1	первосоя- щенникъ	первосвя- щенникъ
359 Ecclesiast1		Эклезіасть	Эклезіасгъ	406 press	9	устрем- лпсься	устремляться
362 ever	5—6	безпре- рывко	безпрерывно	412 real	1	настоцій	настоящій
— „	8	сколько	сколько	415 rid	1	to — get	to get —
— exchange	4	промѣнять, на	промѣнять, на	416 ring	1	перстсиъ	перстень
366 fight	8—9	one's—way	one's way	410 seem	2	not—hear доля;	not — to hear snack, доля;
376 high	20	велиходуш- ный	великодуш- ный	424 smack			
378 illuminate			illuminate	428 stifle	4	задущать	задушать
379 impress	3	облодѣлл	овладѣлп	— stout	2	должій	дюжій
382 intimate	1	намѣкать	намскать	429 strown	1	storw	strow
— issue	5	(отдавать приказъ)	отдавать (приказъ)	— submis- sive	2	покор пвый	покорпвый

9 783337 173074